Sketch-based Interfaces and Modeling

Joaquim Jorge • Faramarz Samavati
Editors

Sketch-based Interfaces and Modeling

Springer

Editors
Joaquim Jorge
Depto. Engenharia Informática
Instituto Superior Técnico
Universidade Técnica de Lisboa
Avenida Rovisco Pais
Lisboa 1049-001
Portugal
jaj@vimmi.inesc-id.pt

Faramarz Samavati
Dept. Computer Science
University of Calgary
University Drive NW 2500
Calgary, Alberta T2N 1N4
Canada
samavati@ucalgary.ca

ISBN 978-1-4471-5730-4 ISBN 978-1-84882-812-4 (eBook)
DOI 10.1007/978-1-84882-812-4
Springer London Dordrecht Heidelberg New York

British Library Cataloguing in Publication Data
A catalogue record for this book is available from the British Library

Cover design: deblik

Printed on acid-free paper

Springer is part of Springer Science+Business Media (www.springer.com)

Foreword

The field of sketch-based interfaces and modeling (SBIM) has had a long history. Since the early 1960s, which saw the birth of interactive computer graphics through Ivan Sutherland's Sketchpad and Jacks' DAC-1 system at General Motors, we have seen researchers developing methods and techniques to let users interact with a computer through sketching, a simple, yet highly expressive medium. Initially, SBIM was not a field in and of itself, but a set of distinct areas where researchers from different backgrounds worked in isolation, without a real community to share ideas. Areas within SBIM included sketch-based modeling, where the goal was to easily create 3D models, and sketch-based interfaces, where the goal was to develop systems for recognizing, for example, hand-writing, command gestures, 2D diagrams, and mathematics. Today, SBIM has emerged as a subfield of computer science that blends concepts from computer graphics, human-computer interaction, artificial intelligence, and machine learning and has brought the two areas of sketching—interface and model specification—together. This synergy was spearheaded by Joaquim Jorge and John Hughes, who started the first SBIM conference in 2004.

Over the years, SBIM has had some great successes (e.g., hand-printing and more recently cursive hand-writing recognition) as well as notable failures where the problem is still intractable in the general case (e.g., 3D sketch understanding). As with most of promising technology, it may take multiple decades for the technology to become mature enough to become viable. Speech recognition is a classic example of this, having taken more than four decades of research and productization before becoming commoditized, and SBIM is just starting to be mature enough to enable us to see that it can be used mainstream. Hand-writing and mathematical expression recognition and simple modeling tools like Google's SketchUp are some examples.

It is interesting to look at the history of using sketching to create graphical models and have the computer recognize hand-written text, mathematics, and diagrams. Any 2D visual language lends itself to sketch-based input, given that it is much easier to enter such languages (e.g., musical scores, mathematics or chemical molecule diagrams) by simply entering them with a pen or stylus than having to convert the language into a encoded 1D form entered on the keyboard. SBIM can trace its roots not just to Ivan Sutherland's seminal Sketchpad but also to his brother Bert Sutherland's system for sketching out logic diagrams and to Robert Anderson's Ph.D. research at Harvard in the late 1960s on mathematics recognition and subsequent evaluation using the RAND tablet, the earliest predecessor to the digitizing tablets of today. It is interesting to note that the areas pioneered by the Sutherlands and Anderson still represent significant research problems today in both recognition and modeling. Fontaine Richardson's Applicon CAD modeling tool was the first commercial product to feature gesture recognition for model elements and commands using a digitizing tablet. There was relatively little research, let alone commercial exploitation, during the 1970s, although Negroponte's Architecture Machine Group at MIT did do some important work on recognizing architectural diagrams. In particular, in 1976 the SIGGRAPH papers by Weinzapfel on Architecture-By-Yourself and by Herot on the HUNCH system began to explore how computers could interpret hand-drawn diagrams and what inference mechanisms and domain knowledge were needed to do so.

In the 1980s and 1990s, we began to see a number of pen-based forerunners to TabletPCs and PDAs, as well as pen-based PC software appear in the market place, commercial implementations inspired by Alan Kay's Dynabook vision of the late sixties. These included Wang FreeStyle, Microsoft Pen Windows, Go's Penpoint, and Apple's Newton. The new devices showed that the commercial sector was starting to see the potential benefits of pen input and gesture-based interfaces. Unfortunately, essentially all these commercial efforts failed for various reasons such as inadequate computing speed and memory, insufficient battery life, and lack of sophisticated recognition technology. Despite these too-early attempts, digitizing tablets continued to be routinely used by artists and designers to create digital ink that remained uninterpreted (e.g., in painting systems) or as a substitute for the mouse with standard WIMP GUIs—robust character, symbol and gesture recognition, let alone sketch understanding, had to wait for more powerful hardware and recognition algorithms.

In the late 1990s we saw two seminal contributions in sketch-based interfaces for 3D modeling. The SKETCH system, developed by Zeleznik et al. in 1996, used a gestural interface and inferencing mechanisms to create 3D objects out of standard 3D geometric primitives such as cuboids, cylinders, and cones for conceptual 3D modeling. In 1999, the Teddy system, developed by Igarashi et al., let users make more free-form, organic 3D models. Both of these interfaces showed that sketch-based interfaces for this type of task is a very natural one since users could make rough drawings of the models they are interested in and have the computer interpret them to generate the 3D geometry. These systems led to a significant amount of new work on sketch-based interfaces for creating and manipulating 3D models.

In the last decade, we have seen an explosion of both sketch-based interfaces and pen-based computing devices. Better and faster hardware coupled with new machine learning techniques for more accurate recognition and more robust depth inferencing techniques for sketch-based modeling have enabled SBIM to enter a new era in research and development. This is one of the main reasons why this is a timely book: it provides us with a very useful collection of state-of-the-art technology from leaders of the SBIM field.

Although great strides have been made, there is still a lot to do to bring SBIM to the mainstream. Faster CPUs, better digitization technology, better battery life are just some of the areas that must be improved from a hardware perspective. More robust recognition algorithms that can handle subtle variability in user hand-writing as well as better depth inferencing in sketch-based modeling are still unsolved problems. Integration with other interaction modalities such as multi-touch and speech recognition to create multi-modal interfaces is now an important research area. Usability analysis of these interfaces is also critically important to advancing SBIM. The current book presents a snapshot of the state of the art in the area. I look forward to the advances that will be made in SBIM in the coming years and I hope that the readers will find inspiration in the valuable collection of articles gathered herein to stimulate their endeavors and advance this important field.

Brown University Andries van Dam

Preface

Sketch-based interfaces date back to Ivan Sutherland's pioneering work. SketchPad, a pen-based system, preceded the ubiquitous mouse by several years. However, SketchPad was too advanced for its day. For many years, this seminal work has remained more of a source of inspiration and awe than a trend to be followed.

Personal computers became sufficiently powerful in the nineties to support research in sketched-based interfaces in Interactive Computer Graphics and Human-Computer Interaction (HCI). People can now interact with drawings, editing and augmenting sketches in many different ways. Indeed, electronic drawings can be parsed and converted to digital objects such as pictures, diagrams and 3D models. Sketching can also be used for editing and animating these objects, a feature not possible on paper. Advances in this area provide the possibility of giving virtual life to simple sketches and effectively use computers to enhance creative thinking. Yet, for all its deceptive simplicity, sketching remains a hard challenge to meet for computer scientists. This is because sketches engage human intellect and abilities in ways that are difficult to approach with machines.

Thus, sketch-based interfaces are the subject of much lively research in recent years. Researchers from many disciplines have contributed to the body of knowledge on sketch-based interfaces. As such, it is difficult to gather a completely inclusive compilation of work done on this topic. Notably, sketching has become a recurring theme at many HCI conferences such as CHI, UIST, IUI, and AVI, and the IEEE Symposium on Visual Languages and Computing (VL/HCC). The Association for the Advancement of Artificial Intelligence (AAAI) held symposia on diagrammatic representations and reasoning, and sketch understanding. Additionally, the graphics community has usually published papers from this area, in conferences such as SIGGRAPH, Eurographics and the SMARTGRAPHICS symposium. Most notably, since 2004, the Eurographics Association has held a series of annual symposia on Sketch-Based Interfaces and Modeling (SBIM).

This book provides an overview of the topics covered in this emerging area of Interactive Computer Graphics, in two main parts. The first part contains chapters related to sketch-based interfaces and pen-based computing. The second part includes chapters about creation and modification of 3D models, covering the use of sketches in graphical and geometrical modeling. We aim to present a collection of works representing recent developments in this area, within the scope of interfaces and modeling, hoping that this book proves to be a valuable resource for students, researchers and academics.

We would like to gratefully thank and acknowledge the many people who have assisted in the preparation of this book and reviewing its chapters.

Joaquim Jorge
Faramarz Samavati

Contents

Chapter 1
Introduction

Faramarz F. Samavati, Luke Olsen, and Joaquim A. Jorge

1.1 Sketch-based Interfaces

Sketch-based interfaces have come a long way since Ivan Sutherland's seminal work. Indeed, Sketchpad [24] spearheaded many techniques in both Computer-Science and Human-Computer Interaction, a system that not only improved on its predecessors but was also an improvement on many of its successors, to quote C.A.R. Hoare [10]. Each generation of sketch-based interfaces can be traced to different hardware devices that shaped their inception and evolution: the lightpen, the digitizing tablet and stylus combination, later the mouse, more recently tablet PCs and multitouch surfaces. These, in combination with the available platform computing power, largely shaped both research and commercial products.

Sketchpad featured an interactive system that allowed users to create engineering drawings using a lightpen, as shown on Fig. 1.1. The calligraphic interface combined sketched input with graphical constraints which were solved by the system to beautify the drawing without the need for explicit commands entered by the user. The GRAIL system, developed by RAND corporation [7] to work with the first tablet digitizing input device, allowed engineers to enter flowcharts using a combination of drawings, text recognition and pen gestures. GRAIL (depicted in Fig. 1.2) used

F.F. Samavati · L. Olsen
Dept. Computer Science, University of Calgary, University Drive NW 2500, Calgary, Alberta T2N 1N4, Canada

F.F. Samavati
e-mail: samavati@ucalgary.ca

L. Olsen
e-mail: ljolsen@ucalgary.ca

J.A. Jorge (✉)
Depto. Engenharia Informática Instituto Superior Técnico, Universidade Técnica de Lisboa, Avenida Rovisco Pais, Lisboa 1049-001, Portugal
e-mail: jaj@vimmi.inesc-id.pt

J. Jorge, F. Samavati (eds.), *Sketch-based Interfaces and Modeling*,
DOI 10.1007/978-1-84882-812-4_1, © Springer-Verlag London Limited 2011

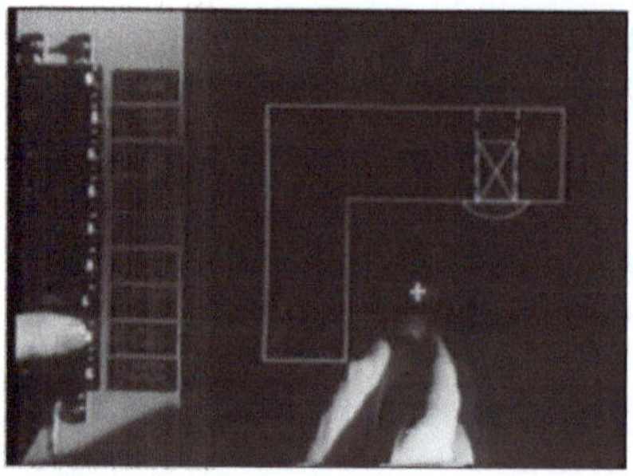

Fig. 1.1 The Sketchpad system in use. It is possible to see the lightpen and button pad on the left. Reproduced from http://www.archive.org

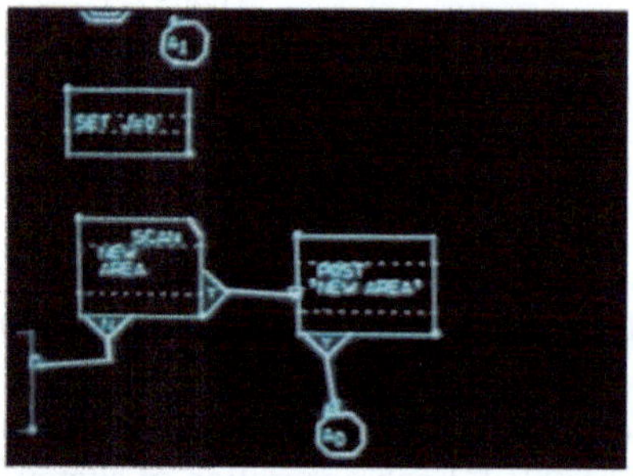

Fig. 1.2 A screenshot of the GRAIL system. Reproduced from http://www.archive.org

a combination of domain knowledge and contextual information to largely do away with the need for explicit commands, illustrating the power of Calligraphic User Interfaces.[1]

While the mouse was invented by Douglas Englebart in the mid-sixties, it did not see widespread use until the Apple Macintosh adopted it as a key component to its desktop user interface two decades later.

The topic of Sketch-Based Interfaces was largely dormant until the early nineties when the first pen-based computers appeared on the market. However, these early platforms were significantly underpowered to tackle handwriting and sketch recognition. By the end of the decade most tablet PC companies had gone out of business. Pen-based interfaces survived in the commercial marketplace thanks to PDAs such as the Apple Newton and the Palm Pilot.

More recently, the advent of multi-touch displays and tablet PCs that combine tactile and pen input has spurred new interest in Calligraphic Interfaces. Also, there is emerging research in three-dimensional applications of sketching in virtual immersive environments, especially in combination with other modalities.

[1]Calligraphic Interfaces, also known as Calligraphic User Interfaces, designate a family of computer applications organized around human-created drawings whether they are used to depict shapes, prepare designs, generate ideas, or simply to enter commands or depictions into a computer [14].

1.1.1 Sketching Issues and Research Topics in HCI

Sketching appears to be a concise, powerful and fast alternative to many conventional input modalities. Indeed, its strengths and weaknesses as a computer input modality come from the very same features. Through sketching people can express, interpret and modify shapes and relationships among drawing elements without much regard to neatness, alignment or precise measurement. However, the ambiguity and imprecision characteristic of free-hand drawings are also a major impediment to developing effective recognizers. Indeed, while other modalities, such as speech recognition and natural language, seem to be making significant strides, sketch recognition has yet to see widespread adoption as an unconstrained input technique. This is probably because the terseness and expressive power of sketches come at the cost of significant human higher cognitive abilities being involved, even more so than for other challenging recognition-based modalities. In their literature survey of sketching in design, Johnson et al. [13] indicate four main challenges to developing both useful and usable general-purpose sketch-based interfaces:

- Native hardware support for pen-based interaction
- Comprehensive robust toolkits for sketch-based systems
- User-friendly methods to train and model recognizable input
- Better interaction techniques for sketch-based systems

The forthcoming sections directly address many of these challenges with the possible exception of developing hardware support for Calligraphic User Interfaces. While hardware support is important, we have deemed it out of scope for this book, which focuses primarily on interfaces and applications proper.

Toolkits are important, but as a software engineering construct they are largely tied to GUI-style interfaces from the late eighties. It may be argued that novel software engineering techniques, methods and artifacts need to emerge to support the new generation of Calligraphic User Interfaces [14].

The third challenge is by and large being addressed by current and ongoing work in the community. Indeed, even if successful at first, hardwired recognizers are hardly the ultimate approach to recognizing sketch input. This is because the endless variations, rich vocabulary and inherent imprecision to user's input make it very difficult to devise simple techniques that satisfactorily handle most cases. Therefore extensible approaches are needed to augment the vocabulary and constructs of a recognition-based interface in powerful yet usable manners.

As for the fourth challenge, recognition-based user interfaces pose interesting problems to HCI researchers. Because sketch input can be ambiguous, the interface should approach it in a different way from the discrete, deterministic techniques so successfully applied to handling mouse and keyboard input. Further, resolving ambiguity can and should be delegated to humans, requiring good interaction design techniques to be brought to bear on the problem. Another very interesting issue in HCI for Calligraphic Interfaces is handling errors which cannot be ascribed to users. Handling these in a graceful if not creative manner is still a vibrant research topic to be addressed by the community.

While most research has focused on the early stages of design and modeling, there is a need for significant progress in terms of interfacing with existing CAD systems, applications and at the final stages of design where more detailed information is entered. Indeed, most of the current applications focus on ideation, whereas little thought has been given to make these ideas and shapes manufacturable.

1.1.2 Recognition

Sketch Recognition is central to Calligraphic Interfaces. This is because it allows applications to become organized around what users draw in a quasi-declarative way, instead of focusing on commands or constructive sequences as many traditional interfaces do. Sketch Recognition is related to both handwriting and gesture recognition, in the sense that it supersedes both. Plamondon and Srihari provide a comprehensive survey on handwriting recognition [21].

Contrary to handwriting or textual recognition, sketches have a non-linear syntax, in that meaning is ascribed to a drawing by looking at shapes and spatial relations rather than sequences, which is the main organizing principle in linear languages. Diagrammatic notations provide excellent means for expressing concepts due to the descriptive power of graphical symbols and spatial arrangements. Graphics Recognition is the subfield of Document Image Analysis and Recognition concerned with interpreting non-textual information present in document images. This field is important because many documents use a diagrammatic notation: i.e., architectural floor plans, mechanical drawings, electronic circuit diagrams, musical scores, flow charts, etc. In particular *sketches*, which roughly express abstract concepts, are a kind of diagram consisting of freehand line drawings. Because of their concise and expressive nature, sketches are a very effective communication mechanism. Thus, online recognition for sketching interfaces has elicited a growing interest among the HCI community [18].

Gesture recognition has been a heavily researched related area. While Ivan Sutherland's work was mostly concerned with a simple set of primitives, Rubine's recognizer allowed single stroke gestures to be learned and later recognized via a simple linear classifier [22], in one of the most cited papers in the field of gesture/symbol recognition. This is because recognition is at the heart of any system that handles sketching. In their comprehensive survey on sketching, Johnson et al. [13] identify some key issues in sketch recognition. These include when to recognize sketches (recognition can distract users from the task at hand); what symbols to recognize; how much of a drawing needs to be recognized; how to segment input—many drawings contain overlapping symbols or strokes. A key issue is how to group strokes in order to recognize what the user meant to draw. Recognizers need this information to perform adequately. Another important issue is what recognition strategy to apply. Many have been proposed over the years with varying degrees of success.

Training recognizers is also an important area. Most interfaces resorting to diagrammatic representations require a rather large vocabulary of symbols (or spatial arrangements of strokes) that needs to be described if we are to develop algorithms or techniques to handle these. Instead of hard-coding these symbols as some have done successfully [8], many systems use a trainable recognizer. However, these need to be provided with good examples of what to recognize.

Another important issue is how to handle recognition errors. Recognition results are often inaccurate or ambiguous; or they return unwanted symbols. This comes both as a curse and an opportunity. Indeed, traditional interfaces assume that errors are somehow the user's fault and worry about how to best convey the appropriate messages to the user. In recognition interfaces, however, it is often best to let the user disambiguate or handle recognition errors in a constructive way to either correct the drawing or retrain the recognizer. Much research still needs to be done in this area.

Finally, two other important areas not addressed above are context and visual languages. Indeed symbols often change meaning depending on the context (other symbols surrounding them) or semantic domain. Both are related to visual languages. Whereas many syntax-driven approaches use some form of visual languages and parsing to extract meaning from diagrams [17] domain-specific knowledge often needs to be specifically coded and addressed at several stages of recognition. Indeed, providing multi-domain recognizers remains an interesting challenge.

A good example of recognition-level research that addresses many of these problems appears in Chap. 2, in which Christine Alvarado approaches multi-domain hierarchical free-sketch recognition using graphical models. We have selected this work because it touches many of the issues in sketch recognition discussed above.

1.1.3 Modes

According to WikiPedia[2] a mode is a "distinct setting within a computer program or any physical machine interface, in which the same user inputs will produce perceived different results than it would in other settings". Thus one important problem in most sketching interfaces is mode switching. Sketching user interfaces interpret input differently depending on which mode the program is in, for instance, drawing applications have input modes such as select, edit object, or input drawing, GUI programs often show which mode they are in by redundant means (cursor, selected entries on a palette, etc.). For example, the cursor will change shape to a pencil to indicate that users can draw when the pencil tool is active. Or it may change to a ruler to indicate that users may enter the corners of a rectangle. In both cases users can press a mouse button and drag the cursor. But the drawing program will parse user input in terms of the active tool. In sketch-based user interfaces sometimes users may not be aware of which mode the program is in, or may be unsure of how to activate the desired mode. Managing modes often distracts people from the task at hand by forcing them to focus on the syntax of the tool they are using rather than their work. This is a significant problem in Calligraphic User Interfaces whose functionality is not as self-disclosing as that of conventional desktop applications.

---

[2]http://en.wikipedia.org/wiki/Mode_(computer_interface), accessed October 2010.

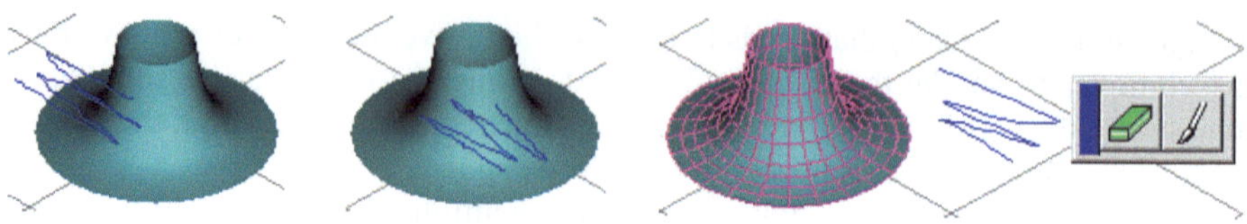

Fig. 1.3 Example of ambiguous input handling in GiDeS. On the left, a stroke which overlaps the outline of a screen object is interpreted as a delete command. In the middle, a stroke totally contained inside a screen object signifies recolor. On the right a scratch gesture totally outside a screen object becomes ambiguous: a menu appears on screen asking the user which of the two meanings should be assumed. Reproduced with permission from [15]

Applications resort to two different approaches to mode switching. In Sketchpad, users changed mode by operating physical buttons with the left hand, while entering drawings with the right hand. In contrast, GRAIL would infer the correct mode by looking at ink drawn by users in the context in which it was drawn. For example, a crossing gesture over a graphical entity would erase it. Text entered inside a box would become a label and a rectangle drawn on an empty area would be recognized as a box. This is fine as long as there are no ambiguous interpretations to a gesture. Some Calligraphic applications such as GiDES [15] handle this by exposing the ambiguity to users and letting them make choices, as can be seen in Fig. 1.3.

In Chap. 3, Eric Saund and Edward Lank approach the problem of minimizing modes in sketch interfaces by using an Inferred Mode protocol. They try to automatically recognize what mode the application should be in according to the user's input in the context of what has been drawn, to the extent that an action can be unambiguously determined.

1.1.4 Sketch-based Applications

There are many research applications that illustrate the power of Sketch-Based Interfaces. Among these we have selected four which address many of the issues highlighted above.

Many sketch-based interfaces parse diagrams to develop simulations of physical or abstract entities. In Chap. 4 Tom Stahovich describes Pen-based user interfaces for engineering and educational applications, in the mechanical and electrical engineering domains. The chapter contributes work on three fundamental sketch understanding problems. The first is pen stroke segmentation, to decompose a pen stroke into geometric primitives. The second, sketch parsing, clusters pen strokes or geometric primitives into groups representing individual symbols. Last, symbol recognition classifies symbols once they have been located by a parser. This chapter provides excellent insights ranging from the low-level details of stroke/ink processing to the high-level issues of symbol recognition and semantic analysis.

In Chap. 5, Joseph LaViola describes MathPad, a system for Mathematical sketching. Diagrams and illustrations are often used to help explain mathematical concepts. Moreover, they are commonplace in math and physics textbooks and provide intuition into abstract principles. Unfortunately, static diagrams generally assist only in the initial formulation of a mathematical problem, not in its analysis or visualization. MathPad describes how to combine on-line recognition with a gestural interface to recognize mathematical formulas and associate variables and values with a physical simulation in order to enter, solve and visualize mathematical expressions. The author describes how to address modes by an ingenuous combination of location-aware gestures, imperative gestures and context in order to make modes largely invisible.

In Chap. 6 Michiel van de Panne and Dana Sharon present an interesting approach to Sketch recognition using flexible parts-based spatial templates. In automatic recognition of drawings for modeling, it is often difficult to describe what is to be recognized in terms of two-dimensional depictions of three-dimensional entities, especially if we want to afford a degree of flexibility to end-users. Their key insight is to use a 2D template for each class of object to be modeled. Templates provide explicit descriptions for optional parts, and thus constitute a compact and scalable approach for modeling many classes of objects as particular layouts of a collection of parts. This helps to avoid the combinatorial explosion that would otherwise occur, by explicitly modeling all possible combinations of parts that might constitute an object. The template structure also provides context for recognizing the parts themselves, making it easier to recognize those parts. Their system matches key points on a sketch to aid in top–down reconstruction, using a branch-and-bound search to identify the template (and corresponding three-dimensional model) that most closely matches a two-dimensional sketch. While their technique looks at first more limited than parsing and is constrained to the template database it provides a seemingly scalable approach to an open-ended problem, in that new templates can in principle easily be learnt from examples.

Finally, in Chap. 7 Manuel João Fonseca and Joaquim Jorge discuss Sketch-based retrieval of vector drawings, describing a Calligraphic User Interface to retrieve clip-art media using a structural approach. Their approach uses topological and geometric information automatically extracted from drawings to derive a multilevel description, which affords a coarse-to-fine comparison between simple sketches and complex vector drawings using a relational graph. Their approach avoids graph matching by using graph spectra as features in a scalable manner. They also show how this retrieval mechanism can be integrated into a 3D sketch-based modeling tools (GiDeS system) applying a paradigm of implicit retrieval, whereby sketched objects are automatically used as queries and returned results are presented as modeling suggestions at the user interface.

1.2 Creation and Modification of 3D Models

Model creation is a major bottleneck in production pipelines, involving complex and diverse shapes with intricate inter-relationships. User interfaces in modeling have traditionally followed the WIMP (Windows, Icons, Menus, Pointer) paradigm.

Though functional and very powerful, they can also be cumbersome and daunting to a novice user, due to numerous commands hidden under layers of functionality. Thus, creating complex models using computers can require considerable expertise and effort. Sketch-based interfaces have also been explored in this context, with the goal of allowing hand-drawn sketches to be used in the modeling process, from rough model creation through fine detail construction. However, mapping 2D sketches to 3D modeling operations is a difficult task, rife with ambiguity. SBIM applications for 3d modeling can be categorized according to how they interpret a sketch, of which there are three primary methods: to create a 3D model, to add details to an existing model, or to deform and manipulate a model.

A model creation system attempts to reconstruct a 3D model from the 2D sketched input. The gamut of creation systems can be divided into two categories, *suggestive* and *constructive*, based on whether or not the input strokes are mapped directly to the output model (in a suggestive system, they are not).

This aligns with the classical distinction between reconstruction and recognition. Suggestive systems first recognize a sketch against a set of templates, and then use the template to reconstruct the geometry. Constructive systems forgo the recognition step, and simply try to reconstruct the geometry. In other words, suggestive systems are akin to visual memory, whereas constructive systems are more rule-based [11].

Because suggestive systems use template objects to interpret strokes, their expressiveness is determined by the richness of the template set. Constructive systems, meanwhile, map input sketches directly to model features; therefore, their expressiveness is limited only by the robustness of the reconstruction algorithm and the ability of the system's interface to expose the full potential.

1.2.1 Suggestive Systems

Suggestive-stroke systems are characterized by the fact that they have some "memory" of 3D shapes built in, which guides their interpretation of input sketches. If a system is designed for character creation, for example, the shape memory can be chosen to identify which parts of a sketch correspond to a head, torso, and so forth. Then the conversion to 3D is much easier, because the shapes and relative proportions of each part is known a priori.

Within the suggestive-stroke category, two main approaches can be uses. In the first approach, the system extrapolates a final 3D shape based on only a few iconic strokes. A classical example is the SKETCH system of Zeleznik et al. [27], which uses simple groups of strokes to define primitive 3D objects. Three linear strokes meeting at a point, for instance, are replaced by a cuboid whose dimensions are defined by the strokes.

In the second approach of suggestive systems, a template objects from a database of template objects [9, 23] is retrieved. Rather than simple primitive objects, the templates are more complete and complex objects. And from the user's perspective, they must provide a complete and meaningful sketch of the desired object, rather than just a few evocative strokes.

This approach is more extensible than extrapolation, because adding new behavior to the system is as easy as adding a new object to the database. Conversely, because the building blocks—the shape templates—are more complex, it may be impossible to attain a specific result by combining the template objects.

The increased complexity on both the input and output sides is reflected in the underlying matching algorithms. A retrieval-based system faces the problem of matching 2D sketches to 3D templates. To evaluate their similarity in 3D would require reconstruction of the sketch, which is the ultimate problem to be solved. Therefore, comparison is typically done by extracting a 2D form the 3D template object.

1.2.2 Constructive Systems

Pure reconstruction is a more difficult task than recognize-then-reconstruct, because the latter uses predefined knowledge to define the 3D geometry of a sketch, thereby skirting the ambiguity problem to some extent (ambiguity still exists in the recognition stage). Constructive-stroke systems must reconstruct a 3D object from a sketch based on rules alone. Because reconstruction is such a difficult and interdisciplinary problem, there have been many diverse attempts at solving it. All the techniques in the second part of this book propose constructive systems.

A common approach for constructive systems is to interactively reconstruct the object as the user sketches. This allows the user to immediately see the result and possibly correct or refine it, and also allows the system to employ more simple reconstruction rules. The most common approach for creating "manufactured objects" is *extrusion*, a term for creating a surface by "pushing" a profile curve through space along some vector (or curve); see Fig. 1.4 for an illustration. This technique is well-suited to creating models with hard edges, such as cubes (extruded from a square) and cylinders (from a circle).

Reconstructing smooth, natural objects requires a different approach. It has been observed that our visual system prefers to interpret smooth line drawings as 3D contours [11]. Accordingly, the majority of constructive SBIM systems choose to interpret strokes as contour lines (see Chaps. 8 to 12).

There are still many objects that correspond to a given contour, so further assumptions must be made to reconstruct a sketch. A key idea in constructive systems is to choose a simple shape according to some internal rules, and let the user refine the model later.

Skeleton-based approaches are a prevalent method for creating a 3D model from a contour sketch. The skeleton is defined as the line from which the closest contour points are equidistant.

The simplest non-trivial skeleton is a straight line. In a symmetric sketch, the skeleton is a straight line aligned with the axis of symmetry. To generate a surface, the sketch can be rotated around the skeleton, creating a surface of revolution (see Chap. 10). A single stroke can also specify the contour, with either a fixed or user-sketched rotation axis to define the surface.

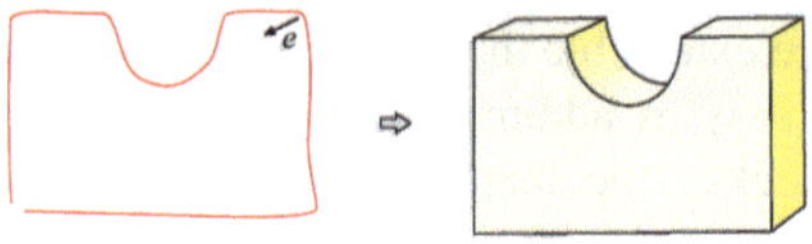

Fig. 1.4 Extrusion is a simple method for reconstructing a contour, by sweeping it along an extrusion vector *e*

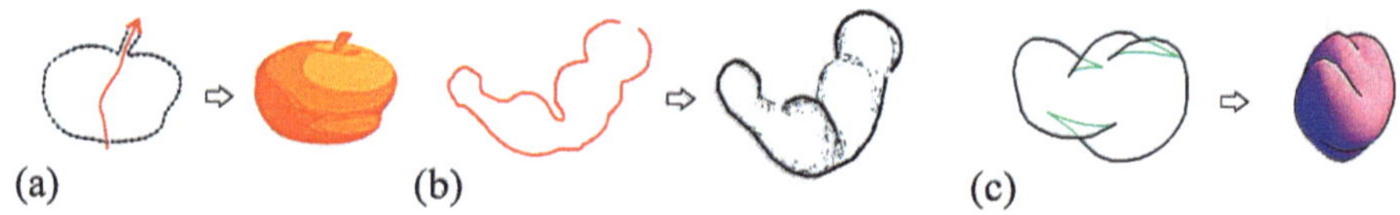

Fig. 1.5 Free-form model creation from contour sketches: **a** rotational blending surfaces have non-branching skeletons [5]; **b** Teddy inflates a sketch about its chordal axis (reproduced with permission from [12]); **c** SmoothSketch infers hidden contour lines (*green lines*) before inflation (reproduced from [16])

In Chap. 10, this idea is extended to a generalized surface of revolution, in which the skeleton is given by the medial axis between two strokes (the authors refer to this construction as *rotational blending surfaces*). The system also allows the user to provide a third stroke, which defines a free-form cross-section, increasing the expressiveness of this construction.

Unfortunately, parametric surfaces—including surfaces of revolution—suffer from topological limitations. The resulting object can always be parameterized over a 2D plane, and the skeletons contain no branches. For contours with branching skeletons, a more robust method is required.

For simple (i.e. non-intersecting) closed contours, inflation is an unambiguous way to reconstruct a plausible 3D model. The Teddy system (Chap. 8), for instance, inflates a contour by pushing vertices away from the chordal axis according to their distance from the contour; see Fig. 1.5b for a typical result.

The skeletal representation of a contour also integrates naturally with an implicit surface representation. In the approach of Alexe et al. [1], spherical implicit primitives are placed at each skeleton vertex; when the primitives are blended together, the result is a smooth surface whose contour matches the input sketch. ShapeShop (Chap. 11) instead uses variational implicit surfaces [25], which use the sketched contour to define constraints in the implicit function.

A different way to reconstruct a contour sketch is to fit a surface that is as smooth as possible. Surface fitting interprets input strokes as geometric constraints of the form, 'the surface passes through this contour.' The outside normal of the contour also constrains the surface normal. These constraints define an optimization problem: of the infinite number of candidates, find one suitable candidate that satisfies the constraints. Additional constraints such as smoothness and thin-plate energy [26] push the system toward a solution. The FiberMesh system (Chap. 9) uses a non-linear optimization technique to generate smooth meshes while also supporting sharp creases and darts.

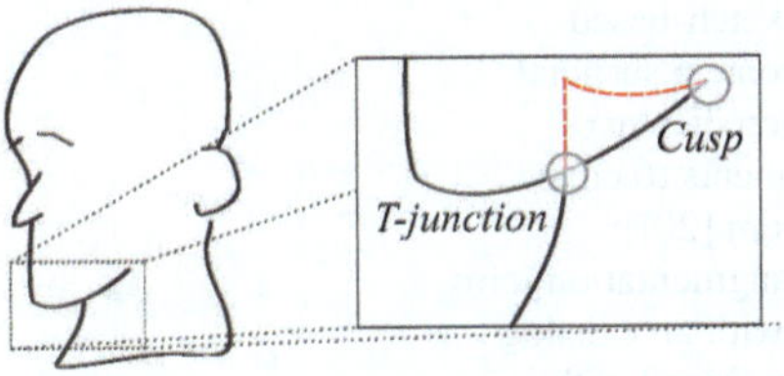

Fig. 1.6 The contour of an object conveys a lot of shape information. *Cutout*: T-junctions and cusps imply hidden contour lines (*red*)

For non-simple contours, such as ones containing self-intersections, a simple inflation method will fail. Recall that the contour of an object separates those parts of the object facing toward the viewer from those facing away. In non-trivial objects, there may be parts of the surface that are facing the viewer, yet are not visible to the viewer because it is occluded by a part of the surface nearer to the viewer. Figure 1.6 shows an example of this: the contour of the neck is occluded by the chin. Note that where the neck contour passes behind the chin, we see a T shape in the projected contour (called a *T-junction*), and the chin contour ends abruptly (called a *cusp*). T-junctions and cusps indicate the presence of a hidden contour; Williams [26] has proposed a method for using these to infer hidden contour lines in an image.

Karpenko and Hughes in Chap. 12 use Williams' algorithm, including support for not only T-junctions but also cusps. They take this approach to reconstruction: a smooth shape is attained by first creating a "topological embedding" and then constructing a mass–spring system (with springs along each mesh edge) and finding a smooth equilibrium state.

1.2.3 Augmentation

Creating a 3D model from 2D sketches is a difficult problem, whose only really feasible solutions lead to simplistic reconstructions. Creating more elaborate details on an existing model is somewhat easier, however, since the model serves as a 3D reference for mapping strokes into 3D. Augmentations can be made in either an *surficial* or *additive* manner.

Surficial augmentation allows users to sketch features on the surface of the model, such as sharp creases [4, 20] (see also Chap. 8) or curve-following slice deformations [28]. After a sketch has been projected onto a surface, features are created by displacing the surface along the sketch. Usually the surface is displaced along the normal direction, suitable for creating details like veins (Fig. 1.7a). The sketched lines may also be treated as new geometric constraints in surface optimization approaches.

Surficial augmentations can often be done without changing the underlying surface representation. For example, to create a sharp feature on a triangle mesh, the existing model edges can be used to approximate the sketched feature and displaced along their normal direction to actually create the visible feature [19, 20].

Additive augmentation uses constructive strokes to define a new part of a model, such as a limb or outcropping, along with additional stroke(s) that indicate where

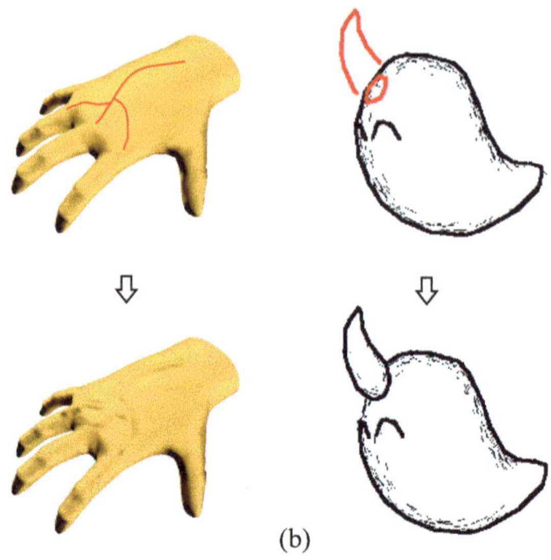

Fig. 1.7 Sketch-based augmentations: **a** surficial augmentation displaces surface elements to create features (from [20]); **b** additive augmentation joins a new part with an existing model (reproduced with permission from [12]). The latter figure also includes surficial features (the eyes)

to connect the new part to the original model (see Chaps. 8 and 9). For example, the extrusion operator in Teddy uses a circular stroke to initiate the operation and define the region to extrude; the user then draws a contour defining the new part, which is inflated and attached to the original model at the connection part (Fig. 1.7b). ShapeShop (Chap. 11) exploits the easy blending afforded by an implicit surface representation to enable additive augmentation, with parameterized control of smoothness at the connection point. The system does not require explicit specification of the connection point, since implicit surfaces naturally blend together when in close proximity. Additive augmentation only affects the original model near the connection point.

The somewhat subjective difference between the two types of augmentation is one of scale: surficial augmentations are small-scale and require only simple changes to the underlying surface, whereas additive augmentations are on the scale of the original model. The distinction can become fuzzy when a system allows more pronounced surficial augmentations, such as Zelinka and Garland's curve analogy framework [28], which embeds 2D curve networks into arbitrary meshes and then displaces the mesh along these curves according to a sketched curve.

1.2.4 Deformation

Besides augmentation, there have been many SBIM systems (including those that have been described in this book) that support sketch-based editing operations, such as cutting, bending, tunneling (creating a hole), contour oversketching, segmentation, and affine transformations. And, like augmentation, sketch-based deformations

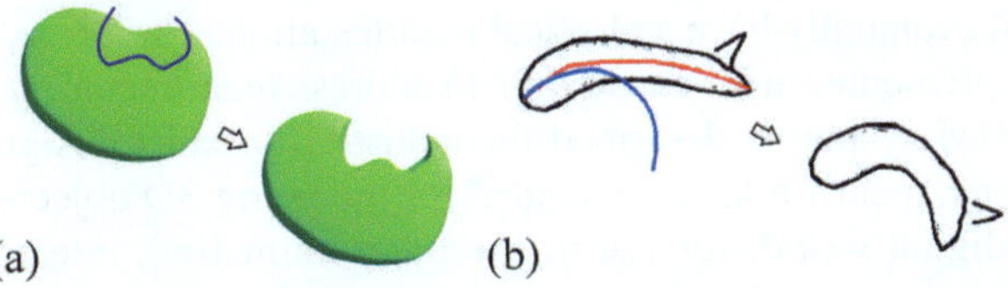

Fig. 1.8 Sketch-based deformations: **a** cutting strokes (*blue*) define a cutting plane along the view direction (Chap. 13); **b** bending a model so that the reference stroke (*red*) is aligned with the target blue stroke (Chap. 8)

have a straightforward and intuitive interpretation because the existing model or scene anchors the sketch in 3D.

To cut a model, the user simply needs to rotate the model to an appropriate viewpoint and draw a stroke where they want to divide the model. The stroke can then be interpreted as a cutting plane, defined by sweeping the stroke along the view direction (Fig. 1.8a). Tunneling is a special case of cutting, in which the cutting stroke is a closed contour contained within a model—everything within the projected stroke is discarded, creating a hole.

Other deformations are based on the idea of oversketching. For example, bending and twisting deform an object by matching a *reference* stroke to a *target* stroke, as shown in Fig. 1.8b. Contour oversketching is also based on matching a reference to a target stroke, but in this case, the reference is a contour extracted from the model itself [19].

In Chap. 9, a handle-based deformation is supported, allowing object contours to be manipulated like an elastic. When a stroke is "grabbed" and dragged, the stroke is elastically deformed orthogonal to the view plane, thereby changing the geometric constraint(s) represented by the stroke. As the stroke is moved, their surface optimization algorithm recomputes a new fair surface interactively.

Model assembly—typically an arduous task, as each component must be translated, rotated, and scaled correctly—is another editing task that can benefit from a sketch-based interface. In Chap. 10, a technique is proposed for applying affine transformations to a model with a single stroke. From a U-shaped transformation stroke, their method determines a rotation from the stroke's principal components, a non-uniform scaling from the width and height, and a translation from the stroke's projection into 3D. By selecting components and drawing a simple stroke, the model assembly task is greatly accelerated.

1.2.5 Modeling Applications

Knowing the nature of the model and the target application helps to infer the third dimension better and enhances the usability of the interface and the quality of the models in SBIM. There are many specific applications in which free-form sketch input is a very useful and powerful interface paradigm. The applications can be classified in two groups. *Computer-aided design* applications are targeted at modeling 3D objects that will eventually have a physical manifestation. Therefore, input sketches need to be complemented with constraints to address manufacturing limitations. In Chap. 13, a SBIM system is described for industrial product design. *Content creation* applications, meanwhile, are intended for modeling 3D objects that will exist usually in the digital world, for use in computer animation, interactive computer games, film, and so on. In this domain, geometric precision is less important than allowing the artist to create free-form surfaces from freehand input. Dressing and hair-styling are two difficult examples in this area. In Chap. 14, several SBIM techniques are presented for designing cloth and hair for a virtual character.

This book provides an overview of the areas covered by Sketch-Based Interfaces and Modeling. We hope that through the discussions and examples provided herein readers will be motivated to further contribute to the research motives in this rapidly evolving and very exciting multidisciplinary area.

References

1. Alexe, A., Gaildrat, V., Barthe, L.: Interactive modelling from sketches using spherical implicit functions. In: Proc. of Int. Conference on Computer Graphics, Virtual Reality, Visualisation and Interaction in Africa (AFRIGRAPH '04), pp. 25–34 (2004)
2. Autodesk Inc.: AutoCAD. http://www.autodesk.com/autocad
3. Autodesk Inc.: Maya. http://www.autodesk.com/maya
4. Biermann, H., Martin, I., Zorin, D., Bernardini, F.: Sharp features on multiresolution subdivision surfaces. Graphics Models (Proc. of Pacific Graphics '01) **64**(2), 61–77 (2001)
5. Cherlin, J.J., Samavati, F., Sousa, M.C., Jorge, J.A.: Sketch-based modeling with few strokes. In: Proc. of Spring Conference on Computer Graphics (SCCG '05), pp. 137–145 (2005)
6. Dassault Systemes: Catia. http://www.catia.com
7. Ellis, T.O., Heafner, J.F., Sibley, W.L.: The grail project: An experiment in man-machine communications. Tech. rep., RAND Corporation (1969)
8. Fonseca, M.J., Pimentel, C., Jorge, J.A.: Cali: An online scribble recognizer for calligraphic interfaces. Tech. Rep. SS-02-08, AAAI (2002)
9. Funkhouser, T., Min, P., Kazhdan, M., Chen, J., Halderman, A., Dobkin, D., Jacobs, D.: A search engine for 3d models. ACM Transactions on Graphics (Proc. of SIGGRAPH '03) **22**(1), 83–105 (2003)
10. Hoare, C.A.R.: Hints on programming language design. SAIL Computer Science Department TR CS-403, October 1973
11. Hoffman, D.D.: Visual Intelligence: How We Create what We See. Norton, New York (2000)
12. Igarashi, T., Matsuoka, S., Tanaka, H.: Teddy: A sketching interface for 3d freeform design. In: Proc. of SIGGRAPH'99, pp. 409–416 (1999)
13. Johnson, G., Gross, M.D., Hong, J., Do, E.Y.L.: Computational support for sketching in design: A review. In: Foundations and Trends in Human Computer Interaction, vol. 2. Now, Hanover (2009). doi:10.1561/1100000013
14. Jorge, J.A.P.: Parsing adjacency languages for calligraphic interfaces. Ph.D. thesis, Rensselaer Polytechnic Institute (1995)
15. Jorge, J.A., Silva, F.N., Cardoso, D.T.: Gides++. In: Proc. of the 12th Annual Portuguese Computer Graphics Meeting, pp. 167–171 (2003)
16. Karpenko, O.A., Hughes, J.F.: Smoothsketch: 3d free-form shapes from complex sketches. In: Proc. of SIGGRAPH '06, pp. 589–598 (2006)
17. Mas, J., Llados, J., Sanchez, G., Jorge, J.: A syntactic approach based on distortion-tolerant adjacency grammars and a spatial-directed parser to interpret sketched diagrams. Pattern Recognition (2010)

18. Narayanan, N.H., Hübscher, R.: Visual language theory: Towards a human computer interaction perspective. In: Visual Language Theory, pp. 85–127. Springer, Berlin (1998)
19. Nealen, A., Sorkine, O., Alexa, M., Cohen-Or, D.: A sketch-based interface for detail-preserving mesh editing. In: Proc. of SIGGRAPH '05, pp. 1142–1147 (2005)
20. Olsen, L., Samavati, F., Sousa, M.C., Jorge, J.: Sketch-based mesh augmentation. In: Proc. of the 2nd Eurographics Workshop on Sketch-Based Interfaces and Modeling (SBIM) (2005)
21. Plamondon, R., Srihari, S.: On-line and off-line handwriting recognition: A comprehensive survey. IEEE Transactions on Pattern Analysis and Machine Intelligence **22**(1), 63–84 (2000)
22. Rubine, D.H.: Specifying gestures by example. In: Proceedings of the 18th Annual SIGGRAPH Conference on Computer Graphics and Interactive Techniques, pp. 329–337. ACM, New York (1991)
23. Shin, H., Igarashi, T.: Magic canvas: interactive design of a 3-d scene prototype from freehand sketches. In: Proc. of Graphics Interface (GI '07), pp. 63–70 (2007)
24. Sutherland, I.: Sketchpad: A man-machine graphical communication system. In: AFIPS Conference Proceedings, vol. 23, pp. 323–328 (1963)
25. Turk, G., O'Brien, J.: Variational implicit surfaces. Tech. rep., Georgia Institute of Technology (1999)
26. Williams, L.R.: Perceptual completion of occluded surfaces. Ph.D. thesis, University of Massachusetts (1994)
27. Zeleznik, R., Herndon, K., Hughes, J.: SKETCH: An interface for sketching 3d scenes. In: Proc. of SIGGRAPH '96. pp. 163–170 (1996)
28. Zelinka, S., Garland, M.: Mesh modeling with curve analogies. In: Proc. of Pacific Graphics '04, pp. 94–98 (2004)

Part I
Sketch-based Interfaces

Chapter 2
Multi-domain Hierarchical Free-Sketch Recognition Using Graphical Models

Christine Alvarado

2.1 Introduction

Consider the following physics problem:

> An 80-kg person is standing on the edge of a 3.6-m cliff. A 3-meter rope is attached to a point directly above his head, and on the end of the rope is a 40-kg medicine ball. The ball swings down and knocks the person off the cliff. Fortunately, there is a (padded) cart at the bottom. How far away from the cliff must the cart be placed in order to catch the person?

The above problem illustrates the central role of pictures and diagrams in understanding. It is almost impossible to read this problem without picturing the scenario in your head, and, for most people, the diagram is essential in solving the problem.

Because of the power of diagrams in thinking and design [8, 12, 56], people rely heavily on hand-sketched diagrams as a quick, lightweight way to put their ideas on paper and help them visualize solutions to their problems. Students, designers, scientists and engineers use sketches in a wide variety of domains, from physical (e.g., mechanical and electrical engineering designs) to conceptual (e.g., organizational charts and software diagrams).

Diagrams drawn on paper are just static pictures, but when drawn on a tablet computer, diagrams have the potential to be interpreted by the computer, and then made interactive. With the rise of pen-based technologies, the number of sketch-based computer tools is increasing. Sketch recognition-based computer systems have been developed for a variety of domains including (but not limited to) mechanical engineering [2, 21, 51], electrical engineering [16], user interface design [9, 34, 42], military course of action diagrams [11, 13], mathematical equations [33, 41], physics [39], musical notation [7, 14], software design [24, 36], note taking (Microsoft OneNote), and image editing [46]. In addition, a few multi-domain recognition toolkits have been proposed [3, 25, 35, 40].

C. Alvarado (✉)
Harvey Mudd College, 301 Platt Blvd., Claremont, CA, USA
e-mail: alvarado@cs.hmc.edu

J. Jorge, F. Samavati (eds.), *Sketch-based Interfaces and Modeling*,
DOI 10.1007/978-1-84882-812-4_2, © Springer-Verlag London Limited 2011

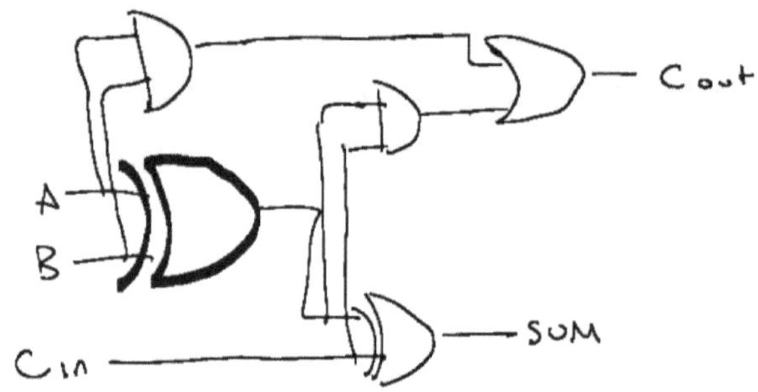

Fig. 2.1 A diagram drawn by a student in a digital design class (stroke thickness altered for illustration)

The problem of two-dimensional sketch recognition is to parse the user's strokes to determine the best set of known patterns to describe the input. This process involves solving two interdependent subproblems: stroke segmentation and symbol recognition. *Stroke segmentation* (or just *segmentation*) is the process of determining which strokes should be grouped to form a single symbol. *Symbol recognition* is the process of determining what symbol a given set of strokes represents.

Despite the growing number of systems, this two-dimensional parsing problem remains a challenging problem for a real-time system. Sketched symbols rarely occur in their canonical form: both noise in the sketch and legal symbol variations make individual symbols difficult to recognize. Furthermore, segmentation and symbol recognition are inherently intertwined. In the sketch in Fig. 2.1, if the system could correctly group the three bold strokes in this sketch, it likely could identify those strokes as an XOR gate using a standard pattern matching technique. Unfortunately, simple spatial and temporal grouping approaches do not work: the three strokes that form the XOR gate are not all touching each other, but they are touching the input and output wires. If the computer somehow can find the correct grouping, it probably will be able to match the strokes to a shape in its library. However, naïvely trying all combinations of stroke groups is prohibitively time-consuming.

Researchers have employed different techniques to cope with these challenges. Some of the systems listed above perform only limited recognition by design. ScanScribe, for example, uses perceptual guidelines to support image and text editing but does not attempt to recognize the user's drawing [46]. Similarly, the sketch-based DENIM system supports the design of web pages but recognizes very little of the user's sketch [42]. Systems of this sort are powerful for their intended tasks, but they do not support a the creative sketch-based design process in more complex domains.

Other recognition systems place restrictions on the user's drawing style in order to make recognition easier. We list four common drawing style restrictions that address these challenges, ordered from most restrictive to least restrictive, and give examples of systems that use each:

1. Users must draw each symbol using a pre-specified pattern or gesture (e.g., Palm Graffiti®, ChemPad [54]).
2. Users must trigger recognition after each symbol (or pause notably between symbols) (e.g., HHreco [28], QuickSet [11]).
3. Users must draw each symbol using temporally contiguous strokes (e.g., AC-SPARC [16]).

4. Some systems place few restrictions on the way users draw, but rely on user assistance or specific domain assumptions to aid recognition. To trigger recognition in MathPad^2, for example, the user must circle pieces of the sketch [39]. The approach presented by Kara and Stahovich performs robust recognition of feedback control system diagrams, but relies on the assumption that the diagram consists of a number of shapes linked by arrows, which is not the case in many other domains [31].

While these previous systems have proven useful for their respective tasks, we aim to create a general sketch recognition system that does not rely on the drawing style assumptions of any one domain. This chapter describes a general-purpose recognition engine that can be applied to a number of symbolic domains by inputting the shapes and commonly occurring combinations of shapes using a hierarchical shape description language, described below. Based on these descriptions, we use a constraint-based approach to recognition, evaluating potential higher-level interpretations for the user's strokes by evaluating their subcomponents and the constraints between them. To achieve recognition robustness and efficiency, we use a combined bottom–up and top–down recognition algorithm that generates the most likely (possibly incomplete) interpretations first (bottom–up) and then actively seeks out lower-level parts of those interpretations that are still missing (top–down).

This chapter presents a synthesis of work presented in [3] and [4], as well as recent work that builds on this prior work. We begin by exploring the challenges of recognizing real-world sketches. Next, we present our approach to recognition, including how we represent knowledge in our system, how we manage uncertainty, and our method of searching for possible interpretations of the user's sketch. Next we analyze our system's performance on real data in two domains. We conclude with a discussion of the major remaining challenge for multi-domain sketch recognition revealed by our evaluation: the problem of efficient and reliable sketch segmentation. We present an emerging technique that attempts to solve this problem.

2.2 The Challenges of Free-Sketch Recognition

Like handwriting and speech understanding, sketch understanding is easy for humans, but difficult for computers. We begin by exploring the inherent challenges of the task.

Figure 2.2 shows the beginning of a sketch of a family tree, with the strokes labeled in the order in which they were drawn. The symbols in this domain are given in Fig. 2.3. This sketch is representative of drawing patterns found in real-world data [5], but it has been redrawn to illustrate a number of challenges using a single example. The user started by drawing a mother and a father, then drew three sons. He linked the mother to the sons by first drawing the shafts of each arrow and then drawing the arrowheads. (In our family tree diagrams, each parent is linked to each child with an arrow.) He will likely continue the drawing by linking the father to the children with arrows and linking the two parents with a line.

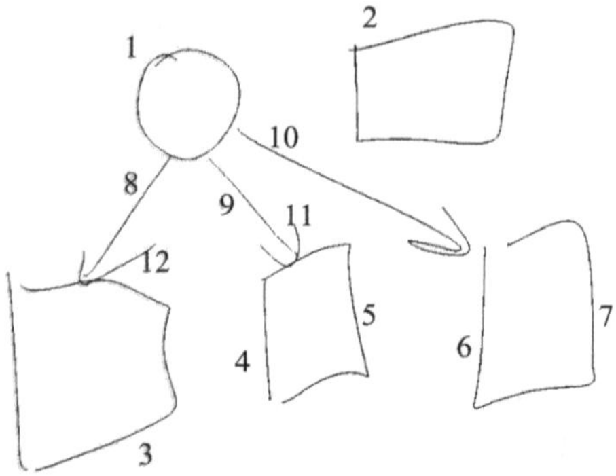

Fig. 2.2 A partial sketch of a family tree

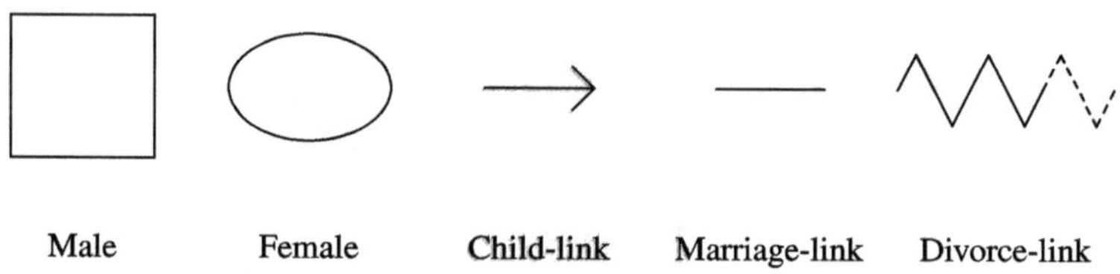

Fig. 2.3 The symbols in the family tree domain

Although relatively simple, this drawing presents many challenges for sketch recognition. The first challenge illustrated in Fig. 2.2 is the incremental nature of the sketch process. Incremental sketch recognition allows the computer to seamlessly interpret a sketch as it is drawn and keeps the user from having to specify when the sketch is complete. To recognize a potentially incomplete sketch, a computer system must know when to recognize a piece of the sketch and when to wait for more information. For example, Stroke 1 can be recognized immediately as a female, but Stroke 6 cannot be recognized without Stroke 7.

The second challenge is that many of the shapes in Fig. 2.2 are visually messy. For example, the center arrowhead (Stroke 11) looks more like an arc than two lines. Next, the stroke used to draw the leftmost quadrilateral (Stroke 3) looks like it is composed of five lines—the top of the quadrilateral has a bend and could be reasonably divided into two lines by a stroke parser. Finally, the lines in the rightmost quadrilateral (Strokes 6 and 7) obviously do not touch in the top-left corner.

The third issue is segmentation: It is difficult to know which strokes are part of which shapes. The shapes in this drawing are not clearly spatially segmented, and naïvely trying different combinations of strokes is prohibitively time-consuming. There are also some inherent ambiguities in how to segment the strokes. For example, lines in our domain indicate marriage, but not every line is a marriage-link. The shaft of the leftmost arrow (Stroke 8) might also have been interpreted as a marriage-link between the female (Stroke 1) and the leftmost male (Stroke 3). In this case, the head of that arrow (Stroke 12) could have been interpreted as a part of the drawing that is not yet complete (e.g., the beginning of an arrow from the leftmost quadrilateral (Stroke 3) to the top quadrilateral (Stroke 2)).

Finally, how shapes are drawn can also present challenges to interpretation. The head of the right-most arrow (part of Stroke 10) is actually made of three lines, two of which are meant to overlap to form one side of the arrowhead. In order to recognize the arrow, the system must know how to collapse those two lines into one, even though they do not actually overlap. Another challenge arises because the same shape may not always be drawn in the same way. For example, the arrows on the left (Strokes 8 and 12, and Strokes 9 and 11) were drawn differently from the one on the right (Stroke 10) in that the user first drew the shaft with one stroke and then drew the head with another. This variation in drawing style presents a challenge for segmentation and recognition because a system cannot know how many strokes will be used to draw each object, nor the order in which the parts of a shape will appear.

Many of the difficulties described in the example above arise from the messy input and visual ambiguity in the sketch. It is the context surrounding the messy or ambiguous parts of the drawing that allows humans to interpret these parts correctly. We found that context also can be used to help our system recover from low-level interpretation errors and correctly identify ambiguous pieces of the sketch. Context has been used to aid recognition in speech recognition systems; it has been the subject of recent research in computer vision [52, 55] and has been used to some extent in previous sketch understanding systems [2, 16, 22, 42, 49, 50]. In the work presented here, we formalize the notion of context suggested by previous sketch recognition systems. This formalization improves recognition of freely-drawn sketches using a general engine that can be applied to a variety of domains.

2.3 Knowledge Representation

The goal of any recognition system is to match its input against an internal representation of a shape or set of shapes and identify the best match or matches (if any) for the given input. However, how each system represents the shape or shapes to be recognized (and consequently how each system matches the input to this internal representation) varies from system to system. For example, one system might represent each shape as a bit-mapped image template of the canonical form of that shape. Then, to perform recognition, that system would apply a series of legal transformations to the input data (e.g., rotation, scaling) to determine whether or not the pixels in the input can be made to line up with the pixels in the template. In contrast, a different system might represent each shape not as an image but as a collection of features extracted from the shapes. Examples of potential features include the ratio between the height and width of the bounding box of the shape, the total length of the strokes in the shape relative to the size of the bounding box, the number of corners in the shape, etc. Recognition in this system would then extract the same features from the input data and determine whether or not the features extracted from the input data are close enough to the features stored for each shape.

While many different representations can be used to perform recognition, the choice of internal shape representation affects the recognition task difficulty. In the example above, recognition using the feature-based approach is more straightforward than the template-matching approach as it involves only a relatively small number of easy to calculate features rather than multiple transformations of the whole input. However, depending on the shapes in the domain, it may be extremely difficult to devise a set of features that reliably separates one shape from another.

Our system represents symbols to be recognized using a probabilistic, hierarchical description language. In choosing our representation, we considered several desired functionalities of our recognition system. First, the system should be extensible to new domains, requiring few training examples. Second, the system should be able to distinguish between legal and illegal shape transformations when performing recognition. Legal transformations include not only rotation, translation and scaling but also some non-rigid shape transformations. For example, the angle between a line in the head of an arrow and the shaft may range from about 10 degrees to about 80 degrees, but an angle greater than 90 degrees is not acceptable. Third, we would like to use this recognition system to compare various techniques for providing recognition feedback to the user, so the system should be able to recognize the sketch as the user draws to allow the system to potentially provide recognition feedback at any point in the drawing process. Finally, the system should be able to cope with the noise inherent in hand-drawn diagrams (e.g., lines that are not really straight, corners that do not actually meet, etc.).

This section describes our hierarchical description language and discusses how this choice of representation allowed us to construct a system that meets the requirements above. We begin by introducing the deterministic properties of the language, then discuss how uncertainty is incorporated into the descriptions. Finally, we discuss the advantages and disadvantages of this choice of representation.

2.3.1 Hierarchical Shape Descriptions

Each shape in the domain to be recognized is described using a hierarchical description language, called LADDER, developed by Hammond and Davis [25]. We introduce the language through examples from the family tree and circuit domains.

We refer to any pattern recognizable in a given domain as a *shape*. *Compound shapes* are those composed of *subshapes*. Compound shapes must be non-recursive. Describing a compound shape involves specifying its subshapes and any necessary *constraints* between those subshapes. As an example, the description of an arrow is given in Fig. 2.4. The arrow has three subshapes—the line that is the shaft and the two lines that combine to make the head. The constraints specify the relative size, position and orientation necessary for these three lines to form an arrow shape (as opposed to just being three arbitrary lines). Once a shape has been defined, other shapes may use that shape in their descriptions. For example, the child-link symbol in the family tree domain (Fig. 2.5) and the current source symbol in the circuit domain (Fig. 2.6) both use an arrow as a subshape.

Shapes that cannot be broken down into subshapes are called *primitive shapes*. The set of primitive shapes includes free-form strokes, lines, arcs and ellipses.

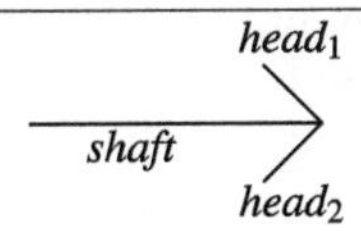

DEFINE ARROW
(Subshapes
(Line *shaft* *head*$_1$ *head*$_2$))
(Constraints
(coincident *shaft*.p_1 *head*$_1$.p_1)
(coincident *shaft*.p_1 *head*$_2$.p_2)
(equalLength *head*$_1$ *head*$_2$)
(larger *shaft* *head*$_1$)
(acuteAngle *head*$_1$ *shaft*)
(acuteAngle *head*$_2$ *shaft*))

Fig. 2.4 The description of the shape "arrow." Once defined, this shape can be used in descriptions of domain-specific shapes, as in Figs. 2.5 and 2.6

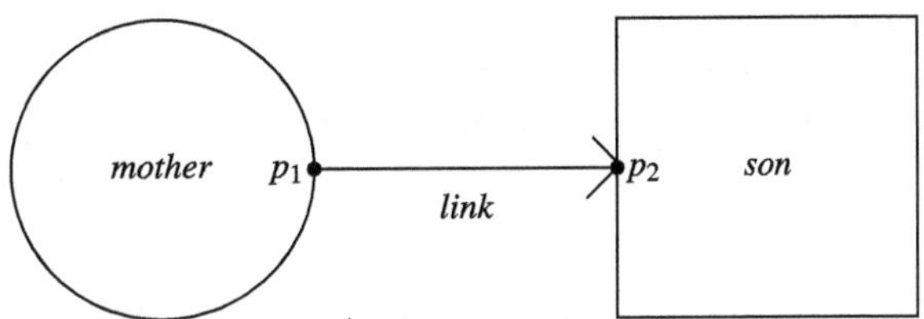

DEFINE FEMALE
(Subshapes
(Ellipse *e*))

DEFINE MALE
(Subshapes
(Quadrilateral *q*))

DEFINE CHILD-LINK
(Subshapes
(Arrow *a*))

DEFINE MOTHER-SON
(Subshapes
(Male *son*)
(Female *mother*)
(Child-Link *link*))
(Constraints
(touches *link.shaft*.p_1 *mother*)
(touches *link.shaft*.p_2 *son*))

Fig. 2.5 Descriptions of several domain shapes (Female, Male and Child-Link) and one domain pattern (Mother–Son) in the family tree domain

Although primitive shapes cannot be decomposed into subshapes, they may have named *subcomponents* that can be used when describing other shapes, e.g., the end-points of a line, p_1 and p_2, used in Fig. 2.4.

Domain shapes are shapes that have semantic meaning in a particular domain. Child-link and current-source are both domain shapes, but arrow and line are not because they are not specific to any one domain. *Domain patterns* are combinations of domain shapes that are likely to occur, for example the child-link pointing from a female to a male, indicating a relationship between mother and son in Fig. 2.5. Compound shape descriptions with no constraints (e.g., the child-link description) are used to rename a generic geometric shape (e.g., the arrow) as a domain shape so that domain-specific semantics may be associated with the shape.

Fig. 2.6 The description of a Current Source from the circuit domain

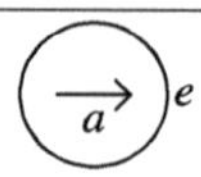

DEFINE CURRENT-SOURCE
(**Subshapes**
(Ellipse *e*)
(Arrow *a*))
(**Constraints**
(contains *e a*))

2.3.2 Handling Noise in the Drawing

The system's goal in recognition is to choose the best set of domain shapes for a given set of strokes. While this task appears to be straightforward, Sect. 2.2 illustrated that ambiguity in the drawing can make recognition more difficult. Here, we describe the language constructs that help the system cope with the inevitable noise and ambiguities in the drawing. We discuss two different types of variation supported by our representation: signal-level noise and description-level variation.

2.3.2.1 Signal-Level Noise: Objective vs. Subjective Measures

Shape descriptions specify the subshapes and constraints needed to form a higher-level shape; however, people rarely draw shapes perfectly or constraints that hold exactly. For example, although a user intends to draw two parallel lines, it is unlikely that these lines will be exactly parallel. We call this type of variation *signal-level noise*.

Because of signal-level noise, low-level shape and constraint interpretations must be based both on the data and on the context in which that shape or constraint appears. Consider whether or not the user intended for the two bold lines in each drawing in Fig. 2.7 to connect. In Figs. 2.7(a) and (b), the bold lines are identically spaced, but the context surrounding them indicates that in Fig. 2.7(b) the user intended for them to connect, while in Fig. 2.7(a) the user did not. On the other hand, the stroke information should not be ignored. The thin lines in Figs. 2.7(b) and (c) are identical, but the distance between the endpoints of the bold lines in these figures indicate that the these lines are intended to connect in Fig. 2.7(b) but not in Fig. 2.7(c).

For each low-level shape and constraint we identify an objectively measurable property that corresponds to that shape or constraint. For example, the property related to the constraint *coincident* is the distance between the two points in question normalized by the length of the lines containing the points in question. This objectively measurable property allows the system to separate the information provided by the stroke data from the information provided by the surrounding context to determine whether or not the constraint actually holds. Section 2.5 discusses precisely how these low-level measurements and the contextual data are combined.

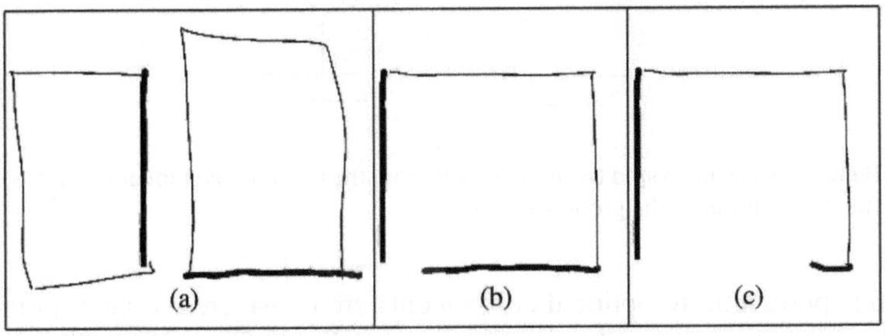

Fig. 2.7 The importance of both data and context in determining whether or not the *bold lines* were intended to connect

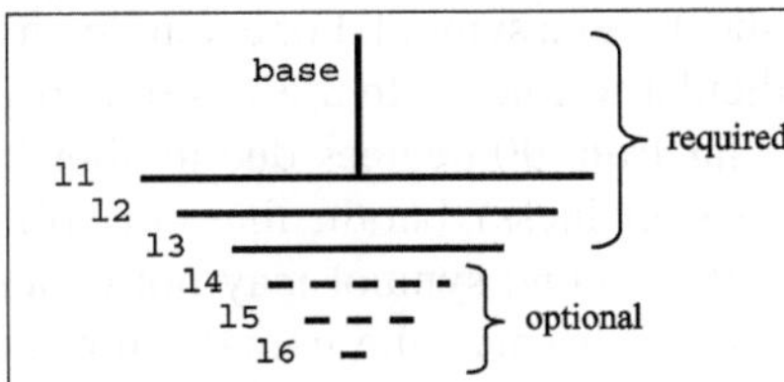

DEFINE GROUND
(Subshapes
(Line *base*)
(Line l_1)
(Line l_2)
(Line l_3)
(*optional* Line l_4)
(*optional* Line l_5)
(*optional* Line l_6))
(constraints omitted))

Fig. 2.8 The ground symbol from the Circuit Diagram domain

2.3.2.2 Description-Level Variation: Optional Components and Constraints

All of the shapes considered so far have been modeled using a fixed number of subshapes and a set of required constraints between those subshapes. These descriptions signify that, when a user draws these symbols, she should draw all of the subparts specified.

In contrast, some shapes have subcomponents that can be omitted legally when they are drawn. For example, consider the ground symbol described in Fig. 2.8. The user may draw up to six horizontal lines, but three of these lines optionally may be omitted. These three lines are flagged as *optional* in the shape description. We call this type of variation *description-level variation.*

Constraints may also be flagged as optional, indicating that they often hold, but are not required in the description of a symbol. For example, we could define the domain shape *wire* as having the single subshape *line* and the optional constraint that the line is horizontal or vertical. This constraint is not strictly required, as wires may be drawn diagonally, but they are often drawn either horizontally or vertically.

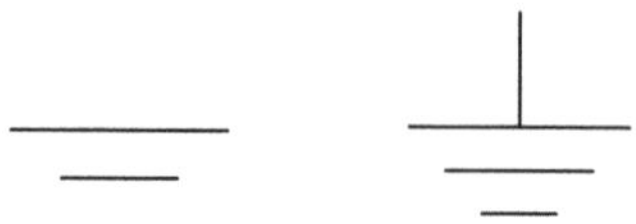

Fig. 2.9 Battery (*left*) and ground (*right*) symbols from the Circuit Diagram domain. Note that the battery symbol is a subset of the ground symbol

Constraints pertaining to optional components are considered to be required if the optional component is present unless they are explicitly flagged as optional.

Understanding the difference between signal-level noise and description-level variation is central to understanding our representation of uncertainty. Signal-level noise is distinguished from description-level variation by considering the user's intent when she draws a symbol. For example, in a ground symbol the *base* line should be perpendicular to line l_1. In a given drawing, the angle between those lines may actually be far from 90 degrees due to signal-level noise (which might be caused by the user's sloppiness), but the lines are still intended to be perpendicular. On the other hand, the ground symbol may not contain line l_6, not because the user was being sloppy, but because the user did not intend to include it when drawing the symbol. We discuss how we model each variation in Sect. 2.5.

2.3.3 Strengths and Limitations

We chose this symbolic, hierarchical representation based on the recognition system guidelines presented in the first part of this section. Here, we consider how this representation supports the creation of a multi-domain free-sketch recognition system. As every representation choice has trade-offs, we also consider the limitations of this approach and briefly discuss how these limitations can be addressed.

The first requirement was that our system must be extensible to new domains, requiring few training examples. To extend the system to a new domain, a user must simply describe the domain shapes and patterns for the new domain. Because the system can use the same hierarchical recognition process, it does not need to be trained with a large number of examples for each new shape. Furthermore, basic geometric shapes can be defined once and reused in a number of domains.

The second requirement was that our system must accept legal non-rigid transformations of sketched symbols without accepting illegal transformations. This requirement is handled by the fact that constraints can be defined to accept a wide range of relationships between shapes. For example, *acuteAngle* refers to any angle less than 90 degrees. Furthermore, only constraints explicitly stated in the shape definition are verified. Constraints that are not specified may vary without affecting the system's interpretation of the shape. For example, the definition of a quadrilateral would not constrain the relative lengths of the lines or the angles between those lines, leaving the system free to interpret any set of four correctly connected lines as a quadrilateral.

The third requirement was that the system be able to recognize a sketch as it is being drawn. To support this goal, our representation in terms of a shape's subcomponents allows the system to detect when it has seen only some of the subcomponents of a given shape. Using these partial interpretations, the system can decide which interpretations are likely complete and which might still be in the process of being drawn. This capability is particularly important when shape descriptions overlap, as in the battery and the ground symbol in the circuit domain (Fig. 2.9). When the user draws what could look like a battery or part of a ground symbol, the system can detect the partial ground interpretation and wait until the user has drawn more strokes to give its final interpretation instead of immediately interpreting the strokes as a battery.

The final requirement was that our system must deal with the noise in hand-drawn diagrams. Our representation allows us to handle signal-level noise by separating low-level objective measurements from judgements about whether or not constraints hold.

Although our representation satisfies the above requirements, it also imposes some restrictions. First, even with a well designed language, specifying shape descriptions may be difficult or time-consuming. Others have developed systems to learn shape descriptions from few examples. In work by Vesselova and Davis [57], as the user draws a shape, the learning system parses the user's strokes into low level components such as lines, arcs, and ellipses. The learner then calculates the existing constraints between these components and uses perceptual cues to deduce which constraints are most important the shape description. Once the system has learned a shape (e.g., a rectangle) it can then use that shape in its description of other shapes (e.g., a house). Hammond and Davis extended this work with an interactive system that helps users debug shape descriptions generating and displaying "near-miss" examples (i.e. shape patterns that vary only slightly from the current description) [27]. The output of both systems is a description of a domain shape in the visual language.

Second, even if we could build a system to learn shape descriptions, some shapes may be difficult or impossible to describe in terms of any simple low-level components or constraints. Those domains with free-form shapes, such as architecture, may have many shapes that cannot be easily described. Our representation is appropriate only for domains with highly structured symbols.

Finally, using this representation it is difficult to represent text or unrecognized strokes. This limitation must be addressed in the recognition system itself. The system should be capable of detecting text or unrecognized strokes and processing them using a different recognition technique or leaving them as unrecognized. Separating text from diagrams is a challenging problem that we do not address here, although recent approaches have proven quite successful at this task [6, 58].

2.4 Recognition Overview

As described above, a core challenge in two-dimensional sketch recognition is the problem of simultaneous segmentation and symbol recognition. Low-level interpretations potentially can help guide the search for possible higher-level interpretations; for example, if the system detects two connected lines, it can first try to match a quadrilateral whose corner lines up with the connection between the lines. However, noise in the input makes it impossible for the system to recognize low-level shapes with certainty or to be sure whether or not constraints hold. Low-level misinterpretations cause higher-level interpretations to fail as well. Trying all possible interpretations of the user's strokes guarantees that an interpretation will not be missed, but it is infeasible due to the exponential number of possible interpretations.

To solve this problem we use a combined bottom–up and top–down recognition algorithm that generates the most likely interpretations first (bottom–up) and then actively seeks out parts of those interpretations that are still missing (top–down). Our approach uses a novel application of dynamically constructed Bayesian networks to evaluate partial interpretation hypotheses and then expands the hypothesis space by exploring the most likely interpretations first. The system does not have to try all combinations of all interpretations, but can focus on those interpretations that contain at least a subset of easily-recognizable subshapes and can recover any low-level subshapes that may have been mis-recognized.

We use a two-stage generate-and-test method to explore possible interpretations for the user's strokes. In the first stage, the system generates a number of *hypotheses*, or possible interpretations for the user's strokes, based on the shape descriptions described in Sect. 2.3. We refer to each shape description as a *template* with one *slot* for each subpart. A *shape hypothesis* is a template with an associated mapping between slots and strokes. Similarly, a *constraint hypothesis* is a proposed constraint on one or more of the user's strokes. A *partial hypothesis* is a hypothesis in which one or more slots are not bound to strokes. Our method of exploring the space of possible interpretations depends on our ability to assess both complete and partial hypotheses for the user's strokes. Section 2.5 describes our hypothesis evaluation technique; Sect. 2.6 describes how these hypotheses are generated.

2.5 Hypothesis Evaluation

We evaluate our shape hypotheses using dynamically constructed Bayesian networks specifically targeted to the task of constraint-based recognition. Our framework is closely related to previously proposed frameworks ([32, 37, 44]) but it was designed to handle the specific problems presented above that arise in the recognition task. Our method offers two advantages over previous constraint-based recognition approaches (e.g., [15, 20, 26]). First, missing data can be treated as unobserved nodes in the network when the system assesses likely hypotheses for the strokes that have been observed thus far. This allows our system to evaluate partial hypotheses (e.g., an arrow with no shaft) in order to interpret drawings as they develop, and to allow the strength of partial hypotheses to guide the interpretation of new strokes as they are processed. Second, the system's belief in a given hypothesis can be influenced both by the stroke data (through the node's children) and the context in which those shapes appear (through the node's parents), allowing the system to cope with noise in the drawing.

2.5.1 Dynamically Constructed Graphical Models

Time-based graphical models, including Hidden Markov Models (HMMs) and Dynamic Bayesian Networks (DBNs), have been applied successfully to time-series data in tasks such as speech understanding. To the extent that stroke order is predictable, HMMs and DBNs may be applied to sketch understanding (see [47] for one approach). Ultimately, however, sketch understanding is different because we must model shapes based on two-dimensional constraints (e.g., intersects, touches) rather than on temporal constraints (i.e., follows), and because our models cannot simply unroll in time as data arrive (we cannot necessarily predict the order in which the user will draw the strokes, and things drawn previously can be changed). Therefore, our network represents spatial relationships rather than temporal relationships.

It is not difficult to use Bayesian networks to model spatial relationships. The difficult part of using Bayesian networks for sketch understanding is that they are traditionally used to model static domains in which the variables and relationships between those variables are known in advance. Static networks are not suitable for the task of sketch recognition because we cannot predict a priori the number of strokes or symbols the user will draw in a given sketch. In fact, there are many tasks in which the possible number of objects and relationships may not be modeled a priori. For example, when reasoning about military activity, the number of military units and their locations cannot be known in advance. For such tasks, models to reason about specific problem instances (e.g., a particular sketch or a particular military confrontation) must be dynamically constructed in response to a given input. This problem is known as the task of *knowledge-based model construction* (KBMC).

A number of researchers have proposed models for the dynamic creation of Bayesian networks for KBMC. Early approaches focused on generating Bayesian networks from probabilistic knowledge bases [18, 19, 23, 45]. A recently proposed representation, called Network Fragments, represents generic template knowledge directly as Bayesian network fragments that can be instantiated and linked together at run-time [37]. Finally, Koller et al. have developed a number of a number of object-oriented frameworks including Object-Oriented Bayesian Networks (OOBNs) [32, 44] and Probabilistic Relational Models (PRMs) [17]. These models represent knowledge in terms of relationships among objects and can be instantiated dynamically in response to the number of objects in a particular situation.

Although the above frameworks are powerful, they are not directly suitable for sketch recognition because they are too general in some respects and too specialized in others. First, with this type of general model, it is a challenge simply to decide how to frame our recognition task in terms of objects, network fragments, or logical statements. Second, because these models are general, they do not make any assumptions about how the network will be instantiated. Because of the size of the networks potentially generated for our task, it is sometimes desirable to generate only part of a complete network, or to prune nodes from the network. In reasoning about nodes that are in the network, we must account for the fact that the network may not be fully generated or relevant information may have been pruned from the network. Finally, these models are too specific in that they have been optimized for

CS hypothesis CS_1
Subshapes:
e → ellipse hypothesis E_1
a → arrow hypothesis A_1
Constraints:
C_1 = (contains `ellipse-fit`(s_1) `shape-fit`(s_2, s_3, s4))

Primitive hypotheses
E_1 = `ellipse-fit`(s_1)
L_1 = `line-fit`(s_2)
L_2 = `line-fit`(s_3)
L_3 = `line-fit`(s_4)

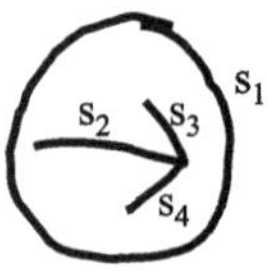

Arrow hypothesis A_1
Subshapes:
shaft → line hypothesis L_1
$head_1$ → line hypothesis L_2
$head_2$ → line hypothesis L_3
Constraints:
C_2 = (coincident `line-fit`(s_2).p1 `line-fit`(s_3).p1)
C_3 = (coincident `line-fit`(s_2).p1 `line-fit`(s_4).p1)
C_4 = (equalLength `line-fit`(s_3) `line-fit`(s4))
C_5 = (shorter `line-fit`(s_3) `line-fit`(s_2))
C_6 = (acuteAngle `line-fit`(s_2) `line-fit`(s_3))
C_7 = (acuteAngle `line-fit`(s_2) `line-fit`(s_4))

Fig. 2.10 A single current source hypothesis (CS_1) and associated lower-level hypotheses. Shape descriptions for the arrow and current source (with labeled subshapes) are given in Figs. 2.6 and 2.4

responding to specific queries, for example, "What is the probability that a particular battery in our military force has been hit?" In contrast, our model must provide probabilities for a full set of possible interpretations of the user's strokes.

2.5.2 Shape Fragments: Evaluating a Single Hypothesis

Briefly, Bayesian networks consist of two parts: a Directed Acyclic Graph that encodes *which* factors influence one another, and a set of Conditional Probability Distributions which specify *how* these factors influence one another.[1] Each node in the graph represents something to be measured, and a link between two nodes indicates that the value of one node is directly dependent on the value of the other. Each node contains a conditional probability function (CPF), represented as a conditional probability table (CPT) for discrete variables, specifying how it is influenced by its parents.

To introduce our Bayesian network model, we begin by considering how to evaluate the strength of a single current source (CS) hypothesis for the stokes in Fig. 2.10. The description of a current source symbol is given in Fig. 2.6. Based on the hierarchical nature of the shape descriptions, we use a hierarchical method of hypothesis evaluation. Determining the strength of a particular current source hypothesis is a

[1] We provide enough background on Bayesian networks to give the reader a high-level understanding of our model. To understand the details, those unfamiliar with Bayesian networks are referred to [10] for an intuitive introduction and [30] for more details.

matter of determining the strengths of its corresponding lower-level shape and constraint hypotheses. A particular current source hypothesis, CS_1, specifies a mapping between the subparts in the current source description and the user's strokes via lower-level hypotheses for the user's strokes (Fig. 2.10). E_1 is an ellipse hypothesis for s_1, A_1 is an arrow hypothesis involving strokes s_2, s_3 and s_4 (through its line hypotheses), and C_1 is a constraint hypothesis that an ellipse fit for stroke s_1 contains strokes s_2, s_3, and s_4. A_1 is further broken down into three line hypotheses (L_1, L_2 and L_3) and six constraint hypotheses ($C_2, \ldots, C_7$) according to the description of the arrow (Fig. 2.4). Thus, determining the strength of hypothesis CS_1 can be transformed into the problem of determining the strength of a number of lower-level shape and constraint hypotheses.

2.5.2.1 Network Structure

The Bayesian network for this recognition task is shown in Fig. 2.11. There is one node in the network for each hypothesis described above, and each of these nodes represents a Boolean random variable that reflects whether or not the corresponding hypothesis is correct. The nodes labeled $O_1, \ldots, O_{11}$ represent measurements of the stroke data that correspond to the constraint or shape to which they are linked. The variables corresponding to these nodes have positive real numbered values. For example, the variable O_2 is a measurement of the squared error between the stroke s_1 and the best fit ellipse to that stroke. The value of O_2 is a real number between 0 and the maximum possible error between any stroke and an ellipse fit to that stroke. The boxes labeled $s_1, \ldots, s_4$ are not part of the Bayesian network but serve to indicate the stroke or strokes from which each measurement, O_i, is taken (e.g., O_2 is measured from s_1). $P(CS_1 = t \mid ev)$ (or simply $P(CS_1 \mid ev)$)[2], where ev is the evidence observed from the user's strokes, represents the probability that the hypothesis CS_1 is correct.

There are three important reasons why the links are directed from higher-level shapes to lower-level shapes instead of in the opposite direction. First, whether or not a higher-level hypothesis is true directly influences whether or not a lower-level hypothesis is true. For example, if the arrow hypothesis A_1 is true, then it is extremely likely that all three line hypotheses, L_1, L_2, L_3, are also true. Second, this representation allows us to model lower-level hypotheses as conditionally independent given their parents, which reduces the complexity of the data needed to construct the network. Finally, continuous valued variables are difficult to incorporate into a Bayesian network if they have discrete valued children. Our representation ensures that the measurement nodes, which have continuous values, will be leaf nodes. These nodes can be pruned when they do not have evidence, thus simplifying the inference process.

Each shape description constrains its subshapes only relative to one another. For example, an arrow may be made from *any* three lines that satisfy the necessary constraints. Based on this observation, our representation models a symbol's subshapes

---

[2]Throughout this section, t means true, and f means false.

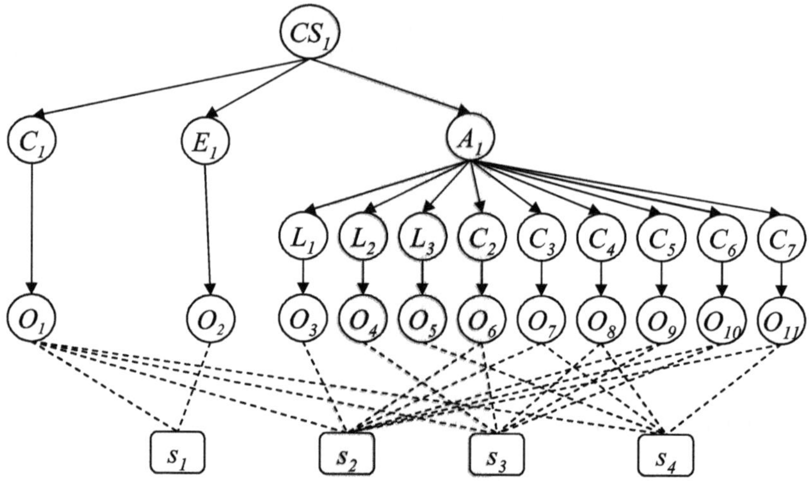

Fig. 2.11 A Bayesian network to verify a single current source hypothesis. Labels come from Fig. 2.10

separately from the necessary constraints between those subshapes. For example, node L_1 represents the hypothesis that stroke s_2 is a line. Its value will be true if the user intended for s_2 to be any line, regardless of its position, size or orientation. Similarly, C_2 represents the hypothesis that the line fit to s_2 and the line fit to s_3 are coincident.

The conditional independence between subshapes and constraints might seem a bit strange at first. For example, whether or not two lines are of the same length seems to depend on the fact that they are lines. However, observation nodes for constraints are calculated in such a way that their value is not dependent on the true interpretation for a stroke. For example, when calculating whether or not two lines are parallel, which involves calculating the different in angle between the two lines, we first fit lines to the strokes (regardless of whether or not they actually look like lines), then measure the relative orientation of those lines. How well these lines fit the strokes is not considered in this calculation.

The fact that the shape nodes are not directly connected to the constraint nodes has an important implication for using this model to perform recognition: There is no guarantee in this Bayesian network that the constraints will be measured from the correct subshapes because the model allows subshapes and constraints to be detected independently. For example, C_3 in Fig. 2.11 indicates that L_2 and L_3 (the two lines in the head of an arrow) must be the same length, not simply that any two lines must have the same length. To satisfy this requirement, The system must ensure that O_6 is measured from the same strokes that O_3 and O_4 were measured from. We use a separate mechanism to ensure that only legal bindings are created between strokes and observation nodes.

The way we model shape and constraint information has two important advantages for recognition. First, this Bayesian network model can be applied to recognize a shape in any size, position and orientation. CS_1 represents the hypothesis that

$s_1, \ldots, s_4$ form a current source symbol, but the exact position, orientation and size of that symbol is determined directly from the stroke data. To consider a new hypothesis for the user's strokes, the system simply creates a copy of the necessary Bayesian network structure whose nodes represent the new hypotheses and whose measurement nodes are linked to a different set of the user's strokes. Second, the system can allow competing higher-level hypotheses for a lower-level shape hypothesis to influence one another by creating a network in which two or more hypotheses point to the same lower-level shape node. For example, the system may consider an arrow hypothesis and a quadrilateral hypothesis involving the same line hypothesis for one of the user's strokes. Because the line hypothesis does not include any higher-level shape-specific constraint information, both an arrow-hypothesis node and a quadrilateral hypothesis node can point to the single line hypothesis node. These two hypotheses then become alternate, competing explanations for the line hypothesis. We further discuss how hypotheses are combined below.

Our model is generative, in that we can use the Bayesian network for generation of values for the nodes in the network based on the probabilities in the model. However, our model is fundamentally different from the standard generative approach used in computer vision in which the system generates candidate shapes (for example, a rightward facing arrow) and then compares these shapes to the data in the image. The difference is that the lowest level of our network represents measurements of the strokes, not actual stroke data. So, although our model can be used to generate values of stroke data measurements, it cannot be used to generate shapes which can be directly compared to the user's strokes. However, because the system can always take measurements from existing stroke data, our model is well suited for hypothesis evaluation.

2.5.2.2 Conditional Probability Distributions

Next, we consider the intuition behind the CPTs for a node given its parents for the hypotheses in Fig. 2.10. We begin by considering the distribution $P(E_1 \mid CS_1)$. Intuitively, we set $P(E_1 = t \mid CS_1 = t) = 1$ (and conversely, $P(E_1 = f \mid CS_1 = t) = 0$), meaning that if the user intended to draw CS_1, she certainly intended to draw E_1. This reasoning follows from the fact that the ellipse is a required component of the CS symbol (and that the user knows how to draw CS symbols). $P(E_1 \mid CS_1 = f)$, on the other hand, is a little less obvious. Intuitively, it represents the probability that the user intended to draw E_1 even though she did not intend to draw CS_1. This probability will depend on the frequency of ellipses in other symbols in the domain (i.e., higher if ellipses are common).

Because CS_1 has no parents, it must be assigned a prior probability. This probability is simply how likely it is that the user will draw CS_1. This probability will be high if there are few other shapes in the domain or if CS symbols are particularly prominent, and low if there are many symbols or if the CS symbol is rare. Exactly how these prior probabilities are determined is beyond the scope of this chapter but is discussed further in [1].

The bottom layer of the network accounts for signal-level noise by modeling the differences between the user's intentions and the strokes that she draws. For example, even if the user intends to draw L_1, her stroke likely will not match L_1 exactly, so the model must account for this variation. Consider $P(O_2 \mid E_1 = t)$. If the user always drew perfect ellipses, this distribution would be 1 when $O_2 = 0$, and 0 otherwise. However, most people do not draw perfect ellipses (due to inaccurate pen and muscle movements), and this distribution allows for this error. It should be high when O_2 is close to zero, and fall off as O_2 gets larger. The wider the distribution, the more error the system will tolerate, but the less information a perfect ellipse will provide.

The other distribution needed is $P(O_2 \mid E_1 = f)$ which is the probability distribution over ellipse error given that the user did not intend to draw an ellipse. This distribution should be close to uniform, with a dip around 0, indicating that if the user specifically does not intend to draw an ellipse, she might draw any other shape, but probably will not draw anything that resembles an ellipse. Discussion of how we determined the conditional probability distributions between primitive shapes and constraints and their corresponding measurement nodes can be found in [1].

2.5.2.3 Observing Evidence from Stroke Data

Finally, we discuss how information from the user's strokes is incorporated into the network to influence the system's belief in CS_1. If we assume that the user is done drawing, the values of $O_1, \ldots, O_{11}$ are fully observable by taking measurements of the strokes. The system can then use those values to infer $P(CS_1 | O_1, \ldots, O_{11})$. If we do not assume the user is done drawing, we may still evaluate $P(CS_1 | ev)$ where the set ev contains all O_i corresponding to strokes the user has drawn so far.

We may model the current source (partial) hypothesis CS_1 even before the drawing is complete. An observation node that does not have an observed value intuitively corresponds to a stroke that the user has not yet drawn. Because observation nodes are always leaf nodes, the missing data have neither a positive nor a negative effect on the system's belief in a given interpretation. CS_1 may be strongly believed even if O_1 is missing. As described in Sect. 2.6, the system uses the strength of incomplete interpretations to help guide the search for missed low-level interpretations.

2.5.3 Recognizing a Complete Sketch

The Bayesian network introduced above can be used to detect a single instance of a CS symbol in any size, position or orientation. However, a typical sketch contains several different symbols as well as several instances of the same symbol.

To detect other shapes in our domain, we may create a Bayesian network similar to the network above for each shape. We call each of these Bayesian networks

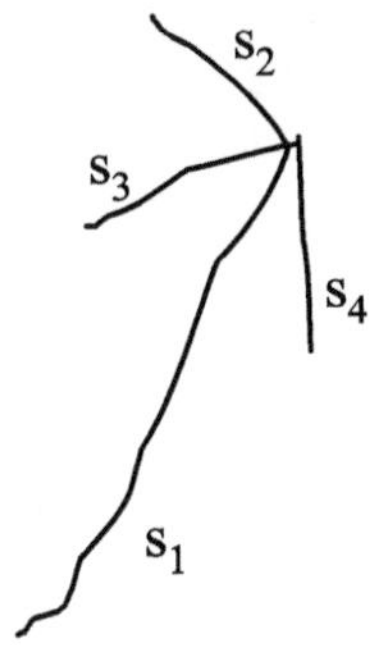

Fig. 2.12 Four strokes, three of which form an arrow. The system might try both s_2 and s_3 as a line in the head of the arrow

a *shape fragment* because these fragments can be combined to create a complete Bayesian network for evaluating the whole sketch.

Above, we assumed that we were given a mapping between the user's strokes and the observation nodes in our network. In fact, the system must often evaluate a number of potential mappings between strokes and observation nodes. For example, if the user draws the four strokes in Fig. 2.12, the system might try mapping both s_2 and s_3 to L_2. As described above, each interpretation for a specific mapping between strokes and observation nodes is called a hypothesis, and each hypothesis corresponds to a single node in the Bayesian network. In this section we discuss how multiple hypotheses are combined to evaluate a complete sketch.

Given a set of hypotheses for the user's strokes, the system instantiates the corresponding shape fragments and links them together to form a complete Bayesian network, which we call the *interpretation network*. To illustrate this process, we consider a piece of a network generated in response to Strokes 6 and 7 in the example given in Fig. 2.2, which is reproduced in Fig. 2.13. Figure 2.14 shows the part of the Bayesian network representing the possible interpretations that the system generated for these strokes. Each node represents a hypothesized interpretation for some piece of the sketch. For example, Q_1 represents the system's hypothesis that the user intended to draw a quadrilateral with strokes 6 and 7. A higher-level hypothesis is compatible with the lower-level hypotheses it points to. For example, if M_1 (the hypothesis that the user intended to draw a male with strokes 6 and 7) is correct, Q_1 (the hypothesis that the user intended to draw a quadrilateral with strokes 6 and 7) and $L_1, \ldots, L_4$ (the hypotheses that the user intended to draw four lines with strokes 6 and 7) will also be correct. Two hypotheses that both point to the same lower-level hypothesis represent competing interpretations for the lower-level shape and are incompatible. For example, A_1, Q_1 are two possible higher-level interpretations for line L_1, only one of which may be true.

Each observation node is linked to a corresponding stroke or set of strokes. In a partial hypothesis, not all measurement nodes will be linked to stroke data. For example, A_1 is a partial hypothesis—it represents the hypothesis that L_1 and L_2 (and, hence, Stroke 6) are part of an arrow whose other line has not yet been drawn. Line nodes representing lines that have not been drawn (L_5 and L_6) are not linked to observation nodes because there is no stroke from which to measure these observations. We refer to these nodes (and their corresponding hypotheses) as *virtual*.

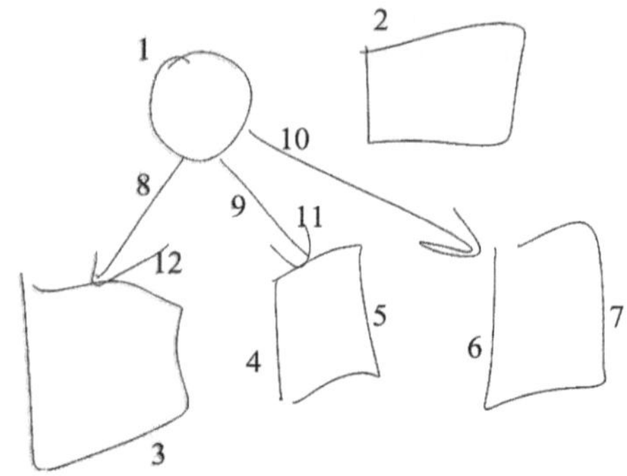

Fig. 2.13 The partial sketch of a family tree from Sect. 2.1

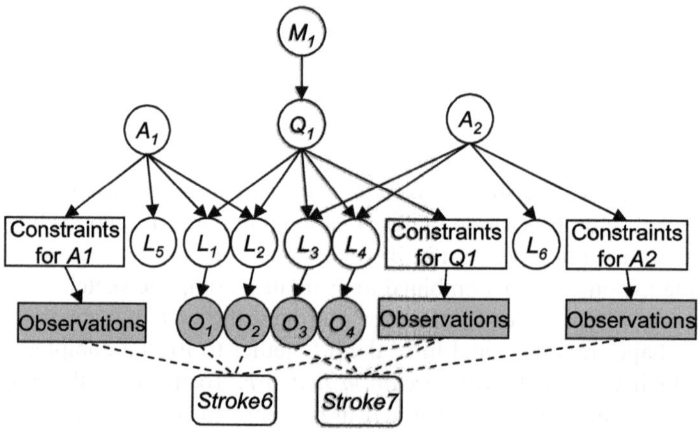

Fig. 2.14 A portion of the interpretation network generated while recognizing the sketch in Fig. 2.13

The probability of each interpretation is influenced both by stroke data (through its children) and by the context in which it appears (through its parents), allowing the system to handle noise in the drawing. For example, there is a gap between the lines in the top-left corner in Q_1 (see Fig. 2.13); stroke data only weakly support the corresponding constraint hypothesis (not shown individually). However, the lines that form Q_1 are fairly straight, raising probabilities of $L_1, \ldots, L_4$, which in turn raise the probability of Q_1. Q_1 provides a context in which to evaluate the coincident constraint, and because Q_1 is well supported by $L_1, \ldots, L_4$ (and by the other constraint nodes), it raises the probability of the coincident constraint corresponding to Q_1's top-left corner.

The fact that partial interpretations have probabilities allows the system to assess the likelihood of incomplete interpretations based on the evidence it has seen so far. In fact, even virtual nodes have probabilities, corresponding to the probability that the user (eventually) intends to draw these shapes but either has not yet drawn this part of the diagram or the correct low-level hypotheses have not yet been proposed because of low-level recognition errors. As we describe below, a partial interpretation with a high probability cues the system to examine the sketch for possible missed low-level interpretations.

2.5.3.1 Linking Shape Fragments

When Bayesian network fragments are linked during recognition, each node H_n may have several parents, $S_1 \dots S_m$, where each parent represents a possible higher-level interpretation for H_n. We use a noisy-OR function to combine the influences of all the parents of H_n to produce the complete CPT for $P(H_n \mid S_1, \dots, S_m)$. The noisy-OR function models the assumption that each parent can independently cause the child to be observed. For example, a single stroke might be part of a quadrilateral or an arrow, but both interpretations would favor that interpretation of the stroke as a line.

The intuition behind Noisy-OR is that each parent that is true will cause the child to also be true unless something prevents it from doing so. The probability that something will prevent a parent $S_i = t$ from causing $H_n = t$ to be true is $q_i = P(H_n = f \mid S_i = t)$. Noisy-OR assumes that all the q_i's are independent, resulting in the following:

$$P(H_n = t \mid S_1, S_2, \dots, S_m) = 1 - \prod_i q_i$$

for each $S_i = t$. We set $q_j = P(H_n = f \mid S_j = t) = 0$ for all parents S_j in which H_n is a required subshape or constraint, and we set $q_k = P(H_n = f \mid S_k = t) = 0.5$ for all parents S_k in which H_n is an optional subshape or constraint. A consequence of these values is that $S_j = t \Rightarrow P(H_n \mid S_1, \dots, S_m) = 1$ for any S_j in which H_n is required, which is exactly what we intended.

Noisy-OR requires that $P(H_n \mid S_1 = S_2, \dots, S_m = f]) = 0$. The result of this requirement is that any shape or constraint has zero probability of appearing if it is not part of a higher-level shape or pattern. This behavior may be what is desired; however, if it is not, we may create an additional parent, S_a, to model the probability that the user intends to draw H_n alone, not as part of a shape or pattern.

2.5.3.2 Missing Nodes

Throughout this process, we have assumed that all of the hypothesized interpretations will exist as a node in the Bayesian network. However, for reasons discussed in Sect. 2.6, there are two reasons a hypothesis might be missing from the network. First, the system does not always initially generate all higher-level interpretations for a shape. Second, the system prunes unlikely hypotheses from the network to control the network's size.

We would like hypotheses that have not yet been generated or that have been pruned nevertheless to influence the strength of the hypotheses in the network. For example, if there are two potential interpretations for a stroke—a line and an arc—and the system prunes the line interpretation because it is too unlikely, the probability of the arc should go up. On the other hand, if the system has only generated an arc interpretation, and has not yet considered a line interpretation, the probability of the arc should remain modest because the stroke might still be a line.

We model nodes not present in the network through an additional parent, S_{np}, for each node H_n in the graph. We define $q_{np} = P(H_n = f \mid S_{np} = t)$ and set $S_{np} = t$. The value of q_{np} takes into account which nodes have been eliminated from the graph and which have not (yet) been instantiated, and it is calculated as follows. Let $T_1, \ldots, T_p$ be the set of shapes that have an element of type H_n as a child but do not exist as parents of H_n in the network. We refer to $T_1, \ldots, T_p$ as *potential parents* of H_n. For example, for node L_1 in Fig. 2.14, this set would contain the single element ML because the marriage-link is the only shape in the family tree domain that has a line as a subshape but is not already a parent of L_1 in the graph. Let $T_1, \ldots, T_i$ be the subset of potential parents that have never appeared as a parent for H_n, and let $T_{i+1}, \ldots, T_p$ be the subset with elements that were once parents for H_n but have been pruned from the network. Then, $q_{np} = \prod_{j=1}^{i} 1 - P(T_j)$. We call $P(T_j)$ the *simple marginal probability* of T_j. It is calculated by calculating the marginal probability based only on the priors of the parents and ancestors of T_j in a network containing exactly one instance of each parent of T_j.

The effect of q_{np} is to allow only those shapes that have not yet been instantiated as parents of H_n to contribute to the probability that $H_n = t$. If the simple marginal probabilities of the missing parents are high, q_{np} will be low, and thus will help raise $P(H_n \mid S_1, \ldots, S_m, S_{np})$. If all the potential parents of H_n have previously been pruned, q_{np} will be 1 and thus have no effect on $P(H_n \mid S_1, \ldots, S_m, S_{np})$.

2.5.4 Implementation and Bayesian Inference

Our system updates the structure of the Bayesian network in response to each stroke the user draws. To perform this dynamic Bayesian network construction, we use an off-the-shelf, open source Bayesian network package for Java called BNJ [61]. Our system manages the hypotheses for the user's strokes as they are generated and pruned. When these hypotheses need to be evaluated (e.g., before they are pruned), our system creates a Bayesian network in BNJ by creating the necessary nodes and links as BNJ Java objects. Our system can then use a number of methods that are built into BNJ for reasoning about the probability of each node.

Generating and modifying the BNJ networks can be time-consuming due to the exponential size of the conditional probability tables (CPTs) between the nodes. We use two techniques to improve the system's performance. First, BNJ networks are only generated when the system needs to evaluate the likelihood of a given hypothesis. This on-demand construction is more efficient than continuously updating the BNJ network because batch construction of the CPTs is often more efficient than incremental construction of these tables. Second, the system modifies only the portion of the BNJ network that has changed between strokes instead of creating it from scratch every time. The process of keeping track of the added and removed hypotheses adds a slight bookkeeping overhead, but this overhead is far less than the work required to regenerate the entire network after each stroke.

To determine the likelihood of each hypothesis, our system uses the BNJ network to find the marginal posterior probability for each node in the network. We experimented with several inference methods including the junction tree algorithm [29, 38], Gibbs sampling, and loopy belief propagation (loopy BP) [43, 59]. Both the junction tree algorithm and loopy BP produced meaningful marginal posterior probabilities, but after some experimentation we were unable to obtain useful results using Gibbs Sampling. We discovered that although the junction tree algorithm gave meaningful results, the networks produced by our system were often too complex for the algorithm to process in a reasonable amount of time. We found that when the junction tree algorithm produced a clique including more than 11 nodes the processing took too long to be acceptable. Unfortunately, for more complicated diagrams and domains, clique sizes greater than 11 were quite common.

Fortunately, we found loopy BP to be quite successful for our task. Although the algorithm is not guaranteed to converge to correct values, we found that on our data the algorithm almost always converged. There were probably only two or three instances in hundreds of tests where the values did not converge. We initialized the messages to 1 and ran the algorithm until node values were stable to within 0.001.

Loopy BP was significantly faster than the junction tree algorithm, but for complex data it was still occasionally slower than we wished. To speed up the system's performance, we added two restrictions. First, we terminated the belief propagation algorithm after 60 seconds of processing if it had not converged by this time. This restriction was needed only about a dozen times in the 80 circuit diagrams we processed, but it prevented the rare case where belief propagation took 20 minutes to converge. Second, we allowed each node to have no more than eight parents (i.e., only eight higher-level hypotheses could be considered for a single hypothesis). This restriction ensured a limit on the complexity of the graphs produced by the system. For the family tree domain, this limitation had no effect on the system's performance because the system never generated more than eight higher-level hypotheses for a lower-level hypothesis. However, in the circuit domain, higher-level hypotheses were occasionally prevented from being considered due to this limitation. For complex domains such as circuit diagrams, we will need to work on finding more efficient inference algorithms to allow the system to process more complex networks in a reasonable amount of time. We will also explore other methods of simplifying the network structure that do not prevent the system from considering possibly correct hypotheses.

2.6 Hypothesis Generation

The major challenge in hypothesis generation is to generate the correct interpretation as a candidate hypothesis without generating too many to consider in real-time.

Our method of evaluating partial interpretations allows us to use a bottom–up/top–down generation strategy that greatly reduces the number of hypotheses considered but still generates the correct interpretation for most shapes in the sketch.

Our hypothesis generation algorithm has three steps.

1. Bottom–up step: As the user draws, the system parses the strokes into primitive objects using a domain-independent recognition toolkit developed in previous work [48]. Compound interpretations are hypothesized for each compound object that includes these low-level shapes, even if not all the subshapes of the pattern have been found.
2. Top–down step: The system attempts to find subshapes that are missing from the partial interpretations generated in step 1, often by reinterpreting strokes that are temporally and spatially proximal to the proposed shape.
3. Pruning step: The system removes unlikely interpretations.

This algorithm, together with the Bayesian network representation presented above, deals successfully with the challenges presented in Sect. 2.2. Using the example in Fig. 2.13, we illustrate how the system generates hypotheses that allow the Bayesian network mechanism to resolve noise and inherent ambiguity in the sketch, how the system manages the number of potential interpretations for the sketch, how the system recovers from low-level recognition errors, and how the system allows for variation in drawing style. For a more detailed description of how we handle specific challenges in hypothesis generation, see [1].

Based on low-level interpretations of a stroke, the bottom–up step generates a set of hypotheses to be evaluated using the Bayesian network mechanism presented in the previous section. In the sketch in Fig. 2.13, the user's first stroke is correctly identified as an ellipse by the low-level recognizer, and from that ellipse the system generates the interpretation `ellipse`, and in turn, partial interpretations (templates) for mother-son, mother-daughter, father-daughter, marriage, partner-female, and divorce. These proposed interpretations have empty slots into which future interpretations will be filled in.

Naive bottom–up interpretation easily can generate too many hypotheses to consider in real-time. We employ three strategies to control the number of hypotheses generated in the bottom–up step. First, when an interpretation can be fit into more than one slot in a higher-level template (e.g., in Fig. 2.14, L1 could be the shaft or either of the lines in the head of A1), the system arbitrarily chooses one of the valid slots rather than generating one hypothesis for each potential fit. Later, the system can shuffle the shapes in the template when it attempts to fit more subshapes.

Second, the system does not generate higher-level interpretations for interpretations that are only partially filled. The lines generated from Strokes 4 and 5 in Fig. 2.13 result in one partial hypothesis—`arrow` (A1)—and two complete hypotheses—`quadrilateral` (Q1) and `marriage-link` (ML1) (Fig. 2.14). Continuing to generate higher-level templates from partial hypotheses would yield a large number of hypotheses (one hypothesis for each higher-level domain pattern involving each existing partial hypothesis). To avoid this explosion, the system continues to generate templates using only the complete hypotheses (in this case, ML1 and Q1).

Third, when the system processes polylines, it assumes that all the lines in a single polyline will be used in one interpretation. While this assumption does not always hold, in practice we find that it is often true and greatly reduces the number of possible interpretations. The system recognizes Stroke 2 as a four-line polyline. The bottom–up step generates only a quadrilateral because that is the only shape in the domain that requires four lines.

The top–down step allows our system to recover from low-level recognition errors. Stroke 3 is incorrectly, but reasonably, parsed into five lines by the low-level recognizer. Because the system does not know about any five-line objects, but does know about things that contain fewer than five lines, it attempts to re-segment the stroke into two lines, three lines and four lines (with a threshold on acceptable error). It succeeds in re-segmenting the stroke into four lines and successfully recognizes the lines as a quadrilateral. Although the four-line fit is not perfect, the network allows the context of the quadrilateral in addition to the stroke data to influence the system's belief in the four-line interpretation. Also note that the five lines from the original segmentation remain in the interpretation network.

The system controls the number of interpretations in the network through pruning, which occasionally causes it to prune a correct hypothesis before it is complete. The top–down step regenerates previously pruned hypotheses, allowing the system to correctly interpret a symbol despite variations in drawing order. The left-most arrow in Fig. 2.2 was drawn with two non-consecutive strokes (Strokes 8 and 12). In response to Stroke 8, the system generates both an arrow partial hypothesis and a marriage-link hypothesis (using the line hypothesis generated for this stroke). Because the user does not immediately complete the arrow, and because the competing marriage-link hypothesis is complete and has a high probability, the system prunes the arrow hypothesis after Stroke 9 is drawn. Later, Stroke 12 is interpreted as a two-line polyline and a new arrow partial hypothesis is generated. The top–down step then completes this arrow interpretation using the line generated previously from Stroke 8, effectively regenerating a previously pruned interpretation.

2.6.1 Selecting an Interpretation

As each stroke is drawn, the sketch system uses a greedy algorithm to select the best interpretation for the sketch. It queries the Bayesian network for the strongest complete interpretation, sets aside all the interpretations inconsistent with this choice, chooses the next most likely remaining domain interpretation, and so forth. It leaves strokes that are part of partial hypotheses uninterpreted. Although the system selects the most likely interpretation at every stroke, it does not eliminate other interpretations. Partial interpretations remain and can be completed with the user's subsequent strokes. Additionally, the system can change its interpretation of a stroke when more context is added.

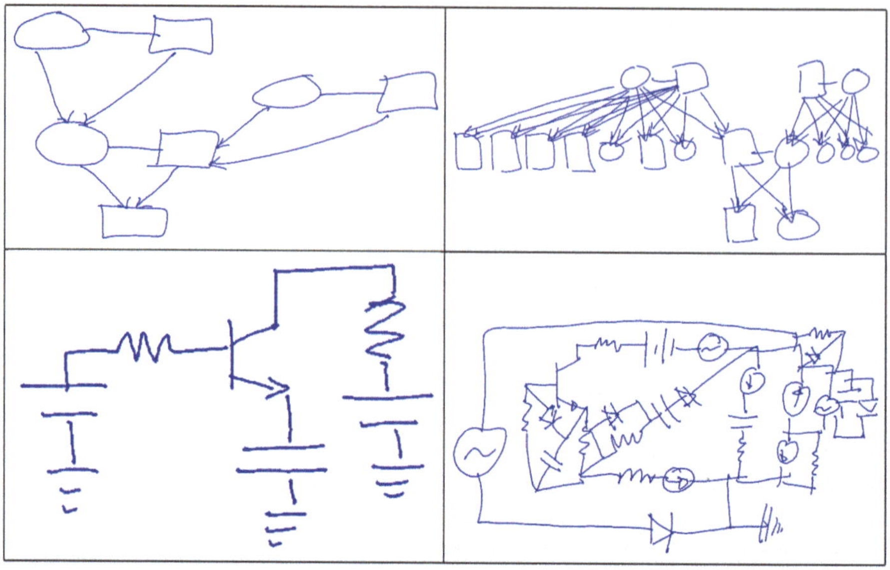

Fig. 2.15 Examples that illustrate the range of complexity of the sketches collected

2.7 Application and Results

Applying our complete system, called SketchREAD (Sketch Recognition Engine for mAny Domains), to a particular domain involves two steps: specifying the structural descriptions for the shapes in the domain and specifying the prior probabilities for the domain patterns and any top-level shapes (i.e., those not used in domain patterns, which, consequently, will not have parents in the generated Bayesian network. See [1] for details on how probabilities are assigned to other shapes). We applied SketchREAD to two domains: family trees and circuits. For each domain, we wrote a description for each shape and pattern in that domain and estimated the necessary prior probabilities by hand. Through experimentation, we found the recognition performance to be insensitive to the exact values of these priors.

We ran SketchREAD on a set of ten family tree diagrams and 80 circuit diagrams we collected from users.[3] Examples of these sketches are given in Fig. 2.15. We present qualitative results, as well as aggregate recognition and running time results for each domain. Our results illustrate the complexity our system can currently handle, as well as the system's current limitations. We discuss those limitations below, describing how best to use the system in its current state and highlighting what needs to be done to make the system more powerful. Note that to apply the system to each domain, we simply loaded the domain's shape information; we did not modify the recognition system.

[3]To collect these sketches we asked users to perform synthesis tasks (i.e. not to copy pre-existing diagrams) and performed no recognition while they were sketching.

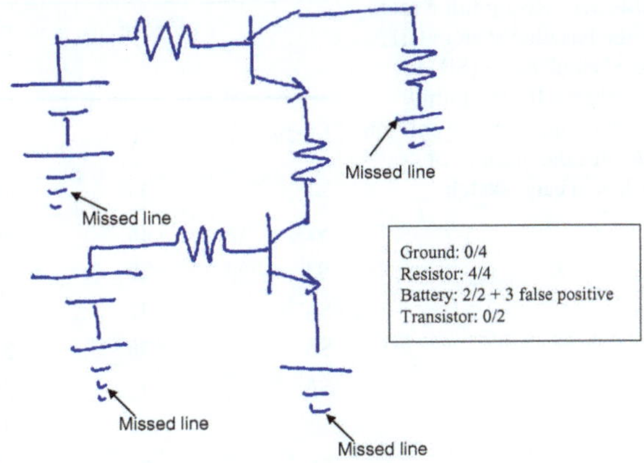

(a) Baseline System

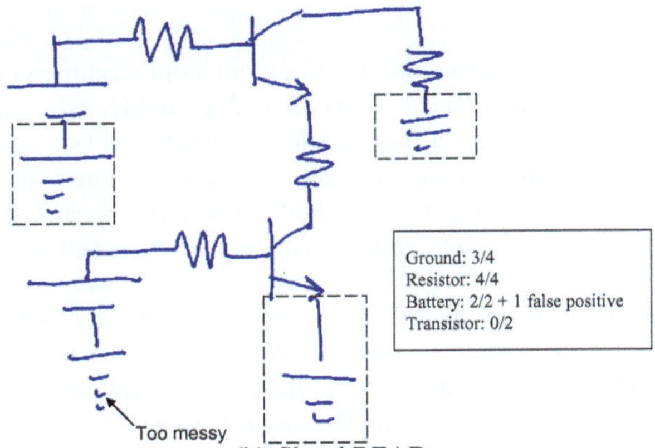

(b) SketchREAD

Fig. 2.16 Recognition performance example. Overall recognition results (# correct/total) are shown in the boxes

Figure 2.16 illustrates how our system is capable of handling noise in the sketch and recovering from missed low-level interpretations. In the baseline case, one line from each ground symbol was incorrectly interpreted at the low-level, causing the ground interpretations to fail. SketchREAD was able to reinterpret those lines using the context of the ground symbol in three of the four cases to correctly identify the symbol. In the fourth case, one of the lines was simply too messy, and SketchREAD preferred to (incorrectly) recognize the top two lines of the ground symbol as a battery.

In evaluating our system's performance, direct comparisons with previous work are difficult, as there are few (if any) published results for this type of recognition task, and those that are published are tested on different (unavailable) datasets. We compared SketchREAD's recognition performance with the performance of a strictly bottom–up approach of the sort used in previous systems [2, 42]. This strictly bottom–up approach combined low-level shapes into higher-level patterns without

Table 2.1 Recognition rates for the baseline system (BL) and SketchREAD (SR) for each sketch for the family tree domain. The size column indicates the number of strokes in each sketch

	Size	#Shapes	% Correct	
			BL	SR
Mean	50	34	50	77
S1	24	16	75	100
S2	28	16	75	87
S3	29	23	57	78
S4	32	22	31	81
S5	38	31	54	87
S6	48	36	58	78
S7	51	43	26	72
S8	64	43	49	74
S9	84	49	42	61
S10	102	60	57	80

top–down reinterpretation. Even though our baseline system did not reinterpret low-level interpretations, it was not trivial. It could handle some ambiguities in the drawing (e.g., whether a line should be interpreted as a marriage-link or the side of a quadrilateral) using contextual information in the bottom–up direction. To encourage others to compare their results with those presented here we have made our test set publicly available at http://rationale.csail.mit.edu/ETCHASketches.

We measured recognition performance for each system by determining the number of correctly identified objects in each sketch (Tables 2.1 and 2.2). For the family tree diagrams SketchREAD performed consistently and notably better than our baseline system. On average, the baseline system correctly identified 50% of the symbols, while SketchREAD correctly identified 77%, a 54% reduction in the number of recognition errors. Due to inaccurate low-level recognition, the baseline system performed quite poorly on some sketches. Improving low-level recognition would improve recognition results for both systems; however, SketchREAD reduced the error rate by approximately 50% independent of the performance of the baseline system. Because it is impossible to build a perfect low-level recognizer, SketchREAD's ability to correct low-level errors will always be important.

Circuit diagrams present SketchREAD with more of a challenge for several reasons. First, there are more shapes in the circuit diagram domain and these shapes are more complex. Second, there is a stronger degree of overlap between shapes in the circuit diagrams. For example, it can be difficult to distinguish between a capacitor and a battery. As another example, a ground symbol contains within it (at least one) battery symbol. Finally, there is more variation in the way people draw circuit diagrams, and their sketches are messier causing the low-level recognizer to fail more often. They tend to include more spurious lines and over-tracings.

Overall, SketchREAD correctly identified 62% of the shapes in the circuit diagrams, a 17% reduction in error over the baseline system. It was unable to handle more complex shapes, such as transistors, because it often failed to generate the

Table 2.2 Aggregate recognition rates for the baseline system (BL) and SketchREAD (SR) for the circuit diagrams by shape

	Total	% Correct		# False Pos	
		BL	SR	BL	SR
AC Source	4	100	100	35	29
Battery	96	60	89	56	71
Capacitor	39	56	69	27	14
Wire	1182	62	67	478	372
Ground	98	18	55	0	5
Resistor	330	51	53	7	8
Voltage Src.	43	2	47	1	8
Diode	77	22	17	0	0
Current Src.	44	7	16	0	0
Transistor	43	0	7	0	14

correct mapping between strokes and pieces of the template. Although the system attempts to shuffle subshapes in a template in response to new input, for the sake of time it cannot consider all possible mappings of strokes to templates. We discuss below how we might extend SketchREAD to improve its performance on complex domains such as circuit diagrams.

We measured SketchREAD's running time to determine how it scales with the number of strokes in the sketch. Figure 2.17 graphs the median time to process each stroke for each domain. The vertical bars in the graph show the standard deviation in processing time over the sketches in each domain. (One family tree diagram took a particularly long time to process because of the complexity of its interpretation network, discussed below. This sketch affected the median processing time only slightly but dominated the standard deviation. It has been omitted from the graph for clarity.) Three things about these graphs are important. First, although SketchREAD does not yet run in real-time, the time to process each stroke in general increased only slightly as the sketch got larger. Second, not every stroke was processed by the system in the same amount of time. Finally, the processing time for the circuit diagrams is longer than the processing time for the family trees.

By instrumenting the system, we determined that the processing time is dominated by the inference in the Bayesian network, and all of the above phenomena can be explained by examining the size and complexity of the interpretation network. The number of nodes in the interpretation network grows approximately linearly as the number of strokes increases. This result is encouraging, as the network would grow exponentially using a naïve approach to hypothesis generation. The increase in graph size accounts for the slight increase in processing time in both graphs. The spikes in the graphs can be explained by the fact that some strokes not only increased the size of the network, but had more higher-level interpretations, creating more fully connected graph structures, which causes an exponential increase in inference time. After being evaluated, most of these high-level hypotheses were immediately pruned, accounting for the sharp drop in processing time on the next

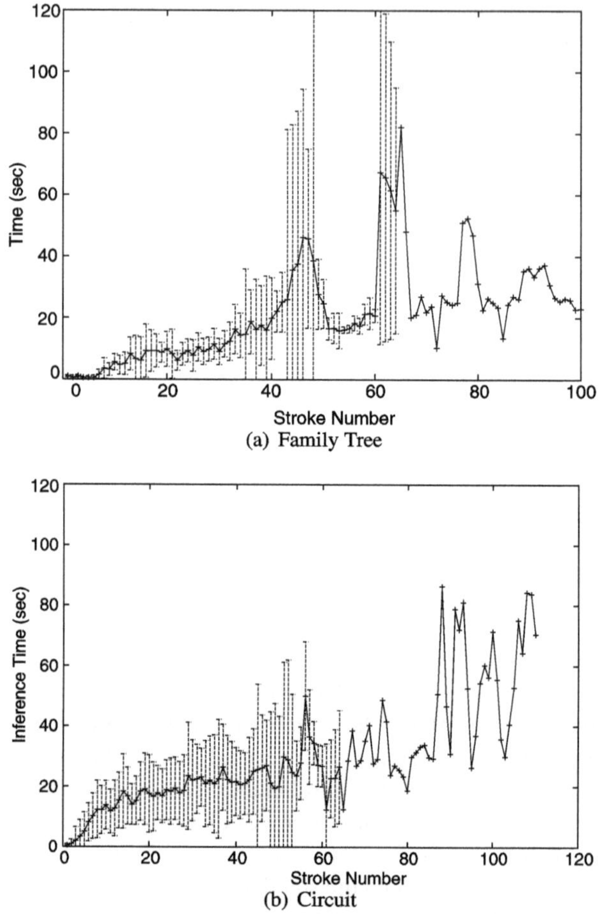

Fig. 2.17 The median incremental time it took the system to process each stroke in the family tree and circuit diagrams. *Vertical bars* show the standard deviation across the sketches in each domain

stroke. Finally, the fact that circuits take longer to process than family trees is related to the relative complexity of the shapes in the domain. There are more shapes in the circuit diagram domain and they are more complex, so the system must consider more interpretations for the user's strokes, resulting in larger and more connected Bayesian networks.

2.8 Remaining Challenges and Extensions

SketchREAD significantly improves the recognition performance of unconstrained sketches. However, its accuracy, especially for complicated sketches and domains, is still too low to be practical in most cases. Here we consider how to improve the system's performance, and in particular, describe a promising method for aiding with segmentation, without placing constraints on the users' drawing style.

First, while SketchREAD always corrected some low-level interpretation errors, its overall performance still depended on the quality of the low-level recognition. Our low-level recognizer was highly variable and could not cope with some users' drawing styles. In particular, it often missed corners of polylines, particularly for symbols such as resistors. Recently proposed, more accurate corner-finding techniques [60] will help address these problems.

Second, although in general SketchREAD's processing time scaled well as the number of strokes increased, it occasionally ran for a long period. The system had particular trouble with areas of the sketch that involved many strokes drawn close together in time and space and with domains that involve more complicated or overlapping symbols. This increase in processing time was due almost entirely to in increase in Bayesian network complexity.

We suggest two possible solutions. First, part of the complexity arises because the system tries to combine new strokes with low-level interpretations to form correct high-level interpretations (e.g., the four lines that make a quadrilateral). These new interpretations were pruned immediately, but they increased the size and complexity of the network temporarily, causing the bottlenecks noted above. In response, we are testing methods for "confirming" older interpretations and removing their subparts from consideration other higher-level interpretations as well as confirming their values in the Bayesian network so that their posterior probabilities do not have to be constantly re-computed. Second, we can modify the belief propagation algorithm we are using. We currently use Loopy Belief Propagation, which repeatedly sends messages between the nodes until each node has reached a stable value. Each time the system evaluates the graph, it resets the initial messages to one, essentially erasing the work that was done the last time inference was performed, even though most of the graph remains largely unchanged. Instead, this algorithm should begin by passing the messages it passed at the end of the previous inference step.

Third, because our recognition algorithm is stroke-based, spurious lines and over-tracing hindered the system's performance in both accuracy and running time. A preprocessing step to merge strokes into single lines would likely greatly improve the system's performance. Also, in the circuit diagram domain, users often drew more than one object with a single stroke. A preprocessing step could help the system segment strokes into individual objects.

2.8.1 Using Single-Stroke Classification to Improve Grouping

Many of the above problems were caused by the difficulty of performing simultaneous segmentation and recognition. In SketchREAD, recognition and segmentation are inherently intertwined: the various hypotheses dictate different stroke segmentations. Using our template-based recognition approach to dictate segmentation means that our system cannot rely on segmentation to limit the number of possible interpretations, nor can it apply vision-based algorithms efficiently to sets of strokes known to comprise a single object. However, as discussed in Sect. 2.2, there is no

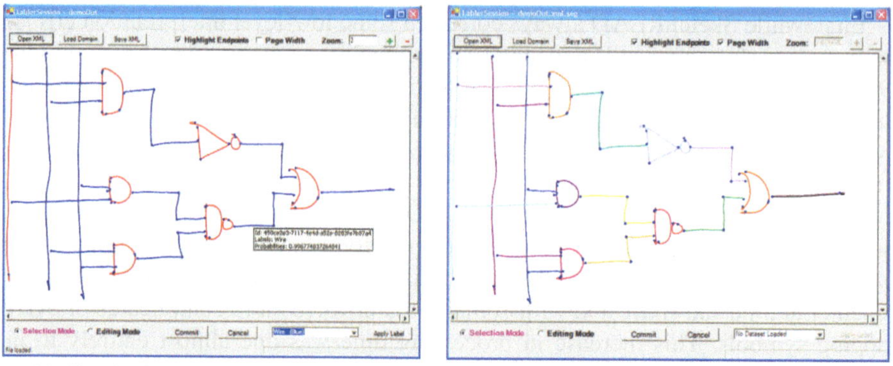

(a) Sketch after stroke-level recognition

(b) Sketch after stroke grouping

Fig. 2.18 Single-stroke recognition and grouping

reliable purely spatial or temporal method to segment strokes into individual objects in freely-drawn sketches.

Recently, researchers have developed a technique to roughly classify single strokes, and this classification be used to inform the process of sketch segmentation. The technique relies on the fact that strokes can be roughly grouped into categories individually by looking at their local properties and their relationships to other strokes in the diagram. For example, in the circuit diagram in Fig. 2.18 the strokes that make up the gates tend to be shorter and have a higher curvature than the strokes that make up the wires. The wire strokes and gate strokes also have a well-defined relationship to one another. Then, once strokes individually are classified as either wires or gates (Fig. 2.18(a)) they are sufficiently separated in both time and space that simple clustering algorithms can successfully group strokes into individual objects (Fig. 2.18(b)), which can then be recognized by any number of sketch recognition algorithms, including the Bayesian network approach presented in this chapter.

Szummer and Qi [53] developed a method for classifying individual strokes based on local and contextual information based using conditional random fields. They illustrate its success on organizational chart diagrams. We have applied their approach to the more complex domain of circuit diagrams and find that it performs quite well.

Briefly, a CRF is an undirected graphical model that represents the conditional probability distribution $P(\mathbf{y} \mid \mathbf{x})$ where $\mathbf{x}$ is a set of input data and $\mathbf{y}$ is a set of labels for these data. The actual CRF consists of a graph $G = (V, E)$ and an associated set of potential functions that together define $P(\mathbf{y} \mid \mathbf{x})$. Each node in V corresponds to an element to label (i.e. the members of $\mathbf{y}$), and each edge in E quantifies a probabilistic dependence between these elements. For more details, see [53].

In our application, the vector $\mathbf{x}$ represents the stroke data while the vector $\mathbf{y}$ represents the labels for each stroke. $P(\mathbf{y} \mid \mathbf{x})$, then, is simply the probability of a given labeling for each stroke, given properties of the stroke data.

We automatically create the graph by creating a node for each stroke and linking nodes for strokes that are spatially or temporally proximal. We find that for some domains, including the digital circuit domain, fragmenting strokes at their corners before creating the graph, as in [53], degrades performance. We consider two types of potential functions: site potentials that measure the compatibility between a stroke and its associated label, and pairwise interaction potentials that measure the compatibility between neighboring labels. Both types of potentials measure compatibility by linearly combining parameters with a set of feature functions and passing the result through a non-linearity (we use the exponential).

After labeling each stroke, we group strokes into individual objects. Even with perfect labels, stroke grouping is not trivial. For example, different wires may overlap in space and the same wire may be separated in time. We use a graph theoretic method for stroke grouping that treats each labeled stroke as a node in a graph, with edges between adjacent strokes. The algorithm then finds the connected components in the graph.

Two strokes are adjacent if their minimum distance is lower than a given threshold. We designed specific distance metrics for the digital circuit domain. Given two strokes, if neither stroke is a wire, then the minimum distance between the strokes is the minimum distance between any two points in the strokes. If either stroke is a wire, the minimum distance between the strokes is the distance from an endpoint to any other point on the other stroke. We use this modified distance because wires frequently overlap even when they are not meant to represent the same component. In both cases, the minimum distance is normalized by the sum of the diagonals of the smallest bounding box around each of the strokes. This normalization provides a unitless measure that is invariant under uniform scaling.

Although this work is still in progress, our initial results in this area are promising. We tested our CRF for single-stroke classification on digital circuit diagrams, classifying strokes as text, wires or gates, and achieve 93% overall accuracy and 77% accuracy in stroke segmentation. Figure 2.18 shows one example result.

2.9 Conclusion

This chapter has presented an approach to multi-domain sketch recognition using dynamically constructed Bayesian networks. We have shown how to use context to improve online sketch interpretation and demonstrated its performance in SketchREAD, an implemented sketch recognition system that can be applied to multiple domains. We have shown that SketchREAD is more robust and powerful than previous systems at recognizing unconstrained sketch input in a domain. The capabilities of this system have applications both in human computer interaction and artificial intelligence. Using and building on this approach, we will be able to explore further the nature of usable intelligent computer-based sketch systems and gain a better understanding of what people would like from a drawing system that is capable of understanding their freely-drawn sketches as more than just strokes. This work provides a necessary step in uniting artificial intelligence technology with novel interaction technology to make interacting with computers more like interacting with humans.

Acknowledgements This work is based on my PhD thesis, supervised by Randall Davis at the Massachusetts Institute of Technology. Recent work is funded by an NSF CAREER award (IIS-0546809).

References

1. Alvarado, C.: Multi-domain sketch understanding. PhD thesis, MIT (2004)
2. Alvarado, C., Davis, R.: Resolving ambiguities to create a natural sketch based interface. In: Proceedings of IJCAI-2001 (2001)
3. Alvarado, C., Davis, R.: Sketchread: A multi-domain sketch recognition engine. In: Proc. UIST (2004)
4. Alvarado, C., Davis, R.: Dynamically constructed Bayes nets for sketch understanding. In: Proceedings of IJCAI '05 (2005)
5. Alvarado, C., Lazzareschi, M.: Properties of real-world digital logic diagrams. In: Proc. of the 1st International Workshop on Pen-Based Learning Technologies (PLT-07) (2007)
6. Bishop, C.M., Svensen, M., Hinton, G.E.: Distinguishing text from graphics in on-line handwritten ink. In: IWFHR '04: Proceedings of the Ninth International Workshop on Frontiers in Handwriting Recognition, pp. 142–147. IEEE Computer Society, Washington (2004)
7. Blostein, D., Haken, L.: Using diagram generation software to improve diagram recognition: A case study of music notation. IEEE Transactions on Pattern Analysis and Machine Intelligence **21**(11) (1999)
8. Buxton, B.: Sketching User Experiences: Getting the Design Right and the Right Design. Morgan Kaufmann, San Mateo (2007)
9. Caetano, A., Goulart, N., Fonseca, M., Jorge, J.: Sketching user interfaces with visual patterns. In: Proceedings of the 1st Ibero-American Symposium in Computer Graphics (SIACG02), pp. 271–279 (2002)
10. Charniak, E.: Bayesian networks without tears: making Bayesian networks more accessible to the probabilistically unsophisticated. Artificial Intelligence **12**(4), 50–63 (1991)
11. Cohen, P.R., Johnston, M., McGee, D., Oviatt, S., Pittman, J., Smith, I., Chen, L., Clow, J.: Quickset: Multimodal interaction for distributed applications. In: ACM Multimedia'97, pp. 31–40. ACM Press, New York (1997)
12. Do, E.Y.L., Gross, M.D.: Drawing as a means to design reasoning. AI and Design (1996)
13. Forbus, K.D., Usher, J., Chapman, V.: Sketching for military course of action diagrams. In: Proceedings of IUI (2003)
14. Forsberg, A.S., Dieterich, M.K., Zeleznik, R.C.: The music notepad. In: Proceedings of UIST '98. ACM SIGGRAPH. ACM, New York (1998)
15. Futrelle, R.P., Nikolakis, N.: Efficient analysis of complex diagrams using constraint-based parsing. In: ICDAR-95 (International Conference on Document Analysis and Recognition), Montreal, Canada, pp. 782–790 (1995)
16. Gennari, L., Kara, L.B., Stahovich, T.F.: Combining geometry and domain knowledge to interpret hand-drawn diagrams. Computers and Graphics: Special Issue on Pen-Based User Interfaces (2005)
17. Getoor, L., Friedman, N., Koller, D., Pfeffer, A.: Learning probabilistic relational models. In: IJCAI, pp. 1300–1309 (1999). http://citeseer.nj.nec.com/friedman99learning.html
18. Glessner, S., Koller, D.: Constructing flexible dynamic belief networks from first-order probabilistinc knowledge bases. In: Symbolic and Quantitative Approaches to Reasoning and Uncertainty, pp. 217–226 (1995)

19. Goldman, R.P., Charniak, E.: A language for construction of belief networks. IEEE Transactions on Pattern Analysis and Machine Intelligence **13**(3) (1993)
20. Grimson, W.E.L.: The combinatorics of heuristic search termination for object recognition in cluttered environments. IEEE Transactions on PAMI **13**(9), 920–935 (1991)
21. Gross, M.D.: The electronic cocktail napkin—a computational environment for working with design diagrams. Design Studies **17**, 53–69 (1996)
22. Gross, M., Do, E.Y.L.: Ambiguous intentions: A paper-like interface for creative design. In: Proceedings of UIST 96, pp. 183–192 (1996)
23. Haddawy, P.: Generating Bayesian networks from probability logic knowledge bases. In: Proceedings of UAI '94 (1994)
24. Hammond, T., Davis, R.: Tahuti: A geometrical sketch recognition system for UML class diagrams. In: AAAI Spring Symposium on Sketch Understanding, 59–68 (2002)
25. Hammond, T., Davis, R.: LADDER: A language to describe drawing, display, and editing in sketch recognition. In: Proceedings of the 2003 International Joint Conference on Artificial Intelligence (IJCAI) (2003)
26. Hammond, T., Davis, R.: Automatically transforming symbolic shape descriptions for use in sketch recognition. In: Proceedings of the Nineteenth National Conference on Artificial Intelligence (AAAI-04) (2004)
27. Hammond, T., Davis, R.: Interactive learning of structural shape descriptions from automatically generated near-miss examples. In: IUI '06: Proceedings of the 11th International Conference on Intelligent User Interfaces, pp. 210–217. ACM, New York (2006)
28. Hse, H., Newton, A.R.: Recognition and beautification of multi-stroke symbols in digital ink. Computers and Graphics (2005)
29. Jensen, F.V., Lauritzen, S.L., Olesen, K.G.: Bayesian updating in causal probabilistic networks by local computations. Computational Statistics Quarterly **4**, 269–282 (1990)
30. Jensen, F.V.: Bayesian Networks and Decision Graphs. Statistics for Engineering and Information Science. Springer, Berlin (2001)
31. Kara, L.B., Stahovich, T.F.: Hierarchical parsing and recognition of hand-sketched diagrams. In: Proc. of UIST '04 (2004)
32. Koller, D., Pfeffer, A.: Object-oriented Bayesian networks. In: Proceedings of the Thirteenth Annual Conference on Uncertainty, Providence, RI, pp. 302–313 (1997)
33. Labahn, G., MacLean, S., Marzouk, M., Rutherford, I., Tausky, D.: Mathbrush: An experimental pen-based math system. In: Dagstuhl Seminar Proceedings, Challenges in Symbolic Computation Software (2006)
34. Landay, J.A., Myers, B.A.: Interactive sketching for the early stages of user interface design. In: Proceedings of CHI '95: Human Factors in Computing Systems, pp. 43–50 (1995)
35. Lank, E.H.: A retargetable framework for interactive diagram recognition. In: Proceedings of the Seventh International Conference on Document Analysis and Recognition (ICDAR'03) (2003)
36. Lank, E., Thorley, J.S., Chen, S.J.S.: An interactive system for recognizing hand drawn UML diagrams. In: Proceedings for CASCON (2000)
37. Laskey, K.B., Mahoney, S.M.: Network fragments: Representing knowledge for constructing probabilistic models. In: Proceedings of UAI '97 (1997)
38. Lauritzen, S.L., Spiegelhalter, D.J.: Local computations with probabilities on graphical structures and their application to expert systems. Journal of the Royal Statistical Society **50**(2), 157–224 (1988)
39. LaViola, J., Zeleznik, R.: Mathpad2: A system for the creation and exploration of mathematical sketches. ACM Transactions on Graphics (Proceedings of SIGGRAPH 2004) **23**(3) (2004)
40. Lu, W., Wu, W., Sakauchi, M.: A drawing recognition system with rule acquisition ability. In: Proceedings of the Third International Conference on Document Analysis and Recognition, vol. 1, pp. 512–515 (1995)
41. Matsakis, N.: Recognition of handwritten mathematical expressions. Master's thesis, Massachusetts Institute of Technology (1999)

42. Newman, M.W., Lin, J., Hong, J.I., Landay, J.A.: DENIM: An informal Web site design tool inspired by observations of practice. Human-Computer Interaction **18**(3), 259–324 (2003)
43. Pearl, J.: Probabilistic Reasoning in Intelligent Systems: Networks of Plausible Inference. Morgan Kaufmann, San Mateo (1988)
44. Pfeffer, A., Koller, D., Milch, B., Takusagawa, K.: SPOOK: A system for probabilistic object-oriented knowledge representation. In: Proceedings of UAI '99, pp. 541–550 (1999)
45. Poole, D.: Probabilistic horn abduction and Bayesian networks. Artificial Intelligence (1993)
46. Saund, E., Fleet, D., Larner, D., Mahoney, J.: Perceptually supported image editing of text and graphics. In: Proceedings of UIST '03 (2003)
47. Sezgin, T.M., Davis, R.: Sketch interpretation using multiscale models of temporal patterns. IEEE Computer Graphics and Applications **27**(1), 28–37 (2007). doi:10.1109/MCG.2007.17
48. Sezgin, T.M., Stahovich, T., Davis, R.: Sketch based interfaces: Early processing for sketch understanding. In: The Proceedings of 2001 Perceptive User Interfaces Workshop (PUI'01), Orlando, FL (2001)
49. Shilman, M., Pasula, H., Russell, S., Newton, R.: Statistical visual language models for ink parsing. In: Sketch Understanding, Papers from the 2002 AAAI Spring Symposium, pp. 126–132. AAAI Press, Stanford (2002)
50. Shilman, M., Viola, P., Chellapilla, K.: Recognition and grouping of handwritten text in diagrams and equations. In: Proceedings of the International Workshop on Frontiers in Handwriting Recognition (IWFHR) (2004)
51. Stahovich, T., Davis, R., Shrobe, H.: Generating multiple new designs from a sketch. Artificial Intelligence **104**(1–2), 211–264 (1998)
52. Strat, T.M., Fischler, M.A.: Context-based vision: Recognizing objects using information from both 2-d and 3-d imagery. IEEE Transactions on Pattern Analysis and Machine Intelligence **13**(10), 1050–1065 (1991)
53. Szummer, M., Qi, Y.: Contextual recognition of hand-drawn diagrams with conditional random fields. In: Proceedings of the 9th Int. Workshop on Frontiers in Handwriting Recognition (IWFHR), pp. 32–37 (2004)
54. Tenneson, D.: Technical report on the design and algorithms of chempad. Technical report, Brown University (2005)
55. Torralba, A., Sinha, P.: Statistical context priming for object detection. In: Proceedings of ICCV '01, pp. 763–770 (2001)
56. Ullman, D.G., Wood, S., Craig, D.: The importance of drawing in the mechanical design process. Computers and Graphics **14**(2), 263–274 (1990)
57. Veselova, O., Davis, R.: Perceptually based learning of shape descriptions. In: Proceedings of the Nineteenth National Conference on Artificial Intelligence (AAAI-04) (2004)
58. Wang, X., Biswas, M., Raghupathy, S.: Addressing class distribution issues of the drawing vs writing classification in an ink stroke sequence. In: SBIM '07: Proceedings of the 4th Eurographics Workshop on Sketch-based Interfaces and Modeling, pp. 139–146. ACM, New York (2007). doi:10.1145/1384429.1384458
59. Weiss, Y.: Belief propagation and revision in networks with loops. Technical report, AI Memo No. 1616, CBCL Paper No. 155, Massachusetts Institute of Technology (1997)
60. Wolin, A., Hammond, T.: Shortstraw: A simple and effective corner finder for polylines. In: Alvarado, C., Cani, M.P. (eds.) Eurographics Workshop on Sketch-Based Interfaces and Modeling (SBIM) (2008)
61. Bayesian network tools in java (bnj). http://bnj.sourceforge.net

Chapter 3
Minimizing Modes for Smart Selection in Sketching/Drawing Interfaces

Eric Saund and Edward Lank

3.1 Introduction

User interface modes are ubiquitous in both mouse–keyboard and pen-based user interfaces for creating graphical material through sketching and drawing. Whether choosing the straight-line or oval tool in Photoshop or PowerPoint, or tapping a toolbar prior to lassoing a word in order to select it in OneNote, users know that, before they can perform the content-relevant action they want, they need to tell the computer the intent of what they are about to do by setting a mode. This chapter reviews our research exploring whether prior setting of modes is always necessary, and whether the future of user interface designs may promise more fluid and direct ways of creating and then selecting and editing words and pictures on a screen.

The purpose of modes is to allow actions performed with a single input device to mean more than one thing. Physical paper permits two fundamental operations, creation of marks, and erasure. For these, the user employs two basic tools, each physically suited to its purpose: a marking tool (pencil, pen, typewriter keys and ribbon) and an erasure tool (eraser, white-out). Computers are more powerful than this. They permit not only creation and deletion, but all manner of modification such as moving, resizing, duplicating, changing colors, changing line quality, changing fonts, controlling depth order, etc.

To effect modification of content, computer authoring and editing tools provide two dominant modes: a creation mode, and a selection mode. Modification of content is performed by first entering selection mode, then selecting graphical content on the screen, and finally performing operations manipulating the selected content.

E. Saund (✉)
Palo Alto Research Center, 3333 Coyote Hill Rd., Palo Alto, CA 94304, USA
e-mail: saund@parc.com

E. Lank
David R. Cheriton School of Computer Science, University of Waterloo, 200 University Ave., West Waterloo, ON, Canada N2L 3G1
e-mail: lank@cs.uwaterloo.ca

J. Jorge, F. Samavati (eds.), *Sketch-based Interfaces and Modeling*,
DOI 10.1007/978-1-84882-812-4_3,

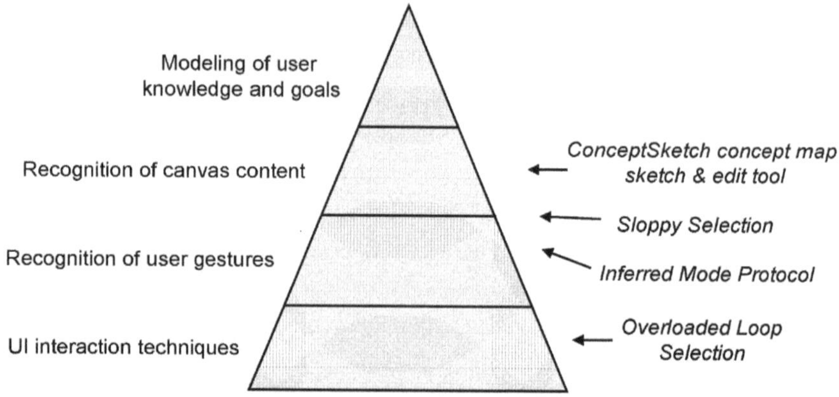

Fig. 3.1 Increasingly sophisticated methods for inferring user intent build on one another. This chapter offers examples highlighting techniques at several levels

Is it possible to design user interfaces that improve the fluidity and precision of the Selection step? Our research indicates that the answer can be yes. The key is to more fully exploit available information about user actions in the context of canvas content, to infer the user's intent. If the user's click, tap, or stroke gesture makes sense only in terms of one particular mode, then the program should allow the user to perform that operation without first explicitly setting the mode, and then post-facto interpret the action in terms of the correct mode.

This may require sophisticated analysis of user's gestures, the visual and semantic structure of canvas content, and even user desires and goals, as shown in Fig. 3.1. Such a project entails risk, for if the program guesses wrong the user interaction can go seriously awry. But when done carefully, the principle can be extended to not only inferring mode but other aspects of user intent, to create new levels of intelligent user interfaces.

This chapter focuses on mode minimization in interfaces via smarter selection techniques. We address three challenges associated with selection:

- How best to incorporate multiple selection techniques into a sketch interface.
- The drawback of requiring mode switching between content creation and selection.
- The challenge of selecting and interacting with salient groups of content.

We address these challenges through the creation of novel interaction techniques contained within a series of experimental graphical creation and editing programs that we have built. The ScanScribe document image editing program eliminates the mode tool palette in a mouse/keyboard image editor by overloading mouse functions for multiple selection methods. The InkScribe draw/edit program for pen computers eliminates prior Draw/Select mode selection through an Inferred Mode interface protocol. A technique we call Sloppy Selection illustrates intelligent object selection by analysis of gesture dynamics coupled with visual segmentation of canvas content. And the ConceptSketch program for creation and editing of Node-Link diagrams shows how recognition of diagrammatic structure supports intelligent object selection by cycling Click/Tap operations. These points in the gesture/canvas-content analysis pyramid are discussed in the subsequent sections of this chapter.

3.2 The Cost of Modes

To motivate minimizing modes in interfaces, it is useful to examine the cost of having a large set of modes. The salient research question is whether some benefit, either in efficiency or accuracy, exists for reducing the set of modes in an interface. To examine this question, we describe our recent work in the cost of mode switching. We first examine the temporal cost of large mode sets, and then explore the effect a large set of modes has on mode switching errors within sketch interfaces.

3.2.1 The Temporal Cost of Modes

Many researchers have studied variations in interaction techniques for stylus input systems that seek to fluidly allow both command and input [2, 5, 9, 17]. This research can be broadly separated into research that seeks to improve the accessibility of software modes versus research that seeks alternatives to modes. While our work primarily falls into the latter category, i.e. in reducing the need for modes within interfaces, improving the accessibility of modes in interfaces is an alternative for improving the fluidity of sketch or graphical applications that contain multiple modes.

One open question is whether or not there exists an "optimal" mode switching technique, and if so, what the performance of that mode switching technique might be. To partially address this question, Li et al. [9] studied five different existing mode switching techniques. These include typical mode switching techniques that have been extensively used, i.e. use of the eraser end of a dual ended stylus, use of the barrel button on an electronic stylus, a press and hold technique similar to the Apple Newton, and use of the non-preferred hand. They also examined a pressure based technique based on work by Ramos et al. on pressure widgets [13]. In this list of mode switching techniques, we note the absence of software widgets to control modes, a result of general recognition of the fact that improvements are needed over software-based modes [10]. Based on experimental data, Li et al. concluded that, of the five techniques, non-preferred hand performed best based upon the metrics of speed (fastest), error rate (second lowest), and user preference (most preferred).

Given the apparent benefit of non-preferred hand mode switching, we explored in detail the specific temporal costs associated with non-preferred hand mode switching [8, 15, 16]. In this work, we looked at the time taken to initiate modes with the non-preferred hand, and the total time taken to perform a simple drawing task, given the need to switch modes. We found that, as the number of modes increased, the total time taken to perform the drawing task increased, and that this increase was a result of an increase in the time required to initiate modes with the non-preferred hand. We discovered [16], using an interface with between two and eight modes, that the cost of manipulating modes in an interface could be modeled using the Hick–Hyman Law [4, 6]. This law predicts a linear relationship between response time and the information entropy, H, associated with n different responses, i.e.

$$RT = a + bH \tag{1}$$

where the information entropy, as defined by Shannon, is

$$H = \sum_{i=1}^{n} p_i \log_2\left(\frac{1}{p_i}\right) \tag{2}$$

where n is the number of alternatives (in our study, the number of modes) and p_i is the probability of the ith alternative.

Figure 3.2, reproduced from [16], depicts the linear relationship between information entropy, H, and time to select a mode, as described in the previous paragraph. To generate this data, we performed an experiment where we presented subjects with a simple line bisecting task, and asked the subjects to draw a line of a specific color, indicated by a mode. We measured the time taken to activate the mode with the non-preferred hand, the time between mode activation and the pen tip touching the surface of the display, and the time taken to perform the drawing task on a tablet computer. Analysis of variance shows that there is a significant main effect of the number of modes on total time ($F_{3,5} = 12.593$, $p < 0.001$) for the task. Analysis of variance for the time to activate modes, i.e. the time to press the appropriate button with the non-preferred hand, shows a significant effect of condition ($F_{3,5} = 22.826$, $p < 0.001$). However, the time interval between mode switch and pen down and the time to perform the drawing task did not vary significantly with number of modes ($F_{3,5} = 1.460$, $p = 0.269$ and $F_{3,5} = 2.360$, $p = 0.101$, respectively).

This work on the cost of mode switching provides evidence that, regardless of the efficiency of any mode switching technique, as you add modes to an interface the cost, measured as the time, to select any individual mode within the interface increases. By reducing the number of modes within an interface, we increase the efficiency of the interface.

3.2.2 Mode Errors: The Mode Problem

In addition to temporal efficiency, the accuracy with which users can manipulate an interface is an important consideration. It seems logical that larger numbers of modes in interfaces increases the likelihood of mode errors. The web site Usability First [20] defines as mode error as:

"A type of slip where a user performs an action appropriate to one situation in another situation, common in software with multiple modes. Examples include drawing software, where a user tries to use one drawing tool as if it were another (e.g.

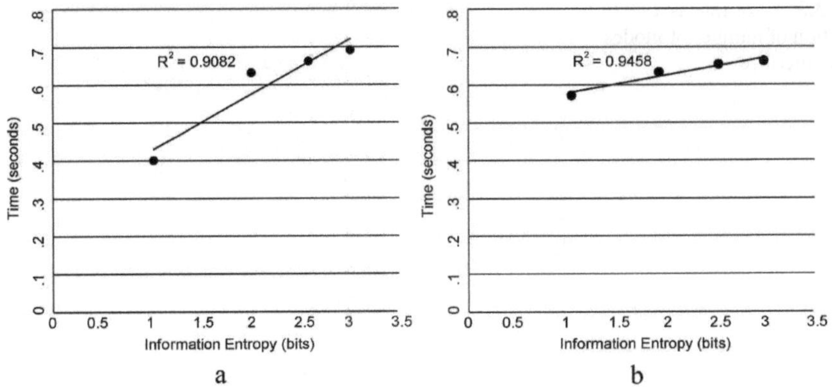

Fig. 3.2 By studying interfaces with two, four, six, eight modes, we show a linear relationship between information entropy, H, and the time taken to select a mode. **a** The case where all modes are equally probable. **b** Varies the probabilities for different modes in the interface

brushing with the Fill tool), or text editors with both a command mode and an insert mode where a user accidentally types commands and ends up inserting text."

Two of the most common mode errors include use of the CAPS-lock and Insert keys on keyboards, both of which alter the effect of keyboard input.

Systems normally mitigate against mode errors by providing some indicator for modes. However, Sellen et al. [19] studied the use of visual feedback and kinesthetic feedback to indicate modes. Visual feedback was provided by changing the shape of the cursor, and kinesthetic feedback by use of a footpedal. In their first study, they used a non-locking piano footpedal, and users were forced to maintain modes. In this experiment, they found that kinesthetic feedback was more effective at preventing mode errors than was visual feedback. They followed this study with a second study that contrasted a locking and non-locking footpedal, and found fewer errors with the non-locking footpedal. Based on Sellen's work, Jef Raskin, in his book *The Humane Interface* [14], advocates a mode switching technique he terms "quasimodes". With quasimodes, as with Sellen et al.'s non-locking footpedal, a user holds down a key to indicate modes.

The non-preferred hand mode switching technique used by Li et al. [9] and by us in our work on the temporal cost of modes [16] is a quasimode, based on Raskin's definition. In Li et al.'s work in two-mode interfaces, non-preferred hand mode switching resulted in an error rate of approximately 1.1%, slightly worse than the using the eraser end of the electronic stylus. One question unanswered by Li et al. is whether a relationship exists between the number of modes and the frequency of mode errors. It seems likely that increasing the number of modes increases the frequency of mode errors: Users are forced to choose one from a larger number of alternatives, giving rise to a higher probability of selecting the incorrect mode from among the set of available modes. However, whether the increase in mode errors as number of modes increases is a logarithmic, linear, or other function of number of modes provides an understanding of the expected cost, in accuracy, of adding addi-

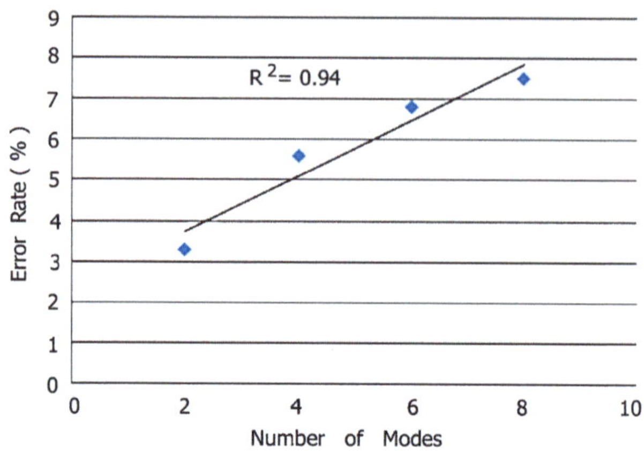

Fig. 3.3 Error rate as a function of number of modes in an interface

tional modes to an interface, and the corresponding benefit associated with reducing the mode set within an interface. To address this question, we examined mode errors as a function of number of modes in a sketch interface in our work modeling the cost of mode switching [16]. We observed error rates of between 3.3% in the two-mode condition and 7.5% in the eight mode condition [16]. Figure 3.3 depicts the mode error rate against number of modes in the interface. In this graph, we see a linear correlation ($R^2 = 0.94$) between number of modes and frequency of mode errors in our experimental task.

Given our results on the relative efficiency and accuracy of interfaces as a function of the number of modes within the interface, we claim that reducing the number of modes is a worthwhile goal. In the following sections, we examine user interface techniques and recognition techniques that we have developed to accomplish this.

3.3 Overloaded Loop Selection: UI Design to Infer Selection Mode

Many graphical editing programs support multiple means for selecting image material through the use of tool palettes. For example, Photoshop offers both a rectangle selection tool and a lasso tool, among others. Selection of one of these tools puts the interface into a distinct Selection mode. The rectangle is faster for selecting isolated objects, but the lasso is capable of "threading the needle" and selecting objects among clutter, and generally of creating oddly shaped selection regions.

We propose that the most straightforward means for amplifying the selection options available to users without requiring attention to a tool palette is to mix them together in a single Select Mode, and infer the user's intent from the gesture they actually produce. We invoke this idea in a technique called Overloaded Loop Selection. The user is free to drag a selection gesture that may take form as either a rectangle or a lasso. Both are displayed simultaneously. If the user proceeds to draw a nearly-closed loop, the rectangle disappears and the lasso region is chosen. But if

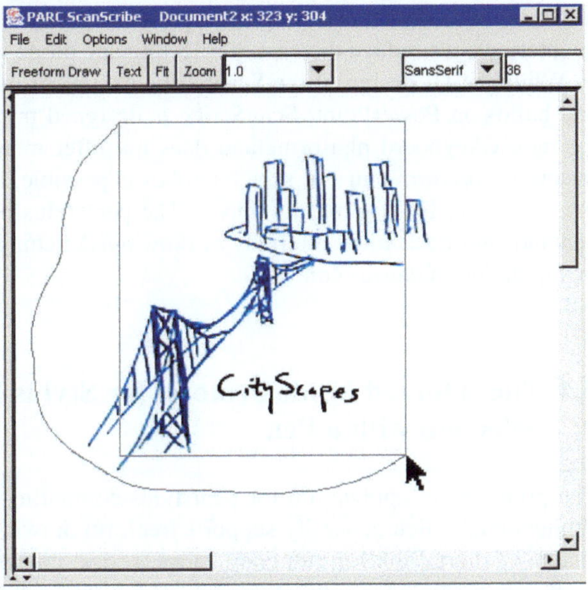

Fig. 3.4 Overloaded loop selection initiated by dragging the mouse with the left button held. Both a selection rectangle and lasso path are active. Closing the path causes the rectangle to disappear, leaving lasso selection. If the button is released while the rectangle is visible, rectangle selection is used instead

the user releases the mouse while the rectangle is displayed, the rectangle selection region is used. See Fig. 3.4.

Overloaded Loop Selection is employed by the ScanScribe document image editor program first introduced at UIST 2003 [18]. ScanScribe takes this idea two steps further. First, in addition to overloading rectangle and lasso selection, Selection Mode supports Cycle Click Selection, which extends the capability to select by clicking the mouse on an object. This is described in Sect. 3.6. Second, ScanScribe supports Polygon selection, by which users are able to select image material by placing and adjusting the vertices of an enclosing polygon. Polygon selection is invoked as a mode, but conveniently so by double-clicking the mouse over a background region, without the need for a separate toolbar.

Overloaded Loop Selection is an example of UI design minimizing prior selection of modes through analysis of the user action alone, without regard to the underlying canvas content. Other examples exist as interface techniques that analyze user action to determine effect in sketch interfaces. Hinckley et al. [5] proposed using a post-gesture delimiter technique, called a "pig-tail", for determining gesture interpretation, and they compared the post-gesture delimiter to using a handle, a timeout, or a button to alter a gesture's "mode". Grossman et al. [3] proposed "hover widgets", where the tracking state of a Tablet PC is used to access modes, and they compared it to using a software button to switch interface modes. Finally, Ramos and Balakrishnan [12] describe a "pressure mark" technique, where the different pressure associated with a mark maps to different interpretations. However, in each of these cases, the need exists to select from among the possible alternative interpretations, either during or after the action. As noted in Sect. 3.2, there is a cost associated with selecting amongst alternatives. By minimizing modes within an interface, we reduce the cost of selecting any mode within the interface.

While the UI design of the ScanScribe document image editor is modeled after and builds on PowerPoint, ScanScribe is designed primarily to be an editing tool for mouse/keyboard platforms and does not offer many options for entering new material. Freeform entry of sketch strokes is possible, but only by explicitly entering a separate Freeform Draw mode. The pen/stylus platform, on the other hand, demands more seamless interplay of drawing/sketching entry and select/command manipulation of canvas content.

3.4 The Inferred Mode Protocol for Stylus Drawing and Selection with a Pen

The prototypical application for pen/stylus computing platforms is the Electronic Whiteboard, which generally supports freeform drawing and handwriting, then selection of digital ink for cut, copy, move, resize, color change, etc. Unconstrained electronic notetaking applications fall within this definition. One of the first electronic whiteboard programs to gain significant contemplation was the Tivoli [11] program for the Xerox Liveboard.

The fundamental problem with pen electronic whiteboard programs is how to support drawing, selection, and commands on selected material through a single pen/stylus channel. The designers of Tivoli experimented with pen barrel buttons, tap-tap gestures, and post-lasso pigtail gestures, among other things, but eventually settled on explicit setting of Draw/Select mode through a side toolbar. Later, the Microsoft Journal program for the TabletPC settled on prior setting of Select mode through either tapping on a toolbar icon or else stationary holding of the pen for a predetermined length of time. All of these methods for mode setting fail to deliver seamless fluid user action. Barrel buttons are awkward to use. Toolbars require redirection of user focus away from the canvas. And stationary hover requires waiting for the hover threshold timeout and also leads to inadvertent entry of Select mode when the user may intending to draw but momentarily simply pausing to think with the pen down. The problem, we believe, is not *how* the user is supposed to set Draw versus Select mode, but that they have to do it at all.

3.4.1 The Mode Problem in Electronic Whiteboard Programs

We illustrate the mode problem through two simple tasks which could be part of a larger document creation/editing session. The purpose of these tasks is not to achieve the final result as efficiently as possible, but rather to simulate the process a user might go through, including changing their mind in midstream and rearranging material they have already placed on the canvas. In Task I (Fig. 3.5a) the user draws

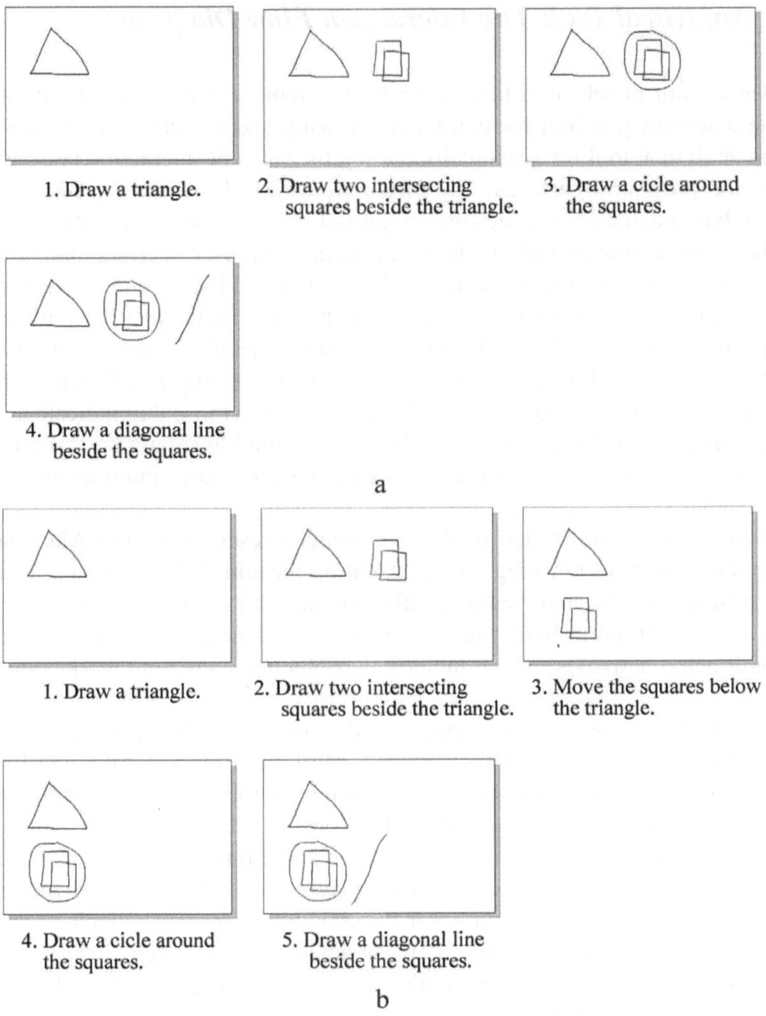

Fig. 3.5 Two simple tasks for a pen drawing/editing platform. **a** Task I involves only draw a series of shapes. **b** Task II involves drawing, then selecting and moving some of the drawn objects (as if the user changed their mind about where to place them), then subsequent additional drawing

a triangle, some overlapping squares, and a diagonal line. In Task II (Fig. 3.5b), they draw these same objects, but midway through, they decide to change the location of the overlapping squares. To do this, they would need to use the drawing tool's edit capabilities to select the squares and drag them to their new desired position on the canvas. This is where the trouble lies. Under a conventional mode-based interface design, the user would enter a selection mode and draw a lasso around the squares to select them. Then, they would have to exit selection mode to return to drawing. If, in the creative moment, these extra UI steps are not completed correctly, the task is thrown off track.

3.4.2 Analytical Tool: The Interaction Flow Diagram

In order to gain insight into how and why the requirement for mode setting can become a serious problem for pen-based drawing and editing systems, we introduce an analytical tool for graphically tracing the steps of interaction between user actions and program interfaces. The *Interaction Flow Diagram* is a form of state diagram, but one that emphasizes the modal state of the program and the operations available to users within each mode. In a conventional user interface state machine diagram, nodes denote internal states of the program and arcs denote possible transitions between them. In the Interaction Flow diagram, nodes are differentiated into three primary types: (1) those that depict internal machine state and information available to the user through the machine's display (rectangles); (2) those that indicate intentional user actions (rounded rectangles); (3) those that indicate a choice or decision point for the user (circles). The Interaction Flow diagram is particularly useful in dissecting user interaction bugs and aspects of user interface design that enable them.

The difference is illustrated in Fig. 3.6, which presents the State Machine diagram and Interaction Flow diagram representing the simple interaction afforded by paper, pencil, and eraser (or equivalently, whiteboard, marker, and eraser). There is no computer program here, the only action object in this diagram is the user's writing/drawing activities, which include two functions, creating marks, and erasing them.

The State Machine diagram represents the use of pencil, eraser and paper as transition among four states: Pencil Poised, Marking, Eraser Poised, and Erasing. The transition arcs reflect the logic of the system, for example the fact that before one can create a mark, one must first hold the pencil, then place its tip to the paper.

The Interaction Flow diagram portrays the interaction in a manner more closely resembling the user's experience. State display nodes, represented by rectangular boxes, indicate information visually (or through other senses) available to the user. In particular, in the quiescent state between actions, the user can see the markings on the page, and they can sense whether the pencil or eraser is poised above the page. Circles indicate deliberative choices, such as between either making a mark or switching to the eraser. The Interaction Flow diagram thus re-configures selected arcs exiting from nodes in the formal State Machine diagram to make explicit certain decisions the user can make at the level of significant functional operations of the tool. Finally, actual user actions are shown as rounded boxes. Often Interaction Flow diagrams package up tedious details of the State Machine diagram. For example, the state transition subgraph of touching, dragging, and lifting the pencil are wrapped into the functional action (rounded box) labeled "draw".

The Interaction Flow diagram in Fig. 3.6b reflects the simplicity of the interaction model for pencil and paper. The current draw/erase mode is always indicated by visual and/or tactile display. The choice to switch modes is always available. To execute a mode switch the user carries out the physical act that brings the desired tool end into position for use. Once in Draw or Erase mode, the system stays in that mode by default. The acts of continuously writing or continuously erasing are

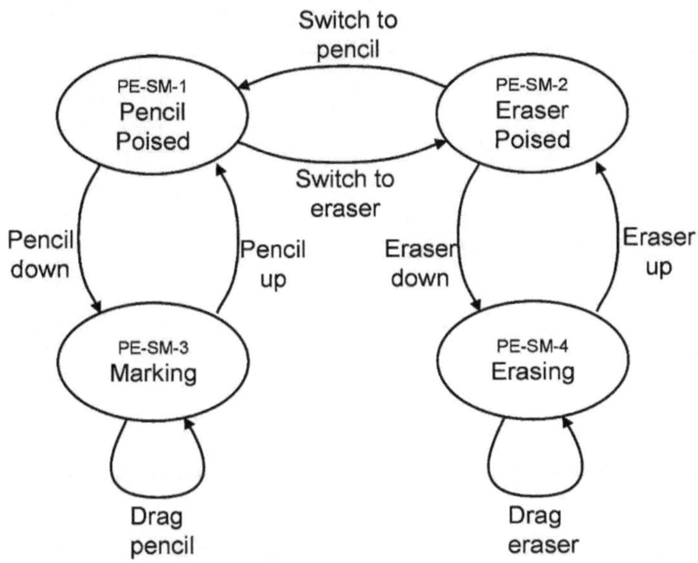

a

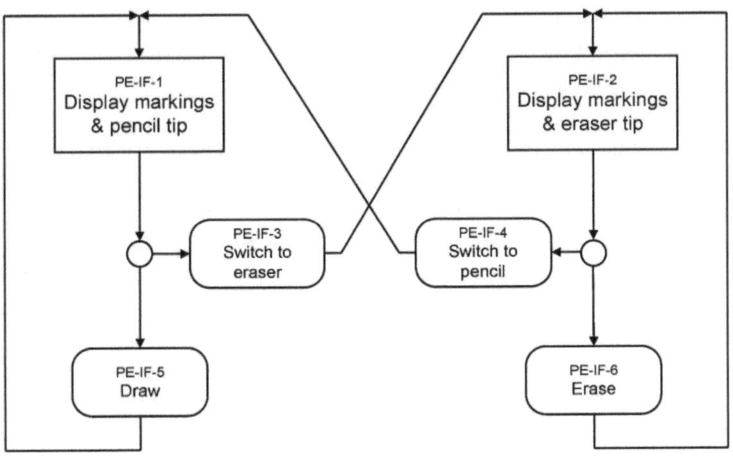

b

Fig. 3.6 **a** State Machine and **b** Interaction Flow diagram for pencil and eraser. Rectangles *represent* a quiescent state of the interface. *Rounded rectangles* represent user actions. *Circles* represent user choices among available actions, given the presentation state

tight loops through states in Fig. 3.6b. When writing fluidly the user may effectively ignore the choice to switch into erase mode. And significantly, for the purpose of managing their interaction with the pencil, the user has no requirement to attend to the information display (i.e. the markings on the surface and the pencil tip in view).

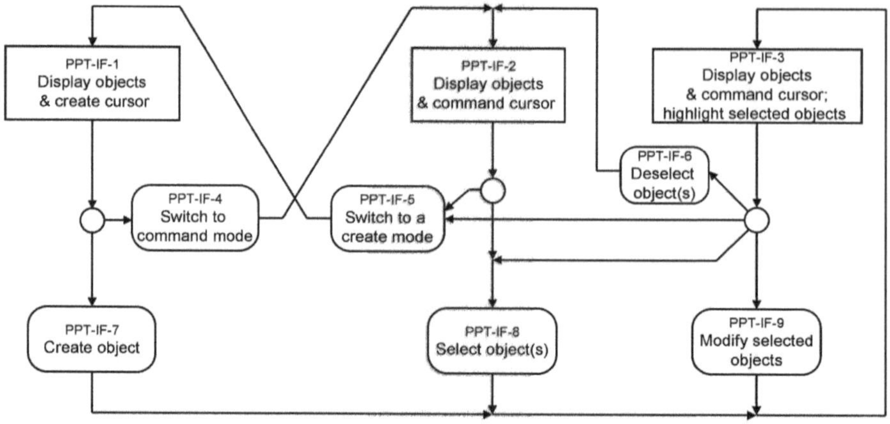

Fig. 3.7 Simplified Interaction Flow Diagram for the PowerPoint structured graphics editor

Rather, they are free to write or draw "open loop," paying attention to the content of their writing instead of the user interface features of the tool.

With the greater functionality of computer programs for creating and editing graphical material comes greater complexity of the user interface. Perhaps the most successful of these is PowerPoint. A simplified User Interaction Flow Diagram for the PowerPoint-style interface is shown in Fig. 3.7.

The fundamental operations here are creation of new text or graphic objects, selection of objects, and modifying selected objects. These are reflected in three state display nodes (rectangular boxes), in Fig. 3.7. When nothing is selected (Node PPT-IF-2), the interface is in Select mode. From here the user has the option of performing a selection operation (PPT-IF-8) or else entering Create/Entry mode by choosing an object type to create by clicking a menu or toolbar icon (PPT-IF-5). Either of these choices results in an internal change of machine state, and also in an augmentation of the display, such as highlighting of selected material (PPT-IF-3), or change from an arrow to crosshair cursor (PPT-IF-1). Once something is selected (PPT-IF-3), the interface enters Command Mode, in which selected material is highlighted. From here the user has a choice to deselect it, modify it, select additional objects, or switch to a create mode.

The default Mode of PowerPoint is Select Mode. PowerPoint permits users to select graphical material by either of two means, by tapping on an object, or by dragging a rectangle which results in selection of all objects entirely enclosed.

3.4.3 Interaction Flow Analysis of Mode-Based Selection and Drawing

The Interaction Flow Diagram provides insight into exactly what can go wrong with prior selection of mode in an electronic whiteboard program. Let us consider in de-

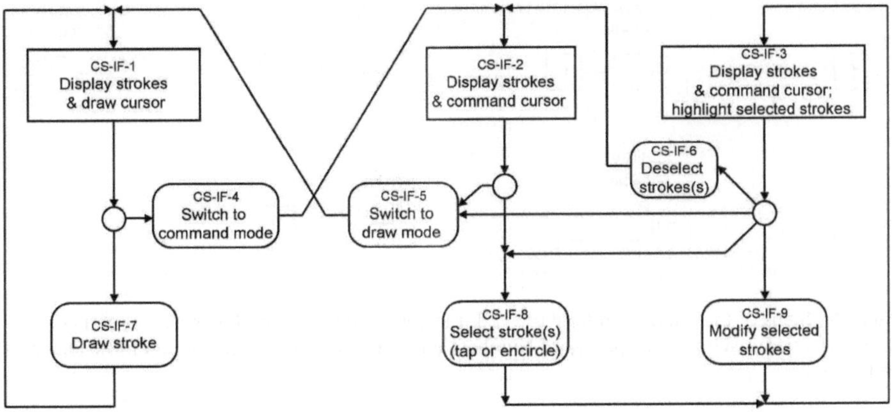

Fig. 3.8 Representative Interaction Flow Diagram for an Electronic Whiteboard program for Pen/Stylus platforms

tail Task I and Task II of Fig. 3.5 in terms of the Interaction Flow for a conventional mode-based Electronic Whiteboard program, such as Tivoli or Microsoft Journal. See Fig. 3.8. This protocol bears strong resemblance to the mouse-based interaction protocol design of PowerPoint and other structured graphics editors. The main difference is that Create/Entry Mode (also known as Draw Mode for a pen/stylus program) and Command Mode are persistent. When in Draw Mode (the leftmost Display/User Action column of the diagram) the act of making repeated marks with the stylus is fluid and unconstrained, just as with a physical pen or pencil. From Draw Mode, the user may switch to Select Mode by an explicit action such as tapping a toolbar item or releasing the stylus barrel button. In Select Mode the user may select objects by tapping or lasso.

Although Draw and Select modes are independent nodes in the Interaction Protocol (CS-IF-1 and CS-IF-2), an Electronic Whiteboard program may or may not actually provide a visible indicator of the current mode. In tablets and electronic whiteboards whose hardware provides pen hover detection, alternative Draw and Select cursors can do this. In purely touch-based stylus systems any visual mode indicator must be placed peripherally if at all. In either case, users are famous for ignoring mode indications rendered via cursor shape.

The mode problem arises when users perform as if the system were in one mode when in fact it is in another. Our sample draw/edit tasks illustrate where the interaction protocol can lead users to make errors. Task I is not a problem. This involves simply adding strokes one after another, in draw mode, as shown in Fig. 3.9.

The interaction flow for *correct* performance of Task II is shown in Fig. 3.10. Note that in order to move the pair of squares the user must first switch to Select mode, then draw a lasso around the squares in order to select them, then drag the selected objects to another position, and finally switch back to Draw mode.

The common interaction bug in this protocol is failure to switch modes before executing the next pen gesture or stroke. Figure 3.11 shows the interaction flow

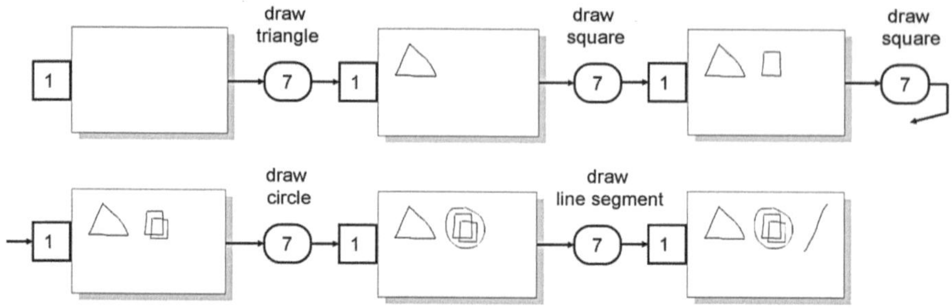

Fig. 3.9 Steps of the interaction flow for Task I under the Interaction Flow protocol of a conventional Electronic Whiteboard program. Numbers indicate nodes of the Interaction Flow Diagram of Fig. 3.8

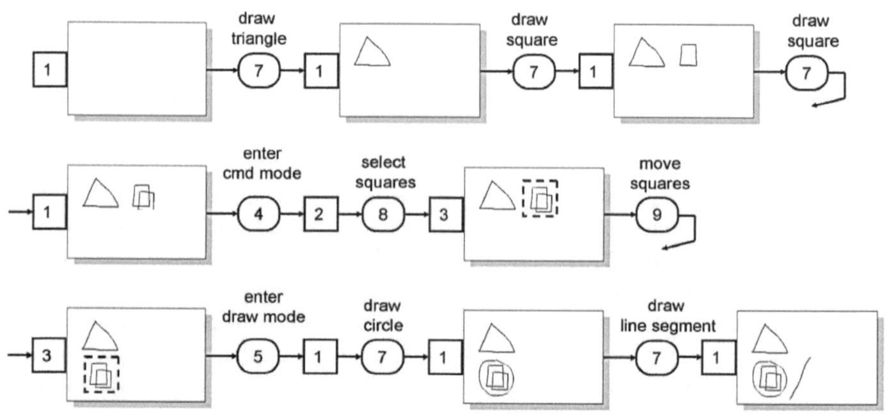

Fig. 3.10 Steps of the interaction flow for correct performance of Task II under the Interaction Flow protocol of a conventional Electronic Whiteboard program. Numbers indicate nodes of the Interaction Flow Diagram of Fig. 3.8

that results from failing to enter Select mode, CS-IF-4. The user behaves as if they are proceeding from Node CS-IF-2, performing what is intended to be a selection gesture. But the program interprets this as a drawn stroke, and renders it as such. Seeing a drawn circle instead of a visual indication of strokes selected, the user is alerted to the problem. He or she must then execute a repair protocol of at least three additional actions, plus devote attention to the display to verify that he or she is back on track, before proceeding with the intended task.

In a similar fashion, by failing to return to Draw mode after performing an edit operation, users are alerted to the problem and must interrupt their flow of interaction in order to recover and re-synchronize their mental model of the interaction with the machine state of the program.

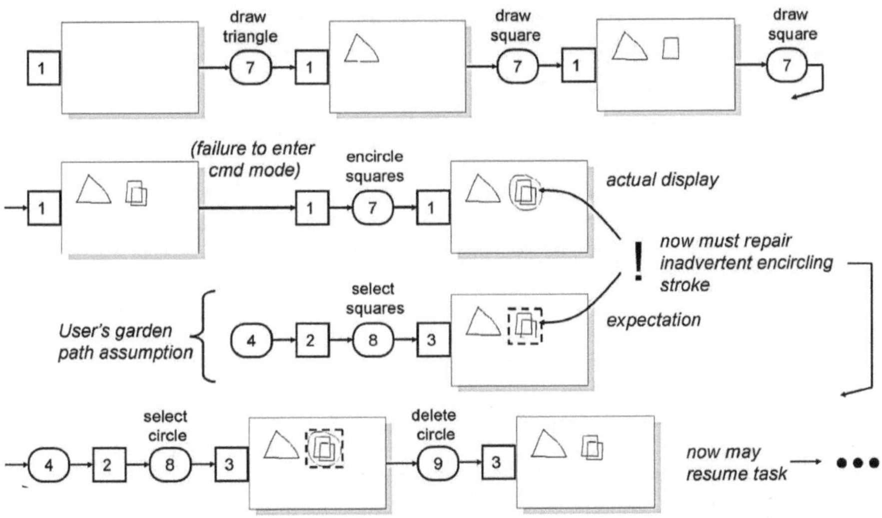

Fig. 3.11 Steps of the interaction flow for disrupted performance of Task II due to a common mode error, under the Interaction Flow protocol of a conventional Electronic Whiteboard program. Numbers indicate nodes of the Interaction Flow Diagram of Fig. 3.8

3.4.4 Inferred Mode Protocol: Inferring Draw/Select Mode

To address the Draw/Select Mode problem for pen/stylus interfaces, we introduced a technique called the Inferred Mode Protocol [17], used in the InkScribe pen-based sketch tool. This protocol allows the user to perform either a draw/entry or lasso selection gesture without a priori specification of mode. The intent of the stroke is inferred from the stroke's shape and its relation to existing canvas content. If the stroke is not closed, or if it is closed but does not enclose any existing material, then it cannot be a lasso selection gesture so is interpreted as new ink. If however it is approximately closed and does enclose markings on the canvas (which can be any combination of digital ink and bitmap image), the gesture is ambiguous. In this case, the interface presents a pop-up menu labeled, "Select?", in a nearby but out-of-the-way location. The user may then elect either to tap the menu item to select the enclosed material, or else simply ignore it and keep writing or drawing.

The Inferred Mode Protocol also supports Cycle Tap Select, described in Sect. 3.6. In doing so, the protocol prohibits the user from drawing dots, or short tap strokes, on top of or very near to existing markings.

The Interaction Flow Diagram for the Inferred Mode Protocol is shown in Fig. 3.12. Note that there are no user action nodes by which the user explicitly switches to a Draw or Command mode. Instead, the logic of mode switching is embedded in the inference of user intent based on the user's actions in context.

At quiescence the user can be faced with one of four visually distinguished situations: nothing is selected (IM-IF-1); nothing is selected but the pop-up menu item saying "Select?" is displayed (IM-IF-2); one or more strokes are selected (IM-IF-3);

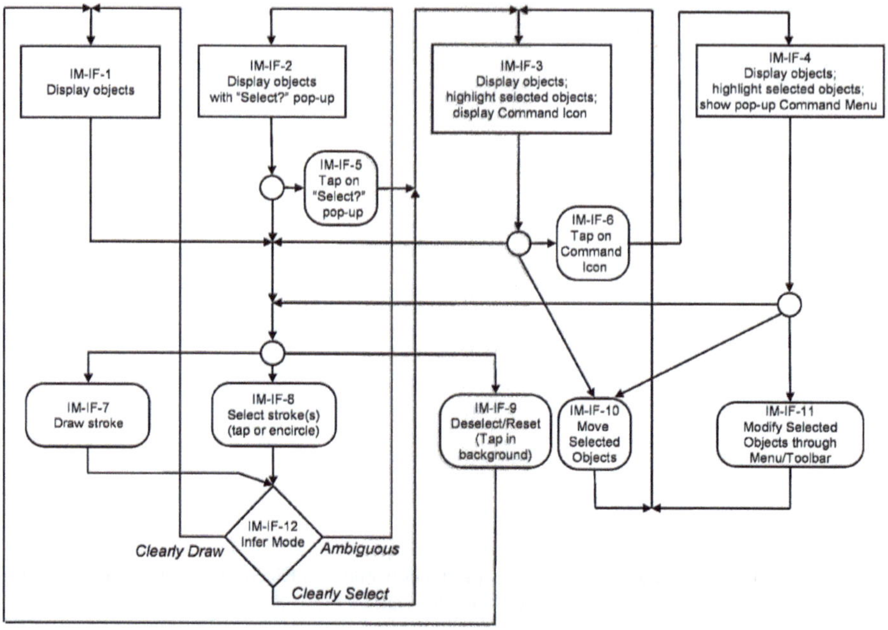

a

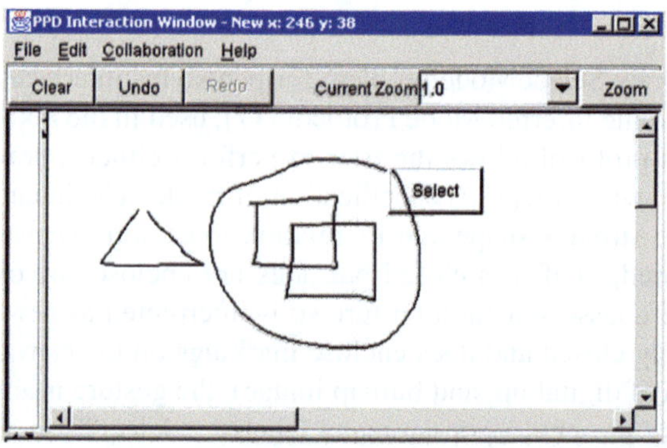

b

Fig. 3.12 Interaction Flow diagram for the Inferred Mode Protocol. The diamond represents the program inferring the user's intended mode. If the intent is ambiguous, a pop-up mediator choice (**b**) is presented which the user may either tap to select encircled material, or ignore and continue writing or drawing

one or more strokes are selected and a command menu is visible (IM-IF-4). From these four possibilities the flow of control converges onto one unified set of choices that are always available regardless of the selection state. Namely, the user can at any time draw more material (IM-IF-7), they can at any time perform a selection gesture

(IM-IF-8), and they can at any time reset the selection status to nothing selected by tapping in the background (IM-IF-9). The final options, to perform a gesture to move or modify selected material (IM-IF-10 and IM-IF-11), are operative only when something is actually selected.

The Inferred Mode Protocol introduces a new type of node to the Interaction Flow notation. This is the Intent Inference node, shown as a diamond (IM-IF-12), which represents a decision process that the system performs on the input gesture drawn at user action nodes IM-IF-7 or IM-IF-8. Note that IM-IF-7 or IM-IF-8 reflect only user intent, not any overtly distinguishable action or state. The purpose of this decision is to determine whether an input pen trajectory is clearly a drawn stroke, clearly a selection operation, or else ambiguous. The decision is made on the basis of certain rules which make use of the machine's prior state, plus the stroke's location, shape, and proximity to other strokes on the canvas. For example, a trajectory creating a closed path is interpreted in the following way:

- If the path encloses no other strokes then it is clearly a drawn stroke.
- If the path encloses at least one other stroke AND some other strokes are selected, then the path is interpreted as a selection gesture that adds the enclosed strokes to the set of selected strokes.
- If nothing is selected and the path encloses at least one other stroke, then the intent is ambiguous. The user could be intending to select the enclosed strokes, or they could simply want to draw a circle around them.

Critically, this gesture interpretation is made after the stroke, and the burden is lifted from the user to specify the correct Draw or Command mode prior to performing the motion. Only if the stroke is ambiguous is the user presented with the "Select?" mediator, at which time they have the choice of tapping the pen to select the enclosed material, or else ignoring it and proceeding to draw either additional digital ink strokes or else an entirely different enclosing gesture to select something else (IM-IF-6).

Figure 3.13 details the interaction flow for Sample Tasks I and II under the Inferred Mode interaction protocol. Tasks I and II are performed identically through the first four actions, where the user executes a circular pen trajectory enclosing the squares. At this point the program cannot know whether the user intends to draw a circle or select the squares it encloses. The system displays the pop-up "Select?" menu item. Here the two tasks diverge. Under Task I, the user ignores the menu item and continues drawing, completing the task with the entry of the final diagonal line. Under Task II, where the user intends to move the squares, they tap on the "Select?" button and the squares become highlighted as selected objects. The user then drags them to the target location, and, without explicitly switching modes, proceeds to complete the task by drawing a circle around the squares, then the final diagonal line.

The Inferred Mode Protocol for pen/stylus interfaces makes minimal use of structure analysis of canvas content, limited simply to determining whether a stroke is approximately closed and if so, whether it encloses existing markings. Further development of intelligent user interfaces involves more sophisticated analysis of the visible canvas in conjunction with the dynamics of the user's stroke.

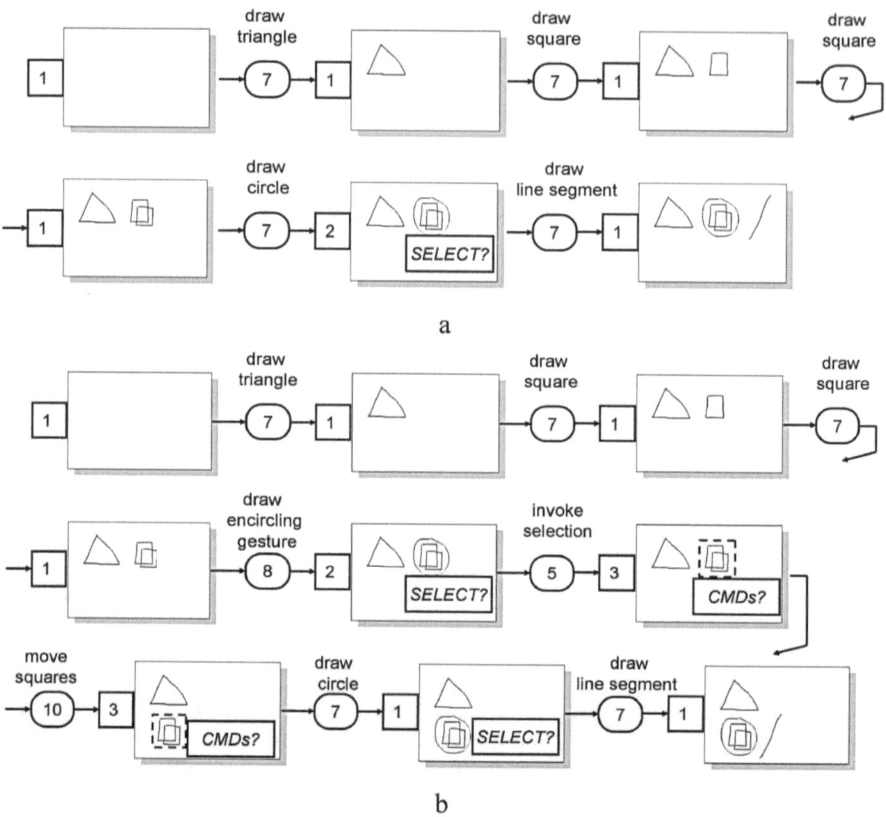

Fig. 3.13 Interaction flow for Task I (**a**) and Task II (**b**) under the Inferred Mode Protocol. Numbers indicate nodes in Fig. 3.12. Note that the user's actions are identical until the point at which they either ignore or tap the pop-up "Select?" button at step IM-IF-3 (3 in the figure)

3.5 Sloppy Selection: Inferring Intended Content of an Ambiguous Selection

Let us assume that the digital ink and bitmap images on a canvas are not arbitrary, random strokes and images, but are meaningful, structured objects. Most instances in which a user intends to cut, copy, move, or otherwise modify material, they do so with respect to this structure. It makes sense to bias interpretation of the user's actions in terms of the coherent objects and groupings present on the canvas. The most commonplace application of this principle applies to the characters, words, lines, and paragraphs comprising text. While always permitting exceptions, selection operations should tend toward selection of these units.

In accordance with this principle, we have suggested a user interface technique for lasso selection called *Sloppy Selection* [7]. Sloppy Selection observes that users' lasso gestures may at times only approximately encircle the object(s) they intend to select. To the extent that the user perceives objects on the canvas as being organized into salient chunks, a quick, approximate selection gesture may be "good enough". Conversely, we assume that if users intend to select arbitrary, non-salient regions of the canvas, they will do so slowly and deliberately. The Sloppy Selection technique thus analyzes the dynamics of the user's lasso gesture to ascertain whether and in what portions of the gesture the user is performing a rough, quick-and-dirty stroke, versus a careful, deliberate partitioning of selected versus excluded material.

In order to implement Sloppy Selection, we must employ a model of user gestures under casual and deliberate intent. We assume that casual, "sloppy" strokes are performed balistically, with a single motor planning event involving minimal mid-course correction. This type of motion is known to follow the minimum jerk principle, from the biological motor control literature. Figure 3.14a illustrates the speed profile of a fast, single-motion lasso gesture. Slowing occurs at locations of highest curvature according to a $2/3$ power law. Conversely, careful, deliberate strokes occur at a much slower speed more closely obeying a "tunnel law" of motion [1], as seen in Fig. 3.14b.

We exploit the difference between fast casual gestures and slow, deliberate gestures by inverting the local speed profile along a gesture to infer what we interpret as an effective selection tolerance width. Where a gesture's speed is less than would be predicted by a minimum jerk motion, we assume that the user is deliberately slowing down to more carefully adjust the gesture path, and therefore the effective tolerance narrows.

To combine the tolerance width with image structure analysis, we first construct candidate salient objects by performing visual segmentation and grouping on the existing canvas digital ink. Then, at the conclusion of a potential selection stroke we analyze the user's inferred selection tolerances. Where a lasso's selection tolerance permits, we divide included from excluded material according to the segmented units. But where the selection tolerance narrows, we split words or stokes literally along the lasso path, as shown in Fig. 3.15.

3.6 Cycle Tap Selection: Exploiting Structure Recognition

The simplest and most direct method of selecting material with a mouse or pen is, respectively, mouse click (typically using the left mouse button) or pen tap. The problem is that this action is ambiguous with respect to the meaningful structure of canvas objects, because any given section of digital ink or fragment of bitmap image may belong to multiple coherent objects. The dominant PowerPoint UI design for graphics interfaces addresses this ambiguity through the use of groups. Primitive objects can be grouped hierarchically into groups that collectively form tree structures. See Fig. 3.16b. Clicking on any primitive object automatically causes selection of the collection of primitive objects descending from the root node of any grouping tree the clicked object belongs to.

In PowerPoint-type UIs, groups are both a blessing and a curse. Once the user has grouped an object, in order to select that object and modify its location or properties, they must first un-group it. At this point, the group structure is lost and to get it

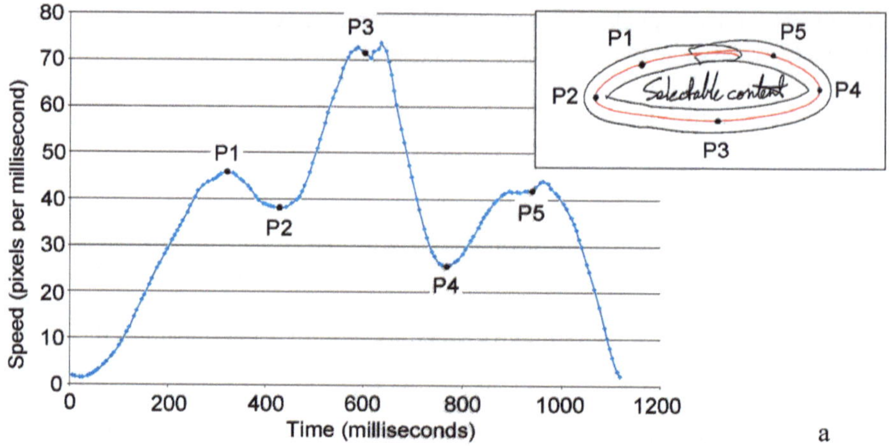

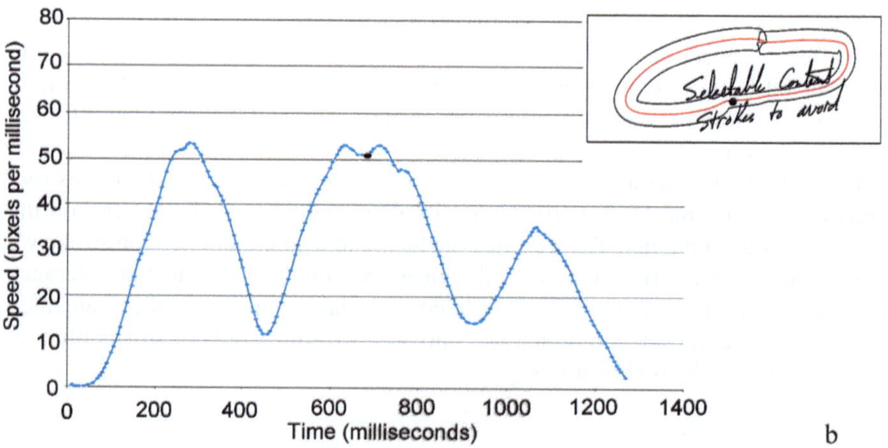

Fig. 3.14 **a** Speed profile for a "sloppy" selection gesture. **b** Speed profile for a "careful" selection gesture. Note the relatively slower speed for the straight section where the gesture is threading between two lines of text

back the user has to reconstruct it manually, which can become quite tedious. Thus, ambiguity and actionable membership in multiple groups as such are not actually supported.

We extend the notion of grouping primitive elements into meaningful larger structures in two stages, each of which carries design for intelligent UIs a step further. These steps are first, lattice groups, and second, automatic group formation through structure recognition.

To permit primitive strokes and bitmap objects to belong to more than one group simultaneously, we reformulate group structure from a hierarchical tree to a lattice. In a lattice, a child node may have more than one parent, and thus may participate in

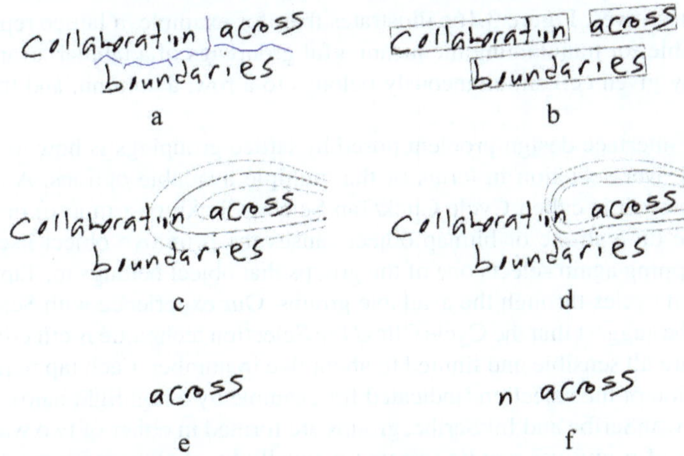

Fig. 3.15 Steps in the sloppy selection gesture interpretation technique. **a, b** Detection of word objects. **c, d**, Inference of gesture carefulness vs. sloppiness. **e, f** Decision whether to select based on word groups or precise gesture path

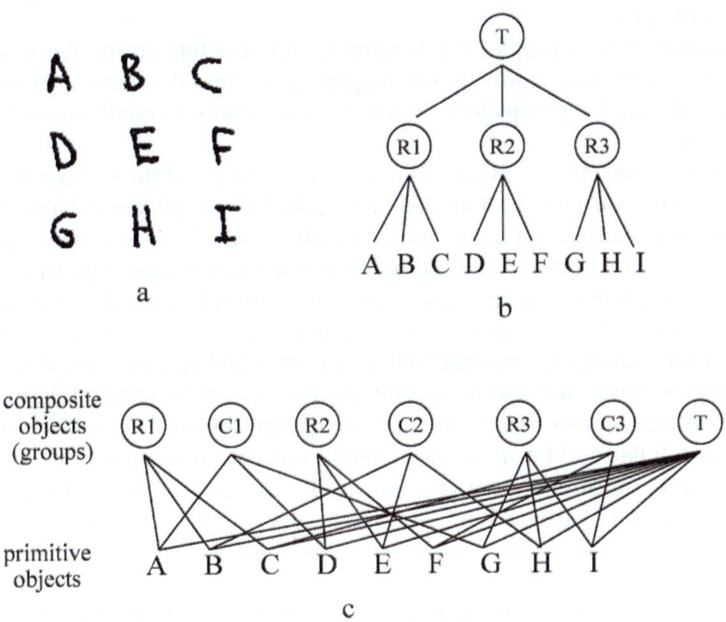

Fig. 3.16 **a** Items arranged in tabular layout. **b** Hierarchical groupings as rows then table. **c** Lattice structure permitting elements to belong to both row and column groups as well as the entire table

more than one group. This idea is taken to an extreme in the ScanScribe document image editor and the InkScribe digital ink sketch creation and editing tool. In these programs, the lattice is flat, consisting of only primitives and a layer representing groups of primitives. Figure 3.16c illustrates that, for example, a lattice representation is sensible for maintaining the meaningful groupings of a tabular arrangement of cells. Any given cell simultaneously belongs to a row, a column, and the entire table.

The user interface design problem posed by lattice groupings is how to give the user control over selection in terms of the multiple available options. A straightforward approach is called Cycle Click/Tap Select. Clicking (a mouse) or tapping (a pen) once on a stroke or bitmap object causes the primitive object itself to be selected. Tapping again selects one of the groups that object belongs to. Tapping repeatedly then cycles through the available groups. Our experience with ScanScribe and InkScribe suggest that the Cycle Click/Tap Selection technique is effective when the groups are all sensible and limited to about five in number. Each tap requires visual inspection of the selection (indicated for example by a highlight halo).

In basic ScanScribe and InkScribe, groups are formed in either of two ways. Any combination of primitives can be selected manually by clicking with the shift key (in ScanScribe for the mouse platform) or tapping individual objects (in InkScribe for the pen/stylus platform). Then, an explicit menu item permits explicit creation of a group. Or, groups may be formed automatically when the user manually selects a collection of primitives, and then performs any operation such as moving, copying, changing color, etc.

This approach to multiple, overlapping group structure forms the basis for a second, more advanced form of meaningful group-based selection of by direct Click/Tap. That is for groups to be formed automatically through automatic structure recognition.

Automatic structure recognition is exemplified in a program we have developed for creating and editing node-link diagrams, called ConceptSketch. Node-link diagrams are the basis for a popular graphical notation, called variously Concept Maps, or Mind Maps, for brainstorming and organizing information through labeled nodes representing cognitive concepts, and (optionally labeled) links depicting relations among concepts. The popularity of concept maps is evidenced by a multitude of free and commercial programs available for creating and editing these diagrams. At this writing, however, none of the available programs offers a truly fluid user interface permitting users to simply draw a concept map in freeform fashion and then select nodes, links, and labels as meaningful objects to rearrange, form and delete new nodes and links. and label or annotate. By design, ConceptSketch is an extension of a basic Electronic Whiteboard that knows about node-link diagrams and automatically recognizes the constructs of this notation automatically as the user creates it.

The key to a powerful concept mapping program is automatic recognition algorithms that can identify and organize the elements of a concept map, including text representing node labels, graphical node indicators, links, arrows, link labels, and arbitrary annotative text and graphics. The recognition strategies we have developed lie beyond the scope of this article. Here, of interest are the user interface techniques for accessing the meaningful diagrammatic objects once they have been recognized.

The Cycle Click/Tap select technique serves this purpose. See Figs. 3.17 and 3.18. In prototypical use, we presume that the user's overall goal is to evolve a

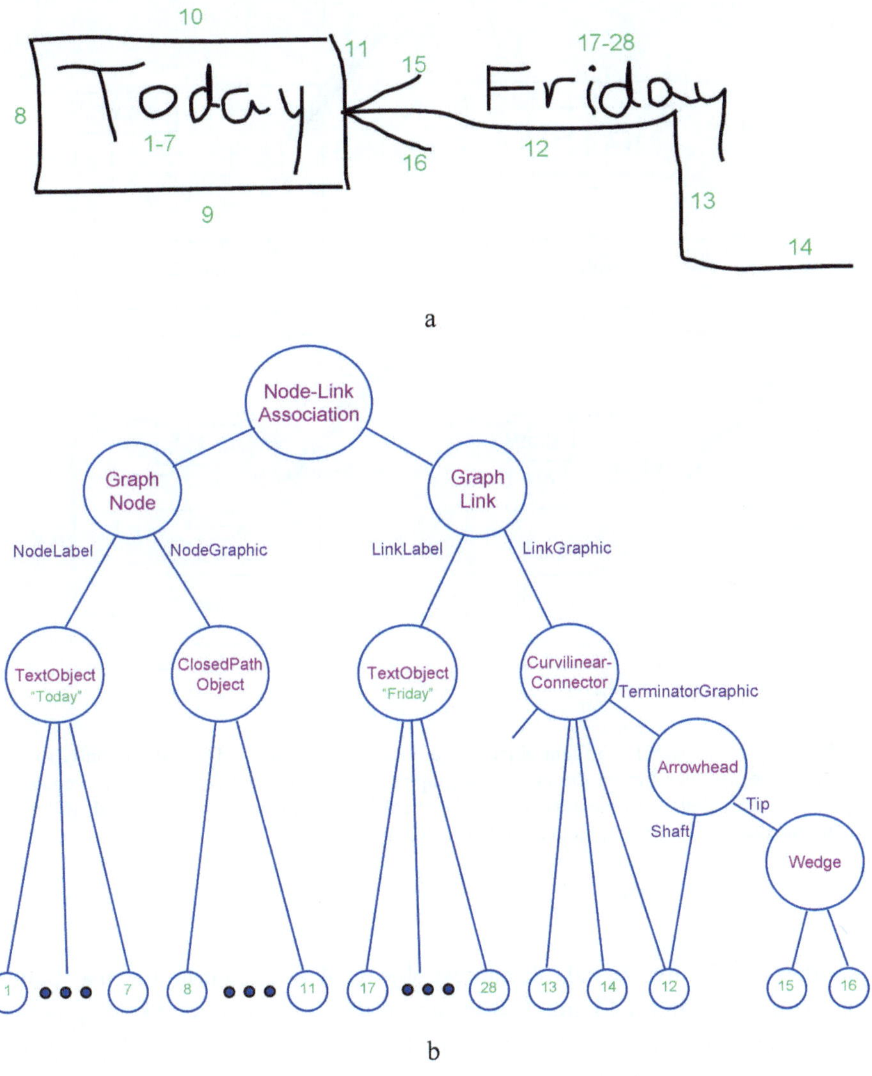

Fig. 3.17 **a** Example sketch. Strokes are labeled in order of input by a pen. **b** Hierarchical graph representing the objects and relations of the sketch in terms of the elements of a Node-Link diagram

rough and malleable sketch into a formalized diagram. The meaningful objects here are: (1) the graphical object representing the concept nodes; (2) the textual labels of these nodes; (3) entire nodes consisting of both node graphics and their textual labels; (4) the curvilinear lines linking concepts; (5) arrows or other terminating graphics of link graphics; (6) textual labels associated with graphical links; (7) entire links consisting of the link lines, their terminator graphics, and their labels; (8) ancillary text; (9) ancillary graphics. To support Cycle Click/Tap select, recognition algorithms need to build structured representations of the canvas that reflect these

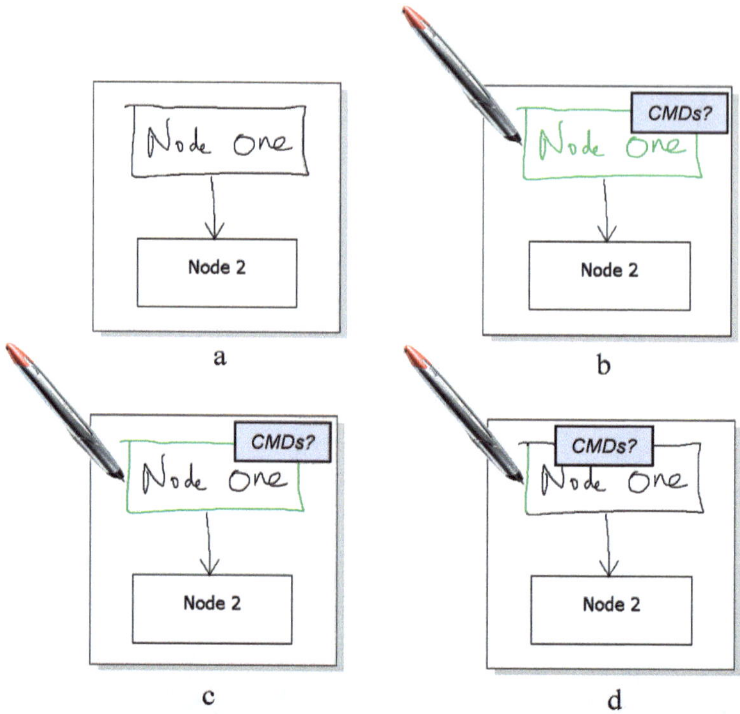

Fig. 3.18 Cycle tap select of salient objects in a node-link diagram. **a** Diagram partially formalized. **b** At the first pen tap on the enclosing graphic, the entire node is selected (the enclosing graphic plus text label). **c** At the next pen tap the enclosing graphic alone is selected. **d** At the next pen tap just the side of the graphic rectangle is selected

groupings of primitive digital ink and text objects. Any given primitive may belong to more than one group. Figure 3.18 illustrates that in the ConceptSketch program, the user may select different levels of structure by repeated tapping. Tapping once on the side of a rectangle forming the enclosing graphic of a node causes that node to be selected, including its text label; tapping again at the same place cycles to selection of just the rectangle; tapping again cycles to selection of just the side of the rectangle.

For creation and editing of Concept Maps using a pen/stylus in ConceptSketch, the Cycle Tap Select protocol is embedded within the Inferred Mode Protocol of Fig. 3.12 in particular, within the Tap selection Node IM-IF-8.

This principle of course applies to all types of graphical structure, across all domains for which effective recognition algorithms can be devised, including circuit diagrams, mathematical notation, physical simulations, engineering and architectural drawings, chemical diagrams, UML diagrams, etc.

3.7 Conclusion

The goal of creating computer tools that anticipate and understand user actions in terms of their purpose and intent is an ambitious one that will not be realized for quite some time. We can however realize some of the lower levels of the pyramid of sophistication that will be required. Our emphasis in this chapter has been on minimizing the requirement that the user pre-specify modes in order to communicate to the program how their subsequent action should be interpreted. We have shown how at the most basic UI level, Overloaded Loop Selection enables multiple methods for selection without the use of a toolbar. We have introduced conservative forms of recognition of a user's gestural intent by considering gestures' paths and dynamics in context of canvas content; these are the Inferred Mode Protocol and the Sloppy Selection technique. And we have shown how recognition of canvas content enables easy selection of meaningful objects through the simple tap/click command, under the Cycle Tap Selection protocol.

We believe that many more techniques will fill in these levels of the pyramid. Indeed, we have taken note of several very interesting contributions by our co-workers in this field. And we look forward to future developments in cognitive modeling of user tasks and goals that will lead to truly intelligent user interfaces.

References

1. Accot, J., Zhai, S.: Beyond Fitts' law: models for trajectory-based HCI tasks. In: Proc. ACM CHI, pp. 295–302 (1997)
2. Accot, J., Zhai, S.: More than dotting the i's—foundations for crossing-based interfaces. In: Proc. CHI '02 (SIGCHI Conference on Human Factors in Computing Systems), pp. 73–80 (2002)
3. Grossman, T., Hinckley, K., Baudisch, P., Agrawala, M., Balakrishnan, R.: Hover widgets: using the tracking state to extend the capabilities of pen-operated devices. In: Proc. ACM CHI, pp. 861–870 (2006)
4. Hick, W.: On the rate of gain of information. Quarterly Journal of Experimental Psychology **4**, 11–36 (1952)
5. Hinckley, K., Baudisch, P., Ramos, G., Guimbretiere, F.: Design and analysis of delimiters for selection-action pen gesture phrases in Scriboli. In: Proc. CHI '05 (SIGCHI Conference on Human Factors in Computing Systems), pp. 451–460 (2005)
6. Hyman, R.: Stimulus information as a determinant of reaction time. Journal of Experimental Psychology **45**, 188–196 (1953)
7. Lank, E., Saund, E.: Sloppy selection: providing an accurate interpretation of imprecise selection gestures. Computers and Graphics **29**(4), 183–192 (2005). Special Issue on Pen Computing
8. Lank, E., Ruiz, J., Cowan, W.: Concurrent bimanual stylus interaction: a study of non-preferred hand mode manipulation. In: GI '06 (Proceedings of Graphics Interface 2006), pp. 17–24, Quebec (2006)
9. Li, Y., Hinckley, K., Guan, Z., Landay, J.: Experimental analysis of mode switching techniques in pen-based user interfaces. In: Proc. CHI '05 (SIGCHI Conference on Human Factors in Computing Systems), pp. 461–470 (2005)
10. Norman, D.: Steps toward a cognitive engineering: Design rules based on analyses of human error. In: Proceedings of the 1982 Conference on Human Factors in Computing Systems, pp. 378–382, Gaithersburg, MA (1982)

11. Pedersen, E., McCall, K., Moran, T., Halasz, F.: Tivoli: an electronic whiteboard for informal workgroup meetings. In: Proc. ACM CHI, pp. 391–398 (1993)
12. Ramos, G., Balakrishnan, R.: Pressure marks. In: Proc. ACM CHI, pp. 1375–1384 (2007)
13. Ramos, G., Boulos, M., Balakrishnan, R.: Pressure widgets. In: Proc. CHI '04 (SIGCHI Conference on Human Factors in Computing Systems), pp. 487–494 (2004)
14. Raskin, J.: The Humane Interface. Addison Wesley, Reading (2000)
15. Ruiz, J., Lank, E.: A study on the scalability of non-preferred hand mode manipulation. In: ICMI '07: Proceedings of the 9th International Conference on Multimodal Interfaces, pp. 170–177, Nagoya, Aichi, Japan (2007)
16. Ruiz, J., Bunt, A., Lank, E.: A model of non-preferred hand mode switching. In: GI '08 (Proceedings of Graphics Interface 2008), pp. 49–56, Windsor, Ontario, Canada (2008)
17. Saund, E., Lank, E.: Stylus input and editing without prior selection of mode. In: Proc. UIST '03 (ACM Symposium on User Interface Software and Technology), pp. 213–216 (2003)
18. Saund, E., Fleet, D., Larner, D., Mahoney, J.: Perceptually-supported image editing of text and graphics. In: Proc. UIST '03 (ACM Symposium on User Interface Software and Technology), pp. 183–192 (2003)
19. Sellen, A., Kurtenbach, G., Buxton, W.: The prevention of mode errors through sensory feedback. Human-Computer Interaction **7**(2), 141–164 (1992)
20. http://www.usabilityfirst.com. June 2008

Chapter 4
Mathematical Sketching: An Approach to Making Dynamic Illustrations

Joseph J. LaViola Jr.

4.1 Introduction

Diagrams and illustrations are often used to help explain mathematical concepts. They are commonplace in math and physics textbooks and provide a form of physical intuition about abstract principles. Similarly, students often draw pencil-and-paper diagrams for mathematics problems to help in visualizing relationships among variables, constants, and functions, and use the drawing as a guide to writing the appropriate mathematics for the problem.

Unfortunately, static diagrams generally assist only in the initial formulation of a mathematical problem, not in its "debugging", analysis or complete visualization. Consider the diagrams in Fig. 4.1. In both cases, a student has a particular problem to solve and draws a quick diagram with pencil and paper to get some intuition about how to set it up. In the diagram on the left of Fig. 4.1, the student wants to explore the difference between the motion of two vehicles, one with constant velocity and one with constant acceleration. In the diagram on the right, the student wants to understand how far an object pushed off a table will fall before it hits the ground and how long it will take to do so. The student can use these diagrams to help formulate the required mathematics to answer various possible questions about these physical concepts.

However, once the solutions have been found, the diagrams become relatively useless. The student cannot use them to check her answers or see if they make visual sense; she cannot see any time-varying information associated with the diagram and cannot infer how parameter changes affect her solutions. The student could use one of many educational or mathematical software packages available today to create a dynamic illustration of her problem, but this would take her away from the pencil and paper she is comfortable with and create a barrier between the mathematics

J.J. LaViola Jr. (✉)
Department of Electrical Engineering and Computer Science, University of Central Florida, Orlando, FL 32816-2362, USA
e-mail: jjl@cs.ucf.edu
url: http://www.eecs.ucf.edu/~jjl

J. Jorge, F. Samavati (eds.), *Sketch-based Interfaces and Modeling*,
DOI 10.1007/978-1-84882-812-4_4, © Springer-Verlag London Limited 2011

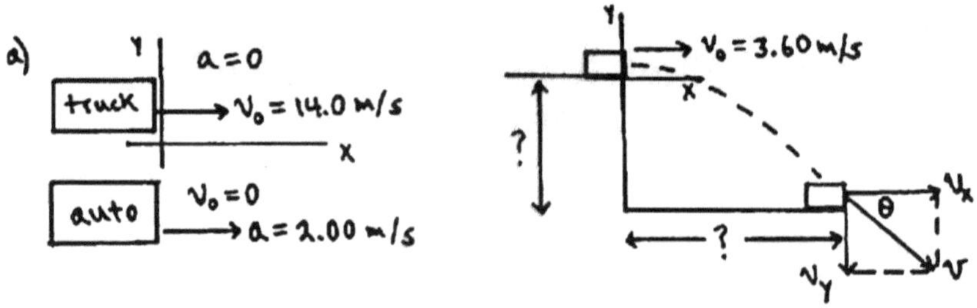

Fig. 4.1 The diagram on the left shows the initial formulation for analyzing the differences between constant velocity and constant acceleration of two vehicles and the diagram on the right shows the initial formulation for exploring how an object falls off a table with some initial velocity (adapted from [4])

she had written and the visualization created on the computer. Because of these drawbacks, statically drawn diagrams have a lack of expressive power that can be a severe limitation, even in simple problems with natural mappings to the temporal dimension or in problems with complex spatial relationships.

4.1.1 Mathematical Sketching

With the advent of pen-based computers, it seems logical that the computer's computational power and the expressivity of pencil and paper could be combined to resolve many of the drawbacks of static diagrams discussed above. Mathematical sketching addresses these problems by combining the benefits of the familiar pencil-and-paper medium and the power of a computer. More specifically, mathematical sketching is the process of making and exploring dynamic illustrations by associating 2D handwritten mathematics with free-form drawings [12, 13]. Animating these diagrams by making changes in the associated mathematical expressions lets users evaluate formulations by their physical intuitions about motion. By sensing mismatches between the animated and expected behaviors, users can often both see that a formulation is incorrect and analyze why it is incorrect. Alternatively, correct formulations can be explored from an intuitive perspective, perhaps to home in on some aspect of the problem to study more precisely with conventional numerical or graphing techniques.

Mathematical sketching incorporates a gestural user interface that lets users modelessly create handwritten mathematical expressions using familiar mathematical notation and free-form diagrams, as well as associations between the two, using only a stylus. Since users must write down both the mathematics and the diagrams themselves, mathematical sketching is not only general enough to apply to a variety of problems, but also supports a deeper mathematical understanding than alternative approaches including, perhaps, professionally authored dynamic illustrations. The ability to rapidly create mathematical sketches can unlock a range of insight, even, for example, in such simple problems as the ballistic motion of a spinning football in a 2D plane, where correlations among position, rotation and their derivatives can be challenging to comprehend.

In this chapter, we will explore the mathematical sketching concept by first discussing some philosophical ideas behind the interaction paradigm. Next, we will examine MathPad[2] [14], an implementation of mathematical sketching, by discussing some important components of the prototype. Finally, we will present a discussion on where mathematical sketching needs to go in the future to make it fully usable in creating dynamic illustrations across a variety of scientific disciplines.

4.2 Philosophical Considerations

Mathematical sketching is the process of making and exploring dynamic illustrations by combining 2D handwritten mathematics and free-form drawings through associations between the two. The first question is: what is a dynamic illustration? For our purposes, a dynamic illustration is a collection of moving pictorial elements used to help explain a concept. These pictorial elements can be pictures, drawings, 3D graphics primitives, and the like. The movement of these pictorial elements can be passive (i.e., someone just watches the animation) or active (i.e., someone interacts with and steers the animation). The concepts that dynamic illustrations help to explain are essentially limitless. They can be used to illustrate how to change the oil in a car, how blood flows through an artery, how to execute a football play, or how to put together a bicycle. They can be used to explain planetary motion, chemical reactions, or the motion of objects though time. Almost any concept can be illustrated dynamically in some way.

In theory, mathematical sketching could be used to make any kind of dynamic illustration. However, devising a general framework to support any type of dynamic illustration is a difficult problem. Thus, we decided to focus on a particular subset of dynamic illustrations to explore the mathematical sketching paradigm. In its current form, mathematical sketching can create dynamic illustrations where objects animate through or as a result of affine transformations. In other words, a mathematical sketch can create a dynamic illustration where objects can translate and rotate or stretch on the basis of other moving objects. These affine transformations are defined using functions of time with known domains or through numerical simulation. Given our current focus, mathematical sketching lets users create dynamic illustrations using simple Newtonian physics for exploring concepts such as harmonic and projectile motion, linear and rotational kinematics, and collisions.

The next part of defining mathematical sketching is writing 2D mathematics. We use the term "2D handwritten mathematics" because the mathematics is written, not typed, and uses common notation that exploits spatial relationships among symbols. For example, the integral of $x^2 \cos(x)$ from 0 to 2 can be written as "`int(x^2*cos(x),x,0,2)`". This one-dimensional representation is used in Matlab, a mathematical software package. A 2D representation such as $\int_0^2 x^2 \cos(x)\,dx$, however, is more elegant, natural, and commonplace. The naturalness of a 2D representation also means that people making mathematical sketches need not learn any new notation when writing the mathematics.

Using 2D handwritten mathematics in mathematical sketching implies that those handwritten symbols must, at some point, be transformed into a representation that the computer can understand. This transformation must take the user's digital ink and recognize it as mathematical expressions and equations. The recognition process must determine what the individual symbols are and how they relate to other symbols spatially. In addition, these recognized expressions and equations must be stored in such a way that they can drive dynamic illustrations using a given programming language. Although the complex process of recognizing mathematical expressions is part of the mathematical sketching process, it touches on the definition of mathematical sketching only indirectly. What is important in terms of mathematical sketching is how users tell the computer to recognize these expressions, and how much user intervention is needed to do so.

The next part of the mathematical sketching definition is making free-form drawings. Free-form drawings in this context are both a blessing and a curse. They are a blessing because they provide the greatest flexibility in what can be drawn: a mathematical sketch can contain simple doodles or articulate line drawings. In addition, if the essence of mathematical sketching is to interact with the computer as if writing with pencil and paper, then free-form drawings are ideal.

With such drawing flexibility, however, come certain disadvantages, arising largely from the nature of mathematical sketching itself. If a mathematical sketch is to contain a precise mathematical specification, then how can such a specification interact fluidly with imprecise free-form drawings to create a cohesive algorithm for deploying a dynamic illustration? What is required is an intermediary between the two, a methodology that transforms the drawings appropriately, so they fit within the scope of the mathematics. The drawings need to be transformed, but we also want to extract some geometrical properties from them to keep them close to their original representations. Thus, a delicate balance is needed between retaining the essence of the drawings and transforming them into something coincident with the mathematics. This transformation methodology, which we call "drawing rectification", is important in achieving plausible dynamic illustrations [2]. From the definition of mathematical sketching, drawing rectification is critical but must be somewhat transparent to the user. In other words, rectification should involve little cognitive effort on the user's part.

The final part of the definition of mathematical sketching is the process of associating mathematics to the drawings. Associations are the key component of mathematical sketching because they are the mechanism for determining which mathematical expressions belong to a particular drawing. Associations do not just determine how drawings should move though time; they are also important in determining other geometric properties such as overall size, length, or width of drawing elements. Without these associations, it is difficult to know precisely how the mathematical specification animates a drawing in terms of what is actually displayed on the screen. For example, even if an object has a certain width and height on the screen, it is difficult to know its dimensions from the mathematical point of view without having users specify them explicitly. In addition, these associations are important in defining internal coordinate systems needed by the mathematical sketch to perform the animation correctly. Default values for a drawing's geometric properties can work in some cases, but not always. The same is true of default coordinate systems.

Associations also have an inherent complication. According to the mathematical sketching definition, an association should associate a set of mathematical expressions with a particular drawing or drawing element. The drawings can then behave accordingly. However, these associations are insufficient without some mathematical semantics. For example, although a set of arbitrary mathematical expressions could be associated perfectly validly to a particular drawing, it would be extremely difficult to determine how the drawing is supposed to behave unless the mathematics has some structure. Once again, we must maintain a delicate balance. On the one hand, we want the associations to infer as much as possible about the mathematical semantics so that the mathematics can be written without artificial restrictions. On the other, we know that associations cannot infer everything, so the mathematics in a mathematical sketch must have some semantic structure. The key is to use a semantic structure that is as close as possible to how people write the mathematics in a pencil-and-paper setting.

4.2.1 Generalizing Mathematical Sketching as a Paradigm

Visualization can be characterized as a process of representing data as images and animations to provide insight into a particular phenomenon. Mathematical sketching is therefore a form of visualization, consisting, as it does, of a subset of the many visualization algorithms, tools, and systems [7]. Mathematical sketching takes data (handwritten mathematics, drawings, and associations) and transforms them into a representation (a dynamic illustration) that can provide insight into a particular phenomenon (the mathematical specification).

More specifically, mathematical sketching can be thought of a method of sketching visualizations. In other words, a pen-based description of a certain concept or phenomenon is transformed into a visualization. This pen-based description can be given as mathematics, drawings, diagrams, gestures, numbers, or even words. Sketching a visualization need not result in a dynamic illustration: the visualization could be static. For example, other work in Brown University's Computer Graphics Lab lets chemists create 3D visualizations of molecules by sketching chemical element symbol names and drawing bonds between them [22] (see Fig. 4.2). In another example, users can sketch numbers in tabular form and then visualize them using a simple graph (see Fig. 4.3). MathPad^2 can also make static sketch-based visualizations. For example, users can write a function (the sketch) and graph it (the visualization). Thus the mathematical sketching paradigm is a tool for creating both static and dynamic visualizations of handwritten mathematical specifications. Perhaps as the ideas of mathematical sketching are extended and developed, it will prove to be a general model for mathematical visualization.

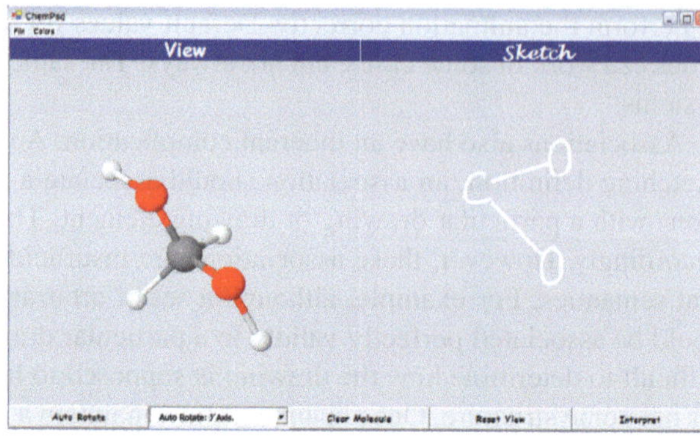

Fig. 4.2 The ChemPad application creates visualizations of molecules by writing chemical element symbol names and drawing bonds between them. Users sketch the molecule on the right (under "Sketch") and view a 3D representation of the molecule on the left (under "View")

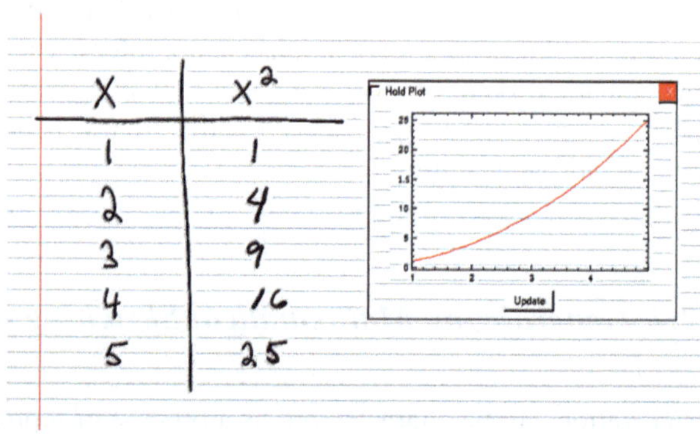

Fig. 4.3 A sketch-based visualization in which numbers in tabular form are visualized with a graph

4.2.2 Observations on Mathematical Sketching

2D mathematical expression recognition is indirectly part of the definition of mathematical sketching. If mathematical sketches are to use 2D handwritten mathematics that must be recognized, then we require a way to tell the computer that recognition needs to occur. Ideally, of course, the system should recognize and parse the expressions online while users are writing. However, people whom we observed writing mathematical expressions in online systems usually paused after writing each symbol to make sure the recognition was correct, a cognitive distraction that took away from what they were doing. More importantly, as early as the 1960s, researchers discovered that users dislike systems that attempt to infer what they are trying to do in the middle of specifying it, since this made the interface very distracting. On the basis of these observations, we chose not to perform online recognition but rather trigger the recognition with an explicit command, so that users could concentrate on the mathematics until the recognition was needed.

Another important issue with mathematical sketching involves free-form drawings. We chose free-form drawings because they are the types of drawings made with pencil and paper. However, with a computer underneath this pencil and paper, it might be reasonable to use standard geometric primitives. The problem with geometric primitives, however, is their limited scope compared to free-form drawings.

Free-form drawings increase the power of a mathematical sketch from an aesthetic point of view. In addition, although geometric primitives could assist in drawing rectification, they do not solve the rectification problem completely, and in order to keep a pencil-and-paper style, these primitives would have to be drawn and recognized, making the internals of mathematical sketching more complex.

Making a mathematical sketch requires associations between mathematics and drawings. There are, of course, many different ways to make these associations. Since illustrations in textbooks and notebooks from mathematics and science classes are usually labeled with variable names and numbers, one logical way to make associations is to use these labels as part of the interaction. Doing this means that associations can be made with little extra cognitive effort, since the labels are already part of the drawing.

Finally, we believe that mathematical sketching makes sense as an approach to making dynamic illustrations. People would rather write mathematics on paper than type it in on a keyboard. Additionally, drawing with pencil and paper is much easier than with a computer. Mathematical sketching thus makes sense because it takes what users can already do with a notebook—write mathematics and make drawings—and extends it to create dynamic illustrations. These illustrations help users not only visualize behaviors but also validate the mathematics they write. Users need only do minimal work beyond what they would normally do, making mathematical sketching a value-added approach.

4.3 The MathPad^2 Prototype

To gain an understanding of how the concept of mathematical sketching can be utilized to make dynamic illustrations, we developed MathPad^2, a prototype Tablet PC application (see Fig. 4.4). In this part of the chapter, we present an overview of the MathPad^2 architecture as well as highlight important software components.

4.3.1 MathPad^2 Architecture

MathPad^2 was developed on a Tablet PC using C# and the Microsoft Tablet PC SDK [10]. This SDK provided a number of useful features for dealing with and maintaining ink strokes: nearest-point and stroke-enclosure tests, transformation routines, and bounding-box functions. As a computational and symbolic back end, we used Matlab via its API for communicating with the Matlab engine from external programs.

The software has the distinct components shown in Fig. 4.5. The main software component is the user interface, which is the major link to other parts of the MathPad^2 system. The user interface component contains the data entry objects for dealing with inking and storage of ink strokes and recognized mathematical expressions. As users make ink strokes on the screen, the gesture analyzer continuously

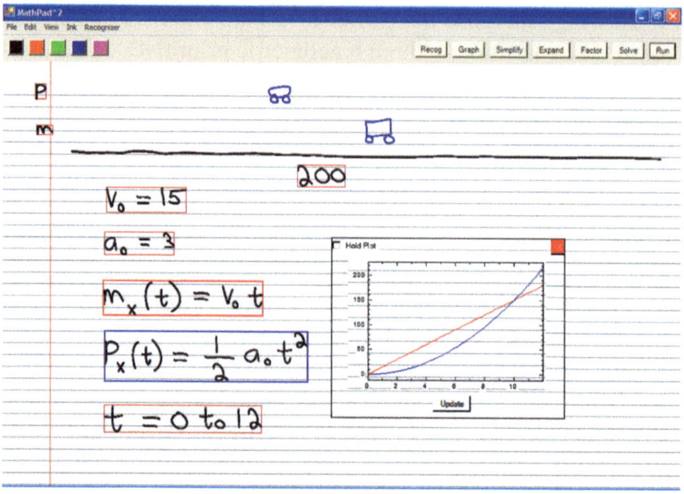

Fig. 4.4 The MathPad^2 prototype. The mathematical sketch shows two cars moving down a road, one with constant velocity and one with constant acceleration. The user writes down the mathematics, draws a road and two cars, and associates the mathematics to the drawing using labels. Running the sketch animates the two cars, illuminating how a car moving with constant acceleration will overtake the car with constant velocity. The sketch also shows a graph of the two equations of motion

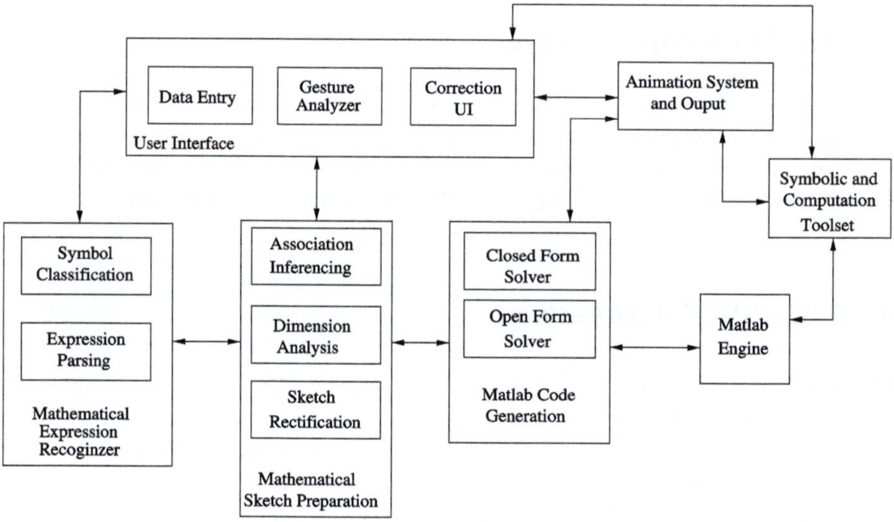

Fig. 4.5 A diagram of the MathPad^2 software architecture

examines them to determine whether they are gestural commands or simply digital ink. If the ink strokes are commands, then the gestural analyzer communicates with other components so that the appropriate actions are performed. The last part of the user interface component is the correction user interface, which lets users make corrections to incorrectly recognized mathematical expressions on a symbol level and on a parsing level.

When users make a mathematical expression recognition gesture, the gestural analyzer sends the ink strokes to the mathematical expression recognizer, which contains the mathematical symbol recognizer and the expression parsing system. The mathematical symbol recognizer is in charge of taking a collection of ink strokes, segmenting them into symbols, and classifying the symbols as particular characters. The expression parser takes the collection of recognized symbols and does a structural analysis pass on them to create mathematical expressions that are sent back to the user interface component.

When users issue a command for a computational or symbolic function, the user interface component sends the appropriate recognized mathematical expressions to the computational and symbolic toolset. This component converts the recognized expressions into a command that is then sent to Matlab for processing. The Matlab engine processes the command and sends the data back to the computational and symbolic toolset, which then sends the results to the animation and output component for display.

When mathematical sketches are created, the user interface component sends ink strokes to the mathematical expression recognizer for processing and, using those results and associated drawing elements, creates a behavior list that is sent to the sketch preparation component. The user interface component also communicates with the association inferencing part of the sketch preparation component in real time whenever implicit associations are made. The sketch preparation component does drawing dimension analysis and drawing rectification, using the data in the behavior list, and also sends the list to the Matlab code generation component. The Matlab code generation component is in charge of using the mathematical specification as well as information from the sketch preparation component to generate Matlab executable code that is sent to the Matlab engine. Once the Matlab engine executes the mathematical sketch code, the data are extracted and sent to the animation system where the animation engine moves any animatable drawing elements based on their mathematical specifications.

4.3.2 The Gestural UI

An important goal of mathematical sketching (see Fig. 4.4) is to facilitate mathematical problem solving without imposing any interaction burden beyond those of traditional media. Since pencil-and-paper users switch fluidly between writing equations and drawing supporting diagrams, a modeless interface is highly desirable. Although a simple freehand drawing pen would suffice to mimic pencil and paper, we want to support computational activities including formula manipulation and animation. This functionality requires extending the notion of a freehand pen, either implicitly by parsing the user's 2D input on the fly or explicitly by letting the user perform gestural operations. We chose an interface that combines both, in an effort to reduce the complexity and ambiguities that arise in many hand-drawn mathematical sketches—we use parsing to recognize mathematical expressions and make associations, and use gestures to segment expressions and perform various symbolic and computational operations.

The challenge then for mathematical sketching's gestural user interface is that its gestures not interfere with the entry of drawings or equations and still be direct and natural enough to feel fluid. We utilize a threefold strategy to accomplish this task. First, we use context sensitivity to determine what operations to perform with a single gesture. Second, we use location-aware gestures so that a single gesture can invoke different commands based on its location and size. Third, we use the notion of punctuated gestures [23], compound gestures with one or more strokes and terminal punctuation, to help resolve ambiguities among gestures, mathematics and drawings. Combining these techniques lets the entire interface be completely modeless and also lets us reduce the gesture set while maintaining a high level of functionality.

One of the important issues is whether the gestures actually make sense, since a completely modeless user interface with a poor gesture set may not work well. Our gesture set was chosen (see Fig. 4.6 for a summary) using two important criteria. First, we wanted our gestures to be easy to perform and learn. Second, we wanted gestures that work and seem logical for multiple commands to be used for all those commands. For example, if a particular gesture makes sense for two or three different operations, then we want that gesture to invoke all those operations. This approach eases learning as well, since users need not remember additional gestures. In the remaining sections, we discuss the design issues the mathematical sketching gestural interfaces; details on the how the gestures are recognized can be found in [10].

4.3.2.1 Writing, Recognizing, and Correcting Mathematics

Writing mathematical expressions in mathematical sketching is straightforward: users draw with a stylus as they would with pencil and paper. The only complication in writing expressions is how errant strokes are corrected. Although the stylus can be flipped over to use its eraser, we found that a gestural action not requiring flipping was both more accurate (because of hardware characteristics of the stylus) and more convenient. We therefore first designed a *scribble erase* gesture in which the user scribbles with the pen back and forth over the ink strokes to be deleted. However, this first implementation created too many false positives: it recognized scribble erase gestures when in fact the user had intended to draw ink and not erase anything. To alleviate this problem we settled on a punctuated gesture because of its relative simplicity and ease of execution. Thus our current definition of scribble erase is the scribble stroke followed directly by a tap. In practice, users found this compound gesture easy to learn, effective in eliminating false positives, and not significantly more difficult or slower than the simple scribble gesture.

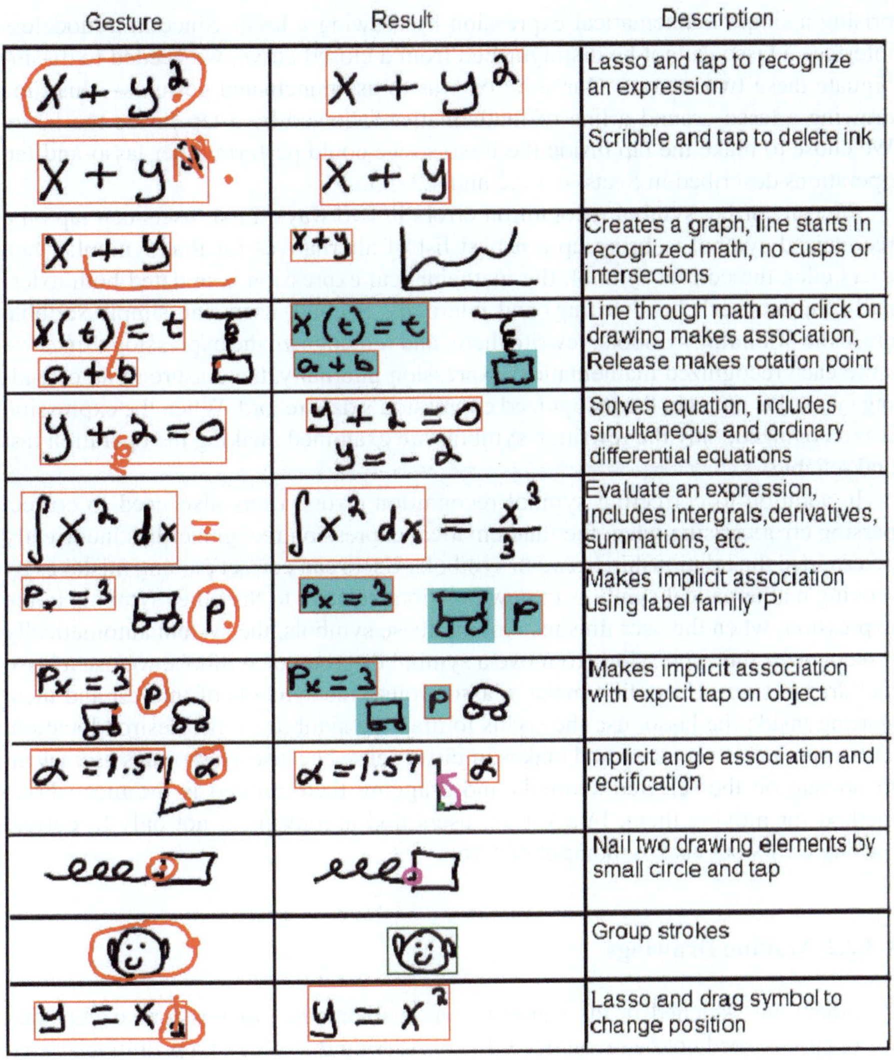

Fig. 4.6 Mathematical sketching gestures. Gesture strokes in the *first column* are shown here in *red*. In the *second column*, *cyan*-highlighted strokes provide association feedback (the highlighting color changes each time a new association is made), and *magenta* strokes show nail and angle association/rectification feedback

Once mathematical expressions are drawn, they must be recognized by the system. Our initial attempt, clicking on a Recognize button that attempted to recognize all mathematics on the page, was problematic because it was hard to algorithmically determine "lines of math" accurately, especially when the expressions were closely spaced, at unusual scales or in unusual 2D arrangements. We therefore chose a manual segmentation alternative by which users explicitly select a set of strokes comprising a single mathematical expression by drawing a lasso. Since in a modeless interface a lasso cannot be distinguished from a closed curve, we needed to disambiguate these two actions. Our solution was to use punctuated gestures—this time drawing a lasso around a line of mathematics followed by a tap inside the lasso. We chose to make the tap inside the lasso so we could perform other lasso-and-tap operations described in Sects. 4.3.2.2 and 4.3.2.5.

We can correct symbol recognition errors in two ways. First, users can tap on a recognized symbol to bring up a n-best list of alternatives for that symbol; when users click the correct symbol, the mathematical expression is updated both externally (in the user's handwriting) and internally. Second, users can simply scribble erase the offending symbols, rewrite them, and rerecognize the expression. Since we store each recognized mathematical expression internally, the erasure of an offending symbol is noted in the recognized expression's data record. When the expression is rerecognized, only the rewritten symbols are examined, making the operation fast and reliable.

In addition to correcting symbol recognition errors, users also need to correct parsing errors arising when the mathematical expression recognizer has incorrectly determined the relationship between symbols. Users can correct parsing mistakes by moving mathematical symbols to new positions relative to the other symbols in the expression; when the user finishes moving these symbols, the system automatically rerecognizes the expression. To move a symbol or group of symbols, we use a lasso and drag gesture. Users first make a lasso around the symbols of interest and then, starting inside the lasso, use the stylus to drag the symbols to the desired location. This approach is very easy and makes intuitive sense because a lasso says users want to operate on the selected symbols and dragging them around is the most direct method for moving them. In addition, users find it convenient not only to correct parsing errors but also to manipulate terms.

4.3.2.2 Making Drawings

Diagrams are sketched in the same way as mathematical expressions except that the diagrams need not be recognized. In considering the value of a primitives-based drawing system against the added interaction overhead of specifying primitives, we decided that our only primitive would be unrecognized ink strokes. We believe that a primitives-based approach would not only require a more elaborate user interface, but would also take away from the pencil-and-paper aesthetic we want to achieve with mathematical sketching.

4.3.2.3 Nailing Diagram Components

In reviewing a broad range of mathematical illustrations, we found that the single low-level behavior of stretching a diagram element can be very powerful. Thus, we support the concept of "nails" to pin a diagram element to the background or pin a point on a diagram element to another diagram element. If either diagram element is moved, the other element either moves rigidly to stay attached at the nail (if it has only one nail) or stretches so that all its nails maintain their points of attachment.

The user creates a nail by drawing a lasso around the appropriate location in the drawing and making a tap gesture inside it (the tap disambiguates the nail gesture from a circle that is part of a drawing). This lasso-and-tap gesture is the same as that used to recognize mathematical expressions. Although we could have used other gestures, such as making a lasso and writing the letter "N" (for nail) to create nails, lasso and tap seemed an attractively more logical gesture since it is analogous to drawing the head of a nail and then hammering it in with the tap.

4.3.2.4 Grouping Diagram Components

Since many drawings involve creating one logical object from a set of strokes (drawing elements), we need to be able to group strokes into composite drawing elements. We can use the same lasso gesture for a grouping operation by drawing a lasso around diagram strokes. We can distinguish the grouping gesture on the basis of tap location. If a stroke is a tap, we check whether the previous stroke completely contains any drawn strokes. If the tap falls within a few pixels of the lasso, then we perform a grouping operation. After the operation, a green box is drawn around the strokes to show that a grouping has been made and to distinguish it from a recognized expression.

Although we could easily define a different gesture for grouping, we believe that maintaining a simple contextually overloaded gesture set is easier for users than the alternative larger gesture set. We explored overloading the mathematical expression recognition gesture and determining whether to make a composite grouping or recognize mathematics by classifying the strokes within a lasso as drawings or text. If the strokes are drawings, they would be grouped; otherwise they would be considered an expression and mathematical recognition would be done. However, this classification is complex and this approach is not yet reliable; more robust algorithms need to be devised for semantic diagram/illustration segmentation.

4.3.2.5 Associations

The most important part of a mathematical sketch is the associations between mathematical expressions and diagrams. Associations are made between scalar mathematical expressions and angle arcs or one of the three special values of a diagram element, its x, y, or rotation coordinate(s).

Implicit Associations Implicit associations are based on the familiar variable and constant names found in mathematics and physics texts. These variable and constant labels appear so regularly in these illustrations that they can clearly be used not for just labeling but for making associations as well. Mathematical sketching supports point and angle associations implicitly and uses the recognized label and linked drawing element to infer associations with other expressions on the page.

To create an implicit point association, users draw a variable name or constant value near the intended drawing element and then use the mathematical expression recognition gesture to recognize the label. The tap location can have two meanings in completing the point association. If the recognition gesture's tap falls within its lasso, then the label is linked to the closest drawing element within some global distance threshold (we use a global distance threshold so that mathematical expressions a significant distance away from a drawing element are not inadvertently associated to that element). If the tap location is outside the lasso, it specifies both the drawing element to be linked to the label and the drawing element's center of rotation (this point is used only for rotational labels). Note that the tap must be located on the drawing element or in the bounding box of a composite drawing element. We have found that users prefer tapping on the drawing element rather than inside the lasso to make a point association, probably because they prefer choosing the drawing element to which mathematics is associated rather than letting the computer choose for them.

To create an implicit angle association, users write a label, then draw an angle arc such that the label is enclosed within the arc and the two ink strokes the arc connects. Then users make a tap whose location on the arc determines the *active line*—the line attached to the arc that will move when the angle changes. The apex of the angle is then marked with a green dot, and the active line is indicated with an arrowhead on the angle arc. Note that we do not detect or support cyclical association relationships, such as the specification of each angle in a triangle.

Explicit Associations For slightly more control over associations and to reduce the density of information in a diagram, associations can also be created explicitly without using variable name labels. The user makes an explicit association by drawing a line through a set of related mathematical expressions and then tapping on a drawing element. After this line is drawn, drawing elements change color as the stylus hovers over them to indicate the potential for an association. This technique provides greater flexibility than the implicit association techniques in two ways. First, explicit associations can specify the precise point of rotation: instead of just tapping on the drawing element (which sets the point of rotation at the center of the drawing element), users can press down on the element to select it, move the stylus, and then lift the stylus to the desired center of rotation, even if it is not on the drawing element. Second, explicit associations are somewhat faster than their implicit counterparts because they do not require users to write down a label first. In addition, users can make an association to a composite drawing element as a whole (e.g., a car) by taping on empty space within the composite's bounding box, or to a part of the composite (e.g., a wheel) by tapping directly on an ink stroke.

4.3.2.6 Supporting Mathematical Toolset

Mathematical sketching also supports mathematical tools for graphing, solving, simplifying, and evaluating recognized functions and equations. The utility of this toolset is twofold. First, it provides traditional tools found in other software packages, so that mathematical sketching becomes a more complete problem-solving and visualization approach. Second, these tools can help in creating mathematical sketches, for example, solving a differential equation to obtain the equations of motion for a sketch or integrating $F = ma$ to find velocity as a function of time.

Graphing Equations Users can graph recognized functions with a simple line gesture that begins on the function and ends at the graph's intended location. The graphing gesture is essentially the same as that used for creating explicit associations, except that it must have a minimum length and its end point must fall outside any of recognized expressions' bounding boxes. The graphing gesture must have a minimum length (about 160 pixels) so that it is not interpreted as a mathematical symbol such as a fraction line. A nice feature of this gesture is that it lets users graph more than one function at a time by making sure that any part of the gesture line (except the end point) intersects an expression's bounding box. The graphing gesture produces a movable, resizable graph widget displaying a plot of the function.

Solving Equations Mathematical sketching also lets users solve equations (see Fig. 4.7. The solver is invoked by a squiggle gesture that resembles the graphing gesture in that its start point must be inside a recognized expression's bounding box, its end point must be outside all expression bounding boxes, and it can intersect multiple recognized expressions along the way. Its distinguishing characteristic is that it must have two self-intersections whereas the graphing gesture must have none. We could have overloaded the graphing gesture and then examined the context of the intersected recognized expressions to determine whether a graphing or solving operation was intended, but it makes more sense to have two distinct gestures for these tasks since graphing and solving are two distinct operations. The squiggle gesture is somewhat arbitrary but users have found it easy to remember and perform. Once a squiggle gesture is recognized, the system presents the solution to users at the end of the gesture.

MathPad^2, can solve single equations, simultaneous equations, and ordinary differential equations (with and without initial conditions) using the same squiggle gesture. When a squiggle gesture is made, the recognized equations intersected by that gesture are examined to determine what type of solving routine to perform. If there is only one recognized equation and it has no derivatives, then we call a single equation solver. If the equation contains derivatives, we call an ordinary differential equation solver. If more than one recognized equation are intersected, we check whether any derivatives are present. If so, the other equations are examined to see if they give valid initial conditions for the differential equation. If so, we call an ordinary differential equation solver. If none of the recognized equations have derivatives, then we call a simultaneous equation solver (we also support simultaneous ordinary differential equations). With this approach users need to remember only one gesture, making the interface much simpler, while making mathematical sketching more powerful.

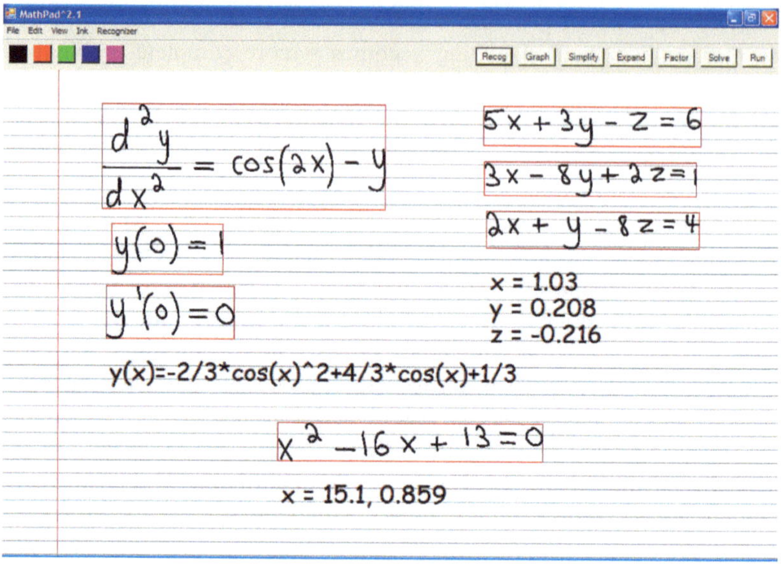

Fig. 4.7 Solutions for a simple equation, an ordinary differential equation, and a set of simultaneous equations all invoked with the same gesture

Evaluating Expressions A variety of different mathematical expressions can be evaluated using the supporting toolset. To evaluate a recognized expression, users make an equal sign and then a tap inside the equal sign's bounding box on the right side of the expression. Choosing an equal sign as part of our evaluation gesture is logical for these types of operations, since users are looking for equivalent mathematical expression representations. In addition, the equal sign is one of the most common mathematical symbols and has an understood meaning.

MathPad^2 supports evaluation of integrals, derivatives, summations, and simplification (see Fig. 4.8 for some examples). The recognized mathematical expression to the left of the equal tap gesture is examined to determine what kind of evaluation to perform. Combinations of summations, derivatives and integrals as well as nth-order operations (e.g., double integrals, triple sums) are also possible. If the recognized expression contains an integral, derivative, or summation then the appropriate evaluation is performed. If none of these are found, then the evaluation defaults to a simplification operation. The benefits of this approach are similar to those of equation solving: users need to remember only one gesture in order to perform different evaluations while the addition improves mathematical sketching's flexibility.

4.3.3 *Mathematical Expression Recognition*

Users write down mathematical expressions as part of the mathematical sketching process and these expressions must be recognized so they can be used later in spec-

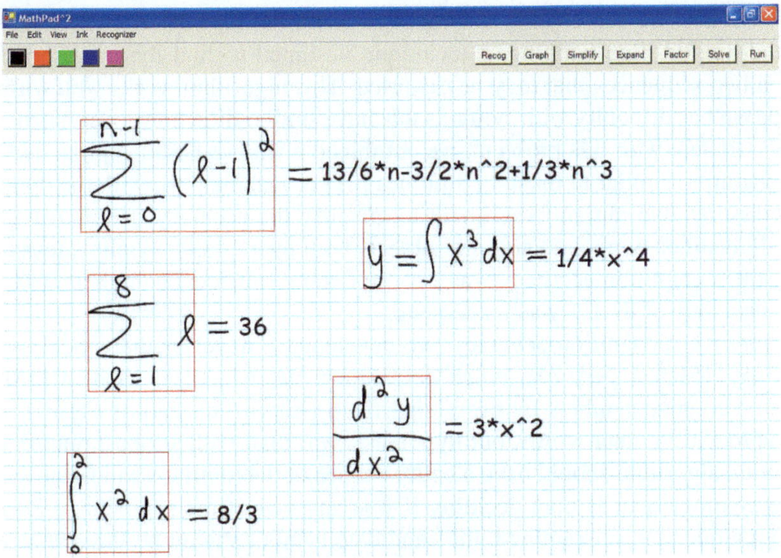

Fig. 4.8 A variety of expressions evaluated using the equal tap gesture

ifying behaviors in a dynamic illustration or in a computational or symbolic operation. Mathematical expression recognition involves two distinct, yet interrelated activities; mathematical symbol recognition and mathematical expression parsing. To present all of the details on our mathematical expression recognizer is beyond scope of this chapter, thus we will only discuss it briefly. A thorough discussion of the general issues involved with mathematical expression recognition and our recognizer, in particular, can be found in [10].

4.3.3.1 Mathematical Symbol Recognition

To recognize mathematical symbols, we chose a writer-dependent approach where each user provides a set of handwriting samples (10 to 20 samples per symbol) for the recognizer to train on. A writer-dependent approach has the advantage that they allow personalized recognizers tailored toward a particular user.

In our earlier implementation of MathPad^2, we used a hybrid approach that combined Li and Yeung's recognition algorithm using dominant points in strokes [17]. "Dominant points in strokes" are defined as the key points in a stroke, including local extrema of curvature, the starting and ending points of a stroke, and the midpoints between these points. The algorithm uses dominant points to extract direction codes for each symbol by looking at the writing direction from one dominant point to another. The direction codes are broken up into 45-degree increments such that each symbol is represented as a sequence of numbers from 0 to 7, with the length of the sequence defined by the number of dominant points in the stroke. Using these direction codes, we can classify a symbol as one of an alphabet of symbols by using band-limited time warping, a technique designed to find the correspondence between two sequences that may be distorted. This algorithm works well for many symbols but has difficulty with symbols that have similar direction codes, such as "(" and "1". To deal with this problem, we combined a feature-based approach using a linear classifier, similar to those in Smithies [21] or Rubine [19], with the dominant point classifier. We ran an experiment to quantify the accuracy of this recognizer (using 48 distinct symbols) using 11 subjects with over 14,000 symbols tested. Although the recognition accuracy was good for some subjects (as high as 98%), the overall accuracy of 87.1% was inadequate.

To improve recognition accuracy, we developed a novel mathematical symbol recognizer [15] that performs much better than the recognizer used in [14]. We chose to recognize symbols by examining them pairwise instead of using a multi-class approach. In other words, our hypothesis was that, with a robust feature set, a recognition algorithm should have a better chance of deciding if a candidate symbol is either symbol A or B than deciding if it is any one of the symbols A–Z. Thus, if every unique pair is examined, the candidate symbol should be the one selected by the most classifiers. This pairwise approach then allows comparisons without the intrusion of another symbol's data outside the pair, which could skew the feature variances in the wrong direction.

One of the issues with this pairwise approach is that the number of comparisons would be $\frac{m(m-1)}{2}$, so m of reasonable size would slow the recognizer down considerably. We had observed through some empirical analysis the Microsoft handwriting recognizer has the correct classification in its n-best list over 99% of the time. Therefore, we incorporated it into our symbol recognizer as a first pass to prune down the number of pairs, making the algorithm much faster.

The key to this approach is to have a robust feature set and a set of associated weights on those features for pairwise discrimination. The weights on these features can be found using a variety of algorithms assuming conditions on the distributions of the features. If the features we use are normally distributed, then approaches found in [19, 21] could be used; however, our features are not necessarily normally distributed. We therefore decided to use AdaBoost [20] to find feature weights because of its invariance to distribution assumptions, its ability to deal with simple classifiers, and its simplicity. AdaBoost takes a series of simple or base classifiers and calls them repeatedly in a series of rounds on training data. Each weak learner's importance or weight is updated after each round on the basis of its performance on the training set. With this recognizer, we obtained an overall accuracy of 95.1%, which is significantly better than our previous approach.

4.3.3.2 Mathematical Expression Parsing

Once the mathematical symbol recognizer classifies a set of ink strokes as a set of particular symbols, these symbols must be structurally analyzed to determine their relationships with one other and parsed to create a coherent mathematical expression. As with mathematical symbol recognition, the parsing system can be writer-independent or -dependent. We chose to make our parser mostly writer-independent since we do utilize ascender and descender information (e.g., an ascender would be "b" while a descender would be "p") from the user's writing samples to help deal with implicit operators (e.g., subscripts, superscripts). With this approach, a key issue is making the spatial relationship rules broad enough to capture how different users write mathematical expressions without making them too broad to maintain accuracy. Unfortunately, there is no set rule of thumb for making these rules. Therefore, we chose the spatial rules based on neatness and consistency criteria. Of course, not all users fit within these criteria, but we felt many of them would and those who did not could adapt to the rules over time.

Our approach to parsing mathematical expressions is based on two methods, a coordinate grammar [3] and procedurally coded syntax rules [16]. We chose a coordinate grammar for ease of implementation and coded syntax rules to help resolve ambiguities and to allow more complex methods for dealing with and reducing parsing decisions. Our coordinate grammar is similar to that in [18] in that we have a set of spatial relationship rules defined separately from our context-free grammar. The spatial relationship rules are used to convert the two-dimensional mathematical expressions into a one-dimensional representation as the expression is parsed with the context-free grammar.

The mathematical expression parsing system takes as input a list of symbols sorted from left to right by location. The algorithm utilizes two types of procedures: *parse* functions and *process* functions. The parse functions parse the symbols according to the context-free grammar. The process functions determine how symbols relate to each other based on their relative locations and contain the spatial relationship rules that determine how symbols interact mathematically. The results from these functions are stored as extra symbol information so the parse functions know exactly what symbols represent and how they relate to one another. The process functions are intermixed with the parse functions and act as helpers, giving them any information they need to parse expressions using the grammar. The parse functions translate the list of symbols into a 1D string representation built upon the context-free grammar. Once the parsing system creates a 1D string, it is sent to the procedurally coded syntax rules for further processing. An example of such a rule is if $5\mathrm{in}(x)$ is recognized, we assume from the similarity of 5 and "s" that a user is trying to write a sine function, and we replace the 5 with an "s".

In addition to constructs such as integrals, derivative and summations, MathPad^2 also supports conditional statements. Conditionals are used as branching instructions in mathematical sketching and are written using a discontinuous function representation. Figure 4.9 shows a conditional expression used in mathematical sketching. The key to parsing conditionals is to break up the lines of mathematics so that each one can be parsed individually and incorporated back into the conditional expression. We tested our parsing algorithm on several hundred mathematical expressions over 11 different subjects. Although some of subjects had their expressions parsed correctly over 98% of the time, the overall average was 90.8%, indicating that we need more work on improving the parsing step.

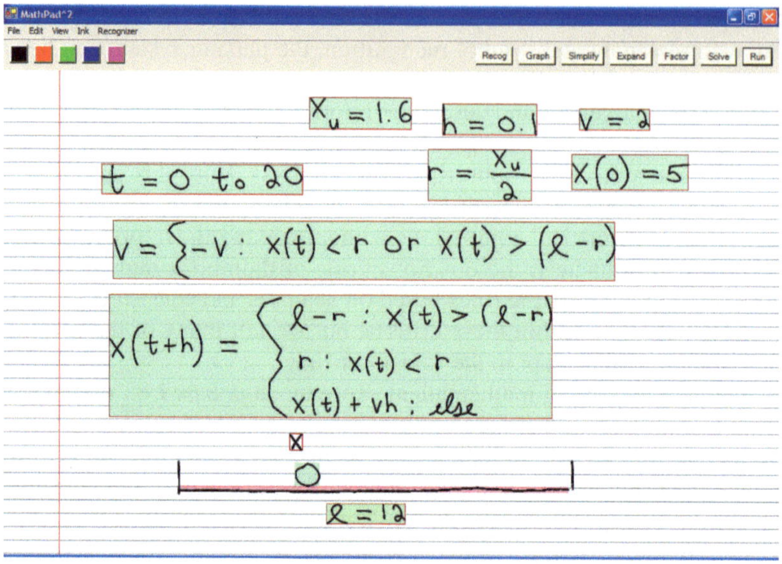

Fig. 4.9 A conditional expression

4.4 Preparing Mathematical Sketches

Mathematical sketches need to be analyzed so that information from the free-form drawings, any associated labels, and the data generated from the mathematics can work together to make dynamic illustrations. This analysis is performed in real time and during a pre-simulation step. The main type of preparation done in real time is association inferencing. When users make an association, mathematical expressions must be attached to a particular drawing element. The pre-simulation step of mathematical sketch preparation, performed just before the sketch animates, gathers important information from the sketch so it can run properly. For a sketch to run properly, dimensional analysis and drawing rectification are required.

4.4.1 Association Inferencing

When users make implicit associations they label drawing elements; we use these labels to determine which written mathematical expressions to associate with a particular drawing element. An expression should be associated with a drawing element if it takes any part in the behavioral specification of that element. Two types of labels can be associated to drawing elements. The first type of labels are constants. As an example, a user might want to associate the number 100 to a horizontal line indicating its length or associate the constant $l = 50$ indicating a building's height. With these types of associations, inferencing is trivial: if a label is a number or equal to a number, the label is the only mathematical expression collected and the association is complete. The second type of labels are variable names which are slightly more complicated since they generally refer to other mathematical expressions. We utilize the *label families* to infer which mathematical expressions should be associated to the labeled drawing element.

A label family is defined by its name, a root string. Members of the label family are variables that include that root string and a component subscript (e.g., x for its x-axis component) or a function specification. For example, if the user labels a drawing element ϕ_o, the inferencing system determines the label family to be ϕ and finds all mathematical expressions having members of the ϕ label family on the left-hand side of the equal sign: ϕ, ϕ_o, $\phi(t)$, $\phi_x(t)$, and so on. The inferencing system then finds all the variable names appearing on the right-hand side, determines their label families, and then continues the search. This process terminates when there are no more variable names to search for. Once all the related mathematical expressions have been found, they are sorted to represent a logical flow of operations that can be executed by a computational engine, and the implicit association is completed.

4.4.2 Drawing Dimension Analysis

Mathematical sketching assumes a global Cartesian coordinate system with the $+x$-axis pointing to the right and the $+y$-axis pointing up. However, the overall scale of the coordinate system—how much screen space is equal to one coordinate unit along either axis—must be defined. Note that individual drawing elements have their own local coordinate systems with the origin at the center of the element. However, these local coordinate systems are all scaled based on the global coordinate dimensions. Mathematical sketch dimensioning is important since the animation system needs to know how to transform data from simulation to animation space. With many mathematical sketch diagrams, enough information is in place to infer the sketch's dimensions, either by using the initial locations of diagram elements or by labeling linear dimensions within a diagram.

When two different drawing elements are associated with expressions so that each drawing element has a different value for one of its coordinates (x or y), then implicit dimensioning can be defined. The distance along the coordinate shared between the two drawing elements establishes a dimension for the coordinate system, and the location of the drawing elements implies the location of the coordinate system origin. For example, for the sketch on the right of Fig. 4.10, at time 0, the value of $h_x(t)$ is 0 and the value of $s_x(t)$ is 10. Thus, we can dimension the x-axis using the distance between the two cars defined by their locations at time 0. The factor used in transforming drawing elements from simulation to animation space is then the distance between the two cars in pixels divided by 10.

Alternatively, if only one drawing element is associated with mathematics or if more than one drawing element is associated with mathematics but they all have the same values at time 0, then the dimension of the coordinate system can still be

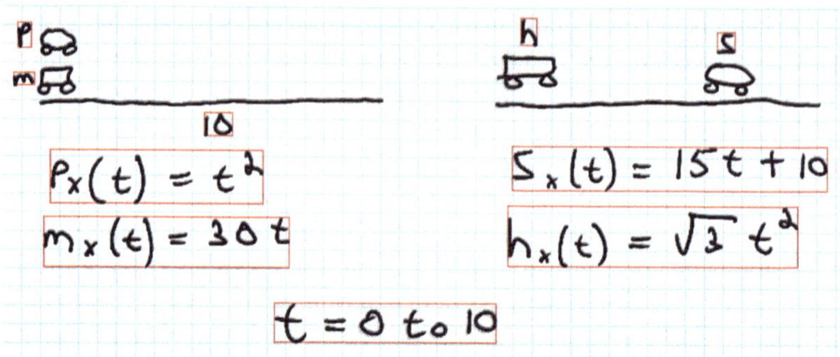

Fig. 4.10 Two methods for inferring coordinate dimensions: the mathematical sketch on the left uses labeling of the ground line, while the one on the right uses the calculated distance between h and s at time $t = 0$

inferred if another drawing element is associated with a numerical label. Whenever a numerical label is applied to a drawing element, it is analyzed: if it is a horizontal or vertical line, the corresponding x- or y-axis dimension is established; otherwise, we apply the label to the best-fit line to the drawing element and then establish the dimensions of both coordinate axes. For example, with the sketch on the left of Fig. 4.10, at time 0 both $h_x(t)$ and $s_x(t)$ are 0, offering no help with defining coordinate dimensions. However, the horizontal line below it is labeled with 10. Therefore, we can dimension the x-axis with 10 and define the simulation-to-animation-space transformation factor to be the width of the line in pixels divided by 10.

Two important issues in drawing dimension analysis must be addressed. First, more than one drawing element may have a line label, so that there are multiple possibilities for a x or y dimension. One approach to this issue is simply to choose the first or last drawing element that defines an x or y dimension. This approach works but is not necessarily ideal; we are currently looking at ways for users to choose drawing elements to use for dimensioning. Second, if not enough information has been specified to define coordinate system dimensions implicitly, then default dimensions are used. This default works for many mathematical sketches but is sometimes insufficient, resulting in drawing elements that hardly move at all or move quickly off the screen. One approach to this problem is to examine the minimum and maximum values that a drawing element obtains during simulation and use it to dimension the coordinate system so that drawings always move appropriately.

4.4.3 Drawing Rectification

Mathematical sketches often have inherent discrepancies between what the mathematics specifies and what the user draws. In other words, because users write precise mathematical specifications and make imprecise free-form drawings, the correspondence mismatch between the two often yields a dynamic illustration that looks incorrect. *Rectification* is the process of fixing the correspondence between drawings and mathematics so that something meaningful is displayed. MathPad^2 supports angle, location, and size rectification which are critical in many of the mathematical sketches created with open-form solutions (see Sect. 4.4.4).

4.4.3.1 Angle Rectification

Mismatches between numerical descriptions of angles and their diagram counterparts are readily discernible. When an angle is associated with mathematics, we rectify the drawing in one of two ways. First, the angle between the two lines connected by the angle arc is computed. Next, the system determines if a mathematical expression corresponding to the angle label already exists. If so, it rotates the active line as determined by the difference between the drawn angle and numerical label, to the correct place based on the mathematical specification. If not, it uses the angle computed from the drawing as the numerical specification of the angle's value. Currently, this angle is represented internally and used during simulation.

Our angle rectification strategy works well when angles are defined by two isolated drawing elements. However, it fails in certain situations. For example, an angle must be defined by two separate drawing elements. If users draw the initial and terminal sides of an angle with one stroke (e.g, the first two sides of a triangle), the angle rectification algorithm cannot handle it. We could deal with this issue by detecting vertices and breaking the stroke into parts. However, the problem gets more difficult when dealing with drawings such as triangles. More details on angle rectification can be found in [10].

4.4.3.2 Location Rectification

User drawings often contain drawing elements placed in relation to other elements. If a drawing element is placed incorrectly with respect to other drawing elements and their mathematical specifications, the dynamic illustration does not look correct and may not present the right visualization. Consider the sketch in Fig. 4.11. The user draws the ball but positions it a bit to the right on the horizontal line. However, to see whether the ball will travel over the fence (a distance of 100 units), the ball should be placed so that it starts at distance zero, which is at the start of the horizontal line. Since this is a 2D sketch, the ball should also be placed at a certain height from the ground. In both cases, we want to place the ball using the initial conditions of the mathematical specification in relation to any labeled drawing elements. In our example, the ball should be at location $(0, 3)$ with respect to the horizontal line, since the initial conditions for its position are defined by $p_x(0)$ and $p_y(0)$. Now the system must rectify the ball's position in order to make a valid correspondence among the ball, the labeled lines, and the mathematics.

To perform location rectification, we begin by looking at all drawing elements associated with functions of time. Each of these elements is checked for explicitly written initial conditions specified by mathematical expressions, found by using the

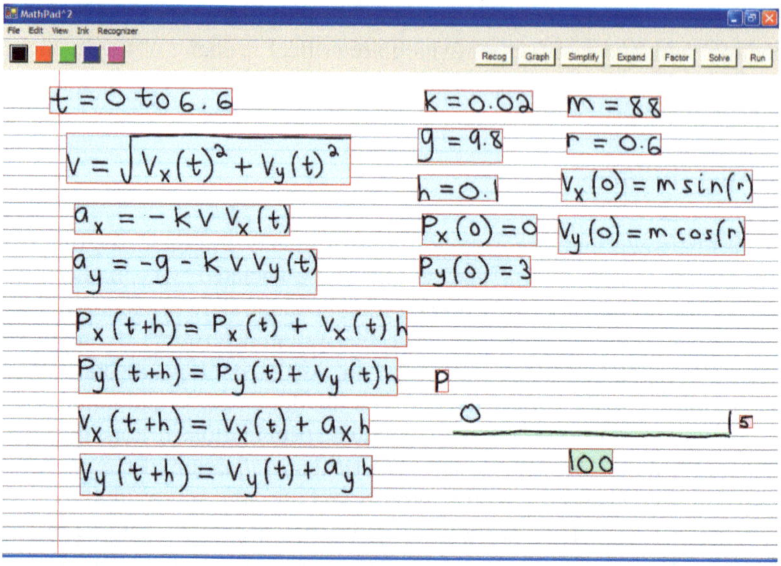

Fig. 4.11 A mathematical sketch created to illustrate projectile motion with air drag (using an open-form solution). If the ball labeled "p" is not positioned correctly with respect to the *horizontal line*, it is difficult to verify whether the mathematics drives the ball over the fence

drawing element's core label. The mathematical expressions associated to the drawing element are examined: if they contain the core label on the left-hand side of the equal sign as a function evaluation, such as the $p_x(0)$ and $p_y(0)$, the right-hand sides of these expressions are taken as the initial condition values. If there is no core label (because an explicit association is used) or no explicitly written initial conditions, we can still find initial conditions for the drawing element by looking at the simulation data's initial values. Once the initial conditions for a drawing element are found, the remaining drawing elements are examined and the information from drawing dimension analysis is used to relocate the drawing element. Drawing elements are relocated based not only on the dimensioning of an axis, but also on the location of the drawing element from which that dimension came, since we want to maintain the relationship between the two. Therefore, we examine each drawing element not associated with a function of time to see if it has a line label and a dimension for the x- or y-axis. If it has a dimension for the x-axis, we look at its start and end x coordinates and choose the smallest. The smallest x coordinate is chosen since we assume the origin along the x-axis is always defined as the leftmost x coordinate of the drawing element. With the x coordinates for the origin o_x, initial condition p_{x0}, and the center of the drawing element d_x we want to relocate, we then calculate a translation factor

$$t_x = -(d_x - o_x) + p_{x0} \cdot sa_x, \tag{1}$$

where sa_x is the dimensioning factor for the x-axis defined in Sect. 4.4.2. t_x is then used to translate the drawing element to its rectified location in the x direction. If the drawing element with the associated line label has a dimension for the y-axis, we use the procedure for x translation to translate the drawing element we want to rectify in the y direction, the only difference being that we choose the bottommost y coordinate of the drawing element with the line label as the origin along the y-axis. Choosing the origin point in this way facilitates an origin with the $+x$-axis pointing to the right and the $+y$-axis pointing up.

Two important issues arise in our location rectification procedure. It is possible that in a 2D mathematical sketch, only one drawing element has a line label, meaning that only the x- or y-axis is dimensioned. Our drawing dimension procedure handles this by simply dimensioning the other axis with the same dimensional information. Since location rectification uses the information from drawing dimension analysis, the relocation of a drawing element will reflect this information. The other important issue is determining what happens when there is more than one x- or y-axis line label, resulting in more than one x or y origin coordinate. In these cases, we assume that when users make drawings they intend to put these elements in approximately the right place. We can thus choose the origin point closest to the drawing element we want to relocate. However, if we make this choice, the x and y dimensions may be taken from another drawing element or elements with line labels. In this situation, the dimensions could be overridden, but this could cause problems if another time-varying drawing element uses those dimensions. If this happens, then separate x and y dimensions are needed for each time-varying drawing element.

4.4.3.3 Size Rectification

The size of a drawing element in relation to other drawing elements or to the written mathematics plays a role in the plausibility of many dynamic illustrations developed with mathematical sketching. The mathematical sketch in Fig. 4.12 illustrates a ball bouncing off a wall in 1D. The mathematics associated with the ball uses the size of the ball to determine when the ball collides with the wall and to update its velocity and location with respect to the wall. The mathematics also precisely specifies the diameter of the ball ($x_u = 1.2$) and specifies how long the horizontal line below the ball should be (which is also used for dimensioning x). Therefore, the ball's behavior is precisely defined. However, the user may or may not draw the ball with diameter 1.2 relative to the horizontal line. If the ball is not drawn at the correct size, the dynamic illustration will not look correct, since the ball either goes through the wall before changing direction or stops and changes direction before it hits the wall. To remedy this situation, the ball must be resized according to the mathematics and its relationship to the x-axis dimension. In this example, since we know the diameter of the ball in simulation space from the variable $x_u = 1.6$, its size in pixels, and its relationship to the horizontal line, we can rectify its size appropriately, as in Fig. 4.12. In this example, location rectification is also important since the ball's location also affects the plausibility of the dynamic illustration.

Resizing drawing elements is slightly more complex than angle or location rectification because drawing elements can be scaled in many different ways. Without

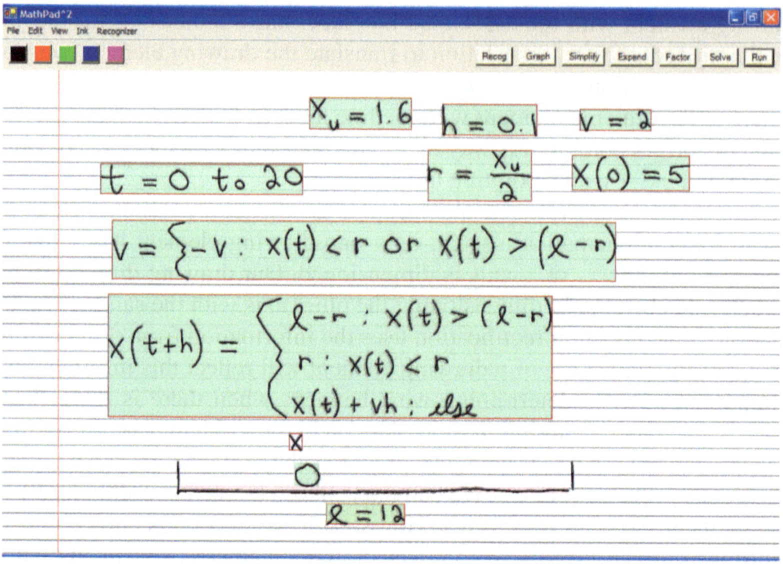

Fig. 4.12 A mathematical sketch showing a ball traveling in 1D, making collisions with two walls (using an open-form solution with a conditional). If the ball (labeled "x") is not the correct size in relation to the x dimension and the mathematics, the illustration will not look correct since the ball will not appear to hit and bounce off the wall

some user intervention, the problem is underconstrained, since a drawing element could be scaled about any point and in any direction (e.g., uniformly, along its x- or y-axis, etc.). To constrain the problem, we first assume that scaling is done about the single or grouped drawing element's center. Second, we assume that a drawing element can be scaled uniformly, along its width, or along its height. These assumptions are somewhat restrictive but work well for most mathematical sketches that require size rectification. The size of a drawing element is specified using its core label subscripted with "u", "w", or "h", respectively. For example, to specify the width of a drawing element we write $x_w = \langle \text{width} \rangle$. Using this notation works when mathematics is associated to a drawing element implicitly or explicitly and does not place any extra burden on users.

To perform size rectification, we first examine all time-varying drawing elements, checking to see if any size information is associated to them. Size information is found by looking at the drawing element's core label and determining if any variable names with the core label have subscripts with "u", "h", or "w". If so, the values assigned to the size variables are extracted from the right-hand side of these equations. Using the information from drawing dimension analysis that gives us the simulation-to-animation-space transformation factors, we then create scaling factors for each drawing element and resize them appropriately. Note that if no core label is present, the algorithm looks for variables starting with "u", "w", or "h", and extracts the values from those equations.

As with location rectification, the complexity of size rectification increases when more than one drawing element has a line label, resulting in more than one choice in dimensioning the x- and/or y-axis. We can deal with this problem, much as in location rectification, by either updating the x- or y-axis dimensions based on which line-labeled drawing element is closer to the drawing element we want to rectify or simply keeping multiple dimensions for each axis and applying them accordingly during animation. Another important concern with our size rectification approach is what happens when the associated mathematics lacks size information. In these cases, it is still possible to infer scale by examining the size of the drawing element in pixels and using the drawing dimensions to create the correct size of the drawing element in simulation space. However, figuring out the type of size rectification to perform (e.g., uniformly, across width or height) would be difficult without some user intervention.

The last concern in our size rectification procedure (and with size rectification in general) is that even with drawing element resizing, a dynamic illustration may not always look precisely correct. The reason for these imperfections is that we let users make free-form drawings.[1] Free-form drawings have an inherent impreciseness on a geometric level that is difficult to take into account when preparing a mathematical sketch for animation. Referring again to Fig. 4.12, we see that the mathematical specification assumes the ball is a perfect circle. Therefore, if users draw the ball as an approximate circle, the ball can still stop slightly before the wall or go past it by a small amount, depending on how the ball is actually drawn. We have found that, in most cases, users do not find these minor imperfections significant and feel the animations are plausible, given that illustrations are based on a sketch.

4.4.4 Translating and Visualizing Mathematical Sketches

In MathPad^2, the mathematical specifications that users write as part of mathematical sketches are essentially small programs that must be translated into the proper format to be executed in a computational engine. The data these programs generate, along with information from the sketch preparation routines, allow the animation engine to animate drawing elements and create a dynamic illustration. However, we want users writing mathematical specifications to perceive them not as a program that requires an ordered list of instructions, but rather as a collection of mathematical statements that they might write in their notebooks to solve a problem. This collection of mathematical statements should be order-independent from the user's perspective and not have the rigid structure required by conventional programming languages. To facilitate a more notational style, the mathematical specifications used in mathematical sketching do not require variable declarations: users simply write variables and constants without any regard to whether they are integers or reals. The

[1] Angle and location rectification suffer from this permissiveness to a lesser extent.

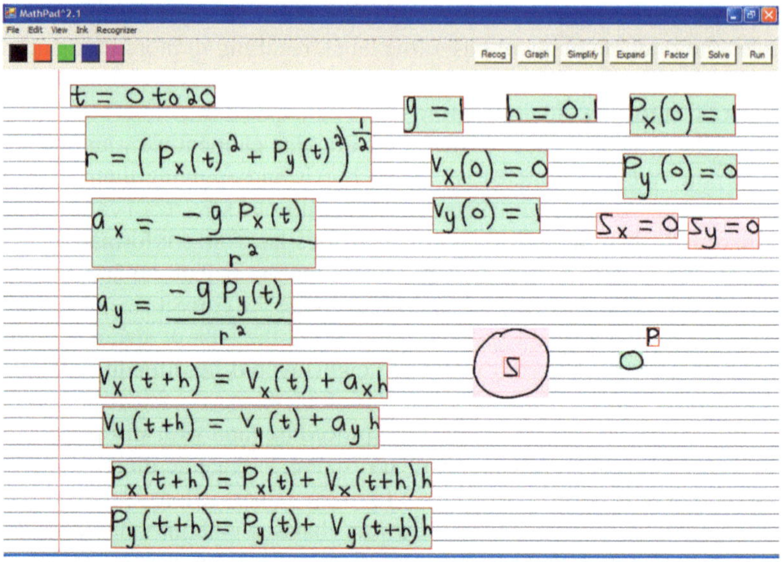

Fig. 4.13 Using an open-form solution, the mathematical sketch shows an illustration of orbital motion

mathematical specifications also need not be written linearly: users can write their specifications anywhere on the page, as they might in a notebook.

MathPad^2 supports mathematical sketches that use both closed-form (see Fig. 4.4 and open-form solutions. With closed-form solutions, the movement of a drawing element can be defined with functions whose output is known for any point in time. Thus, a closed-form function of time can be evaluated for any time t and the result easily returned. Unfortunately, not all types of mathematical and physical phenomena can be modeled with closed-form solutions. With open-form solutions, movement of a drawing element is not known in advance and needs to be simulated using a numerical technique. Thus, the movement data for a particular drawing element are determined incrementally. Examples of mathematical sketches that employ open-form solutions are shown in Figs. 4.11, 4.12, and 4.13 and create dynamic illustrations for 2D projectile motion subject to air resistance, a ball colliding with two walls, and orbital motion, respectively. Translating mathematical sketches that use closed-form solutions is fairly straightforward and is discussed in [10]. Thus, here we focus on how sketches using open-form solutions are translated.

There are many different notations for writing open-form solutions (e.g., using subscripts or index variables). Our initial approach was to use subscript notation. However, after consulting several elementary physics textbooks, we chose a notation (see Fig. 4.13) that we felt was more appropriate for our intended user base, high school and first year college students.

Before any processing can be done on an open-form solution, it must first be recognized as one. Using our notation, a function's current value is determined, in part, from its previous values. Thus, the left-hand sides of expressions that fit

Fig. 4.14 Code generated from the mathematical specification in Fig. 4.12. Note that since indexing into arrays in Matlab start at 1, the initial condition $x(0) = 5$ written in the sketch is translated to $x(1) = 5$

```
h = 0.1
x_u = 1.6
v = 2
r = x_u/2
l = 12
x(1) = 5
for i = 2:200
  if (x(i-1) < r | x(i-1) > (l-r))
    v = -v;
  end
  if (x(i-1) > (l-r))
    x(i) = l-r;
  elseif (x(i-1) < r)
    x(i) = r;
  else
    x(i) = x(i-1) + v*h;
  end
end
```

this criteria have as input parameter $t + \langle\text{variable}\rangle$ where the "variable" is a time increment: for example, $p_x(t+h) = p_x(t) + a^2$. The mathematical expressions associated with a given drawing element are examined; if any of them have $t + \langle\text{variable}\rangle$ on the left-hand side of the equal sign and the time increments (i.e., the symbol to the right of the "$t+$") are all the same variable, we assume an open-form solution.

Open-form solutions have a preprocessing and computation step. In the preprocessing step, user-defined function names and their parameters are extracted from the mathematical expressions associated to drawing elements. We need to know these names to translate the expressions to Matlab-compatible strings and to convert them into proper functions with appropriate indexing. Once the function names and parameters are extracted, the preprocessing step looks for iteration constructs, extracting information from them used in the computation step, and converting mathematical expressions to Matlab-compatible strings. The last part of the preprocessing routine deals with the initial conditions. If a user-defined function has a number as a parameter (i.e., $p_x(0)$), we assume it defines an initial condition for that function.

For each animatable drawing element, the computation step first determines which user-defined functions should be included within an iteration construct by examining their parameters. Using the time increment variable found when the mathematical sketch was examined to see if it was an open-form solution, the number of iterations is calculated using $\lceil\frac{(T_{\text{final}} - T_{\text{initial}})}{\Delta t}\rceil$, where Δt is the time increment variable. With this information the Matlab code is constructed (see Fig. 4.14) and executed and the data are stored in arrays named after the user-defined functions in the mathematical specification. Once the data are generated, the animation engine uses them to animate the dynamic illustration.

4.5 Moving Forward with Mathematical Sketching

Because mathematical sketching is a relatively large-scale interaction paradigm, a significant amount of future work can be explored. This section presents a research agenda for mathematical sketching in the context if improving the MathPad^2 prototype.

4.5.1 The Computational and Symbolic Toolset

Graphing mathematical expressions is currently restricted to two-dimensional line plots. Extending graphing functionality to support other types of graphs such as histograms, 3D line plots, and contour and surface plots in 2D and 3D would increase mathematical sketching's flexibility. Adding these new types of graphs would not add much complexity to the interface. Using the graphing gesture, the system could analyze the mathematical expressions to determine what type of graph to create. In some cases, several types of graphs could be made for a given mathematical expression: adding a simple marking [9] or flow menu [6] to the graph gesture would let users choose which type of plot they wanted if multiple plot styles were available. Mathematical sketching also needs to support plotting function families. For example, a solution to an ordinary differential equation is a family of functions based on the constants in the solution. If initial conditions are provided, the solution is simply one function (assuming no other constants are present). Having the system choose a reasonable range for these constants so the general solution to an ordinary differential equation can be visualized would greatly improve mathematical sketching. Users could also specify these ranges for more interactive control. Another limitation of mathematical sketching's current graphing approach is that a function's domain is predefined in the graph. Users can adjust a function's domain in the graph widget by writing in the values, but an automatic way to choose an appropriate domain might be more useful. One approach to finding an appropriate domain would be use the zeros of the function as a guide, but this approach would work well only in some cases.

More flexibility in expression evaluation and equation solving will also increase the power of mathematical sketching. Currently, users make an equal and tap gesture next to a recognized mathematical expression and the expression's context determines whether integration, summation, differentiation, or simplification should be performed. Extending expression evaluation to support additional numerical calculations as well as other symbolic manipulation such as factoring, Fourier transforms, and Taylor series expansions would make it difficult simply to rely on the expression's context for its evaluation. Using either marking or flow menu techniques as part of the equal and tap gesture would help to distinguish among the multitude of different evaluation options while still maintaining the user interface's fluidity. In equation solving, mathematical sketching assumes it will solve for x, y, z, and w if these variables are present in the equations. However, users may want to define

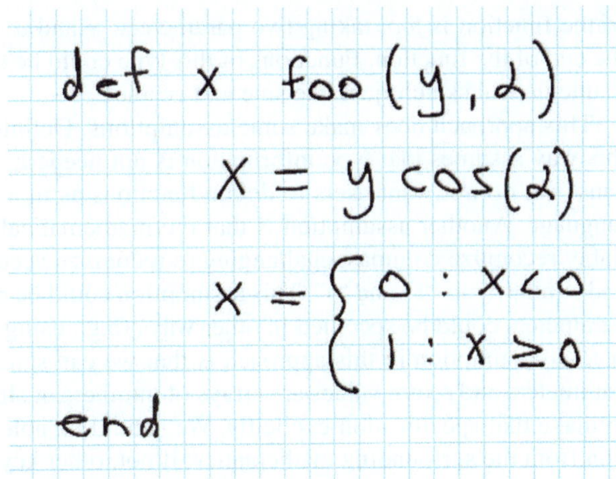

Fig. 4.15 How a user might specify a user-defined function. The *def* and *end* keywords signify the start and end of the function respectively

a set of equations with unknown constants and solve in terms of them. Improving the interface for invoking equation-solving operations would let users choose what variables to solve and thus provide more flexibility. A way to support this additional functionality would be to turn the equation-solving gesture into a compound gesture by which users could explicitly write in the variables to solve for, resorting to a default scenario if no variables are written.

4.5.2 Functions and Macros

Letting users define their own functions and macros would make mathematical sketching more powerful because users could build libraries of specific reusable functions. For example, a user could create a Runge–Kutta function for use in sketches requiring open-form solutions, or define a function to encapsulate a rotation or scaling operation. Users can already define simple functions when making mathematical sketches to a certain extent, but they cannot store them and reuse them at will.

The key issue in user-defined functions and macros is how and at what level they are specified in mathematical sketching. In general, users should be able to specify the function name, its input parameters, the statements that make up the function, and its output parameters. These user-defined functions and macros could also become relatively sophisticated in terms of whether function parameters can be passed by value or by reference.

One approach to defining functions and macros is to use a keyword to indicate that a function is going to be defined and a keyword to indicate where the function ends, as in Fig. 4.15. Important information about the function could then be extracted. In Fig. 4.15, users write the *def* keyword to indicate that they want to define a new function. The x on that line indicates the return variable and the name of the function is *foo*, taking two parameters, y and α. The *end* keyword signifies the end of the function. Functions of this type could be stored and used in any other mathematical sketch (just like sine and cosine).

This approach does make some assumptions. Defining functions and macros in this way assumes that type information is not needed; this assumption is valid because we do not want users to define functions as in a conventional programming language. Another assumption is that the mathematical symbol recognizer can reliably recognize commas, challenging to recognize accurately because of their size and similarity to "1" and ")". This assumption could be relaxed since other the input parameters could be specified in other ways (e.g., using ":" or a parameter widget). A final assumption in this approach is that we can safely determine whether input parameters and return values are arrays of numbers or simply scalars without having to make that specification explicitly. We should be able to determine this information from the surrounding mathematics; if not, other keywords could be introduced. Adding user-defined storable functions and macros like the one shown in Fig. 4.15 would require a moderate software development effort, although there will be some challenging design decisions to make in dealing with more complicated function specifications.

User-defined functions and macros could be used on the mathematical sketch level as well. Users could encapsulate small sketches for use in building up more complex ones. The problem with this functionality is that many complex physical and mathematical problems cannot be easily broken down into simpler pieces. This key issue makes encapsulating small sketches to make more complex ones a very difficult research problem, and more work is needed to determine the utility of using simple mathematical sketches as building blocks for more complicated ones.

4.5.3 Moving to 3D

Mathematical sketching currently supports two-dimensional dynamic illustrations: drawing elements can rotate and translate in the x or y directions. Mathematical sketching could be made more powerful by extending it to support three-dimensional dynamic illustrations. Supporting three-dimensional dynamic illustrations has some interesting implications. First, because we are adding another dimension, mathematical specifications will become more complex, and support for partial derivatives will be needed. Second, users' drawings become more complex because they will be done in perspective. Third and most importantly, drawing dimension analysis and drawing rectification must be extended to deal with three dimensions. In addition, many people have difficulty making 3D drawings which can make mathematical sketch preparation even more difficult to perform. The last two implications assume that three-dimensional dynamic illustration support would be a direct extension of two-dimensional mathematical sketching. Users would write mathematics, make 3D drawings and make associations between the two. Since making 3D drawings can be difficult, one way to simplify creating 3D dynamic illustrations is to used 3D geometric primitives created using simple pen gestures, possibly using techniques from Sketch [24] or Teddy [8]. This approach goes against our free-form drawing aesthetic in mathematical sketching, but from a usability standpoint 3D geometric primitives seem very helpful and make drawing rectification much easier to deal with. If we use 3D geometric primitives, supporting 3D dynamic illustrations will be a fairly straightforward but significant software development effort. However, if users can draw 3D diagrams as part of a mathematical sketch, then the problem gets more difficult because of the issues involved with rectifying and understanding a 3D diagram, resulting in a significantly challenging research area.

4.5.4 Interactivity

Mathematical sketching is a highly interactive activity. However, when users create mathematical sketches, all they can do is run the sketch and watch the animation. An interesting area of further research is to provide higher levels of interactivity during a dynamic illustration. Letting users interact with the dynamic illustration while it is running would make possible a more extensive exploration into mathematical and physical concepts in a variety of different situations. For example, users could explore collisions by grabbing one object and moving it into another object, or could move a cylinder through a flow field to observe how its movement affects flow.

This increased interactivity would require additional constructs such as methods for labeling drawing elements as interactively movable. Internally, some of the mathematical sketching components would have to be modified. Currently, mathematical sketching acts like a compiled program: data are generated from the mathematical specifications using Matlab and are then used to animate drawing elements. Letting users interact with dynamic illustrations as they run would require a more interpretive approach: the data would need to be generated one frame at a time because users would influence drawing element behavior in real time. This type of interactivity would work only with open-form solutions because drawing elements' positions and orientations would not be known in advance. Converting to an interpretive scheme would require a moderate software development effort, and creating the additional user interface constructs required to specify interactivity and actually interact with the dynamic illustration is a moderately difficult research problem, given that there are many different ways to construct a more interactive dynamic illustration. For example, we could use special gestures to indicate what drawing elements should be interactive or make it part of the mathematical specification with a predefined function combined with our association mechanism.

4.5.5 Generating Mathematics from Drawings

Users have often commented that they would like their drawings to generate mathematics. Specifically, many users have wanted to draw a function and have MathPad^2

create a mathematical representation for the drawing. This functionality would be useful in many different circumstances, especially when users have a good idea of what a function looks like but have no way to represent it mathematically. At a minimum, it would be trivial to find a polynomial that approximates the function based on the drawing points. In fact, if a function has n points we can find a $(n-1)$st-order polynomial that fits the function exactly (assuming continuity). We could also do various forms of curve fitting using splines, piecewise polynomials, or least squares. These techniques would not necessarily provide an exact mathematical representation for the drawing, but they might be sufficient in some cases. Users could provide guidance to the system on what types of functions to look for (e.g., exponential, sine wave, etc.). Using a curve fitting technique would require a moderate software development effort because there are many known techniques for doing this type of task. Finding more exact functions for a given drawing is a difficult research problem, but is certainly an interesting area for future work.

Another way to generate mathematics from drawings is to use a vector gesture to define vectors and attach them to drawing elements describing the element's initial trajectory. For example, in a 2D projectile motion example, a user could make a vector gesture and attach it to a ball: the length of the gesture would indicated the ball's speed and the angle between the vector and the horizontal would indicate the ball's initial angle. These values could then be presented to users as mathematical expressions. The ball's speed and initial angle would be modified by moving the vector and would be reflected in the generated mathematical expressions. This approach would give users an alternative way to make parts of a mathematical specification associated with a drawing element.

When users want to change a parameter in a mathematical specification, they erase the value, write in a new one, and recognize the whole expression again. We could make this task easier for users by providing a mechanism for changing parameters quickly, say by invoking a slider widget that attaches itself to a parameter expression so users could interactively update the parameter value. To create these sliders, users could draw a line of sufficient length and put a large dot somewhere on it. Next users would tap in the bounding box of the mathematical expression they want to modify. Users could then move the large dot back and forth to change the parameter value accordingly. This technique is another example of a plausible approach to generating mathematics (i.e., constants) from drawings.

4.5.6 Adding Specific Underlying Mathematical Engines

One of the major principles of mathematical sketching is that users should specify all of the necessary mathematics to make a dynamic illustration. This principle is in direct contrast with Alvarado's ASSIST system [1], which needs no mathematics specifications (only the drawings) to make a dynamic illustration. The ASSIST system does not need any mathematical specifications because it has an underlying 2D motion simulator. This approach has significant merit but we feel that specifying at least some of the mathematics is important in understanding and exploring various mathematical and physical concepts. The interaction between users' mathematical specifications and specific underlying mathematical engines is thus an interesting area for future work.

Consider the effect on a ball moving along a plane of a series of objects each with different attracting and repelling forces. To make this dynamic illustration, an open-form solution is needed. However, a user could start with $F = ma$ and derive a differential equation for the motion of the ball and then employ a numerical technique to make the dynamic illustration. In some cases, going as far as the differential equation suffices for the user, who could make the associations as usual and run the mathematical sketch. The difference in this situation is that a physics engine uses the information in the sketch to construct the data required to run the dynamic illustration. With this hybrid approach, users must still derive mathematical specifications for given drawing elements but can let an underlying mathematics engine do the work that the users might not be interested in. Given the possibly complex interactions between the underlying mathematics engine and user-derived mathematical specifications, this hybrid approach is a challenging research problem.

4.5.7 Alternate Forms of Dynamic Illustration

Mathematical sketching currently lets users create dynamic illustrations by animating drawing elements with rigid body transforms and simple stretching. It would be interesting to explore other types of dynamic illustrations with different aesthetics. For example, dynamics can be visualized through changing colors. Consider heat dissipation across a rectangular plate. We can approximate the solution in closed form with the mathematics shown in Fig. 4.16.

One approach to visualizing the heat dissipating through the metal plate is based on color-coding, as in Fig. 4.17. The idea behind this illustration is to let users define their own types of visualizations that are not necessarily movement based. Users could define the grid points and the domain as shown in the two figures and supply a rule for how the values of u should change at each point in time. In this example, a user specifies that when $u = 0$ the dots should be red and when $u = 1$ the dots should be blue. Using this rule, mathematical sketching would interpolate between the two extreme cases depending on the value of u at any time t in locations (x, y) for some domain. Having the illustration change colors is just one way to define these types of illustrations; we could also define glyphs that would change size during the simulation. This type of dynamic illustration is an interesting area for future work because it moves out of the traditional translation- and rotation-style animations that mathematical sketching currently supports. Providing a mechanism for user-defined visualizations would be a significantly challenging research problem from a user interface point of view, since a pen-based visualization language would need to be defined.

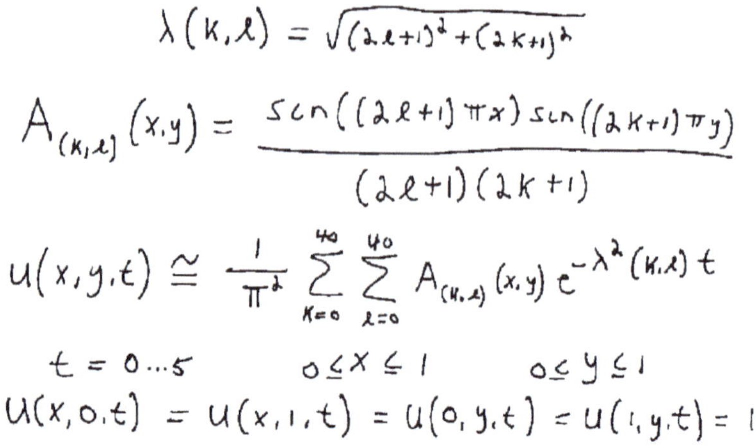

Fig. 4.16 An approximate solution to the heat equation on a rectangular metal plate

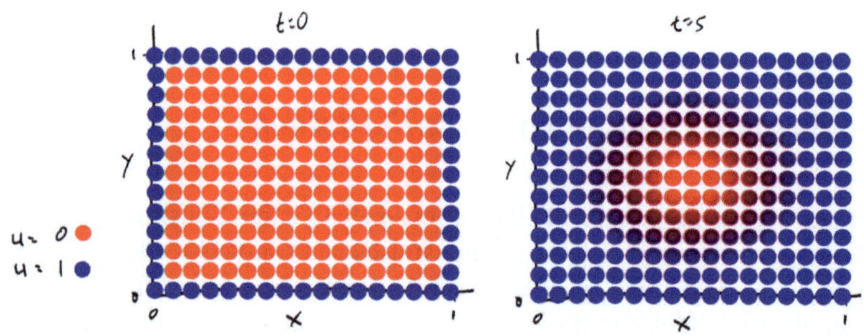

Fig. 4.17 Two snapshots of a dynamic illustration showing heat dissipating across a metal plate given the mathematics in Fig. 4.16. As the illustration runs, the dots change color to show temperature changes

4.5.8 Evaluation

Understanding how mathematical sketching affects users is an important area that must be explored at the usability and pedagogical levels. We have already conducted initial usability evaluations of MathPad^2 by examining the user interface's intuitiveness and the application's perceived usefulness [11]. We asked seven subjects to perform tasks such as making mathematical sketches, graphing functions, evaluating expressions, and solving equations. The usability study's results suggest that the MathPad^2 user interface is generally intuitive, with subjects picking up the interface with relative ease. With only minimal training, most gestures are easy to remember and use. One exception was the equation-solving gesture. Some subjects had trouble remembering this gesture and performing it accurately. This indicates that this gesture is not as intuitive as the others. Although most subjects performed the tasks with little trouble, a few had some difficulty, stemming primarily from problems with mathematical expression recognition, indicating that we need better recognition accuracy. However, these subjects also said they were willing to accept these recognition problems, given MathPad^2's functionality. Finally, subjects thought the application was a powerful tool that beginning physics and mathematics students could use to help solve problems and better understand scientific concepts. For details on this evaluation see [12].

Other usability evaluations on mathematical sketching usability should be conducted. For example, it has been shown for handwriting recognition that the relationship between recognition rates and user acceptance depends on the perceived cost-to-benefit ratio in a specific task [5]. Thus, an interesting research question would be see whether these results extend to mathematical sketching. From a pedagogical perspective, understanding whether a tool like MathPad^2 can change students' perceptions about calculus and physics and whether it helps students better understand mathematics and physics concepts is an important research goal. Rigorous classroom assessments are needed to prove that mathematical sketching is a viable approach to learning.

4.6 Conclusion

In this chapter, we have presented mathematical sketching, an interaction paradigm for creating and exploring dynamic illustrations. By combining handwritten mathematics with free-form drawings, users can make personalized visualizations of a variety of mathematical and physical phenomena. These dynamic illustrations overcome many of the limitations of static drawings and diagrams found in textbooks and student notebooks by allowing verification of the mathematics in users' solutions. In addition, the animations generated from the mathematical specifications give intuition about the behavioral aspects of a given problem. Mathematical sketching is unique among the approaches to making dynamic illustrations with computers because it requires users to write down mathematics to drive their illustrations, thus becoming a powerful extension to pencil and paper.

Acknowledgement Thanks to Robert Zeleznik, Andries van Dam, John Hughes, and David Laidlaw for valuable discussions on mathematical sketching.

References

1. Alvarado, C.J.: A natural sketching environment: bringing the computer into early stages of mechanical design. Master's Thesis, Department of Electrical Engineering and Computer Science. Massachusetts Institute of Technology, May 2000
2. Barzel, R., Hughes, J., Wood, D.N.: Plausible motion simulation for computer graphics animation. In: Proceedings of the Eurographics Workshop on Computer Animation and Simulation'96, pp. 183–197. Springer, Berlin (1996)

3. Chan, K., Yeung, D.: An efficient syntactic approach to structural analysis of on-line handwritten mathematical expressions. Pattern Recognition **33**(3), 375–384 (2000)
4. Ford, L.A.: Student Solutions Manual to Accompany University Physics. Addison-Wesley, Reading (1992)
5. Frankish, C., Hull, R., Morgan, P.: Recognition accuracy and user acceptance of pen interfaces. In: Proceedings of the Conference on Human Factors in Computing Systems (ACM SIGCHI 1995), pp. 503–510. ACM Press, New York (1995)
6. Guimbretière, F., Winograd, T.: FlowMenu: Combining command, text, and data entry. In: Proceedings of the ACM Symposium on User Interface Software and Technology (UIST 2000), pp. 213–216. ACM Press, New York (2000)
7. Hansen, C., Johnson, C. (eds.): The Visualization Handbook. Elsevier Academic, Dordrecht (2005)
8. Igarashi, T., Matsuoka, S., Tanaka, H.: Teddy: A sketching interface for 3D freeform design. In: Proceedings of the 26th Annual Conference on Computer Graphics and Interactive Techniques, pp. 409–416. ACM Press/Addison-Wesley, New York (1999)
9. Kurtenbach, G., Buxton, W.: User learning and performance with marking menus. In: Proceedings of the ACM Conference on Human Factors in Computing Systems (CHI'94), pp. 258–264. ACM Press, New York (1994)
10. LaViola, J.: Mathematical sketching: a new approach to creating and exploring dynamic illustrations. Ph.D. Dissertation, Brown University, Department of Computer Science, May 2005
11. LaViola, J.: An initial evaluation of a pen-based tool for creating dynamic mathematical illustrations. In: Eurographics Workshop on Sketch-Based Interfaces and Modeling 2006, pp. 157–164, September 2006
12. LaViola, J.: An initial evaluation of MathPad^2: a tool for creating dynamic mathematical illustrations. Computers and Graphics **31**(4), 540–553 (2007)
13. LaViola, J.: Advances in mathematical sketching: moving toward the paradigm's full potential. IEEE Computer Graphics and Applications **27**(1), 38–48 (2007)
14. LaViola, J., Zeleznik, R.: MathPad^2: a system for the creation and exploration of mathematical sketches. ACM Transactions on Graphics (Proceedings of SIGGRAPH 2004) **23**(3), 432–440 (2004)
15. LaViola, J., Zeleznik, R.: A practical approach to writer-dependent symbol recognition using a writer-independent recognizer. IEEE Transactions on Pattern Analysis and Machine Intelligence **29**(11), 1917–1926 (2007)
16. Lee, H., Wang, J.: Design of a mathematical expression recognition system. Pattern Recognition Letters **18**, 289–298 (1997)
17. Li, X., Yeung, D.: On-line handwritten alphanumeric character recognition using dominant points in strokes. Pattern Recognition **30**(1), 31–44 (1997)
18. Martin, W.J.: A fast parsing scheme for hand-printed mathematical expressions. Artificial Intelligence Memo No. 145, Massachusetts Institute of Technology (1967)
19. Rubine, D.: Specifying gestures by example. In: Proceedings of SIGGRAPH'91, pp. 329–337. ACM Press, New York (1991)
20. Schapire, R.: A brief introduction to boosting. In: Proceedings of the 16th International Joint Conference on Artificial Intelligence, pp. 1401–1406 (1999)
21. Smithies, S., Novins, K., Arvo, J.: A handwriting-based equation editor. In: Proceedings of Graphics Interface'99, pp. 84–91 (1999)
22. Tenneson, D.: Interpretation of molecule conformations from drawn diagrams. Ph.D. Dissertation, Brown University, Department of Computer Science, May 2008
23. Zeleznik, R., Miller, T.: Fluid inking augmenting the medium of free-form inking with gestures. In: Graphics Interface 2006, pp. 155–162, June 2006
24. Zeleznik, R.C., Henrdon, K.P., Hughes, J.F.: SKETCH: An interface for sketching 3D scenes. In: Proceedings of the 23rd Annual Conference on Computer Graphics and Interactive Techniques, pp. 163–170. ACM Press, New York (1996)

Chapter 5
Pen-based Interfaces for Engineering and Education

Thomas F. Stahovich

5.1 Introduction

"In many disciplines, sketches have great utility as a problem-solving tool, as they provide a suitable medium for recording elusive thoughts, visualizing and testing emerging ideas, and for compactly and efficiently representing various types of information such as spatial, temporal and causal relationships" [18].[1] Sketches are particularly useful in the early stages of design, where their fluidity and ease of construction enable creativity and the rapid exploration of ideas [37]. In a seminal study of the importance of drawing in mechanical design, Ullman et al. [40] demonstrated that sketches are a particularly useful form of graphical representation and that "CAD systems must allow for sketching input."

Despite the evidence suggesting that sketching is an essential part of engineering design, most contemporary engineering software still cannot work effectively from sketch input [18]. With recent advances in machine-interpretation techniques, it is now becoming possible to create practical interpretation-based interfaces for engineering software. In this chapter, we report on our efforts to create interpretation techniques to enable pen-based engineering applications. We describe work on two fundamental sketch understanding problems. The first is sketch parsing, the task of clustering pen strokes or geometric primitives into individual symbols. The second is symbol recognition, the task of classifying symbols once they have been located by a parser.

We have used the techniques that we have developed to construct several pen-based engineering analysis tools. These are used here as examples to illustrate our methods. We have also begun to use our techniques to create pen-based tutoring

[1] This chapter is a compilation of material from a variety of previously published articles and contains extensive quotes from those sources. Footnotes are used to indicate the sources of the material in each section.

T.F. Stahovich (✉)
University of California, Riverside, CA 92521, USA
e-mail: stahov@engr.ucr.edu

J. Jorge, F. Samavati (eds.), *Sketch-based Interfaces and Modeling*,
DOI 10.1007/978-1-84882-812-4_5,

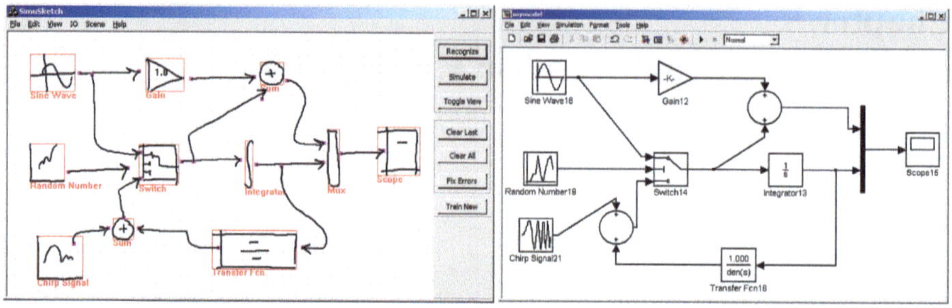

Fig. 5.1 *Left*: Sim-U-Sketch, *Right*: Simulink model derived from the sketch. (From [14]; used with permission)

systems that scaffold students in solving problems in the same way they would ordinarily solve them with paper and pencil. The chapter concludes with a brief discussion of these systems.

5.2 Sketch Parsing

Sketch parsing is the task of grouping a user's pen strokes into the intended symbols without requiring the user to indicate when one symbol ends and the next one begins.[2] (In the literature, the terms "sketch parsing" and "sketch segmentation" are used synonymously. We prefer the former to prevent confusion with the term "pen stroke segmentation.") Figure 5.1 shows a parsing example in which the identified stoke groups are enclosed in rectangles. Parsing, which is a prerequisite step to recognition, is a difficult problem, in part, because the number of stroke groups to consider increases exponentially with the number of strokes. Furthermore, even when a sketch contains only a small number of strokes, brute force enumeration of stroke groups often results in groups that resemble domain shapes but which were not intended as such by the drawer. To avoid these difficulties, many current systems require the user to explicitly indicate the intended partitioning of the ink by pressing a button on the stylus or by pausing between symbols [8, 27]. Alternatively, some systems require each object to be drawn in a single pen stroke [20]. However, these sorts of constraints typically result in a less than natural drawing experience.

Researchers have explored a wide variety of techniques for parsing sketches and other graphical images. For example, Saund et al. [33] present a system that uses Gestalt principles to determine the salient objects represented in a line drawing. Their work concerns only the grouping of the strokes and does not employ recognition to determine if the identified groups are the intended ones. Notowidigdo and Miller [28] describe a system for interpreting structured diagrams such as flow charts, but their techniques are intended for off-line computation. Jacobs [13] describes a system to recognize objects with straight-line perimeter representations.

[2]The material in this section is derived from [18].

The system uses a number of heuristic rules to group edges that likely come from a single object, and then uses simple recognizers to identify the objects represented by the edges. However, because the technique requires straight line segments and sharp corners, it may not be well-suited to informal, hand-drawn sketches.

There has been recent progress on techniques specifically intended for on-line parsing of hand-drawn ink. For example, Shilman et al. [36] present an approach to ink parsing that relies on a manually-coded visual grammar. The grammar defines composite objects hierarchically in terms of lower-level objects. The lowest-level objects—individual pen strokes—must be recognizable in isolation (with Rubine's method [31]), although ambiguity can be tolerated. In more recent work, Shilman and Viola [35] have improved upon this approach by first generating a multitude of candidate stroke groups, and then evaluating each candidate using a fast bitmap-based recognizer. Alvarado and Davis [1] describe a parsing approach based on dynamically constructed Bayesian networks. The approach is general purpose in that it can be applied to a wide variety of sketches and diagrams, but processing time can be long. Inspired by the advances in speech recognition, some approaches require visual objects to be drawn with a predefined sequence of pen strokes [34, 42]. While useful at reducing computational complexity, the strong temporal dependency of these methods forces the user to remember the correct order in which to draw the pen strokes.

In this section, we present two parsing methods that we have developed in our work. The first relies on a mark–group–recognize architecture in which easily-recognizable "marker symbols" are used to help locate the remaining symbols. The second uses geometric information, especially "ink density," and domain knowledge to locate symbols.

5.2.1 Mark–Group–Recognize

Our mark–group–recognize parsing technique is based on the existence, in many domains, of "marker symbols"—symbols that can be easily extracted from a continuous stream of pen strokes and that help separate the remaining pen strokes into clusters representing individual symbols.[3] We have used this technique to implement two different sketch-based engineering applications. The first application, called Vibrosketch [18], is a tool for analyzing vibratory systems comprised of masses, springs, and dampers (Fig. 5.2). For this problem, masses and ground symbols serve

[3]The material in this section and its subsections is derived from Kara, L.B., Stahovich, T.F.: Hierarchical parsing and recognition of hand-sketched diagrams. In: UIST '04: Proceedings of the 17th annual ACM Symposium on User Interface Software and Technology, pp. 13–22. ACM, New York (2004). doi:10.1145/1029632.1029636 [14]. A preliminary version of this work appeared in Kara, L.B., Stahovich, T.F.: Sim-U-Sketch: a sketch-based interface for SimuLink. In: AVI '04: Proceedings of the Working Conference on Advanced Visual Interfaces, pp. 354–357. ACM, New York (2004). doi:10.1145/989863.989923 [16].

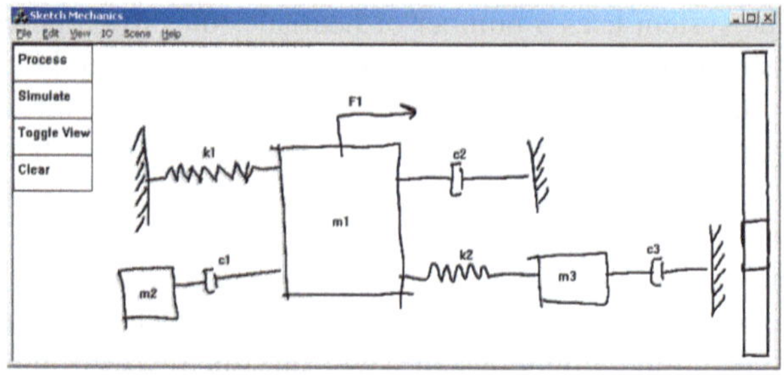

Fig. 5.2 Vibrosketch interface

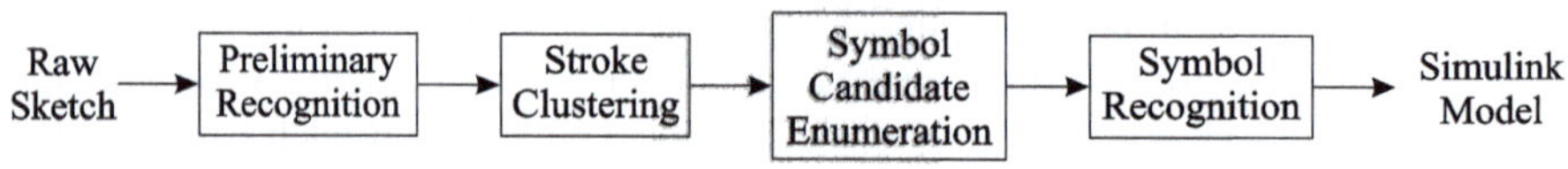

Fig. 5.3 Sim-U-Sketch architecture

as markers. The second application, which we will use here as a detailed illustration of the approach, is called Sim-U-Sketch (Fig. 5.1) [14, 16]. This system is a sketch-based front-end to Matlab's Simulink package, a tool for analyzing feedback control systems and other similar dynamic systems. For this problem, arrows serve as markers.

Sim-U-Sketch's architecture is shown in Fig. 5.3. The first processing step is to identify the arrows, which have geometric and kinematic characteristics that enable them to be easily extracted from a continuous stream of strokes. The arrows are then used to efficiently cluster the remaining pen strokes into distinct groups corresponding to individual symbols. Next, informed by the results of the clustering algorithm, the system employs contextual knowledge to generate a set of candidate interpretations for each of the clusters. Finally, the image-based symbol recognizer described in Sect. 5.3.3 is used to classify each cluster. The remainder of this section describes these steps in more detail (for complete details see [14]).

It is important that the marker symbols be recognized with high accuracy because the overall parsing accuracy depends on this. Also, the marker symbol recognizer must be computationally efficient, as it is used to process every stroke in a sketch. For these reasons, we use special-purpose recognizers for identifying marker symbols. By contrast, general purpose recognizers are used to classify the clusters once they are located.

The design of our arrow recognizer is based on observations suggesting that arrows are often drawn with one or two pen strokes and are frequently drawn from tail to head. Our arrow recognizer[4] handles two-stroke arrows by joining the last point of the first stroke to the first point of the second stroke so that both kinds of arrows effectively become single pen strokes. The (equivalent) single pen stroke is resampled to produce 36 evenly spaced points. The cosine of the angle between adjacent

[4]The version of Sim-U-Sketch described in [14] used a heuristic arrow recognizer. Here we describe an improved arrow recognizer. This description is derived from [24].

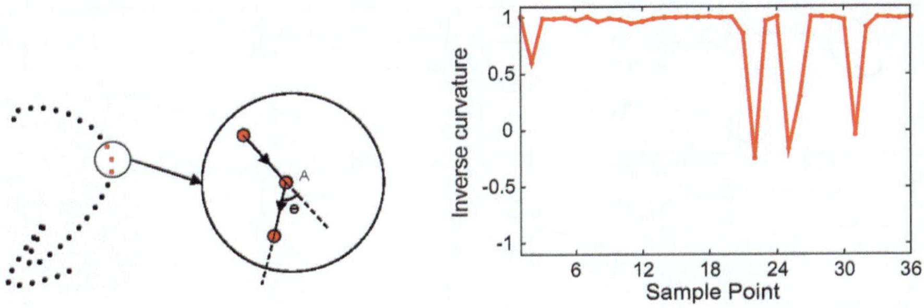

Fig. 5.4 *Left*: Resampled arrow. Inverse curvature at point A is $\cos(\theta)$. *Right*: Inverse curvature of the arrow. (Adapted from [24]; used with permission)

segments is then computed, as shown in Fig. 5.4. The cosine is inversely related to the curvature. For example, if two consecutive segments are nearly collinear, the cosine is close to 1.0. If there is a large discontinuity, such as a 90° bend, the cosine is close to 0.0. For this reason, the cosine of the angle between adjacent segments is called "inverse curvature."

Figure 5.4 shows the inverse-curvature representation of a typical arrow. Notice that the inverse curvature is approximately 1.0 for most points on the arrow, but is much smaller (in this case, less than 0.0) for the three discontinuities at the head of the arrow. It is these discontinuities that enable the technique to identify arrows.

The inverse-curvature values are provided as inputs to a neural network. To make the approach insensitive to the shape of the arrow shaft, the first 18 inverse-curvature values are actually discarded. The neural network thus has 18 inputs describing the head portion of the arrow. The output of the neural network is the classification of the (equivalent) pen stroke as either an arrow or a non-arrow.

Once the arrows have been identified, the next step is to group the remaining strokes into different clusters, representing different symbols. The key idea behind stroke clustering is that strokes are deemed to belong to the same symbol only when they are spatially proximate. The challenge is reliably determining when two pen strokes should be considered close together. Here, we rely on the arrows to help make this determination. In network diagrams, each arrow typically connects a source object at its tail to a target object at its head. Hence, different clusters can be identified by grouping together all the strokes that are near the same end of a given arrow. In effect, two strokes are considered spatially proximate if the nearest arrow is the same for each.

Figure 5.5 shows an example of the stroke clustering process. The process begins by assigning each non-arrow stroke to the nearest arrow. Here distance is measured between the median point of the stroke and either the tip or tail of the arrow, whichever is closer. Strokes assigned to the same arrow end are grouped to form a stroke cluster. Clusters with partially or fully overlapping bounding boxes are merged. Finally, each arrow tip or tail that is not assigned to a cluster is linked to the nearest cluster.

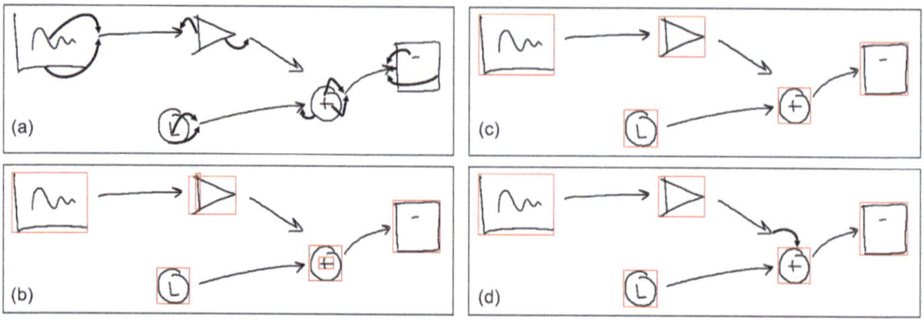

Fig. 5.5 The stroke clustering process. **a** Each stroke is assigned to the nearest arrowhead or tail. **b** Strokes assigned to the same arrow are grouped into clusters. **c** Clusters with overlapping bounding boxes are merged. **d** Arrows that received no strokes are attached to the nearest cluster. (From [14]; used with permission)

Once the clusters have been located, they are sent to our image-based symbol recognizer (Sect. 5.3.3) for classification. However, to reduce recognition cost and chances for confusion, the system first uses contextual knowledge to reduce the number of possible interpretations for each cluster. More specifically, the program considers only those interpretations that are consistent with the number of arrows going in and out of a cluster. For example, while the sum and clock symbols look quite similar (the two circular symbols in Fig. 5.5), a sum must have at least two incoming arrows while a clock must have none. With this additional knowledge, our symbol recognizer will never consider the sum and clock as two competing interpretations.

5.2.2 *Enumerate–Recognize–Prune*

Our second parsing technique is intended for network-like diagrams consisting of symbols linked together by connectors.[5] This technique uses geometric information to efficiently enumerate candidate symbols, which are sent to a recognizer for classification. Domain knowledge is then used to prune the list of candidate symbols, resulting in the final interpretation of the sketch.

We have used this parsing technique to implement AC-SPARC [9], a sketch-based circuit analysis tool, and thus our discussion here is focused on the interpretation of circuit sketches. AC-SPARC, which is shown in Fig. 5.6, can interpret a free-hand sketch of an analog circuit, and from this generate an input file for the SPICE circuit analysis tool [41].

AC-SPARC's interpretation process is described in Fig. 5.7. The first step is ink segmentation, the task of decomposing each pen stroke into its constituent geometric primitives. Our segmentation technique uses pen speed and curvature information

[5]The material in this section and its subsections is derived from [9].

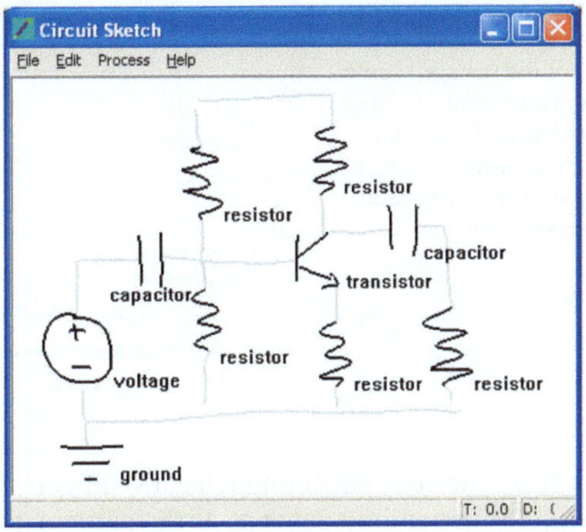

Fig. 5.6 AC-SPARC: a sketch-based interfaces to the SPICE electric circuit analysis program. (From [9]; used with permission)

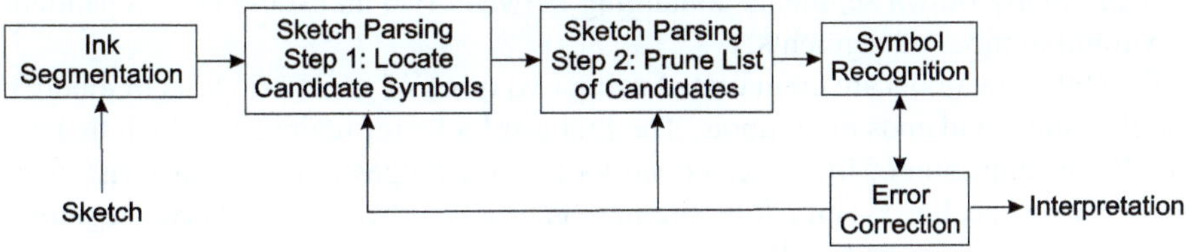

Fig. 5.7 Architecture of AC-SPARC

to identify segment points ("corners"). (See [38] for details of the segmenter.) It is common for a single pen stroke to contain multiple symbols; performing segmentation enables the system to find each of the symbols contained within a stroke. Once the ink has been segmented, geometric tests are used to locate candidate symbols, which are then classified using the feature-based recognizer described in Sect. 5.3.2. Knowledge about circuits is then used to prune the list of candidate symbols to produce an interpretation of the circuit. In a final processing step, additional domain knowledge about circuits is used to automatically correct errors made in the previous processing steps.

5.2.2.1 Parsing Step 1: Enumerating Candidate Symbols

The first parsing step is to enumerate the candidate symbols. To do this efficiently, our technique assumes that the user finishes drawing one symbol (circuit component) before drawing a connector (wire) or another symbol. Our observations of people drawing electrical circuits suggest this assumption is reasonable. Therefore, when locating candidate symbols, we consider only consecutively drawn segments. As an additional means of reducing computation, we have found that it is possible to establish limits for the number of segments that a symbol may contain. The lower

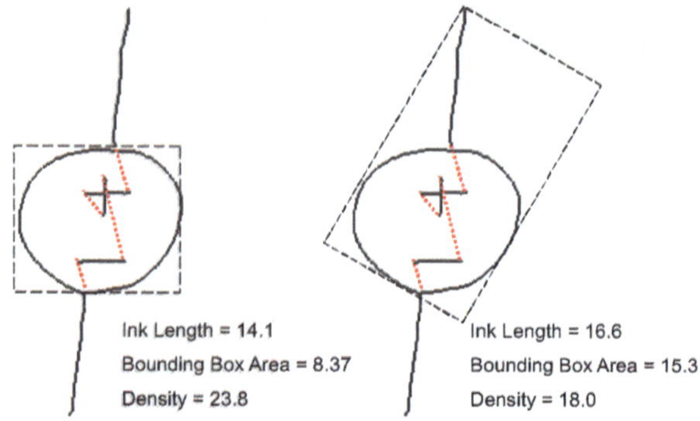

Fig. 5.8 Density decreases when a segment is added to the end of the voltage source symbol. Hidden ink is shown by *dotted lines*. Bounding boxes are shown by *dashed rectangles*. (From [9]; used with permission)

limit is two, since it is uncommon that a symbol is represented by a single line or arc segment. The upper limit depends on the particular user's drawing style, but for analog circuits is typically between 6 and 12. Candidate symbols are, therefore, groups of sequentially-drawn segments containing between two and some user-dependent maximum number of segments.

Candidate symbols are enumerated using two types of geometric tests to identify possible starts and ends of symbols. The first test looks for regions in which there is a high concentration of ink. The second looks for changes in the characteristics of the segments, such as when a long segment is followed by a much shorter segment. These tests are described in detail below.

Ink Density Locator: Symbols usually consist of a high concentration of ink, while the ink of connectors is often more spread out. Our ink density approach identifies candidate symbols by searching for regions of high ink density. More specifically, *we search for sequences of segments having the property that the addition of another segment to either end of the sequence causes a decrease in density*, as this is an indication of adding a connector segment. We define *ink density* as the ratio of the square of the ink length to the area of the oriented bounding box of the ink:

$$\text{density} = \frac{\text{ink\_length}^2}{\text{bounding\_box\_area}}. \tag{1}$$

Here, in addition to the actual ink shown on the screen, the ink length also includes the *hidden ink*, which we define as the ink that would occur if the user did lift the stylus while drawing. For example, the hidden ink of a voltage source is shown by the dotted lines in Fig. 5.8. Including the hidden ink accentuates the density of symbols drawn with multiple strokes, thus making them easier to identify. We square the ink length so that it scales the same way as bounding box area, thus making the density parameter insensitive to uniform scaling.

Ink density analysis uses a forward-backward algorithm to find the start and end segments of candidate symbols. In the forward step, the approach starts with a given segment and considers increasingly long sequences of consecutively drawn segments. Each time a segment is added to the sequence, the density is computed. If there is a decrease in density of 20% or more, it is quite possible that a connector

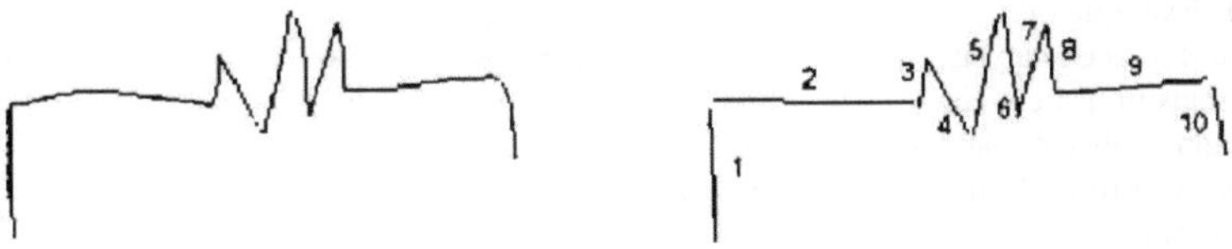

Fig. 5.9 A hand-drawn resistor (*left*) and the segmented ink (*right*). (From [9]; used with permission)

segment was added to the sequence. In this case, the previous segment is deemed a possible end of a symbol. This may not be the best end, however, and thus additional segments continue to be added to the sequence until the user-dependent maximum number of segments is reached. Each time there is a decrease in density of 20%, another candidate end segment is identified.

In the backward step, ink density analysis is once again applied. For each possible end segment, prior segments are added one at a time until the user-dependent maximum number of segments is reached. The changes in density are monitored with each addition. The segment drawn after the segment whose addition causes the largest decrease in density is selected as the start segment for the given end segment. The sequence is now considered a candidate symbol. If there is no segment whose addition to the beginning of the sequence causes a decrease in density, then the sequence is discarded as it likely consists only of connector segments.

All sequences that survive this analysis are considered candidate symbols. It is possible to find additional candidates by repeating the analysis by, in essence, reversing time. A backward step is performed first, and candidate start segments are located by searching for decreases in density greater than 20%. A forward step is then applied to find the best end segment for each start segment.

Consider applying this approach to the resistor shown in Fig. 5.9. For sake of example, we assume that the forward step begins from Segment 5. The initial sequence consists of Segments 5 and 6. Adding Segments 7, 8, 9, and 10 results in density changes of +87.4%, −5.1%, −35.5%, and +10.1% respectively. Only the addition of Segment 9 produces a density decrease greater than 20%, and thus only Segment 8 is a possible end segment. In the backward step, the sequence initially consists of Segments 8 and 7. Segments are then added to the start of this sequence until Segment 2 is reached. This results in density changes of +42.9%, +20.7%, +13.0%, −2.1%, and −23.0%. The addition of Segment 2 causes the biggest decrease in density, and thus Segment 3 is considered the best start segment for the sequence that ends with Segment 8. The result is a candidate symbol consisting of Segments 3–8, which in fact corresponds to the intended resistor. Note that the approach was able to successfully locate the resistor despite the fact the forward step began in the middle of the symbol.

Segment Difference Locator: There are usually large differences between a connector and the first segment of a symbol, and between the last segment of a symbol and the subsequent connector. Our segment difference locator finds symbols by identifying those differences. For each segment in the sketch, the locator computes

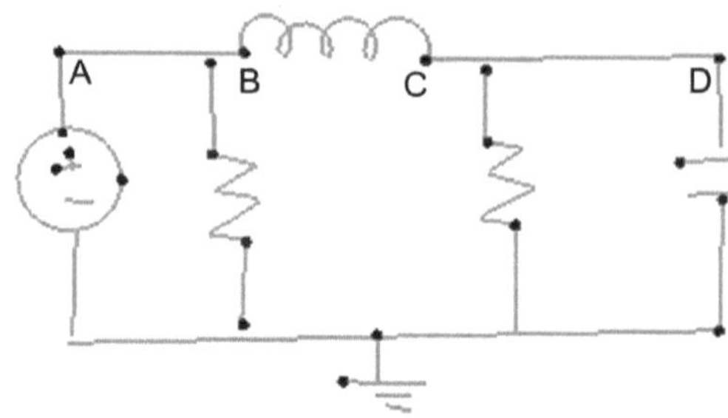

Fig. 5.10 Example of segment difference analysis. Possible transitions between symbols and connectors are show as *dots*. (From [9]; used with permission)

four characteristics and compares them to those of the segment before it. These characteristics include: (1) Segment type: line vs. arc; (2) Segment length: the lengths of two segments are considered different if one is more than 40% longer than the other; (3) Segment orientation: if the acute angle between two segments differs by 65° or more, they are considered different in this characteristic; (4) Intersection type: classified as none, endpoint-to-endpoint ("L"), endpoint-to-midpoint ("T"), or midpoint-to-midpoint ("X"). We define a good candidate symbol to be a group of segments that are similar in these four characteristics but which differ from the other segments touching the group. For example, the inductor in Fig. 5.10 is easily distinguishable as a series of short arc segments, with longer line segments, representing wires, on either side.

We consider any pair of consecutively drawn segments that differs in two or more characteristics to be a possible transition between a symbol and a connector. The point between such a pair of segments is referred to as a "segment difference point." Figure 5.10 shows all such points for a typical circuit sketch. Candidate symbols are defined to be sequences of segments, bounded by two segment difference points, containing between two and the user-dependent maximum number of segments. Note that the points bounding candidate symbols need not be consecutive, and thus candidates can overlap. For instance, candidate symbols for Fig. 5.10 include the sequences of segments between points A and C, A and D, B and C, B and D, and so on. While this approach finds many valid symbols, it also locates many non-symbols, as described in the next section.

5.2.2.2 Parsing Step 2: Pruning Using Domain Knowledge

Not all of the symbols enumerated by our symbol locators are valid symbols. The final parsing step is to use domain-specific information to prune out the candidates that are unlikely to be symbols. This is done using several heuristics. However, before the pruning begins, each candidate symbol must first be classified with a symbol recognizer (we use the one in Sect. 5.3.2), as the results of classification are used in the heuristics. The basic approach is to collect information supporting and refuting the fact that a group of segments is a symbol. The following is a summary of the heuristics we use for the electric circuit domain.

Some of the indications that a group of segments may be an electrical component include: (1) The ink density of the candidate component is high. (2) The probability of a match between the candidate component and the class identified by the recognizer is high. (3) Two segments touching the candidate component are collinear. This is a good indication of a component because many components are drawn with collinear wires connected on each side. Some of the indications that a group of segments may not be an electrical component include: (1) The candidate component has the wrong number of connections for the component it has been classified as. For example, a ground symbol should have only one connection and a resistor should have two. (2) The bounding box of the candidate component is thin. (3) The average length of the segments in a candidate component is long. This characteristic is useful because components often contain many short segments, while wires are frequently long segments.

Each candidate is assigned a heuristic score, which is initially zero. Points are added for positive indications, and are subtracted for negative indications. For a candidate to be considered a component, its heuristic score must be above a threshold. Additionally, because two symbols cannot share segments, any candidate overlapping another candidate with higher heuristic score is pruned. Any segments not identified as part of a symbol are considered to be connectors.

5.2.2.3 Automated Error Correction

Once the parsing and recognition steps are complete, the system knows the locations of the symbols, and the connections between them. At this point, the system can use domain-specific knowledge to correct parsing and recognition errors. Here we summarize our approach for circuits.

One indication that there may be a parsing problem in an electric circuit is that a large number of consecutively drawn segments have been identified as wires. It is uncommon for a user to draw wires this way, thus suggesting that a component has been missed. In such situations, the system first tries to find the missed component by lowering the threshold for heuristic pruning. If a component is still not found, a miss-classification may have caused the parser to err. In this case, the system considers lower ranked classifications for any candidate components that contain the wire segments in question. If the score of one of those candidates is now above the heuristic threshold, the system keeps that candidate and its new classification.

Another indication of a problem is that a component has the wrong number of connections. For example, if a ground symbol has two connections, there may be an interpretation error. This is often a result of an incorrect classification by the recognizer. The problem is sometimes fixed by selecting the second choice of the recognizer. Otherwise, we assume that the problem is due to the sketchiness of the drawing—two segments that were intended to intersect did not, or two segments that were not supposed to intersect did. To fix this, the component's segments, and the nearby wire segments, are extended or shortened until the correct number of connections is found.

5.3 Recognition

Researchers have developed a wide range of techniques for recognizing hand-drawn shapes and symbols. Existing techniques vary in the type of representation used.[6] For example, some techniques use a feature-based description of shape, while others use a structural description capturing both the geometry and topology of a shape. Existing techniques also vary in a number of important performance characteristics such as insensitivity to scaling and rotation, accuracy, speed, and tolerance for over-stroking. Additionally, some techniques are limited to single-stroke shapes, while others can handle multi-stroke shapes.

Many existing approaches to symbol recognition rely on feature-based representations. For example, Fonseca et al. [8] use features such as the smallest convex hull that can be circumscribed around the shape, the largest triangle that can be inscribed in the hull, and the largest quadrilateral that can be inscribed. Because their classification relies on aggregate features of the pen strokes, it might be difficult to differentiate between similar shapes. Rubine [31] describes a trainable gesture recognizer designed for gesture-based interfaces. The recognizer is applicable only to single-stroke symbols, and is sensitive to the drawing direction and orientation. Pereira et al. [30] have extended Rubine's method to multi-stroke symbols. However, such symbols must be drawn with a consistent set of strokes. Additionally, they have developed a graph-based symbol recognizer, but it is not trainable. Matsakis [25] describes a system for converting handwritten mathematical expressions into a machine-interpretable typesetting command language. Each symbol requires a multitude of training examples, where each example must be preprocessed to eliminate variations in drawing directions and stroke orderings. However, the preprocessing makes their approach sensitive to rotations.

In addition to feature-based methods, researchers have also explored a variety of other representations and approaches. For example, Sezgin and Davis [34] present a technique based on hidden Markov models. The approach requires shapes to be drawn with a consistent pen stroke ordering. Hammond and Davis [11] developed a recognizer that relies on hand-coded shape descriptions. Shilman et al. [36] present a sketch recognition approach that requires a manually encoded visual grammar. A large corpus of training examples is used to learn the statistical distributions of the geometric parameters used in the grammar, resulting in a statistical model. Composite objects are defined hierarchically in terms of lower-level, single-stroke symbols, which are recognized using Rubine's method [31]. Gross' [10] approach relies on a 3×3 grid inscribed in the symbol's bounding box. The sequence of grid cells visited by the pen distinguishes each symbol. Because of the coarse resolution of a 3×3 grid, this approach may not be able to handle symbols with small features. Hse and Newton [12] developed a recognizer based on Zernike moments. However, a preprocessing step in which the image size is normalized may make the approach sensitive to orientation.

[6] The material in this section is derived from [22].

In this section, we present three recognition techniques we have developed. Our graph-based recognizer uses an attributed relational graph representation to describe both the geometry and topology of a symbol. With this approach, symbol recognition is a graph-matching problem. Our graph-based recognizer is insensitive to orientation, non-uniform scaling, and drawing order. Our feature-based recognizer distills the geometry and topology of a symbol to a set of features and thus avoids the cost of graph matching. As a result, our feature-based recognizer is faster than our graph-based recognizer, although some accuracy is sacrificed to achieve this. Our image-based recognizer represents symbols as down-sampled bitmaps. Symbol recognition relies on template matching techniques. Our image-based recognizer can learn from single training examples and is particularly useful for "sketchy" symbols such as those with substantial over-stroking.

5.3.1 Graph-based Recognizer

Our graph-based recognizer [21, 22] is a trainable, multi-stroke symbol recognizer for pen-based user interfaces.[7] The approach is insensitive to orientation, non-uniform scaling, and drawing order. Symbols are represented internally as attributed relational graphs describing both the geometry and topology of the symbols. Symbol definitions are statistical models, which makes the approach robust to variations common in hand-drawn shapes. Symbol recognition requires finding the definition symbol whose attributed relational graph best matches that of the unknown symbol. Much of the power of the approach derives from the particular set of attributes used, and our metrics for measuring similarity between graphs. One challenge addressed in this work is how to perform the graph matching efficiently. We developed five approximate matching techniques: stochastic matching, which is based on stochastic search; error-driven matching, which uses local matching errors to drive the solution to an optimal match; greedy matching, which uses greedy search; hybrid matching, which uses exhaustive search for small problems and stochastic matching for larger ones; and sort matching, which relies on geometric information to accelerate the matching.

5.3.1.1 Representation

The nodes in our attributed relational graph (ARG) representation describe the geometric primitives comprising a shape. Each node is characterized by the type of the primitive—line or arc—and its relative length. The primitives are obtained from the raw pen strokes via the speed-based pen stroke segmenter described in [38]. The

[7]The material in this section and its subsections is derived from [22]. An earlier version of this material also appeared in [21], which is "©Eurographics Association 2006; Reproduced by kind permission of the Eurographics Association."

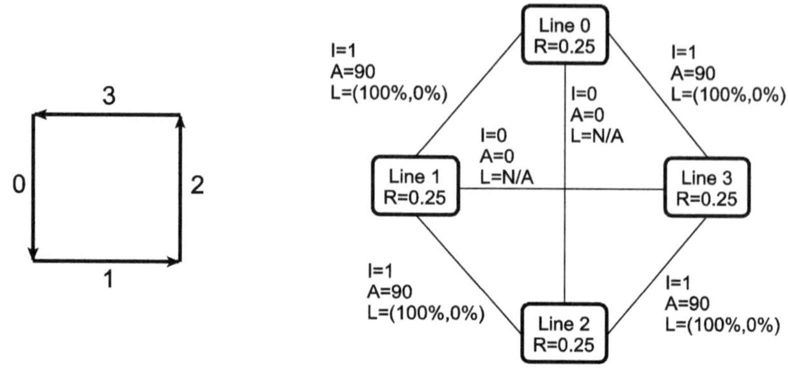

Fig. 5.11 *Left*: An ideal square drawn with a single, counter-clockwise pen stroke. *Arrows* show the direction of drawing. *Right*: The corresponding ARG. I = number of intersections, A = intersection angle, L = intersection location, R = relative length. (Adapted from [22]; used with permission)

relative length of a primitive is defined as the ratio of its length to the total length of the primitives comprising the symbol. For example, each of the four line segments in a perfect square would have a relative length of 0.25. Defining length on a relative basis results in a scale-independent recognizer.

The edges in an ARG represent the geometric relationships between the primitives. Each pair of primitives is characterized by the number of intersections between them, the relative locations of the intersections, and for lines, the angle of intersection. When extracting intersections from a sketch, a tolerance of 10% of the length of the primitives is used to allow for cases in which an intersection was intended but one of the primitives was a little too short. Intersection locations are measured relative to the lengths of the two primitives. For example, if the beginning of one line segment intersects the midpoint of another, the location is described by the coordinates (0%, 50%). The intersection angle is defined as the acute angle between two line segments. It is defined for both intersecting and non-intersecting line segments. Defining an intersection angle for non-intersecting segments allows the program to represent the topology of symbols with disconnected parts. Intersection angle is undefined for an intersection between an arc and another primitive.

Figure 5.11 shows an example of an ARG for an ideal square. Each side of the square has a relative length of 0.25 and intersects two other sides with an intersection angle of 90°. Because of the drawing directions used in this example, all intersections are located at the end of one line segment and the beginning of another.

A definition for a symbol is created by constructing an "average" ARG from a set of training examples. (Additional details of the training process are described in Sect. 5.3.1.4.) The number of nodes in a definition is taken to be the most frequently occurring number of nodes in the training examples. Each node in the definition is assigned the primitive type that occurred most frequently for that node in the training data. The number of intersections assigned to a pair of primitives is determined in an analogous fashion. A pair of primitives is assigned two intersections if at least

Table 5.1 Error metrics and corresponding weights. (From [22]; used with permission)

Error Metrics (E_i)	Weight (w_i)
E_1: Primitive count error	20%
E_2: Primitive type error	20%
E_3: Relative length error	20%
E_4: Number of intersections error	15%
E_5: Intersection angle error	15%
E_6: Intersection location error	10%

70% of the examples had two. If less than 70% had two intersections, but there was at least one intersection 70% of the time, the pair is assigned one. Otherwise, the pair is assigned zero intersections. The remaining properties of the ARG—relative length, intersection angle, and intersection location—are continuous valued properties. These are characterized by the means and standard deviations of the values from the training examples.

5.3.1.2 Measuring Similarity

During recognition, it is necessary to compare the ARG of the unknown symbol to that of each definition symbol to find the best match, and hence the classification of the unknown. The match between an unknown and a definition is quantified in terms of a weighted sum of the error metrics listed in Table 5.1. The weights, which are based on empirical studies, reflect the relative importance of the various error metrics for discriminating between symbols. For the purposes of recognition, the dissimilarity score is converted to a *Similarity Score* in the obvious way:

$$\text{Similarity Score} = 1 - \sum_{i=1}^{6} w_i E_i \tag{2}$$

where the E_i are the error metrics and the w_i are the weights listed in Table 5.1.

The error metrics for relative length, intersection angle, and intersection location involve comparing properties of the unknown symbol to distributions of those properties encoded in a definition. For example, it is necessary to compare the relative length of each primitive in the unknown to the mean and standard deviation of the relative length of the corresponding primitive in the definition. Ordinarily, this is done with a Gaussian probability density function. As an alternative, we have developed a modified probability density function (MPDF) that is better suited to our recognition task:

$$P(x) = \exp\left[-\frac{1}{50.0} \cdot \frac{(x-\mu)^4}{\sigma^4}\right]. \tag{3}$$

Here, μ and σ are the mean and standard deviation of the features from the training examples. This function was designed empirically such that its top is flatter than the

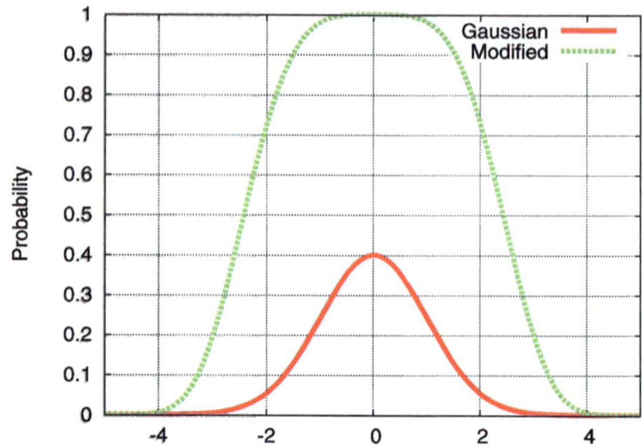

Fig. 5.12 Gaussian probability density function and modified probability density function for $\mu = 0$ and $\sigma = 1$. (From [22]; used with permission)

Gaussian probability density function for the same μ and σ. This makes it easier to detect matches that are in the "vicinity" of the definition. For comparison, Fig. 5.12 shows both the Gaussian probability density function and our modified probability density function for $\mu = 0$ and $\sigma = 1$.

The six error metrics used for computing the similarity score are described in the following sections. Here we use the term "unknown" to refer to the symbol to be recognized, or equivalently, the ARG of that symbol. Likewise, the term "definition" refers to the ARG of a definition symbol. Note also that each metric is normalized to the range [0, 1] so that the weights in Table 5.1 have predictable influences.

Primitive Count Error: The primitive count error is the difference between the number of nodes in the unknown and definition ARGs, normalized by the minimum number of nodes:

$$E_1 = \min\left(1.0, \frac{|N_{\text{U}} - N_{\text{D}}|}{N_{\min}}\right) \tag{4}$$

Here, N_{U} and N_{D} are the numbers of nodes in the unknown and definition ARGs, respectively, and $N_{\min} = \min(N_{\text{U}}, N_{\text{D}})$. We normalize by $N_{\min}$ to quantify the significance of the mismatch in the primitive count. The fewer primitives there are, the more significant a given mismatch is. The error saturates at one so that all errors have the same range of [0, 1].

Primitive Type Error: The primitive type error is the number of node pairs with mismatched types, normalized by the minimum number of nodes:

$$E_2 = \frac{\sum_{i=1}^{N_{\min}} [1 - \delta(\text{Type}(U_i), \text{Type}(D_i))]}{N_{\min}}. \tag{5}$$

Here, U_i is a node from the unknown, D_i is the corresponding node from the definition, $\text{Type}(X)$ is a function that returns the primitive type (arc or line) of node X, and $\delta(p, q)$ is one when $p = q$, and zero otherwise.

Relative Length Error: Each primitive from the unknown should have a relative length similar to that of the corresponding primitive from the definition. If not, an error is assigned. Here, similarity is measured using the MPDF defined in (3). The error is computed as

$$E_3 = \frac{\sum_{i=1}^{N_{\min}} [1 - P(R(U_i))]}{N_{\min}} \tag{6}$$

where $R(U_i)$ is the relative length encoded in node U_i of the unknown ARG, and $P(x)$ is evaluated using the mean and standard deviation from the corresponding node in the definition. Note that whereas $P(x)$ is the probability of match, $1 - P(x)$ is the probability of mismatch.

Number of Intersections Error: A pair of primitives in the unknown should have the same number of intersections as the corresponding pair in the definition. If not, an error is assigned. The total error is computed as

$$E_4' = \frac{\sum_{i=1}^{N_{\min}-1} \sum_{j=i+1}^{N_{\min}} |I(U_i, U_j) - I(D_i, D_j)|}{\min(M_{\mathrm{U}}, M_{\mathrm{D}})} \tag{7}$$

where $I(X, Y)$ is the number of intersections between the primitives in nodes X and Y, and M_{U} and M_{D} are the numbers of edges in the unknown and definition ARGs, respectively. This error is normalized by the number of potentially intersecting pairs of primitives. However, because a pair of primitives can intersect as many as two times, E_4' has a range of [0, 2]. So that all error metrics have the same range of [0, 1], the value of E_4' is "squashed" with:

$$S(x) = \frac{1}{1 + \exp[6(1 - x)]} \tag{8}$$

This squash function, was chosen such that small differences are attenuated while larger ones are preserved. Using the squash function, the "Number of Intersections Error" is defined as

$$E_4 = S(E_4') \tag{9}$$

Intersection Angle Error: The intersection angle of a pair of lines in the unknown should be similar to that of the corresponding pair of lines in the definition. (Intersection angle is defined only for pairs of lines.) If not, an error is assigned. Here, similarity is again measured using the MPDF defined in (3). The error is computed as the sum of the intersection angle errors normalized by the number of line pairs the unknown and definition have in common:

$$E_5 = \frac{\sum_{i=1}^{N_{\min}-1} \sum_{j=i+1}^{N_{\min}} [1 - P(A_{ij})]}{\sum_{i=1}^{N_{\min}-1} \sum_{j=i+1}^{N_{\min}} \mathrm{Lines}(U_i, U_j, D_i, D_j)} \tag{10}$$

Here, A_{ij} is the angle at which the primitive from node i of the unknown intersects the primitive from node j of the unknown. $P(A_{ij})$ is evaluated using the mean and standard deviation from the corresponding pair of primitives from the definition. Note that if the two primitives are not lines, A_{ij} is undefined and $P(A_{ij})$ is taken to be one. Lines(U_i, U_j, D_i, D_j) is one when all of the arguments are nodes representing lines, and zero otherwise.

Intersection Location Error: The locations of the intersections between a pair of primitives from the unknown should be similar to those of the corresponding pair of primitives from the definition. If not, an error is assigned. Here, similarity is again measured using the MPDF defined in (3). Because intersection location is defined by two coordinates, the MPDF is applied twice for each intersection. The total error is computed as

$$E_6 = \frac{\sum_{i=1}^{N_{\min}-1} \sum_{j=i+1}^{N_{\min}} \sum_{k=1}^{I(D_i,D_j)} ([1 - P(L_i^k)] + [1 - P(L_j^k)])}{\sum_{i=1}^{N_{\min}-1} \sum_{j=i+1}^{N_{\min}} 2 \cdot I(D_i, D_j)} \tag{11}$$

where (L_i^k, L_j^k) is the coordinates of the kth intersection between the primitives from nodes i and j of the unknown. $I(D_i, D_j)$ is the number of intersections between the primitives from nodes i and j of the definition. In cases where a pair of primitives intersect in the unknown but not in the definition, or vice versa, both $P(L_i^k)$ and $P(L_j^k)$ are set to zero. This error is normalized by twice the number of intersections, as two coordinates can contribute error to each intersection.

5.3.1.3 Graph Matching

The previous section described how to compute the similarity between two graphs. This assumed that each node in the unknown ARG was assigned to a specific node in the definition. This is a graph-matching, or graph-isomorphism problem. If the user always draws each symbol with a consistent number of primitives and a consistent drawing order, the graph-matching problem is trivial. In this case, drawing order would directly provide the correct node-pair assignments. In practice, however, users do not always maintain a consistent drawing order. Furthermore, the problem is made more difficult because of noise, such as extra or missing nodes in the unknown (i.e., extra or missing geometric primitives).

We have developed several efficient, approximate matching techniques to find the best match between two ARGs. Here we describe three of them. For complete details, please see [22]. Most of our techniques rely on search-based methods that begin with an initial node-pair assignments based on drawing order. Assignments are then swapped until the best match is obtained. The quality of the match at each iteration is determined using the similarity score in (2). Our various methods differ in the way they select the assignments to swap at each iteration.

If the two graphs being matched do not have the same number of nodes, the smaller one is "padded" with empty nodes. This ensures that every node in one graph has a match with a unique node in the other, and hence that every node is considered by the swapping process. When evaluating the error metrics, a pairing

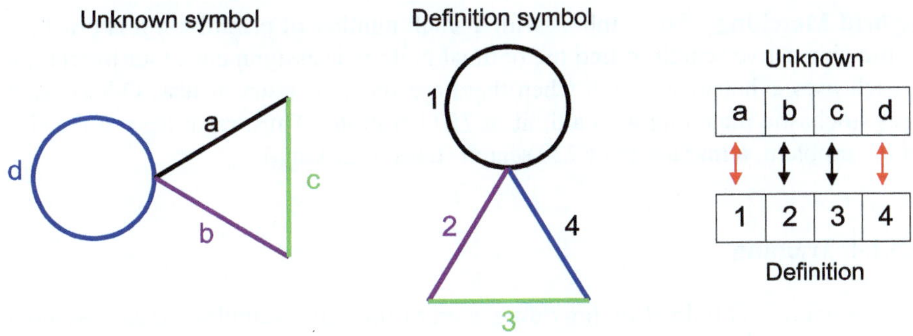

Fig. 5.13 Graph matching: assignments **b**-**2** and **c**-**3** are correct, while **a**-**1** and **d**-**4** are not. (Adapted from [22]; used with permission)

with an empty node produces the maximum possible local error. For example, the addition of empty nodes does not reduce the primitive count error, E_1.

Figure 5.13 illustrates the typical search process. For ease of explanation, the figure shows hypothetical symbols rather than ARGs. Finding the correct node-pair assignments is equivalent to finding the correct assignment of the primitives of the unknown to the primitives of the definition. Here, the primitives of the definition symbol are numbered according to a typical drawing order. Likewise, the primitives of the unknown are labeled with letters indicating the order in which they were actually drawn. Based on drawing order, primitive **a** of the unknown is initially assigned to primitive **1** of the definition, **b** is assigned to **2**, and so on. It is clear that assignments **b**-**2** and **c**-**3** are correct, while **a**-**1** and **d**-**4** are not. Swapping the latter to produce the assignments **d**-**1** and **a**-**4** is what is needed. The success of this swap can be measured by the resulting increase in the similarity score.

Stochastic Matching This approach to graph matching is based on stochastic search. To begin, the initial node-pair assignments are saved as the current best. Then, three node-pair assignments, which we will call A, B, and C, are randomly selected. A and B are swapped producing assignments A' and B'. B' is then swapped with C. If the new similarity score is better than the current best score, the new assignments are saved as the new current best. This process is repeated a fixed number of times, and the current best node-pair assignments are returned as the best match.

Greedy Matching This approach uses greedy search to find good node-pair assignments. The program first considers the best assignment for the first node of the unknown. If there are n nodes, the program considers all $n - 1$ cases in which the first node pair is swapped with another. Whichever assignment produces the best similarity score is selected for the first node, and this node pair is removed from further consideration. This is repeated for the second node pair and so on. In all, $O(n^2)$ sets of node-pair assignments are considered. The entire search process can be repeated for increased accuracy. We have found that one repetition produces a significant improvement in accuracy, but additional repetitions achieve diminishing returns.

Hybrid Matching For symbols with a small number of primitives, it is practical to use exhaustive search to find the optimal node-pair assignments. Our hybrid approach uses exhaustive search when there are six node pairs or less. Otherwise it uses stochastic matching with a limit of 720 iterations. Thus, regardless of the size of the problem, a maximum of 720 search states is explored.

5.3.1.4 Training

The recognizer is trained by providing a set of training examples for each symbol class. As described in Sect. 5.3.1.1, the program constructs an "average" ARG for each class. This entails another graph-matching problem. To learn a definition, the program must match the ARGs of the various training examples to one another. This task is different from the previous matching problem because a similarity score cannot be computed until after a definition has been learned.

We have explored two solutions to this problem. The first is to require the training examples to be drawn with a consistent drawing order. In this case, the matching problem is avoided as the drawing order uniquely identifies the nodes in the ARG. The second approach requires the user to draw symbols with a consistent orientation. With this approach, all examples of a given symbol are scaled to a unit square and translated to the origin. One of the examples is selected as a reference. The nodes of the other examples are matched with the nodes of the reference example using geometric proximity. Specifically, each primitive in an example is matched with the nearest primitive in the reference example.

5.3.2 Feature-based Recognizer

The previous section described our graph-based recognizer, which uses an attributed relational graph to represent both the geometry and topology of a symbol. With that recognizer, symbol recognition involves solving a graph-matching problem. Our feature-based recognizer avoids the cost of graph matching by reducing the topology and geometry of a symbol to a set of features. Our feature-based recognizer is thus much faster than the graph-based recognizer, although it does sacrifice some accuracy to achieve this.[8]

With our feature-based recognizer, a symbol is described by nine features. These include the number of: pen strokes, line segments, arc segments, endpoint ("L") intersections, endpoint-to-midpoint ("T") intersections, midpoint ("X") intersections, pairs of parallel lines, and pairs of perpendicular lines. The final feature is the average distance between the endpoints of the segments, normalized by the maximum distance between any two endpoints. This feature helps differentiate between objects containing non-uniformly scaled versions of the same segments. For example, the

[8]The material in this section is derived from [9].

average distance between the endpoints of a square is larger than that of a rectangle. We assume that each feature value is normally distributed. The mean and standard deviation for each feature is learned from a set of training examples.

An unknown symbol is classified by comparing its features to the observed distributions of the features for each of the learned definitions, D_i. The unknown is classified by the definition that best matches it. Mathematically, the goal is to find the definition D^* that has the highest probability of matching S:

$$D^* = \arg\max P_i(D_i \mid S) \tag{12}$$

We assume that all definitions are equally likely to occur, and hence we set the prior probabilities of the definitions to be equal. We also assume that the nine geometric features x_j are independent of one another. Otherwise, a much larger number of training examples would be required for classification. According to Bayes' Rule, the definition that best classifies the symbol is therefore the one that maximizes the likelihood of observing the symbol's individual features:

$$D^* = \arg\max_i \Pi_j P(x_j \mid D_i) \tag{13}$$

As stated above, we assume each statistical definition model $P(x_j \mid D_i)$ to be a Gaussian distribution with mean $\mu_{i,j}$ and standard deviation $\sigma_{i,j}$:

$$P(x_j \mid D_i) = \frac{1}{\sigma_{i,j}\sqrt{2\pi}} \exp\left[\frac{-(x_j - \mu_{i,j})^2}{2\sigma_{i,j}^2}\right] \tag{14}$$

Since we are assuming that the features are independent, this is referred to as a naïve Bayesian classifier. This type of classifier is commonly thought to produce optimal results only when all features are truly independent. This is not a proper assumption for our problem, since some of the features we use are interrelated. For example, the number of intersections in a symbol frequently increases with the number of lines and arcs. However, Domingos and Pazzani [5] showed that the naïve Bayesian classifier does not require independence of the features to be optimal. While the actual probabilities of match may not be accurate, the rankings of the definitions will most likely be so.

Because of our assumption of a Gaussian distribution, definitions in which the training examples show no variation in one or more features cause difficulty during recognition. This situation is a common occurrence because a small number of training examples are often used, and because eight of the features used for classification can assume only discrete values. To prevent definitions from becoming overly rigid in this way, we require that all features, with the exception of the continuously valued average distance between endpoints, have a standard deviation of at least 0.3. This significantly increases recognition rates, especially when only a few training examples have been used.

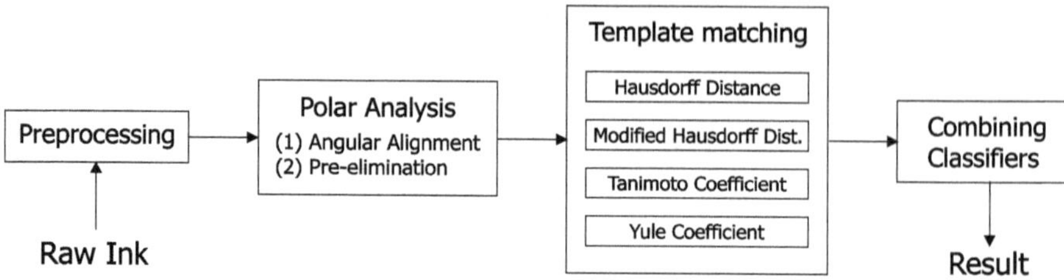

Fig. 5.14 Architecture of Image-based Recognizer

5.3.3 Image-based Recognizer

For our image-based recognizer [15, 17], symbols are internally represented as binary bitmaps, called "templates."[9] This representation has a number of desirable characteristics. For example, it avoids the need for stroke segmentation and thus avoids issues with segmentation errors. Similarly, the approach is well suitable for recognizing "sketchy" symbols such as those with substantial over-stroking.

The classification of an unknown symbol is determined by comparing it to definition symbols using an ensemble of four different classifiers (template matchers). The scores of the individual classifiers are aggregated to produce a combined score for each definition. The definition with the best combined score is assigned to the unknown symbol.

Template matching techniques are sensitive to orientation. Thus, when two templates are compared, it is necessary that they have the same orientation. In many systems, this is achieved by incrementally rotating one pattern relative to the other until the best correspondence is obtained. This approach, however, is too expensive for real-time applications. We have developed a much more efficient technique based on a polar coordinate representation. The technique is based on the fact that rotations in screen coordinates become translations in polar coordinates. Hence, finding the optimal rotational alignment in screen coordinates reduces to determining the shift between patterns in polar coordinates.

The recognition architecture consists of four sequential layers as shown in Fig. 5.14. The first step is preprocessing, where the input symbols are cropped, size-normalized and quantized into templates. If the system is in training mode, the template becomes a definition and is added to the database of existing definitions. If the system is in recognition mode, the template is passed to the next stage where it is matched against the definitions.

In the first step of recognition, the unknown symbol is transformed into a polar coordinate representation, which allows the program to efficiently determine which orientation of the unknown best matches a given definition. During this process, definitions that are found to be markedly dissimilar to the unknown are pruned out and the remaining ones are kept for further analysis. In the second step, recognition

[9]The material in this section and its subsections is derived from [17].

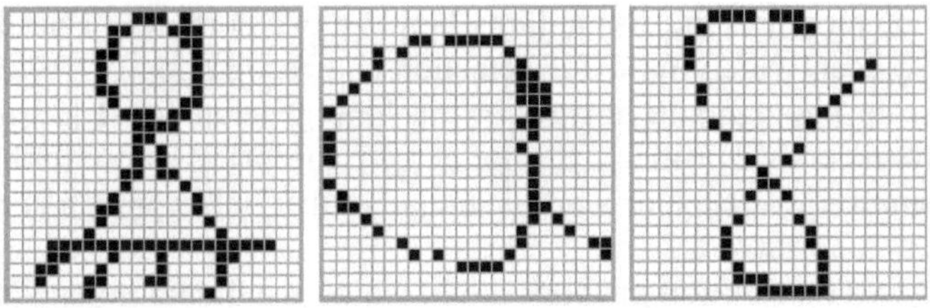

Fig. 5.15 Examples of symbol templates. *Left*: a mechanical pivot, *Middle*: 'a', *Right*: '8'. The templates are shown on 24×24 grids to better illustrate the quantization. (From [17]; used with permission)

switches to screen coordinates where the surviving definitions are analyzed in more detail using an ensemble of four different classifiers. Each classifier outputs a list of definitions ranked according to their similarity to the unknown. In the final step of recognition, results of the individual classifiers are pooled together to produce the recognizer's final decision.

As shown in Fig. 5.14, the analysis in the polar coordinates precedes the analysis in the screen coordinates. However, for clarity of presentation, we begin the discussion with our template representation and the four template matching techniques, since some of those concepts are necessary to set the context for the analysis in the polar coordinates.

5.3.3.1 Representation

Symbols are internally represented as binary bitmap images, which we call "templates." When constructing a template, it is first necessary to frame the image. To do this, a coordinate-aligned bounding box is constructed. The shortest dimension of the bounding box is then expanded, without changing the location of the box's center, to produce a square. The result is that the shape is centered in a square frame, without necessarily filling it. This preserves the original aspect ratio so that one can distinguish between, say, a circle and an ellipse. The frame is then sampled to produce 48×48 binary bitmap. This quantization significantly reduces the amount of data to consider while preserving the pattern's distinguishing characteristics. This resolution has proven to be a good compromise between accuracy and efficiency. Figure 5.15 shows examples of typical templates.

5.3.3.2 Template Matching with Multiple Classifiers

Template matching, in its simplest form, is the process of superimposing two digital images and applying a measure of similarity. While most template-based recognition systems are designed around a single similarity measure, we use four different methods to enhance recognition accuracy. The first two are based on the Hausdorff distance, which measures the dissimilarity between two point sets. Hausdorff-based methods have been widely used for detection and recognition of "rigid" objects, such as those in photographic images or machine generated text [32]. A few researchers have recently considered the use of the Hausdorff distance for hand-drawn pattern recognition [3, 26]. Our work is unique in that our approach is rotation invariant.

Our other two recognition methods are based on the Tanimoto and Yule coefficients. Unlike the Hausdorff methods, these methods measure the similarity between patterns and output their results in the form of correlation coefficients. The Tanimoto coefficient is extensively used in chemical informatics [7]. The Yule coefficient has been proposed as a robust measure for binary template matching [39]. To the best of our knowledge, the Tanimoto and Yule measures have not previously been applied to handwritten pattern recognition.

In the following paragraphs we detail these four classification methods and explain the modifications we used to better suit them to hand-drawn symbol recognition.

Hausdorff Distance: The Hausdorff distance between two point sets A and B is defined as

$$H(A,B) = \max\big(h(A,B), h(B,A)\big) \tag{15}$$

where

$$h(A,B) = \max_{a \in A}\Big(\min_{b \in B} \|a - b\|\Big). \tag{16}$$

$\|a - b\|$ represents a measure of distance (e.g., the Euclidean distance) between two points a and b. $h(A,B)$ is referred to as the directed Hausdorff distance from A to B and corresponds to the maximum of all the distances one can measure from each point in A to the closest point in B. If $h(A,B) = d$, then every point in set A is at most distance d away from some point in B. $h(B,A)$ is the directed distance from B to A and is computed in a similar way. Note that in general $h(A,B) \neq h(B,A)$. The Hausdorff distance is defined as the maximum of the two directed distances.

In its original form, the Hausdorff distance is overly sensitive to outliers. The *Partial* Hausdorff distance proposed by Rucklidge [32] eliminates this problem by ranking the points in A according to their distances to points in B in descending order, and assigning the distance of the kth ranked point as $h(A,B)$. The partial Hausdorff distance from A to B is thus given by:

$$h^k(A,B) = \mathop{k\text{th}}_{a \in A} \min_{b \in B} \|a - b\|. \tag{17}$$

The partial Hausdorff distance softens the distance measure by discarding points that are maximally far away from the other point set. In our implementation, we discard the most distant 6% of the points.

Whether it is based on the maximum or the kth ranked directed distance, calculation of $h(A,B)$ involves computing, for each point in A, the distance to the nearest point in B. We use a distance transform to do this efficiently. A distance transform is a morphological operation that converts a binary bitmap image into an image in which each pixel encodes its distance (we use the Euclidean distance) to the nearest black pixel in the same image. The resulting image is called a distance map and serves as look-up table for the closest distances. Note that the distances maps for the definition symbols can be computed off-line and saved. Also, we use the distance maps to accelerate the computation of the other classifiers.

Modified Hausdorff Distance: The Modified Hausdorff Distance (MHD) [6] replaces the max operator in the directed distance calculation by the average of the distances:

$$h_{\text{mod}}(A, B) = \frac{1}{N_a} \sum_{a \in A} \min_{b \in B} \|a - b\| \tag{18}$$

where N_a is the number of points in A. The modified Hausdorff distance is then defined as the maximum of the two directed average distances:

$$\text{MHD}(A, B) = \max\big(h_{\text{mod}}(A, B), h_{\text{mod}}(B, A)\big) \tag{19}$$

Although $h_{\text{mod}}(A, B)$ may appear similar to $h^k(A, B)$ with $k = 50\%$, the difference is that the former corresponds to the mean directed distance while the latter corresponds to the median. Dubuisson and Jain argue that for object matching purposes, the average directed distance is more reliable than the partial directed distance mainly because as the noise level increases, the former degrades gracefully whereas the latter exhibits a pass/no-pass behavior.

Tanimoto Coefficient: The Tanimoto coefficient between two binary images A and B is defined as

$$T(A, B) = \frac{n_{ab}}{n_a + n_b - n_{ab}} \tag{20}$$

where n_a is the total number of black pixels in A, n_b is the total number of black pixels in B, and n_{ab} is the number of overlapping black pixels.

Intuitively, $T(A, B)$ specifies the number of matching pixels in A and B, normalized by the union of the two point sets. By definition, $T(A, B)$ yields values between 1.0 (maximum similarity) and 0.0 (minimum similarity). In the form given above, the similarity between two images is based solely on the matching black pixels. However, for images that contain mostly black pixels, the discrimination power of $T(A, B)$ may vanish. In such situations, coincidence of white pixels can be used as a measure of similarity:

$$T^{\text{C}}(A, B) = \frac{n_{00}}{n_a + n_b - 2n_{ab} + n_{00}} \tag{21}$$

where n_{00} is the number of matching white pixels. The denominator is the number of pixels that are white in at least one of the images. $T^{\text{C}}(A, B)$ is called the Tanimoto coefficient complement. It represents the number of matching white pixels normalized by the union of the white pixels from the two images. The two expressions can be combined to form the Tanimoto similarity coefficient [7]:

$$T_{\text{sc}}(A, B) = \alpha \cdot T(A, B) + (1 - \alpha) \cdot T^{\text{C}}(A, B) \tag{22}$$

where α is a weighting factor between 0.0 and 1.0. Ideally, if the number of black pixels in an image is small compared to the number of white pixels, the similarity decision should be based on matching black pixels. In this case, $T(A, B)$ should be emphasized by means of a large α. In the converse case, similarity should be based on matching white pixels, which means $T^{\mathrm{C}}(A, B)$ should be emphasized by means of a small α.

This effect can be achieved by linking α to the relative number of black pixels as follows:

$$\alpha = 0.75 - 0.25 \cdot \left(\frac{n_a + n_b}{2 \cdot n} \right) \tag{23}$$

where n is the image size in pixels. The term in parentheses is the total number of black pixels divided by the total number of pixels in the two images. The form of this relationship is adapted from [7] such that α is small when the number of black pixels is high and vice versa. We selected the two constants in the equation so that α is generally high, in the range $[0.5, 0.75]$ to be precise. This bias favors $T(A, B)$ over $T^{\mathrm{C}}(A, B)$. The choice is justified by the fact that hand-drawn symbols usually consist of thin lines (unless excessive over-tracing is done) producing rasterized images that contain fewer black pixels than white. Hence, for our applications, the Tanimoto coefficient should be controlled more by $T(A, B)$ than by $T^{\mathrm{C}}(A, B)$.

Similarity measures that are based exclusively on the number of overlapping pixels, such as the Tanimoto coefficient, often suffer from slight misalignments of the rasterized images. We have found this problem to be particularly severe for hand-drawn patterns where rasterized images of ostensibly similar shapes are almost always disparate, either due to differences in shape, or more subtly, due to differences in drawing dynamics. To make the Tanimoto coefficient insensitive to typical variations in hand-drawn shapes, we use a thresholded matching criterion that considers two pixels to be overlapping if they are separated by a distance less than 1/15th of the image's diagonal length. For a 48×48 image grid, this translates into 4.5 pixels, i.e., two points are considered to be overlapping if the distance between them is less than 4.5 pixels.

Yule Coefficient: The Yule coefficient, also known as the coefficient of colligation, is defined as

$$Y(A, B) = \frac{n_{ab} \cdot n_{00} - (n_a - n_{ab}) \cdot (n_b - n_{ab})}{n_{ab} \cdot n_{00} + (n_a - n_{ab}) \cdot (n_b - n_{ab})} \tag{24}$$

where the term $(n_a - n_{ab})$ corresponds to the number of black pixels in A that do not have a match in B. Similarly, $(n_b - n_{ab})$ is the number of black pixels in B that do not have a match in A.

$Y(A, B)$ produces values between 1.0 (maximum similarity) and -1.0 (minimum similarity). Unlike the original form of the Tanimoto coefficient, the Yule coefficient simultaneously accounts for the matching black and white pixels via the terms n_{ab} and n_{00}. However, like the Tanimoto coefficient, it is sensitive to slight misalignments between patterns. We therefore employ a thresholded matching criterion similar to the one we use with the Tanimoto method.

Tubbs [39] originally employed this measure for generic, noise-free binary template matching problems. By using a threshold, we have made the technique useful when there is considerable noise, as is the case with hand drawn shapes.

Combining Classifiers: Our recognizer compares the unknown symbol to each of the definitions using the four classifiers explained above. The next step in recognition is to identify the true class of the unknown by synthesizing the results of the component classifiers. However, the outputs of the classifiers are not compatible in their original forms because: (1) The first two classifiers are measures of *dissimilarity* while the last two are measures of *similarity*, and (2) the classifiers have dissimilar ranges.

To establish a congruent ranking scheme, we first transform the Tanimoto and Yule similarity coefficients into distance measures by reversing (negating) their values. This process brings the Tanimoto and Yule coefficients in parallel with the Hausdorff measures in the sense that the numerical scores of all classifiers now increase with increasing dissimilarity. Next, to eliminate the range differences among classifiers, we normalize the values of all four classifiers to the range 0 to 1 using a linear transformation function. For each classifier, the transformation maps the distance scores to the range [0,1] while preserving the relative order established by that classifier. Finally, having standardized the outputs of the four classifiers, we combine the results using a method similar to the sum rule introduced by Kittler et al. [19]. For each definition symbol, we compute a combined normalized distance by summing the normalized distances obtained from the constituent classifiers. The unknown pattern is then assigned to the class having the minimum combined normalized distance.

5.3.3.3 Handling Rotations

Before an unknown template can be compared to a definition template, the two must be brought into the same orientation. We use a techniques based on a polar coordinate representation to do this efficiently. The polar coordinates of a point in the x–y plane are given by the point's radial distance, r, from the origin and the angle, θ, between that radius and the x axis. The well known relations are:

$$r = \sqrt{(x - x_o)^2 + (y - y_o)^2} \tag{25}$$

and

$$\theta = \tan^{-1}\left(\frac{y - y_o}{x - x_o}\right) \tag{26}$$

where (x_o, y_o) is the origin.

A symbol originally drawn in the screen coordinates (x–y plane) is transformed into polar coordinates by applying these formulas to each of the data points. To make this representation scale-independent, we normalize the r values using the "ink length" of the symbol, which is defined at the total distance the pen tip travels

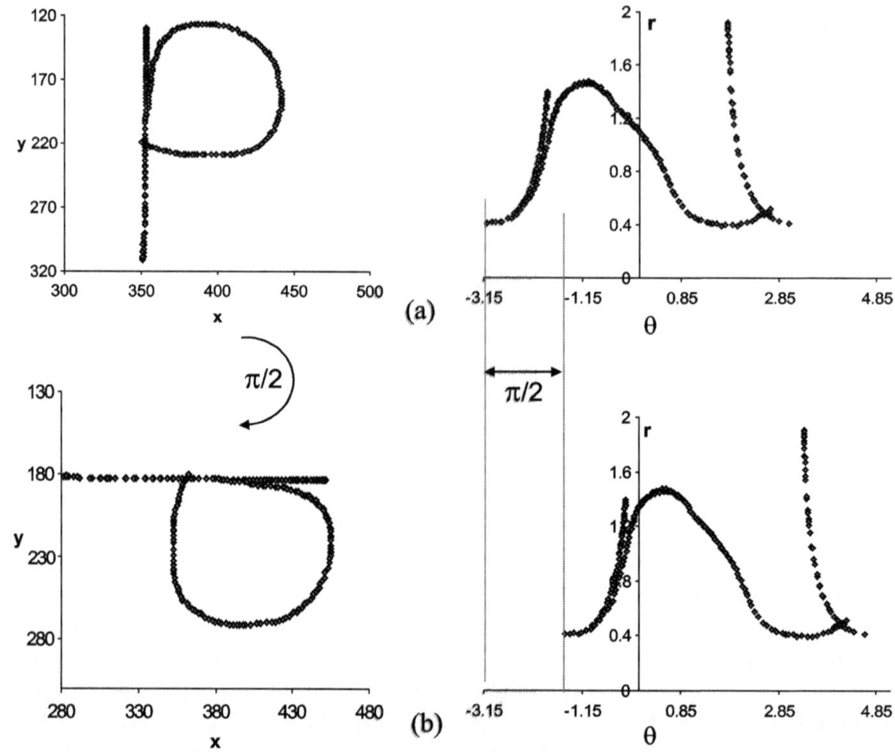

Fig. 5.16 **a** *Left*: Letter 'P' in screen coordinates. *Right*: in polar coordinates. **b** When the letter is rotated in the x–y plane, the corresponding polar transform shifts parallel to the θ axis. (From [17]; used with permission)

on the writing surface. Figure 5.16a illustrates a typical transformation. As shown in Fig. 5.16b, when a pattern is rotated in the x–y plane, the corresponding polar image slides parallel to the θ axis by the same angular displacement.

To find the angular offset between two polar images, we use a slide-and-compare algorithm in which one image is incrementally displaced along the θ axis. At each displacement, the two images are compared to determine how well they match. The displacement that results in the best match indicates how much rotation is needed to best align the original images. Because the polar images are 48×48 quantized templates, we can use the template matching techniques described earlier to match the polar images. We use the modified Hausdorff distance (MHD) as it is slightly more efficient than the regular Hausdorff distance, and it performs slightly better than the Tanimoto and Yule coefficients in polar coordinates.

One difficulty with the polar transform is that data points near the centroid of the original screen image are sensitive to the precise location of the centroid. To remedy this, we introduce a weighting function $w(r)$ that attenuates the influence of pixels near the centroid. Using this function, the directed MHD becomes

$$h_{\text{mod\_weighted}}(A, B) = \frac{1}{N_a} \sum_{a \in A} w(a_r) \cdot \min_{b \in B} \|a - b\| \tag{27}$$

where a_r represents the radial coordinate of point a in the quantized polar image A. The directed distance from B to A, $h_{\text{mod\_weighted}}(B, A)$, is calculated similarly, and the maximum of the two directed distances is the MHD between A and B. Our weighting function has the form:

$$w(r) = r^{0.10}. \tag{28}$$

This function asymptotes near 1 for large values of r, and falls off rapidly for small values of r.

Once the angular difference between two patterns is determined with the polar coordinate analysis, the patterns can then be aligned in the x–y plane by a single rotation. The aligned templates can then be compared using the template matching techniques described earlier.

The degree of match between two polar images provides a reasonable estimate of the match of the original screen images. In fact, if it were not for the imprecision of the polar transform for small r values, the recognition process could be performed exclusively in the polar plane. Despite this, we have found that the correct definition for an unknown is typically among the definitions ranked in the top 10% by the polar coordinate matching. Thus, we typically discard 90% of the definitions before considering the match in screen coordinates.

5.4 Educational Applications

Our Sim-U-Sketch (Fig. 5.1), Vibrosketch (Fig. 5.2), and AC-SPARC (Fig. 5.6) systems were originally intended as experimental platforms for developing easy-to-use engineering analysis tools. However, these systems also have value as educational tools. In engineering education, it is common for students to use sophisticated software tools like SPICE [41]. But the complexity of the interfaces often limits the usefulness of the tools, as students often spend more time learning to use the software than thinking about the essential concepts. Our systems, by contrast, enable students to operate analysis tools by simply drawing the same kinds of sketches and diagrams they see in lecture. This allows students to focus on problem solving rather than how to use the software.

While our pen-based analysis tools are useful for education, they do not have tutoring functionality. In our more recent work, we have explicitly focused on the use of pen-based technology for creating intelligent tutoring systems. "In particular, our goal is to create computational techniques to enable natural, pen-based tutoring systems that scaffold students in solving problems in the same way they would

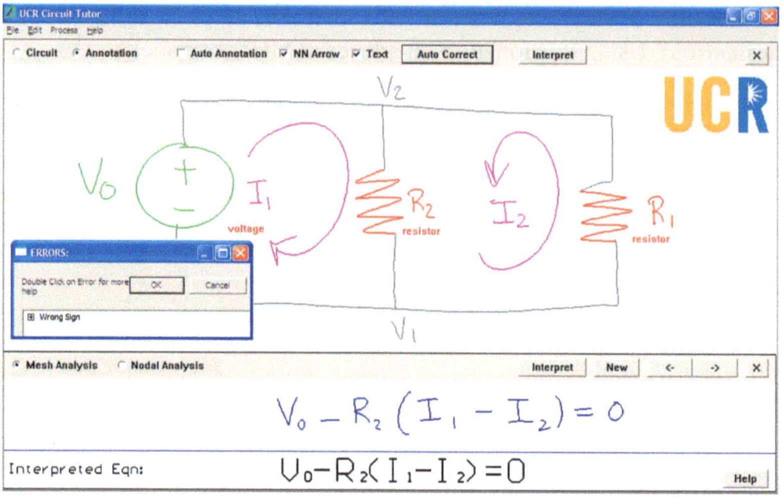

Fig. 5.17 Kirchhoff's Pen used for mesh analysis. The system informs the student of a sign error

ordinarily solve them with paper and pencil" [4]. This goal is consistent with recent research comparing student performance across different user interfaces showing that "as the interfaces departed more from familiar work practice..., students would experience greater cognitive load such that performance would deteriorate in speed, attentional focus, meta-cognitive control, correctness of problem solutions, and memory" [29].

"As one step toward our goal, we have developed Kirchhoff's Pen [4], a pen-based tutoring system that teaches students to apply Kirchhoff's voltage and current laws. Kirchhoff's voltage law (KVL) states that the sum of the voltages around any closed loop, or "mesh," is zero. Kirchhoff's current law (KCL) states that the sum of the currents into an electrical node is zero. Kirchhoff's Pen is built on top of our AC-SPARC system." [4]

To use Kirchhoff's Pen, the student begins by either sketching a circuit schematic or loading a predrawn circuit. The student then "annotates the circuit to indicate the component labels, mesh currents, and nodal voltages, ... and writes the appropriate equations in a window at the bottom of the screen. The system interprets the equations, compares them to the correct equations (which are automatically derived from the circuit), and provides feedback about errors. Figure 5.17 shows an example of the system being used for mesh analysis. The equation at the bottom of the screen is intended to describe the mesh on the left side of the circuit. However, the student has made a sign error: the $R_2 I_2$ term should be negative, but was written as positive. The system identifies the error" and guides the student in fixing it [4].

As another step toward our goal, we have built Newton's Pen [24], a pen-based statics tutor designed for the LeapFrog FLY pentop computer.[10] Statics is the subdiscipline of engineering mechanics concerned with the equilibrium of objects subjected to forces. The FLY is based on Anoto [2] digital paper technology and has an embedded 96 MHz ARC processor. The FLY is used in conjunction with paper preprinted with a specially designed dot pattern. Newton's pen runs entirely on the FLY's embedded processor, which created significant challenges because of the limited memory and computational power available (there is only about 4k bytes of RAM available). The platform also presented substantial user interface design challenges because audio is the only form of dynamic output: The system has a speech synthesizer and can play recorded sound clips.

"Newton's Pen scaffolds students in the construction of free body diagrams and equilibrium equations. Problems are solved on digital paper preprinted with user interface objects, such as "HELP" and "DONE" buttons. Figure 5.18a shows a worksheet for drawing a free body diagram. To begin, the student taps the pen on the "START FBD" button, and the system prompts the student to draw the free body diagram in the space provided. After each graphical element is drawn, the system provides interpretive audio feedback. If the student makes a problem-solving error, or the input is not recognized, the system informs the student via synthesized speech. The student can tap "HELP" at any time for audio hints about what to do next, or for guidance after an error. When the student completes the free body diagram, he or she hits the "DONE" button, and is directed to write the equilibrium equations on the worksheet in Fig. 5.18b" [23]. The system interprets the equations and provides audio feedback if there are errors.

User studies with Kirchoff's Pen and Newton's Pen have shown that these systems are effective educational tools. The studies involved novice undergraduates who had been exposed to the relevant lecture material (Kirchoff's laws or statics) but had not yet attempted homework problems. Prior to using our system, the students were given pretests which indicated they had little understanding of the material. After about one hour with our systems, most students were able to comfortably solve problems. Attitudinal surveys of the students suggested that they were quite pleased with the systems and would use them in their courses if they were available.

5.5 Conclusion

This chapter has described our techniques for sketch parsing and symbol recognition. We have used these techniques to implement practical pen-based engineering analysis tools and effective pen-based tutoring systems. Despite the usefulness and usability of these systems, there are many significant problems left to be solved. For

[10] This paragraph is derived from [24]. An earlier version of this material also appeared in Lee, W., de Silva, R., Peterson, E.J., Calfee, R.C., Stahovich, T.F.: Newton's Pen: a pen-based tutoring system for statics. In: SBIM '07: Proceedings of the 4th Eurographics Workshop on Sketch-Based Interfaces and Modeling, pp. 59–66. ACM, New York (2007). doi:10.1145/1384429.1384445 [23].

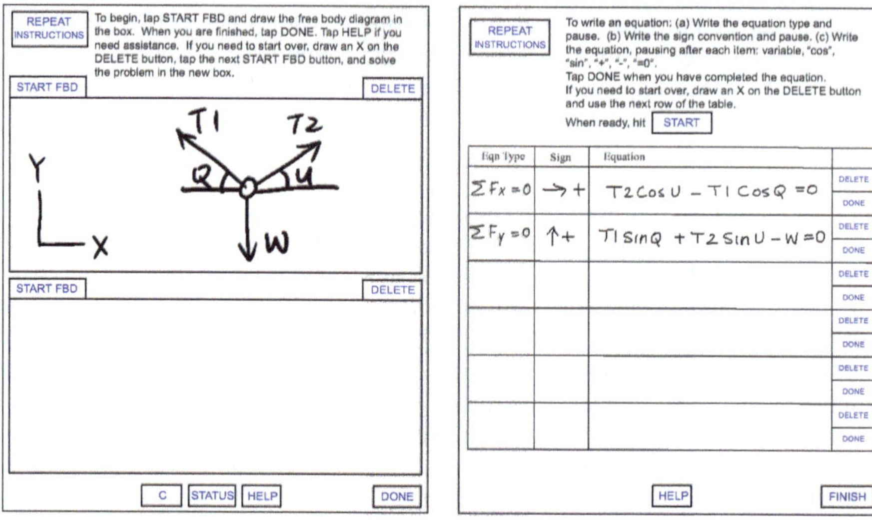

Fig. 5.18 **a** Worksheet for drawing free body diagrams. **b** Worksheet for writing equilibrium equations. (From [24]; used with permission)

example, our techniques often rely on domain knowledge to achieve high accuracy. This is particularly true of AC-SPARC, which uses knowledge of circuits both for parsing and for automatic error correction. Our ongoing work is focused on generalizing our techniques, making them more domain independent and applicable to an even wider range of problems. However, it is likely that some amount of domain knowledge will always be necessary to achieve high performance. For instance, it would be challenging even for a human to understand a crudely-drawn sketch without some contextual knowledge. For the same reasons, sketch interpretation systems will always rely on domain knowledge, and possibly domain-specific techniques.

Our goal is to create user interfaces that are substantially more natural to use than traditional mouse-and-windows-based interfaces. Pen-based interfaces are clearly a step in the right direction. However, human communication is frequently multimodal and often includes sketching, gesturing, and speaking. Another important research direction is the creation of user interfaces that can understand these modalities and use them simultaneously. This will not only result in more natural interfaces, but will also result in more robust systems, as the various modalities will enable mutual disambiguation.

In recent years, pen-based computing hardware has become ubiquitous—now even inexpensive mobile phones have pen or touch interfaces. However, most pen-based devices use the pen (or finger) simply for pointing. Achieving the real value of such devices requires recognition-based interfaces. We have begun to explore such interfaces for engineering and education, but there is a vast range of domains yet to be explored. Our initial successes give us confidence that much can be accomplished in these other domains.

Acknowledgements The author gratefully acknowledges Microsoft Research and Leapfrog Enterprises, Inc. for their support of this work. This chapter describes the hard work and important contributions of many graduate students including David Tyler Bischel, Ruwanee de Silva, Leslie Gennari, Levent Burak Kara, WeeSan Lee, Eric Peterson, and Ryan Rusich.

References

1. Alvarado, C., Davis, R.: Dynamically constructed Bayes nets for multi-domain sketch understanding. In: International Joint Conference on Artificial Intelligence (2005)
2. Anoto group AB. http://www.anoto.com/
3. Cheung, K.W., Yeung, D.Y., Chin, R.T.: Bidirectional deformable matching with application to handwritten character extraction. IEEE Transactions on Pattern Analysis and Machine Intelligence **24**(8), 1133–1139 (2002)
4. de Silva, R., Bischel, D.T., Lee, W., Peterson, E.J., Calfee, R.C., Stahovich, T.F.: Kirchhoff's pen: a pen-based circuit analysis tutor. In: SBIM '07: Proceedings of the 4th Eurographics Workshop on Sketch-Based Interfaces and Modeling, pp. 75–82. ACM, New York (2007). doi:10.1145/1384429.1384447
5. Domingos, P., Pazzani, M.: Beyond independence: Conditions for the optimality of the simple Bayesian classifier. In: Machine Learning, pp. 105–112. Morgan Kaufmann, San Mateo (1996)
6. Dubuisson, M.P., Jain, A.K.: A modified Hausdorff distance for object matching. In: 12th International Conference on Pattern Recognition, Jerusalem, Israel, pp. 566–568 (1994)
7. Fligner, M., Verducci, J., Bjoraker, J., Blower, P.: A new association coefficient for molecular dissimilarity. In: The Second Joint Sheffield Conference on Chemoinformatics, Sheffield, England (2001)
8. Fonseca, M.J., Pimentel, C., Jorge, J.A.: Cali—an online scribble recognizer for calligraphic interfaces. In: AAAI Spring Symposium on Sketch Understanding, pp. 51–58 (2002)
9. Gennari, L., Kara, L.B., Stahovich, T.F., Shimada, K.: Combining geometry and domain knowledge to interpret hand-drawn diagrams. Computers & Graphics **29**(4), 547–562 (2005). doi:10.1016/j.cag.2005.05.007
10. Gross, M.D.: Recognizing and interpreting diagrams in design. In: ACM Conference on Advanced Visual Interfaces, pp. 88–94 (1994)
11. Hammond, T., Davis, R.: Ladder, a sketching language for user interface developers. Computers & Graphics **29**(4), 518–532 (2005)
12. Hse, H.H., Newton, A.R.: Recognition and beautification of multi-stroke symbols in digital ink. Computers & Graphics **29**(4), 533–546 (2005)
13. Jacobs, D.W.: The use of grouping in visual object recognition. Technical Report 1023, MIT AI Lab (1988)
14. Kara, L.B., Stahovich, T.F.: Hierarchical parsing and recognition of hand-sketched diagrams. In: UIST '04: Proceedings of the 17th annual ACM Symposium on User Interface Software and Technology, pp. 13–22. ACM, New York (2004). doi:10.1145/1029632.1029636
15. Kara, L.B., Stahovich, T.F.: An image-based trainable symbol recognizer for sketch-based interfaces. In: AAAI Fall Symposium Series 2004: Making Pen-Based Interaction Intelligent and Natural (2004)
16. Kara, L.B., Stahovich, T.F.: Sim-U-Sketch: a sketch-based interface for SimuLink. In: AVI '04: Proceedings of the Working Conference on Advanced Visual Interfaces, pp. 354–357. ACM, New York (2004). doi:10.1145/989863.989923
17. Kara, L.B., Stahovich, T.F.: An image-based, trainable symbol recognizer for hand-drawn sketches. Computers & Graphics **29**(4), 501–517 (2005). doi:10.1016/j.cag.2005.05.004
18. Kara, L.B., Gennari, L., Stahovich, T.F.: A sketch-based tool for analyzing vibratory mechanical systems. Journal of Mechanical Design **130**(10), 101101 (2008). doi:10.1115/1.2965595

19. Kittler, J., Hatef, M., Duin, R.P.W., Matas, J.: On combining classifiers. IEEE Transactions on Pattern Analysis and Machine Intelligence **20**(3), 226–239 (1998)
20. Landay, J.A., Myers, B.A.: Sketching interfaces: Toward more human interface design. IEEE Computer **34**(3), 56–64 (2001)
21. Lee, W., Kara, L.B., Stahovich, T.F.: An efficient graph-based recognizer. In: Eurographics Workshop on Sketch-Based Interfaces and Modeling (2006)
22. Lee, W., Kara, L.B., Stahovich, T.F.: An efficient graph-based recognizer for hand-drawn symbols. Computers & Graphics **31**(4), 554–567 (2007). doi:10.1016/j.cag.2007.04.007
23. Lee, W., de Silva, R., Peterson, E.J., Calfee, R.C., Stahovich, T.F.: Newton's Pen: a pen-based tutoring system for statics. In: SBIM '07: Proceedings of the 4th Eurographics Workshop on Sketch-Based Interfaces and Modeling, pp. 59–66. ACM, New York (2007). doi:10.1145/1384429.1384445
24. Lee, W., de Silva, R., Peterson, E.J., Calfee, R.C., Stahovich, T.F.: Newton's pen: A pen-based tutoring system for statics. Computers & Graphics **32**(5), 511–524 (2008). doi:10.1016/j.cag.2008.05.009
25. Matsakis, N.E.: Recognition of handwritten mathematical expressions. Master thesis, MIT (1999)
26. Miller, E.G., Matsakis, N.E., Viola, P.A.: Learning from one example through shared densities of transforms. In: Proceedings of the IEEE Conference on Computer Vision and Pattern Recognition, pp. 464–471 (2000)
27. Narayanaswamy, S.: Pen and speech recognition in the user interface for mobile multimedia terminals. Ph.D. thesis, University of California at Berkeley (1996)
28. Notowidigdo, M., Miller, R.C.: Off-line sketch interpretation. In: AAAI Fall Symposium Series 2004: Making Pen-Based Interaction Intelligent and Natural (2004)
29. Oviatt, S., Arthur, A., Cohen, J.: Quiet interfaces that help students think. In: UIST '06, pp. 191–200 (2006)
30. Pereira, J.P., Branco, V.A., Silva, N.F., Cardoso, T.D., Ferreira, F.N.: Cascading recognizers for ambiguous calligraphic interaction. In: 2004 Eurographics Workshop on Sketch-Based Interfaces and Modeling, pp. 63–72 (2004)
31. Rubine, D.: Specifying gestures by example. Computer Graphics **25**, 329–337 (1991)
32. Rucklidge, W.J.: Efficient Visual Recognition Using the Hausdorff Distance. Lecture Notes in Computer Science, vol. 1173. Springer, Berlin (1996)
33. Saund, E., Mahoney, J., Fleet, D., Larner, D., Lank, E.: Perceptual organisation as a foundation for intelligent sketch editing. In: AAAI Spring Symposium on Sketch Understanding, pp. 118–125 (2002)
34. Sezgin, T.M., Davis, R.: HMM-based efficient sketch recognition. In: International Conference on Intelligent User Interfaces (IUI'05), New York (2005)
35. Shilman, M., Viola, P.: Spatial recognition and grouping of text and graphics. In: EUROGRAPHICS Workshop on Sketch-Based Interfaces and Modeling (2004)
36. Shilman, M., Pasula, H., Russell, S., Newton, R.: Statistical visual language models for ink parsing. In: AAAI Spring Symposium on Sketch Understanding, pp. 126–132 (2002)
37. Shpitalni, M., Lipson, H.: Classification of sketch strokes and corner detection using conic sections and adaptive clustering. ASME Journal of Mechanical Design (1995)
38. Stahovich, T.F.: Segmentation of pen strokes using pen speed. In: AAAI 2004 Fall Symposium: Making Pen-Based Interaction Intelligent and Natural (2004)
39. Tubbs, J.D.: A note on binary template matching. Pattern Recognition **22**(4), 359–365 (1989)
40. Ullman, D.G., Wood, S., Craig, D.: The importance of drawing in the mechanical design process. Computers & Graphics **14**(2), 263–274 (1990)
41. Vladimirescu, A., Newton, A.R., Pederson, D.O.: SPICE Version 2g.0 User's Guide. Dept. of Electrical Engineering and Computer Sciences, University of California, Berkeley (1980)
42. Yasuda, H., Takahashi, K., Matsumoto, T.: A discrete HMM for online handwriting recognition. International Journal of Pattern Recognition and Artificial Intelligence **14**(5), 675–688 (2000)

Chapter 6
Flexible Parts-based Sketch Recognition

Michiel van de Panne and Dana Sharon

6.1 Introduction

The automatic recognition of drawings or sketches is an important problem to solve. Computers and interfaces which could see such diagrams as being more than raw lists of pixels or stroke coordinates would open up many new possibilities for more intelligent interfaces and document processing. The recognition problem is perhaps easiest when the elements to be recognized have a fully predetermined structure, such as consistently drawn versions of the letter 'A' or an arrowhead. At the other end of the spectrum, humans are able to do quite well at recognizing objects that have extreme variability in their depictions. For example, we can recognize drawn people or trees despite the many potential variations in shape, pose, choice of drawn features, and drawing style. In this chapter we present two sketch-recognition techniques that aim at the middle of this spectrum by seeking to recognize drawings that exhibit *structured, parts-based variation.* Figure 6.1 shows examples of the types of drawings that can be recognized using these techniques. The objects can exhibit significant variation in how they are drawn. They can also have optional parts, such as the pupils, eyebrow strokes, and beards for the faces of row a, and the presence or absence of handles and engines-on-the-wings for the object drawings of row b.

The type of recognition discussed in this chapter is distinct from diagram recognition, another common type of sketch recognition problem, e.g., [7], in several ways. Diagrams are often modeled using a fixed vocabulary of symbols, each with a fixed or restricted drawn representation, e.g., boxes and arrows, or electrical components and wires. In the class of objects we are interested in, objects can have a highly variable drawn representation, and the relative spatial location of parts plays a key role in the recognition process. The recognition problem we tackle is also significantly different from the problem of interpreting 3D structure from 2D drawings.

M. van de Panne (✉) · D. Sharon
Department of Computer Science, University of British Columbia, 2366 Main Hall, Vancouver, BC, Canada V6T 124
e-mail: van@cs.ubc.ca

J. Jorge, F. Samavati (eds.), *Sketch-based Interfaces and Modeling*,
DOI 10.1007/978-1-84882-812-4_6,

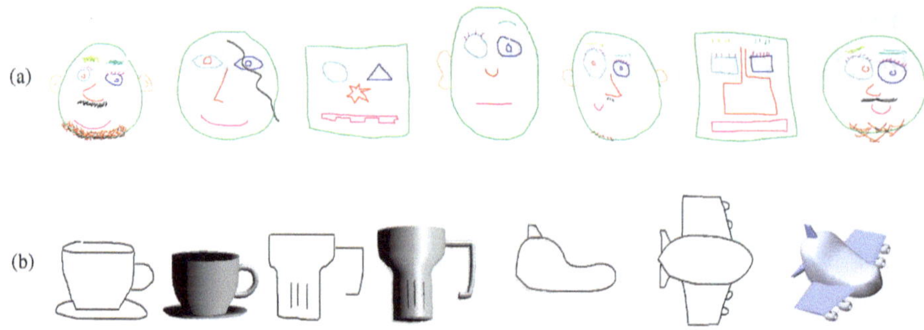

Fig. 6.1 Examples of parts-based sketch recognition. **a** Face drawings that can be successfully recognized, as illustrated by the color-coding of the drawn lines. **b** Drawings of cups and airplanes that can be successfully recognized, as illustrated by the resulting 3D models

A key to the recognition algorithms we present is the use of a 2D template for each class of objects to be modeled. The templates provide explicit support for optional parts, and therefore offer a compact and scalable approach for modeling many classes of objects. Recognizing a whole object in terms of being a particular layout of a collection of parts helps avoid the combinatorial explosion that would otherwise be required if explicitly modeling all possible combinations of parts that might constitute an object. The template structure also provides context for the recognition of the parts themselves, which might not otherwise be sufficiently unique in order to be recognized in isolation. As a trivial example, the arm of a stick-figure drawing of a human cannot be distinguished from a leg without knowing some of the contextual information provided by the surrounding lines.

We present two recognition algorithms in this chapter, each of which has its own specific form of template model. The first is a *hierarchy of parts (HOP)* model, which assumes that each drawn object has a single 'body' part with an attached hierarchy of optional parts. Recognition for this case proceeds by treating the drawn strokes as a graph and looking for pieces of the graph that are similar in both structure and shape. The second is a *constellation of parts (COP)* model, which assumes that there are a core set of possibly-disconnected parts, and the recognition is based in large part on identifying parts by their relative location with respect to each other.

6.1.1 Algorithm Design Issues

Recognition algorithms can be developed around many possible assumptions and approaches. Together, these form the design space for the sketch-recognition algorithm. In what follows, we provide various means by which sketch-recognition algorithms can be classified, and where our two proposed techniques are placed with respect to these.

6.1.2 Image-based vs. Stroke-based

Drawings can be treated as images, which offers the potential advantage of being able to adapt computer vision methodology and algorithms. However, extracted edges and connectivity information play an important role in many vision-based recognition algorithms, and this is even more the case for drawings where there is little in the way of color, texture, or other image-patch information to exploit. As a result, our proposed techniques directly work with the given strokes as sets of connected, ordered points.

6.1.3 Use of Timing Information

Given a decision to work with strokes, we need to decide which stroke attributes to work with. If the strokes are captured when drawn, i.e., with a pen-based interface, timing information is available, which can then be exploited in support of recognition. For example, the strokes used to draw a particular symbol by a particular user might usually drawn in a given order. The timing information within a stroke can be used to help identify corner points at which a stroke could be segmented. However, there can always be valid exceptions to a model based on usual stroke ordering and timing. This information may also be specific to individual users or particular object variations. Human observers can also readily recognize objects in drawings without having observed the timing and ordering of the drawing process. By relying on timing information, the source of some recognition failures may be highly opaque to the user given that this information is not directly visible in a drawing. The recognition algorithms proposed in this chapter do not use timing or ordering information.

6.1.4 Top–Down vs. Bottom–Up

Two basic approaches for recognition are to: (i) search for models that are compatible with given evidence, i.e., bottom–up, or (ii) search for evidence that would be compatible with a given model, i.e., top–down. Given the large space of possible assignments of strokes or stroke-segments to possible parts of possible objects, it is important to find methods that quickly constrain the search. Our proposed methods generally use a top–down approach. We make some assumptions regarding stroke segmentation and connectivity, which can be thought of as a type of bottom–up interpretation. This greatly simplifies the recognition process, but we note that it can also be the source of unrecoverable errors because it may commit to one particular segmentation or grouping of strokes, where the best interpretation may require an alternate segmentation or grouping.

6.1.5 Object Template Representation

Recognition requires prior knowledge of some form of the expected class of shapes or the expected arrangement of drawn features that constitute a drawn object. This is most commonly represented in terms of a template. Templates can encode the mean shapes of objects or object parts, or they can encode a likelihood distribution over possible shapes. Template information can be user-defined or learned from example. The two recognition algorithms described in this chapter each have their own unique template representation. The hierarchical parts model uses the mean shapes of parts and implements hard constraints on the relative location of parts with respect to each other. In contrast, the constellation parts model uses a probabilistic approach for modeling both the shapes of parts and the locations of parts.

6.1.6 Degree of Supported Variation

Recognition algorithms can often be simplified if it is assumed that the drawing contains no extraneous strokes and the required parts are fixed and known in advance, i.e., there is no notion of optional parts. Making these assumptions allows the recognition problem to search for a solution in the space of all possible one-to-one mappings between drawn features or strokes and template features or strokes. If these assumptions cannot be made, the space of possible solutions is often significantly enlarged because it is now possible that any given stroke may simply be noise or not be part of a good interpretation. Similarly, a top–down search can also no longer rely on every template part actually being instanced in a drawing. Both algorithms that follow support spurious strokes and optional parts.

6.1.7 Search Algorithm

Recognition algorithms can vary in many ways. Some algorithms can provide 'any-time results', i.e., they can return the current best match at any time, which is a useful feature in settings where fast, non-optimal recognition is more important than slow, optimal recognition. The recognition results may consist of fine scale point-to-point correspondences or, alternatively, at a coarser scale such as part labels assigned to strokes of the input drawing. Algorithms can vary significantly in their scalability. The algorithms presented in the remainder of this chapter have been demonstrated on drawn objects that have from 5–50 strokes, and up to 10 labels.

6.1.8 Recognition as Search

Recognition can be treated as a search process, where the goal is to find the best interpretation of the strokes in a drawing, in the set of all possible interpretations.

The recognition methods proposed in this chapter are no different. As a prelude to describing them in detail, we first consider the operation of simple search algorithms on a well-posed recognition problem. For this, we define a drawing as consisting of n strokes and having a corresponding set of n labels that need to be assigned in a one-to-one mapping to the strokes. Each drawn stroke has a number of local known attributes, such as its total arc length, bounding-box perimeter, mean orientation, centroid, etc. Let us assume that, for each label, there is a known likelihood distribution for each attribute, the simplest version of which is to assume an independent Gaussian distribution for each attribute.

A first algorithm to consider is to find, for each stroke, the most likely label according to the attributes of the stroke. This is the simplest form of bottom–up search, and treats each stroke in an independent fashion. Alternatively, one could perform a type of top–down search, namely finding, for each label, the stroke that most likely corresponds to that label. The obvious pitfall of both of these algorithms is that they fail to enforce the one-to-one mapping we require between the strokes and labels. Enforcing this constraint requires considering the set of all possible label-to-stroke assignments, of which there are $n!$ combinations, and considering each of these with respect to the overall objective, such as maximizing the product of the individual label-to-stroke likelihoods (equivalently, maximizing the sum of the log likelihoods). Fortunately, branch-and-bound techniques can be applied to significantly reduce the search space.

The parts-based recognition problems we tackle have additional features which further complicate the problem as depicted thus far. First, the assignment of labels to strokes will depend not only on the stroke attributes, but also on the location of the stroke relative to other labeled strokes. For example, a good indication that a stroke represents the nose is that it lies below the eyes and above the mouth. The challenge here is that the assignments of labels to strokes become further interdependent. Second, the one-to-one mapping of labels to strokes is too restrictive. We wish to support having multiple strokes for some labels, e.g., a sketched eyebrow or beard, having parts be optional, e.g., eyelashes, and being able to support drawings that can contain spurious strokes, i.e., which do not participate in the final recognition. The two methods presented in this chapter are developed specifically to cope with these extra constraints.

6.2 Related Work

Recognizing single strokes in isolation is perhaps the simplest version of sketch understanding and can be used to support interfaces that use pen gestures as commands [12]. Recognizing multi-stroke visual structure is significantly more complex, given that the interpretation of strokes is dependant on its local context. One approach is to treat it as a graph isomorphism problem [9], where it is applied to the recognition of human stick figures using a known model of connectivity.

Diagram recognition has been a significant focus for many methods. The search is often anchored by first finding well-defined symbols, such as drawn characters or electrical component symbols [7]. The search can then be further constrained by exploiting the known structure of the given application domain or object classes. Algorithms often include a mix of top–down and bottom–up procedures that are informed by some domain knowledge, or are statistically informed based on the observed stroke order [14] or the interpretation assigned to neighboring strokes [11]. Diagram recognition and their comparative evaluation [10] still leave many unresolved issues in terms of building robust-yet-flexible systems. The sketch-recognition component of our problem can also be thought of as being "diagrammatic". However, our 2D templates have features that are specifically tailored to our problem domain, such as the notion of part hierarchies, optional parts, and one-of-N part selection. We consider handwriting recognition as a distantly-related problem.

A probabilistic approach to sketch stroke interpretation is proposed in [1]. This uses domain-specific libraries of 'Bayesian network fragments' that describe shapes and domain patterns. Several mechanisms to control the size of the space of hypotheses are presented, and the technique is applied to the domain of electrical circuit diagram recognition. Qi et al. [11] proposes the use of conditional random fields for labeling box-and-line diagrams for particularly difficult ambiguous examples where constraints must propagate in order to find the most likely interpretation. Perceptually based shape descriptions are used to help infer the recognition of image structure in [13]. Our work looks at recognition problems that do not require connectivity between parts and considers object sketches that can exhibit considerable variability.

Image-based techniques can also be used to help identify sketches or parts of sketches. Shape contexts [2] can be used to match sketch images to a fixed set of prototype template images. Image-based classifiers are applied in [15] in order to determine likely interpretations for subsets of strokes. An A* search procedure is used to search among the space of possible subset of strokes in order to find a maximum-likelihood interpretation for the image. This is applied to a graphic symbol set of 13 symbols.

Constellation models, also known as pictorial structure models, are composed of a set of local parts, each of which has an appearance model, and a geometry model that defines preferred relative locations or distances of the parts [5]. They are well suited to applications such as face recognition, where features such as the nose, eyes, and mouth have particular local features and also have relatively well-defined distances to each other. The model is further developed in [4], where it is applied to identify both faces and body configurations from images. The model continues to be extended, with an emphasis on learning pictorial structure models automatically from example images of object classes. More generally, this can be viewed as an example of *statistical relational learning*.

An agent-based approach is presented in [8], although this relies on a predefined grammar for the description of the components. The work of [6] is similar to ours in that it uses a constellation-type model and a probabilistic framework. Our work differs in a number of respects, including application to a different domain, using different and larger individual and pairwise feature sets, supporting flexible object classes with optional parts, and a staged search strategy.

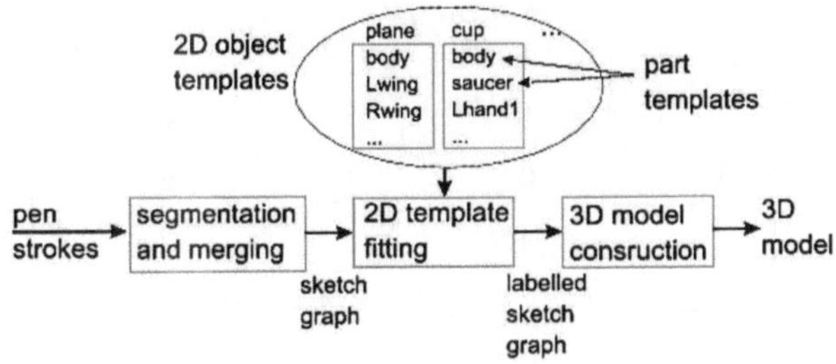

Fig. 6.2 Hierarchy-of-parts method overview

6.3 Hierarchy-of-Parts Models

Many drawings of objects can be modeled as a hierarchy of parts. For example, an airplane drawing may consist of a fuselage (airplane body) with attached wings, and possibly engines attached to the wings. Such a hierarchy also suggests a recognition strategy that begins by locating the root part, e.g., the airplane fuselage in our example, and then proceeds by searching for child parts. Conveniently, knowledge about the spatial relationships between parent-and-child can be exploited to help restrict the search. For example, finding the fuselage of an airplane provides significant clues about where to look for the wings. Optional parts can be supported as long as they are leaf nodes in the part hierarchy.

In the method to be presented, both the templates and the input drawing are represented as graph structures. Strokes are treated as graph edges and stroke end-points are treated as nodes. The nodes can have multiple incident edges from nearby stroke end-points. Finding a part then consists of searching for a well-matched instance of a given part in the graph structure that represents the drawing. In particular, given a tentative correspondence between a template graph and the larger drawing graph, the shapes of the edges which comprise a part should be similar to the shapes of their corresponding counterparts in the drawing.

The end application of our hierarchy-of-parts model is the creation of 3D models from the correctly labeled drawing. As will be elaborated shortly, this assumes the existence of a procedure that constructs a 3D model from sets of measurements taken from a labeled 2D drawing.

A more detailed overview of the method is given in Fig. 6.2 and a specific example of the recognition process is given in Fig. 6.3. The input pen strokes are first preprocessed in order to produce a graph structure. The preprocessing steps consist of (1) adding nodes at the start and end of each stroke; (2) adding nodes at corners and points of local curvature maxima; and (3) merging all nodes that are within a threshold distance of each other. The segmented strokes become the edges of the graph. The resulting sketch graph will not necessarily be fully connected because some parts such as windows and eyes can be drawn in isolation. We also choose not to segment strokes at T-junctions; these typically occur when sub-parts are attached to main object parts and our sketch recognition does not require graph connectivity for the recognition of such sub-parts. Figures 6.3a and b show the strokes of an input sketch and the resulting sketch graph.

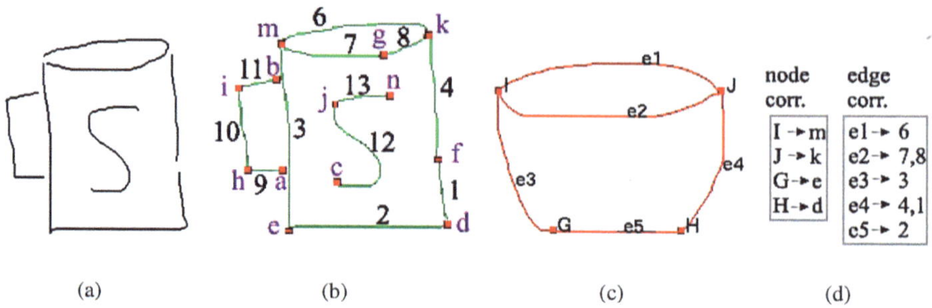

Fig. 6.3 The recognition process. **a** Original sketch, consisting of five strokes; **b** graph computed from sketch strokes; **c** cup-body template graph; **d** computed best-fit correspondences

Given a sketch graph, the next step fits a series of 2D templates to the sketch graph. This happens at two levels: at the higher level, multiple object templates are fitted to the sketch graph and scored for their fit. At a lower level, each object template consists of multiple part templates. The object template supports flexible instantiation of the part templates. Parts may be deemed as mandatory or optional. A choose-one-of-N option may also be specified. For example, a cup template can specify that it may have an optional right handle, which can be either rounded or square, as modeled by two separate templates. The ability to support this type of information distinguishes our approach from other shape recognition approaches that support only a flat hierarchy, i.e., given N fixed templates, find the best-fit template.

Both object and part templates are represented as graphs with pre-specified node locations. Just as in a sketch graph, template graph edges are sketched curves. The actual process of matching part templates is thus accomplished using a search over node correspondences, which are then scored using a curve-matching metric on the best-fit curve correspondences that the node correspondences induce. Figure 6.3c shows a cup-body template and Fig. 6.3(d) lists the best-fit correspondences that were computed for it. These correspondences thus define the labeling of the sketch graph.

Given a best-fit object template and all the instanced part templates that participated in the fit, the last step constructs a 3D model from the labeled 2D sketch. This is done by extracting measurements from the 2D sketch, such as wing length or cup height, as well as by fitting spline curves to particular stroke segments. For example, we use a multi-segment spline curve to smoothly approximate the sides of the airplane fuselage and the shape of the rounded cup handle. Given a priori knowledge of the object class and the extracted measurements that describe this particular desired instance, a 3D model can be constructed. Adding a new object class to the system requires designing a 2D object template, consisting of multiple part templates, as well as developing a procedural means of constructing the 3D shape from the labeled sketch.

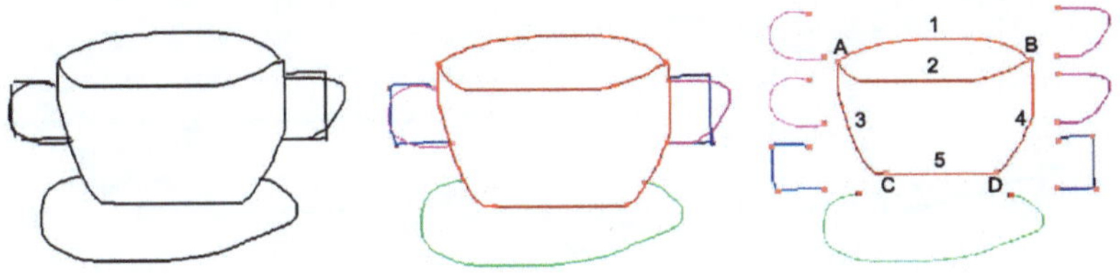

(a) (b) (c)

Fig. 6.4 Construction of the cup template. **a** Sketched strokes; **b** strokes grouped by part **c** the cup-body template and its four key-points five curves, drawn with its child parts separated for clarity. The left-side handles, right-side handles, and saucer are parented by the cup-body curves 3, 4, and 5, respectively

6.3.1 Recognition Algorithm

In describing the algorithm, we first describe the 2D templates and their construction. We then describe how template graphs are matched to the sketch graph using a search over possible correspondences. We define curve feature vectors which are used to evaluate the correspondences. Lastly, we give further details about the hierarchical structure of the templates.

6.3.2 Template Construction

Like the sketch graph, an object template is a graph, consisting of nodes which represent key points on the object, and edges, which represent curves of particular shapes that are expected to be found in a sketch. An example of an object template for a cup is shown in Fig. 6.4. An object template is itself constructed using a sketch, where each stroke becomes an edge in the resulting template graph.[1] Nodes are added at the start and end of each stroke and then merged with nearby neighbors. Figure 6.4a shows the initial sketch for the template. The resulting template graph is shown in Fig. 6.4b. The coloring of this figure also illustrates the next step, which consists of creating multiple part templates from the global template.

Individual part templates are subgraphs of the global template graph. A simple graphical user interface supports their construction. Using a mouse, the user selects a set of edges that constitute a desired part template. The nodes and edges of this subgraph are then saved as the part template definition. Lastly, a hierarchy is established among the parts by designating an edge of an existing part template to serve as the *parent edge* of the new part template. This serves the dual purpose of introducing a hierarchical order for search and instantiating the model parts, as well as a means to encode knowledge about the relative location of parts.

[1] Stroke segmentation is turned off when drawing the template graph.

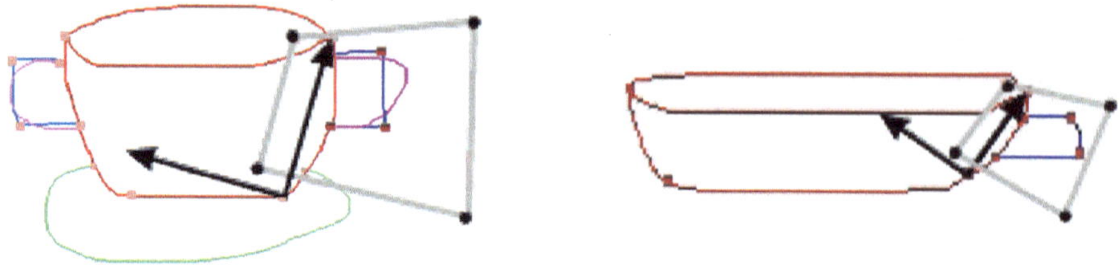

Fig. 6.5 Transformation of the bounding polygon for the right-cup handle. The template is shown on the left, and a sketch on the right. The right-hand edge of the cup-body template serves as the parent edge for this part

Creating a 2D template for a new class of objects requires careful thought, although its actual construction can be done in about 15–20 minutes using the GUI. The template should represent a stereotypical example of the desired class of objects. The template parts also need to provide the information necessary for the appropriate 3D reconstruction of the various parts.

Also associated with the parent edge is a *bounding polygon* (BP), which serves to represent the area in which to search for a part template during the sketch recognition. We use a convex quadrilateral to represent the BP. The BP is specified during the design of a part template by dragging its vertices to the desired locations in the template sketch window. The polygon lives in a coordinate system that is defined by the parent edge. One of the two nodes associated with the edge becomes the origin of this coordinate system, and the other node locates the point $(1, 0)$. As shown in Fig. 6.5, this allows the BP to be transformed to the sketch coordinate system once the parent edge has been labeled in the sketch. If the parent edge is not labeled in the sketch, i.e., the parent part was not instantiated, then there will be no attempts to fit the part templates which use that parent edge. The BP provides the sketch-recognition algorithm with necessary information about the expected relative location of parts and thus serves to greatly constrain the search space of possible correspondences.

The part templates that are at the root of the part hierarchy, such as the plane or cup body, do not have a parent edge. For these parts, the part template explicitly stores an expected location for the graph nodes that comprise the part. By using a normalized coordinate system that is defined by the axis-aligned bounding box of the template sketch, normalized coordinates are computed for each node. The bounding box of a drawn sketch serves to instantiate this normalized coordinate system for the sketch and thereby provides a set of expected locations for the nodes. As shown in Fig. 6.6, the sketch-recognition algorithm will only search for correspondences for a template graph node within a given radius of the expected location. This radius is defined in normalized coordinates (we use $r = 0.3$) and thus typically maps to an elliptical region in the sketch.

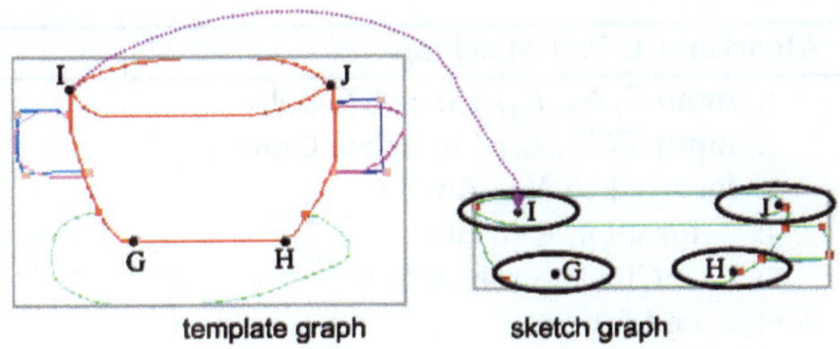

Fig. 6.6 Expected locations in the sketch graph are computed for the template graph nodes of the cup body using a normalized coordinate system based on the bounding box

6.3.3 Template Matching

Given a sketch graph and a set of object templates, the recognition system must determine the template that best fits the given sketch. An object template is in turn made up of multiple part templates, and thus the core of the recognition algorithm is built around a procedure for matching (finding) a given part template to the sketch. A best-fit solution consists of (1) corresponding sketch graph nodes for each template graph node; (2) corresponding *paths* through the object sketch graph for each template edge; and (3) a score that denotes the quality of the fit.

The matching process is summarized in Algorithm 1. As a whole, it consists of iteratively generating and scoring different sets of correspondences between template graph nodes and sketch graph nodes. A total of N_{iter} of such generate-and-score are attempted and the best-scoring configuration is retained. For a given generated set of node correspondences (lines 4–6), a best-fit correspondence is computed for each template edge (lines 8–12). Each template edge, such as the left-hand side of the cup body, should correspond to a *path* in the sketch graph that may traverse multiple connected sketch-graph edges. The sketch strokes may be over-segmented when constructing the sketch graph, or because a particular feature may have been drawn using multiple strokes. Both of these cases can be observed in the example shown in Fig. 6.3.

There may be multiple paths between a given pair of nodes in the sketch graph. It then needs to be determined which of these paths best corresponds to the given template edge. The pathset(n_a, n_b) function determines a set of possible paths, $\mathbb{P}$, between nodes n_a and n_b in the sketch graph using a depth-first graph traversal. In order to limit the number of possible paths, which can become large for a highly connected sketch graph, we bound the search to paths whose ratio of arclength to straight-line distance is less than twice this same ratio as computed for the template edge that we are seeking to match.

Each path $p \in \mathbb{P}$ is tested for similarity with the given template edge that we seek to match (line 10). This is accomplished by computing a *curve feature vector*, $\mathbb{F}$, for the template curve e_{t} and for each path p, and computing a match score $\mathbb{M}(\mathbb{F}(e_{\text{t}}), \mathbb{F}(p))$ based upon these feature vectors. The details of how $\mathbb{F}$ and $\mathbb{M}(\mathbb{F}_1, \mathbb{F}_2)$ are computed are given in the following section.

Several methods could be used to arrive at appropriate choices of node correspondences to be evaluated (lines 4–6). One choice would be to systematically evaluate all permutations of assignments of the N_{t} template nodes to the N_{s} sketch nodes.

Algorithm 1: Part Matching

input $\mathbb{S}(N_s, E_s)$ {Sketch Graph}
input $\mathbb{T}(N_t, E_t)$ {Template Graph}
for $i = 1$ to N_{iter} **do**
  for all $n_t \in N_t$ **do**
    $C[n_t] \leftarrow \text{select}(N_s)$
  end for
  score $\leftarrow 0$
  for all $e_t \in E_t$ **do**
    $\mathbb{P} \leftarrow \text{pathset}(C[n_1(e_t)], C[n_2(e_t)])$
    $p \leftarrow \text{bestMatchPath}(e_t, \mathbb{P})$
    score $\leftarrow$ score $+ \mathbb{M}(e_t, p)$
  end for
  if score $>$ bestScore **then**
    update bestScore and best correspondences
  end if
end for

While this approach is guaranteed to find globally-optimal correspondences, it suffers from a combinatorial explosion. Our system currently employs a stochastic local search method, beginning a search by using a uniform random assignment of sketch nodes to template nodes. Randomized local changes to the current set of correspondences are then evaluated and accepted or rejected in a greedy fashion. If a local maxima is reached, the current best solution is updated if necessary, and the search is restarted at another randomized point in the space of all possible correspondences. We limit the total number of iterations to $N_{iter} = 2000$.

6.3.4 Curve Matching

In order to determine if a given path through the sketch graph is similar in shape to a desired edge of the template that we seek to locate in the sketch, we first define a curve feature vector $\mathbb{F}$ over paths or edges. This is defined as $\mathbb{F} = [f_1 \ f_2 \ f_3]^T$, where $f_1 = \theta$, $f_2 = a/d$, $f_3 = A/d^2$, θ is the angle of the straight line between the curve end-points with respect to the horizontal, a is the arclength of the curve, d is the straight-line distance between the end-points, and A is the signed area between the curve and the straight line. The key parameters are illustrated in Fig. 6.7. Feature f_1 encodes preferences for desired angles, as our sketch-recognition scheme is not rotation-invariant. Features f_2 and f_3 encode information about the type of curve that connects the end-points and provide useful distinctions between a curve that passes above or below the straight line, as well as how much the curve meanders.

We note that a limitation of the curve feature vector is that two curves that are symmetric with respect to the perpendicular bisector of the end-points will have the

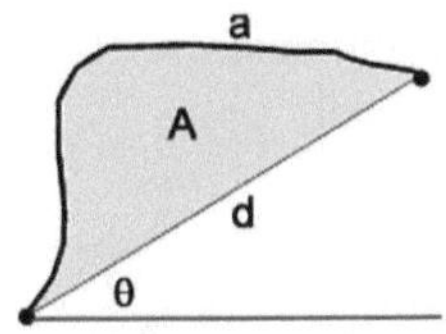

Fig. 6.7 Key parameters used to compute the curve feature vector: arclength a, straight-line distance d, angle θ, and area A

same curve feature vector. Also, the curve-feature vector is potentially problematic for closed curves. For this reason, closed curves are automatically segmented into open curves. An axis-aligned box is computed for the stroke. If $w > h$, the curve is segmented at the points where $x_{\min}$ and $x_{\max}$ occur. Otherwise, the curve is segmented where $y_{\min}$ and $y_{\max}$ occur.

The matching function that compares two curve feature vectors is defined as $\mathbb{M}(F_a, F_b) = k\sum_i w_i g(\sigma_i, f_{i_a} - f_{i_b})$, where $g(\sigma, x) = e^{-0.5(x/\sigma)^2}$ and $k = 1/\sum_i w_i$. The w_i values provide a relative weighting of the feature vector components.[2] The matching function provides a maximum score of 1 for curves that are highly similar, and a score of zero for those that are very dissimilar. σ_i provides a means of scaling the feature vector elements (or rather their differences) to provide a meaningful level of sensitivity.[3] As described in Algorithm 1, the match scores of all curves that make up a part template are summed in order to yield a total match score for the part template.

6.3.5 Template Hierarchy

Object templates are specified in a simple script file and consist of an ordered list of part templates T_j to be matched to the sketch graph, $\mathbb{S}$, as well as an instancing threshold, α_j. The thresholds provide a means to allow parts that have a low best-match score to not be instanced as part of the model. This provides control to the template designer as to whether or not a scribble drawn to the right of the cup should be interpreted as a cup-handle anyhow (low threshold), or as a scribble that is to be ignored (high threshold).

Part templates also provide support for one-of-N matching. For example, it may be possible to interpret a cup-handle as either a rounded handle or a square handle, each of which has its own part template and its own associated 3D-model-construction method. A comma-separated list of part-template names in the object template has a one-of-N semantics, meaning that all the templates in the list should be considered, but only the best-fitting template should be retained.

The scores of part templates can be combined to compute an overall object template score. Currently, we compute a score based on the mean scores of the instantiated part templates. The object template scores allow a sketch to be fitted with all

---

[2] We use $w_1 = 2, w_2 = 1, w_3 = 1$.

[3] We use $\sigma_1 = 22°, \sigma_2 = 0.25, \sigma_3 = 0.1$.

the possible object templates, with only the best-fit object template being used to instantiate the 3D model.

6.3.6 Application to 3D Model Construction

Once the sketch recognition is complete, a 3D model is constructed in a procedural fashion. This procedural construction is hard-coded for each object class. We have found that this is generally the most time-consuming aspect of adding a new object class. We now discuss the construction rules used for each object class.

The cup construction proceeds as follows. A centerline is estimated from the axis-aligned bounding box for the cup-body strokes. A spline is fitted to the sketched curves segments that make up the right side. A surface of revolution is then constructed from the centerline and the fitted spline. The saucer is similarly constructed as a surface of revolution from a spline that is fitted to the appropriate sketched curves. The 3D handle is constructed by sweeping a predefined 3D cross-section along a spline that is fitted to the sketched handle. Adjustments are made to the positions of the saucer and the handle(s) so that these parts are contacting the body even if there are gaps that exists in the sketch. Unrecognized strokes that are drawn over the region of the cup body are projected onto the cup body as annotations, as shown in Fig. 6.1b.

Our airplane model assumes the existence of two recognized sketches of traditional orthographic views: a side view and a top view. These each have their own separate template. The information from both labeled sketches is then combined in the model building process. The system can also accept a top view alone, in which case default assumptions are made about the fuselage and the tail.

The airplane fuselage has a default cross-sectional shape that is uniformly scaled as it is swept along the spline curves defined by the fuselage side, top, and bottom curves. The wings and horizontal stabilizers are constructed using a swept-airfoil cross-section. The tail fin has a similar swept construction. Engines are instanced as copies of a single 3D engine model, scaled and translated to match the top-view sketch. Left–right symmetry is enforced in the final model. The model building process must also resolve any conflicts between the top view and the side view, such as the length of the fuselage. This is handled by scaling one of the views so that the fuselage lengths matches the other view.

The 3D fish model consists of a body, dorsal fin, anal fin, a pair of pectoral fins, and a pair of pelvic fins. Top and bottom splines are fitted to the top and bottom of the body, starting at the front tip of the fish and ending at the top and bottom of the caudal fin, respectively. A default elliptical cross-sectional shape is then swept from front-to-back along these splines, undergoing uniform scaling as necessary. This swept surface is tapered to end with zero-width at the beginning of the caudal fin, which is identified as the narrowest part of the right-half of the fish. All the fins, including the caudal fin, are modeled as polygons. The pectoral and pelvic fins are tilted at predefined angles away from the body.

Table 6.1 List of template parts used to build the cup, plane, and fish templates. n and e denote the number of nodes and edges in the part template graphs, respectively

plane	n	e	cup	n	e	fish	n	e
body	2	2	body	4	5	body	3	3
Lwing	4	3	saucer	2	1	topfin	2	1
Rwing	4	3	RHr1	2	1	midfin	2	1
Ltail	4	3	RHr2	2	1	eye	2	2
Rtail	4	3	LHr1	2	1	botfin1	2	1
Leng	2	1	LHr2	2	1	botfin2	2	1
Reng	2	1	RHs	4	3			
Leng2	2	1	LHs	4	3			
Reng2	2	1						

6.3.7 Results and Discussion

The current recognition process requires on the order of one second to match an object template hierarchy against a sketch, as measured on an 800 MHz TabletPC. The current sketching interface consists of a sketch area, an area for displaying the resulting 3D model, and a button panel. The user draws their desired sketch in the sketch area and hits a 'Recognize' button. The interface supports a progressive workflow if this is desired. The recognition and model building can thus be invoked at any time for whatever parts that have currently been drawn. One caveat is that parts such as the handles of the cup cannot be recognized in isolation. The parent part must first be successfully instantiated.

We have tested the system using three classes of objects: cups, planes, and fish. Table 6.1 gives the list of part templates used for each object template. While many of the examples we show illustrate some kind of symmetry, we note that this is not a requirement of the system.

The most effective mode of use for our system is one in which the user can tell the system which class of objects is being drawn, and thus the system knows in advance which object template hierarchy to match against the drawn sketch. Another mode that we support is to have the system do a linear search through each of the available object templates in turn and then instantiate the 3D object corresponding to the best-fit object template.

Images can be loaded into the background to use as a reference for tracing a particular airplane, cup, or fish. At the same time, the model building can extract a texture map from the background image if this is desired. This thus supports quick-and-dirty construction of models from photographs.

The cup template represents the prototypical view that is commonly used to draw or photograph a cup. A variety of cups and mugs modeled using our system are shown in Fig. 6.8. The template supports left and right rounded handles and square handles. A second left and right rounded handle can also be recognized, which can serve to either define inside and outside edges for the handle, or as a second rounded handle. In our implementation, it is the model building process that distinguishes

Fig. 6.8 The cup template graph, and sketches of cups and wine glasses shown together with the synthesized 3D models

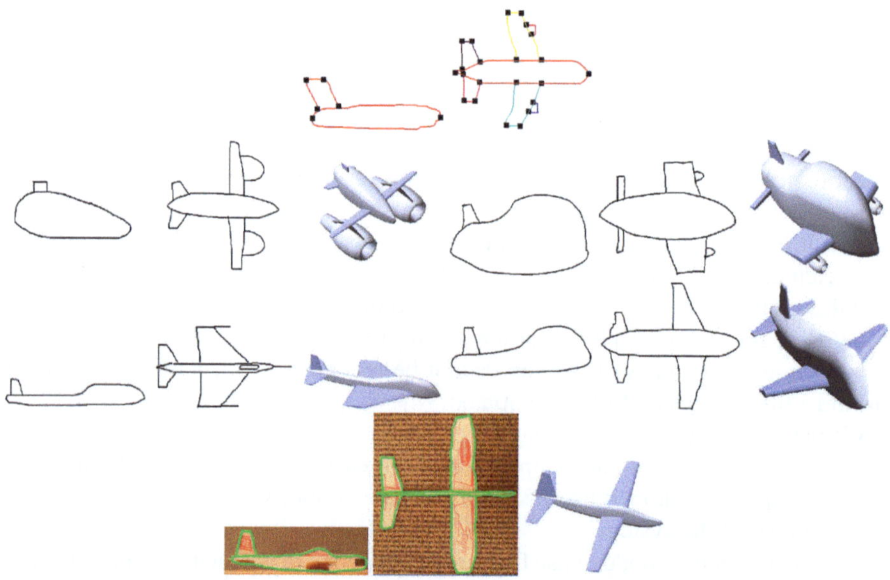

Fig. 6.9 The airplane side-view and top-view templates, and five examples of input-sketches shown together with the resulting 3D models

between these two cases. For single-curve handles, a default handle width and cross-section is assumed. For double-curve handles, a rounded-rectangular cross-section is assumed that has fixed depth but varies in width according to the drawn curves.

Figure 6.9 show a number of sketches and the resulting 3D airplane models. The current implementation assumes that the side-view sketch is drawn and recognized first. The 3D model is then instanced when the top-view sketch is drawn and recognized.

Figure 6.10 shows two examples of fish that have been constructed by tracing over photographs of fish. The texture is then lifted from the images and applied to the 3D models.

Fig. 6.10 The fish template and two fish models that were created by tracing over photographs

6.3.8 Failure Modes

Our system has a number of failure modes. First, the curve feature vector and the distance metric associated with it does not always function as desired. For example, element f_1, which represents the angle of the straight line between the curve's endpoints, is a very meaningful feature for the fuselage lines of an airplane, which are expected to be horizontal, but is a weak feature for the identification of the fish fins, which can occur at various points on the body. Second, the bounding box attached to the parent part edge can be a fairly weak indicator of expected part location because of its binary nature. A more smoothly-varying model of expected location, as found in some pictorial structure models, would perhaps provide better performance.

Some sketches are also not recognized because of sloppiness in sketches that results in disconnected strokes. Increasing the threshold distance within which sketch-graph nodes are merged allows for more of such gaps to be bridges, but this comes at the expense of losing further detail in the drawn parts because strokes which were intended to be distinct may be merged together. The key points in the curves that become the nodes of the sketch graph are not always extracted as desired. The curve feature vector currently has no notion of the smoothness of the curve, and thus smooth template curves may be matched to jagged paths through the sketch graph without penalty, assuming that the remaining curve features match well.

6.3.9 Comparison with Template Editing

For any given 3D model generated by our system, the same result could also in principle be achieved by directly editing the original template curves. We suggest drawing is often easier than template manipulation. Consider the case of the cup template, which has four handles and a saucer, as shown in Fig. 6.4. A great many control points would need to be repositioned to create the mugs and vases shown in Fig. 6.8, whereas it can be drawn in a matter of seconds. The user also has to understand what control points are, why there are two left handles and two right handles, has to delete three of these, and then move the control points on the remaining handle in order to achieve the squarish right handle that is finally desired. Second, a recognition-based approach minimizes what the user needs to know and hides the underlying representation and assumptions used to construct the 3D model.

6.3.10 Scalability

Our solution is scalable with the addition of more templates. To be efficient with a large number of templates would require a separate object-classification step in order to identify a small set of candidate object classes to which the full template match could then be applied. While our system still has robustness issues, it can support large within-class variations. For example, our cup template can model a large variety of cup or mug types and shapes (Figs. 6.1b and 6.8). Similarly, our airplane template supports a significant variety of shapes (Figs. 6.1b and 6.9). With respect to the use of templates, it is clear that some form of prior knowledge is essential for sketch or line-drawing recognition, and we choose to embody this prior knowledge in our 2D templates.

The recognition success improves if users have some familiarity with the template. At the start of the project, we collected sketch data on a TabletPC with purposely-vague instructions by asking users with no knowledge of the templates to "draw a cup," or "draw a plane." Many of the resulting cup sketches can be correctly used by our system to build the expected 3D models. However, many of the original airplane drawings can not be processed without some errors.

6.4 Constellation of Parts Models

As its name would imply, the constellation of parts model places some emphasis on the overall picture formed by the spatial location of parts with respect to each other. Thus, even in situations where the parts themselves may be nondescript, e.g., a nose drawn as a single point, a constellation model can label the parts by using knowledge of the expected spatial relations between the parts. For example, in a drawing of a face, the nose can be expected to lie between the eyes and mouth. An example constellation model of a face object is shown in Fig. 6.11.

The information required to assign a label to a part may lie partly with its shape and partly with its spatial location relative to other parts. Statistical models provide a principled way to combine these different types of clues. Recognition is modeled as finding the maximum-likelihood interpretation of the data (the drawing) with respect to the model (the relevant statistical parameters as derived from training data). We use statistical models for part shapes and for pairwise relations between parts.

The constellation of parts (COP) model is different in several respects from the hierarchy-of-parts (HOP) model. Unlike the graph-based representation used in HOP, there is no reliance on connectivity information. Parts in a COP model can be fully disconnected. The COP model supports optional parts by defining them in relation to all the mandatory parts. A limitation is that the label assigned to one optional part cannot serve as a clue to help label another optional part; optional parts cannot 'see' each other. A particular limitation of the COP model is that we currently assume each drawn stroke to be a part. Later we describe possible ways of removing this limiting assumption.

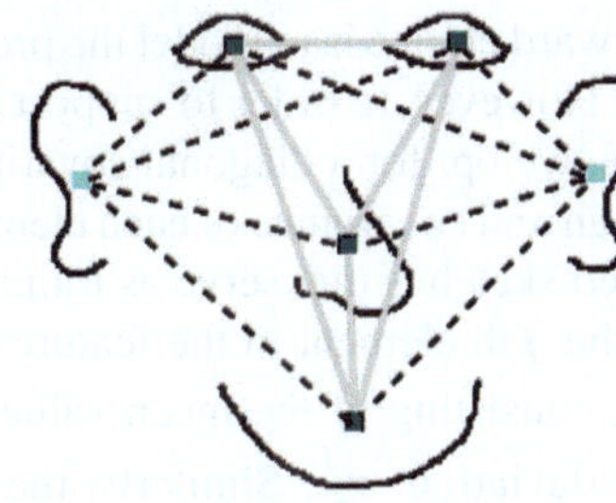

Fig. 6.11 Example constellation model for a sketched face, showing the pairwise interactions. In this example, the left eye, right eye, mouth, and nose are mandatory and thus have complete pairwise interactions. The left ear and right ear are optional and thus have pairwise interactions with all mandatory parts but not with each other

We define a four-element feature vector for individual object parts: $\mathcal{F} = [x\ y\ d\ \beta]$ where (x, y) are the location of the center of the axis-aligned bounding-box (AABB) of a stroke, as measured in image coordinates normalized to $x, y \in [0, 1]$; d is the normalized coordinate length of the AABB diagonal; and $\beta = \cos(\phi)$, with ϕ being the angle of the AABB diagonal with respect to the x-axis.

Similarly, we choose a four-element feature vector for part pairs defined by $\mathcal{G}_{ab} = [\Delta x_{ab}\ \Delta y_{ab}\ D_{ab}\ D_{ba}]$, where $\Delta x = x_a - x_b$ and $\Delta y = y_a - y_b$ define the relative positions of the AABB centers of strokes a and b in normalized coordinates, D_{ab} is the minimum distance between the end-points of stroke a and any point on stroke b, and D_{ba} is the minimum distance between the end-points of stroke b and any point on stroke a. In general, $\mathcal{G}_{ab} \neq \mathcal{G}_{ba}$.

Full constellation models do not scale well with the number of parts, n, since they result in $O(n^2)$ pairwise features. We choose to alleviate this by characterizing each label as mandatory or optional. Individual features are computed for both mandatory and optional parts. However, pairwise features are only computed if one or both of the labels in the pair corresponds to a mandatory part. In general it is possible to further reduce the number of pairwise features by searching for subsets that yield good recognition performance [3].

The sketch-recognition process has two phases, the first of which searches the space of possible mandatory label assignments, and the second, which searches for optional labels for the remaining unlabeled strokes. In this way the mandatory labels provide contextual location information necessary for assigning appropriate labels to the potentially large number of optional parts. We describe the search algorithm in the following section.

6.4.1 Learning the Model

An object class model is represented using a probability distribution over the features, e.g., object parts and object part pairs, as learned from a set of example labeled sketches. A straightforward choice is to model the probability distributions using multi-variate Gaussians. However, in order to support recognition from a small number of training examples, we opt for a diagonal covariance matrix. Thus we independently compute the mean and covariance of each element of the feature vectors $\mathcal{F}$ and $\mathcal{G}$ for the set of labeled sketches that serve as training data. More explicitly, the probabilistic model for the fth element in the feature vector of a label ℓ is defined by the parameters θ_ℓ^f, consisting of the mean value for the feature element, μ_ℓ^f, as well as the standard deviation, σ_ℓ^f. Similarly, the pair feature parameters, $\theta_{\ell j}^f$, are given by $\langle \mu_{\ell j}^f, \sigma_{\ell j}^f \rangle$.

6.4.2 Labeling Likelihood

The best match is determined by finding the most likely stroke labeling, as measured according to the model parameters learned from the example drawings. The probability of a given labeling L is given by the product of the individual stroke labeling likelihoods, further multiplied by the product of all labeled stroke pair likelihoods. This can be expressed as:

$$P(L \mid \theta) = \prod_{i=1}^{N} \prod_{\ell=1}^{M} P(\mathcal{F}_i \mid \theta_\ell)^{\delta_{i\ell}} \prod_{j=1}^{m} \prod_{k=1}^{N} P(\mathcal{G}_{ik} \mid \theta_{\ell j})^{\delta_{kj}} \tag{1}$$

In the above expression, the assignment of strokes to labels is modeled as a label-assignment matrix δ, with $\delta_{i\ell} = 1$ if stroke i is assigned label ℓ, and $\delta_{i\ell} = 0$ otherwise. The exponentiation using the δ values is thus a notational convenience for compactly representing stroke-label assignments. All terms having an exponent of $\delta = 0$ evaluate to 1 and thus effectively drop out of the likelihood computation. The label-assignment matrix has imposed upon it the appropriate restriction that each stroke can be assigned only one label, and that mandatory labels should map to a unique stroke. N is the number of strokes, M is the number of labels, and m is the number of mandatory labels. $P(\mathcal{F}_i \mid \theta_\ell)$ models the likelihood of stroke i having label ℓ. Similarly, $P(\mathcal{G}_{ik} \mid \theta_{\ell j})$ models the likelihood of the stroke pair (i, k) having the labeling (ℓ, j). The above omits the normalizing constant $P(\theta)$, which does not affect the ML solution. We assume a uniform prior on the likelihood of parts appearing in a sketch.

The interior of the first term, $P(\mathcal{F}_i \mid \theta_\ell)^{\delta_{i\ell}}$, represents the probability of stroke i having label ℓ. This is computed for all strokes, as given by the outside product. The interior of the second term, $P(\mathcal{G}_{ik} \mid \theta_{\ell j})^{\delta_{kj}}$, represents the probability of stroke i in relation to all the mandatory parts, as measured by the pairwise feature vectors. Thus if a stroke is labeled as a right ear but it is located below the mouth, then it is this term that will give that labeling a low likelihood. Pairwise relations are computed with respect to all mandatory parts, as given by the outside product. The inside product is a notational convenience for expressing the stroke-label assignment for the mandatory strokes.

6.4.3 Recognition Algorithm

A maximum-likelihood (ML) search procedure finds the most plausible labeling for all strokes that appear in the image. For a simple application of a constellation model having n strokes and m independent object part labels, there are m^n possible assignments that could in principle be explored, and each assignment configuration requires evaluating $O(n^2)$ pairwise interactions. Further complications arise because some strokes may not have plausible labels, and some object parts (i.e., labels) may not be found in a given sketch, or may have multiple instances. In order to allow for these complications, and to alleviate the computational cost associated with the exponential number of matches, the search over possible label assignments has two phases.

The first search phase involves labeling strokes that correspond only to the mandatory object parts and then committing to those labels. This is followed by a linear search through the optional labels for the recognition of the remaining unlabeled strokes. Both search phases use the same objective function, namely the likelihood as described in the previous section.

The search over possible label assignments is carried out using a branch-and-bound search tree. Each node in the search tree represents a partial labeling of the sketch. A node at depth i in the tree has found corresponding strokes for labels 1 through i. Each node in the tree has a current assigned likelihood which is determined from the product of individual stroke-label likelihoods for the i assigned labels, as well as all the pairwise interaction likelihoods among all labeled parts.

To advance the search, a node is extended by evaluating all possible assignments of mandatory label $i+1$ to unlabeled strokes. During the search, the algorithm tracks the cost of the best (most likely) known complete assignment of mandatory labels. The cost is used to bound branches of the search. Each completed search branch can potentially result in a better bound to restrict the remaining search.

Branches of the search tree can only be bounded once a complete assignment of mandatory labels is found. If the number of strokes or mandatory labels is high, finding complete assignments is prohibitively slow. We employ two approaches to further constrain the search: multipass thresholding and hard constraints.

With multipass thresholding, we bound branches of the search before encountering a full labeling. If a node's likelihood, as computed by its current partial set of label assignments, is lower than a specified threshold α, that search branch is terminated. We use multiple passes, beginning with an optimistic threshold. That is, at first, we assume all feature likelihoods in a match will be very high. This can result in an overly restrictive search that may lead to no complete labellings being found. However, this is quick to compute in comparison to a full search, or a search with a more pessimistic bound.

Upon failure to find a successful complete label assignment, each successive pass of the branch-and-bound search uses a progressively more pessimistic assumption until complete solutions are found. The first complete solutions found are then used as a good bound for a final search pass wherein the threshold can be as pessimistic as is desired. We begin with a threshold corresponding to $P(\mu + 1.3\sigma)$ for each feature element likelihood, and on each successive pass we scale this by $2/3$. Multipass thresholding makes the search feasible for a large number of strokes and mandatory labels and also results in fast labeling for 'good' sketches while supporting more extensive searches through the hypothesis space for assigning labels to more ambiguous sketches.

In lieu of a threshold based on the likelihood-to-date for the partial assignments, an alternative that we have found to be equally successful is to threshold based on individual part and pair likelihoods. Thus, a branch is terminated when it involves any individual likelihood that falls below a threshold β. For the examples shown in the paper, this is the type of multipass thresholding that we apply.

Hard constraints can be seen as a variant on the type of thresholding just described. For a particular object class, it may be the case that one feature label should always satisfy a particular relation with respect to another. For example, the nose could be required to always be located above the mouth in a face sketch. For our implementation, we infer *above*, *below*, *left*, and *right* relationships from the example sketches wherever they can be found. Thus, if the nose AABB center appears above the mouth AABB center in all the example sketches, this will be added as a hard constraint. An object class may have many such constraints between labeled parts.

6.4.4 Results and Discussion

We have tested the method on the five classes of objects listed in Table 6.2. These have 7–15 labels and have been tested on drawings having 3–200 strokes. We use on the order of 20–60 training examples for each class. Figures 6.1a, 6.12, 6.13, 6.14, and 6.15 show training sketches and successful test sketches. The recognition time is typically 0.01–2.5 s for the shown examples, with most of this time being spent on initialization. During initialization, a feature vector $\mathcal{F}$ is pre-computed for all strokes and another feature vector $\mathcal{G}$ for all stroke pairs of the input sketch. For an example face sketch containing 171 strokes, the recognition takes a total of 1.97 seconds, with 80% of the computation time spent on initialization, 18% on searching for mandatory labels, and 2% on finding labels for the optional parts. Spurious strokes can be rejected by placing a threshold on the fit of optional stroke labels.

Hard constraints, as described previously, may significantly reduce recognition times. However, when they are automatically inferred from training data, the system may falsely register the existence of a hard constraint. For example, few training sketches may result in the system falsely believing that the left eye is always below a right eyelash. However, such a situation could easily occur in a cartoon-style face sketch or a somewhat asymmetric sketch. This could be viewed as an indication that more training data are required.

Figure 6.16 shows a set of failure examples, meaning that one or more strokes are mislabeled. Recognition can go wrong in several ways: (1) inability to find suitable mandatory strokes because of the hard constraints; (2) mislabeling of a mandatory stroke, leading to havoc with the remaining strokes; (3) mislabeling of optional

Table 6.2 Object classes

Class	Mandatory labels	Optional labels
faces	5	10
flowers	2	5
sailboats	3	5
airplanes	3	4
characters	7	8

Fig. 6.12 **a** Flower sketch training examples. The mandatory labels are *pot, stem, stigma*; the optional labels are *saucer, petal, leaf, and sepal.* **b** Flower sketches recognized using our system

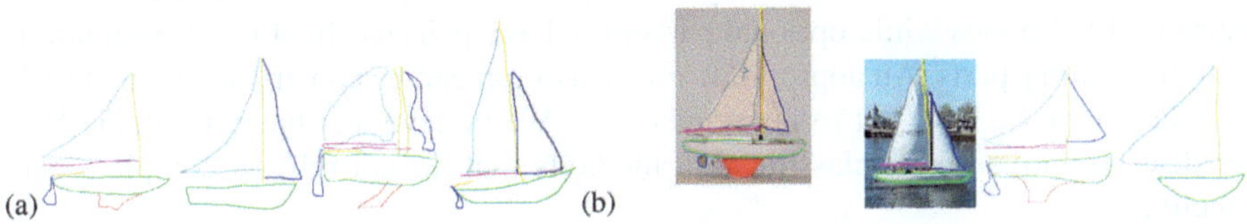

Fig. 6.13 **a** Sailboat sketch training examples. The mandatory labels are *hull, main-sail, mast*; the optional labels are *jib, boom, keel, rudder, tiller*. **b** Sailboat sketches recognized using our system

strokes. In practice, errors of type (1) are rare and imply a lack of training data. Errors of type (2) can occur if unusual strokes occur that affect the overall bounding box and therefore result in atypical normalized coordinates. This might occur for adding overly long or bushy hair in face sketches, or certain atypical stems in flower sketches. Errors of type (3) most commonly occur when there are few mandatory strokes, such as for the sailboats or flowers. The model does not currently give any consideration to relationships between optional parts. Lastly, other mislabelings can be attributed to impoverished probability distribution models and inadequate feature vectors.

In order to evaluate the utility of the multipass thresholding technique, we test the recognition of sketches with and without thresholding. Table 6.3 shows the results of this experiment. In all cases, the multipass thresholding results in significantly lower computation times. Most notable is a 103-stroke face sketch which took only 1.242 seconds to recognize with thresholding, yet without thresholding, failed to find a labeling within 9 hours.

Table 6.3 Computation times for recognition algorithm with and without the multipass technique

Class	Num strokes	With multipass (s)	Without multipass (s)
face	103	1.242	>9 hours
flower	54	0.46	0.98
sailboat	8	0.02	0.03
airplane	21	0.08	0.1
character	18	0.12	126.69

Our system assumes a uniform prior for the a priori likelihood of optional parts. This decision stems in part from our expectation that a small number of training sketches will not necessarily reflect the probability of parts appearing in future sketches. Thus, the identity of parts depends solely on their shape and fit as modeled by the constellation model.

We define the recognition of a sketch to be the labeling of the individual parts of a sketch that is of a known object class. If the class of the input sketch is unknown, the maximum-likelihood fit could be determined for each of a list of object classes in order to provide information about the object class. The ML log-likelihoods that come from each class are not directly comparable, however, because object classes differ in their number of mandatory parts. Mandatory parts have fully connected pairwise likelihoods while optional parts only have pairwise likelihoods in relation with mandatory parts. An appropriate normalization can be constructed to deal with this, although we have yet to investigate this. We believe that there are likely better discriminative object-classification methods that do not rely on complete part labeling.

It may be possible to further improve on the mean search time for the branch-and-bound algorithm by using variants of the A* algorithm. This involves expanding non-terminal nodes in the search in an order sorted by their cost-to-date. However, much of the leverage of A* comes from the ability to generate a suitable always-optimistic cost-to-go function. Unfortunately this provides little leverage given that it is possible that the remaining unlabeled strokes could perfectly match the mean features.

We have presented a system that adapts *constellation* or *pictorial structure* models from the computer vision literature for flexible sketch recognition. Adaptations include support for optional parts, the use of an efficient multipass branch-and-bound search for exploring the space of possible interpretations, and the construction of individual and pairwise features suitable for sketch recognition.

In the current system we have only experimented with a limited number of individual and pairwise features. It is likely that features other than those we have proposed will be useful in producing a more robust system. Given a large set of possible features and appropriate data sets, it should be possible to run an offline process that determines the k most informative features (individual and pairwise). How to best represent the probability distributions for a given set of features is a further open problem. Our model of independent, normally-distributed features is well

(a)

(b)

Fig. 6.14 **a** Character sketch training examples. The mandatory labels are *head*, *torso*, *thigh*, *shin*, *foot*, *upper-arm*, *lower-arm*; the optional labels are *hat*, *neck*, *hand*, *nose*, *eye*, *pupil*, *mouth*, *ear*. **b** Character sketches recognized using our system

(a)

(b)

Fig. 6.15 **a** Airplane sketch examples. The mandatory labels are *fuselage*, *left-wing*, *right-wing*; the optional labels are *left-stabilizer*, *right-stabilizer*, *left-engine*, *right-engine*, *propeller*, *window*, *tail-fin*. **b** Airplane sketches recognized using our system

suited for systems relying on only a small set of example labeled sketches. However, multi-variate Gaussian models or mixtures of Gaussians may provide better results for larger data sets, at the expense of requiring a larger number of labeled examples.

Fig. 6.16 Failure modes of our system. Mislabeling can be caused by lack of training sketches and inadequate features

6.5 Conclusions

Parts-based models allow for significant flexibility in recognizing sketches which are neither 'diagrammatic' (in the sense of circuit diagrams or box-and-arrow diagrams) nor necessarily representative of 3D models. Recognition for these models needs to rely on strong prior information about the expected object classes. Object and parts-of-object recognition can naturally be described as a search problem, with the goal of finding assigned labels for parts that are mutually compatible, as defined by the template model.

There remains significant work to be done in this area. Robustness, efficiency, model flexibility, and scalability can all likely be improved upon. Parts and part hypotheses should ideally share the same representations as objects. This is not the case for the algorithms we have presented. Currently, working with a large number of strokes (> 50) remains problematic when seeking to maintain interactive recognition. Gestalt principles may provide a promising approach for grouping strokes into parts or objects, which would greatly help the flexibility and speed of the recognition approaches. The described recognition processes are largely top–down: HOP uses a fixed-order traversal of the template part hierarchy, while COP searches through the space of mandatory label assignments in a fixed order to construct the search tree. In both cases this ignores bottom–up information that could be used to reorder the search to begin with the strokes which have likely bindings to particular labels, thereby strongly constraining the search early on.

It is intriguing to speculate that there may eventually be a convergence among techniques for diagram recognition, parts-based drawing recognition, 3D reconstruction from 2D drawings, and the broad range of computer vision problems.

References

1. Alvarado, C., Davis, R.: Sketchread: a multi-domain sketch recognition engine. In: UIST '04 ACM Symposium on User Interface Software and Technology, pp. 23–32 (2004)
2. Belongie, S., Malik, J.: Shape matching and object recognition using shape contexts. IEEE Transactions on Pattern Analysis and Machine Intelligence **24**(24), 509–522 (2002)
3. Crandall, D., Felzenszwalb, P.F., Huttenlocher, D.P.: Spatial priors for part-based recognition using statistical models. In: Proceedings of CVPR, pp. 10–17 (2005)
4. Felzenszwalb, P.F., Huttenlocher, D.P.: Pictorial structures for object recognition. International Journal of Computer Vision **61**(1), 55–79 (2005)
5. Fischler, M.A., Elschlager, R.A.: The representation and matching of pictorial structures. IEEE Transactions on Computers **22**(1) (1973)

6. Kaelbling, L.P., Lozano-Perez, T.: Learning three-dimensional shape models for sketch recognition. Technical Report, MIT CSAIL, January 2005
7. Kara, L.B., Stahovich, T.F.: Hierarchical parsing and recognition of hand-sketched diagrams. In: Proceedings of UIST'04 (2004)
8. Mackenzie, G., Alechina, N.: Classifying sketches of animals using an agent-based system. In: Proceedings of the 10th International Conference CAIP. Springer Lecture Notes in Computer Science, vol. 2756, pp. 521–529. Springer, Berlin (2003)
9. Mahoney, J.V., Fromherz, M.P.J.: Three main concerns in sketch recognition and an approach to addressing them. In: AAAI Spring Symposium on Sketch Understanding (2002)
10. Oltmans, M., Alvarado, C., Davis, R.: Etcha sketches: Lessons learned from collecting sketch data. In: Making Pen-Based Interaction Intelligent and Natural. AAAI Fall Symposium (2004)
11. Qi, Y., Szummer, M., Minka, T.P.: Diagram structure recognition by Bayesian conditional random fields. In: IEEE International Conference on Computer Vision and Pattern Recognition (CVPR) (2005)
12. Rubine, D.: Specifying gestures by example. In: SIGGRAPH '91, pp. 329–337 (1991)
13. Saund, E., Mahoney, J., Fleet, D., Larner, D., Lank, E.: Perceptual organization as a foundation for intelligent sketch editing. In: AAAI Spring Symposium on Sketch Understanding (2002)
14. Sezgin, T.M., Davis, R.: HMM-based efficient sketch recognition. In: Proceedings of the International Conferences on Intelligent User Interfaces (IUI'05), pp. 281–283, 9–12 January 2005. ACM Press, New York (2005)
15. Shilman, M., Viola, P.: Spatial recognition and grouping of text and graphics. In: Eurographics Workshop on Sketch-Based Interfaces and Modeling (2004)

Chapter 7
Sketch-based Retrieval of Vector Drawings

Manuel J. Fonseca, Alfredo Ferreira, and Joaquim A. Jorge

7.1 Introduction

Ready made components or previously created objects are often re-used when creating new documents. Typically, users find these elements manually by browsing a set of directories or categories, or more recently resorting to some kind of information retrieval system. Although there are different types of retrieval systems the most useful ones rely on information automatically extracted from content rather than those that require manual insertion of meta-data to support further searching.

Content-based retrieval of pictorial data, such as digital images, drawings or graphics, rely mainly on their content. Raster (bitmap) images are typically described using primitive features such as color, shape and texture, which can be automatically extracted using simple processing techniques [24].

Vector drawings, on the other hand, have a richer description, a more complex structure and a natural hierarchy requiring different techniques from those developed for raster images.

Currently there are several solutions to retrieve vector drawings. Some rely only on contours [1]; others only deal with simple figures [13, 16, 19]; and those that support more complexity perform queries using existing examples rather than using sketch-based interaction [14, 20, 23].

A solution for searching and retrieving drawings should offer a simple and efficient query mechanism based on sketches. Users should be able to easily convey the idea of what they want to find taking advantage of their visual memory and sketching abilities. To that end, a solution must be based on algorithms and techniques

M.J. Fonseca (✉) · A. Ferreira · J.A. Jorge
INESC-ID/TU Lisbon, R. Alves Redol, 9, 1000-029 Lisboa, Portugal
e-mail: mjf@inesc-id.pt

A. Ferreira
e-mail: alfredo.ferreira@inesc-id.pt

J.A. Jorge
e-mail: jaj@inesc-id.pt

J. Jorge, F. Samavati (eds.), *Sketch-based Interfaces and Modeling*,
DOI 10.1007/978-1-84882-812-4_7,

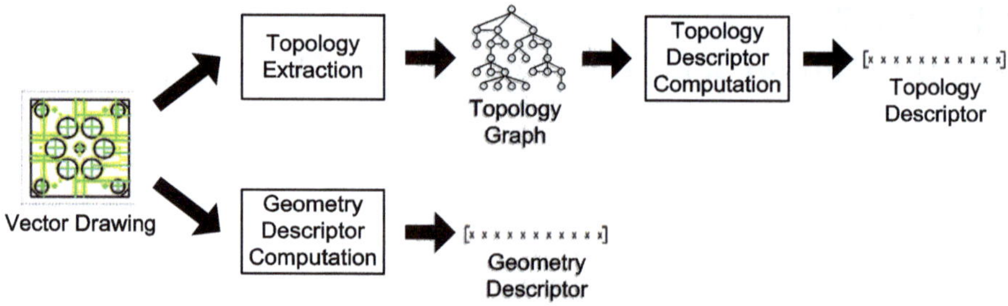

Fig. 7.1 Block decomposition to describe drawing content, using topology and geometry

developed for sketch-based interfaces using shape and/or pattern recognition. The solution described here for sketch-based retrieval of vector drawings relies on a recognition library called CALI [9], which was developed to identify hand-drawn sketches and to support creation of calligraphic interfaces. It was later adapted to produce descriptors, which identify the geometry of drawings and sketched queries by using internal geometric features in the form of a vector.

In this chapter, we describe a solution for sketch-based retrieval of complex vector drawings that describe content with topology and geometry. In Sect. 7.2 we start by describing the mechanism used to extract information from content and the multilevel description scheme to support partial matching. Section 7.3 describes two applications. One for retrieving technical 2D drawings and another for clip art figures. In Sect. 7.4 we describe the new paradigm of implicit retrieval, which combines sketch-based modeling techniques with retrieval methods to enrich the modeling process. Finally, Sect. 7.5 presents some conclusions.

7.2 Feature Extraction from Sketches and Drawings

As we mentioned before, vector drawings require different approaches from raster images, which rely mainly on color and texture information. Simple vector drawings are usually described using only shape contour information. However, complex drawings, such as, technical 2D and 3D CAD drawings or clip arts contain several entities, which would be ignored by just using their contour. Moreover, the way these visual elements are spatially arranged convey relevant information that must be used to describe a drawing's content. Additionally, query-by-example and sketch-based queries require different techniques for interpretation and comparison with stored drawings. Thus, to describe the content of sketched queries and complex vector drawings we developed an approach that uses **Topology**—a global feature that describes the spatial arrangement of drawings, and **Geometry**—a local feature, which describes the shape of the visual entities present in the drawing (see Fig. 7.1).

In this section we describe the topological information extracted from drawings and the mechanism used to convert it into feature vectors. Afterward, we present the approach used to code the geometry of the visual elements in the drawing.

7.2.1 *Topology*

Content-Based Retrieval systems use information extracted from objects and spatial relationships. Thus spatial information should be preserved during the classification process so that users can easily retrieve those drawings from the database. The approach presented here not only preserves topological information, but uses it to index drawings in a database. We choose to index by topology because it is a global feature of drawings providing us with a good characteristic to distinguish figures from each other. This way the searching process starts by selecting drawings with a similar topology to the sketched query (reducing the number of candidate results) and then computes the geometric similarity between them.

Extracted topological information is combined in a Topology Graph. This graph describes the global topology among all elements in a drawing. On the one hand, using graphs to describe topology is a good solution, but on the other, comparing graphs is a complex task. Since graph isomorphism is a Nondeterministic Polynomial time complete (NP-complete) problem [30], we try to avoid its computation, by reducing the problem to the calculation of distances between descriptors. To that end, we map topology graphs into multidimensional vectors and perform comparisons between these to find similar graphs.

Additionally, to make the comparison of simple sketches and complex drawings possible, we create several topological descriptors from the same topology graph of a figure. Each descriptor represents a subpart or level of detail of the drawing. In this way, we end up with several descriptors for a single figure. This allows comparison of different complexity queries with various representations of the same drawing and facilitates partial matching.

In the remainder of this section, we identify the more relevant topological relationships and show how they are combined to create a topology graph. Next, we demonstrate how topology graphs are mapped into multidimensional vectors and present the multilevel description scheme to describe complex drawings hierarchically by level of detail. Finally, we introduce an improvement to the topology graph in order to code spatial proximity between visual elements of drawings.

Topological Relationships Spatial relationships may be classified into *directional* and *topological* relations. The most frequently used directional relationships are `North`, `South`, `East`, `West`, `NorthEast`, `NorthWest`, `South East` and `SouthWest`. For topological relationships Egenhofer [3, 4] presented a set of eight relations between two planar regions, namely `Disjoint`, `Meet`, `Overlap`, `Contain`, `Inside`, `Cover`, `Covered-By` and `Equal` as illustrated in Fig. 7.2.

We decided to restrict spatial relationships to those that are independent of translation and rotation of drawings. We only consider topological relationships as using directional does not guarantee independence of transformation. Moreover, to both make our approach less restrictive and the topology graph simpler we simplified the topological relationships defined by Egenhofer. For this we used his neighborhood graph for topological relationships, depicted in Fig. 7.3 (left) [4], to create our simplification shown in Fig. 7.3 (right). Our set of topological relationships groups

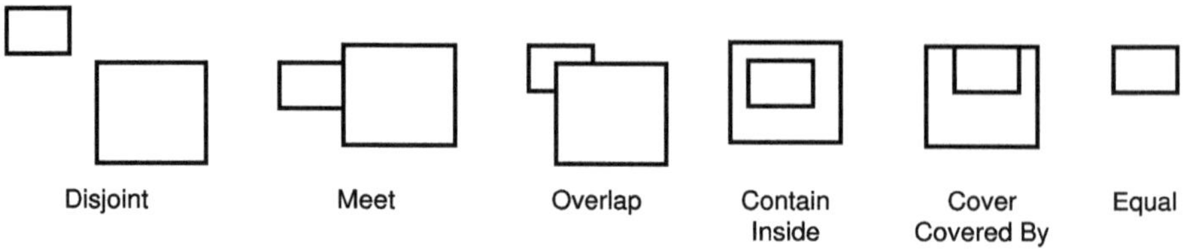

Fig. 7.2 Topological relationships defined by Egenhofer

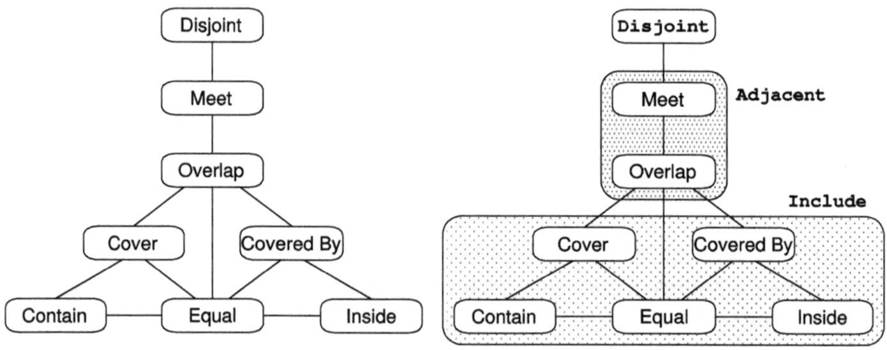

Fig. 7.3 Topological relationships originally defined by Egenhofer (*left*) and our simplified version (*right*)

neighbor relations yielding only three topological relationships between two polygons: `Disjoint` , `Include` and `Adjacent`.

Two polygons are **Disjoint** if all intersections among all faces are empty. If polygon P1 contains completely polygon P2 or P1 equals P2 then P1 **Includes** P2. And finally, if two polygons meet or if they intersect then they are considered **Adjacent**.

By reducing the number of relationships, we made our approach less restrictive and, more importantly, the topology graph will be simpler, as we shall see below. Furthermore, by using only these three relationships, we guarantee the stability of graphs when drawings are changed. Therefore, similar drawings will be described by similar topology graphs.

Leung developed an approach [15] where he further reduced the number of relations using only inclusion. We think this simplification is excessive because inclusion alone is not enough to correctly describe topological relationships between objects and increases the number of collisions among graphs, i.e. similar graphs for different drawings.

Topology Graph One of the best ways to describe the spatial arrangement between visual elements is through the use of graphs, where nodes represent the visual entities and edges code their relationships. In our approach, topological relationships extracted from drawings are compiled in a **Topology Graph**, where "vertical" edges mean `Inclusion` and "horizontal" connections mean `Adjacency`, as illustrated in Fig. 7.4.

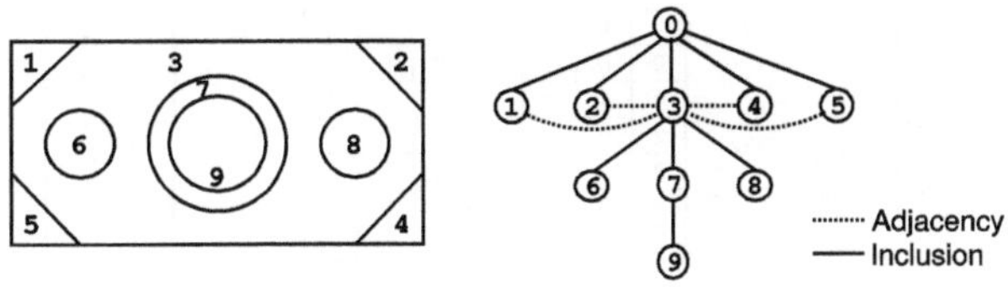

Fig. 7.4 Vector Drawing (*left*) and correspondent topology graph (*right*) describing the spatial arrangement

The topology graph has a well defined structure, being very similar to a rooted tree with side connections. It always has a root node representing the whole drawing. Children from the root represent the dominant blocks (polygons) from the drawing, i.e. blocks that are not contained in any other block. The next level of the graph describes polygons contained by the blocks identified before. This process is applied recursively until we get the complete hierarchy of blocks. As a conclusion, we can say that each graph level adds more drawing details. So, by going down in the depth of the graph, we are "zooming in" to drawing details. This feature of the topology graph will be explored later on by the multilevel description mechanism.

From Topology Graphs to Descriptors As mentioned above the graph matching problem is reduced to the computation of distances between descriptors. To achieve this we use graph spectra [2] to map graphs into vector descriptors. The spectrum of a graph G (which consist of n eigenvalues, where n is the number of nodes) is computed from the eigenvalues of its adjacency matrix, A. We choose to use the spectrum of the graph, because it is one of its most discriminating properties.

Since the spectrum of a graph is a graph invariant, it is natural to think that it would provide a polynomial algorithm to decide whether two graphs are isomorphic and thereby solve the graph isomorphism problem. However, graph spectrum is not a *complete invariant*. A graph invariant ϕ is said to be complete if, for any graphs G, H, the equality $\phi(G) = \phi(H)$ implies that G is isomorphic to H. Although, isomorphic graphs have the same spectrum, two graphs with the same spectrum need not be isomorphic.

According to Cvetković [2] and Shokoufandeh [27] the use of graph spectrum as an indexing method is valid since: (1) it captures local topology, (2) is invariant to subgraph re-order and (3) is stable as small changes in the graph produce little changes in its spectrum. Resulting descriptors however are not unique. More than one graph can have the same spectrum giving rise to collisions similar to those in hashing schemes. Shokoufandeh et al. [27] argue that these collisions occur rather infrequently, a claim verified by our experiments [5]. Using 100,000 randomly generated graphs versus a set of 10 candidate similar graphs we have observed that collisions with descriptors of very different graphs still allow us to reliably retrieve the most likely graphs.

Figure 7.5 presents the block diagram for computing a topology descriptor. First, we compute the adjacency matrix of the graph, second we compute its eigenvalues and finally we sort the absolute values to obtain the topology descriptor. Resulting descriptors are multidimensional points, where dimension depends on graph (and drawing) complexity. Very complex drawings will produce descriptors with high dimensions, while simple drawings will produce descriptors with low dimensions.

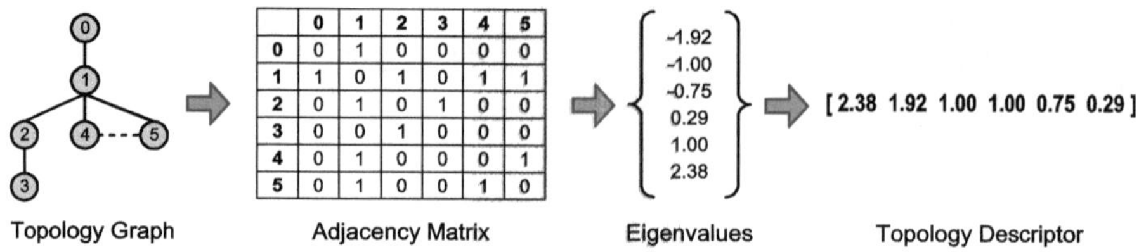

Fig. 7.5 Block diagram for topology descriptor computation

We assume that topology graphs are undirected graphs thus yielding symmetric adjacency matrices and assuring that eigenvalues are always real. Furthermore, by computing the absolute value and sorting it decreasingly we exploit the fact that the largest eigenvalues are more informative about the graph structure. Additionally, the largest eigenvalues are stable under minor perturbation of the graph structure, making topological descriptors also stable.

Multilevel Description As we have seen previously, the topological organization of a drawing is described using a topology graph that is mapped to a multidimensional descriptor. This way we get a descriptor for each graph (drawing) and we can compute the similarity between graphs by calculating a distance between the correspondent descriptors. However, including complex drawings in the database implies the requirement for making a query based on a simplification. Users may not remember or want to sketch the complete drawing or object. Thus, we need a mechanism to make the task of sketching queries for complex drawings easier.

One possible solution is to describe drawings considering just their contour, as some approaches do [1]. However, these techniques discard all the details inside the contour ignoring a lot of information relevant to describe drawing content. The solution presented here describes drawings not only as a whole but also as small pieces suitable for users to search using simple sketches.

To that end, the topology graph is divided in several parts (corresponding each to a subpart of the drawing) and a topological descriptor is computed for each. This way we can search complex drawings by just sketching subparts of it.

Although this solves the problem of finding subparts of drawings, another still exist. Complex drawings have lots of details that users sometimes forget to draw when sketching a query. To overcome this we developed a multilevel description scheme to describe drawings hierarchically by levels of detail allowing the use of rough approximations of drawings as queries [5, 11]. To that end we compute several topological descriptors for each drawing one for each level of detail. At the end, we have one descriptor per level allowing the matching between a query and several representations of the same drawing.

To compute descriptors for subparts of drawings and for different levels of detail we resort to the topology graph (see Fig. 7.4). For subparts, we recursively divide the graph into various subgraphs and then we compute descriptors for each. To describe different levels of detail we exploit the "tree-like" structure of our topology graph and compute a descriptor for each level of the graph. Looking at Fig. 7.6 we can

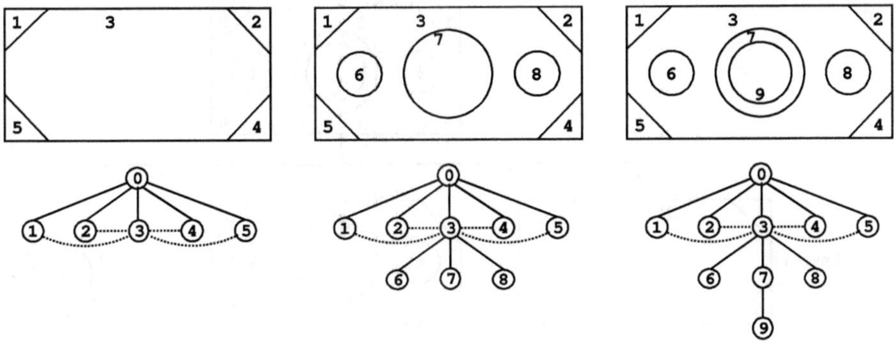

Fig. 7.6 Different levels of detail and the correspondent graph of topology

Fig. 7.7 Subpart of the drawing with two levels of detail and the correspondent graph of topology

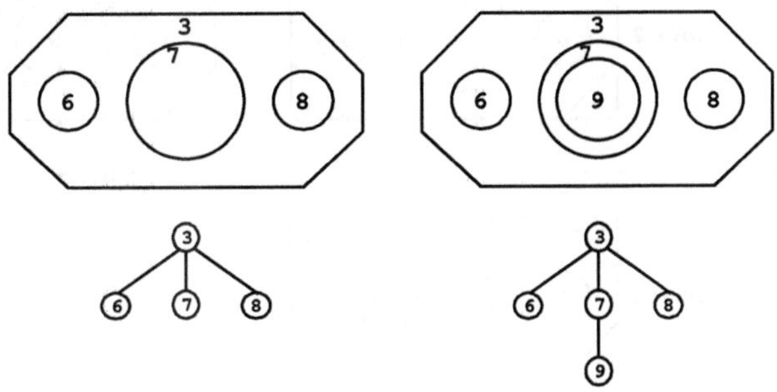

see that by going down in the structure of our topology graph, we are adding more detail to the drawing. In this figure we can identify three different graphs one for each degree of detail. So if we now compute a descriptor for each of these levels we end up with three ways to search for the current drawing, using more or less detail.

This approach also has the merit of allowing classification of subparts of drawings by computing descriptors for subgraphs. Figure 7.7 illustrates the subgraphs extracted and their corresponding part of the drawing. We recursively apply the description by levels of detail to these subgraphs. The result of this process is a set of graphs and subgraphs that describe both the topology at different levels of detail and the different subparts of a drawing. After this multilevel description we have descriptors for the parts of the drawing shown in Fig. 7.8, and consequently we can search for the (complete) drawing by sketching any of these representations.

Spatial Proximity While this solution produces good results, in some cases they could be improved if we take into account the distance between the visual elements in a drawing. Recently we devised a new mechanism to include proximity into the topology graph [28]. The goal is to be able to differentiate between a drawing with two polygons which are close together and a drawing with two polygons that are far apart, as illustrated in Fig. 7.9.

To code proximity in the topology graph, we associate weights to the adjacency links of the graph. While in the initial solution we only have an adjacency link when

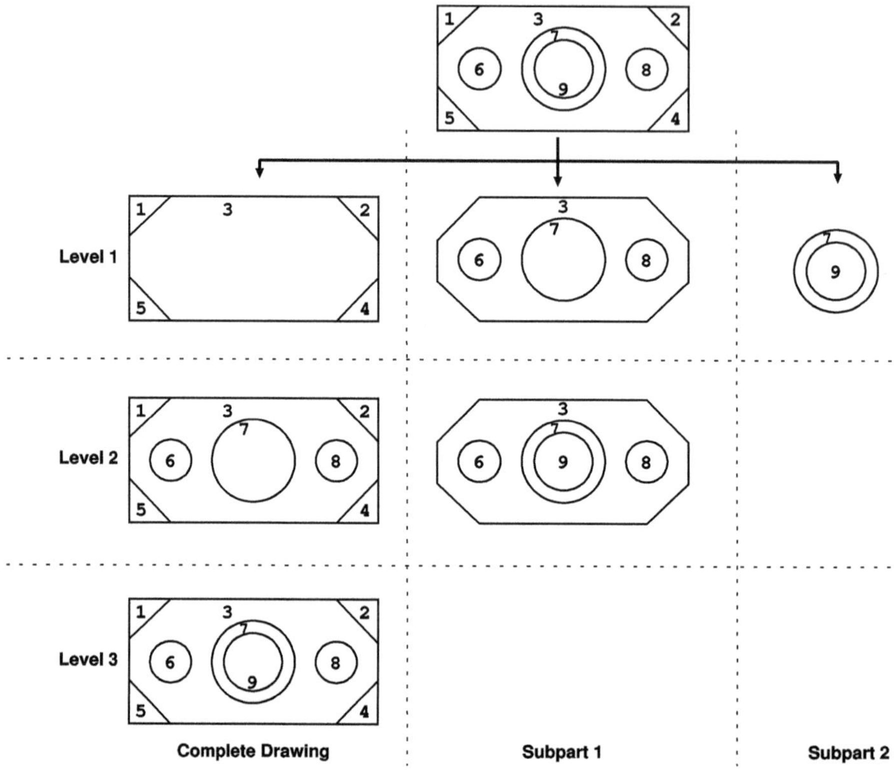

Fig. 7.8 Several representations for a given drawing (on top), using our multilevel description technique

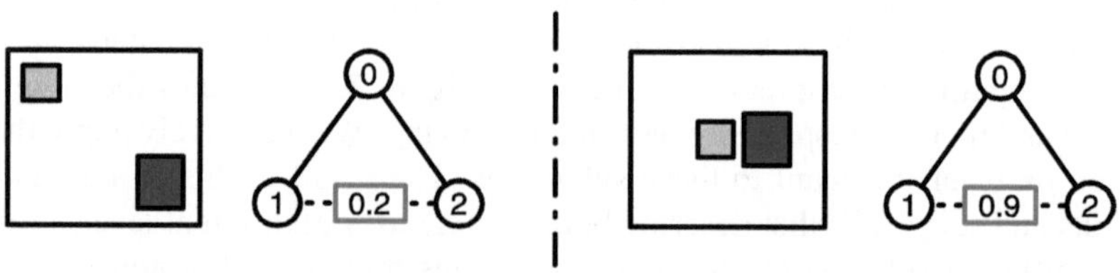

Fig. 7.9 Using the adjacency weight to differentiate between far and near objects

two primitives are connected, now we compute the (normalized) distance between two elements and use this value as the weight of the link. This distance is normalized by using the diagonal of the bounding box of the parent object that contains the two elements.

Figure 7.10 shows the representation of the proximity information in the graph and in the adjacency matrix, through the use of weights.

This change in the weights of the topology graph does not affect the stability and robustness of eigenvalues, as ascertained by Sarkar and Boyer in their study [26].

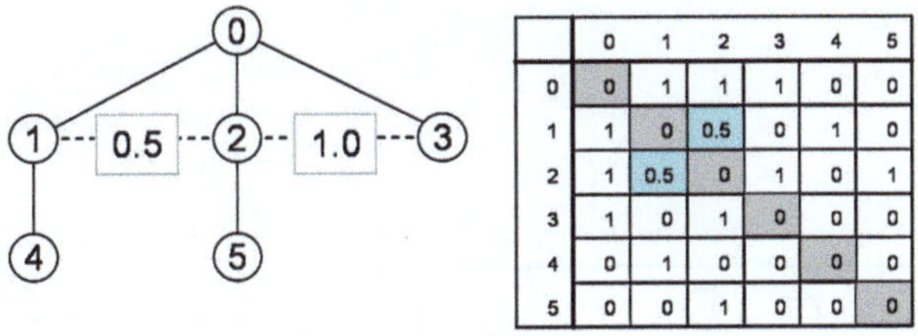

Fig. 7.10 Graphical representation of the adjacency weights in the graph and in the matrix

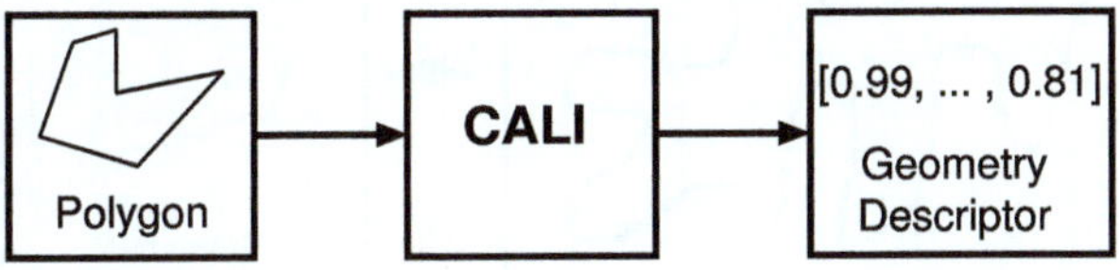

Fig. 7.11 Block diagram for computing the geometric descriptor

7.2.2 Geometry

While topology conveys global information about the drawing, the shape of an object represents local characteristics which can be used to narrow down the search.

To describe the geometry of entities from vector drawings and from sketched queries, we use a general, simple, fast and robust recognition approach called CALI [7, 9]. This was initially devised for recognition in calligraphic interfaces. However, since CALI performed well in recognizing hand-drawn input, we generalized that approach by using it to classify any shape for retrieval. Thus, instead of using CALI to identify specific shapes or gestures from sketches (e.g., rectangles, circles, lines, etc.) we compute a set of geometric attributes from which we derive features such as area and perimeter ratios from special polygons and store them in a multidimensional vector (geometric descriptor), as illustrated in Fig. 7.11.

Indeed, our approach can be thought of as a two-stage process. First we evaluate the geometric characteristics of a shape. Then we convert these into affine-invariant geometric features by simple arithmetic operations which combine these attributes with known commensurable values for simple convex primitives, such as quadrilaterals and triangles. More importantly, using geometric features instead of polygon classification allows us to index and store potentially unlimited families of shapes in a scalable manner.

To obtain a complete description of geometry in a drawing, we apply this method to each geometric entity from the drawing, yielding a set of geometric descriptors.

Our geometric description method uses a set of global geometric properties extracted from drawing entities. We start the calculation of geometric features by computing the *Convex Hull* of the provided element. Then we compute three special polygons from the convex hull: the *Largest Area Triangle* and the *Largest Area Quadrilateral* inscribed in the convex hull, and finally, the *Smallest Area Enclosing Rectangle*, as illustrated in Fig. 7.12.

Finally, we compute the ratios between area and perimeter from each special polygon. We experimentally evaluated all these ratios, as described in detail in [7, 8] before we reach the set of features listed in Table 7.1. This set of features

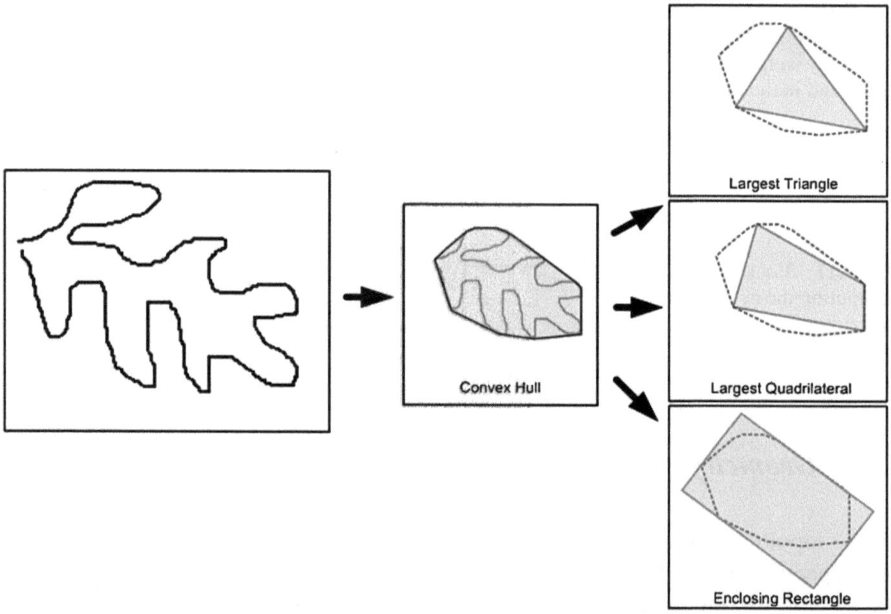

Fig. 7.12 Special polygons of a geometric entity

Table 7.1 List of relevant geometric features extracted from polygons and sketches

Feature	Description
A_{ch}	Area of the convex hull
A_{er}	Area of the (non-aligned) enclosing rectangle
A_{lq}	Area of the largest quadrilateral
A_{lt}	Area of the largest triangle
H_{er}	Height of the (non-aligned) enclosing rectangle
P_{ch}	Perimeter of the convex hull
P_{er}	Perimeter of the enclosing rectangle
P_{lq}	Perimeter of the largest quadrilateral
P_{lt}	Perimeter of the largest triangle
T_l	Total length, i.e. perimeter of original polygon
W_{er}	Width of the (non-aligned) enclosing rectangle

allows the description of shapes independently of their size, rotation, translation or line type. Such features can be used to classify drawings or hand-sketched queries.

Then, we combine these geometric features to produce a feature vector that describes the shape of visual entities (geometric descriptor). Figure 7.13 shows the geometric features that compose the feature vector. To decide whether two shapes are similar we just compare their feature vectors. Experiments have shown that our approach works well if individual features are stable and robust [8].

$$\left[\frac{P_{ch}}{T_l} \quad \frac{A_{ch}}{P_{ch}^2} \quad \frac{H_{er}}{W_{er}} \quad \frac{A_{lq}}{A_{er}} \quad \frac{A_{ch}}{A_{er}} \quad \frac{A_{lq}}{A_{ch}} \quad \frac{A_{lt}}{A_{lq}} \quad \frac{A_{lt}}{A_{ch}} \quad \frac{P_{lq}}{P_{ch}} \quad \frac{P_{lt}}{P_{ch}} \quad \frac{P_{ch}}{P_{er}}\right]$$

Fig. 7.13 Geometric feature vector created by the CALI library, using the geometric features described in Table 7.1

Experimental evaluation [12], using a database of general fish contours, revealed that this method outperforms well know algorithms, such as Zernike moments [18], Fourier descriptors [22] or grid-based methods [17], amongst others.

7.3 Application Examples for 2D Drawings

This section describes three prototypes developed using this approach based on topological and geometric information. One application is for retrieving 2D technical drawings of molds, SIBR [11], the other two help users in retrieving clip art figures, BajaVista [6] and Indagare [28, 29]. We selected these two types of media objects to search for because both are well structured figures and are complex enough to represent a good testbed for this approach. Technical drawings are characterized by very rich topological information and their visual elements are mostly basic geometric shapes. Clip art drawings however present more generic visual entities and a poorer spatial organization. Indeed, during user evaluation we observed that users, while searching for clip art drawings, typically draw a small number of shapes and consequently do not specify topology but mainly geometry [28].

Figure 7.14 depicts a screen-shot of the calligraphic interface of the SIBR application used to retrieve 2D technical drawings [11]. On the left we can see the sketch and on the right the results returned by the implied query. These results are ordered from top to bottom with the most similar on top. As we can see, although the sketched query is very simple the system was able to identify similar complex drawings. This is due mainly to the use of our hierarchical and multilevel description structure for topological information.

The BajaVista prototype [6] can index and retrieve clip art drawings by content, either using sketches or querying by example. Figure 7.15 depicts a screen-shot of this application. On the top left we can see the sketch of a candle and on the bottom results returned by the implied query. These results are ordered from left to right, with the most similar on the left. The system also allows users to select one of the results to submit as a query (query by example), since our classification scheme handles graphics and sketches in the same manner.

These two prototypes were evaluated using medium-size databases. The SIBR prototype was tested on a database containing one hundred elements, while the database used to test BajaVista indexed 968 drawings. Tests with both prototypes showed effective results when searching for both technical or clip art drawings in a short time (less than a second). Furthermore users were satisfied that returned results matched their expectations. Indeed, while in the first instance we presented the five top drawings in each case, feedback from tests convinced us to increase the displayed set to ten or twenty. Surprisingly, users assigned greater importance to being

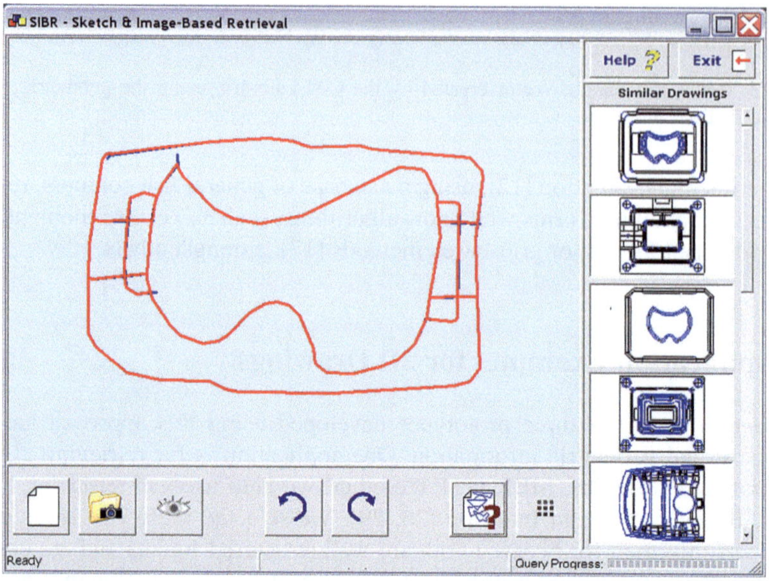

Fig. 7.14 Sketch-based retrieval prototype for technical drawings (SBIR). Users specify queries using sketches and candidate results are presented on the right, with the most similar on top

Fig. 7.15 First clip art finder prototype (BajaVista). Similar results to the sketch are presented at the bottom, the best candidate being the first on the left

able to retrieve the desired result among the top 10 or 20 elements than finding the two "best" candidates. Indeed, we were told by users that they preferred recall over precision (at least in this limited sense). Additionally, users liked very much the in-

Fig. 7.16 Second clip art finder prototype (Indagare), using proximity information and a new algorithm to compare geometry

teraction paradigm (sketches as queries) in contrast to more traditional approaches based on query by example.

Recently, we carried out a study with a new prototype to retrieve clip art drawings called Indagare [28, 29]. It is based on the approach described here but with two differences from the previous two prototypes. Indagare uses the topology graph with proximity information and includes a new geometry matching algorithm that takes advantage of the way users sketch queries to search for clip art drawings i.e. geometry rather than topology.

This new prototype (see Fig. 7.16) is a web search engine where users can search for drawings using sketches, query by example and keywords. Results are presented with the most similar in the top-left quadrant. Experimental evaluation of this prototype revealed increases of around 30% in the precision [29], in comparison to the original approach used in BajaVista that uses first topology and then geometry to compare drawings.

7.4 Toward 3D Modeling Using Implicit Retrieval

Since 3D objects have a well defined structure the retrieval approach described for 2D drawings can be applied with some minor adaptations. However, instead of developing a system to simply retrieve 3D objects, we integrated the retrieval mechanism in the sketch-based modeling workflow, creating a new modeling paradigm [10]. In this new modeling paradigm queries are automatically created while users sketch their 3D models. Instead of users explicitly defining and submitting queries, the system permanently collects users' sketches and uses them as (implicit) queries to the retrieval module suggesting the use of similar 3D objects from databases of components or other objects. **Implicit retrieval** describes the process of using the editing tool to create and execute queries automatically without user intervention. In this way, the modeling system is always "looking" at users' actions and whenever it detects changes to an object it searches the database and proposes similar drawings.

We applied this paradigm in two modeling prototypes. One for the creation of 3D technical objects where existing objects are suggested to the user when he creates something similar to objects in a database. The other is for the creation of Lego models and returns Lego parts while users are sketching their dimensions.

7.4.1 Modeling 3D Technical Objects

In this section we briefly describe the modeling tool where we integrated the retrieval module. We present its interaction paradigms the expectation lists and the method of creating 3D objects. Then, we describe a seamless way of integrating the retrieval component, queries and returned results into the modeling tool through expectation lists and implicit retrieval.

Overview of the Modeling Tool The 3D sketch-based modeling tool GIDeS is a system for creating geometric models through Calligraphic Interaction [21]. Its main goal is to improve on the usability of CAD systems at the early stages of product design. To this end it combines different paradigms: First, a *calligraphic* sketching metaphor provides for a paper-like interaction. Second, dynamic menus—*expectation lists*—try to expose the state of the application without interfering with the task. Third, an incremental drawing paradigm allows precise drawings to be progressively constructed from sketches through simple constraint satisfaction. Finally, reducing instruction set and command usage allow for a simple and learnable approach in contrast with the complexity of present-day interactive systems.

To deal with ambiguous input the GIDeS system uses expectation lists, a kind of non-intrusive context-based dynamic menus that free users from memorizing modeling gestures and constructs. Whenever users' strokes are ambiguous, the application displays a menu with icons that correspond to two or more possible different interpretations of the input. Figure 7.17 illustrates how expectation lists deal with ambiguity and exploit it to the user's benefit. In this case the designer sketched a stroke that resembles an ellipse. The resulting expectation list suggests an accurate ellipse as its default option as well as other possible interpretations. Users can then select one of the proposals or continue drawing, in which case the default option is selected.

3D Object Description GIDeS allows construction of 3D objects from 2D interaction. In order to integrate our retrieval mechanism into the modeling tool, we must have a logical database with the description of all existing 3D objects that can be searched and included during a modeling task. Thus, for each 3D object we must

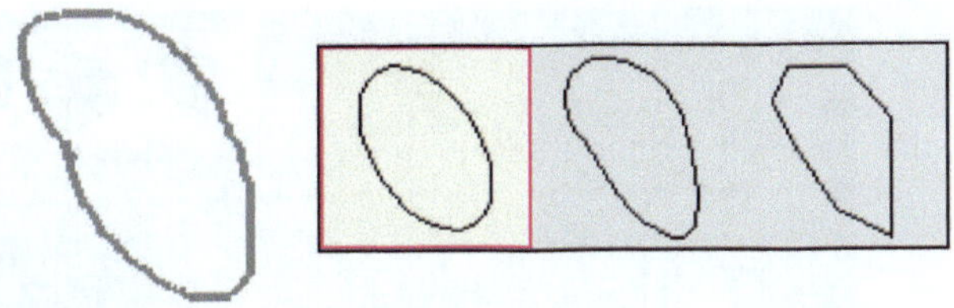

Fig. 7.17 Sketched figure and the Expectation list. Users can select one of the possible interpretations or continue to sketch

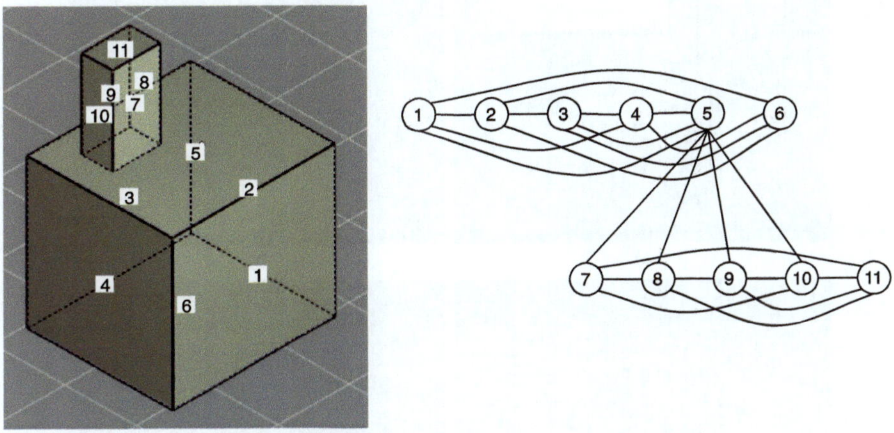

Fig. 7.18 3D object (*left*) and correspondent faces graph, used to compute the signature of the object

compute a signature that describes it. While for 2D drawings we used topological and geometric information to compute descriptors for 3D objects we are using the spatial relationship between faces and edges in a boundary representation.

Thus, for each 3D object we create a graph describing face organization and another graph describing the connections between edges. Then, from these two graphs we compute descriptors using graph eigenvalues [2], as we did for topology graphs of 2D drawings. However, since face and edge graphs (see Fig. 7.18) do not have the same structure of the topology graphs described before (see Fig. 7.4), we are not able to apply our multilevel method, which allows describing subparts of objects. Thus, as we did for 2D drawings 3D objects are described using multidimensional feature vectors and the similarity between them is converted into the computation of a distance between descriptors.

Finally, to match the query with existing objects in the database we compute descriptors for the query and search both sets of signatures separately (one with information about face graphs and the other with information about edge graphs). To compute the final similarity between the query and objects in the database we combine both similarity measures one from the face graph and another from the edge graph.

Query Formulation and Execution Figure 7.19 shows a modeling sequence in the GIDeS tool, where the user is sketching an object and the system is suggesting

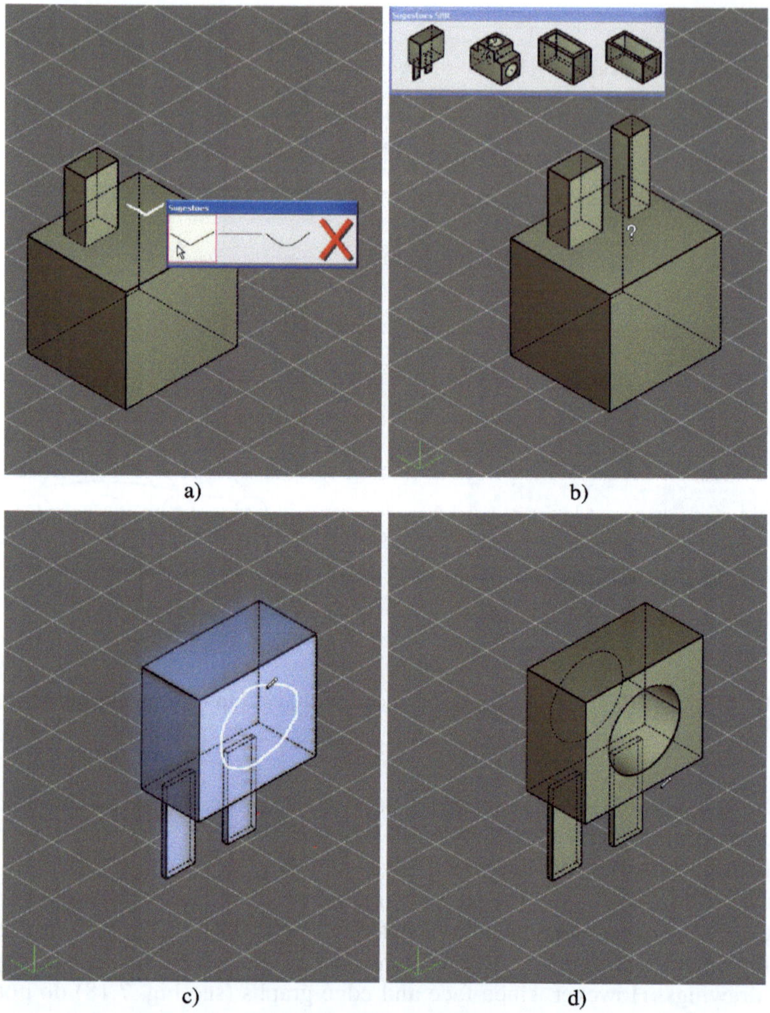

Fig. 7.19 Modeling sequence using the suggestions mechanism and implicit retrieval

results through the expectation list. This figure illustrates the two types of hints provided by the GIDeS system, modeling and editing suggestions and implied elements from the retrieval component. On Fig. 7.19(a) we have the suggestion of simple geometric 2D lines, while Fig. 7.19(b) we have the new type of cues provided by the implicit retrieval module. Figure 7.19(c) shows the retrieved object being modified using the normal GIDeS modeling operations, while Fig. 7.19(d) presents the final 3D object. Through this interaction paradigm users can freely create 3D models using sketches or select one of the suggested (retrieved) objects and continue to model on top of it. The main advantage of this scheme is that it is less intrusive than other approaches and users do not have to switch context to search for the de-

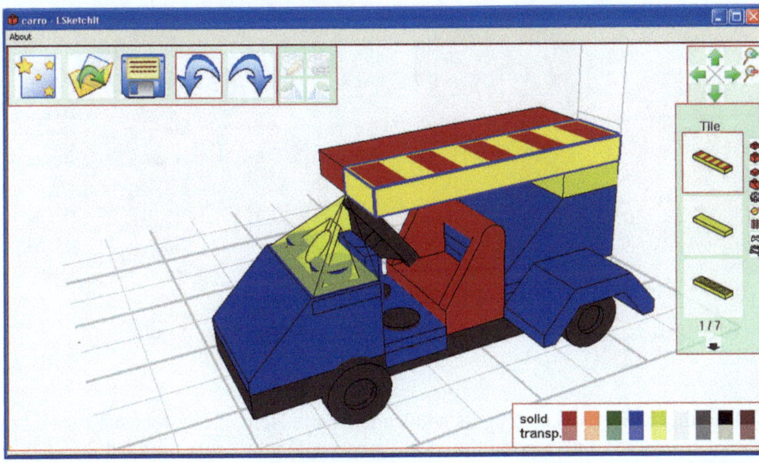

Fig. 7.20 General overview of the LSketchIt application, showing the suggestion list on right, the color palette on the bottom and the Lego model on the center

sired element to include. Moreover, this exploits the familiar interaction paradigm to provide queries as an extension of drawing in a natural manner.

7.4.2 Modeling Lego Scenes

Here we describe a sketch-based solution to create Lego models LSketchIt [25], which also uses the implicit retrieval paradigm (see Fig. 7.20). Users can easily add parts to Lego scenes using simple sketches that are converted into implicit queries to the database of Lego parts. Contrary to other sketch-based retrieval methods described before, this system uses a simple retrieval approach based mainly on the 3D dimensions of the Lego parts and on its category. To include a part into a scene users specify one or more dimensions of it using sketches and the system automatically creates the query, submits it and suggests (retrieves) a list of possible parts that matches the specifications.

In the remainder of this section we describe how this retrieval mechanism works and how we created the parts database.

Part Library Existing LEGO parts belong to the LEGO Company and are not freely available. To overcome this, we used the open-source LeoCAD library. Each part in the library has: name, dimensions and category associated to it. These are very useful for our retrieval mechanism, since it relies mainly on this information. For organization purposes we divided the parts into nine main groups (Plates, Bricks, Tile, Slope Brick, Technic, Space, Train, Other Bricks and Accessories). These groups can be used to filter out returned results or to help users browsing the entire collection of parts.

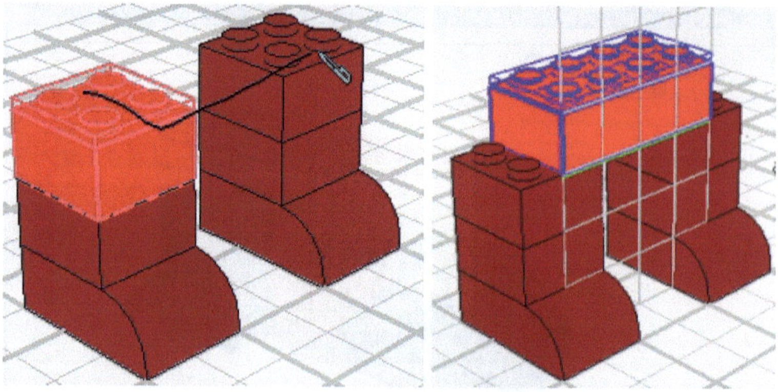

Fig. 7.21 Inserting a part by sketching its width and length. Here, the system suggests a brick that satisfies these dimensions. Other possibilities are presented in the suggestion list

Fig. 7.22 Refinement of the part to insert by sketching (a triangle) over an existing part

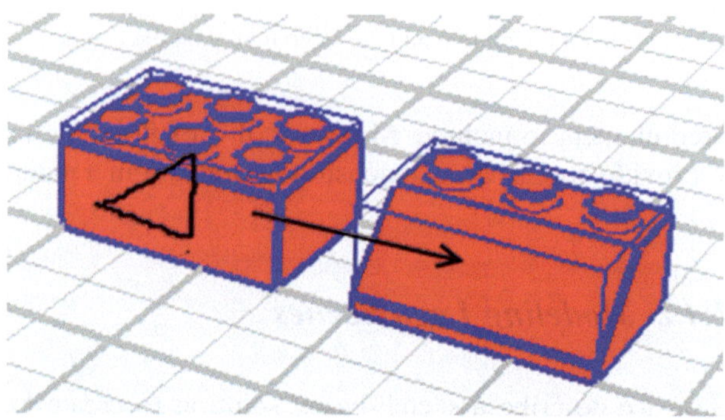

Retrieval Mechanism The search mechanism relies mainly on the information about dimensions and categories of parts that are stored in the library. When users want to use a part they can sketch one dimension (e.g., width, length or height) or more than one dimension (e.g., width and length), while modeling (see Fig. 7.21). Then, the retrieval system compares dimensions defined using sketches with the parts stored in the database and returns a set of results that are displayed in the suggestion list organized by categories.

To enrich the modeling process we allow over sketching of gestures on parts to refine the selection and find specific types of parts. For instance, if we draw a triangle inside the retrieved or selected brick, the system will refine the query, showing only bricks with slopes (see Fig. 7.22). Table 7.2 shows the different combinations of gestures and the produced result.

Results Presentation All existing applications for LEGO creation typically present the search results in an exhaustive text list. This way of presenting information is very uncomfortable and has a low usability as it forces users to recall rather than recognize. Users must preview several items in the text list before selecting one. To overcome this, we use a suggestion list to present returned results, allowing

Table 7.2 List of gestures available to refine the part to insert. Users can sketch over the part or outside the selected part, producing different results

Gesture	Outside part	Inside part
Line		Pin
Circle	Tyre, Wheel, Round	Side, Hole
Rectangle	Baseplate, Plate, Brick	
Triangle	Slope Brick	

users to quickly recognize the desired part. Users can also reduce the number of suggested results, by selecting the desired type of part (Plates, Bricks, Tile, etc.), clicking on the small icons listed vertically on the right of the screen in Fig. 7.20.

7.5 Conclusions

Content based retrieval of vector drawings is a research area with some activity but it is not too widely explored. In recent years researchers have dedicated more effort to content based retrieval of (raster) images. Although, there has been a lot of work developed for images these approaches can not be applied to vector drawings because they have a more complex structure and hierarchy.

In this chapter we described an approach for sketch-based retrieval of vector drawings that describes their contents using Topology (information about the spatial organization of drawings entities) and Geometry (information about shape). This mechanism also includes a new multilevel description scheme for describing drawings and subparts of drawings with different levels of detail. This technique allows partial matching and the comparison between simple sketched queries and complex drawings stored in a database.

We also described applications to retrieve complex drawings (technical and clip art drawings), which were subject to user evaluation. Users provided good feedback about the systems very often highlighting the positive aspect of using sketches to specify what they want to find.

Finally, we presented the paradigm of implicit retrieval that integrates the retrieval mechanism into the workflow of the modeling process. It allows users to freely model objects using sketches, while the system takes the responsibility to automatically generate queries (implicitly) from the created models and also to present the returned results as modeling suggestions.

References

1. Berchtold, S., Kriegel, H.P.: S3: Similarity in CAD database systems. In: Proceedings of the International Conference on Management of Data (SIGMOD'97), pp. 564–567. ACM Press, Tucson (1997)
2. Cvetković, D., Rowlinson, P., Simic, S.: Eigenspaces of Graphs. Cambridge University Press, Cambridge (1997)

3. Egenhofer, M.J.: A formal definition of binary topological relationships. In: Litwin, W., Schek, H. (eds.) Third International Conference on Foundations of Data Organization and Algorithms (FODO'89). Lecture Notes in Computer Science, vol. 367, pp. 457–472. Springer, Berlin (1989)
4. Egenhofer, M.J., Al-Taha, K.K.: Reasoning about gradual changes of topological relationships. In: Frank, A., Campari, I., Formentini, U. (eds.) Theory and Methods of Spatio-Temporal Reasoning in Geographic Space. Lecture Notes in Computer Science, vol. 639, pp. 196–219. Springer, Berlin (1992)
5. Fonseca, M.J.: Sketch-based retrieval in large sets of drawings. Ph.D. thesis, Instituto Superior Técnico/Technical University of Lisbon (2004)
6. Fonseca, M.J., Barroso, B., Ribeiro, P., Jorge, J.A.: Retrieving ClipArt images by content. In: Proceedings of the 3rd International Conference on Image and Video Retrieval (CIVR'04). Lecture Notes in Computer Science, vol. 3115, pp. 500–507. Springer, Berlin (2004)
7. Fonseca, M.J., Jorge, J.A.: Using fuzzy logic to recognize geometric shapes interactively. In: Proceedings of the 9th International Conference on Fuzzy Systems (FUZZ-IEEE'00), vol. 1, pp. 291–296. San Antonio, USA (2000)
8. Fonseca, M.J., Jorge, J.A.: Experimental evaluation of an on-line scribble recognizer. Pattern Recognition Letters **22**(12), 1311–1319 (2001)
9. Fonseca, M.J., Pimentel, C., Jorge, J.A.: CALI: an online scribble recognizer for calligraphic interfaces. In: Proceedings of the 2002 AAAI Spring Symposium—Sketch Understanding, pp. 51–58. Palo Alto, USA (2002)
10. Fonseca, M.J., Ferreira, A., Jorge, J.A.: Towards 3D modeling using sketches and retrieval. In: Proceedings of the first Eurographics Workshop on Sketch–Based Interfaces and Modeling, pp. 127–136. EG, Grenoble (2004)
11. Fonseca, M.J., Ferreira, A., Jorge, J.A.: Content-based retrieval of technical drawings. International Journal of Computer Applications in Technology (IJCAT) **23**(2–4), 86–100 (2005)
12. Fonseca, M.J., Ferreira, A., Jorge, J.A.: Generic shape classification for retrieval. In: Proceedings of the 6th IAPR International Workshop on Graphics Recognition (GREC'05), pp. 291–299 (2005)
13. Gross, M., Do, E.: Demonstrating the electronic cocktail napkin: a paper-like interface for early design. In: Proceedings of the Conference on Human Factors in Computing Systems (CHI'96), pp. 5–6 (1996)
14. Hou, S., Ramani, K.: Structure-oriented contour representation and matching for engineering shapes. Computer Aided Design **40**(1), 94–108 (2008)
15. Leung, H.W.H.: Representations, feature extraction, matching and relevance feedback for sketch retrieval. PhD Thesis, Carnegie Mellon University, Pittsburgh, Pennsylvania, USA (2003)
16. Liang, S., Sun, Z.X., Li, B., Feng, G.H.: Effective sketch retrieval based on its contents. In: Proceedings of Machine Learning and Cybernetics, vol. 9, pp. 5266–5272 (2005)
17. Lu, G.J., Sajjanhar, A.: Region-based shape representation and similarity measure suitable for content-based image retrieval. Multimedia Systems **7**, 165–174 (1999)
18. Mehtre, B.M., Kankanhali, M.S., Lee, W.F.: Shape measures for content based image retrieval: a comparison. Information Processing and Management **33**(3), 319–337 (1997)
19. Namboodiri, A.M., Jain, A.K.: Retrieval of on-line hand-drawn sketches. In: Proceedings of the 17th International Conference on Pattern Recognition (ICPR'04), vol. 2, pp. 642–645. IEEE Computer Society, Washington (2004)
20. Park, J., Um, B.: A new approach to similarity retrieval of 2D graphic objects based on dominant shapes. Pattern Recognition Letters **20**, 591–616 (1999)
21. Pereira, J.P., Jorge, J.A., Branco, V.A., Ferreira, F.N.: Calligraphic interfaces: mixed metaphors for design. In: 10th International Workshop on the Design, Specification and Verification of Interactive Systems (DSV-IS'03). Funchal, Madeira, Portugal (2003)
22. Persoon, E., Fu, K.S.: Shape discrimination using Fourier descriptors. IEEE Transactions on Systems, Man and Cybernetics **7**(3), 170–179 (1977)
23. Pu, J., Ramani, K.: On visual similarity based 2d drawing retrieval. Journal of Computer Aided Design **38**(3), 249–259 (2006)

24. Rui, Y., Huang, T.S., Chang, S.F.: Image retrieval: current techniques, promising directions, and open issues. Journal of Visual Communication and Image Representation **10**(1), 39–62 (1999)
25. Santos, T., Ferreira, A., Dias, F., Fonseca, M.J.: Using sketches and retrieval to create LEGO models. In: Proceedings of the Eurographics Workshop on Sketch-Based Interfaces and Modeling 2008 (SBIM'08), pp. 89–96. EG, Annecy (2008)
26. Sarkar, S., Boyer, K.: Quantitative measures of change based on feature organization: eigenvalues and eigenvectors. Tech. rep., Image Analysis Research Lab, University of South Florida (1996)
27. Shokoufandeh, A., Dickson, S., Siddiqi, K., Zucker, S.: Indexing using a spectral encoding of topological structure. In: IEEE Conference on Computer Vision and Pattern Recognition (CVPR'99), pp. 2491–2497. IEEE Computer Society, Los Alamitos (1999)
28. Sousa, P., Fonseca, M.J.: Sketch-based retrieval of drawings using topological proximity. In: Proceedings of the 14th International Conference on Distributed Multimedia Systems, Special Track on Sketch Computing (DMS'08), pp. 276–281. Boston, USA (2008)
29. Sousa, P., Fonseca, M.J.: Geometric matching for clip-art drawing retrieval. Journal of Visual Communication and Image Representation (JVCI) **20**(2), 71–83 (2009)
30. Ullmann, J.R.: An algorithm for subgraph isomorphism. Journal of the ACM (JACM) **23**(1), 31–42 (1976)

Part II
Sketch-based Modeling

Chapter 8
A Sketching Interface for Freeform 3D Modeling

Takeo Igarashi

8.1 Introduction

Although much progress has been made over the years on 3D modeling systems, they are still difficult and tedious to use when creating freeform surfaces. Their emphasis has been the precise modeling of objects motivated by CAD and similar domains. An important contribution in the field was the SKETCH system [34], which introduced a gesture-based interface for the rapid modeling of CSG-like models consisting of simple primitives.

We extended these ideas to create a sketching interface for designing 3D freeform objects and developed a prototype system called Teddy [15]. The essential idea is the use of freeform strokes as an expressive design tool. The user draws 2D freeform strokes interactively specifying the silhouette of an object, and the system automatically constructs a 3D polygonal surface model based on the strokes (Fig. 8.1). The user does not have to manipulate control points or combine complicated editing operations. Using our technique, even first-time users can create simple, yet expressive 3D models within minutes. In addition, the resulting models have a hand-crafted feel (such as sculptures and stuffed animals) which is difficult to accomplish with most conventional modelers. Examples are shown in Fig. 8.2.

This chapter describes the sketching interface and the algorithms for constructing 3D shapes from 2D strokes in Teddy. The geometric representation we used is a standard polygonal mesh to allow the use of numerous software resources for post-manipulation and rendering. However, the interface itself can be used to create other representations such as volumes [30] or implicit surfaces [21].

Like SKETCH [34], Teddy was designed for the rapid construction of approximate models, not for the careful editing of precise models. To emphasize this design goal and encourage creative exploration, we used the real-time pen-and-ink rendering described in [18], as shown in Fig. 8.1. This also allowed real-time interactive

T. Igarashi (✉)
The University of Tokyo and JST ERATO, Tokyo, Japan
e-mail: takeo@acm.org

J. Jorge, F. Samavati (eds.), *Sketch-based Interfaces and Modeling*,
DOI 10.1007/978-1-84882-812-4_8, © Springer-Verlag London Limited 2011

Fig. 8.1 Teddy in use on a display-integrated tablet

Fig. 8.2 Painted models created using Teddy and painted using a commercial texture-map editor

rendering using Java on mid-range PCs without dedicated 3D rendering hardware at that time.

An immediate application of Teddy is as a plug-in for existing modeling packages. However, Teddy's ease of use has the potential to open up new application areas for 3D modeling beyond standard usage model. Possibilities include rapid prototyping in the early stages of design, educational/recreational use for non-professionals and children [20], and real-time communication assistance on pen-based systems. We report on a case study where a high school teacher used our system to teach 3D concepts in geography.

Teddy is available as a Java applet at the following web site http://www-ui.is.s.u-tokyo.ac.jp/~takeo/teddy/teddy.htm.

8.2 Related Work

A typical procedure for geometric modeling is to start with a simple primitive such as a cube or a sphere, and gradually construct a more complex model through successive transformations or a combination of multiple primitives. Various deformation techniques [17, 27] and other shape-manipulation tools [9] are examples of transformation techniques that let the user create a wide variety of precise, smooth shapes by interactively manipulating control points or 3D widgets.

Another approach to geometric modeling is the use of implicit surfaces [4, 19]. The user specifies the skeleton of the intended model and the system constructs smooth, natural-looking surfaces around it. The surface inflation technique [29] extrudes the polygonal mesh from the skeleton outward. In contrast, our approach lets the user specify the silhouette of the intended shape directly instead of by specifying its skeleton.

Some modeling systems achieve intuitive, efficient operation using 3D input/output devices [7]. 3D devices can simplify the operations that require multiple operations when using 2D devices.

Our sketching interface is inspired by previous sketch-based modeling systems [8, 34] that interpret the user's freeform strokes and interactively construct 3D rectilinear models. Our goal is to develop a similar interface for designing rounded freeform models.

Williams published a method for constructing a 3D shape by inflating the inside of a given 2D silhouette [32, 33]. He used it to add shading effect to 2D drawings as well as to generate a 3D polygonal model. Our work is built on his seminal contribution and extended it to a more complete modeling system based on sketching.

The use of freeform strokes for 2D applications has recently become popular. Some systems [10, 16] use strokes to specify gestural commands and others [3] use freeform strokes for specifying 2D curves. These systems find the best matching arcs or splines automatically, freeing the users from explicit control of underlying parameters.

Since the first introduction of our system, many different variants have been explored in the research community. They mainly experimented with different representations for a 3D model, such as voxels to support topology changes [22], subdivision surfaces to create smoother surface [14], implicit surfaces to achieve smooth connection between components [1, 25], hierarchical representations to support subsequent editing [25] and animation [14], and mesh optimizations to support editing by the constraints on the surface [20]. Some of these are described in the following chapters of this book.

8.3 User Interface

Teddy's physical user interface is based upon traditional 2D input devices such as a standard mouse or tablet. We use a two-button mouse with no modifier keys. Unlike traditional modeling systems, Teddy does not use WIMP-style direct manipulation techniques or standard interface widgets such as buttons and menus for modeling operations. Instead, the user specifies his or her desired operation using freeform strokes on the screen, and the system infers the user's intent and executes the appropriate editing operations. Our videotape shows how a small number of simple operations let the users create very rich models.

In addition to gestures, Teddy supports direct camera manipulation using the secondary mouse button based on a virtual trackball model [13]. We also use a few button widgets for auxiliary operations, such as save and load, and for initiating bending operations.

8.4 Modeling Operations

This section describes Teddy's modeling operations from the user's point of view; details of the algorithms are left to the next section. Some operations are executed immediately after the user completes a stroke, while some require multiple strokes. The current system supports neither the creation of multiple objects at once, nor operations to combine single objects. Additionally, models must have a spherical topology; e.g., the user cannot create a torus. An overview of the model construction process is given first, and then each operation is described in detail.

The modeling operations are carefully designed to allow incremental learning by novice users. Users can create a variety of models by learning only the first operation (creation), and can incrementally expand their vocabulary by learning other operations as necessary. We have found it helpful to restrict first-time users to the first three basic operations (creation, painting, and extrusion), and then to introduce other advanced operations after these basic operations are mastered.

8.4.1 Overview

Figure 8.3 introduces Teddy's general model construction process. The user begins by drawing a single freeform stroke on a blank canvas (Figs. 8.3(a, b)). As soon as the user finishes drawing the stroke, the system automatically constructs a corresponding 3D shape (c). The user can now view the model from a different direction (d). Once a model is created, it may be modified using various operations. The user can draw a line on the surface (e–g) by drawing a stroke within the model silhouette. If the stroke is closed, the resulting surface line turns red and the system enters "extrusion mode" (h–i). Then the user rotates the model (j) and draws the second stroke specifying the silhouette of the extruded surface (k–m). A stroke that crosses the silhouette cuts the model (n–o) and turns the cut section red (p). The user either clicks to complete the operation (q) or draws a silhouette to extrude the section (r–t). Scribbling on the surface erases the line segments on the surface (u–w). If the user scribbles during the extrusion mode (x–y), the system smoothes the area surrounded by the closed red line (z–z′).

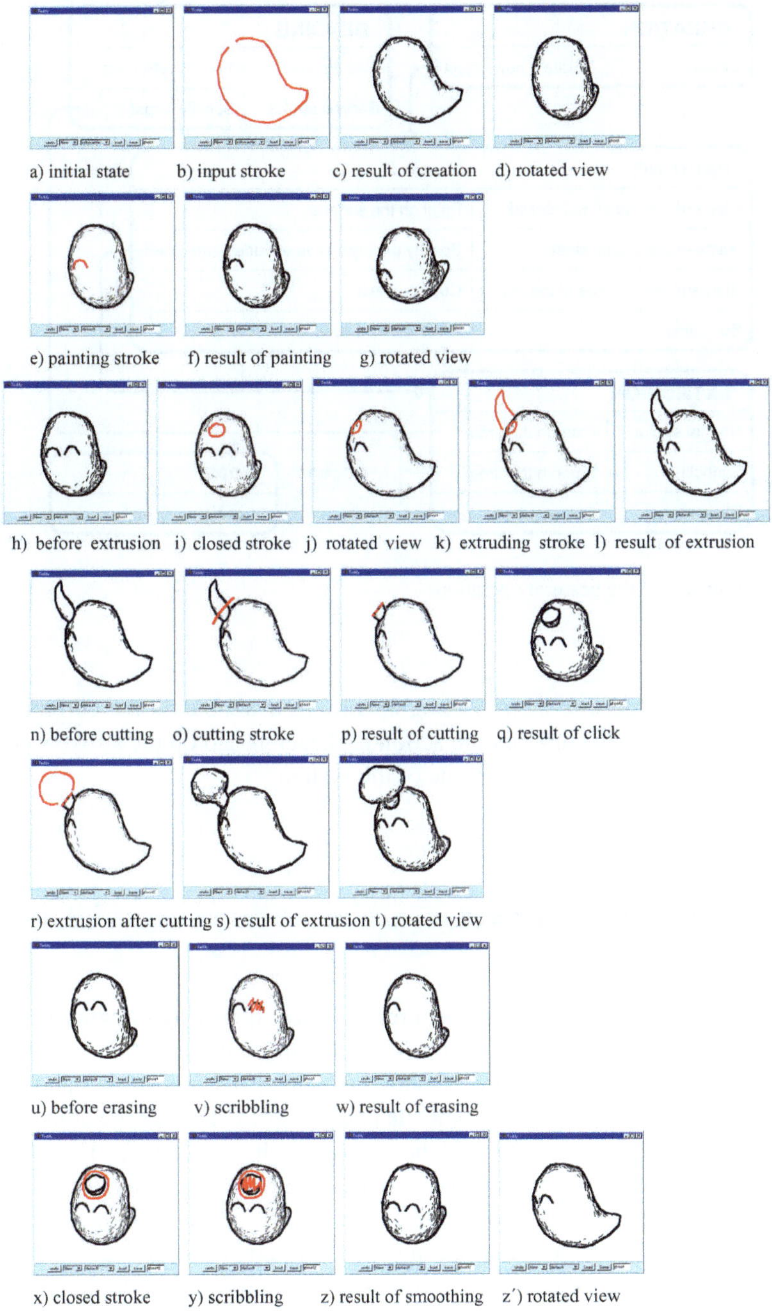

Fig. 8.3 Overview of the modeling operations

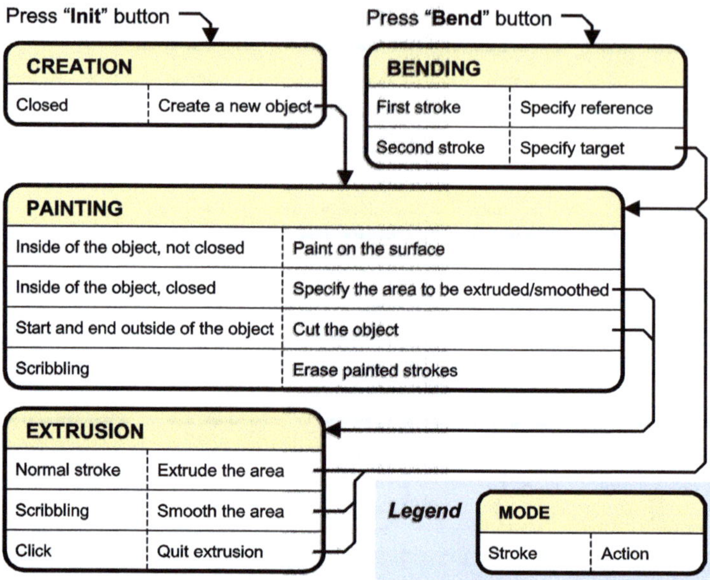

Fig. 8.4 Summary of the gestural operations

Figure 8.4 summarizes the modeling operations available on the current implementation. Note that the appropriate action is chosen based on the stroke's position and shape, as well as the current mode of the system.

8.4.2 Creating a New Object

Starting with a blank canvas, the user creates a new object by drawing its silhouette as a closed freeform stroke. The system automatically constructs a 3D shape based on the 2D silhouette. Figure 8.5 shows examples of input strokes and the corresponding 3D models. The start point and end point of the stroke are automatically connected, and the operation fails if the stroke is self-intersecting. The algorithm to calculate the 3D shape is described in detail in Sect. 8.5. Briefly, the system inflates the closed region in both directions with the amount depending on the width of the region: that is, wide areas become fat, and narrow areas become thin. Our experience so far shows that this algorithm generates a reasonable-looking freeform shape. In addition to the creation operation, the user can begin model construction by loading a simple primitive. The current implementation provides a cube and a sphere, but adding more shapes is straightforward.

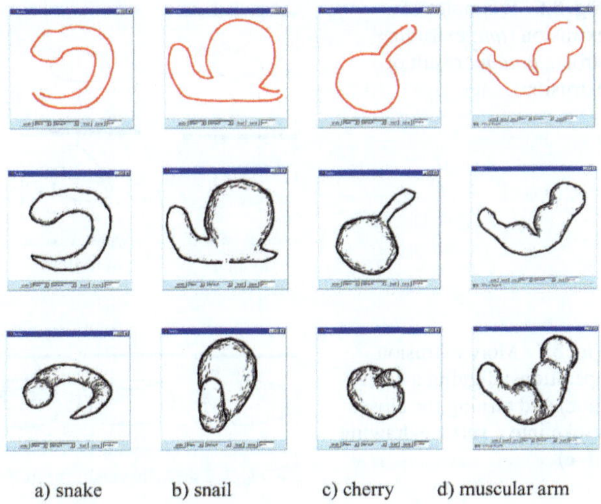

Fig. 8.5 Examples of creation operation (*top*: input stroke, *middle*: result of creation, *bottom*: rotated view)

8.4.3 Painting and Erasing on the Surface

The object surface is painted by drawing a freeform stroke within the object's silhouette on the canvas (the stroke must not cross the silhouette) [11]. The 2D stroke is projected onto the object surface as 3D line segments, called surface lines (Fig. 8.3(e–g)). The user can erase these surface lines by drawing a scribbling stroke[1] (Fig. 8.3(u–w)). This painting operation does not modify the 3D geometry of the model, but lets the user express ideas quickly and conveniently when using Teddy as a communication medium or design tool.

8.4.4 Extrusion

Extrusion is a two-stroke operation: a closed stroke on the surface and a stroke depicting the silhouette of the extruded surface. When the user draws a closed stroke on the object surface, the system highlights the corresponding surface line in red, indicating the initiation of "extrusion mode" (Fig. 8.3(i)). The user then rotates the model to bring the red surface line sideways (Fig. 8.3(j)) and draws a silhouette line to extrude the surface (Fig. 8.3(k)). This is basically a sweep operation that constructs the 3D shape by moving the closed surface line along the skeleton of the silhouette (Fig. 8.3(l)). The direction of extrusion is always perpendicular to the object surface, not parallel to the screen. Users can create a wide variety of shapes using this operation, as shown in Fig. 8.6. They can also make a cavity on the surface

[1] A stroke is recognized as scribbling when $sl/pl > 1.5$, where sl is the length of the stroke and pl is the perimeter of its convex hull.

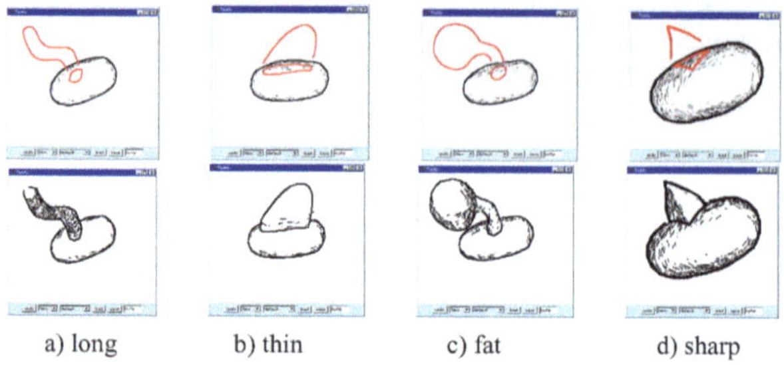

Fig. 8.6 Examples of extrusion (*top*: extruding stroke, *bottom*: result of extrusion)

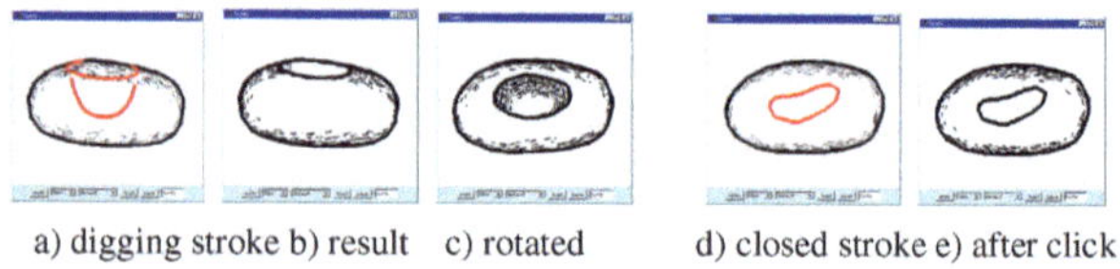

Fig. 8.7 More extrusion operations: digging a cavity (**a–c**) and turning the closed stroke into a surface drawing (**d–e**)

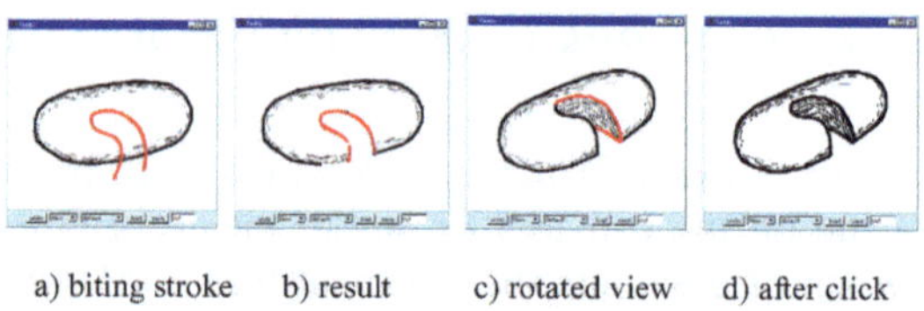

Fig. 8.8 Cutting operation

by drawing an inward silhouette (Fig. 8.7(a–c)). The current implementation does not support holes that completely extend to the other side of the object. If the user decides not to extrude, a single click turns the red stroke into an ordinary painted stroke (Fig. 8.7(d–e)).

8.4.5 *Cutting*

A cutting operation starts when the user draws a stroke that runs across the object, starting and terminating outside its silhouette (Fig. 8.3(o)). The stroke divides the object into two pieces at the plane defined by the camera position and the stroke. What is on the screen to the left of the stroke is then removed entirely (Fig. 8.3(p)) (as when a carpenter saws off a piece of wood). The cutting operation finishes with a click of the mouse (Fig. 8.3(q)). The user can also 'bite' the object using the same operation (Fig. 8.8).

The cutting stroke turns the section edges red, indicating that the system is in "extrusion mode". The user can draw a stroke to extrude the section instead of a click (Figs. 8.3(r–t), 8.9). This "extrusion after cutting" operation is useful to modify the shape without causing creases at the root of the extrusion.

Fig. 8.9 Extrusion after cutting

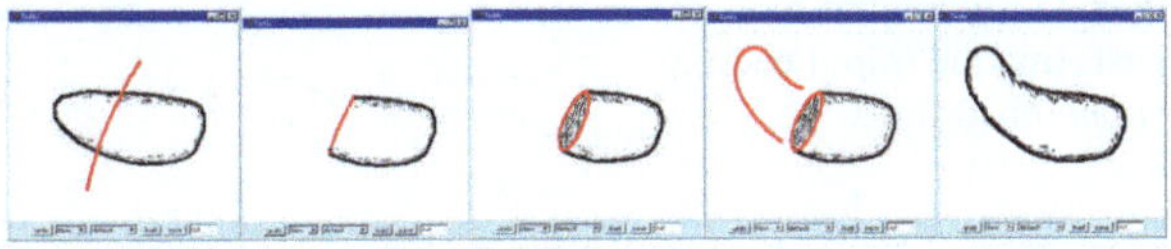

a) cutting stroke b) result c) rotated d) extruding stroke e) result

Fig. 8.10 Smoothing operation

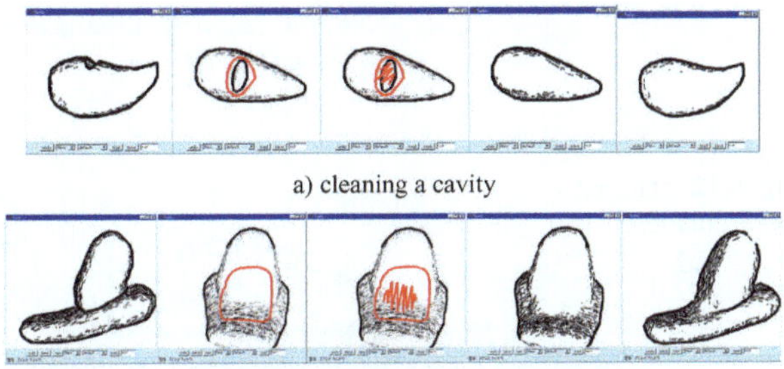

a) cleaning a cavity

b) smoothing a sharp edge

8.4.6 Smoothing

One often smoothes the surface of clay models to eliminate bumps and creases. Teddy lets the user smooth the surface by drawing a scribble during "extrusion mode." Unlike erasing, this operation modifies the actual geometry: it first removes all the polygons surrounded by the closed red surface line and then creates an entirely new surface that covers the region smoothly. This operation is useful to remove unwanted bumps and cavities (Figs. 8.3(x–z′), 8.10(a)), or to smooth the creases caused by earlier extrusion operations (Fig. 8.10(b)).

8.4.7 Transformation

We are currently experimenting with an additional "transformation" editing operation that distorts the model while preserving the polygonal mesh topology. Although it functions properly, the interface itself is not fully gestural because the modal transition into the bending mode requires a button push. This operation starts when the user presses the "bend" button and uses two freeform strokes called the reference stroke and the target stroke to modify the model. The system moves vertices of the polygonal model so that the spatial relation between the original position and the target stroke is identical to the relation between the resulting position and the reference stroke. This movement is parallel to the screen, and the vertices do not move perpendicular to the screen. This operation is described in [6] as warp; we do not discuss the algorithm further.

Transformation can be used to bend, elongate, and distort the shape (Fig. 8.11). We plan to make the system infer the reference stroke automatically from the ob-

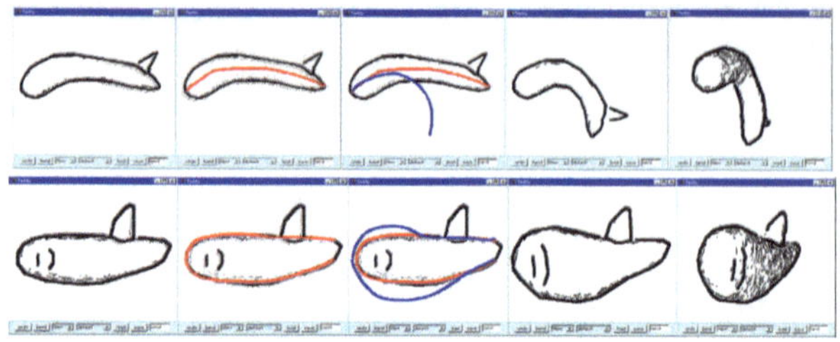

Fig. 8.11 Examples of transformation (*top*: bending, *bottom*: distortion)

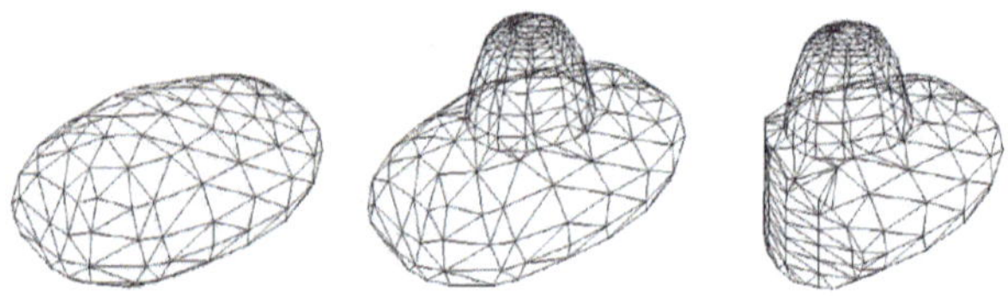

Fig. 8.12 Internal representation

ject's structure in order to simplify the operation, in a manner similar to the mark-based interaction technique of [3].

8.5 Algorithm

We next describe how the system constructs a 3D polygonal mesh from the user's freeform strokes. Internally, a model is represented as a polygonal mesh [31]. Each editing operation modifies the mesh to conform to the shape specified by the user's input strokes (Fig. 8.12). The resulting model is always topologically equivalent to a sphere. We developed the current implementation as a prototype for designing the interface; the algorithms are subject to further refinement and they fail for some illegal strokes (in that case, the system indicates the problem and requests an alternative stroke). However, these exceptional cases are fairly rare, and the algorithm works well for a wide variety of shapes.

Our algorithms for creation and extrusion are closely related to those for freeform surface construction based on skeletons [4, 19], which create a surface around user-defined skeletons using implicit surface techniques. While our current implementation does not use implicit surfaces, they could be used in an alternative implementation.

In order to remove noise in the handwriting input stroke and to construct a regular polygonal mesh, every input stroke is re-sampled to form a smooth polyline with uniform edge length before further processing [5].

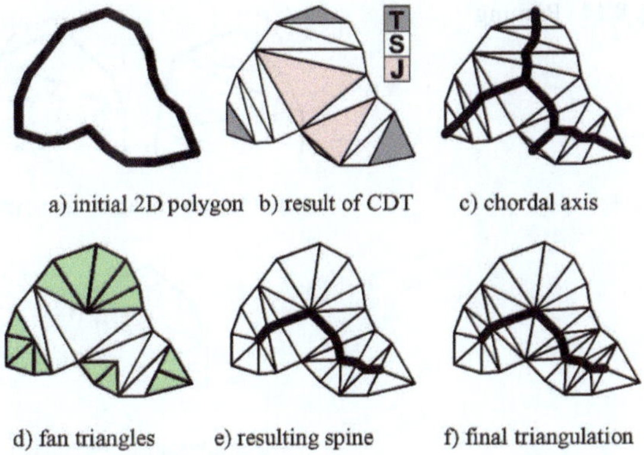

Fig. 8.13 Finding the spine

8.5.1 Creating a New Object

Our algorithm creates a new closed polygonal mesh model from the initial stroke. The overall procedure is this: we first create a closed planar polygon by connecting the start point and end point of the stroke, and determine the spine or axes of the polygon using the chordal axis introduced in [24]. We then elevate the vertices of the spine by an amount proportional to their distance from the polygon. Finally, we construct a polygonal mesh wrapping the spine and the polygon in such a way that sections form ovals.

When constructing the initial closed planar polygon, the system makes all edges a predefined unit length (see Fig. 8.13(a)). If the polygon is self-intersecting, the algorithm stops and the system requests an alternative stroke. The edges of this initial polygon are called external edges, while edges added in the following triangulation are called internal edges.

The system then performs a constrained Delaunay triangulation of the polygon (Fig. 8.13(b)). We then divide the triangles into three categories: triangles with two external edges (terminal triangle), triangles with one external edge (sleeve triangle), and triangles without external edges (junction triangle). The chordal axis is obtained by connecting the midpoints of the internal edges (Fig. 8.13(c)), but our inflation algorithm first requires the pruning of insignificant branches and the re-triangulation of the mesh. This pruning algorithm is also introduced in [24].

To prune insignificant branches, we examine each terminal triangle in turn, expanding it into progressively larger regions by merging it with adjacent triangles (Fig. 8.14(a–b)). Let X be a terminal triangle; then X has two exterior edges and one interior edge. We erect a semicircle whose diameter is the interior edge, and which lies on the same side of that edge as does X. If all three vertices of X lie on or within this semicircle, we remove the interior edge and merge X with the triangle that lies on the other side of the edge.

If the newly merged triangle is a sleeve triangle, then X now has three exterior edges and a new interior edge. Again, we erect a semicircle on the interior edge and check that all vertices are within it. We continue until some vertex lies outside the semicircle (Fig. 8.14(c)), or until the newly merged triangle is a junction triangle. In

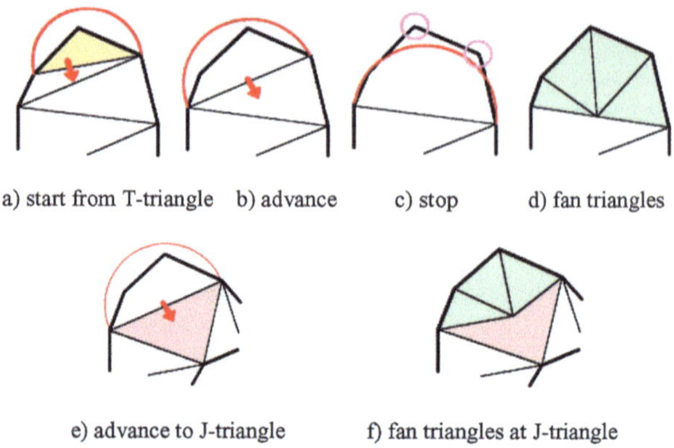

Fig. 8.14 Pruning

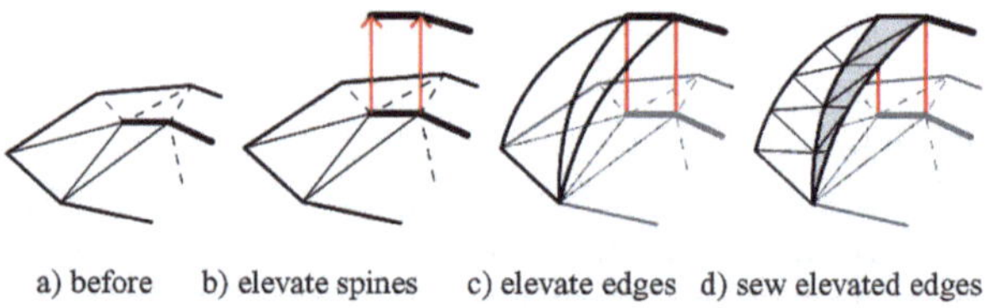

Fig. 8.15 Polygonal mesh construction

the first case, we triangulate X with a "fan" of triangles radiating from the midpoint of the interior edge (Fig. 8.14(d)). In the second case, we triangulate with a fan from the midpoint of the junction triangle (Fig. 8.14(e–f)). The resulting fan triangles are shown in Fig. 8.13(d). The pruned spine is obtained by connecting the midpoints of remaining sleeve and junction triangles' internal edges (Fig. 8.13(e)).

The next step is to subdivide the sleeve triangles and junction triangles to make them ready for elevation. These triangles are divided at the spine and the resulting polygons are triangulated, so that we now have a complete 2D triangular mesh between the spine and the perimeter of the initial polygon (Fig. 8.13(f)).

Next, each vertex of the spine is elevated proportionally to the average distance between the vertex and the external vertices that are directly connected to the vertex (Fig. 8.15(a, b)). Each internal edge of each fan triangle, excluding spine edges, is converted to a quarter oval (Fig. 8.15(c)), and the system constructs an appropriate polygonal mesh by sewing together the neighboring elevated edges, as shown in Fig. 8.15(d). The elevated mesh is copied to the other side to make the mesh closed and symmetric. Finally, the system applies mesh refinement algorithms to remove short edges and small triangles [12].

8.5.2 Painting on the Surface

The system creates surface lines by sequentially projecting each line segment of the input stroke onto the object's surface polygons. For each line segment, the system first calculates a bounded plane consisting of all rays shot from the camera through

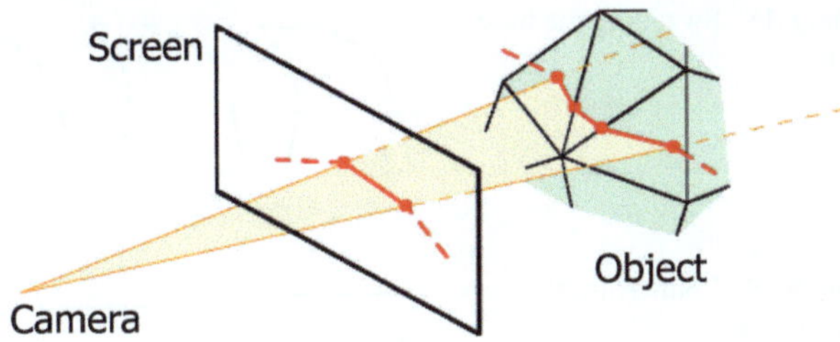

Fig. 8.16 Construction of surface lines

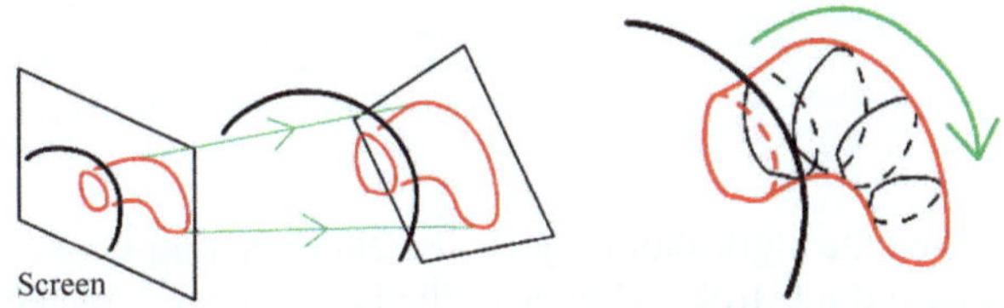

Fig. 8.17 Extrusion algorithm

the segment on the screen. Then the system finds all intersections between the plane and each polygon of the object, and splices the resulting 3D line segments together (Fig. 8.16). The actual implementation searches for the intersections efficiently using polygon connectivity information. If a ray from the camera crosses multiple polygons, only the polygon nearest to the camera position is used. If the resulting 3D segments cannot be spliced together (e.g., if the stroke crosses a "fold" of the object), the algorithm fails.

8.5.3 Extrusion

The extrusion algorithm creates new polygonal meshes based on a closed base surface line (called the base ring) and an extruding stroke. Briefly, the 2D extruding stroke is projected onto a plane perpendicular to the object surface (Fig. 8.17(a)), and the base ring is swept along the projected extruding stroke (Fig. 8.17(b)). The base ring is defined as a closed 3D polyline that lies on the surface of the polygonal mesh, and the normal of the ring is defined as that of the best matching plane of the ring.

First, the system finds the plane for projection: the plane passing through the base ring's center of gravity and lying parallel to the normal of the base ring.[2] Under the above constraints, the plane faces toward the camera as much as possible (Fig. 8.17(a)).

[2]The normal of the ring is calculated as follows: Project the points of the ring to the original XY-plane. Then compute the enclosed "signed area" by the formula: $A_{xy} = 0.5 \times \sum_{i=0}^{n-1}(x[i] \times y[i+1] - x[i+1] \times y[i])$ (indices are wrapped around so that $x[n]$ means $x[0]$). Calculate A_{yx} and A_{zx} similarly, and the vector $v = (A_{yz}, A_{zx}, A_{xy})$ is defined as the normal of the ring.

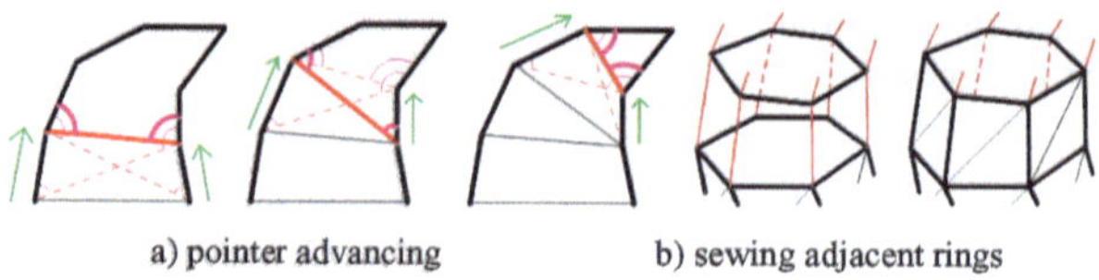

Fig. 8.18 Sweeping the base ring

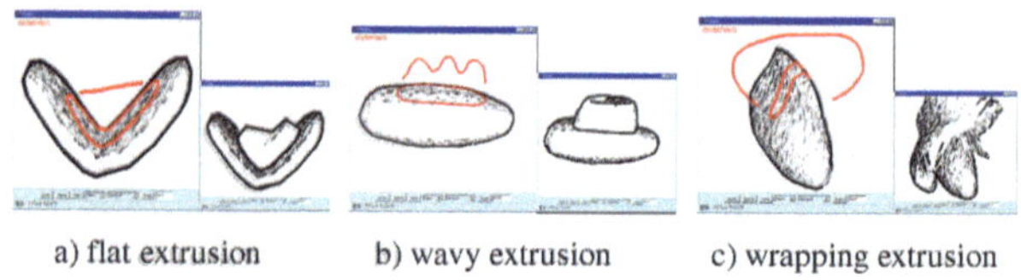

Fig. 8.19 Counterintuitive extrusions

Then the algorithm projects the 2D extruding stroke onto the plane, producing a 3D extruding stroke. Copies of the base ring are created along the extruding stroke in such a way as to be almost perpendicular to the direction of the extrusion, and are resized to fit within the stroke. This is done by advancing two pointers (left and right) along the extruding stroke starting from both ends. In each step, the system chooses the best of the following three possibilities: advance the left pointer, the right pointer, or both. The goodness value increases when the angle between the line connecting the pointers and the direction of the stroke at each pointer is close to 90 degrees (Fig. 8.18(a)). This process completes when the two pointers meet.

Finally, the original polygons surrounded by the base ring are deleted, and new polygons are created by sewing the neighboring copies of the base ring together [2] (Fig. 8.18(b)). The system uses the same algorithm to dig a cavity on the surface.

This simple algorithm works well for a wide variety of extrusions but creates counterintuitive shapes when the user draws unexpected extruding strokes or when the base surface is not sufficiently planar (Fig. 8.19).

8.5.4 Cutting

The cutting algorithm is based on the painting algorithm. Each line segment of the cutting stroke is projected onto the front and back facing polygons. The system connects the corresponding end points of the projected edges to construct a planar polygon (Fig. 8.20). This operation is performed for every line segment, and the system constructs the complete section by splicing these planar polygons together.

Finally, the system triangulates each planar polygon [26], and removes all polygons to the left of the cutting stroke.

8.5.5 Smoothing

The smoothing operation deletes the polygons surrounded by the closed surface line (called a ring) and creates new polygons to cover the hole smoothly. First, the

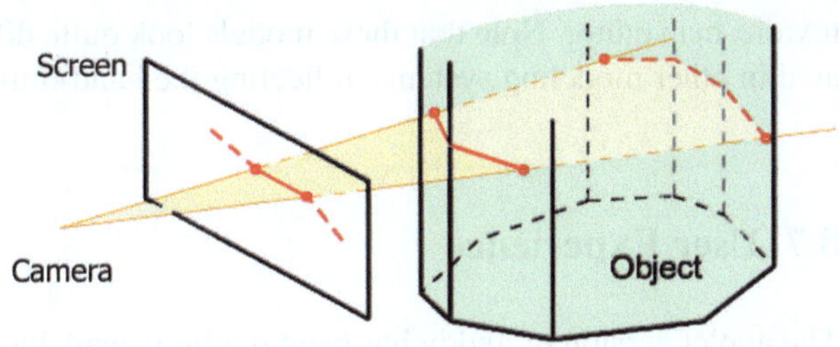

Fig. 8.20 Cutting

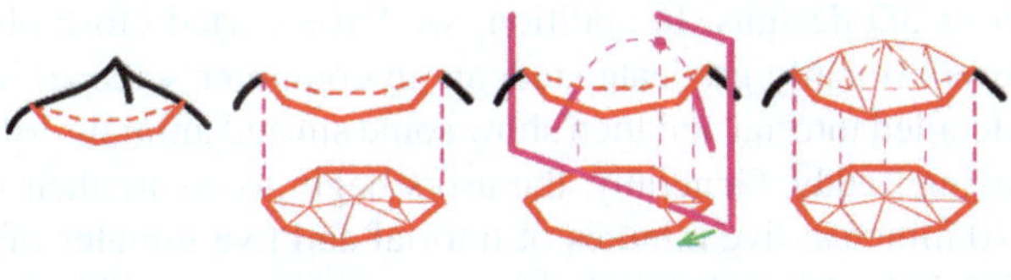

Fig. 8.21 Smoothing algorithm

system translates the objects into a coordinate system whose Z-axis is parallel to the normal of the ring. Next, the system creates a 2D polygon by projecting the ring onto the XY-plane in the newly created coordinate system, and triangulates the polygon (Fig. 8.21(b)). (The current implementation fails if the area surrounded by the ring contains creases and is folded when projected on the XY-plane.) The triangulation is designed to create a good triangular mesh based on [26]: it first creates a constrained Delaunay triangulation and gradually refines the mesh by edge splitting and flipping; then each vertex is elevated along the Z-axis to create a smooth 3D surface (Fig. 8.21(d)).

The algorithm for determining the Z-value of a vertex is as follows: For each edge of the ring, consider a plane that passes through the vertex and the midpoint of the edge and is parallel to the Z-axis. Then calculate the z-value of the vertex so that it lies on the 2D Bézier curve that smoothly interpolates both ends of the ring on the plane (Fig. 8.21(c)). The final z-value of the vertex is the average of these z-values.

Finally, we apply a surface-fairing algorithm [28] to the newly created polygons to enhance smoothness.

8.6 Implementation

Our prototype is implemented as a 13,000 line Java program. We tested a display-integrated tablet (Mutoh MVT-14, see Fig. 8.1) and an electric whiteboard (Xerox Liveboard) in addition to a standard mouse. The mesh construction process is completely real-time, but causes a short pause (a few seconds) when the model becomes complicated. Teddy can export models in OBJ file format. Figure 8.2 shows some 3D models created with Teddy by an expert user and painted using a commercial texture-map editor. Note that these models look quite different from 3D models created in other modeling systems, reflecting the hand-drawn nature of the shape.

8.7 User Experience

The applet version of Teddy has been publicly available since 1999. Feedback from the users indicates that Teddy is quite intuitive and encourages them to explore various 3D designs. In addition, we have started close observation of how first-time users (mainly graduate students in computer science) learn Teddy. We start with a detailed tutorial and then show some stuffed animals, asking the users to create them using Teddy. Generally, the users begin to create their own models fluently within 10 minutes: five minutes of tutorial and five minutes of guided practice. After that, it takes a few minutes for them to create a stuffed animal such as those in Fig. 8.2 (excluding the texture).

Our technique has been used in several commercial products including video games (Nintendo Gamecube and Sony Playstation 2) and 3D modeling packages. In the games, the users create their own characters using our techniques and use them in the following battles and adventures. The modeling packages used our technique in two ways, one is for expert users to create initial model to be modified later using standard mesh editing tools and one is for novice users (mainly children) to create simple 3D models.

We also run a case study in a geography class in a high school (Fig. 8.22). A teacher needs to teach various 3D concepts such as mountains and valleys in geography, but it is often difficult to explain these concepts using 2D medium such as blackboards. One can also use videos and physical props, but these tools lacks the informal style seen in sketching in backboards, which is very important in educational purposes. Our technique can naturally extend sketching activities into three dimensions.

In the class, the teacher described various concepts in geography one by one using our tool. He first showed a mountain model and carved multiple U-shaped valleys, eventually revealing a characteristic shape called a horn (Fig. 8.22(a)). He next showed a simple flat terrain model and carved flat valleys successively to create a river terrace (Fig. 8.22(b)). He also explained the concept of ocean trench using our system (Fig. 8.22(c)). The teacher usually explains it using 2D illustration on a blackboard, but many students wrongly misunderstand that the ocean trench is just a hole, not a trench when seeing the 2D cross section. One of the most convincing examples was teaching the concept of contour lines using our technique (Fig. 8.22(d)). The teacher first shows a 3D model of a mountain and draws several horizontal lines in the side view, saying that these lines indicate equal heights. The teacher then changes the viewpoint to see the mountain and the lines from the top. This way, the students understand the relationship between the closed lines on the map (contour lines) and the 3D geometry. Students answered that 3D sketching helped understanding complicated 3D concepts in a follow-up questionnaire.

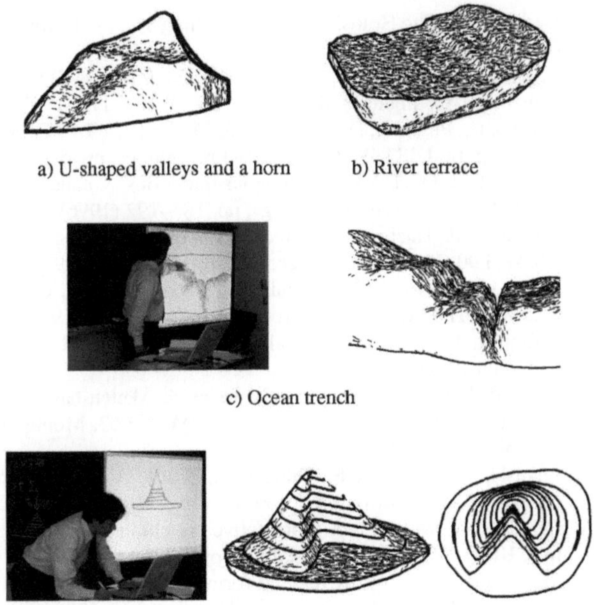

a) U-shaped valleys and a horn b) River terrace

c) Ocean trench

d) Contour lines

Fig. 8.22 Teaching geography using three dimensional sketching

8.8 Conclusions

This chapter introduced a sketching interface for designing freeform 3D models. The user interactively sketches the silhouette of the desired 3D model and the system automatically constructs a reasonable, rotund 3D model. The user can also cut the model or add part on top of the model using sketching operation. The proposed system use simple mesh representation and achieve inflation via skeleton extraction based on constrained Delaunay triangulation.

References

1. Alexe, A., Barthe, L., Gaildrat, V., Cani, M.: A sketch-based modelling system using convolution surfaces. Rapport de recherch, IRIT-2005-17-R, IRIT, Université Paul Sabatier, Toulouse, Juillet 2005
2. Barequet, G., Sharir, M.: Piecewise-linear interpolation between polygonal slices. In: ACM 10th Computational Geometry Proceedings, pp. 93–102 (1994)
3. Baudel, T.: A mark-based interaction paradigm for free-hand drawing. In: UIST'94 Conference Proceedings, pp. 185–192 (1994)
4. Bloomenthal, J., Wyvill, B.: Interactive techniques for implicit modeling. In: 1990 Symposium on Interactive 3D Graphics, pp. 109–116 (1990)
5. Cohen, J.M., Markosian, L., Zeleznik, R.C., Hughes, J.F., Barzel, R.: An interface for sketching 3D curves. In: 1999 Symposium on Interactive 3D Graphics, pp. 17–21 (1999)
6. Correa, W.T., Jensen, R.J., Thayer, C.E., Finkelstein, A.: Texture mapping for cell animation. In: SIGGRAPH 98 Conference Proceedings, pp. 435–456 (1998)

7. Deering, M.: The Holosketch VR sketching system. Communications of the ACM **39**(5), 54–61 (1996)
8. Eggli, L., Hsu, C., Elber, G., Bruderlin, B.: Inferring 3D models from freehand sketches and constraints. Computer-Aided Design **29**(2), 101–112 (1997)
9. Grimm, C., Pugmire, D., Bloomental, M., Hughes, J.F., Cohen, E.: Visual interfaces for solids modeling. In: UIST '95 Conference Proceedings, pp. 51–60 (1995)
10. Gross, M.D., Do, E.Y.L.: Ambiguous intentions: A paper-like interface for creative design. In: UIST'96 Conference Proceedings, pp. 183–192 (1996)
11. Hanrahan, P., Haeberli, P.: Direct WYSIWYG painting and texturing on 3D shapes. In: SIGGRAPH 90 Conference Proceedings, pp. 215–224 (1990)
12. Hoppe, H., DeRose, T., Duchamp, T., McDonald, J., Stuetzle, W.: Mesh optimization. In: SIGGRAPH 93 Conference Proceedings, pp. 19–26 (1993)
13. Hultquist, J.: A virtual trackball. In: Glassner, A. (ed.) Graphics Gems, pp. 462–463. Academic Press, San Diego (1990)
14. Igarashi, T., Hughes, J.F.: Smooth meshes for sketch-based freeform modeling. In: ACM Symposium on Interactive 3D Graphics, ACM I3D'03, Monterey, California, 27–30 April 2003, pp. 139–142 (2003)
15. Igarashi, T., Matsuoka, S., Tanaka, H.: Teddy: A sketching interface for 3D freeform design. In: SIGGRAPH 99 Conference Proceedings (1999)
16. Landay, J.A., Myers, B.A.: Interactive sketching for the early stages of user inter-face design. In: CHI'95 Conference Proceedings, pp. 43–50 (1995)
17. MacCracken, R., Joy, K.I.: Free-form deformations with lattices of arbitrary topology. In: SIGGRAPH 96 Conference Proceedings, pp. 181–188 (1996)
18. Markosian, L., Kowalski, M.A., Trychin, S.J., Bourdev, L.D., Goldstein, D., Hughes, J.F.: Real-time nonphotorealistic rendering. In: SIGGRAPH 97 Conference Proceedings, pp. 415–420 (1997)
19. Markosian, L., Cohen, J.M., Crulli, T., Hughes, J.F.: Skin: A constructive approach to modeling free-form shapes. In: SIGGRAPH 99 Conference Proceedings (1999)
20. Nealen, A., Igarashi, T., Sorkine, O., Alexa, M.: FiberMesh: Designing freeform surfaces with 3D curves. ACM Transactions on Computer Graphics (Proceedings of SIGGRAPH 2007) **23**(3), 41 (2007)
21. Nishimura, H., Hirai, M., Kawai, T., Kawata, T., Shirakawa, I., Omura, K.: Object modeling by distribution function and a method of image generation. Transactions of the Institute of Electronics and Communication Engineers of Japan **J68-D**(4), 718–725 (1985)
22. Owada, S., Nielsen, F., Nakazawa, K., Igarashi, T.: A sketching interface for modeling the internal structures of 3D shapes. In: Proceedings of 3rd International Symposium on Smart Graphics, 2–4 July 2003. Lecture Notes in Computer Science, pp. 49–57. Springer, Heidelberg (2003)
23. Pausch, R., Burnette, T., Capeheart, A.C., Conway, M., Cosgrove, D., DeLine, R., Durbin, J., Gossweiler, R., Koga, S., White, J.: Alice: Rapid prototyping system for virtual reality. IEEE Computer Graphics and Applications **15**(3), 8–11 (1995)
24. Prasad, L.: Morphological analysis of shapes. CNLS Newsletter **139**, 1–18 (1997)
25. Schmidt, R., Wy-vill, B., Sousa, M.C., Jorge, J.A.: ShapeShop: Sketch-based solid modeling with BlobTrees. In: 2nd Eurographics Workshop on Sketch-Based Interfaces and Modeling, pp. 53–62 (2005)
26. Shewchuk, J.R.: Triangle: engineering a 2D quality mesh generator and Delauny tri-angulator. In: First Workshop on Applied Computational Geometry Proceedings, pp. 124–133 (1996)
27. Singh, K., Fiume, E.: Wires: A geometric deformation technique. In: SIGGRAPH 98 Conference Proceedings, pp. 405–414 (1998)
28. Taubin, G.: A signal processing approach to fair surface design. In: SIGGRAPH 95 Conference Proceedings, pp. 351–358 (1995)
29. van Overveld, K., Wyvill, B.: Polygon inflation for animated models: a method for the extrusion of arbitrary polygon meshes. Journal of Visualization and Computer Animation **18**, 3–16 (1997)

30. Wang, S.W., Kaufman, A.E.: Volume sculpting. In: 1995 Symposium on Interactive 3D Graphics, pp. 109–116 (1995)
31. Welch, W., Witkin, A.: Free-form shape design using triangulated surfaces. In: SIGGRAPH 94 Conference Proceedings, pp. 247–256 (1994)
32. Williams, L.: 3D paint. In: 1990 Symposium on Interactive 3D Graphics, pp. 225–233 (1990)
33. Williams, L.: Shading in two dimensions. In: Graphics Interface '91, pp. 143–151 (1991)
34. Zeleznik, R.C., Herndon, K.P., Hughes, J.F.: SKETCH: An interface for sketching 3D scenes. In: SIGGRAPH 96 Conference Proceedings, pp. 163–170 (1996)

Chapter 9
The Creation and Modification of 3D Models Using Sketches and Curves

Andrew Nealen and Marc Alexa

9.1 Introduction

This chapter describes interfaces and algorithms that support a potentially untrained user's intent to communicate a mental model of 2D/3D shape to a digital computer; FiberMesh for the creation, and SilSketch for the modification of 3D shapes. FiberMesh is a system for designing freeform surfaces with a collection of 3D curves. The user first creates a rough 3D model by using a sketching interface. The user-drawn strokes stay on the model surface and serve as handles for controlling the geometry. For a given set of curves, the system automatically constructs a smooth surface embedding by applying functional optimization. SilSketch is an over-sketching interface for feature-preserving surface mesh editing. The user sketches a stroke that is the suggested position of part of a silhouette of the displayed surface. The overall algorithm has been designed to enable interactive modification of the surface—yielding a surface editing system that comes close to the experience of sketching 3D models on paper.

While machines are equipped with clearly defined interfaces for video input (cameras, scanners) and output (monitors, projectors), human beings are not. In fact there is quite an imbalance at work here; while one could argue that the human visual system is currently superior to the video-in of a machine, we lack a clear definition of the human video-out. The most common ways of communicating and/or creating 2D/3D shapes are either using hand-drawn 2D sketches, or modeling 3D shapes with malleable materials such as clay. Unfortunately, these means of communication and creation are generally limited to a small subset of artistically trained individuals. In the following we describe our interfaces and algorithms, which are

A. Nealen (✉)
Rutgers University, 110 Frelinghuysen Road, Piscataway, NJ 08854, USA
e-mail: andy@nealen.net

M. Alexa
TU Berlin, Einsteinufer 17, 10587 Berlin, Germany
e-mail: marc.alexa@tu-berlin.de

J. Jorge, F. Samavati (eds.), *Sketch-based Interfaces and Modeling*,
DOI 10.1007/978-1-84882-812-4_9, © Springer-Verlag London Limited 2011

designed to assist the user with meaningful and intuitive operations and thereby alleviate the described shortcomings.

9.2 FiberMesh: Designing Freeform Surfaces with 3D Curves

Current tools for freeform design, and the resulting design process, can be roughly categorized into two groups. The group of professional modeling packages makes use of parametric patches or subdivision surfaces [1, 31], where the user has to lay out the coarsest level patches in an initial modeling stage, and then modify control points to generate details. Because it is difficult for inexperienced users to generate the control structure for an intended shape from scratch, a group of research tools [19, 20, 23, 24, 36] as well as character editors in entertainment media such as videogames [15, 30] are built around intuitive modeling metaphors such as sketching, trying to hide the mathematical subtleties of surface description from the user. However, some of these tools lack a high-level control structure, making it difficult to iteratively refine the design, or re-use existing designs.

We try to bridge the gap by using curves, a universally accepted modeling metaphor, as an interface for designing a surface. Notice that curves appear in both tools mentioned above: they appear as parameter lines, or seams where locally parameterized patches meet; they are sketched to generate or modify shape, or they are extracted from the current shape and used as handles. Also note that traditional design is mostly based on drawing characteristic curves.

Yet, design is a process. We cannot expect a user to draw the control (or characteristic) curves of a shape into free space. Our first fundamental idea is to let the user *define control curves by drawing them onto the shape* in its current design stage. These curves can be used as handles for deformation right after their definition, as in other tools, or at any other time in the design process. Of course, the effect of control curves can be modified (i.e. smooth vs. sharp edge), they can be removed from the current design, and there are no restrictions on their placement and topological structure. Specifically, they may be connected to or intersect other curves, or not.

The second fundamental principle is that *the shape is defined by the control curves* at any stage of the design process. While we found it important to serve the process of construction—indeed, the curves themselves define the topology of the surface—the result should be independent of when a control curve was modified. We achieve this by defining the surface to minimize certain functions of its differentials [32, 45], while constraining it by the control curves.

The system allows the user to design practical models such as 3D characters (Fig. 9.1), by introducing a high-level user interface for curve control.

It is crucial that both the modification of curves as well as the computation of surface geometry allow for an interactive and smoothly responding system. For this we build on the recent advances in discrete Laplacian [4, 5, 40, 46] and other higher-order or non-linear functionals for surface processing [6, 18, 44]. One of the key driving forces is the use of highly efficient sparse linear solvers [9, 42]. They can

Fig. 9.1 Modeling results using FIBERMESH. The user interactively defines the control curves, combining sketching and direct manipulation, and the system continuously presents fair interpolative surfaces defined by these curves (dark = *smooth curve*, light = *sharp curve*)

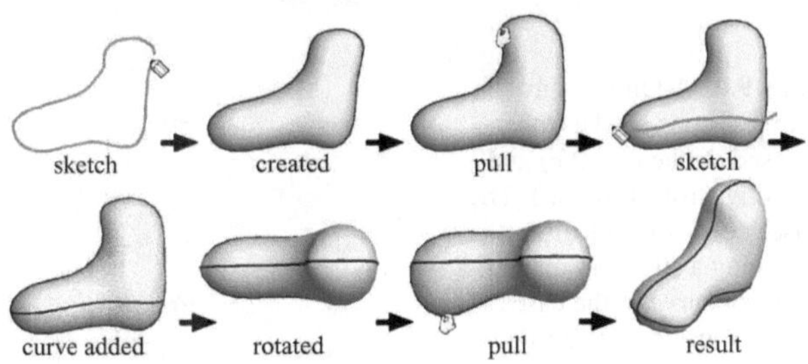

Fig. 9.2 An example modeling sequence

efficiently solve matrix systems of tens of thousands of entries, which makes it possible to process interesting 3D meshes in real-time.

9.2.1 User Interface

From the user's point of view, the system can be seen as an extension to a freeform modeling system based on silhouette sketching, such as Teddy [20]. The user interactively draws the silhouette of the desired geometry and the system automatically constructs a (rotund) surface via functional optimization, such that its silhouette matches the user's sketch. However, the user's original stroke *stays* on the model surface and serves as a handle for further geometry control. The user can manipulate these curves interactively and the surface geometry changes accordingly. In addition, the user can freely add and remove control curves on the surface. These extensions enable the design of far more elaborate shapes than those possible with sketching alone. Figure 9.2 shows an overview of the process.

In a sense, the modeling process is similar to traditional modeling methods, such as parametric patches and subdivision surfaces: the user also defines nets of curves

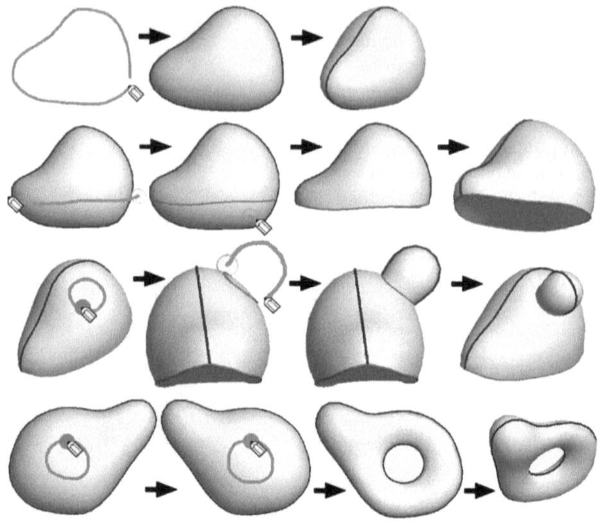

Fig. 9.3 Sketching operations (from top to bottom): creation, cut, extrusion and tunnel

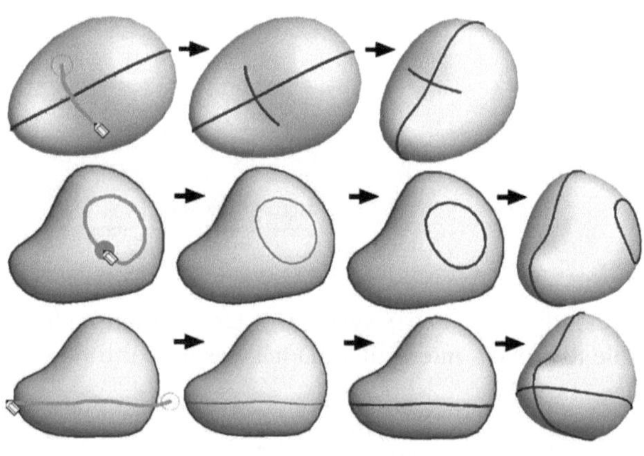

Fig. 9.4 Adding control curves: open stroke (*top*), closed stroke (*middle*) and cutting stroke (*bottom*). The user needs to click after drawing a stroke to make it a control curve in the cases of closed stroke and cutting stroke

and the system automatically generates a smooth surface based on these. An advantage of this interface is that the user does not need to worry about the topology of the curves. Traditional methods require the user to cover the entire surface with triangle or quad regions. This method is much more flexible: curves need not be connected to other curves and much fewer curves can represent simple geometry. It is also important that, instead of providing individual points as an interface, our interface treats curves as continuous entities. We believe this can help smooth the "skill transfer" from 2D drawing to 3D modeling.

9.2.1.1 Sketching Tool

The system provides five kinds of sketching operations: creation, cut, extrusion, tunnel (Fig. 9.3), and add-control curve (Fig. 9.4). When the user draws a closed stroke

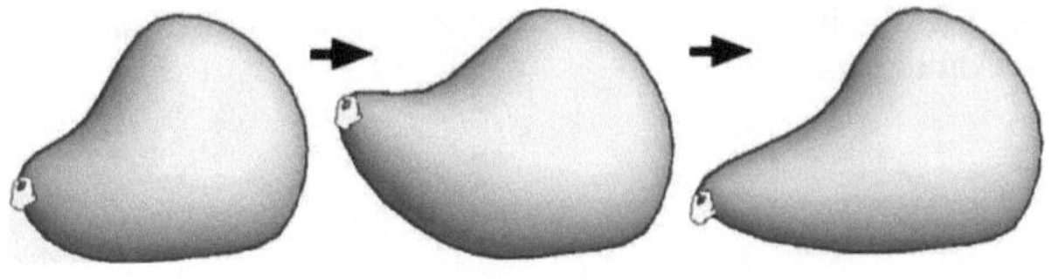

Fig. 9.5 Pulling a curve. The deformed curve segment is determined by how much of it the user peels off

on a blank canvas, the system automatically inflates the closed area and presents an initial 3D model. The user draws a stroke crossing the model to cut it. Drawing a closed stroke on the object surface followed by a silhouette stroke creates an extrusion. If the user draws another closed loop on the opposite side of the surface, the system generates a tunnel. These operations are borrowed from the original Teddy system, but the difference is that the user's original strokes stay on the model surface as control curves. These control curves literally define the surface shape (as positional constraints in the surface optimization), and the user can modify the shape by deforming these control curves. New control curves can be added by drawing an open stroke on the object surface, drawing a closed stroke followed by clicking, and by drawing a cutting stroke followed by clicking (Fig. 9.4). The last method is very useful during the early stages of model creation, since it allows the user to quickly generate a convenient handle to adjust the amount of inflation (or *fatness*).

The control curves are divided into two types: smooth curves (dark) and sharp curves (light). A smooth curve constrains the surface to be smooth across it, while a sharp curve only places positional constraints with C^0 continuity.

9.2.1.2 Deformation Tool

The deformation tool lets the user grab a curve at any point and pull it to the desired location. The curve deforms accordingly, preserving local details as much as possible (see Fig. 9.5 and Sect. 9.2.2.1). Editing operations are always applied to the control curves, not directly to the surface. If the user wants more control, new control curves must be added on the surface. Explicit addition of control curves exposes the surface structure in a clear way, and the curves serve as a convenient handle for further editing.

We use a peeling interface for the determination of the deformed curve segment (region of interest, ROI) [21]. The size of the curve segment to be deformed is proportional to the amount of pulling.

9.2.1.3 Rubbing Tool

The rubbing tool is used for smoothing a curve. As the user drags the mouse back and forth (rubs) near the target curve, the curve gradually becomes smooth. The more the user rubs, the smoother the curve becomes (Fig. 9.6). This tool is very important because the curves resulting from sketching can contain noise, and localized deformation might introduce jaggy parts.

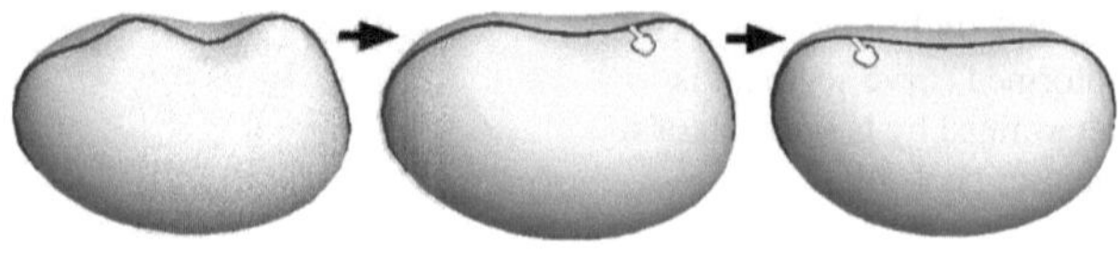

Fig. 9.6 Rubbing (smoothing) a curve

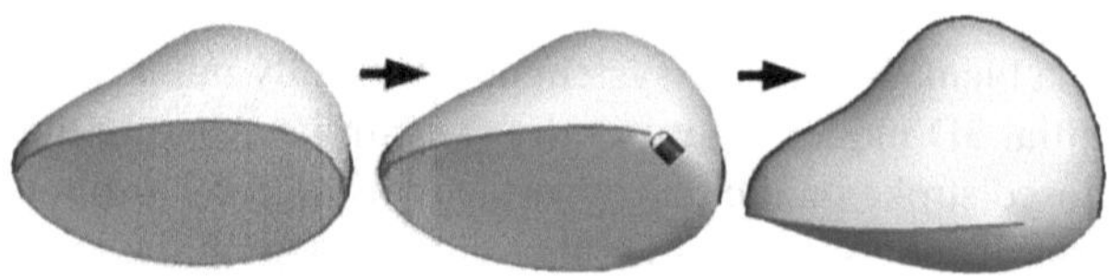

Fig. 9.7 Erasing a control curve (*left*: before erasing, *middle*: immediately after erasing, *right*: after surface optimization)

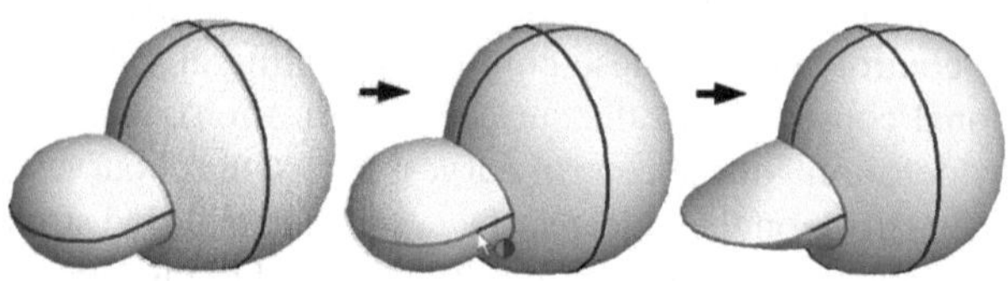

Fig. 9.8 Changing the curve type (*left*: before the change, *middle*: immediately after the change, *right*: after surface optimization)

9.2.1.4 Erasing Tool and Type Change Tool

The erasing tool works as a standard curve segment eraser: the user drags the cursor along a control curve to erase it. This is equivalent to removing constraints that define the surface. The system optimizes the surface when the user finishes an erasing operation (releases the mouse button, Fig. 9.7). The type change tool is for changing the type of a control curve. Like the erasing tool, the user drags the cursor along a curve to change the property. If the curve is a sharp curve, it converts it to a smooth curve (or curve segment), and vice versa (see Fig. 9.8).

9.2.2 Algorithm

To implement the described interface we propose an algorithm that consists of two main steps: curve deformation and surface optimization. The additional steps, mesh construction and remeshing (Sect. 9.2.2.3), only occur at the end of the modeling operations creation, extrusion, cut, and deformation.

Instead of solving for both curve positions and fair surface simultaneously, we have found that decoupling the curve deformation from the surface optimization step is fast, intuitive, produces aesthetically pleasing results, and supports our fundamental principle of defining shape by control curves. The user first deforms (pulls) the curve(s) using the deformation tool (Sect. 9.2.2.1), after which the new curve positions are fed to the surface optimization step as positional constraints (Sect. 9.2.2.2). During curve pulling, these two operations are performed sequentially to achieve interactive updates of both the curves and the surface they define.

9.2.2.1 Curve Deformation

The user interface for curve deformation is a usual direct manipulation method: the user grabs and drags a point on a curve, and the curve deforms smoothly within the peeled region of interest (ROI). The current implementation always moves the grabbed point parallel to the screen.

The algorithm we use is a variant of detail-preserving deformation methods using differential coordinates [38], combined with co-rotational methods [13]. Geometry is represented using differential coordinates, and the final result is obtained by solving a sequence of linear least-square problems, subject to boundary (positional) constraints. The main challenge in this framework is the computation of appropriate rotations for the differential coordinates. One approach is to explicitly compute rotations beforehand, typically by smoothly interpolating the prescribed orientation constraints defined by the user [29, 46–48]. These methods are not applicable in our setting because the user should only need to drag a vertex without specifying rotations. Another approach is to implicitly compute rotations as a linear combination of target vertex positions [14, 40]. Our technique is similar to these methods, but we explicitly represent rotation matrices as separate free variables. This is due to the fact that neighboring vertices along a curve are nearly collinear and inappropriate for deriving rotations from them.

Conceptually, what we want to solve is the following error minimization problem:

$$\begin{aligned}\operatorname*{arg\,min}_{\mathbf{v},\mathbf{R}} \Bigg\{ & \sum_i \left\|\mathbf{L}(\mathbf{v}_i) - \mathbf{R}_i\delta_i\right\|^2 + \sum_{i\in C_1} \left\|\mathbf{v}_i - \mathbf{v}_i'\right\|^2 + \sum_{i,j\in E} \|\mathbf{R}_i - \mathbf{R}_j\|_F^2 \\ & + \sum_{i\in C_2} \|\mathbf{R}_i - \mathbf{R}_i'\|_F^2 \Bigg\}, \end{aligned} \tag{1}$$

where $\mathbf{L}(\cdot)$ is the differential operator, $\mathbf{v}_i$ represents the vertex coordinates, $\mathbf{R}_i$ represents rotations associated with these vertices in the deformed curve, $\|\cdot\|_F$ is the Frobenius norm, E is the set of curve edges, C_1 and C_2 are the sets of constrained vertices, and primed values are given constraints. The first term minimizes the difference between the resulting differential coordinates and the rotated original differential coordinates δ_i. The second term represents positional constraints (we use three constrains: two at the boundary of the ROI and one at the handle). The third term ensures that the rotations are smoothly varying along the curve [2, 14, 41], and the last term represents rotational constraints (we use two constraints at the boundary of the ROI). These four terms also need to be appropriately weighted to obtain visually pleasing results. We have omitted these weights in the above equation for simplicity.

A problem with this approach is that $\mathbf{R}$ is not linear. Unconstrained transformation includes shearing, stretching, and scaling, which is undesirable for our application. Similar to Laplacian Surface Editing [40], we therefore use a linearized rotation

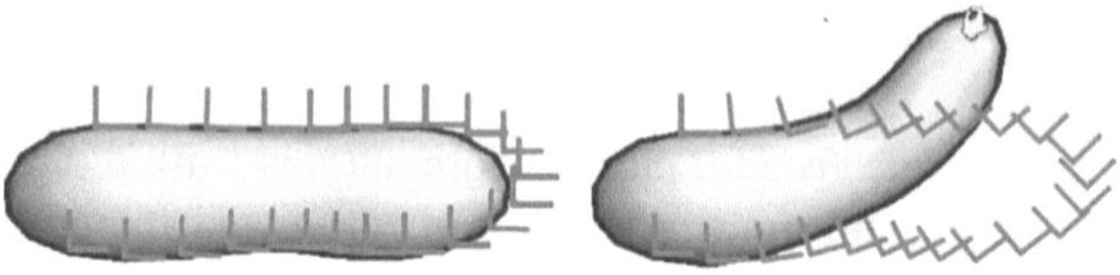

Fig. 9.9 Rotated local coordinate frames (*light grey*) after curve deformation by pulling a single vertex

matrix to represent small rotations. In order to accommodate large rotations, we iteratively compute the gross rotation by concatenating small delta rotations obtained by solving a linear system at each step.

In summary, what we solve in each step is the following minimization problem:

$$\arg\min_{\mathbf{v},\mathbf{r}} \left\{ \sum_i \left\| \mathbf{L}(\mathbf{v}_i) - \mathbf{r}_i \mathbf{R}_i \delta_i \right\|^2 + \sum_{i \in C_1} \left\| \mathbf{v}_i - \mathbf{v}_i' \right\|^2 + \sum_{i,j \in E} \| \mathbf{r}_i \mathbf{R}_i - \mathbf{r}_j \mathbf{R}_j \|_F^2 + \sum_{i \in C_2} \| \mathbf{r}_i \mathbf{R}_i - \mathbf{R}_i' \|_F^2 \right\}, \tag{2}$$

where $\mathbf{R}_i$ is the gross rotation obtained from the previous iteration step and fixed in each minimization step. $\mathbf{r}_i$ is a linearized incremental rotation represented as a skew symmetric matrix with three unknowns,

$$\mathbf{r}_i = \begin{bmatrix} 1 & -r_{iz} & r_{iy} \\ r_{iz} & 1 & -r_{ix} \\ -r_{iy} & r_{ix} & 1 \end{bmatrix}.$$

As a whole, this minimization problem amounts to the solution of a sparse linear system and it returns optimal vertex positions and delta rotations $\mathbf{r}_i$. We update target gross rotations as $\mathbf{R}_i \leftarrow \mathbf{r}_i \mathbf{R}_i$, and also orthonormalize them using polar decomposition [14]. Figure 9.9 shows the resulting gross rotations obtained using three iterations of this algorithm.

One remaining issue is the choice of differential coordinates L. We have tested two options: first-order differentials (L_0) and second-order differentials (L_1)

$$L_0 = \mathbf{v}_i - \mathbf{v}_{i-1}, \qquad L_1 = \mathbf{v}_i - \frac{1}{|N_i|} \sum_{j \in N_i} \mathbf{v}_j.$$

L_1 seems to be the popular choice for surface deformation. However in our case, we found that L_1 is not appropriate for the estimation of rotations because it almost always degenerates (i.e. is close to zero) in a smooth curve. On the other hand, L_0 always has certain length in an appropriately sampled curve and serves as a reliable guide for estimating rotations. One problem with L_0-based geometry computation is that it causes C^1 discontinuities on the boundaries of the ROI. Therefore, we first use L_0 for the iterative process of rotation estimation, and then switch to L_1 for computing the final vertex positions using the estimated rotations.

Fig. 9.10 The results of least-square meshes (*left*) and our non-linear solution (*right*) for a planar curve

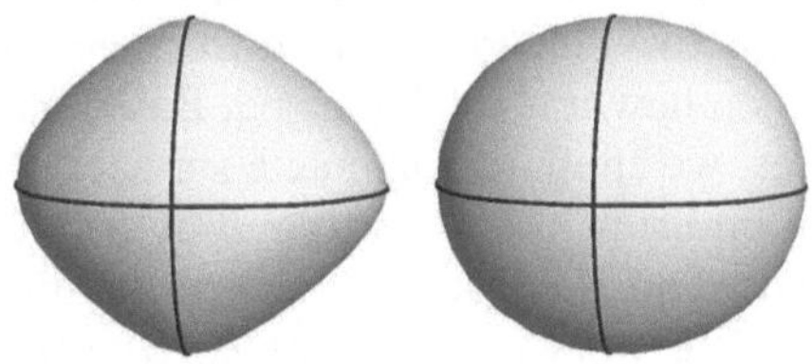

Fig. 9.11 Least-square mesh (= linearized thin-plate surface $\Delta^2\mathbf{x} = 0$, *left*) and the results of our non-linear solution (*right*)

9.2.2.2 Surface Optimization

It is important to provide real-time visual feedback to the user during control-curve deformation. This constraint necessitates the use of a fast surface optimization algorithm. An intuitive choice appears to be some discrete surface defined as the solution of a sparse linear system [5, 38]. If we kept the system matrix constant during interaction, updating the positions would only require back-substitution, which is very fast. Unfortunately, in our setting we have encountered a shortcoming inherent to these algorithms, which is due to the absence of normal constraints along the curves. Specifically, if the positional constraints lie in a subspace, the solution will also be constrained to lie in this subspace. In our tool, the initially sketched curve is planar, so the resulting mesh geometry is also planar, see Fig. 9.10 [33]. Even in the presence of non-planar positional constraints, surfaces from Sorkine et al. [39] or the linearized thin-plate surfaces of Botsch and Kobbelt [4] seem to concentrate curvature near the curves, see Fig. 9.11 (left column).

Therefore, we have chosen to implement a solution which generates a fair surface S that interpolates the control curves by means of non-linear functional optimization, also known as (non-linear) variational surface design. There are a variety of possible objective functions to choose from. Welch and Witkin [45] compute surfaces that minimize the integral of squared principle curvatures κ_1 and κ_2

$$E_{\mathrm{p}} = \int_S \left(\kappa_1^2 + \kappa_2^2\right) dA, \tag{3}$$

which is also known as thin-plate energy, while Bobenko and Schröder's [3] surfaces minimize the closely related Willmore energy

$$E_{\mathrm{w}} = \int_S (\kappa_1 - \kappa_2)^2 \, dA, \tag{4}$$

implemented as a flow. They use this flow for smoothing and hole filling. Moreton and Séquin's [32] surfaces minimize variation of curvature

$$E_c = \int_S \left(\frac{d\kappa_n}{d\hat{e}_1}\right)^2 + \left(\frac{d\kappa_n}{d\hat{e}_2}\right)^2 dA, \tag{5}$$

which is the integral of squared partial derivatives of normal curvature κ_n with respect to the directions $\hat{e}_1$, $\hat{e}_2$ of principal curvatures.

Each objective function has its own strengths and weaknesses, which also heavily depend on how it is implemented. Based on these previous results and our own experiences, we chose to compute a surface, which results from a sequence of optimization problems. This is inspired by a surface construction method presented by Schneider and Kobbelt [37]. The partial differential equation (PDE) governing fairness in their work is defined as $\Delta_B H = 0$, where Δ_B is the discrete Laplace–Beltrami operator, and $H = (\kappa_1 + \kappa_2)/2$ is the mean curvature. Their basic idea is to factorize this fourth-order problem into two second-order problems and solve them sequentially. First they compute target mean curvatures (scalars) that smoothly interpolate the curvatures specified at the boundary, and then move the vertices, one vertex at a time, to satisfy the target curvatures.

However, the second stage of their technique is not fast enough to provide interactive updates of the geometry when the user pulls the curve. In addition, we are lacking curvature information at the boundaries. Our idea for a faster computation is to cast both second-order problems as sparse linear systems that use a constant system matrix. This allows factoring the matrices once and then performing only back-substitution during the iterations.

In particular, in the first second-order system we replace the geometry dependent Laplace–Beltrami operator by the uniformly discretized Laplace operator and solve the following least-square minimization problem:

$$\arg\min_c \left\{ \sum_i \|\mathbf{L}(c_i)\|^2 + \sum_i \|c_i - c_i'\|^2 \right\}, \tag{6}$$

where $\mathbf{L}(\cdot)$ denotes the discrete graph Laplacian, to obtain a set of smoothly varying Laplacian magnitudes (LMs) $\{c_i\}$, which approximate scalar mean curvature values. The first term requires that the neighboring LMs vary smoothly and the second term requires the LMs at all vertices to be near the current LM c_i'. In the first iteration we set target LMs only for the constrained curves using the scalar curvatures along these curves. Unlike the work of Schneider and Kobbelt [37], where the curvature is fixed at the boundary, these initial target LMs are likely to change in subsequent iterations.

To obtain a geometry that satisfies these target LMs we use the uniformly discretized Laplacian as an estimator of the *integrated* mean curvature normal [44]. The integrated target Laplacian $\delta_i = A_i \cdot c_i \cdot \mathbf{n}_i$ per vertex is given as the product of an area estimate A_i for vertex i, the target LM c_i and an estimate of the normal $\mathbf{n}_i$ from the current face normals. Then new positions could then be computed by solving the following global least-square system:

$$\arg\min_{\mathbf{v}} \left\{ \sum_i \|\mathbf{L}(\mathbf{v}_i) - \delta_i\|^2 + \sum_{i \in C} \|\mathbf{v}_i - \mathbf{v}'_i\|^2 \right\}, \tag{7}$$

where the first term requires that the vertex Laplacians are close to the integrated target Laplacians, and the second term places positional constraints on all vertices in the control-curve set C.

However, our assumption that the uniformly discretized Laplacian is a reasonable estimate for the integrated mean curvature normal does not hold when the edges around a vertex are not of equal length. Rather than using a geometry dependent discretization, which would require recomputation of the system matrix in each iteration, we try to achieve equal edge lengths by prescribing target edge vectors. For this, we first compute desired scalar edge lengths, similar to the computation of desired target LMs, by solving

$$\arg\min_{e} \left\{ \sum_i \|\mathbf{L}(e_i)\|^2 + \sum_i \|e_i - e'_i\|^2 \right\}, \tag{8}$$

for a smooth set $\{e_i\}$ of target average edge lengths, from the current set of the average lengths e'_i of edges incident on vertex i. Again, we start the iterations by using only the edge lengths along the given boundary curve. Note that the matrix for this linear system is identical to the system for computing target LMs, so that we can re-use the factored matrix.

From these target average edge lengths, we derive target edge 3-vectors η_{ij} for a subset B of the edges in the mesh

$$\eta_{ij} = (e_i + e_j)/2 \cdot (\mathbf{v}_i - \mathbf{v}_j)/\|\mathbf{v}_i - \mathbf{v}_j\|. \tag{9}$$

Using this set of target edge vectors, we modify the linear system in (7) to derive the updated vertex positions as follows:

$$\arg\min_{\mathbf{v}} \left\{ \sum_i \|\mathbf{L}(\mathbf{v}_i) - \delta_i\|^2 + \sum_{i \in C} \|\mathbf{v}_i - \mathbf{v}'_i\|^2 + \sum_{(i,j) \in B} \|\mathbf{v}_i - \mathbf{v}_j - \eta_{ij}\|^2 \right\}. \tag{10}$$

We have found that it is sufficient to only constrain edges incident to the constrained curves, because setting the uniformly discretized Laplacian equal to vectors in normal direction automatically improves inner fairness at all free vertices [35].

The two-step process, consisting of solving for target LMs and edge lengths and then updating the positions, is repeated until convergence. In practice, we observed that the computation converges rather quickly, in approximately five to ten iterations. The system needs to repeatedly solve a few sparse linear systems, but the expensive matrix factorizations are required only once at the beginning (because left-hand side matrices remain unchanged during iteration). The system only needs to run back-substitutions during the iterations, which is very fast. See Fig. 9.12 for an overview of one iteration.

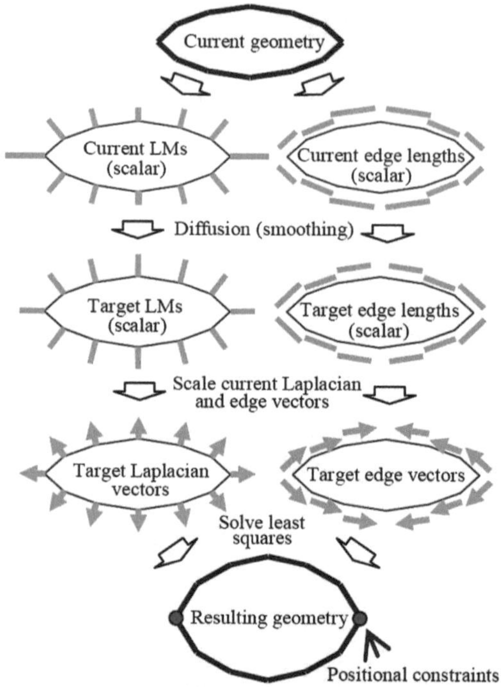

Fig. 9.12 A single iteration of our surface optimization algorithm

While the algorithm described above is stable and robust, it is not entirely independent of tesselation, since we use the uniformly weighted graph Laplacian as an approximation of the integrated mean curvature normal to avoid matrix factorization in every iteration. To overcome this, we could compute a minimal energy surface as Schneider and Kobbelt [37] propose. As an experiment with a non-linear solution that is independent of surface tesselation, we have implemented the inexact Newton method for Willmore flow described in [44]. We have found that our algorithm tends to generate very similar results if the discretization is near-regular and that, as expected, there are situations where unequal edge lengths along the fixed boundaries would benefit from the discretization-independent solution. However, not only are these techniques significantly slower to an extent that makes them unsuitable for most interactive editing situations, we have also encountered that the solution can become unstable when using insufficient boundary constraints, that is, curves without normals (this is expected and mentioned in [44]).

9.2.2.3 Meshing Implementations

The system generates a new mesh after the creation, cut, and extrusion operations. In the case of cut, the system flattens the intersection (it is always developable) and generates a 2D mesh inside of it. In the cases of creation and extrusion, the system generates a 2D mesh on the image plane within the region surrounded by

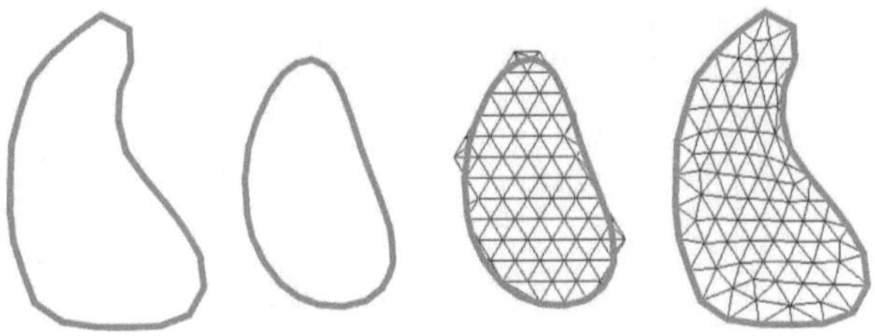

Fig. 9.13 Initial mesh generation. The sketch curve (*left*) is resampled, smoothed (*2nd from left*) and intersected with a regular triangular grid (*3rd from left*), resulting in the mesh topology used for surface optimization (*right*)

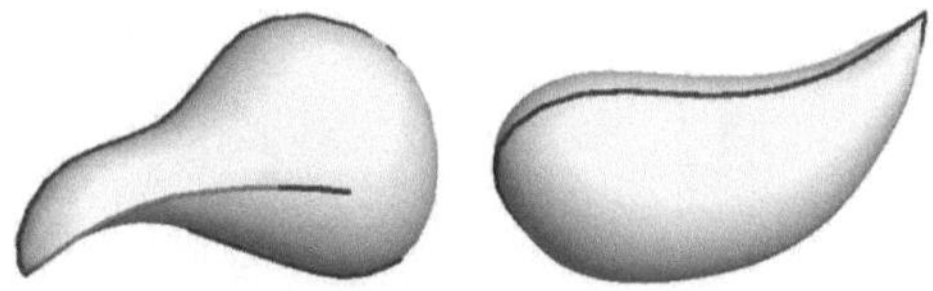

Fig. 9.14 Open sharp curve (*left*) and point-sharp curve (*right*)

the input stroke. The system first resamples the input stroke and then smoothes it by moving each vertex to the mid point of adjacent vertices. It is possible to skip this process, but the resulting mesh is nicer for our purpose because it ends up generating more triangles in high curvature areas. The resampled stroke is intersected with a regular triangular grid mesh, and each point of the resampled stroke is connected to the nearest grid vertex. Both front and back sides are created from the same 2D mesh and stitched together at the common boundary (Fig. 9.13). Note that this merely defines the mesh connectivity, not the actual geometry, which is computed subsequently as described in the previous section.

9.2.3 Results

Figure 9.14 shows shapes that are difficult to model with implicit representations [25, 36, 43]. CSG operations allow the user to represent *closed* sharp curves along a boundary [36], but it is problematic to represent an *open* sharp curve starting in the middle of a smooth surface. It is also difficult to represent *point sharp* (e.g., the tip of a cone) using the standard implicit representation. Both can be modeled with our system (Fig. 9.14).

Figures 9.15 and 9.16 show some more complex results obtained with our modeling tool. While the models shown in Fig. 9.1 each took a trained user approximately 5–10 minutes to create, those depicted in Figs. 9.15 and 9.16 took between 10 minutes (arm) and 1 hour (torso).

We have conducted an informal user study to test FIBERMESH. We trained first-time novice users for approximately 10–15 minutes, and then let them create some models (Fig. 9.17). We also asked a professional 2D animation artist to evaluate our system (Fig. 9.18). To quote the artist:

> "One great thing about this system is that one can start doodling without having a specific goal in mind, as if doodling on paper. One can just create something by drawing a stroke, and then gradually deform it guided by serendipity, which is very important for creative

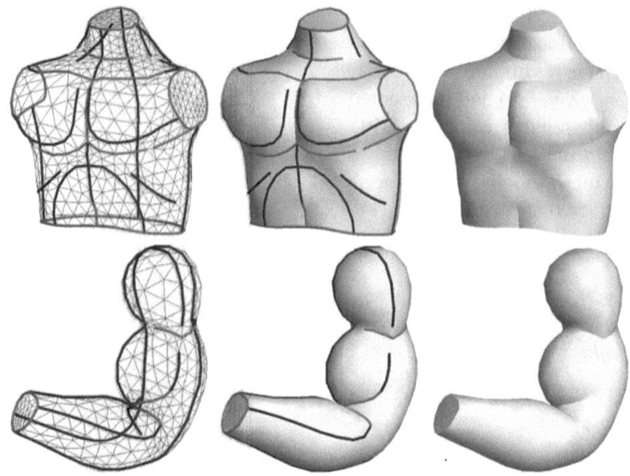

Fig. 9.15 Some results obtained using FIBERMESH

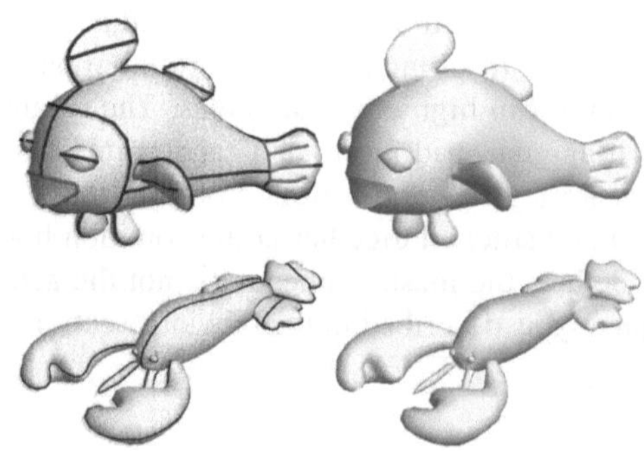

Fig. 9.16 Some *fishy* results obtained with the FIBERMESH tool

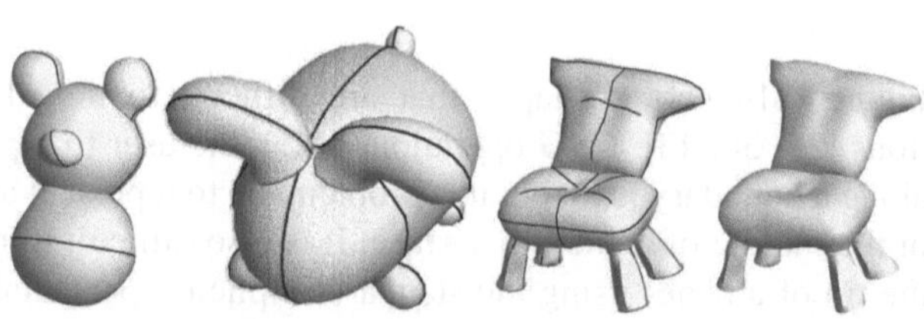

Fig. 9.17 Results obtained from first-time novice users. Model creation took 10, 10 and 20 minutes, respectively

> work. Traditional modeling systems (parametric patches and subdivision surfaces) require a specific goal and careful planning before starting to work on the model, which can hinder the creative process."

Furthermore, we have learned that (a) FIBERMESH indeed supports the skill transfer from traditional 2D sketching to 3D modeling, (b) while the system does require some practice, the amount is reasonable and acceptable and (c) creating separate models first and then merging, as well as animation tools would be very useful.

Our implementation is written in Java running on the Windows platform. Mesh processing routines are written in Java, but sparse matrix solvers are written in native code (linked via JNI). On an Intel Pentium M 1 GHz machine, factorization

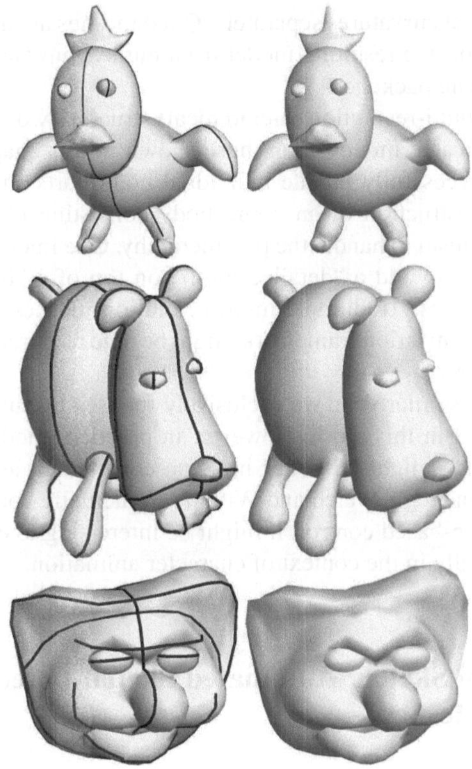

Fig. 9.18 Creations from a professional 2D animation artist. Modeling took 10, 20 and 20 minutes, respectively

takes less than a second, and interactive curve deformation (including surface optimization) works in 10–15 fps in most of our examples (600–2000 vertices). We currently process the entire mesh as a single system throughout the deformation, which causes some slowdown when the model becomes complicated. Note though, that it is straightforward to handle larger meshes by editing only a subset of the mesh, while fixing the rest.

9.2.4 Discussion

Our current implementation uses a curve only as a series of positional constraints. However, we can expect that curves have more information. For example, when an artist defines a shape with curves, it is often the case that these curves indicate the principal curvature direction of the surface. It is also natural to expect that the character lines form curvature extrema. It might be possible to obtain better (more intuitive and aesthetically pleasing) surfaces by taking these issues into account during optimization. One interesting direction to explore would be to create a quad mesh that follows the direction of the curves. Quad meshes naturally represent principal curvature directions and would make it possible to handle minimum and maximum principal curvatures separately. Quad meshes are also desirable when the user wants to export the resulting model from our system and continue editing it in a standard modeling package.

A multi-resolution (hierarchical) structure would be necessary to construct more complicated models than those shown in this chapter. Our current implementation can successfully handle individual body parts such as torso, finger, and face, but the construction of an entire body consisting of these parts would require some mechanism to handle the part hierarchy. One interesting approach would be to allow the user to add a "detailed mesh" on top of a "base mesh" as in multi-resolution approaches. Traditional multi-resolution meshes require fixed mesh topology, but our optimization framework might be able to introduce a topologically more flexible structure.

In a similar vein, we exclusively focused on surface-based control (curves on the surface) in this work. However, in practical modeling purposes, a skeleton-based approach might be better in some cases, such as a modeling of simple tube-like arms and legs. Welch and Witkin [45] actually combined surface-based control and skeleton-based control. It might be interesting to explore further into this direction, especially in the context of character animation.

9.3 SilSketch: Automated Sketch-based Editing of Surface Meshes

The process of generating 3D shapes in engineering or content creation typically goes through several *design reviews*: renderings of the shapes are viewed on paper or a screen, and designers indicate necessary changes. Oftentimes designers sketch replacements of feature lines onto the rendering. This information is then taken as the basis of the next cycle of modifications to the shape.

We have designed a surface mesh editing system motivated by design reviews: given nothing but the over-sketch of a feature line, it automatically deforms the mesh geometry to accommodate the indicated modification. Building on existing mesh deformation tools [34, 40], the main feature of this chapter is the *automatic* derivation of all necessary parameters that these systems require as input in *real-time*.

In particular, Laplacian Surface Editing [40], but also most other recent mesh deformation techniques [6, 46] require the selection of: handle vertices, the displacement for these handle vertices and a region of interest (ROI), representing the part of the mesh to be modified to accommodate the displaced handle vertices. For our system, we need to compute this information from the over-sketched feature line alone; and we do this in fractions of a second. The steps described below comprise our system (see also Fig. 9.19):

1. Based on the screen projection of the shape, a subset of pixels lying on potential feature lines is identified. These pixels are then segmented and converted to image-space polylines as the set of candidate feature lines.

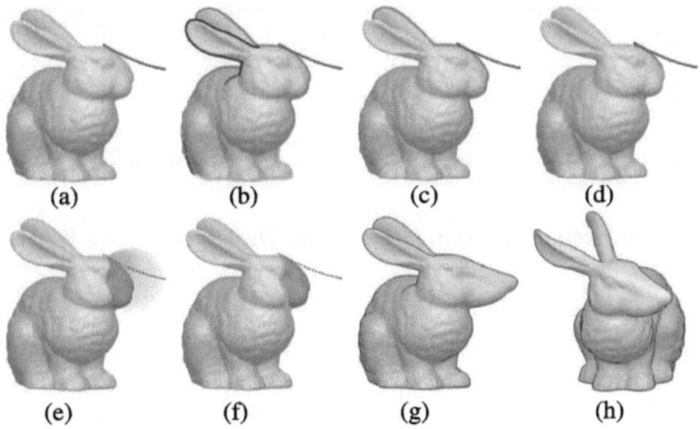

Fig. 9.19 Algorithm pipeline. *Top row*, from left to right: **a** user sketch, **b** image-space silhouettes, **c** retained silhouettes after proximity culling, **d** handle estimation; *Bottom row*, left to right: **e** correspondences and ROI estimation by bounding volumes, **f** setup for Laplacian Surface Editing, **g** and **h** deformation result. Note that the user only sees **a, g** and **h**

2. The user sketch is matched against all polylines to find the corresponding part on a feature line.
3. Based on the correspondence in image-space, a set of handle vertices in the surface mesh is selected. The image-space projection of these vertices covers the detected part of the feature line.
4. New positions for the handle vertices are derived from the displacements in image-space between the projection of the handle vertices and the user's sketch; these are the necessary displacements.
5. A part of the surface mesh around the handle vertices, computed by region growing, is defined as the ROI.

Note that in steps 3, 4, and 5 we compute the necessary input for shape deformation, while steps 1 and 2 are required to identify the input, based only on the user sketch.

Deriving the parameters for mesh deformation from sketches only is not new: Kho and Garland [27] derive ROI and handle vertices from sketching onto the projected shape, essentially implying a skeleton for a cylindrical part. A second stroke then suggests a modification of the skeleton, and the shape is deformed according to the deformed skeleton. However, according to Hoffman and Singh [17], we recognize objects mainly by a few feature lines, namely silhouettes and concave creases. Since the process of paper-based sketching relies exactly on these features, we feel it is more natural to use them as the basis for our over-sketching mesh deformation tool. In particular, this requires positional constraints defined on mesh edges and finding the correspondence between a pre-selected silhouette of the mesh and the over-sketched silhouette. In our earlier work [34] the user manually selects the ROI and a part of one of the silhouettes as a pre-process. In the work presented here, all these manual selections are now automated; the user only provides a single stroke, from which handle and ROI are estimated (Figs. 9.19 and 9.20).

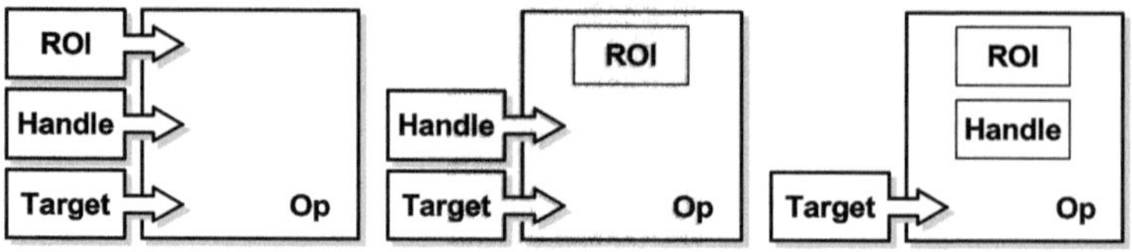

Fig. 9.20 Required user interaction (from left to right): Nealen et al. [34], Kho and Garland [27], and our approach

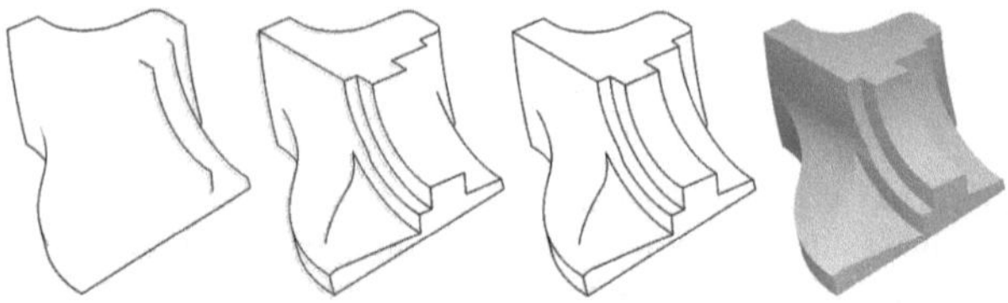

Fig. 9.21 Depth map discontinuities (*left*), normal map discontinuities (*2nd left*), combined discontinuities (*3rd left*), flat shaded scene (*right*)

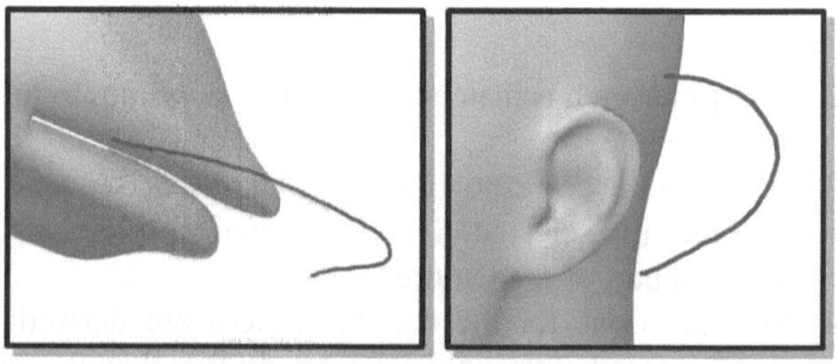

Fig. 9.22 Handle estimation due to the similarity of handle candidate (*light grey* partial object silhouette) and targeted deformation (*dark grey* sketch)

We have also observed that computing silhouettes from the mesh representation (i.e. in object-space) has problems: the silhouette path on the mesh might fold onto itself when projected to image-space—specifically, a point of the silhouette in image-space could map to several pieces of the silhouette on the mesh. As a result, the mapping from the sketch to handle vertices could be ill-defined. More generally, the complexity of the silhouette path on the surface is not necessarily reflected in its image-space projection, making a reasonable mapping from the sketch to vertices on the mesh difficult.

Because of these problems we detect silhouettes in image-space, and then try to identify vertices in the mesh that would map onto the detected region in image-space. Image-space silhouettes are usually obtained using edge detection filters on the depth map and/or normal map of the shape [16]. Typically, the conversion from raster-based edge pixels to vector-based polylines is then achieved by applying some morphological operations (e.g. thinning) and finally tracing (e.g. chain codes). We have decided to restrict the set of feature lines to discontinuities in the depth map. This approach shows a feasible trade-off between quantity of feature lines vs. their significance (see Fig. 9.21).

Matching a segment of a silhouette in image-space to the user sketch requires a metric, defining the distance between polylines. This metric should resemble human perception of similarity. We have found that the important features are proximity to the candidate feature lines and intrinsic shape (see Fig. 9.22). By intrinsic shape we mean similarity regardless of position and orientation in space. To maximize this intrinsic shape similarity we use a method by Cohen and Guibas [8].

We determine the handle mesh vertices corresponding to the silhouette segment by selecting vertices that are close to the handle in image-space. The displacements for these vertices are derived from displacements in image-space.

We consider defining the ROI as a form of mesh segmentation, for which various geometry-based methods are described (see [22, 26]). These methods are only restricted by the requirement for interactive response times. Generally, topologically growing the ROI from the handle vertices is a feasible method.

Once we have defined handle vertices, their transformed target positions and the region of interest, the application of Laplacian surface editing is straightforward. Note that the user only provides 2D input and we have found that preserving the scale in depth leads to more intuitive results than scaling isotropically in 3D. Interestingly, several of the refinements of Laplacian Surface Editing (such as [40]) favor isotropic scaling. For this reason, here we use an approach in the spirit of [28], where local transformations of each frame are estimated a priori.

9.3.1 Interface

Our user interface consists of a single rendering window with an orthogonal projection, embedded controls for navigation, and the capability of drawing viewport-aligned strokes (enabled by default). Holding some meta key activates the embedded navigation controls, with which the user can drag the mesh along the horizontal and vertical axis, rotate it by tapping beside it and dragging the mouse, and scale the current projection by clicking and dragging two invisible sliders on the left and right screen boundaries.

If the user has determined an appropriate view, placing a sketch near the silhouette implies a deformation. The system identifies the appropriate parameters (see following sections) and then displays the result. The user has the option to approve this deformation or to apply refinements by over-sketching the new silhouette path.

The user sketches the desired deformation result as a view-dependent polyline. This polyline simply consists of tracked mouse events, and we apply the Douglas-Peucker algorithm [11] to obtain a simplified version.

9.3.2 Image-Space Silhouettes

In this section, we describe how to retrieve image-space 2D polylines that describe discontinuities in the depth map (and therefore silhouettes) of the scene using two steps of detection and extraction. We developed a method that exploits the properties of a synthetic scene (= absence of noise) to speed up our algorithm, rather than relying on well established methods like the Canny edge detector [7] or morphological operations.

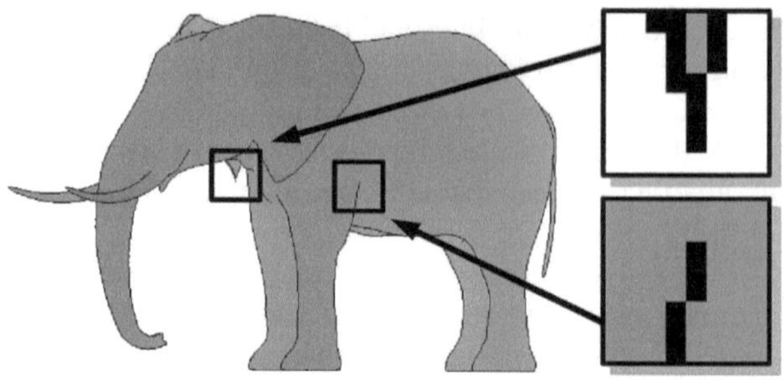

Fig. 9.23 Depth map with binary overlay from (11) (*left*), degenerated silhouette feature (*top*, *right*), silhouette caused by a surface crease (*bottom*, *right*)

9.3.2.1 Silhouette Detection

We determine discontinuities in the depth map by applying a 4-neighborhood Laplacian edge detection filter on each pixel p, along with some threshold θ_p:

$$\mathrm{sil}(p) := D^2_{xy}\big[\mathrm{depth}(p)\big] > \theta_p. \tag{11}$$

We retrieve only edge pixels that describe the foreground of a discontinuity, since we map the depth range of the scene to (near, far) [0, 1] and use θ_p as a threshold for the *signed* filter response. Depending on the choice of θ_p (we recommend 0.005), the binary images retrieved consist of continuous silhouette paths (Fig. 9.23, left). Note though, that these paths can be more than a single pixel wide, especially in areas of high curvature.

9.3.2.2 Silhouette Extraction

For the subsequent handle estimation (Sect. 9.3.3), we need to convert the silhouette pixel paths into a set of image-space polylines. Aiming for simplicity and speed, we developed a greedy segmentation algorithm that relies only on local criteria for silhouette tracing.

The basic idea of tracing connected components of the silhouettes is that silhouette pixels in the image are neighbors on a silhouette segment if they have similar depth. In other words, two neighboring silhouette pixels a and b are depth continuous if

$$\mathrm{cont}(a, b) := \big\|\mathrm{depth}(a) - \mathrm{depth}(b)\big\| < \theta_n. \tag{12}$$

Remember that the silhouette pixels form a path that could be wider than a single pixel, making the conversion to a polyline ambiguous. Some approaches use the morphological operation of thinning to correct this problem. However, applying morphological operations on the binary silhouette image may result in silhouette paths that are continuous in 2D, but discontinuous in depth. This is illustrated in Fig. 9.24b: the silhouette terminates on pixel f_c if n_7 is removed by erosion, and $\|\mathrm{depth}(f_c) - \mathrm{depth}(n_0)\|$ exceeds θ_n. In this case, n_7 is exactly the pixel that

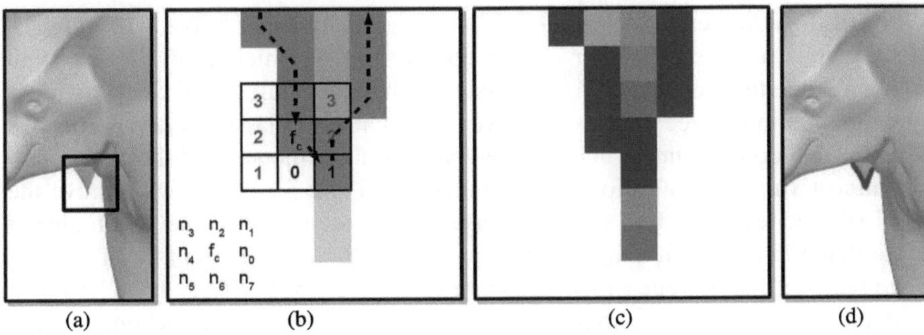

Fig. 9.24 Tracing the silhouette path near a degenerate feature (from left to right): **a** Elephant's ear, **b** tracing step ($f_c \rightarrow n_7$) with priority map, neighborhood index (*bottom left*) and a degenerate feature in *light grey* (which is removed in a pre-processing step), **c** final silhouette path (*dark pixels*), **d** extracted silhouette

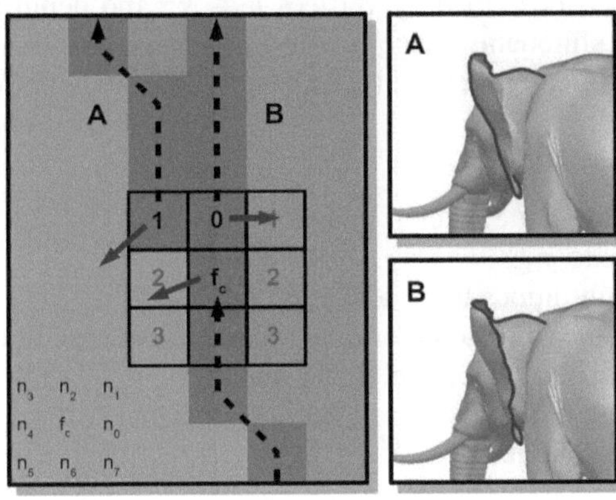

Fig. 9.25 Maintaining depth map gradient orientation. Path A shows how our tracing algorithm maintains depth map gradient orientation with respect to the tracing direction (gradients shown as arrows per pixel). If we disregard these gradients, the tracing algorithm will track a bogus silhouette, in this case path B, due to the preferred tracing direction. Note though, that the silhouette part from path B, which is missing in path A, will be a separate silhouette segment after all silhouettes have been traced

stitches the silhouette together. Instead of developing depth sensitive morphological operations, we solve this issue by using a local tracing criterion.

The idea for the local tracing is to favor silhouette paths with lower curvature in image-space—that is, straight silhouettes are favored over ones with sharp corners. The criterion is implemented as a priority map relative to the direction from which we entered the current silhouette pixel (see Figs. 9.24 and 9.25: a smaller number in the mask around f_c indicates higher priority). Based on the priority mask, silhouette edge paths are formed by selecting from depth continuous silhouette pixels.

However, correctly identifying endpoints of silhouette paths requires extra attention. A silhouette path ends in surface creases; and it might appear to end in sharp creases of the silhouette (see Fig. 9.23). It also ends in image-space when the silhouette is obstructed by another part of the surface, in which case it connects to another silhouette (see Fig. 9.25). Our basic tracing algorithm would correctly identify endpoints in surface creases, however, it might also classify sharp corners as endpoints and could connect unconnected parts of the silhouettes if they happen to have almost similar depth. To avoid terminating in sharp corners, we remove the tips of silhouettes. Note that surface creases are surrounded by pixels with almost similar depth in the depth image, while tips of the silhouette are not (see Fig. 9.23). So we remove tips by repeatedly removing silhouette pixels if they have less than two depth continuous 8-neighbors in the depth image (see Fig. 9.24, second image). As an additional criterion for identifying connected silhouette pixels we use consistency of the surface normals along the silhouette (see Fig. 9.25). As we are only interested in the orientation of the normals, it is sufficient to consider the gradients of the depth map.

In detail, our silhouette extraction algorithm creates silhouette polylines $S : \{(v_1, d_1), \dots, (v_n, d_n)\}$ described by vertices $v_i \in \mathbb{R}^2$ and depth values $d_i \in \mathbb{R}$, by scanning the binary silhouette image row by row, and extracting feature paths for any encountered silhouette pixel $f_c : (v_c, d_c)$ according to the following algorithm:

1. Create $S = \emptyset$.
2. Append f_c to S.
3. Determine next silhouette pixel f_n, where
   (a) f_n is adjacent to f_c
   (b) f_n is depth continuous to f_c according to (12)
   (c) f_n maintains the orientation of depth map gradients with respect to the current tracing direction (see Fig. 9.25), and
   (d) the tracing direction turn caused by f_n is minimal.
4. Mark f_c as a non-silhouette pixel.
5. Assign f_n to f_c.
6. Repeat on 2. until $f_c = \text{NIL}$.

Note that (a) and (b) are determined by (11), and (12) respectively, whereas (c) ensures continuity of the normals along the silhouette paths (Fig. 9.25). Furthermore, (d) is the tracing criterion, navigating the tracing algorithm through silhouette paths wider than a single pixel.

Since scanning the silhouette image row by row typically encounters a silhouette somewhere inside its path, the tracing algorithm is applied twice for any initial pixel, in opposite directions.

9.3.3 Handle Estimation

To derive the actual handle polyline (a subset of all silhouette polylines), we introduce an estimation metric which reflects the likelihood that an arbitrary silhouette segment is a good handle with respect to the user sketch (target polyline). As pointed out before, this scoring function relies on both proximity and similarity.

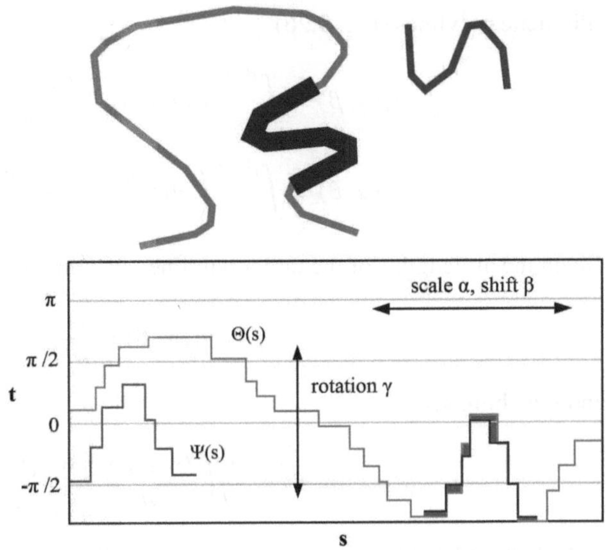

Fig. 9.26 *Top*: the short, *medium grey* target polyline, *light grey* silhouette, and best match (*dark grey/thick*) shown as a subset of the silhouette polyline. *Bottom*: arclength vs. cumulative turning angle representations of target $\Psi(s)$, silhouette $\Theta(s)$, and best-match polylines (*bottom*)

First, we substitute the silhouette polylines by simplified delegates (polylines as well, see [11]), and reduce the silhouettes by culling according to a proximity criterion (see Figs. 9.19b and c).

The criterion on similarity is derived from the *Polyline Shape Search Problem (PSSP)* described by Cohen and Guibas [8]. First, we compute Turning Angle Summaries (TASs) $\{(s_0, t_0), \ldots, (s_n, t_n)\}$ from the edges $\{e_0, \ldots, e_n\}$ of the target and silhouette polylines by concatenating tuples of edge lengths s_i and cumulative turning angles t_i, where

$$s_i = \| e_i \|, \qquad t_i = \begin{cases} \measuredangle(e_0, 0) & \text{if } i = 0, \\ \measuredangle(e_{i-1}, e_i) + t_{i-1} & \text{if } i > 0. \end{cases} \tag{13}$$

Please note that these summaries lack the representation of absolute coordinates, but they do retain the polyline arclength. Furthermore, rotating a polyline relative to its head results in a shift of its TAS along the turning angle axis, whereas isotropic scaling results in stretching its TAS along the arclength axis (see Fig. 9.26).

We match the target polyline onto a single silhouette polyline, described by its (isotropic) scale α and position (shift) β, by matching their Turning Angle Summaries (Fig. 9.26). The match result $M_{\text{PSSP}} : (\alpha, \beta, \gamma, R_{*\text{mod}})$ is described by a prescribed α and β, an optimal rotation γ, and the matching score $R_{*\text{mod}}$. Optimal rotation and matching score are computed by a modified version of the scoring function from [8]. Using finite sums of differences, I_1 and I_2 describe the linear and squared differences between the piecewise constant TASs $\Psi(s)$ of the target and $\Theta(s)$ of the silhouette polylines (Fig. 9.26):

$$I_1(\alpha,\beta)=\int_{s=\beta}^{\beta+\alpha}\left(\Theta(s)-\Psi\left(\frac{s-\beta}{\alpha}\right)\right)ds,$$
$$I_2(\alpha,\beta)=\int_{s=\beta}^{\beta+\alpha}\left(\Theta(s)-\Psi\left(\frac{s-\beta}{\alpha}\right)\right)^2ds. \tag{14}$$

Given the arclength l of the target polyline, we compute optimal rotation

$$\gamma=\gamma_*(\alpha,\beta)=\frac{I_1}{\alpha l}, \tag{15}$$

and matching score

$$R_{*\mathrm{mod}}(\alpha,\beta)=\frac{1}{\alpha l}\left(\frac{I_2(\alpha,\beta)}{\alpha l}-\left(\frac{I_1(\alpha,\beta)}{\alpha l}\right)^2\right). \tag{16}$$

Cohen and Guibas retrieve matches for all segments (α,β) by using a topological sweep algorithm [12] to match the respective Turning Angle Summaries in scale/position space. However, since this approach needs $O(m^2n^2)$ time for m silhouette edges and n target edges, we decided to probe only a discrete number of sample segments in (16) in $O(m+n)$ time per segment. Specifically, we match the target polyline to sample segments of a silhouette polyline by discretely sampling α and β respectively.

For the proximity criterion we compute the distances of corresponding endpoints of the two polylines, retrieving a near and far value $\mathrm{Prox}_{\mathrm{near}}$, $\mathrm{Prox}_{\mathrm{far}}$. Then we apply a final scoring function on the obtained per-silhouette match results:

$$R:=1/(1+w_1\mathrm{Prox}_{\mathrm{near}}+w_2\mathrm{Prox}_{\mathrm{far}}+w_3R_{*\mathrm{mod}})^2. \tag{17}$$

Iterating over all silhouettes, we select the segment with the highest score, and extract the deformation handle from the respective full-res silhouette by using (α,β) of its matching record M_{PSSP}.

9.3.4 Finding Handle/Target Correspondences

Given the polylines of deformation handle and target, we need to determine the corresponding mesh vertices and their transformed positions, respectively.

Using both the image-space handle pixels, as well as the corresponding depth map, we construct an object-space bounding volume for each handle pixel (see Fig. 9.27). A mesh vertex is classified as a handle vertex if it lies in the union of these bounding volumes.

The transformed positions for these handle vertices are computed by mapping their handle-relative positions onto the target polyline. Specifically, we determine

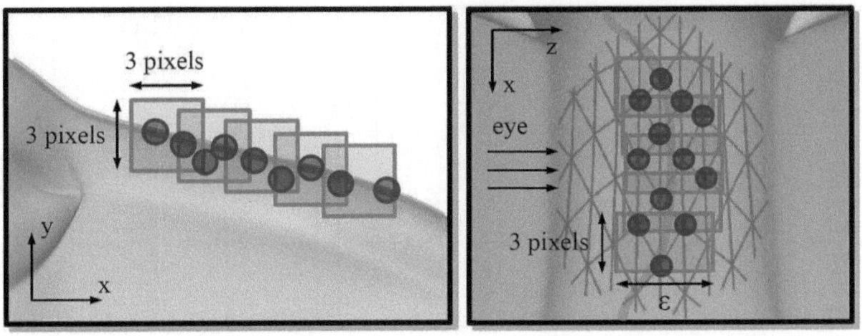

Fig. 9.27 Mesh vertices that are classified as handle members (*circles*) using one bounding volume (*grey box*) for each image-space handle pixel. *Left*: view from the editor, *right*: view from top (silhouette indicated as a *light grey line* in both views)

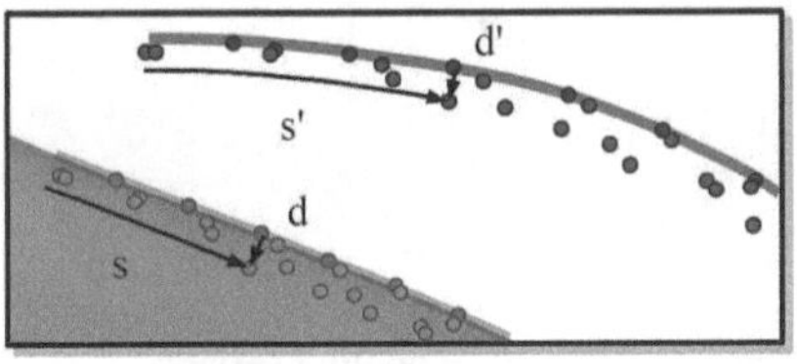

Fig. 9.28 Mapping of handle-relative arclength position s and displacement d (*light grey*) onto the target polyline (*dark grey*)

the position (s, d) for each handle vertex, where the arclength position s is given by its orthogonal projection of length d. Both handle and target polylines are parameterized uniformly in [0, 1] and the target position (s', d') is scaled accordingly (see Fig. 9.28).

9.3.5 ROI Estimation

To complete the deformation setup, we have to select the final ROI of the mesh according to some context sensitive criterion. We grow the ROI from the handle vertices. To control the expansion, we constrain the ROI to lie within a union of bounding volumes, which consists of one volume per handle vertex.

Specifically, we create a union of spheres, where each sphere center is located at the position of the respective handle vertex. Each sphere radius is set to the Euclidean distance $d_{h,s}$ between handle vertex and its transformed position. We have experimented with a variety of functions $r_s = f(d_{h,s})$, but have found that using $r_s = d_{h,s}$ already yields satisfying results: when the user sketch is far from the handle, using a larger sphere results in a larger ROI, yielding more deformable material (Fig. 9.29), which is a reasonable heuristic. To determine the ROI, we define the handle vertices to be the initial ROI vertex set, and grow this set by subsequently adding vertices of the mesh that are (a) adjacent to the current ROI border, and (b) are inside the union of spheres.

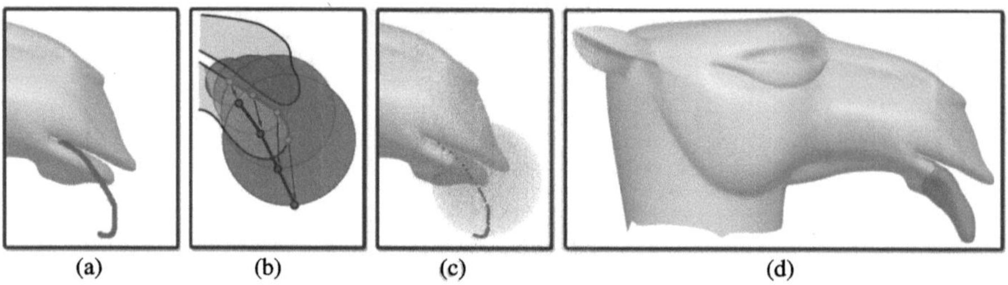

Fig. 9.29 Automatic ROI selection (from left to right): **a** After the user places a sketch, the handle is estimated and correspondences are established. **b** From these correspondences, the ROI is grown within the union of spheres, starting from the handle vertices (lower lip). **c** Shows this for the camel lip example. **d** We use the obtained vertex sets *handle*, *transformed handle* and *ROI* as input to the Laplacian surface editing algorithm. See text for more details

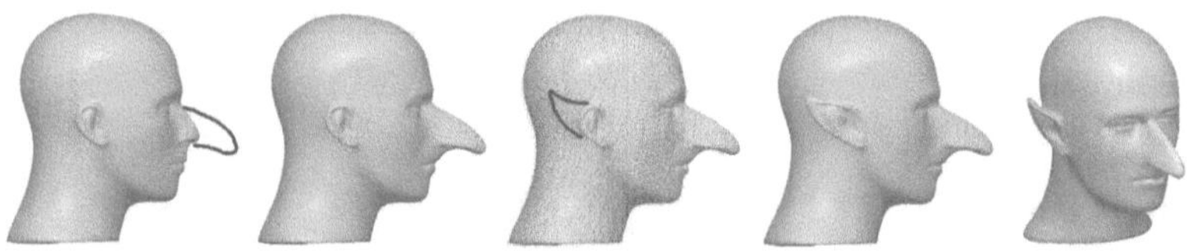

Fig. 9.30 The MANNEQUIN modeling session

9.3.6 Results

The modeling session shown in Fig. 9.30 illustrates ease of use: after the user places a stroke, the system responds interactively, presenting a deformation that generally corresponds to the user's intent. All algorithmic details, which are shown in various figures in this chapter, are absent from the actual user interface.

Table 9.1 shows some timings obtained on a Intel Core 2 Duo 6600 processor with 2.4 GHz and 2 GB memory. Extracting and segmenting the image-space silhouettes (column *Sil*) takes between 5–20% of the processing time. Handle estimation and finding handle/target correspondence (column *Handle*) depends on the density of silhouettes, as well as the number of model vertices (= 5–25% overall). The column *LSE size* shows the dimensions of the sparse linear system (= number of ROI vertices), which is factored (FacLSE) and solved (SolveLSE) every time the user places a new stroke. This works interactively for ROIs up to a few thousand vertices. Of course we can also re-use the factorization. Note that in all cases, our algorithms (Sil + Handle + ROI) use less time than LSE setup, factorization and solve (FacLSE + SolveLSE).

9.3.7 Discussion

Each of the steps in our approach presents a trade-off between fidelity and speed. And while the requirement of real-time interaction certainly restricts the algorithmic

Table 9.1 Some timings of our system

Model	Feature	Sil*	Handle*	ROI	FacLSE	SolLSE*	Sum	LSE size
Bunny	Ear	109	297	15	1032	500	1953	4911^2
CamelHead	Lip	110	250	15	250	140	765	1533^2
Mannequin	Nose	188	219	15	485	156	1063	2013^2
	Ear	94	62	16	609	156	937	3627^2

All timings in ms

*Unoptimized code

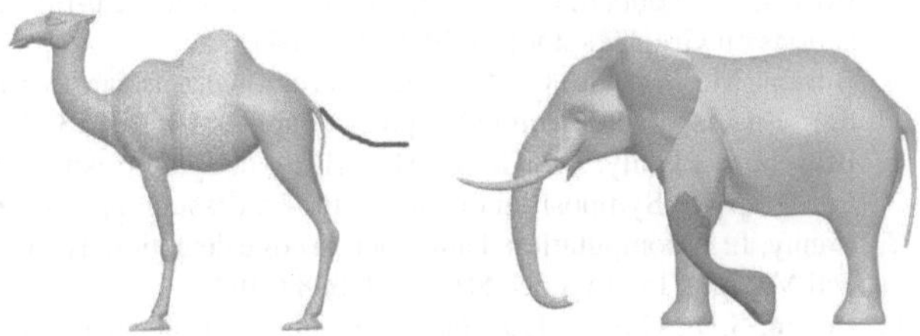

Fig. 9.31 *Left*: ambiguous handle estimation at the CAMEL's tail. *Right*: unnatural deformation of the ELEPHANT's leg due to the limitation of Laplacian surface editing regarding large rotations

possibilities, it should also be clear that almost all over-sketches are potentially ambiguous, even in the case of communication among humans—so it is unlikely that an algorithm could consistently guess correctly according to the user's expectation (Fig. 9.31).

We find that the extraction and segmentation of feature lines (silhouettes) works in almost all practical cases. It might be interesting to extend the extraction to discontinuities in the normals of the shape, or even to more subtle feature lines such as suggestive contours [10]. Another set of feature lines, though invisible from the rendering but known to more experienced users, are the projections of skeleton curves used in models rigged for animation. The information deduced by our system could then be fed into modeling systems controlled by skeletons.

Finally, as the system is almost generic with regard to the type of surface representation and the deformation tool, it would be very interesting to also try this approach in other settings.

9.4 Conclusion

Creating 3D shapes and characters from scratch is still an inherently difficult task. Many previous attempts rely on the fact that the user has some domain knowledge and/or is familiar (to a certain degree) with the intricate mathematical subtleties of the modeling tool, thus rendering these systems unusable for inexperienced users. The work presented in this chapter eases the use of 3D modeling tools for first-time users, and expands the possibilities for experienced modelers. By utilizing various abstractions, such as silhouettes and other general surface curves—and their 2D projections—we have strived to make our modeling interfaces feel more like traditional 2D painting, sketching, and manipulation.

References

1. 3ds Max: Autodesk (2008). http://www.autodesk.com/3dsmax
2. Allen, B., Curless, B., Popović, Z.: The space of human body shapes: reconstruction and parameterization from range scans. ACM Transactions on Graphics **22**(3), 587–594 (2003)
3. Bobenko, A.I., Schroeder, P.: Discrete Willmore flow. In: Eurographics Symposium on Geometry Processing, pp. 101–110 (2005)
4. Botsch, M., Kobbelt, L.: An intuitive framework for real-time freeform modeling. ACM Transactions on Graphics **23**(3), 630–634 (2004)
5. Botsch, M., Sorkine, O.: On linear variational surface deformation methods. IEEE Transactions on Visualization and Computer Graphics **14**(1), 213–230 (2008)
6. Botsch, M., Pauly, M., Gross, M.: PriMo: coupled prisms for intuitive surface modeling. In: Eurographics Symposium on Geometry Processing, pp. 11–20 (2006)
7. Canny, J.: A computational approach to edge detection. IEEE Transactions on Pattern Analysis and Machine Intelligence **8**(6), 679–698 (1986)
8. Cohen, S.D., Guibas, L.J.: Partial matching of planar polylines under similarity transformations. In: SODA: ACM-SIAM Symposium on Discrete Algorithms (A Conference on Theoretical and Experimental Analysis of Discrete Algorithms) (1997)
9. Davis, T.A.: UMFPACK V4.3—an unsymmetric-pattern multifrontal method. ACM Transactions on Mathematical Software **30**(2), 196–199 (2004)
10. DeCarlo, D., Finkelstein, A., Rusinkiewicz, S., Santella, A.: Suggestive contours for conveying shape. ACM Transactions on Graphics **22**(3), 848–855 (2003)
11. Douglas, D., Peucker, T.: Algorithms for the reduction of the number of points required to represent a hne or its caricature. The Canadian Cartographer **10**(2), 112–122 (1973)
12. Edelsbrunner, H., Guibas, L.J.: Topologically sweeping an arrangement. In: STOC '86: Proceedings of the Eighteenth Annual ACM Symposium on Theory of Computing, pp. 389–403 (1986)
13. Felippa, C.: Nonlinear finite element methods (2007). www.colorado.edu/engineering/CAS/courses.d/NFEM.d/
14. Fu, H., Au, O.K.C., Tai, C.L.: Effective derivation of similarity transformations for implicit Laplacian mesh editing. Computer Graphics Forum **26**(1), 34–45 (2007)
15. Gingold, C.: SPORE's magic crayons. In: Game Developers Conference (2007)
16. Hertzmann, A.: Introduction to 3D non-photorealistic rendering: Silhouettes and outlines. In: Non-Photorealistic Rendering. SIGGRAPH 99 Course Notes (1999)
17. Hoffman, D.D., Singh, M.: Salience of visual parts. Cognition **63**, 29–78 (1997)
18. Huang, J., Shi, X., Liu, X., Zhou, K., Wei, L.Y., Teng, S.H., Bao, H., Guo, B., Shum, H.Y.: Subspace gradient domain mesh deformation. ACM Transactions on Graphics **25**(3), 1126–1134 (2006)
19. Igarashi, T., Hughes, J.F.: Smooth meshes for sketch-based freeform modeling. In: ACM Symposium on Interactive 3D Graphics, pp. 139–142 (2003)
20. Igarashi, T., Matsuoka, S., Tanaka, H.: Teddy: A sketching interface for 3D freeform design. In: ACM SIGGRAPH, pp. 409–416 (1999)
21. Igarashi, T., Moscovich, T., Hughes, J.F.: As-rigid-as-possible shape manipulation. ACM Transactions on Graphics **24**(3), 1134–1141 (2005)
22. Ji, Z., Liu, L., Chen, Z., Wang, G.: Easy mesh cutting. Computer Graphics Forum **25**(3), 283–291 (2006)
23. Kara, L.B., Shimada, K.: Sketch-based 3D shape creation for industrial styling design. IEEE Computer Graphics and Applications **27**(1), 60–71 (2007)

24. Karpenko, O.A., Hughes, J.F.: SmoothSketch: 3D free-form shapes from complex sketches. ACM Transactions on Graphics **25**(3), 589–598 (2006)
25. Karpenko, O.A., Hughes, J.F., Raskar, R.: Free-form sketching with variational implicit surfaces. Computer Graphics Forum **21**(3), 585–594 (2002)
26. Katz, S., Tal, A.: Hierarchical mesh decomposition using fuzzy clustering and cuts. In: SIGGRAPH '03: ACM SIGGRAPH 2003 Papers, pp. 954–961 (2003)
27. Kho, Y., Garland, M.: Sketching mesh deformations. In: Proceedings of Symposium on Interactive 3D Graphics and Games, pp. 147–154 (2005)
28. Lipman, Y., Sorkine, O., Cohen-Or, D., Levin, D.: Differential coordinates for interactive mesh editing. In: International Conference on Shape Modeling and Applications, pp. 181–190 (2004)
29. Lipman, Y., Sorkine, O., Levin, D., Cohen-Or, D.: Linear rotation-invariant coordinates for meshes. ACM Transactions on Graphics **24**(3), 479–487 (2005)
30. Maxis: SPORE ™, Electronic Arts (2008). www.spore.com
31. Maya: Autodesk (2008). http://www.autodesk.com/maya
32. Moreton, H.P., Séquin, C.H.: Functional optimization for fair surface design. In: ACM SIGGRAPH, pp. 167–176 (1992)
33. Nealen, A., Sorkine, O.: A note on boundary constraints for linear variational surface design, Technical Report, TU Berlin (2007)
34. Nealen, A., Sorkine, O., Alexa, M., Cohen-Or, D.: A sketch-based interface for detail-preserving mesh editing. ACM Transactions on Graphics **24**(3), 1142–1147 (2005)
35. Nealen, A., Igarashi, T., Sorkine, O., Alexa, M.: Laplacian mesh optimization. In: ACM GRAPHITE, pp. 381–389 (2006)
36. Schmidt, R., Wyvill, B., Sousa, M.C., Jorge, J.A.: Shapeshop: Sketch-based solid modeling with blobtrees. In: Eurographics Workshop on Sketch-Based Interfaces and Modeling, pp. 53–62 (2005)
37. Schneider, R., Kobbelt, L.: Geometric fairing of irregular meshes for free-form surface design. Computer Aided Geometric Design **18**(4), 359–379 (2001)
38. Sorkine, O.: Differential representations for mesh processing. Computer Graphics Forum **25**(4), 789–807 (2006)
39. Sorkine, O., Cohen-Or, D.: Least-squares meshes. In: Shape Modeling International, pp. 191–199 (2004)
40. Sorkine, O., Lipman, Y., Cohen-Or, D., Alexa, M., Rössl, C., Seidel, H.P.: Laplacian surface editing. In: Eurographics Symposium on Geometry Processing, pp. 179–188 (2004)
41. Sumner, R., Popović, J.: Deformation transfer for triangle meshes. ACM Transactions on Graphics **23**(3), 399–405 (2004)
42. Toledo, S.: TAUCS: A Library of Sparse Linear Solvers. Tel Aviv University, Tel Aviv (2003)
43. Turk, G., O'brien, J.F.: Modelling with implicit surfaces that interpolate. ACM Transactions on Graphics **21**(4), 855–873 (2002)
44. Wardetzky, M., Bergou, M., Harmon, D., Zorin, D., Grinspun, E.: Discrete quadratic curvature energies. CAGD (2007). doi:10.1016/j.cagd.2007.07.006
45. Welch, W., Witkin, A.: Free-form shape design using triangulated surfaces. In: ACM SIGGRAPH, pp. 247–256 (1994)
46. Yu, Y., Zhou, K., Xu, D., Shi, X., Bao, H., Guo, B., Shum, H.Y.: Mesh editing with Poisson-based gradient field manipulation. ACM Transactions on Graphics **23**(3), 644–651 (2004)
47. Zayer, R., Rössl, C., Karni, Z., Seidel, H.P.: Harmonic guidance for surface deformation. Computer Graphics Forum **24**(3), 601–609 (2005)
48. Zhou, K., Huang, J., Snyder, J., Liu, X., Bao, H., Guo, B., Shum, H.Y.: Large mesh deformation using the volumetric graph Laplacian. ACM Transactions on Graphics **24**(3), 496–503 (2005)

Chapter 10
Sketch-based Modeling and Assembling with Few Strokes

Aaron Severn, Faramarz F. Samavati, Joseph J. Cherlin, Mario Costa Sousa, and Joaquim A. Jorge

10.1 Introduction

In traditional illustration, the depiction of 3D forms is usually achieved by a series of drawing steps using few strokes. The artist initially draws the outline of the subject to depict its overall 3D form and shape features. This initial outline is known as *constructive curves* and usually illustrates very simple geometric forms. Outline details and internal lines are then progressively added to suggest features such as curvatures, wrinkles, slopes, folds, etc. [6, 10, 12]. We were inspired by three methods used in traditional illustration to depict the overall basic shape of the subject: the spiral, scribble and bending methods (Fig. 10.1, top, middle, bottom, respectively).

Using the *spiral method*, shape depiction is achieved by the use of quickly formed spiral strokes connecting the constructive curves, creating a visual blend of the overall volume between the constructive curves. Spiral strokes are helpful when irregular

A. Severn · F.F. Samavati · M. Costa Sousa
Department of Computer Science, University of Calgary, University Drive NW 2500, Calgary, Alberta T2N 1N4, Canada

A. Severn
e-mail: aaron.severn@gmail.com

F.F. Samavati
e-mail: samavati@ucalgary.ca

M. Costa Sousa
e-mail: smcosta@ucalgary.ca

J.J. Cherlin
Liquid Entertainment, 999 Main St., Redwood City, CA 94063, USA
e-mail: jcherlin@gmail.com

J.A. Jorge (✉)
Depto. Engenharia Informática Instituto Superior Técnico, Universidade Técnica de Lisboa, Avenida Rovisco Pais, Lisboa 1049-001, Portugal
e-mail: jaj@vimmi.inesc-id.pt

J. Jorge, F. Samavati (eds.), *Sketch-based Interfaces and Modeling*,
DOI 10.1007/978-1-84882-812-4_10, © Springer-Verlag London Limited 2011

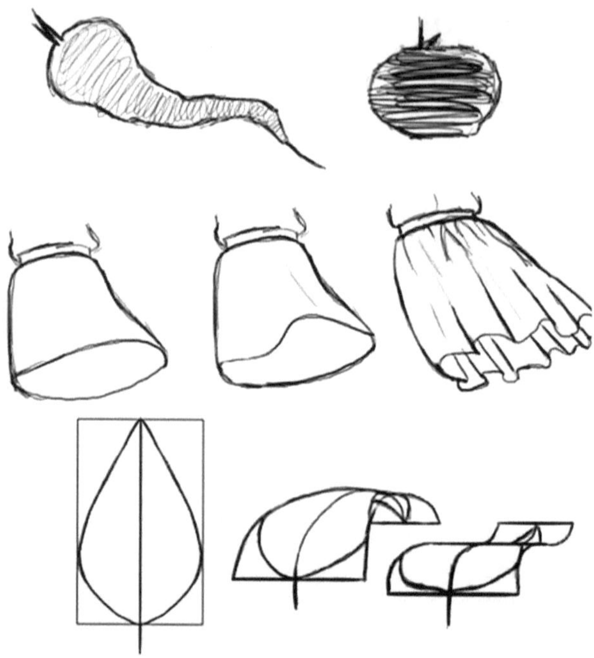

Fig. 10.1 Traditional hand-drawn techniques for progressive shape depiction [6, 10, 12] (*top row*) spiral, (*middle row*) scribble, (*bottom row*) bending methods. Illustrated by Dia Hadley, Animator, Liquid Entertainment

rounded forms are involved, such as fruits, vegetables, or when modeling human and animal bodies due to their predominantly rounded shapes.

The *scribble method* involves the use of continuous strokes placed between constructive curves. The scribbled strokes are typically used to depict specific folds, bumps, etc., across the subject. In Fig. 10.1 (middle row), a single scribbled stroke applied at each drawing step defines the fold pattern at the boundary end of the skirt.

The *bending* (or distortion) method illustrates how artists visualize adding unique variations to an initial sketch or visual idea of the subject. These variations aid in depicting the overall shape of subjects which naturally present a large variety of twists, turns, and growth patterns, such as botanical and anatomical parts. Though this method is not present during the process of creating a finished drawing, it is useful when conceptualizing or contemplating a form.

Another common method used by artists to communicate visual form is the rendering of cross sections. These cross sections allow us to get a better grasp of the nature of the shape being portrayed. Cross sections are generally not present in finished drawings, but are used to communicate the general idea about a shape, focusing on the internal features such as curvatures, folds, and discontinuities. Examples of cross sections from an art book can be seen in Figs. 10.2 and 10.3. Inspired by such cross-sectional illustration techniques, we have found that cross sections can also be used to communicate a shape using a computer modeling program, and lend themselves nicely to a sketch-based design framework and methodology.

When we model 3D forms it is usually necessary to assemble elements or to reposition all or part of a model. Sketch-based methods using few strokes are also applicable to the transformation of models in a 3D modeling system, not only giving

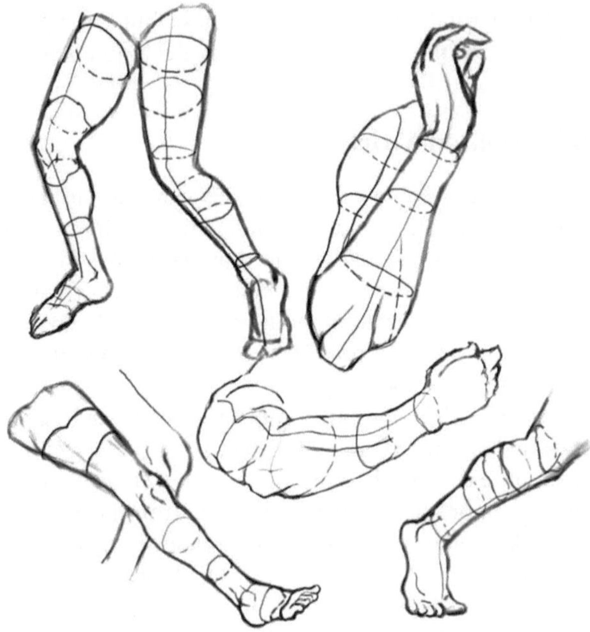

Fig. 10.2 This figure illustrates various shapes by using cross sections. Though these cross sections would not be present in a finished work, they are used to provide guidelines (constructive curves) for subsequent drawing steps and refinement in the illustration production pipeline. These cross-section guidelines are useful when describing form to an artist, and in our case, to a modeling program. Illustrated by Dia Hadley, Animator, Liquid Entertainment

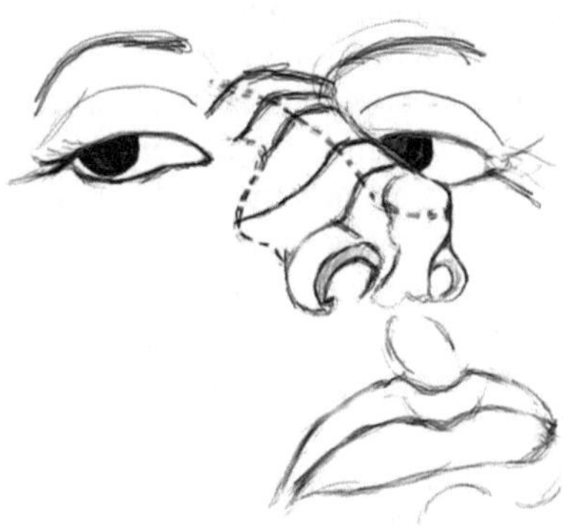

Fig. 10.3 This figure illustrates the form of the nose by using cross sections as guidelines (constructive curves). Illustrated by Dia Hadley, Animator, Liquid Entertainment

a better visual impact and more intuitive interface, but also approximating our regular and natural drawing metaphor and stylization [14, 32]. We have found that using simple strokes to define transformations is a useful addition to existing methods.

In this chapter we present a sketch-based modeling system inspired by artistic illustration techniques. We discuss methods that facilitate rapid modeling of a wide variety of free-form 3D objects, constructed, edited, transformed, and assembled from just a few freely sketched strokes. We present two parametric surfaces, rotational and cross-sectional blending, constructed after two and three strokes, respectively. These surfaces can be deformed by a single stroke input and modified by cross-section over-sketching. We also present a sketch-based approach to perform transformations in our modeling system using a single stroke. We interpret the translation, rotation, and non-uniform scaling from principle component analysis of the stroke and the idea of an active model to guide pivot-based transformations.

10.2 Related Work

Sketch-based systems are a relatively new area in modeling. Their main feature is to allow the creation and/or manipulation of 3D models by using strokes extracted from user input and/or existing drawing scans. Refer to [20] for a complete classification of sketch-based systems. Our model creation system fits in the sketch-based category of gestural modeling, in which hand gestures are used as commands for generating and editing 3D shapes from 2D segments. Next, we review selected works within this category.

SKETCH [32] combines mouse gestures and simple geometric recognition to create and modify 3D models. To this end SKETCH uses a gesture grammar to create simple extrusion-like primitives in orthogonal view. It is also possible to specify CSG operations and define quasi-free form shapes in a limited manner.

Quick-Sketch [9] is based on parametric surfaces. The system creates extrusion primitives from sketched curves, which are segmented into line and circle primitives with the help of constraints. They also consider surfaces of revolution and ruled surfaces for creating more free-form shapes. In all cases, a combination of line segments, arcs and B-Spline curves are used for strokes. Although this system can be used for sketching engineering parts and some simple free-form objects, it is hard to sketch more complicated free-form objects such as in Fig. 10.1.

Teddy [14] is a sketch-based system that allows the user to easily create free-form 3D models. The system automatically creates a surface, by inflating regions defined by closed strokes. Strokes are inflated, using chordal axis transform, so that portions of the mesh are elevated based on their distance from the stroke's chordal axis. Teddy also allows users to create extrusions, pockets, and cuts to edit the models in quite flexible ways. Sharp features or creases cannot be inserted directly on the models except through cuts.

Owada et al. [19] proposed a sketch-based interface similar to Teddy for modeling 3D solid objects and their internal structures. Sketch-based operations similar to those in Teddy are used to define volume data. The authors take advantage of a spatially-enumerated representation for performing volume editing operations including extrude and sweep. Extruding connects a volumetric surface to a new branch, or can be used to punch holes through the surface. Sweep allows creating a second surface on top of the original. This is accomplished by drawing the cross section of where the two surfaces are to meet, and a sweep path to define the place of the second surface. By hiding portions of a model, and then using extrusions, the user can specify hollow regions inside an object. While the volume representation is used to advantage, this system is also not suitable for editing sharp features or creases.

Karpenko et al. [16] use Variational Implicit Surfaces [29] for modeling blobs. They organize the scene in a tree hierarchy thus allowing users to edit more than one object at a time. Also, their system allows constrained move operations between tree nodes. Another interesting feature is using guidance strokes for merging shapes. Like Teddy, this system is not clearly suited to editing sharp features or creases into objects.

BlobMaker [5] is a system for free-form modeling using variational implicit surfaces. This system also uses variational implicit surfaces as a geometrical representation for free-form shapes. Shapes are created and manipulated using sketches on a perspective or parallel view. The main operations are inflate, which creates 3D forms from a 2D stroke, merge which creates a 3D shape from two implicit surface primitives and oversketch which allows redefining shapes by using a single stroke to change their boundaries or to modify a surface by an implicit extrusion. This system improves on Igarashi et al. [14] and Karpenko et al. [16] by performing inflation independently of screen coordinates and using a better approach to merging blobs. Like other systems previously reviewed, BlobMaker does not provide tools to create sharp features.

Ijiri et al. [15] present a sketch-based system for specialized editing of leaf-like objects combining free-form modeling with bending operations. Sketch-based modeling is also used, together with floral diagrams and inflorescences, to provide the positional information for assembling individual flower components. However, the interface is limited to modeling floral features such as leaves or petals using specific interaction idioms.

Varley et al. [30] present a method to generate a 3D mesh based on user-input strokes. Their method assumes that the 3D mesh the user wishes to generate is geometrically similar to a pre-defined template. The camera position and orientation are estimated based on the spatial layout of the strokes and the template. The authors discuss various methods of extracting meshes using the camera and stroke information, including reconstruction using assumptions of mirror symmetry, and reconstruction using planar constraints. They again use the template to determine where each of these reconstruction methods is applicable. The mesh is ultimately constructed as a collection of Coon's patches or by a method of B-Rep reconstruction using similar stroke data. The authors also present a novel stroke capturing algorithm which they use in both their B-Rep and 3D mesh methods. This algorithm allows the user to draw strokes in a style similar to the one many artists and engineers use when they sketch on paper. In this style, many shorter sub-strokes are used to compose each stroke. They refer to the group of sub-strokes as a "bundle of strokes", and their algorithm interprets each 'bundle' as a single stroke. In their method, only intersecting strokes are considered to be part of the same bundle.

Schmidt et al. [25] present a sketch-based modeling system, called ShapeShop, using Hierarchical Implicit Volume Models as an underlying shape representation. Sketched 2D contours are inflated into rounded three-dimensional implicit volumes and these basic shapes are combined with sketch-based modeling operations, using standard blending and CSG operators.

Several other works have explored the use of simple sketch-based stroke indicators or commands for specifying linear transformations for modeling 3D objects. Pereira et al. [22] present a calligraphic sketching metaphor for a CAD/drawing system (GIDeS) providing a paper-like interaction for various modeling operations

Fig. 10.4 Stroke capture: unfiltered stroke (*left*), after applying the reverse Chaikin filter (*middle*) and the final stroke showing its control points (*right*)

including translation. Gomis et al. [11] use strokes for indicating 2D symmetry operators in a calligraphic editor for tile and textile design. Igarashi and Hughes [13] present a sketch-based indicator approach for placing clothes on a 3D character and manipulating them. The user paints free-form marks on the clothes that are then placed around the body so that corresponding marks match.

Schmidt et al. [26] present an interface for 3D object manipulation using transient 3D widgets that are invoked by sketching context-dependent strokes. Widgets are automatically aligned to axes and planes determined by the user's stroke, and pivot-points can also be sketched.

The systems we have reviewed fall roughly into three categories. (1) Extrusion-based systems such as Sketch, GIDeS, and Quick-Sketch are able to create simple ideal solids and duct-like shapes, but are not suited for editing free-form objects. (2) Blob editing systems allow users to create soft blobby surfaces, but are not very good for creating blade-like shapes or patches. Finally, (3) reconstruction-based systems [18, 30] are better suited for creating 3D solids from wire-frame drawings and thus better at creating mechanical engineering parts, but not free-form objects.

This chapter is based on an extension of Cherlin et al. [4] that includes the transformation strokes of Severn et al. [27].

10.3 Stroke Capture

The first stage of a sketch-based parametric surface modeling system is to capture and parameterize raw data created from an input device such as a pen or mouse. Our approach is to extract a uniform B-spline curve from the data (Fig. 10.4, left).

Let $P = \{p_i, i = 0, \dots, n\}$ denote the data points with the same order created by the input device. Using these points as the control points of a B-spline curve can create a simple parametrization for the data set. However, this method causes three problems. First, the points are very noisy due to the shaky nature of handling the input devices. In addition, this noise is inherited by the curve as well. Second, the points are irregularly distributed along the drawing path due to variations in drawing speed. Third, there will be a very large number of points because the input device sends data at a high frequency, many times per second.

Classical approaches to stroke capturing filter the noise and parameterize the stroke in separate steps. The first pass applies point reduction and dehooking, while the second step uses line segment approximation [7, 21]. We choose to use a more simple method of stroke capture that yields a smooth and compact approximation to the input stroke.

We would like to fit a B-spline curve with a low number of control points to our stroke data. B-splines have a guaranteed degree of continuity, which resolves the difficulty due to noise. The problem of point distribution is easily solved with B-splines because it is straightforward to evenly sample points along the B-spline by stepping along the curve.

To find the B-spline curve, one may use least squares to obtain the optimal curve [9, 24]. However, even in the best case scenario, the least squares model must be converted to a linear system of equations which must be solved.

Multiresolution representation for B-spline curves provides a good approach for solving this problem. In this representation, P is efficiently decomposed into a low resolution approximation $Q = \{Q_i, i = 0, \dots, m\}$ and a set of details vectors $D = \{d_i, i = 0, \dots, n - m\}$. Now we can use Q as control points of a B-spline curve which creates a smoother curve from the original approximation by P. In fact, D captures the high-energy part of the curves which is mostly noise. In practice, we may have to use several levels of decompositions to obtain a suitable result.

In particular, reverse subdivision approach for multiresolution [3, 23] provides a very fast and simple multiresolution representation for common B-spline schemes. In this approach, for finding Q from P, it is sufficient to apply a simple *reverse subdivision* mask that is equivalent to a local least square approximation. Therefore, this approach uses a pre-solved least square mask (instead of solving it recurrently).

We have particularly used reverse Chaikin subdivision (when a quadratic B-spline is desirable) to efficiently create a denoised B-spline with evenly spaced control points. The reverse Chaikin mask (short version) is $[\frac{-1}{4}\ \frac{3}{4}\ \frac{3}{4}\ \frac{-1}{4}]$ [23]. To reduce the number of points from $p_0, p_1 \dots p_n$ to $q_0, q_1 \dots q_m$:

$$q_j = -\frac{1}{4}p_{i-1} + \frac{3}{4}p_i + \frac{3}{4}p_{i+1} - \frac{1}{4}p_{i+2} \tag{10.1}$$

where the step size of i is two. The cardinality of the coarse points is *almost* half that of the fine points.

We re-apply the reverse Chaikin filter to the control points, to yield a coarser set of control points. Each time the reverse subdivision is applied to the control points, the resulting curve becomes smoother, although it deviates further from the original stroke as shown in Fig. 10.5. We have found in our experiments that running the subdivision three times provides sufficient denoising while the deviation from the input stroke is not noticeable. These results were obtained on a monitor with in 1280×1024 pixel resolution, and using an optical mouse or Wacom drawing tablet as the input device. Figure 10.4 shows this process.

When a cubic B-spline is desirable a reverse of cubic B-spline subdivision (see [3]) can be used. A reason for using the reverse scheme is to have a smoother stroke, though the downside is that the stroke deviates more from the original input. However, as mentioned before, we observed that our approach preserves the intent of the sketched shape. This is a very important goal in SBIM: "what you sketch is what you get" in the final model.

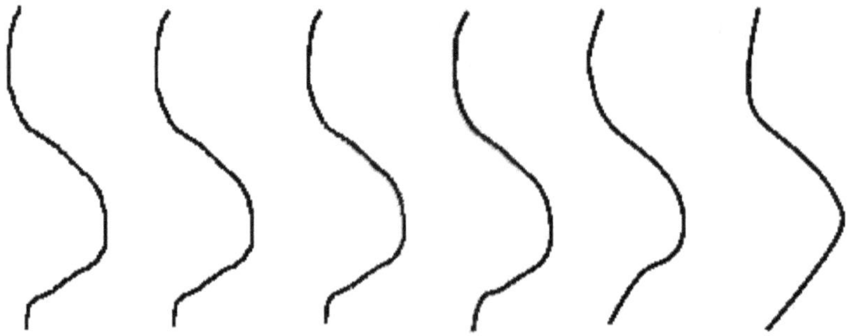

Fig. 10.5 An unfiltered stroke is shown in (**a**). **b–f** show successive applications of the reverse Chaikin subdivision. Each time the subdivision is applied, the curve is smoother but deviates from the original, unfiltered stroke

10.4 Creation Phase

As we discussed in Sect. 10.1, our goal is to create parametric surfaces from sketching a small number of strokes. Some types of parametric surfaces are naturally good selections for this purpose. For example, a surface of revolution can be easily constructed from a single 2D curve. The user only needs to sketch a curve and identify an axis of rotation. Extruded surfaces are another good example, since only a curve and an extrusion vector must be specified. However, surfaces of revolution or from extrusions can only make a limited set of shapes and it is not possible to create the artistic conventions illustrated in Fig. 10.1. B-spline surfaces (uniform, non-uniform and NURBS) are more general than those mentioned above and are more suited to free-form modeling. B-splines are a very effective and powerful surface modeling technique. However, they are not traditionally defined by curves but instead via control points.

In this work, we introduce two kinds of parametric surfaces: *rotational blending* and *cross-sectional blending*, matching and conforming to the artistic description of objects (Fig. 10.1). Using these surfaces, we are able to model many different types of existing and conceptual objects with very few strokes.

10.4.1 Rotational Blending Surface

This surface was inspired by the traditional spiral method for preliminary sketching (Fig. 10.1). In this method, the artist depicts the basic 3D form of the subject by quickly sketching spirals or any ring-shaped curves to visually blend the 3D masses between the two constructive curves [12].

This type of surface requires the user to enter two curves (as shown in Fig. 10.6). The curves represent the exterior contour edges of a 3D form. We approximate this form by defining a parametric description of a rotational blending surface.

Fig. 10.6 A rotational blending surface created with two strokes

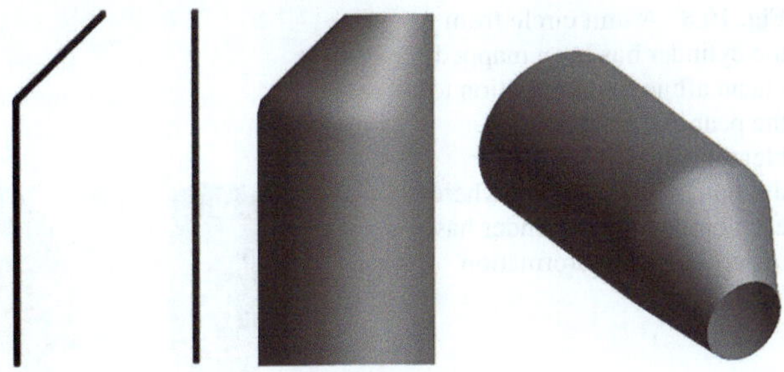

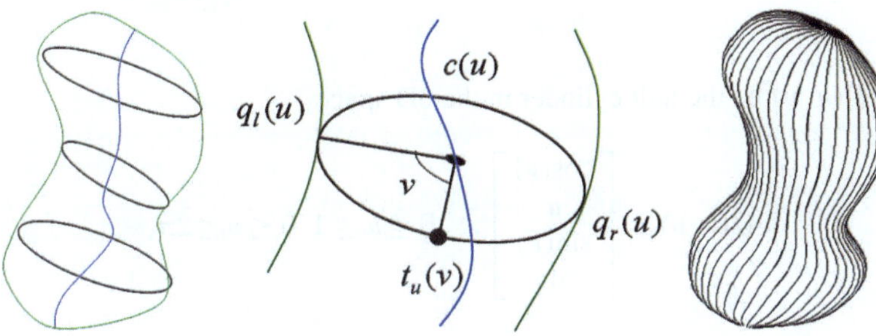

Fig. 10.7 A rotational blending surface. The *left* and *middle images* show the constructive curves (*green*), $q_l(u)$ and $q_r(u)$, the center curve $c(u)$ (*blue*), and a circular slice of the surface, denoted $t_u(v)$. The *right image* shows a completed surface overlaid with the blending curves formed by holding v constant

Let $q_l(u)$ and $q_r(u)$ be the coplanar 2D curves (strokes) defined by the user. Due to our stroke capturing method, $q_l(u)$ and $q_r(u)$ are B-spline curves. We use $q_l(u)$ and $q_r(u)$ as constructive curves of the rotational blending surface. Let $\wp$ denote the plane of the curves and $c(u)$ be the curve formed by the midpoint of $q_l(u)$ and $q_r(u)$ at each u (Fig. 10.7). Assuming that $t_u(v)$, for fixed u, parameterizes the circle perpendicular to $\wp$ with center $c(u)$ and passing through $q_l(u)$ and $q_r(u)$ at each u

$$t_u(0) = q_l(u),$$
$$t_u(\pi) = q_r(u),$$
$$t_u(2\pi) = q_l(u).$$

Figure 10.7 illustrates how the curve $t_u(v)$ is generated from the constructive curves. The desired surface $S(u, v)$ is formed by all the circles $t_u(v)$ along $c(u)$ when u varies. For fixed v and variable u, a set of curves are generated, blending $q_l(u)$ to $q_r(v)$ in a rotational fashion (Fig. 10.7, right).

In order to define $S(u, v)$ in a more formal way, we show that $S(u, v)$ can be formed by a series of affine transformations on the circular cross sections of a cylin-

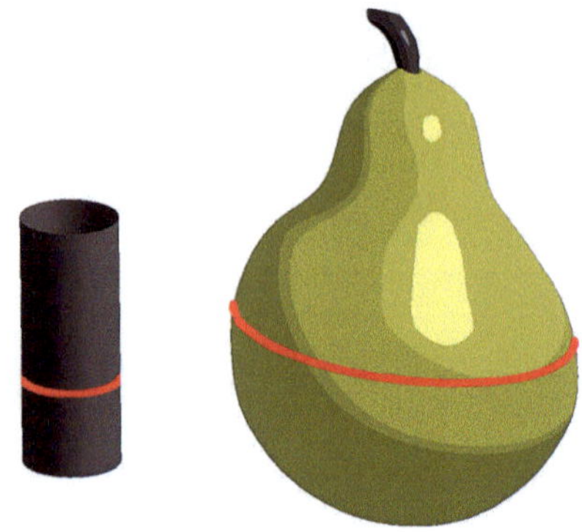

Fig. 10.8 A unit circle from the cylinder has been mapped via an affine transformation to the pear. All rotational blending circles can be thought of as a cylinder where each circle in the cylinder has undergone a transformation

der. Let $Q(u, v)$ be the unit cylinder in the 3D space

$$Q(u,v) = \begin{bmatrix} \cos(v) \\ u \\ \sin(v) \\ 1 \end{bmatrix}, \quad 0 \le u \le 1, 0 \le v \le 2\pi,$$

and let us define

$$p_l(u) = Q(u, \pi), \tag{10.2}$$

$$p_r(u) = Q(u, 0), \tag{10.3}$$

$$p_c(u) = \frac{1}{2} p_l(u) + \frac{1}{2} p_r(u). \tag{10.4}$$

In our construction of $S(u, v)$, $p_l(u)$ is mapped to $q_l(u)$, $p_r(u)$ to $q_r(u)$ and $p_c(u)$ to $c(u)$. For any fixed u, we have a unit circle in $Q(u, v)$ and a general circle in $S(u, v)$ and we wish to map the unit circle to the general one (shown in Fig. 10.8). This can be done by applying an affine transformation $M_s(u)$ to $Q(u, v)$,

$$S(u, v) = M_s(u) Q(u, v). \tag{10.5}$$

Notice $M_s(u)$ consists of two affine transformations,

$$M_s(u) = M_2(u) M_1(u)$$

where $M_1(u)$ is a scaling about $p_c(u)$ with the following parameters:

$$\text{scale}_x = \|q_r(u) - q_l(u)\|,$$

$$\text{scale}_y = 1,$$

$$\text{scale}_z = \|q_r(u) - q_l(u)\|.$$

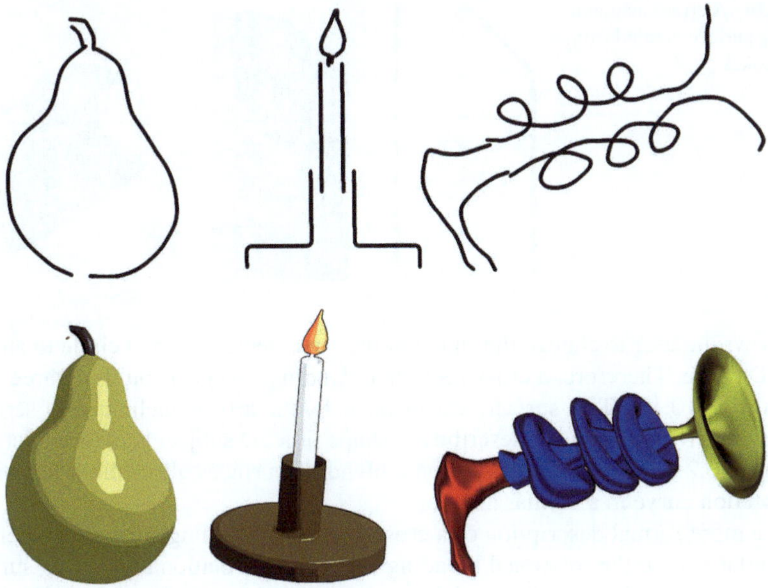

Fig. 10.9 A variety of shapes can be generated using few strokes (*top row*) by solely using rotational blending surfaces. The pear, candle and laser gun were created with respectively, four, eight and six strokes

And $M_2(u)$ is a frame transformation [1] from $(p_c(u), x, y, z)$ to $(c(u), x'(u), y'(u), z)$ where

$$x'(u) = \frac{q_r(u) - q_l(u)}{\|q_r(u) - q_l(u)\|},$$

and $y'(u) = z \times x'(u)$.

The rotational blending surface shows a good flexibility and can create a variety of models, as shown in Fig. 10.9. In addition, as an important advantage, the surface follows the input strokes. This shows that the surface is acting in a predictable way and respects the user's intention. Furthermore, when the constructive curves have corner points or sharp features, the final surface will also have sharp features and rotational creases, as shown in the candle in Fig. 10.9.

10.4.2 Cross-Sectional Blending Surfaces

Although the rotational blending surface is the default surface generator in our system, it can not construct every type and variation of free-form surface, as it can only create rounded objects. In order to increase the flexibility of our surface generator, as well as keep the number of input strokes very small, we introduce our second type of parametric surface. It is a simple modification of the rotational blending surface

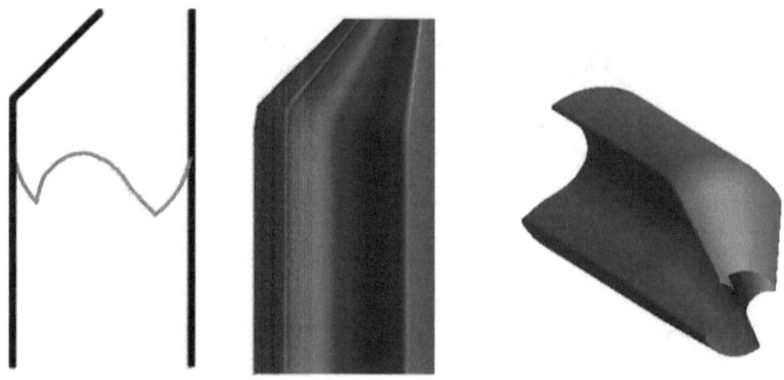

Fig. 10.10 A cross-sectional blending surface created from three strokes

that allows the user to change the shape of the cross section from a circle to an arbitrary 2D curve. Therefore, a cross-sectional blending surface is built on three given strokes (Fig. 10.10). This surface was inspired by the artistic technique of scribble, for drawing cross sections to describe the shape of a 3D subject [12] (see Sect. 10.1 and Figs. 10.2 and 10.3). Cross-sectional blending surfaces allow the user to add a cross-section curve in a similar manner.

For a more formal description of a cross-sectional blending surface, we define it in a similar way to the rotational blending surface. For rotational blending surfaces we used a mapping from a cylinder (circular cross sections) to the surface. For cross-sectional blending surfaces, we use a mapping from a ruled surface (created from the arbitrary cross section $t(v)$) to the final surface. The cross-section curve

$$t(v) = \begin{bmatrix} x(v) \\ z(v) \end{bmatrix}, \quad 0 \le v \le 2\pi$$

is directly defined from the third stroke. The ruled surface $Q(u, v)$ is created by moving $t(v)$ along the u direction:

$$Q(u, v) = \begin{bmatrix} x(v) \\ u \\ z(v) \\ 1 \end{bmatrix} \quad 0 \le v \le 2\pi, 0 \le u \le 1.$$

We define $p_l(u)$, $p_r(u)$, and $p_c(u)$ exactly as (10.2), (10.3) and (10.4). Again, we use $M_s(u)$ for transforming the generic cross section $t(v)$ to be fit to $q_l(u)$ and $q_r(u)$ as well as to be normal to the drawing plane. Consequently, the cross-sectional blending surface $S(u, v)$ is created in a similar manner as the result from (10.5) for the rotational blending surface.

Figures 10.11 and 10.12 show the model of a leaf and a sword blade, respectively, created using cross-sectional blending surfaces.

10.5 Editing Phase

The parametric surfaces described in the previous sections are used to create basic shapes that can then be edited. This is very similar to the artistic design process of

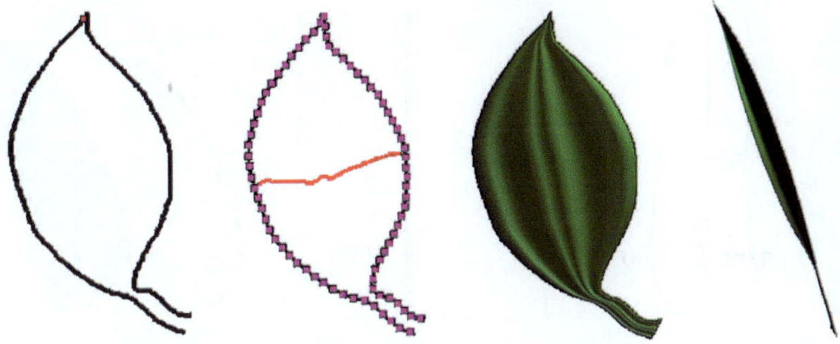

Fig. 10.11 From left to right: sketching two constructive strokes (*black*), one cross-sectional stroke (*red*) and the resulting leaf model in front and side views

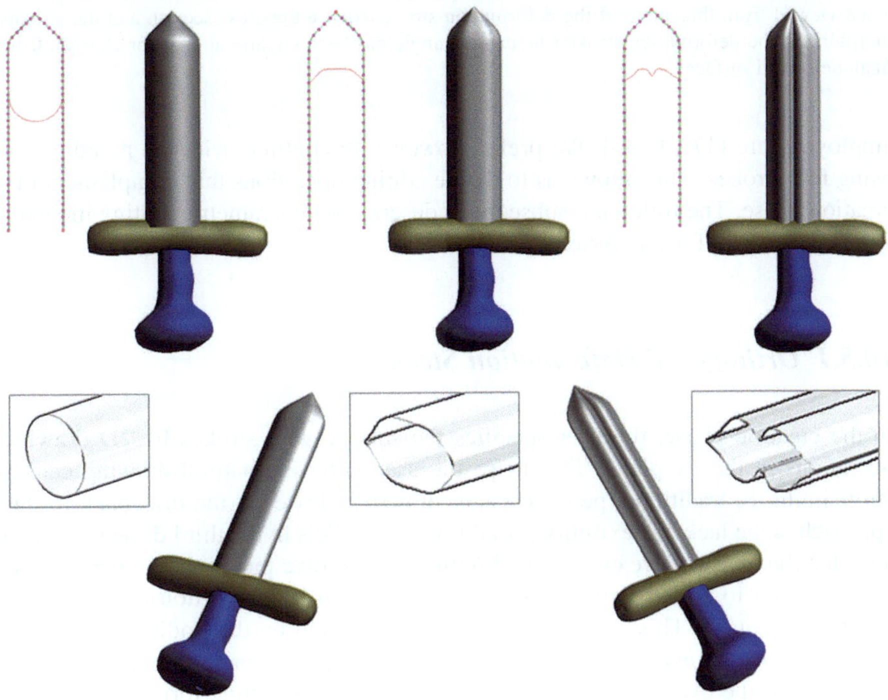

Fig. 10.12 Modeling a sword blade using cross-sectional blending surfaces. *Top row*, left to right: drawing the constructive curves only (*dotted lines*) results in a perfectly rounded object. Sketching the cross-sectional outline (*red line*) results in a better, sharper, faceted blade. *Bottom row*: the sword in a different view. Notice the final surfaces, with sharper features

progressive drawing refinement, which is prevalent in various sketching techniques [6, 12] (Sect. 10.1, Fig. 10.1). We are free to use either parametric or mesh representations at the editing stage. Consequently, any technique for mesh editing can be also

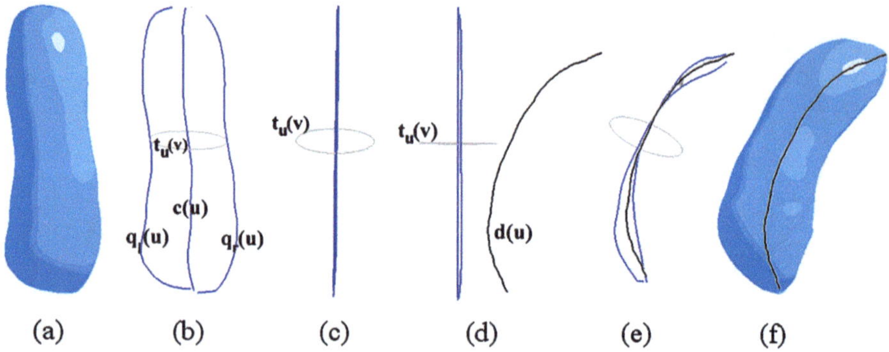

Fig. 10.13 The orthogonal deformation stroke in action. **a** the surface we wish to deform; **b** its constructive curves $q_l(u)$, $q_r(u)$, the center curve $c(u)$, and a cross section of the surface $t_u(v)$; **c** the surface as viewed from the side, notice that $q_l(u)$, $q_r(u)$ and $c(u)$ are all the same, straight line when viewed from this angle; **d** the deformation stroke $d(u)$; **e** the cross section and the strokes morphing to the deformation stroke (the camera angle has been slightly altered for clarity); **f** the final, deformed surface

employed here [17, 30, 33]. We prefer, however, to continue with the paradigm of using few strokes. This allows us to define editing operations that complement our creation phase. The following subsections describe two parametric editing methods which are crucial for our system.

10.5.1 Orthogonal Deformation Stroke

In the creation phase, the user specifies the surface with strokes by 2D drawing operations in the xy plane. This helps the user to have a natural drawing canvas very similar to traditional pen-and-paper drawing. However, the drawback to this approach is the lack of flexibility for editing our models in the third dimension, and also that the constructive curves are 2D. In order to solve this problem, we propose a mechanism to allow the user to deform the model in a direction orthogonal to the drawing plane. This editing technique was inspired by the traditional bending (or distortion) method [12] (Sect. 10.1, Fig. 10.1). In this method, the artist adds variations to the overall 3D shape of the subject and its outline form by distorting few strokes [6].

We begin by rotating the model so that we can see it from the side. Let $\wp'$ be the new view plane. Note that all three curves $q_l(u)$, $q_r(u)$ and $c(u)$ form an identical vertical line segment $l(u)$ in this plane. The user enters the deformation stroke $d(u)$ in $\wp'$ as illustrated in Figs. 10.13 and 10.14. From the user perspective, this stroke shows the skeleton (the axis) of the deformed surface.

Based on our discussion in Sect. 10.4, the original surface $S(u, v)$ is formed by moving the cross-section curve $t_u(v)$ along $c(u)$ (see Figs. 10.7 and 10.13). Note that this is true for both surfaces of the creation phase. We use the deformation

Fig. 10.14 *Left*: perspective view of three deformation strokes (in *white*) applied to the single leaf model of Fig. 10.11. *Right*: artistic composition using our system illustrating the shape and color progression of autumn leaf. The stem was modeled as a rotational blending surface. The leaf of Fig. 10.11 is placed at the top of the stem. The other three leaves are deformations of this top leaf using three different orthogonal deformation strokes

stroke $d(u)$ to transform cross sections of $S(u, v)$ to a new set of curves that create the deformed surface $\hat{S}(u, v)$. More specifically, for every fixed u, we transform the cross-section curve $t_u(v)$ to a new curve $\hat{t}_u(v)$. The appropriate transformation is determined by the relative situation of $c(u)$ (or $l(u)$) and $d(u)$ in the new view plane $\wp'$. For this, let $(l(u), T_l(u), V)$ denote the source frame formed at $l(u)$. In this notation, $T_l(u)$ is the unit tangent vector of $l(u)$ and V is the view vector. The destination frame is $(d(u), T_d(u), V)$, where $T_d(u)$ is the unit tangent vector of $d(u)$. Let $M(u)$ be the transformation that maps the source frame to the destination frame for every u. If we assume that both $\hat{t}_u(v)$ and $t_u(v)$ are represented in the homogeneous

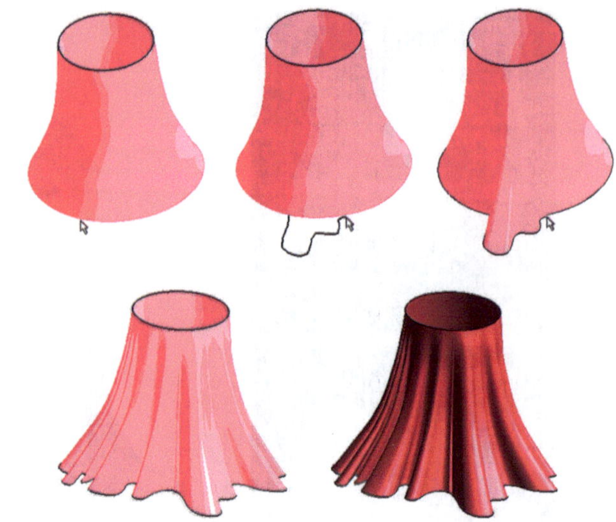

Fig. 10.15 A skirt modeled with cross-sectional oversketch. *Top row*, left to right: starting with a simple tube, the user selects a cross section of the surface. Next, the user redraws a section of it and this edits the surface. *Bottom row*: the surface is rotated and drawn upon further, and the results are shown with both toon and Gouraud shading for clarity

coordinate system, then we have

$$\hat{t}_u(v) = M(u)t_u(v). \tag{10.6}$$

Again by changing u, the resulting curves $\hat{t}_u(v)$ construct the deformed surface $\hat{S}(u, v)$ as illustrated in Figs. 10.13 and 10.14.

10.5.2 Cross-Sectional Oversketch

Cross sections and their strokes have significant impact on the forms of our parametric surfaces. We use an over-sketch technique to edit the cross sections, including circles for rotational blending surfaces, in the editing phase that is related to the traditional scribble method (Sect. 10.1, Fig. 10.1). It is very simple to return back to the original view(where the cross section was drawn) and change the cross section's stroke. However, there is a certain limitation due to the 2D mode of interaction. For example, it is hard to control the behavior of the cross-section curve near to the intersections. Therefore, it is better to allow the user to change the cross-section stroke for any view. In this method, the user can rotate the object and change the view, and then can select a cross section on the surface. This is done by setting the parameter u (Sect. 10.4.1) proportional to the mouse position. Then we highlight the corresponding cross section $t_u(v)$ on the surface that forms a visible interaction. At this stage, we map the changes given by the user to the cross section. This is an operation that allows the user to edit a surface by *oversketching*. As shown in Fig. 10.15, we simply insert the new portion of the stroke, and delete the old one. This new stroke (including parts of the original one and the new oversketched stroke) is re-processed as described in Sect. 10.3.

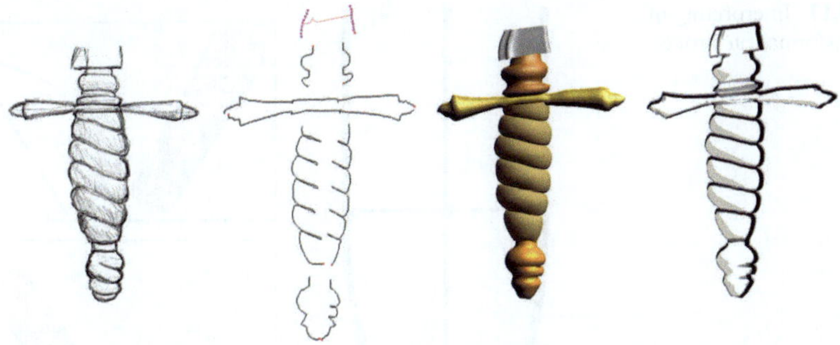

Fig. 10.16 Modeling a dagger handle from an existing drawing. From left to right: starting with the existing drawing *Gunner's Dagger* (Copyright 1998–2004 Rio Aucena. Used with permission), the user sketches 11 strokes to model five specific parts of the original drawing. The blade is modeled as a cross-sectional blending surface (3 strokes) and the other four parts are modeled as rotational blending surfaces (2 strokes per surface). The final model is then rendered with both Gouraud and non-photorealistic shading

10.6 Transformation Stroke

Traditional systems usually support transformations through a click and drag interface (with support from 3D widgets in some cases), where translation, rotation, and scaling are divided into three distinct operations, or by defining complicated relationships between models. A simple mouse click in 3D is not enough to provide a reasonable three-dimensional transformation. Existing 2D interfaces for 3D environments present difficulties that make even simple manipulations surprisingly hard to perform [28]. Assembling two models, for instance, can involve a sophisticated set of transformations until the alignment of the models is as desired. In this section, we present a sketch-based approach to perform transformations in a modeling system using a single stroke. This is a justifiable effort because a stroke provides more information than a simple mouse click.

Our transformation stroke supports manipulation of arbitrary models, freely and with respect to other models, in a three-dimensional environment. Strokes are provided by moving the mouse along the intended stroke path. The mouse position is sampled at discrete intervals to create a polyline representation of the stroke. For the transformation stroke, it is not necessary to extract control points, for the raw data points are enough. Our goal is to find a general method that can specify the transformation without any (or with a minimized amount of) specific knowledge about the type of models we are transforming. This assumption helps us having a method general enough to be fit in any graphics system or modeling technique. On the other hand, it makes the problem harder and introduces several ambiguities

Our system supports an *active model*, which can be selected by the user if desired. If an active model is selected, transformation strokes will use it as a visual-spatial reference for aspects of the transformation that are difficult to interpret using two-dimensional input, such as the desired depth of a model.

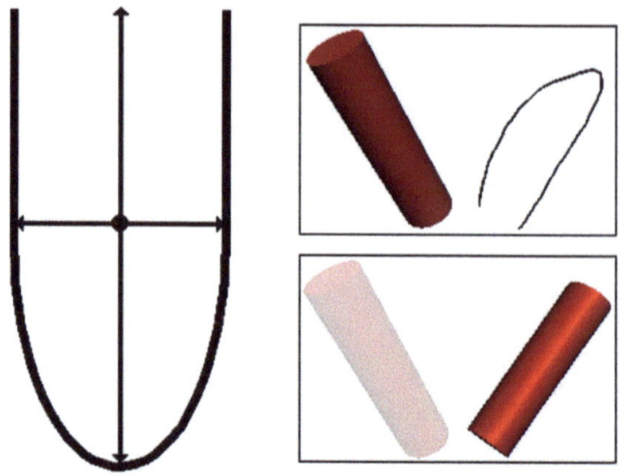

Fig. 10.17 Interpreting of the transformation stroke

10.6.1 Stroke Interpretation

A 2D stroke is not enough to determine all parameters and degrees of freedom of a 3D transformation. We need natural and simple interpretations for ambiguities. We use a U-shaped stroke to represent the object and its orientation, with the height of the U being greater than its width (Fig. 10.17). We need to determine three sets of information from our stroke: the target position of the model; the target orientation; and the target scale. To obtain this information we determine four measurements from the stroke. We find a vector from the base to the top of the U-shaped stroke (Fig. 10.17) (the major axis) and determine its magnitude, which will be used to determine the target scale. We then find a vector perpendicular to the major axis on the plane of the stroke, the *minor axis*, and determine its magnitude, also for use in scaling transformation. We follow by using the center of the stroke to determine the target position, and the orientation of the major axis for the target orientation.

The major and minor axes of the stroke are computed using principle component analysis [8]. We compute the covariance matrix

$$M = \frac{1}{n}\sum_{i=0}^{n-1}(P_i - C)(P_i - C)^{\mathrm{T}}$$

where n denotes the number of points in the input stroke, P_i denotes the points of the stroke, and C denotes the mean of those points. Since the stroke lies in the xy-plane, M is a 2×2 matrix. The principle components, which will form the axes of the stroke, are the eigenvectors of M. These two orthogonal vectors are the axes of maximum and minimum variance, thus indicating the orientation of the stroke. We determine the magnitude of both axes by projecting each of the points of the stroke onto each of the axes to determine how far the stroke extends in each direction. By taking the midpoint of the extents along each axis, we can determine the center of the stroke (Fig. 10.18).

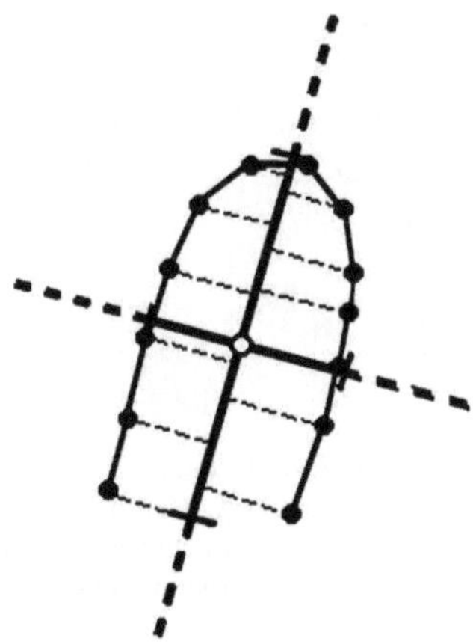

Fig. 10.18 Stroke extents are determined by projecting each stroke point onto the computed axes, the stroke center is at the midpoint along each axis

10.6.2 Translation

We determine translation by moving the center of a model to the center of the stroke, such that the stroke specifies the target position. We compute the center of the model as the center of an axis-aligned bounding box around the model since this is the fastest and easiest approach, and typically gives good results. Alternately, it could also be computed as the center of an oriented bounding box, the center of mass, or any other means that is appropriate.

Since the stroke is defined only on the xy-plane, this simple translation does not deal with the depth of the model. We make use of two heuristics for resolving this issue. The first is to simply maintain the current depth of the model. The second involves determining the position relative to another model, which we call the *active model*, and using its depth.

10.6.2.1 Active Model

The intended depth for a transformation can be determined by using an active model as a visual-spatial reference. The depth of this active model will of course vary across its surface. We therefore interpret the desired behavior in three different ways.

- If the start and end points of the stroke lie over the active model (Fig. 10.19) then we determine the depth from the intersection of the stroke and the model on the viewing plane. To do this, we cast two rays from the view point, through the start and end points of the stroke, to determine where the rays enter and exit the active model. We then take the average of these four points and use its resulting depth as the new depth of the model that is being transformed. This method allows the user to define a region of interest in the active model, to which the transformed model should be moved.
- If the start and end points do not lie over the active model, then there is no intersection; we therefore approximate the desired depth using the center of a bound-

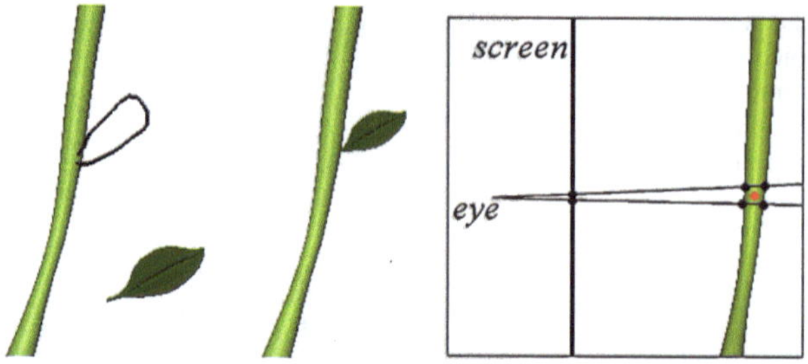

Fig. 10.19 When the stroke starts and ends over the active model (the stem) the depth of the active model in the vicinity of the stroke is used in the translation. *Inset*: the local depth (at the *red point*) is computed by averaging the entry and exit points of two rays cast from the view point (eye), through the start and end of the stroke on the screen plane, and into the model

Fig. 10.20 A transformation stroke is used to translate the cylinder forward in the screen using the torus as an active model, providing visual-spatial reference (*top*). The *insets* (*bottom*) show a top view of how the new depth of the cylinder is determined from the active model (the torus)

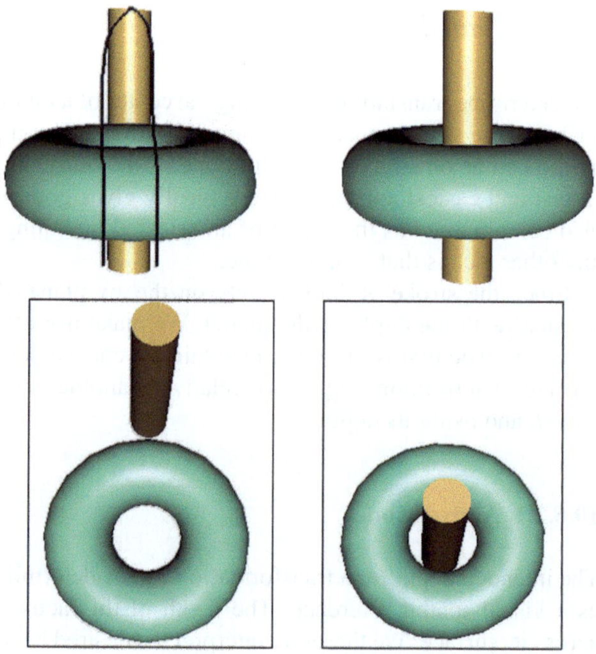

ing box around the active model (Fig. 10.20). Here, the active model is used as a visual-spatial reference for establishing the depth.

- The user is allowed to select a point on the surface of the active model (the active point), and if this point is selected, it will define the desired depth (Fig. 10.21).

After a depth reference is determined, we project the stroke center to the desired depth, using an appropriate projection to match up with the viewing transformation, and then compute the translation from the center of the model to the center of stroke at that depth.

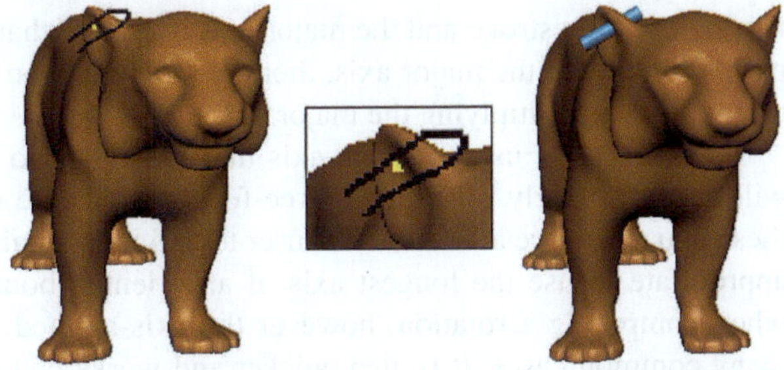

Fig. 10.21 An active point can be used when the center of the model does not provide an accurate enough depth. Here, the active point is on the left ear

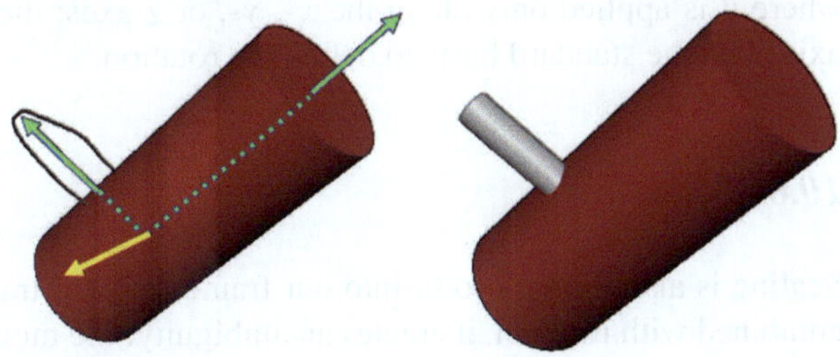

Fig. 10.22 Stroke-based rotation. The main axis of the model is aligned to the main axis of the stroke

10.6.3 Rotation

When determining the rotation, we have more degrees of freedom than what can be expressed in a stroke, thus we must choose an appropriate interpretation for addressing ambiguities. The intention of our rotation is to align the longest axis of the model to the stroke's major axis. This approach gives a logical and predictable result that in practice is easily achieved and used. In our default interpretation, we assume that the model will be axis-aligned in some direction, so that the longest axis of an axis-aligned bounding box will yield a meaningful orientation. This is often true for manufactured objects such as pipes or nails, but can also be true for natural objects. We determine the longest axis out of the x-, y-, and z-axes using an axis-aligned bounding box which, in the case of our system, has already been computed around each model. We use two different methods for finding the axis of rotation. In the first, the axis of rotation is the cross product of the longest axis of the model and the major axis of the stroke, and the angle of rotation is the angle between these two axes (Fig. 10.22). In the second method, we can simply use the normal to the screen as the direction of the axis. In the first method, the proportion of the source and the target axes is important, while in the second method the orientation of the model toward the viewer is kept unchanged.

We would like to be able to predict which direction the model will be oriented based on the direction of its main axis and some property of the stroke. Here, we choose the curved portion of the U-stroke to indicate which way the major axis is pointing. Principle component analysis produces a vector in the first or fourth quadrant (having a positive x coordinate) for the axis of maximum variance, so there is a risk that our stroke's major axis will be oriented in the opposite direction to the one we want. To determine whether or not this is the case, we project the start and a middle point of the stroke onto the major axis. If the dot product between the first point of the stroke and the major axis is greater than the dot product between a middle point and the major axis, then our axis must be reversed, so we correct the orientation by multiplying the major axis by -1.

In some cases, using a main axis that is aligned to either the x-, y-, or z-axis will perform poorly, since many free-form models are not axis-aligned. To handle these situations, we also allow the user to define the main axis directly. It may seem appropriate to use the longest axis of an oriented bounding box around a model when computing a rotation, however the axis-aligned approach performs well in many common cases. It is also quicker and works better with our scaling method, where it is applied only along the x-, y-, or z-axes; therefore, we prefer to use an axis from the standard basis to define the rotation.

10.6.4 Scaling

Scaling is also difficult to fit into our framework for transformation strokes. When combined with rotation, it creates an ambiguity: the model could either be scaled to the dimensions suggested by the stroke (without rotation) or it could be rotated first and then scaled. Also, since our two-dimensional strokes are intended to represent the non-uniform scaling of a three-dimensional we are missing information along one axis.

We have resolved the first problem by choosing to always rotate first and then scale. This choice is appropriate since it results in a close aspect ratio between the original model and the transformed version, which is typically what the user would expect (less surprising result). The second problem is resolved by assuming that the model should only be stretched or compressed along the longest axis, while the aspect ratio between the other two axes should be maintained. We only need two scaling factors to define such a scale, which is what we have from the stroke.

Initially, we use the magnitude of the stroke's major axis to scale along the longest axis of the model. This is the same axis that we used to rotate the model. The scale factor will be the magnitude of the stroke's major axis divided by the magnitude of the longest model axis. This scale either stretches or compresses the model to the same length as the stroke.

Next, we determine the aspect ratio of the two remaining axes, v_0 and w_0, which is calculated as $a = |v_0|/|w_0|$. We intend to scale the diagonal of the rectangle defined by v_0 and w_0 to the magnitude of the stroke's minor axis (we call it magnitude d) (Fig. 10.23). Thus, we can solve for the scaled magnitude of v_0 and w_0 as follows:

$$|w| = \sqrt{d^2/(a^2+1)},$$

$$|v| = a \cdot |w|$$

where v and w represent the scaled vectors. We then compute the scaling factors as $|v|/|v_0|$ and $|w|/|w_0|$, respectively.

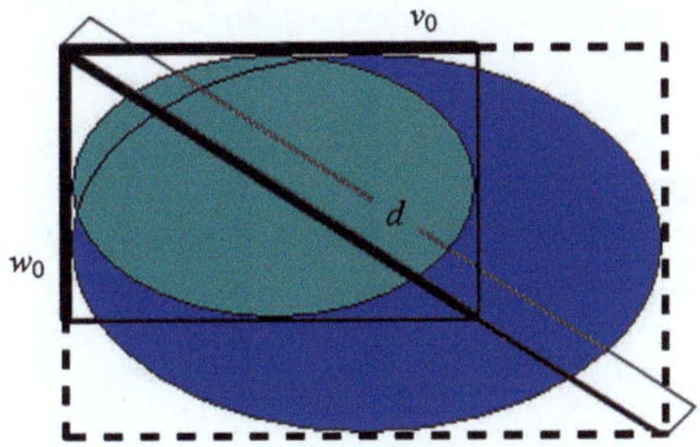

Fig. 10.23 Scaling the shorter two sides, v_0 and w_0. The diagonal of v_0 and w_0 is computed and then scaled to the width of the stroke. This same scaling factor is then used to scale v_0 and w_0

10.7 Results and Discussion

10.7.1 Gestural Modeling

We developed a prototype sketch modeling system in order to generate results using the sketch-based techniques presented here. All the results were generated on an AMD Athlon 2800 with a GeForce 5900 XT, 512 MB card, with quad meshes from our parametric representation rendered in OpenGL.

We created 3D models using few strokes representing subjects of cartoon styles (Figs. 10.9, 10.12, 10.15, 10.16, 10.24, 10.25) and botanical illustrations (Figs. 10.11, 10.14, 10.26, 10.27). We were able to construct models with sharp corners (e.g. candle in Fig. 10.9), facets (e.g. sword in Fig. 10.12), and bumps (e.g. pumpkin in Fig. 10.24).

We observed that, in many cases, some models such as the pear, candle, laser gun, sword, leafy stalk, and pumpkin were particularly fast to create (around less than a minute) using rotational and/or cross-sectional blending surfaces. More complex models took longer because they relied more upon the assembly of parts (fitting each surface together), which eventually lead to our work on stroke-based transformations. We initially implemented standard techniques for assembling 3D parts, in which the user directs translation and rotation by clicking and dragging with the mouse. We found this kind of assembly interface to be the major bottleneck of our content creation process. When creating models of the wizard, the fox, and the caped character (Figs. 10.24 and 10.25), and for the yellow berries (Fig. 10.27), we observed that over 60% of the time was spent on assembling the parts. The wizard took about an hour to create, of which about 35 minutes were spent assembling the parts. Clicking and dragging each surface so that it fit exactly right with the other surfaces was tedious and difficult to do with the mouse or pen. The yellow berries took around two hours to create with approximately 80 minutes spent on assembling the leaves and berries to the stem.

We also noticed that we were able to create many of our models more quickly than we could have hand-drawn and shaded the same subjects. For instance, the constructive lines (contour) of a pear took the same amount of time on computer as on paper, but the computer-generated pear is quicker to create because it can be automatically shaded. A drawing done by hand has to be shaded manually, for instance, by slanting the pencil and using its side or by hatching.

Fig. 10.24 Cartoon-like shapes. From top to bottom with total number of strokes sketched by the user in parenthesis: paprika (2) and tangerine (2) (both sketched directly, inspired by the spiral method drawings in Fig. 10.1), pumpkin (5), caped character (19), wizard (57), and snoopy (10)

Fig. 10.25 Cartoon-like shapes. A cartoon fox took 13 strokes for modeling it, while a cartoon radish, took 15 strokes

10.7.2 Transformation Stroke

We have used our transformation stroke to position and resize 3D objects in a wide variety of modeling experiments. Figure 10.28 depicts a scene where ten statues were positioned on a landscape using only ten strokes. We made use of the active model feature to position the models so that their bases are located on the part of the terrain lying under the stroke end points. Since precise positioning of the statues is unnecessary to create the desired scene (and may even be detrimental to the realistic, given the presence of variability in the real-world) a sketch-based approach works well.

Transformation strokes can be used to quickly place models. We have used them to assemble larger models from their parts, for both natural objects such as the tree structure in Fig. 10.29, created from a single simple primitive; the vine in Fig. 10.30, made up of a leaf and stem created using our gestural modeling system; and mechanical parts such as the various assembled gears in Fig. 10.31. Note that the gears were placed without using scaling, since the parts were already precisely and properly scaled.

Our method is best suited to models that have a well defined main axis, which is true of many real world objects. This property can be seen in man-made objects, such as nails and cars, as well as in natural objects like leaves and trees (Fig. 10.32). The ability to specify a user-defined main axis extends the usefulness of our transformation stroke to additional objects; however, those where no reasonable main axis exists, such as spherical objects, present difficulties.

Fig. 10.26 *Rose*, modeled in 23 strokes. The petals and the three stems were generated in 2 strokes, each using rotational blending surfaces. Each leaf was generated with 3 strokes using cross-sectional blending surfaces (Fig. 10.11), distorted (Sect. 10.14), and interactively placed at the stem using standard rotation/translation modeling tools similar to the ones found in Maya [2]. Bottom image: (*left*) the two strokes sketched for the rose petals; (*middle* and *right*) real botanical illustrations were used as templates for sketching over the leaves (two middle leaves [31] and a sample from a painting)

10.8 Conclusions

We have presented a sketch-based system that allows interactive modeling of many free-form 3D objects with few strokes. Our techniques draw on conventional drawing methods and workflows to derive interaction idioms that should be familiar to illustrators. We have developed algorithms for parametric surfaces using rotational and cross-sectional blending. Although we were inspired by traditional pencil and pen & ink drawing techniques, our methods allow either subtle or incremental (as with paper) or large-scale changes to the objects.

Fig. 10.27 *Pyramidalis Fructu Luteo* (yellow berries), modeled in 33 strokes. The berries and the stem were generated in 2 strokes, each using rotational blending surfaces. Each leaf was generated with three strokes using cross-sectional blending surfaces (Fig. 10.11). *Bottom left image*: The user sketched directly over nine specific parts of a real botanical illustration of yellow berries (Copyright 2004 Siriol Sherlock. Used with permission.): one stem, three leaves and five berries (*right image*). In the model, all leaves and berries are instances of these nine sketched-based objects. Each of the leaf instances was properly distorted (Sect. 10.14) and both leaves and berries were then placed at the stem by the user with standard modeling tools

Our results with cartoon-like features show that it is possible to model quite convoluted shapes with a small number of strokes. Our stroke capture method is efficient and leads to a B-spline curve, which is suitable for 2D or 3D design. The stroke capturing method yields the control points that are used in most other modeling systems, so it is highly compatible with existing methods.

We described two flexible parametric surfaces that allow the user to model 3D objects quickly and easily. Although our surfaces are designed specifically for sketch-based modeling, they could be used in other modeling applications, as well as be

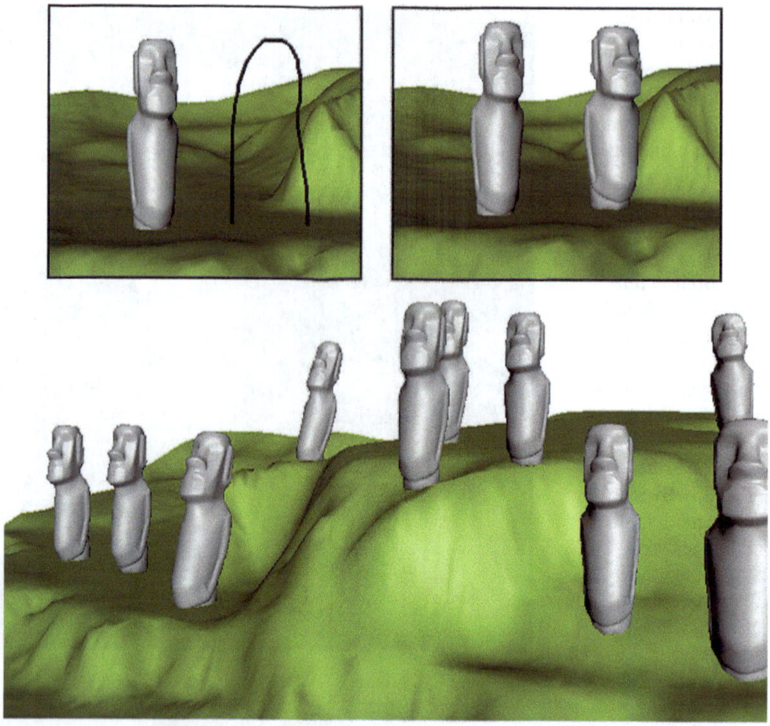

Fig. 10.28 A scene created in a few minutes with transformation strokes. Starting at the *top left image*, the user sketches a single stroke indicating the intended position (translation) and scale of the statue. This allows fast instantiations of 3D objects

integrated into existing modeling systems. These surfaces yielded good results, and were efficient enough to run in real-time.

When combined with our editing operations, the parametric surfaces can be used to design an even greater range of shapes. Our editing operations were specifically designed to complement our parametric surfaces. Although they are tied somewhat to our parametric definitions, similar editing operations could be devised that operate under the same principle for other types of surfaces.

Our stroke-based method for performing transformations is capable of interpreting the desired translation, rotation, and non-uniform scaling in many common situations. By building a complex transformation from a single stroke, we allow for quicker and easier manipulation of models than was previously possible with a mouse. We have found this to be beneficial when assembling complex models made out of many parts. Our transformation stroke is relatively easy to implement and does not involve a high computational cost.

There are many avenues for future research. Sketch-based modeling techniques can be combined with commercial packages, allowing the sketching process to be further refined by observing how sketch modeling complements other types of mod-

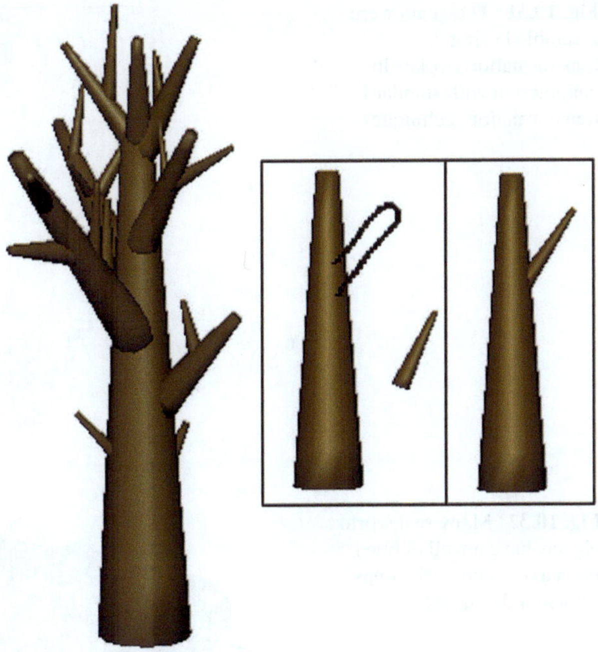

Fig. 10.29 A tree structure is constructed by positioning copies of a branch primitive using strokes

Fig. 10.30 Many leaves can be quickly added to a stem to produce a vine branch. The leaf and stem models were created using our gestural modeling techniques

eling. More typical modeling techniques could be modified so they would better fit with sketch-based modeling, and vice versa.

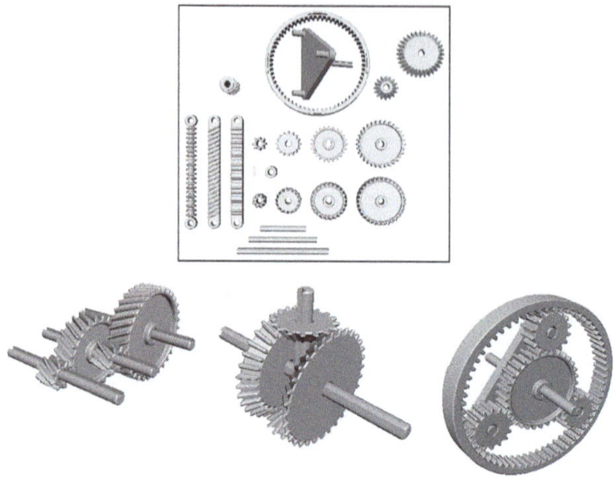

Fig. 10.31 The gears were assembled using transformation strokes in conjunction with standard transformation techniques

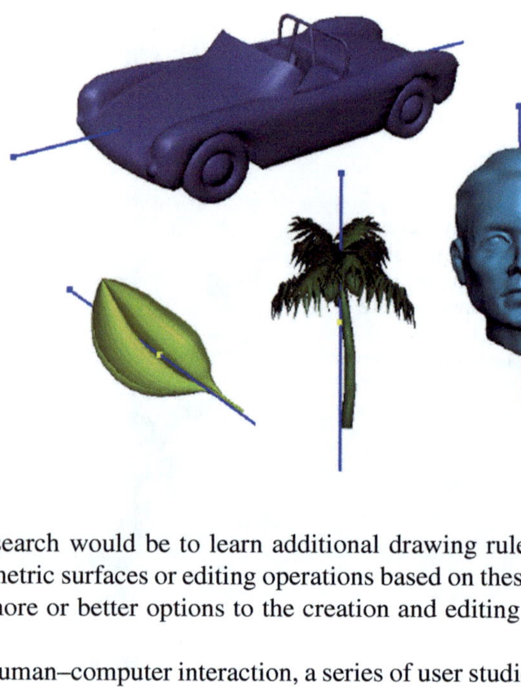

Fig. 10.32 Many real world objects have a well defined main axis, such as the ones shown in this figure

Another direction of research would be to learn additional drawing rules from artists and define new parametric surfaces or editing operations based on these rules. This would mean adding more or better options to the creation and editing phases of the modeling pipeline.

As with any method of human–computer interaction, a series of user studies need to be carried out. The user base would have to be artists. It would be interesting to know what artists, who have never used a 3D modeling program, thought of our sketch-based modeling system, and also what artists who have used other commercial packages thought of it as well. It would also be important to measure how fast an artist could learn to use our sketch-based modeling system versus how long it takes an artist to learn the various existing commercial modeling packages.

We have proposed two main types of parametric surfaces that were made to fit in with our sketching operations. If new sketching operations are developed, new types of surfaces might also have to be developed. These surfaces could include features not available with our current system. Another good feature would be the ability to blend with nearby surfaces, much as an implicit surface can. Yet, another good ability would be parametric surfaces specifically designed for efficient sketch-based Constructive Solid Geometry (CSG) operations.

While our transformation stroke interprets many of the desired user manipulations, it is not yet comprehensive. Our stroke is best suited for models with a well defined main axis, and while this encompasses a wide variety of models, further work is required to produce a transformation stroke that will interpret the user's intentions under more general circumstances. Although using a bounding box's axes and the major axis of the stroke can provide a useful default interpretation of the user's intension, it is not always correct, and requires additional information that might be directly provided by the user. However, it would be better if all necessary properties could be determined automatically by the system.

Many aspects of our system involve choosing an appropriate interpretation among a variety of possibilities. These choices have a profound impact on the behavior of our transformation strokes, in particular for rotation and scaling. While we have attempted to choose the best interpretation for all ambiguous situations, some other interpretation may prove to be more appropriate. These alternate interpretations require further study to determine the best choice. Once again, user studies need to be conducted to determine the best interpretations and to assess the overall effectiveness of the method.

References

1. Angel, E.: Interactive Computer Graphics: A Top-Down Approach Using Opengl, 3rd edn. Addison Wesley Professional, Reading (2002)
2. AutodeskMaya: Anatomy for Artists. Autodesk, Inc., San Rafael (2006). http://www.autodesk.com
3. Bartels, R.H., Samavati, F.F.: Reversing subdivision rules: Local linear conditions and observations on inner products. Journal of Computational and Applied Mathematics **119**(1–2), 29–67 (2000)
4. Cherlin, J.J., Samavati, F., Sousa, M.C., Jorge, J.A.: Sketch-based modeling with few strokes. In: Proc. of the 21st Spring Conference on Computer Graphics (SCCG '05) (2005)
5. de Araujo, B., Jorge, J.: Blobmaker: Free-form modelling with variational implicit surfaces. In: Proc. of the 12th Portuguese Computer Graphics Meeting, pp. 17–26 (2003)
6. Dease, C., Grint, D., Kennedy, D.: Complete Drawing Course (The Diagram Group). Sterling, New York (1999)
7. Douglas, D., Peucker, T.: Algorithms for the reduction of the number of points required to represent a digitized line or its caricature. Canadian Cartographer **10**(2), 112–122 (1973)
8. Duda, R.O., Hart, P.E.: Pattern Classification and Scene Analysis. Wiley, New York (1973)
9. Eggli, L., Hsu, C., Bruderlin, B., Elber, G.: Inferring 3d models from freehand sketches and constraints. Computer-Aided Design **29**(2), 101–112 (1997)
10. Goldstein, N.: The Art of Responsive Drawing. Prentice-Hall, New York (1999)
11. Gomis, J.M., Albert, F., Contero, M., Naya, F.: Calligraphic editor for textile and tile pattern design system. In: Proceedings of SmartGraphics '04. Lecture Notes in Computer Science, vol. 3031, pp. 114–120. Springer, Berlin (2004)

12. Guptill, A.: Rendering in Pencil. Watson-Guptill, New York (1977)
13. Igarashi, T., Hughes, J.F.: Clothing manipulation. In: 15th Annual Symposium on User Interface Software and Technology (UIST '02), pp. 91–100 (2002)
14. Igarashi, T., Matsuoka, S., Tanaka, H.: Teddy: A sketching interface for 3d freeform design. In: Proc. of SIGGRAPH '99, pp. 409–416 (1999)
15. Ijiri, T., Owada, S., Okabe, M., Igarashi, T.: Floral diagrams and inflorescences: interactive flower modeling using botanical structural constraints. ACM Transactions on Graphics (Proc. of SIGGRAPH '05) **24**(3), 720–726 (2005)
16. Karpenko, O., Hughes, J., Raskar, R.: Free-form sketching with variational implicit surfaces. Computer Graphics Forum **21**(3), 585–594 (2002)
17. Lawrence, J., Funkhouser, T.: A painting interface for interactive surface deformations. In: Proc. of Pacific Graphics '03, pp. 141–150 (2003)
18. Naya, F., Jorge, J.A., Conesa, J., Contero, M., Gomis, J.M.: Direct modeling: from sketches to 3d models. In: Proc. of the 1st Ibero-American Symposium in Computer Graphics, pp. 109–117 (2002)
19. Ohwada, S., Nielsen, F., Nakazawa, K., Igarashi, T.: A sketching interface for modeling the internal structures of 3d shapes. In: Proc. of the 4th International Symposium on Smart Graphics, LNCS, vol. 2733, pp. 49–57. Springer, New York (2003)
20. Olsen, L., Samavati, F., Sousa, M., Jorge, J.: Sketch-based modeling: a survey. Computers & Graphics **33**, 85–103 (2009)
21. Park, J., Kwon, Y.B.: An efficient representation of hand sketch graphic messages using recursive Bezier curve approximation. In: Image Analysis and Recognition. Lecture Notes in Computer Science, vol. 3211/2004, pp. 392–399 (2004)
22. Pereira, J.P., Jorge, J.A., Branco, V.A., Ferreira, F.N.: Calligraphic interfaces: Mixed metaphors for design. In: Interactive Systems: Design, Specification and Verification, DSV-IS 2003 Proc., pp. 154–170 (2003)
23. Samavati, F.F., Bartels, R.H.: Local filters of b-spline wavelets. In: Proceedings of International Workshop on Biometric Technologies (BT 2004). University of Calgary, Canada (2004)
24. Samavati, F., Mahdavi-Amiri, N.: A filtered b-spline models of scanned digital images. Journal of Science **10**(4), 258–264 (2000)
25. Schmidt, R., Wyvill, B., Sousa, M., Jorge, J.: Shapeshop: Sketch-based solid modeling with blobtrees. In: 2nd Eurographics Workshop on Sketch-Based Interfaces and Modeling, pp. 53–62 (2005)
26. Schmidt, R., Singh, K., Balakrishnan, R.: Sketching and composing widgets for 3d manipulation. Computer Graphics Forum (Proc. of Eurographics '08) **27**(2), 301–310 (2008)
27. Severn, A., Samavati, F.F., Sousa, M.C.: Transformation strokes. In: Proc. of Eurographics Workshop on Sketch-Based Interfaces and Modeling, pp. 75–82 (2006)
28. Tolba, O., Dorsey, J., McMillan, L.: A projective drawing system. In: ACM Symposium on Interactive 3D Graphics, pp. 25–34 (2001)
29. Turk, G., O'Brien, J.: Shape transformation using variational implicit surfaces. In: Proc. of SIGGRAPH '99, pp. 335–342 (1999)
30. Varley, P., Suzuki, H., Mitani, J., Martin, R.: Interpretation of single sketch input for mesh and solid models. International Journal of Shape Modeling **6**(2), 207–240 (2000)
31. West, K.: How to Draw Plants: The Techniques of Botanical Illustration. The Herbert Press, Coventry (1983)
32. Zeleznik, R., Herndon, K., Hughes, J.: Sketch: An interface for sketching 3d scenes. In: Proc. of SIGGRAPH '96, pp. 163–170 (1996)
33. Zorin, D., Schroder, P., Sweldens, W.: Interactive multiresolution mesh editing. In: Proc. of SIGGRAPH '97, pp. 259–268 (1997)

Chapter 11
ShapeShop: Free-Form 3D Design with Implicit Solid Modeling

Ryan Schmidt and Brian Wyvill

11.1 Introduction

Implicit modeling has been used since the early 1980s as an alternative to mainstream solid-modeling techniques. Beyond Boolean composition, implicit modeling integrates blending and deformation operators which allow complex free-form solid models to be more easily described. Recent advances have alleviated some of the major technical problems, such as visualization speed and surface control. In this chapter we describe how to combine these new techniques with a sketch-based 3D modeling interface, resulting in a powerful tool for quickly creating solid models. Our system, called *ShapeShop*, has been used as a testbed to investigate a range of problems, from real-time visualization [36], sweep surfaces [35], surface parameterization [38], and implicit surface deformation [41], to higher-level design and usability issues such as structured visualization [39] and 3D manipulation [40]. Sketch-based 3D modeling is the common thread which ties all these various problems together [33, 34, 37, 46].

Much like the seminal Teddy system [18], ShapeShop is a tool for incrementally creating a 3D model using simple 2D sketches. From this starting point, many other sketch and pen-based interaction techniques have been adapted and integrated into the system. ShapeShop borrows liberally from work in sketching assistance [7, 17], gestural systems [48], crossing interfaces [2], and suggestive modeling [16]. One long-term aspect of the ShapeShop project is to evaluate how these non-traditional techniques can be effectively combined within a complex interface.

R. Schmidt (✉)
Dept. of Computer Science, University of Toronto, 10 King's College Road, Rm. 3302, Toronto, Ontario M5S 3G4, Canada
e-mail: rms@dgp.toronto.edu

B. Wyvill
Department of Computer Science, University of Victoria, Engineering/ Computer Science Building (ECS), Room 504, STN CSC, PO Box 3055, Victoria, BC, Canada V8W 3P6
e-mail: blob@cs.uvic.ca

J. Jorge, F. Samavati (eds.), *Sketch-based Interfaces and Modeling*,
DOI 10.1007/978-1-84882-812-4_11, © Springer-Verlag London Limited 2011

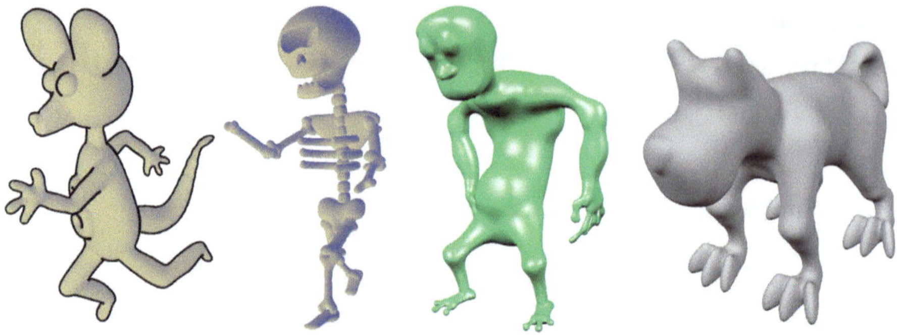

Fig. 11.1 Character models designed by an expert ShapeShop user (the first author), progressing from the earliest versions of the software (*left*) to the most recent releases (*right*)

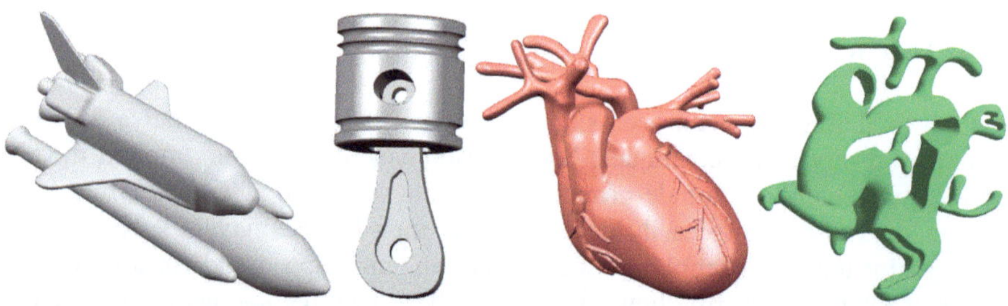

Fig. 11.2 ShapeShop provides an expressive set of sketch-based implicit modeling techniques which support a variety of modeling styles, from high-level conceptual design and CAD-style solid modeling to free-form biological modeling, and even "3D doodling"

The most fundamental difference between ShapeShop and its predecessors is in the use of procedural shape modeling techniques, particularly the hierarchical implicit volume representation known as the BlobTree [45]. As with many other problems in computer science, utilizing a structured, hierarchical framework allows designers to interact with complex models more effectively. In addition, the BlobTree combines traditional CAD-style solid modeling with organic free-form blending in a single interface, greatly enhancing the range of models which can be constructed via sketching (Figs. 11.1 and 11.2). ShapeShop also takes a non-purist approach to sketch-based interface design—functionality is exposed using traditional 2D widgets if suitable alternatives have not yet been developed. As a result, designers can express levels of model complexity not yet reachable using "pure" sketch-based tools. Examples of such models are sprinkled throughout the following chapter, in which ShapeShop's interface techniques, modeling tools, and implementation details are described.

Another notable aspect of the ShapeShop project is that due to extensive development carried out since 2004, the software is quite capable. Many of the results mentioned above are exposed in the current development versions, which are (ir)regularly released on the internet at http://shapeshop3d.com.

Although still very much "research software", ShapeShop has been extended to the point where working artists have found a use for it in their production pipelines.

Fig. 11.3 3D sculptures created by first modeling in ShapeShop, and then importing the surface mesh into Modo [23] for texturing and rendering. Images ©Corien Klapwijk

Some digital sculptors have also taken an interest in ShapeShop, and a few such works are shown in Fig. 11.3. The feedback we have received from this small but growing community of active users is highly informative. The chapter closes with insights gathered from this feedback, as well as issues encountered during the design and development of ShapeShop.

11.2 The ShapeShop Interface

A screenshot of the ShapeShop user interface is shown in Fig. 11.4. The system is implemented using a combination of Microsoft's MFC C++ application framework and custom OpenGL widgets. The main interface window is a single-pane model view. Two additional windows are used to manipulate the scene—a tree view for interacting with the current BlobTree hierarchy, and a list view for changing parameters of a selected tree node. Standard menus and toolbars are also used to control functionality which has not yet been exposed in the sketch-based interface.

Various interface components are embedded in a Heads-Up Display (HUD) rendered on top of the model view. The Expectation List dynamically responds to sketches drawn by the user, offering possible model interactions. The Parameter Toolbar offers interactive manipulation of the most commonly-used parameters of the selected node. Similarly, the Options Toolbar provides access to frequently changed scene parameters, and the View Toolbar provides camera control.

11.2.1 Pencil-based Interaction

ShapeShop has been designed primarily to support use on direct-input displays, such as the touch-sensitive SmartBoard (Fig. 11.5). These devices lack any sort of modal

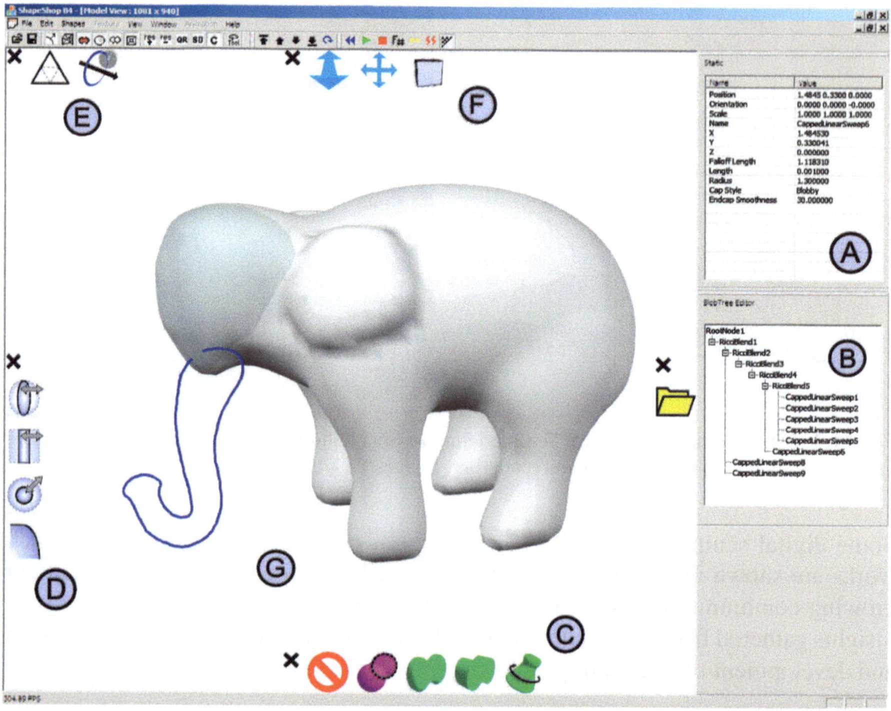

Fig. 11.4 The various major interface elements in ShapeShop include the (A) Parameter Editor, (B) BlobTree Editor, (C) Expectation List, (D) Parameter Toolbar, (E) Options Toolbar, (F) View Toolbar, and (G) Model View

switch (buttons). Hence, we think of the interaction style in ShapeShop as *pencil-based* rather than *pen-based*, as most pen-based systems incorporate physical mode switches such as buttons on the pen barrel. Restricting ourselves to pencil-based interaction does complicate the interface, as tasks commonly initiated with physical mode switches must be converted to alternate schemes. In addition, since traditional 2D interface widgets can be difficult to use with pen or touch input, we adopt the stroke-based widget interaction techniques of CrossY [2]. For example, a button is "pressed" by drawing a stroke across it.

An obvious drawback is that we have heavily overloaded the meaning of such strokes. For example, the user may intend to interact with a 2D widget, make a gestural command, or specify the 2D silhouette of many possible 3D shapes. To resolve this ambiguity, we apply three stages of interpretation. First, visible 2D and 3D widgets that take continuous input are given a chance to capture the current stroke as it is being drawn. Next, uncaptured strokes are tested against visible widgets for crossing actions, and then against the small set of gestures that the system understands.

If no widget or gesture interactions are detected, the system assumes that a 3D construction or editing operation is desired. These actions are presented to the user via the Expectation List, a dynamic toolbar utilized in several other sketch-

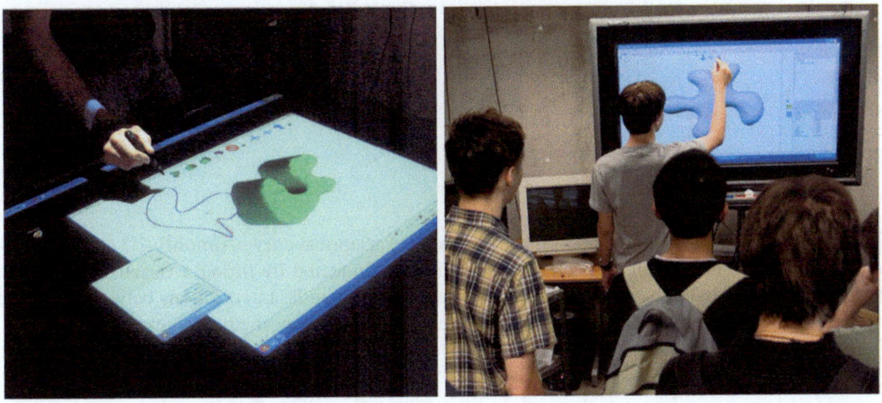

Fig. 11.5 Our *pencil-based* modeling interface is designed to support non-modal input devices, like these touch-sensitive horizontal tabletop and digital whiteboard displays

ing tools [3, 13, 16]. Context-dependent rules are used to populate the Expectation List, by comparing the current sketch with the underlying 3D model. For example, a closed contour generates several sweep-surface options, but hole-cutting options are only produced if the contour intersects the current surface. Note that Expectation Lists in previous systems have generally contained small images of what the updated surface would look like for each expectation list icon. For complex models the user may be required to carefully inspect each image to find the desired action. Instead, we use color-coded iconic representations which may be more easily recognized.

11.2.2 Sketching Assistance

Two-dimensional sketches form the basis for 3D shape creation in ShapeShop. To aid the user in the 2D drawing task, ShapeShop includes techniques that assist with the creation of smooth 2D contours. Our approach is inspired by Baudel's oversketching techniques [7] and the *interactive beautification* tools found in the Pegasus system [17]. See [27] for a recent survey of these and related techniques.

A fundamental limitation of most standard input devices is that they provide only point samples to the operating system. These discrete data can be converted to a polyline by connecting temporally-adjacent point samples. However, in the case of curves the polyline is only an approximation to the smooth curve the user desires. In our system we do not create an approximate polyline, but instead fit a smooth 2D variational implicit curve [32, 43] to the discrete samples. Curve normals derived from the discrete polyline are used to generate the necessary off-curve constraint points [10]. Variational curves provide many benefits, such as automatic smoothing and gap-closing with minimal curvature (Fig. 11.6).

While this approach is most effective for closed curves, it can also be applied to open curves in some cases. If the fit variational curve extends beyond the sketching

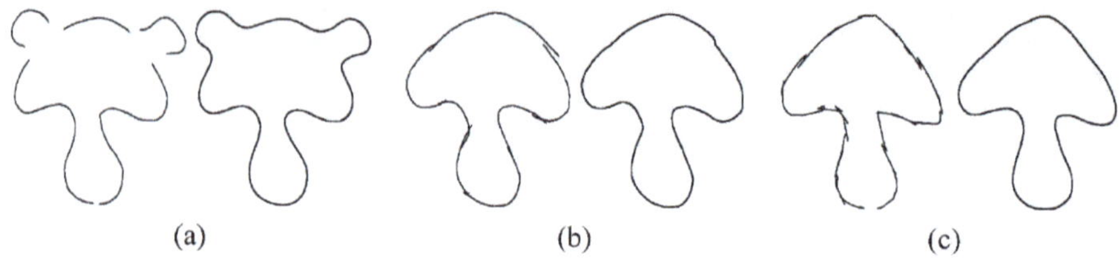

Fig. 11.6 The gap-filling and smoothing properties of variational curves simplify 2D curve sketching. In (**a**), multiple disjoint strokes are automatically connected by fitting a variational curve to the input samples. In (**b**), smoothing parameters are used to handle intersections between multiple strokes. Rough self-intersecting sketches can be automatically smoothed, as shown in (**c**)

Fig. 11.7 Examples of the *eraser* gesture (**a**) and *smooth* gesture (**b**). These gestures manipulate the parameters used to compute the final variational curve (*dashed line*)

area, we assume the curve is open and clip it to lie within the endpoints of the sampled polyline. However, as ShapeShop is a volume modeling interface, closed contours are required to perform most of the creation and editing actions.

ShapeShop supports sketch-based editing of the set of point samples, but not the final variational curve. To simultaneously visualize these two different components, we render the current variational curve in black and the sketched polyline in transparent blue (Fig. 11.7). Three gestural commands are available to assist users when drawing 2D sketches. The first, *eraser*, is initiated with a "scribble", as shown in Fig. 11.7(a). An oriented bounding box is fit to the scribble vertices and used to remove point samples from the current 2D sketch. The variational curve is re-computed using the remaining samples.

The second gestural command is *smooth*, initiated by circling the desired smoothing region a minimum of two times. Each point sample has a smoothing parameter associated with it which is incremented if the point is contained in the circled region. The variational curve is then re-computed with the new smoothing parameters (Fig. 11.7(b)). This gesture can be applied multiple times to the same point samples to further smooth the 2D sketch. Finally, we include an *undo* gesture, input as a quick stroke straight to the left, which removes the most recent stroke.

We have found these techniques to be very effective for creating smooth 2D sketches. This in turn improves the efficiency of 3D modeling, since fewer corrections need to be made to the 3D shape. One current limitation is that sharp creases in the input sketch are lost, since the underlying variational curve is always C^2 continuous. A useful extension to our technique would be to automatically detect sharp edges, and re-introduce them into the smoothed variational curves.

Fig. 11.8 Blobby inflation converts the 2D sketch shown in **a** into the 3D volume **b** such that the 2D sketch lies on the 3D silhouette. The width of the inflated volume can be manipulated interactively, shown in (**c**). Sketched 2D curves can also be used to create **d** linear sweeps and **e** surfaces of revolution

11.2.3 Sketch-based Modeling Operations

ShapeShop supports construction of three basic types of shapes derived from sketched 2D contours—"blobby" inflation in the style of Teddy [18], linear sweeps, and surfaces of revolution. Based on these three shapes, sketch-based cutting and blending operations are implemented using BlobTree composition operators.

A key benefit of utilizing the BlobTree shape representation is that the current volume is procedurally defined by an underlying model tree which represents both a scene graph and a full construction history. Single primitives, as well as entire portions of the tree, can be modified or removed at any time. Exposing this flexibility through a sketch-based interface can be quite difficult, and much research remains to be done on intuitive techniques for editing volumetric scene graphs. In ShapeShop, the designer can use gestural commands and 3D widgets to manipulate individual BlobTree nodes, however more complex operations like tree re-structuring require the use of a traditional tree-view widget (Fig. 11.4). In our experience, designers find it difficult to understand the link between this text-based tree view and the actual model structure. An abstraction which simplified this tree view while still preserving the considerable power it provides would be highly desirable.

11.2.3.1 Blobby Inflation

As in many other sketch-based modeling tools [3, 18, 20, 25, 28, 42], the primary shape-creation operation in ShapeShop is *inflation*, where a closed 2D contour is then inflated into a "blobby" 3D shape. This operation can be easily accomplished using implicit sweeps with the blobby endcap style, as described in Sect. 11.3.3. The 2D sketch (Fig. 11.8a) is projected onto a 3D plane parallel to the current view plane, and then inflated in both directions (Fig. 11.8b). After creation, the width of the primitive can be manipulated interactively with a 2D widget (Fig. 11.8c). The inflation width is functionally defined and could be manipulated to provide a larger difference between thick and thin sections. One advantage of the implicit representation is that holes and disjoint pieces can be handled transparently.

Fig. 11.9 Cutting can be performed **b** across the object silhouette or **c** through the object interior. Holes can be interactively translated and rotated. Intersection with other holes is automatically handled, as shown in (**d**). Hole depth can also be modified to create cut-out regions (**e**)

11.2.3.2 Sweep Surfaces

The sweep-surface representation underlying our blobby inflation scheme also supports linear sweeps (Fig. 11.8d) and surfaces of revolution (Fig. 11.8e). Linear sweeps are created in the same way as blobby shapes, with the sweep axis perpendicular to the view-parallel plane. The initial length of the sweep is proportional to the screen area covered by the bounding box of the 2D curve, but can be interactively manipulated with a 2D widget. Surfaces of revolution are created by revolving the sketch around an axis lying in the view-parallel plane. As in the case of linear sweeps, the revolution template can contain holes, and revolutions with both spherical and toroidal topology can be created.

Aside from Cherlin et al.'s advanced revolution technique [11], most sketch-based systems have not included these additional types of shapes. While blobby inflation is highly useful for many modeling tasks, linear sweeps and revolutions are invaluable in situations such as mechanical modeling. In particular, surfaces of revolution are a class of shape that cannot be approximated with blobby inflation.

11.2.3.3 Cutting

Since the underlying BlobTree is a true volumetric model, cutting operations can be easily implemented using CSG operators. Designers can either cut a hole through the object or remove volume by cutting across the object silhouette. Since the "hole" is internally represented as a linear sweep, no additional implementation is necessary to support cutting. In addition, the designer may interactively transform this subtracted sweep at any time, effectively dragging the hole around through the surface. Interactive controls are also available to modify the depth of cutting operations. An example is shown in Fig. 11.9. This CSG-based cutting operation is both more precise and less restrictive than in existing systems. Note that although only sharp edges are demonstrated in Fig. 11.9, ShapeShop includes various "soft" CSG difference operators which generate filleted edges of varying smoothness.

11.2.3.4 Blending

ShapeShop relies on the easy-to-implement implicit blending techniques supported by the BlobTree to allow the designer to increase the volume of the current object.

Fig. 11.10 The sketch-based blending operation **a** creates a new blobby inflation primitive and **b** blends it to the current volume. The blending strength can be interactively manipulated, the extreme settings are shown in (**c**) and (**d**). The blend region is re-computed automatically when the blended primitives move, as shown in (**e**)

As demonstrated in Fig. 11.10, this action is initiated by sketching a contour across the silhouette or interior of the current shape. Selecting the resulting suggestion creates a new blobby primitive which is blended with the current model. The width of the new primitive can be manipulated with a slider, as can the amount of blending. Again, as the blend is a dynamic composition of two implicit volumes, either can be transformed interactively (Fig. 11.10(e)).

Various other tools have explored implicit blending [3, 20] or discrete fairing [25] in a sketch-based context. However, the style of dynamic implicit blending available in ShapeShop is highly useful in practice, and one of the features that professional 3D artists find most desirable when first being introduced to the system.

One issue neglected thus far is how to fix the depth of the view-parallel 3D plane onto which a sketched contour is projected. Unlike Teddy's extrusions, we try to infer the correct depth from context, rather than require the user to mark the surface. Without any prior evidence, the plane is assumed to pass through the origin. However, if the sketched strokes overlap the 2D projection of the surface, we center the projection plane at the average depth value along the strokes. If a part is selected, only its surface is considered. This technique is reasonably effective in practice, and one can learn to manipulate the viewpoint and stroke to generate a good initial guess. However, minor errors are common and major errors sometime occur, requiring 3D manipulation. We are currently exploring efficient techniques for allowing the designer to more explicitly specify the depth of newly created primitives.

11.2.3.5 Surface Drawing

Perhaps the most straightforward type of sketch-based interaction is drawing curves directly on an existing 3D surface. Such techniques have long been used in traditional modeling systems [4], and are a basis for operations in many sketch-based systems [18, 24, 25]. ShapeShop supports such a "surface-drawing" technique, useful for adding detail and creating arbitrary 3D structures. The operation is very simple—rays through the 2D strokes are intersected with the current implicit volume, and a solid tube-like volume represented by a 3D implicit polyline

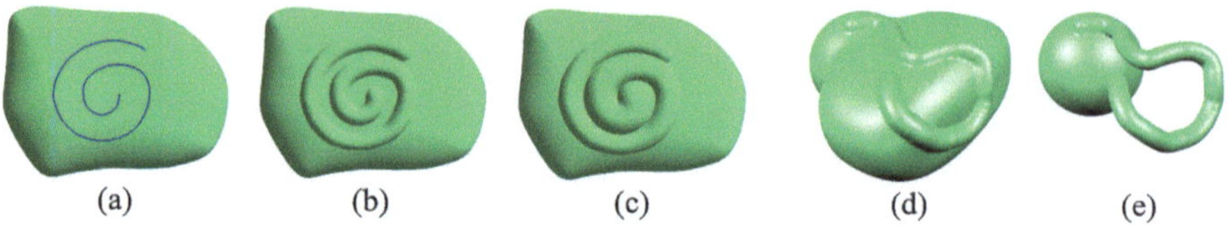

Fig. 11.11 Surface drawing is specified by a 2D sketch, as shown in (**a**). Blended skeletal implicit point primitives are placed along the line at intersection points with the model, shown in (**b**). In (**c**) the radius of the points is increased and then tapered along the length of the 2D curve. Temporary construction surfaces (**d**) can be used to create more complex 3D curves (**e**)

primitive is generated. Interactive controls are provided to manipulate both the surface radius and linear scaling (tapering) along the polyline. Results are shown in Fig. 11.11(a–c).

With Surface Drawing, any pair of implicit primitive and composition operator can be used as a type of "brush" to add detail to the current surface. Implementing these alternative tools within the BlobTree framework is very straightforward. In addition, since each surface-drawing stroke is represented independently in the model hierarchy, individual surface details can be modified or removed using the existing modeling interface. Of course, as the surface is dynamically polygonized, interactive visual fidelity must be limited at levels which often do not resolve fine details. This does unfortunately limit the use of surface drawing in practice.

Surface drawing also readily demonstrates another extremely useful property of utilizing the BlobTree as an underlying shape representation for sketch-based modeling. As shown in Fig. 11.11(d–e), surface drawing can be applied to a temporary *construction* surface, which is then erased, resulting in free-floating geometry which does not lie on a planar space curve. The same technique can be used to fix the depth of sketched primitives without excessive manual positioning. These temporary construction surfaces are a novel property of ShapeShop which was not designed into the system, but simply emerged out of the non-linear hierarchical editing capabilities of the BlobTree. One potentially fruitful area of future research would be to explore more explicit support for construction surfaces in sketching systems.

11.2.4 Selection and Transformation

Procedurally defined BlobTree volumes inherently support non-linear editing of internal tree nodes. However, before a primitive can be manipulated it must be selected. One option is to cast a ray into the set of primitives and select the first-hit primitive. This technique is problematic when dealing with blending surfaces, since the designer may click on the visible surface but no primitive is hit.

Picking in ShapeShop is implemented by intersecting a ray with the current volume, and then selecting the primitive which contributes most to the total field value at the intersection point. This algorithm selects the largest contributor in blending situations, and selects the subtracted primitive when the user clicks on the inside

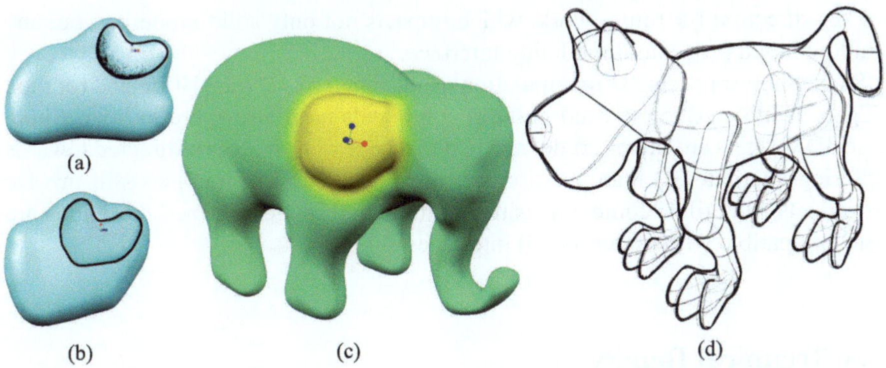

Fig. 11.12 Internal volumes can be directly rendered using pen-and-ink stippling (**a**) or transparency (**b**). Portions of the surface can also be highlighted to show the influence region of a selection (**c**). Visual Scaffolding techniques provide an integrated display of all the primitives making up a model (**d**), but do not convey the structure of the BlobTree

of a hole surface. However, selecting the maximum contributor can result in non-intuitive behavior in cases where a small primitive is blended with a larger one, as the larger primitive may contribute more to the field at all points on the surface. In this case, the user must use the BlobTree Editor tree view (Fig. 11.4) to select the desired node. An un-implemented but sensible alternative would be to cycle through the possible selections using multiple taps.

This selection system only allows for selection of primitives. To select composition nodes we implement a *parent* gesture, which selects the parent of the current node. The *parent* gesture is entered as a straight line towards the top of the screen. No similar child-selection gesture has been implemented because it is unclear how to disambiguate which child is desired in cases where a node has multiple children. A selected primitive or composition node can be removed using the *eraser* gesture described in Sect. 11.2.2. Removing a composition node is equivalent to cutting a branch from the model tree—all children are also removed. More complex tree traversal and manipulation, such as re-arranging nodes, currently require the use of the BlobTree Editor tree view.

We have experimented with several rendering modes to display the shape of selected primitives, which are often completely contained within the current volume (Fig. 11.12). These techniques effectively convey the shape of the selected volume, but the semantics of the local BlobTree structure are completely opaque. Visualization of structured hierarchical 3D models, in a manner suitable for intuitive direct manipulation, is a challenging and relatively open problem. Obvious approaches like transparency or cut-away views do not scale well to complex nested trees. One possible approach we have recently explored involves *visual scaffolding*, a rendering style which mimics the construction geometry sketched by artists to help produce correct proportions and perspective in pencil-and-paper drawing [39]. However, this technique only addresses visualization of the BlobTree primitives; no support for display or interaction with composition nodes was provided (Fig. 11.12(d)). This is a key direction for future work, which impacts not only solid modeling, but any dataflow-based procedural modeling interface.

ShapeShop supports 3D manipulation using standard 3D translation and rotation widgets. Compared to the fluid gestural commands used elsewhere in ShapeShop, these 3D widgets are rather crude, and hence recent work has been directed towards exploring alternate 3D manipulation schemes [40]. These techniques still involve 3D widgets, but utilize context-sensitive gestural and suggestive methods which are more compatible with sketch-based interfaces.

11.3 Technical Details

The technical details underlying the various components of the ShapeShop system span many areas of computer graphics and human-computer interaction. In the following text we focus the discussion on the critical shape modeling aspects relating to hierarchical implicit volume modeling. Even that is quite a large subject, far too extensive to describe here in any depth. Hence, we limit ourselves to a very brief overview of the basics, and refer the interested reader to [33] for detailed information and discussion of open problems in this area.

11.3.1 Hierarchical Implicit Volume Modeling

Consider a function f that, when applied to a point $\mathbf{p} \in \mathbb{R}^3$, produces a scalar value $f(\mathbf{p}) \in \mathbb{R}$. A surface $\mathcal{S} \in \mathbb{R}^3$ can then be defined by the equality

$$f(\mathbf{p}) = v \tag{1}$$

where $v \in \mathbb{R}$ is a scalar value. This surface $\mathcal{S}$ is an *iso-contour* of the *scalar field* produced by $f(\mathbf{p})$, and v is the *iso-value* that produces $\mathcal{S}$. In computer graphics, $\mathcal{S}$ is commonly known as an *implicit surface*. One example is the *distance field*, defined with respect to some geometric entity T, such as a point or a curve:

$$d_{\mathsf{T}}(\mathbf{p}) = \min_{\mathbf{q} \in \mathsf{T}} |\mathbf{q} - \mathbf{p}|. \tag{2}$$

Intuitively, $d_{\mathsf{T}}(\mathbf{p})$ is the shortest distance from $\mathbf{p}$ to T. Hence, $d_{\mathsf{T}}(\mathbf{p}) = 0$ describes the set of points $\mathbf{p}$ lying on T, while non-zero iso-values define offset surfaces. By mapping values to grayscale, we can visualize a 2D slice of the field (Fig. 11.13(a)).

Distance fields can be used directly for 3D modeling, however they have several limitations—they do not necessarily define closed surfaces, may be discontinuous, and have infinite extent. As we shall soon see, these are problematic if we wish to functionally combine implicit surfaces. Instead, we can apply a second function g to the distance field, which is known as a *falloff* or *potential* function. We use

$$g(d) = \left(1 - d^2/r^2\right)^3. \tag{3}$$

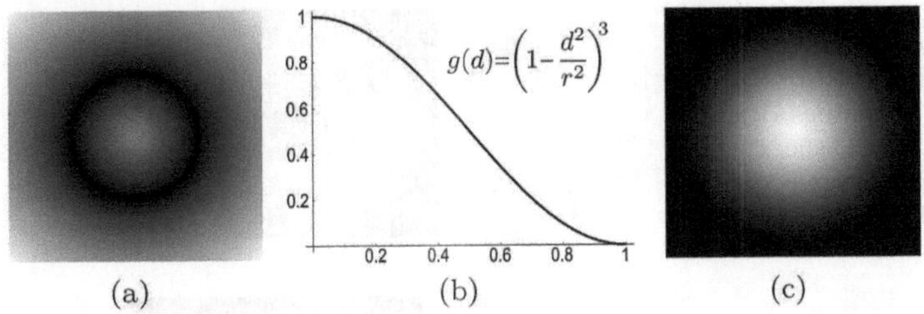

Fig. 11.13 The 2D distance field from a circle is shown in (**a**), with distance values mapped to grayscale—brighter values indicate larger distances. Skeletal primitives are created by applying a potential field (**b**) to a distance field, resulting in a bounded field such as in (**c**), which visualizes the value of $g \circ d(\mathbf{p})$ when the skeleton is a single point

As shown in Fig. 11.13(b), this function smoothly decreases from 1 to 0. When composed with a distance field, the resulting field $f(\mathbf{p}) = g \circ d_{\mathsf{T}}(\mathbf{p})$ is *bounded*, meaning that there is a finite region within which all non-zero values, as well as the iso-surface, are guaranteed to be contained (Fig. 11.13(c)). This type of implicit surface is known as a *skeletal primitive*, because T is the *skeleton* of the iso-surface.

Skeletal primitives provide other guarantees as well. Assuming T is convex, the field is necessarily continuous, and is closed by definition. Hence, given an *iso-value* v, skeletal primitives also define implicit *volumes*:

$$\mathcal{V} = \{\mathbf{p} : f(\mathbf{p}) \geq v\}. \tag{4}$$

The volumetric property is quite useful. For example, (4) provides a trivial point containment test. Implicit volumes can also be trivially composed via *Boolean operations*. The union of two implicit volumes f_1 and f_2 can be described by a new scalar field, generated by functional composition [31]:

$$(f_1 \cup f_2)(\mathbf{p}) = \max\bigl(f_1(\mathbf{p}), f_2(\mathbf{p})\bigr). \tag{5}$$

The power of this operation, and similar ones for *intersection* and *subtraction* or *difference*, is that they are *closed* under the space of all possible implicit volumes, meaning the can be applied repeatedly, each time producing another implicit volume (Fig. 11.14). Hence, implementing solid-modeling techniques such as *Constructive Solid Geometry* (CSG) is nearly trivial with implicit volumes. The CSG Tree is represented as a hierarchy of functional compositions such as (5), with skeletal primitives at the leaf nodes (see Fig. 11.19 for a simple example).

Solid modeling is not limited to CSG. Another useful class of operation is the construction of smooth transitions between two surfaces, often known as a *blend*. Functional blend operators can be defined for implicit volumes, such as Ricci's blend operator [31] (Fig. 11.14(c)):

$$(f_1 \uplus f_2)(\mathbf{p}) = \bigl(f_1(\mathbf{p})^s + f_2(\mathbf{p})^s\bigr)^{\frac{1}{s}} \tag{6}$$

which allows the user to control blend smoothness via the parameter s (as $s \rightarrow \infty$, $\uplus \rightarrow \cup$). Like the CSG operators, this blend operator is independent of the complexity of the implicit surface, and simply produces another implicit volume. We

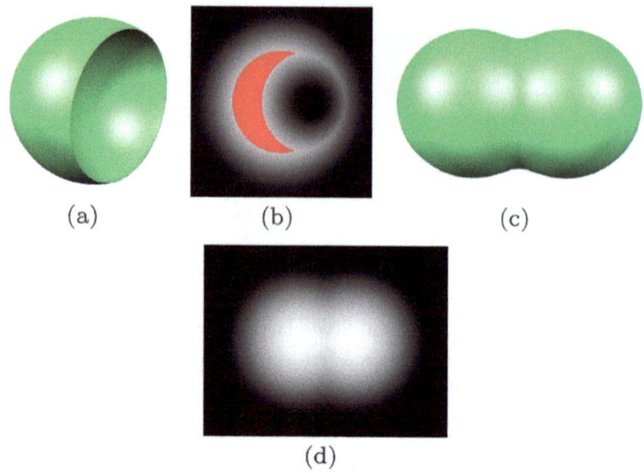

Fig. 11.14 An implicit sphere is subtracted from another using a CSG Difference operation (**a**), and blended in (**c**). 2D slices through the respective 3D scalar fields are shown in (**b**) and (**d**)

can now see why *bounded* fields such as those produced by skeletal primitives are so important—each input field to (6) can only affect the blended surface within its bounding region. This local influence preserves a "principle of least surprise" that greatly improves the usability of constructive implicit modeling.

The BlobTree hierarchical modeling framework is an extension of the traditional CSG Tree which encapsulates techniques for constructive solid modeling with skeletal primitives [45]. In addition to CSG and blending, the BlobTree system includes support for functional warping and deformation, texturing, and animation. See [15] for a thorough description of the full BlobTree system. The BlobTree implementation used in ShapeShop is relatively non-traditional, in that only functionality relating specifically to shape modeling has been implemented, largely to reduce computational costs. For example, even basic BlobTree color support would quadruple the memory requirements involved in the Hierarchical Spatial Caching described in Sect. 11.3.4.

11.3.2 BlobTree Visualization

As noted in the previous section, an implicit surface is defined as an iso-contour of a scalar field, $f(\mathbf{p}) = v$. Unlike a parametric definition, this equation does not directly provide points on the surface. Instead, visualization algorithms must search through space to determine where the surface lies.

Perhaps the simplest technique for visualizing implicit surfaces is polygonization. We use a continuation polygonization algorithm, which initially finds points on the surface by marchings outwards from internal *seed points* defined by the primitives. Space is then subdivided into small cubes, and the cubes intersecting the surface are incrementally enumerated using a stack and hash table [44]. This minimizes the number of field evaluations, and hence is more efficient for polygonizing functional surfaces than the popular *Marching Cubes* algorithm [22], which

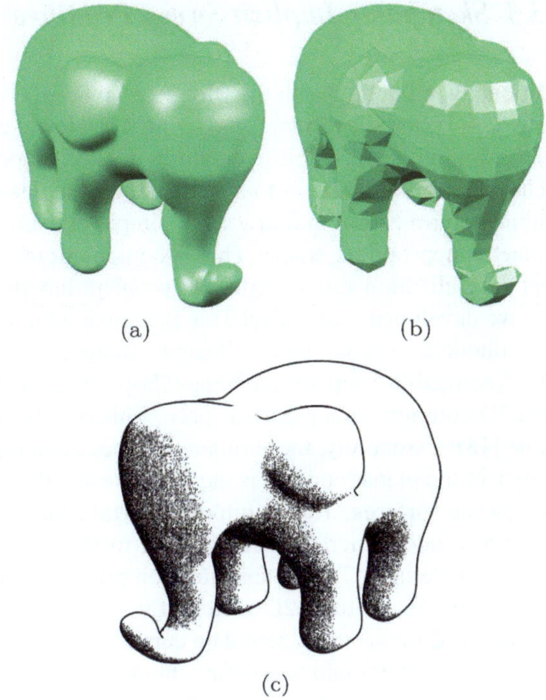

Fig. 11.15 Implicit surfaces can be visualized by dynamically tessellating the surface (**a**). However, to ensure real-time feedback, the mesh fidelity must be dramatically lowered (**b**). Based on this coarse mesh, we can generate high-fidelity pen-and-ink renderings at little extra cost (**c**)

performs a brute-force enumeration of all cubes inside a fixed volume. Ideally these algorithms produce the same mesh, although we cannot guarantee that a seed point exists inside each disconnected component, and hence the continuation approach can sometimes miss parts of the surface.

To interactively visualize BlobTree models in ShapeShop, the polygonization algorithm is performed in real-time, using an optimized version of Bloomenthal's code [8]. Two modified versions of this polygonizer are also available. The first simply adds the crease-finding techniques described in the Extended Marching Cubes work [21]. The second provides support for local updates, where mesh re-computation is limited to the regions in which the current model has changed. The extra contextual information that must be stored to support partial re-meshing does introduce significant overhead, however, smaller local updates are so much more efficient that the benefits largely outweigh this cost.

Despite expending significant effort in our attempts to optimize our polygonizer, we still must sacrifice visual fidelity to ensure interactive feedback rates, even for moderately simple models. Hence, we have begun to explore other visualization techniques. By combining a coarse mesh with local refinement techniques, we can provide real-time pen-and-ink-style rendering at a higher level of visual fidelity, but within the same computation budget as lower quality real-time polygonization (Fig. 11.15). See [39] for technical implementation details.

11.3.3 Sketchable Implicit Sweep Primitives

Traditionally, modeling with the BlobTree involved composition of fixed geometric primitives—spheres, cylinders, and so on [45]. However, in a sketch-based modeling tool, we would like to be able to create an inflated shape with a silhouette that closely matches an arbitrary 2D contour sketched by the designer. One approach is to use numerical optimization to find a set of simple primitives which, when blended, will produce an appropriate shape. This is computationally impractical [9], although a recent specialization for the inflation problem has made it more tractable [1]. Instead, we developed a new BlobTree primitive which supports direct manipulation of the silhouette contour, so that it can be matched directly to a given 2D sketch.

As described in Sect. 11.2.3, ShapeShop's creation tools allow the user to sketch closed 2D contours on a plane in space. This contour is then *inflated* into some 3D volume [18]. Essentially, these inflated shapes are a type of sweep surface or extrusion, where the planar contour is the *template* and the plane normal is the *trajectory*. While sweep surfaces are ubiquitous in surface modeling [30], implicit sweep representations have generally been limited to star-shaped templates [12] which are procedurally defined. To create an implicit primitive whose silhouette contour could be matched to an arbitrary 2D sketch, it was necessary to develop sweep primitives which allowed for arbitrary template curves.

In the implicit domain, we define the desired primitive by sweeping a bounded, continuous 2D template scalar field $f_{\mathcal{C}}$, whose iso-contour v approximates the sketched closed contour $\mathcal{C}$, along the trajectory $\mathcal{T}$. As with other BlobTree primitives, the general approach is to apply a falloff function to the distance field of the curve, hence $f_{\mathcal{C}} = g \circ d_{\mathcal{C}}$, where $d_{\mathcal{C}}$ is the 2D distance field defined by $\mathcal{C}$ and g is as in (3). Note that as the surface of other BlobTree primitives is defined at $v = 0.5$, the values of $d_{\mathcal{C}}$ must be shifted so that the v contour aligns with the 0-contour of the distance field. The shifted distance $d'_{\mathcal{C}}$ is then:

$$d'_{\mathcal{C}} = \min\bigl(g^{-1}(v) + d_{\mathcal{C}}, 0\bigr). \tag{7}$$

The bounded template field $f_{\mathcal{C}}$ is then defined as

$$f_{\mathcal{C}} = g \circ d'_{\mathcal{C}}. \tag{8}$$

This formulation produces a template with the desired iso-contour, but the distance field of a non-convex $\mathcal{C}$ contains C^1 discontinuities (Fig. 11.16(a)). These discontinuities will be swept in 3D and produce undesirable artifacts when the sweep primitive is blended with other shapes [33]. Hence, it is necessary to generate a "smoothed" distance field, which approximates $d_{\mathcal{C}}$ but remains continuous.

To create such a smooth distance field, we utilize variational interpolation, also known as *thin-plate splines* approximation. Essentially, a C^2 interpolating thin-plate spline is fit to a set of constraint points placed at samples of $\mathcal{C}$ [47]. To ensure that the solution passes through the sample points, inner and outer *normal constraints* are added at short distances along the normals to $\mathcal{C}$ at the on-curve samples (Fig. 11.17(a)).

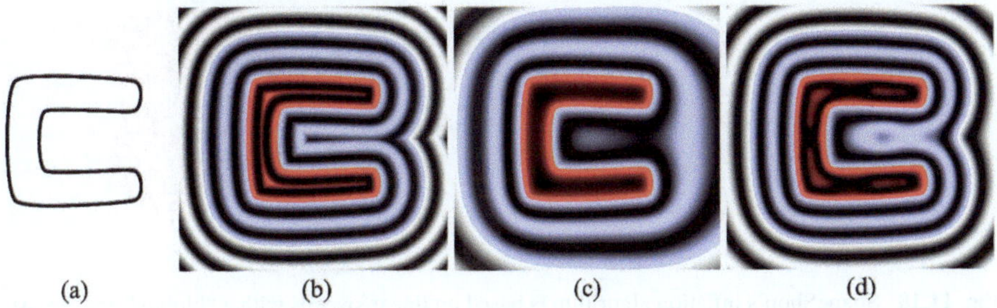

Fig. 11.16 Scalar fields generated using a non-convex curve (**a**). The exact distance field (**b**) has C^1 discontinuities inside and outside the curve. Standard variational interpolation with normal constraints provides a poor approximation in concave regions, and is difficult to bound (**c**). Our approach (**d**) smoothly approximates the distance field away from the surface

Fig. 11.17 *Normal constraints* (**a**) at a point $\mathbf{c}_i$ are added at short offset Δs from the curve $\mathcal{C}$, along the curve normal $\mathbf{n}_i$. *Boundary constraints* (**b**) are placed at a constant distance from $\mathcal{C}$ to improve the distance field approximation and ensure that the field $f_\mathcal{C}$ is bounded within a known distance

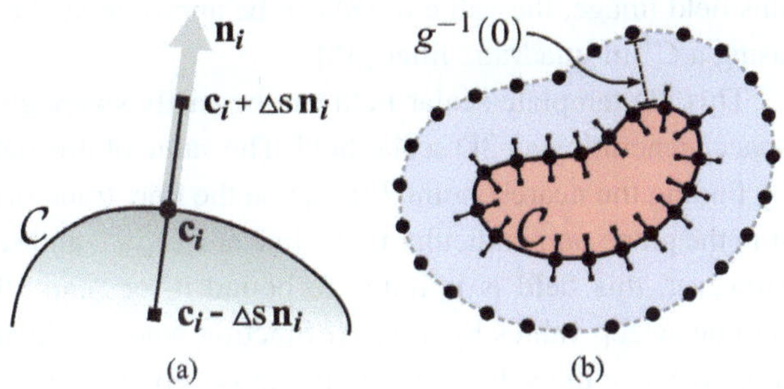

Normal constraints only constrain the solution near $\mathcal{C}$—the rest of the field is unconstrained, resulting in a poor approximation to the distance field (Fig. 11.16). This is problematic if the field is to be bounded by applying a falloff function, as a time-consuming spatial search is required to determine the non-zero region of the resulting field. With the true distance field, the bounding zero-contour lies along the distance contour $d_\mathcal{C} = g^{-1}(0)$, the bounds of which can be reliably computed. Hence, to predictably bound our approximate distance field, we add *boundary* constraints which force the variational field to approximate this outer contour. In addition, we add constraints along two interior contours in the distance field, one at $g^{-1}(0.5v)$, which is approximately half-way between $\mathcal{C}$ and the zero-contour, and another at $g^{-1}(1.5v)$, which lies inside $\mathcal{C}$. The purpose of these extra constraints is to further reduce error in the distance field approximation. To sample these contours, we compute the distance transform of $\mathcal{C}$ on a 512^2 pixel image, and trace the discrete iso-contours in the image. As shown in Fig. 11.16, these constraints greatly improve the distance field approximation, while maintaining global C^2 continuity.

One drawback of this approach is that the evaluation of the variational field which approximates the distance field is $O(N)$ in the number of constraint points, so evaluating (8) is quite expensive. However, since we are only interested in the final bounded field, we can pre-compute its values on a regular grid, or *field image*. From

Fig. 11.18 ShapeShop's inflation algorithm is based on linear sweeps with a "blobby" endcap (**a**). Flat endcaps with filleted edges (**b**) or sharp creases (**c**) are also supported, increasing the range of shapes which can be modeled

this field image, the value of (8) can be approximated at any point in constant time using a C^1 bi-quadratic filter [35].

This 2D template scalar field can be easily swept along a line $L(t) = \mathbf{o} + t\mathbf{d}$ in space, generating an 3D scalar field. The value of this field is defined at a 3D point $\mathbf{p}$ by finding the nearest point $L(t_{\text{near}})$ on the line, transforming $\mathbf{p}$ into 2D coordinates $\mathbf{u}$ in the plane perpendicular to the line at $L(t_{\text{near}})$, and sampling the 2D field image. However, this field is infinite. To bound it, or "cap" the sweep, we multiply the infinite sweep values by a falloff function whose value ranges from 1 at $t = 0$ to 0 at $t_{\max}$. Since the values of the infinite sweep vary inside the template, they reach 0 at different distances along the line, producing an endcap which is wider in regions further from the sketched contour, giving the impression of a shape which has been inflated. The falloff function can be modulated to vary the width of the shape, and also to produce different effects such as completely flat endcaps with smooth or sharp transitions (Fig. 11.18).

In a traditional surface or solid-modeling environment, limiting the available primitives to linear sweeps and surfaces of revolution would be highly restrictive. However, by the simple addition of implicit blending, ShapeShop is capable of expressing a wide range of complex shapes. While the description here has been necessarily brief, the interested reader is referred to [35] and [33] for a more thorough discussion, including details on creating implicit sweeps with circular and arbitrary trajectories. The latter seems particularly useful in a sketch-based tool, although it has yet to be integrated into ShapeShop. We also note that a variety of other approaches to implicit inflation have been explored, based on blending point primitives [1], 3D variational interpolation [3, 20], and convolution surfaces [1, 42]. The main limitation with all of these methods, including the technique described here, is that they produce continuous fields which cannot represent any sharp corners in the sketch. We have proposed one solution for restricted cases [35], but the general problem remains unaddressed.

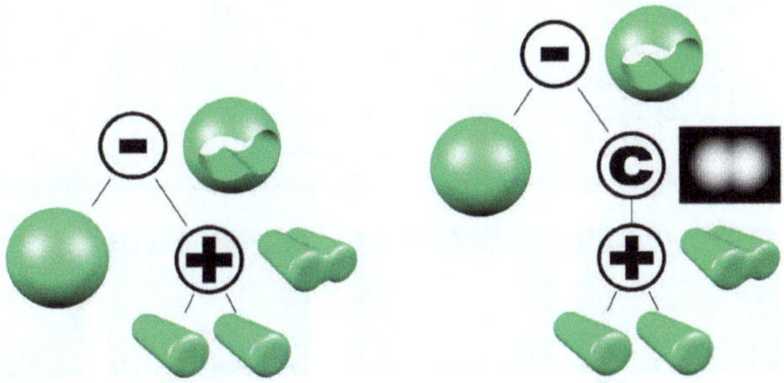

(a) (b)

Fig. 11.19 In (**a**), two cylinder primitives are blended, and then subtracted from a sphere. In (**b**), a cache node is inserted above the blend node. Once filled, the cache short-circuits evaluation of the blend subtree, replacing an $O(m)$ traversal with an $O(1)$ tri-linear interpolation

11.3.4 Hierarchical Spatial Caching

One of the major limitations of hierarchical implicit modeling techniques like the BlobTree is that the complexity of the hierarchy grows with the complexity of the model. Hence, the recursive evaluations of the tree which are required to sample the scalar field defining the implicit volume become increasingly expensive. Unfortunately, implicit surface visualization methods rely on sampling the value and gradient of this field many times for each output mesh vertex. In profiling implicit surface polygonizers, we observed that for even moderately complex models, over 95% of the computation time is spent recursively evaluating the BlobTree. The cost of these evaluations must be reduced to ensure that the designer is not hampered by non-interactive visual feedback.

Inspired by promising results in [6], the *Hierarchical Spatial Caching* method was introduced [36] to address the interactivity problem. The fundamental idea behind this technique is to dynamically insert spatial caches into the BlobTree as *cache nodes*. These nodes approximate the scalar field of their subtree using a set of regular discrete samples which are computed as needed. This reduces the cost of evaluating the subtree from $O(m)$ to amortized $O(1)$ (Fig. 11.19).

Unlike previous approaches [6, 14], the sample values at grid vertices are not precomputed, but rather evaluated as needed (Fig. 11.20). This lazy evaluation provides a significant benefit, as full evaluation of high-resolution grids is computationally intensive. In addition, if surface-tracking visualization algorithms are used, only cache samples near the surface are required. In this case most of the samples in a fully evaluated grid will never be used—particularly if they will be invalidated in the next frame as the user drags a primitive across the screen.

The resolution of spatial caches is key to visual fidelity—too low a resolution, and the subtree's scalar field will not be adequately reconstructed, while oversampling results in wasted computation. In practice, we err on the side of caution and use a fixed grid resolution of 128^3. An obvious improvement would be to utilize adaptively-sampled grids, as in [14]. Unfortunately, adaptive methods have high initial overhead, which is impractical when the cache is being discarded each frame, and to date also lack even basic C^0 continuity (see [33] for details).

A related issue is the positioning of cache nodes, which should be sparsely distributed throughout the tree, ideally above subtrees which define semantic "parts".

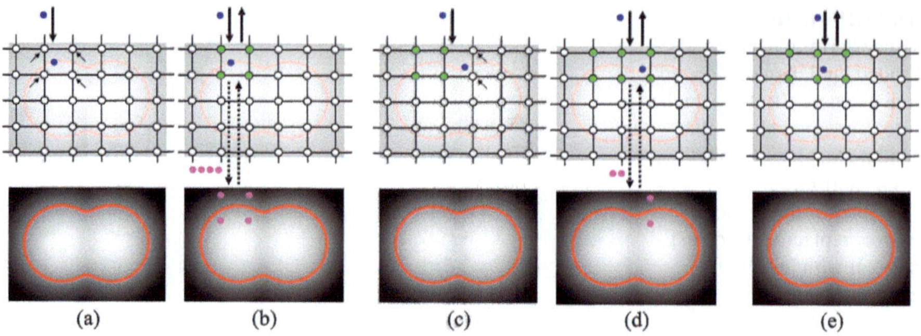

Fig. 11.20 In (**a**), the field values necessary to reconstruct the value at the incoming query point (in *blue*) are unavailable. The child field must be evaluated four times, once for each cache value (**b**). In (**c**), two cache values are missing and must be evaluated in the child field (**d**). Finally, in (**e**) all cache values are available. The incoming value query can be directly approximated in $O(1)$ time, no $O(m)$ evaluations of the child field are necessary

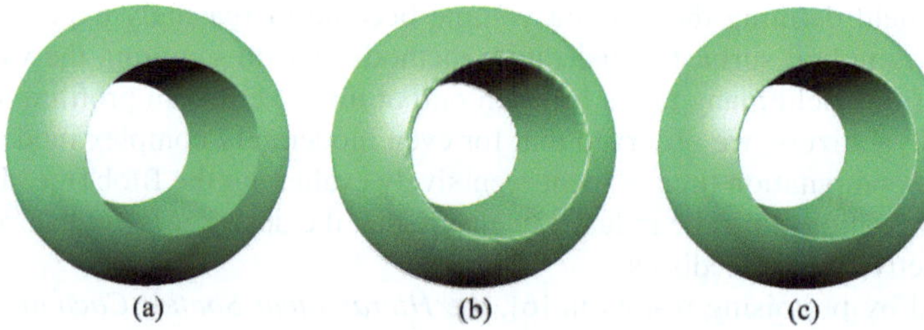

Fig. 11.21 Comparison of representation of a sharp edge without caching (**a**), with a cache resolution of 128^3 (**b**), and 256^3 (**c**). The Extended Marching Cubes polygonizer is used, producing a clear sharp edge in (**a**), but having no effect in (**b**) and (**c**) due to gradient smoothing at the crease

Since it is preferable that the designer not have to manually place cache nodes, ShapeShop uses simple heuristics to position cache nodes near the top of the tree. As with the sampling resolution, these ad-hoc solutions are effective in practice, but more principled approaches would be beneficial, and remain open problems.

In test cases simulating interactive modeling actions, hierarchical Spatial Caching results in an order-of-magnitude reduction in the computation necessary to triangulate a BlobTree model. This is a critical enhancement, making BlobTree modeling practical for use in interactive systems like ShapeShop. However, there are some drawbacks [33]. In particular, spatial approximation tends to smooth out sharp creases in the surface. This is a standard problem with surfacing implicit models, but recent polygonizers can use the field gradient to reconstruct sharp edges [21]. Unfortunately the interpolating filters to reconstruct smooth scalar fields from a sampled grid also smooth out the gradients, preventing sharp features from being recovered (Fig. 11.21). A solution to this problem will require the development of schemes which are sensitive to the properties of the scalar fields they are approximating.

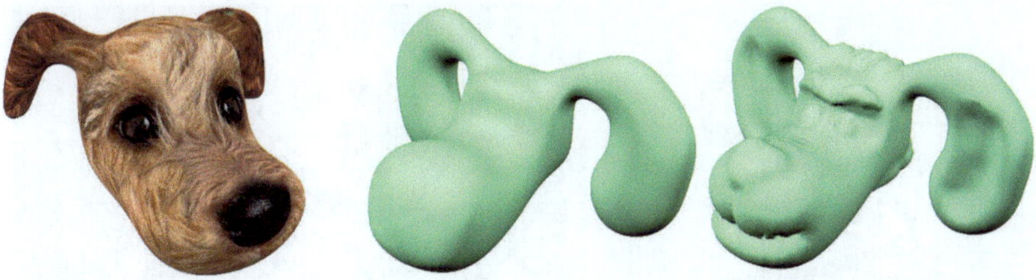

Fig. 11.22 Additions to the ShapeShop modeling system have included decal texturing (*left*) and mesh-based procedural surface editing layers (*right*)

11.4 The ShapeShop System

As with much of the research described in this book, one of our basic assumptions is that sketch-based interfaces will ultimately lead to more efficient and expressive 3D modeling tools. However, in our experience, working artists and designers have a hard time imagining how sketch-based tools could fit into their design pipelines. We have found that many artists do experiment with SBM research software that is publicly released, but these systems are regarded more as curiosities rather than real tools, as such systems (sensibly) tend to focus on demonstrating novelty rather than striving for production quality. Unfortunately, without user demand, the industrial 3D tool-makers with whom we have interacted remain skeptical of sketch-based modeling techniques. Hence, one of our goals with ShapeShop was to develop the system to the point where it could potentially be useful to real users.

ShapeShop was first made public at the SBIM Workshop in 2005, and included most of the techniques described here, as well as a few more which have since been removed. This was one of our early lessons—unlike systems with traditional interfaces, where one can always "just add another menu item", the designers of interfaces based on gestures and context-sensitivity must be much more self-critical, and willing to sacrifice infrequently-used tools if the system is to remain usable.

This initial version also lacked save/load capabilities, which severely limited the utility of the software. When demonstrating the system to artists, however, their biggest concern was texturing. Like many SBM systems, the output of ShapeShop is an unstructured triangle mesh, and hence manually assigning meaningful UV coordinates can be a time-consuming process. This lead to the development of decal texturing [38], shown in Fig. 11.22, which was released in ShapeShop V2 at SIGGRAPH 2006. This version also included saving and loading, making the system far more practical for real users.

Between the steady trickle of e-mail feedback, and posts discussing ShapeShop on web-based community forums, we have learned that working 3D designers are experimenting with ShapeShop in their professional workflows. Some of this exploration is purely artistic, such as the 3D sculptures displayed in Fig. 11.23, which were created by an artist who frequents the ShapeShop web forums. We have been contacted by bespoke jewelers, children's toy makers, elementary school teachers,

Fig. 11.23 3D sculptures created by first modeling in ShapeShop, and then importing the surface mesh into Modo [23] for texturing and rendering. Images ©Corien Klapwijk

and traditional-media artists who are using ShapeShop to experiment with 3D modeling. Much of this experimentation is short-lived, as the initial excitement tends to fade once the many limitations of the system become clear. Still, the comments we receive from users who have tried the software are almost uniformly positive, indicating a high level of interest in sketch-based modeling techniques.

There is one particular method in which 3D designers are integrating ShapeShop into their pipeline that warrants further explanation. As brush-based displacement painting systems like Z-Brush [29] and Modo [23] have become more capable, it is now common practice to build a basic model in traditional software, and then import it into these tools, where realistic levels of detail can be much more easily created. ShapeShop and other SBM software are quite effective in the initial blocking or massing stages, where they are more efficient than traditional control-point interfaces. We have attempted to encourage this workflow by adding mesh refinement tools to ShapeShop, as initial mesh quality is a necessity for these sculpting tools. However, it may be interesting to explore a more specific focus on this particular workflow, as it has significant implications for sketch-based modeling systems.

11.5 Discussion

In the previous sections, we have described the fundamental components of the ShapeShop sketch-based modeling system. From 2D drawing assistance to pen-based interaction to hierarchical, procedural shape representation, ShapeShop incorporates many aspects of our own research and that of others. By continually developing the software and releasing it "into the wild", we have received extensive feedback from working 3D designers. This experience has given us much insight into the advantages and shortcomings of our work.

The use of a structured, procedural hierarchy to represent the sequence of sketched operations is perhaps the largest advantage of ShapeShop over its contemporaries. Not only does this permit greater complexity, it also allows designers to tweak and refine indefinitely. The response of 3D artists to this capability has been extremely positive. By utilizing implicit volumetric techniques, ShapeShop avoids the artificial distinction between "CAD-style" and "free-form" modeling that most tools make. The implicit approach also greatly enhances the ability to quickly explore a wide range of design variations (Fig. 11.24). Although iterative design is extremely common, few systems provide any specific support, and hence it is often very costly in 3D. Ultimately, we would like to reduce the burden on the designer when they wish to pick-and-choose from multiple variations.

Construction surfaces are another powerful feature of the procedural approach used in ShapeShop. Again, we have not designed in any specific support for construction surfaces, but are in the process of exploring how to do so. The use of a procedural hierarchy also introduces many new challenges. We have yet to find a straightforward way to even visualize the model tree in an intuitive and understandable way, let alone interact with it. In our informal observation of users, this is one of the most problematic areas of the system. Even computer graphics graduate students schooled in CSG techniques have trouble manipulating the model tree via an abstract tree-view widget.

Although ShapeShop simplifies many modeling tasks, the design space is ultimately constrained to shapes that can be practically constructed by blending sweeps and revolutions. Research is in progress to lift this limitation, such as the implicit push-and-pull deformations recently introduced [41]. The *Surface Tree* mesh-based procedural layered editing technique [34], has also been implemented in ShapeShop, providing powerful but non-implicit surface manipulation tools (Fig. 11.22).

Finally, a frequent comment from academia is that sketch-based modeling systems like ShapeShop must be proven through controlled evaluation, as has become standard practice for proposing novel interaction techniques in the field of human-computer interaction. However, those techniques can be reasonably tested in isolation, as the evaluation is largely based on human performance metrics. Such approaches are not applicable to evaluating the fitness of a complex SBM system, which in many cases integrates a wide range of novel interactions. Furthermore, we are not particularly interested in pure modeling speed, but rather a trade-off between efficiency and expressiveness, which is more difficult to measure. Direct comparisons to professional 3D modeling systems are also not particularly useful. Novice users must be trained for many hours to do anything productive in a complex modeling tool, while professional users have personal workflows so highly-optimized that any comparison to a new interface is hopelessly biased. And as there is so little in common between traditional and sketch-based interfaces, the most that can be learned from test subjects is personal preferences.

In some sense, we consider the public release of ShapeShop to be the ultimate test of usefulness. However, like the few attempts at evaluating SBM systems that have been performed [5, 19, 26], we have found that user response is essentially uniformly positive. Without variation, these data do not really tell us anything, except

Fig. 11.24 Design iterations generated by adding detail to an initial base model (*left*). Volumetric implicit techniques free the designer from having to manage issues like model structure or discrete topology when exploring model variations. For example, the pig nose on the far right was simply drawn on top of the original dog nose

that the subjects have no basis for comparison and are probably only responding to the novelty of the system. We have also found that an initial positive response should not be taken to imply usefulness of the system in practice; once the novelty wears off, designers are apt to return to the tools they are more familiar with. Hence, we believe that the question of how to sensibly evaluate sketch-based modeling systems has yet to be answered, and is perhaps the most important open problem in the area.

References

1. Alexe, A., Gaildrat, V., Barthe, L.: Interactive modelling from sketches using spherical implicit functions. In: Proceedings of AFRIGRAPH 2004, pp. 25–34 (2004)
2. Apitz, G., Guimbretiére, F.: Crossy: a crossing-based drawing application. In: Proceedings of ACM UIST 2004, pp. 3–12 (2004)
3. Araújo, B., Jorge, J.: Blobmaker: Free-form modelling with variational implicit surfaces. In: Proceedings of 12th Encontro Português de Computação Gráfica (2003)
4. Autodesk Inc.: Autodesk Maya 2008 (2008). http://www.autodesk.com/maya
5. Bae, S.H., Balakrishnan, R., Singh, K.: ILoveSketch: as-natural-as-possible sketching system for creating 3d curve models. In: Proceedings of the ACM Symposium on User Interface Software and Technology (UIST), pp. 151–160 (2008)
6. Barthe, L., Mora, B., Dodgson, N., Sabin, M.: Interactive implicit modelling based on c^1 reconstruction of regular grids. International Journal of Shape Modeling **8**(2), 99–117 (2002)
7. Baudel, T.: A mark-based interaction paradigm for free-hand drawing. In: Proceedings of UIST '94, pp. 185–192 (1994)
8. Bloomenthal, J.: An implicit surface polygonizer. In: Graphics Gems IV, pp. 324–349. Academic Press, San Diego (1994)
9. Bloomenthal, J. (ed.): Introduction to Implicit Surfaces. Morgan Kaufmann, San Diego (1997). ISBN 1-55860-233-X
10. Carr, J.C., Beatson, R.K., Cherrie, J.B., Mitchell, T.J., Fright, W.R., McCallum, B.C., Evans, T.R.: Reconstruction and representation of 3d objects with radial basis functions. In: Proceedings of ACM SIGGRAPH 2001, pp. 67–76 (2001)
11. Cherlin, J.J., Samavati, F.F., Costa Sousa, M., Jorge, J.A.: Sketch-based modeling with few strokes. In: Proceedings of the Spring Conference on Computer Graphics (2005)
12. Crespin, B., Blanc, C., Schlick, C.: Implicit sweep objects. Computer Graphics Forum **15**(3), 165–174 (1996)
13. Fonseca, M.J., Ferreira, A., Jorge, J.A.: Towards 3d modeling using sketches and retrieval. In: Proceedings of the First Eurographics Workshop on Sketch-Based Interfaces and Modeling (2004)

14. Frisken, S., Perry, R., Rockwood, A., Jones, T.: Adaptively sampled distance fields: A general representation of shape for computer graphics. In: Proceedings of SIGGRAPH 2000, pp. 249–254 (2000)
15. Galbraith, C.: Modeling natural phenomena with implicit surfaces. PhD thesis, Department of Computer Science, University of Calgary (2005)
16. Igarashi, T., Hughes, J.F.: A suggestive interface for 3d drawing. In: Proceedings of ACM UIST 2001, pp. 173–181 (2001)
17. Igarashi, T., Matsuoka, S., Kawachiya, S., Tanaka, H.: Interactive beautification: a technique for rapid geometric design. In: Proceedings of ACM UIST '97, pp. 105–114 (1997)
18. Igarashi, T., Matsuoka, S., Tanaka, H.: Teddy: A sketching interface for 3d freeform design. In: Proceedings of ACM SIGGRAPH 99, pp. 409–416 (1999)
19. Kara, L.B., Shimada, K., Marmalefsky, S.D.: An evaluation of user experience with a sketch-based 3d modeling system. Computers & Graphics **31**(4), 580–597 (2007)
20. Karpenko, O., Hughes, J., Raskar, R.: Free-form sketching with variational implicit surfaces. Computer Graphics Forum **21**(3), 585–594 (2002)
21. Kobbelt, L.P., Botsch, M., Schwanecke, U., Seidel, H.P.: Feature-sensitive surface extraction from volume data. In: Proceedings of ACM SIGGRAPH 2001, pp. 57–66 (2001)
22. Lorensen, W.E., Cline, H.E.: Marching cubes: a high resolution 3d surface construction algorithm. Computer Graphics (Proceedings of SIGGRAPH 87) **21**, 163–169 (1987)
23. Luxology LLC.: Modo 302, July 2008. http://www.luxology.com
24. Nealen, A., Sorkine, O., Alexa, M., Cohen-Or, D.: A sketch-based interface for detail-preserving mesh editing. ACM Transactions on Graphics **24**(3), 1142–1147 (2005)
25. Nealen, A., Igarashi, T., Sorkine, O., Alexa, M.: Fibermesh: Designing freeform surfaces with 3d curves. ACM Transactions on Graphics **26**(3), 41–1419 (2007)
26. Oh, J.Y., Stuerzlinger, W., Danahy, J.: Sesame: Towards better 3d conceptual design systems. In: Proceedings of the 6th conference on Designing Interactive systems, pp. 80–89 (2006)
27. Olsen, L., Costa Sousa, M., Samavati, F.F., Jorge, J.: A taxonomy of modeling techniques using sketch-based interfaces. In: Eurographics 2008 STAR Reports (2008)
28. Owada, S., Nielsen, F., Nakazawa, K., Igarashi, T.: A sketching interface for modeling the internal structures of 3d shapes. In: Proceedings of the 4th International Symposium on Smart Graphics, pp. 49–57 (2003)
29. Pixologic Inc.: Zbrush 3.1 (2008). http://www.pixologic.com
30. Requicha, A.A.G.: Representations for rigid solids: theory, methods and systems. Computing Surveys **12**(4), 437–464 (1980)
31. Ricci, A.: A constructive geometry for computer graphics. Computer Graphics Journal **16**(2), 157–160 (1973)
32. Savchenko, V., Pasko, A., Okunev, O., Kunii, T.: Function representation of solids reconstructed from scattered surface points and contours. Computer Graphics Forum **14**(4) (1995)
33. Schmidt, R.: Interactive modeling with implicit surfaces. Master's thesis, Department of Computer Science, University of Calgary (2006)
34. Schmidt, R., Singh, K.: Sketch-based procedural surface modeling and compositing using surface trees. Computer Graphics Forum **27**(2), 321–330 (2008)
35. Schmidt, R., Wyvill, B.: Generalized sweep templates for implicit modeling. In: 3rd International Conference on Computer Graphics and Interactive Techniques in Australasia and Southeast Asia (GRAPHITE 2005), pp. 187–196 (2005)
36. Schmidt, R., Wyvill, B., Galin, E.: Interactive implicit modeling with hierarchical spatial caching. In: Proceedings of International Conference on Shape Modeling and Applications (SMI 2005), pp. 104–113 (2005)
37. Schmidt, R., Wyvill, B., Costa Sousa, M., Jorge, J.A.: ShapeShop: Sketch-based solid modeling with blobtrees. In: Proceedings of the 2nd Eurographics Workshop on Sketch-Based Interfaces and Modeling, pp. 53–62 (2005)
38. Schmidt, R., Grimm, C., Wyvill, B.: Interactive decal compositing with discrete exponential maps. ACM Transactions on Graphics **25**(3), 605–613 (2006)
39. Schmidt, R., Isenberg, T., Jepp, P., Singh, K., Wyvill, B.: Sketching, scaffolding, and inking: a visual history for interactive 3d modeling. In: Proceedings of NPAR '07, pp. 23–32 (2007)

40. Schmidt, R., Singh, K., Balakrishnan, R.: Sketching and composing widgets for 3d manipulation. Computer Graphics Forum **27**(2), 301–310 (2008)
41. Sugihara, M., de Groot, E., Wyvill, B., Schmidt, R.: A sketch-based method to control deformation in a skeletal implicit surface modeler. In: Proceedings of SBIM 2008 (2008)
42. Tai, C.L., Zhang, H., Fong, J.C.K.: Prototype modeling from sketched silhouettes based on convolution surfaces. Computer Graphics Forum **23**(1), 71–83 (2004)
43. Turk, G., O'brien, J.F.: Modelling with implicit surfaces that interpolate. ACM Transactions on Graphics **21**(4), 855–873 (2002)
44. Wyvill, G., McPheeters, C., Wyvill, B.: Data structures for soft objects. Visual Computer **2**(4), 227–234 (1986)
45. Wyvill, B., Guy, A., Galin, E.: Extending the CSG Tree. Warping, blending and boolean operations in an implicit surface modeling system. Computer Graphics Forum **18**(2), 149–158 (1999)
46. Wyvill, B., Foster, K., Jepp, P., Schmidt, R., Costa Sousa, M., Jorge, J.A.: Sketch based construction and rendering of implicit models. In: Proceedings of the First Eurographics Workshop on Computational Aesthetics in Graphics, Visualization and Imaging 2005, pp. 67–74 (2005)
47. Yngve, G., Turk, G.: Robust creation of implicit surfaces from polygonal meshes. IEEE Transactions on Visualization and Computer Graphics **8**(4), 346–359 (2002)
48. Zeleznik, R.C., Herndon, K.P., Hughes, J.F.: SKETCH: an interface for sketching 3d scenes. In: Proceedings of ACM SIGGRAPH 96, pp. 163–170 (1996)

Chapter 12
Inferring 3D Free-Form Shapes from Complex Contour Drawings

Olga Karpenko and John F. Hughes

12.1 Introduction

There is an emerging need for non-expert users to create 3D computer models. One example of that is communication: if one wanted to explain a concept to a colleague that involved a 3D shape, it would be nice if one could just sketch the shape on the computer screen the same way one would sketch it on paper and then, once the sketch is interactively turned into a 3D shape, rotate it to explain the idea. Other applications include initial design of characters for computer games and animation, rough industrial design of free-form objects, and interfaces for searching 3D mesh repositories. Commercial modeling software tools like Maya are very powerful and let users create fine, detailed models, but are hard to learn and not well suited for non-expert users and hard to use even for professionals. By contrast, sketch-based modeling interfaces are simple, easy-to-learn interfaces that rely on perceptually significant aspects of models for input—letting a user sketch contours, for example, to indicate shape.

When our visual system is presented with a sketch, it makes nearly-instant inferences about the shape in the drawing. As one can see in Fig. 12.1, even simple contour drawings convey shape very well. The inference mechanism is partly based on expectation—when we see something that looks like an elephant's trunk, for instance, it is easy to infer that the nearby long narrow parts must be tusks. But other aspects depend on local cues—a contour that ends, or that disappears behind another—and a broader view that helps us integrate these local cues into a coherent whole [8]. Dual to this recognition ability is our ability to learn to draw contours of

O. Karpenko (✉)
University of California, Berkeley, USA
e-mail: oakarpenko@gmail.com

J.F. Hughes
Brown University, Providence, RI, USA
e-mail: jfh@cs.brown.edu

J. Jorge, F. Samavati (eds.), *Sketch-based Interfaces and Modeling*,
DOI 10.1007/978-1-84882-812-4_12,

Fig. 12.1 This cartoon-like illustration shows how even simple contour drawings convey shape very well. It also demonstrates that even contours of the simplest drawings contain junctions

objects in a way that lets us communicate their shape to others. While drawing *well* can be difficult, even children can draw easily recognizable shapes. On the other hand, while drawing outlines or contours is relatively easy, we know few people who can reliably draw the hidden contours of even simple shapes.

The main advantage of modeling interfaces based on drawing is that they allow a user to draw what he or she is thinking of directly. One can create the shape interactively by applying a sequence of editing gestures like in Teddy [10], but the more information the user can convey by a single-view sketch, the better, since the experience is more similar to drawing on paper and thus more natural. The main challenge is that inferring a shape from a complex contour-sketch is a hard problem in general. Teddy's inflation algorithm is a good step, but limited to simple closed curve contours. SmoothSketch [14, 16], described in this chapter, makes inflation possible for the more complex drawings that contain various junctions, although it is by no means a final answer. Such a final answer may never be found, though—it is easy to draw contour sets that are so complicated that different viewers make different inferences about them. The best one can hope for is to create plausible shapes for a fairly large class of contours on which users agree on the interpretation. That is what SmoothSketch does.

SmoothSketch is not a *system* like Teddy; it is an *inflation component* that can be used in a free-form-sketching interface like Teddy. We believe that a sketching program should let the user and the computer share the work, each doing what it does best. The computer can infer a plausible shape from a moderately complex contour like the ones shown in this chapter. Then, to create more complex objects or to, say, modify the thickness of the inflated models, a user would use various gestures like the ones available in Teddy and other sketch-based systems. Currently, SmoothSketch supports editing of the existing intermediate shape representation, hidden contours, and it lets the user select an alternative topological interpretation from the list of suggestions.

In finding a shape consistent with a user's drawing, we are solving an *underspecified* problem: if the user draws a circle, perhaps s/he is imagining a sphere behind which is hidden Michaelangelo's sculpture of David. While that is a *possible* interpretation of the drawing, it is not the one our system will find; instead, we will create a spherical blob. Thus our inference process is always making choices. When, for

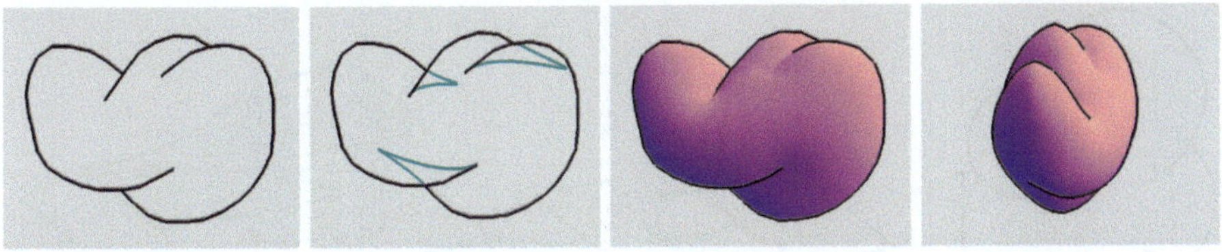

Fig. 12.2 The user draws the visible contours of a shape; our program infers the hidden contours, including hidden cusps, and then creates a fairly smooth 3D shape matching those contours. The 3D shape can be viewed from any direction

instance, we take a user's contour drawing and guess the locations of hidden parts of the contour, we have already made a choice to assume that the hidden parts of the contour are topologically as simple as possible. The reader should keep this in mind. When we say "we want to find the location of the hidden cusp" (a cusp is a feature of a contour) we are really saying "having assumed a topologically simple hidden contour, we want to choose a location for the hidden cusp that is consistent with the visible contour, and seems to be in a probable location." This suggests a probabilistic interpretation: we can imagine the set of all possible surfaces in space, and assign each a probability; we are then seeking, among all surfaces consistent with the user's drawing, the "most probable." While this formulation is useful to keep in mind, we lack any real knowledge of how probably different surfaces might be, so it is currently hopeless to try to solve the entire problem in this probabilistic framework. But as you will see during the discussion of contour completion, we use probabilistic approaches where possible.

12.2 Overview and Background

Our system takes a user's contour-drawing of a smooth, compact, oriented, embedded surface-without-boundary (which we will call a *good* surface) and determines a 3D surface whose contours match those that the user drew. Figure 12.2 shows an example of a typical user drawing and the shape inferred. Because this is an underdetermined problem—is a circle a contour drawing of a pancake? a sphere? a cigar viewed end-on?—we make several assumptions. First, we assume orthographic projection. Secondly, the contours must be *oriented*, i.e., drawn so the surface lies on the left. Thus to draw a torus, a user would draw a counter-clockwise outer stroke and a clockwise inner stroke. This assumption helps us resolve some of the ambiguities in the drawing.

We also assume that the projection is *generic* [8]: the view is not accidental and no probability-zero events occur. The contours can be quite complex: in particular, they can contain two types of singularities: T-points and cusps. Informally, a T-point is where one contour disappears behind another piece of surface. A cusp is where a contour disappears behind its own surface.[1] T-points and cusps are the only types

[1]For a formal definition of a T-point and a cusp see Sect. 12.4.

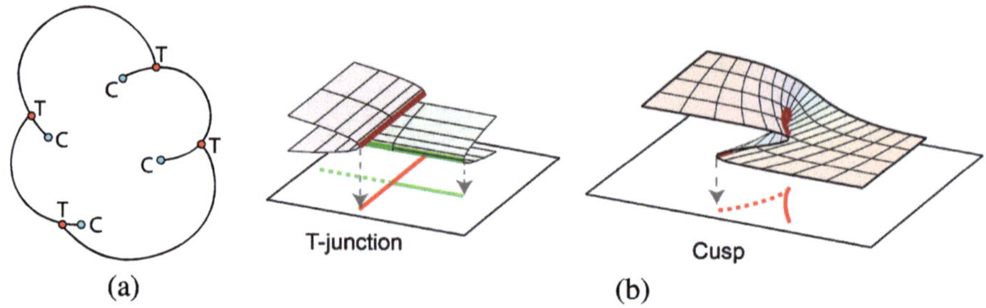

Fig. 12.3 **a** A drawing with the tee points and cusps marked. **b** Contour components: T-junctions and cusps

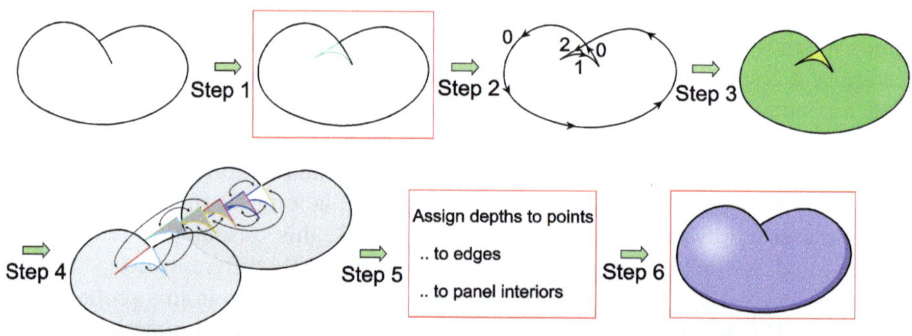

Fig. 12.4 Steps involved in creating a 3D shape from a contour drawing of a kidney bean. The roadmap is based on Williams' framework. Operations highlighted in red are novel contributions of SmoothSketch

of singularities that occur in an arbitrary generic contour of a smooth surface (see Fig. 12.3).

Williams' thesis [33] and subsequent work lay out a plan for finding a surface fitting a given collection of visible contours.[2]

The framework consists of three stages:

1. *Figural Completion*: Complete the drawing by inferring the hidden contours, and provide a Huffman labeling for it [9]. This corresponds to steps 1 and 2 in Fig. 12.4.
2. *Paneling Construction* [6]: Convert the completed drawing to an abstract topological surface, and map this surface to $\Re^2$ so that the "folds" of the mapping match the contours of the drawing (steps 3 and 4 in Fig. 12.4).
3. *Smooth Embedding*: Lift this mapping to a smooth embedding in $\Re^3$ whose projection is the mapping to $\Re^2$ (steps 5 and 6 in Fig. 12.4).

[2]The reader interested in implementing the ideas of this chapter will need first to become acquainted with Williams' work.

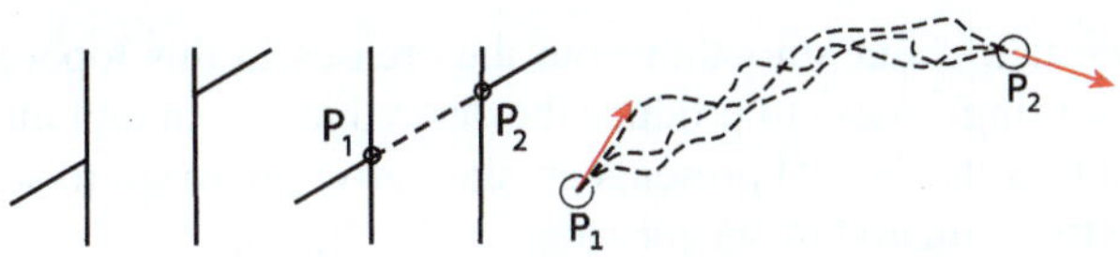

Fig. 12.5 How can we join the two tee points on the left? With an optimal completion, as shown in the middle. Optimality is determined by choosing, among all C^1 random walks from P_1 to P_2, the most likely one, under a simple probabilistic model. Mumford [21] shows such curves are elastica, which had been studied by Euler

Some steps of this framework were just theoretical for smooth closed surfaces without boundary. In SmoothSketch, we proposed solutions to the steps highlighted in red, turning this framework into a practical system. We now give an overview of each of these steps and explain how SmoothSketch is built on top of previous work.

The problem of figural completion was solved by several researchers for the case of "anterior surfaces"—roughly the front-facing parts of scenes, which generically have no cusps. In particular, Williams and Jacobs [35], and Mumford [21], describe an approach to completing the hidden contours, which generically join tee points in the drawing (see Fig. 12.5). To join a pair of tees, they consider all C^1 random walks (i.e., random walks in which the tangent direction θ changes by an amount X at each point, where X is a Gaussian random variable) starting at the first tee, headed in the right direction, and ending at the second, and assign to each a probability based on the product of the probabilities of each angle-change and $e^{-\lambda}$, where λ is the length of the curve. They posit that the maximum-likelihood random walk is a good candidate for the completion; when multiple pairs of tees might be joined, they choose pairings which have largest likelihoods.

We extend this approach, in Sect. 12.5, to the cases where a T-point must be joined to a cusp, or two cusps must be joined. To determine which visible endpoints (tees or cusps) should be joined to which, we use a greedy search similar to Nitzberg et al. [24].

In step 2 Huffman [9] labels are assigned to the contours. Labels indicate the number of surfaces in front of the contour (visible contours have label zero); the surface on which the contour lies is to the left when you traverse it in the direction shown by the arrow. After the figural completion stage is complete, the 2D drawing is cut into flat regions along the boundaries (for the kidney bean example, see green and yellow regions in Fig. 12.4) and Williams' algorithm is used to create multiple copies (panels) of these regions. Williams' algorithm also specifies which edges of these panels have to be glued to one another and the relative order of the panels (steps 3 and 4 in Fig. 12.4). This representation gives a topological reconstruction of the 3D shape.

To create smooth embedding, we take the results of the paneling construction—an abstract manifold and a continuous mapping f of it to $\Re^2$ and embed it one dimension at a time: first assigning depth to the vertices (that generally correspond to projections of T-s and cusps), then to the edges, and finally to the interiors of the panels (step 5). This algorithm is described in Sect. 12.7. The result is a topological embedding (i.e., a 1-1 continuous map from the surface into $\Re^3$). Finally, in Sect. 12.8 we talk about smoothing out the creases in this topological embedding by a mass–spring system to produce the desired fairly smooth mesh in 3-space (step 6). Karpenko's thesis [14] presents an alternative approach to step 6 based on minimizing the total squared mean curvature.

12.3 Related Work

Shape from Drawings. The problem of inferring 3D shape from 2D drawings has been studied in a great many forms; if one extends it to include determining drawings from images as a first step, it occupies much of the computer vision literature. We will only describe the work most closely related to SmoothSketch.

Much early shape-from-drawing work applied to blueprint-like drawings of machined surfaces. The important features of such shapes are sharp bends, like the edges of a cube—and their trihedral intersections. The techniques applicable in that area are therefore rather different from those used in this paper.

Pentland and Kuo [25] presented a system that infers simple 3D curves and surface patches from 2D strokes by minimizing the energy of the corresponding *snakes*.

A classic paper in this area is by Huffman [9], who developed two labeling schemes—one for objects made from planar surfaces, one for smooth objects—and proved that their complete contour drawings must have the corresponding sorts of labeling. Williams [33, 34] did the defining work in inverting the smooth-surface labeling scheme, as described in the previous section.

Bellettini et al. [2] proposed a variational model for reconstructing a smooth surface from its contour containing self-occlusions.

Another direction of research explored creating 3D effects on drawings without explicitly reconstructing a 3D shape. Williams [32] generates interesting 3D shading effects on 2D images without reconstructing a 3D geometry by applying a variety of complex shading techniques. Johnston [12] computes lighting on 2D drawings by estimating surface normals from the drawing.

Contour Completion. Huffman labelings are for complete contour projections—the projections of both the visible and invisible parts of an object's contours. Given a drawing of the visible parts of a contour, we must infer where the invisible parts lie. Kanizsa's work [13] on contour completion (and its relationship to the mechanisms of the human visual system) forms the basis for much of the later work in the area. A solution proposed first by Grenander [5] was to use a stochastic process to model the space of all possible edges. Mumford proves that elastica that arise in the completion problem described in Sect. 12.2 could be modeled by a white noise stochastic process. Williams [35] approximates the solution by considering a sampling of the space of all random walks (with varying $\Delta\theta$—the direction of the walk) starting from the first point with the first direction and coming to the second point with the second direction, and taking the random walk with the highest probability as the best path connecting two edges.

Although contour completion is a well-studied research topic, many problems are still open; in Sect. 12.5 we propose our solution, inspired by the work of Williams and Mumford, to the problem of finding a hidden cusp for a cusp-contour completion case.

Sketching Interfaces. Several gestural interfaces for sketching 3D shapes have been developed for different classes of models. For rectilinear objects, the Sketch system described by Zeleznik et al. [36] lets a user create and edit models through gestural interface, where geometric aspects of gestures determine numerical parameters of the objects. These ideas were extended by several research groups [26, 29].

For free-form objects, Igarashi's Teddy [10] was the first interface for free-form modeling via sketching. In it, a user inputs a simple closed curve and the system creates a shape matching this contour. Then the user can add details by editing the mesh with operations like extrusion, cutting and bending, all done gesturally. The Smooth Teddy [11] system allowed the user to organize shapes into a hierarchy and included algorithms for beautification and mesh refinement. Nealen et al. [23] recently extended Teddy into FiberMesh—a system for modeling surfaces with 3D curves.

Karpenko et al. [17] described a system for creating shapes from free-form sketches; the primitive objects were variational implicit surfaces, which facilitated operations like surface blending. ShapeShop [28] uses hierarchical implicit volume models to let a user interactively edit complex models via a sketching interface. Alexe et al. [1] extract the skeleton from the sketch and then construct a convolution surface. None of these systems handle complex strokes containing tees and cusps.

Nealen et al. [22] presented a sketch-based interface for Laplacian mesh editing where a user draws reference and target curves on the mesh to specify the mesh deformation.

Recently, Cordier and Seo [3] also explored the problem of inferring free-form shapes of drawings of occluding contours. They restricted themselves to contours containing only tee junctions, but allowed multiple objects. They first compute the 2D skeleton of the sketch, then solve the constrained optimization problem to find the corresponding 3D skeleton and create the 3D shape using the work of Alexe et al. [1]. Only objects with circular cross-sections can be reconstructed with their system.

12.4 Notation and Problem Formulation

Much of the material that follows relies on ideas from differential geometry and combinatorial and differential topology. We refer the reader to the books of Guillemin and Pollack [7] and Koenderink [19, 20] for clear expositions of the necessary background.

Suppose that S is a smooth, closed, compact, orientable surface-without-boundary (i.e., a *good* surface) embedded in the $z > 0$ halfspace of $\Re^3$. The orthogonal projection of S onto the $z = 0$ plane will have a compact image. We assume

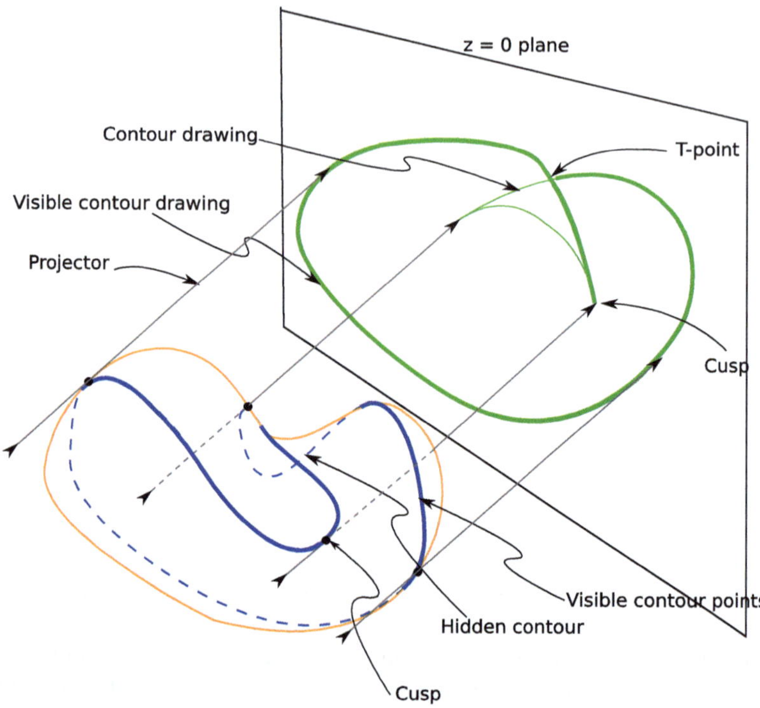

Fig. 12.6 (Adapted from Williams' [34].) The contour, in blue, of a good surface embedded generically in 3-space projects to a contour drawing, in *green*; the visible contour (drawn bold) projects to the visible-contour drawing. A point where the projector is tangent to the contour projects to a cusp in the contour drawing. The restriction of the projection to just the contour is 1-1 except at finitely many points, where two contours cross in the drawing; these are called T-points

that the embedding and this projection are *generic*. If the projector through the point $s \in S$ lies in the tangent plane at s, then s is called a *contour point*; if the projector first meets S at s, then s is a *visible*-contour point (see Fig. 12.6). The projection of C to the $z = 0$ plane is the *contour drawing* of S; the projection of V to the $z = 0$ plane is the *visible-contour drawing* of S.

The projection from the contour to the contour drawing is an embedding at most points; the exceptions are *crossings*, where two contours meet, and *cusps*. A cusp is a point $s \in S$ where the projector through s is tangent to C at s. The projection of a cusp appears as a point where the contour drawing "reverses direction" (see Fig. 12.7, left); we use the term "cusp" to refer both to the cusp and its projection. When an arc of the visible contour drawing reaches a crossing, it appears as a T*-point*: one part of the contour becomes invisible there.

For a generic smooth surface and viewpoint, tees and cusps of the contour will be isolated, as will curvature zeroes of the contour; this guarantees a unique osculating plane at a cusp, which means the projected contour must reverse direction rather than emanating from the cusp in any other direction (see Fig. 12.7, left).

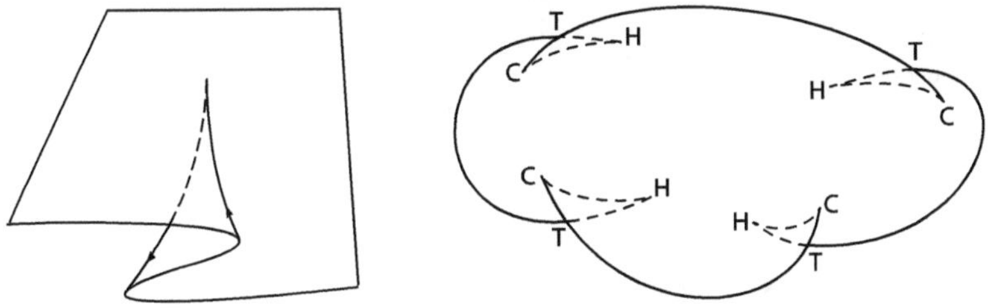

Fig. 12.7 (*Left*) The generic projection of a contour at a cusp reverses direction at the cusp. (*Right*) A drawing with the tee points and cusps marked; hidden contours and hidden cusps that must be inferred are shown in *dotted lines*

The "bean" example (Fig. 12.6) is something of an archetype for the method described in this chapter, in the sense that it is the simplest shape that has a cusp. The way that this single visible cusp is processed is the key to processing more general drawings, hence we use the bean as an example throughout.

In Fig. 12.7 (right) we show in solid lines a typical input drawing; in dotted lines are the projections of invisible contours. Certain hidden contour points are also cusp points; the visible cusps are marked with a "C" while the hidden cusps are marked with an "H".

Note that the user input is the part of the contour drawn in solid lines. Everything marked by a dashed line is a part of a *hidden* contour and needs to be inferred by our program.

With this terminology, our goal is to take a user-provided directed visible-contour drawing of a good surface as above and to determine a surface S whose visible contours match the given drawing.

12.5 Figural Completion for Smooth Surfaces

Given the visible-contour drawing, in the $z = 0$ plane, for a good surface in $\Re^3$, we describe an approach to completing the drawing, i.e., adding hidden contours so that the resulting drawing can be Huffman-labeled. The approach works in a large number of cases, although not all. The existence of this algorithm raises a question: what drawings are completable? In [14] we partially solve this problem by exhibiting a large class of drawings that admit such extensions; the general problem of characterizing extendable visible-contour drawings remains open, however.

We assume that visible contours are oriented, that is, a user always draws contours so that the surface is to the left of the contour. We also assume that the hidden contours do not intersect each other or visible contours except at junctions.

To complete hidden contours, we consider all visible-contour endpoints, and estimate the likelihood of a hidden contour joining each possible pair. Following Nitzberg et al. [24], we pair up points using their greedy algorithm, testing multiple configurations for (a) probability, and (b) consistency (i.e., can they be Huffman-

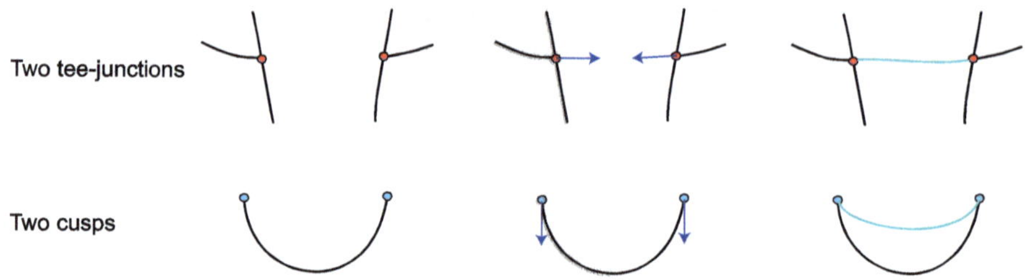

Fig. 12.8 The figure shows how tangent directions and Bézier completion curves are computed when two tee points or two cusps are paired up

labeled?). The probabilistic model presented here is only meant to be suggestive, and not a model of actual probabilities.

12.5.1 Preprocessing an Input Stroke and Guessing T-points and Cusps

User input is gathered from an input device (a mouse in our case). A user indicates when a stroke begins and ends by pressing or releasing a mouse button. Since during the input of each stroke, the 2D points arrive at an arbitrary rate, we re-sample these points so that they are not very close to each other.

We identify the visible cusps and tee points on a drawing using the following simple algorithm:

- We can determine T-points as stroke endpoints that "touch" some other segment ("touch" means "lie within 12 pixels").
- All other endpoints are initially classified as cusps. Some of them are "real" visible cusps and some of them are "regular" endpoints. "Regular endpoints" are points that are close to each other and belong to the same stroke; a user just happened to draw the stroke in several segments. We can classify endpoints as "regular" if the distance between them is small and the tangents are similar.

12.5.2 Pairwise Completion

First, for each pair of endpoints of the visible contour we compute an initial estimate of the probability that they are connected by a hidden contour. Each endpoint has a location and associated direction for the completion curve. For T-points or "regular" points, the direction is given by the tangent ray of the visible contour; for cusps it is the opposite (see Fig. 12.8).

To compute the likelihood of joining two tees or two cusps, we compute an energy function for the pairing, inversely proportional to the likelihood. The energy

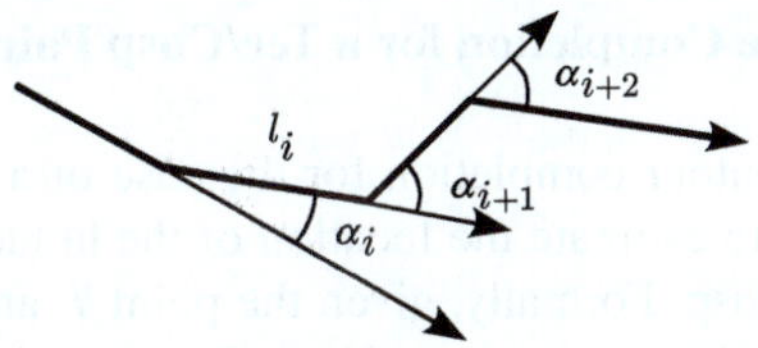

Fig. 12.9 The energy of the polyline approximating the Bézier spline is computed as a product of the sum of angle changes between the consecutive segments and the exponent of the sum of the segment lengths

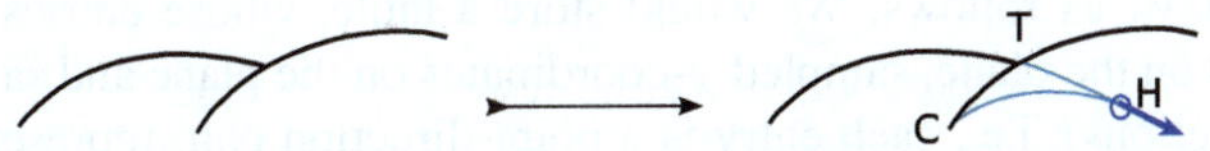

Fig. 12.10 When we have a T-point and a cusp to match it to, we seek the location of a hidden cusp such that the two hidden contour parts joining our points to the hidden cusp have the highest probability

function of the pairing is a sum of two energy functions $E = E_{\text{curve}} + E_{\text{end points}}$, where E_{curve} is the energy of the curve that would connect them were they to be matched and $E_{\text{end points}}$ is the energy corresponding to the heuristic defined by the endpoint tangent directions. We approximate the elastica curve with a Bézier spline connecting the endpoints given their tangent vectors (see Fig. 12.8). The Bézier curve is defined by the two endpoints and the points displaced from the endpoints along the tangent vectors. The distance by which the endpoints are displaced along the tangents is $\frac{1}{3}$ of the distance between the endpoints. The Bézier curve is then uniformly sampled and the energy function of the resulting polyline is computed as follows (see Fig. 12.9):

$$E_{\text{curve}} = e^{\sum_i l_i} \cdot \sum_i \Delta\theta_i$$

where l_i is the length of the ith segment of the polyline, and $\Delta\theta_i$ is the absolute value of the angle change between two consecutive segments of the polyline. $E_{\text{end points}}$ corresponds to another heuristic similar to [24], where we use the tangents at the endpoints to estimate the likelihood of the matches. Intuitively, if the tangent directions at the two endpoints are very similar, it is likely for them to be paired even if the length of the curve connecting them would be long (think of a fat snake whose tail passes behind its body). Similarly, if the tangents at the endpoints are very different, it should be pretty unlikely for them to be paired up. Let ϕ be the angle between the tangents at the endpoints. Then,

$$E_{\text{end points}} = \begin{cases} 0 & \phi \leq 0.3, \\ 1.0 & 0.3 < \phi < 2.5, \\ Ce^{\phi} & \phi \geq 2.5. \end{cases}$$

12.5.2.1 Computing the Completion for a Tee/Cusp Pairing

To compute a hidden contour completion for the case of a tee/cusp match (shown in Fig. 12.10), we need to estimate the location of the hidden cusp and the tangent direction at the hidden cusp. Formally, given the point T and the tangent vector V_t at T, the cusp point C and tangent vector V_c at C, we need to compute the position H and the tangent vector V_h of the hidden cusp (see Fig. 12.11). Following the work of Williams [35] (done for the case of hidden contours connecting tee junctions), we use the probabilities of directional random walks to estimate H and V_h.

Ideally, we would like to simulate two sets of directional random walks to estimate H and V_h as follows. We would store a table, whose entries are sampled x-coordinates on the plane, sampled y-coordinates on the plane and sampled angles (defining directions); i.e., each entry is a point-direction pair, representing a small box of points and a small range of angles.

To fill in the table, we would start a directional random walk from the point T with the direction V_t. At each step we would vary the angle by $\Delta\theta$ chosen from a $(0, 1)$ Gaussian distribution. After a fixed number of steps (chosen for each random walk from an exponential distribution with mean 60), a walk would end up at a point on the plane with some direction. Then we would increment the table cell corresponding to this point and direction by one. After simulating many random walks, we would divide every value in the table by the total number of random walks. So, each cell of the table would contain an estimate of the probability that a directional random walk starting from T with V_t ends at the point and with the direction defined by this cell.

The same process would be repeated for C and V_c with a new table of probabilities. In the end, we would have two tables: one for T and V_t, and the other for C and V_c. For each point and direction on the plane these tables would contain probabilities that the corresponding random walk will end up there. To guess a location of a hidden cusp, we could multiply the probabilities in the corresponding cells in two tables and take the point and direction with the highest product probability. This point/direction pair would be the estimate of the location and the direction of a hidden cusp.

To get a reasonable estimate of the hidden-cusp location, we would need to run each of two random walks about 10^6 times, which means that our system would not be interactive. To overcome this problem, we precompute a table of probabilities as follows (see Fig. 12.11, right):

- Fix the first point at $(0, 0)$ and the direction at angle 0.
- For (α, ϕ) defining the second point (on a unit circle) and its direction, store the resulting point (which is a hidden cusp and calculated as the point where two random walks meet with the highest probability) and the direction at this point (x, y, θ).

Now we can rotate and translate the coordinate system formed by an arbitrary tee/cusp pair so that the tangent vector at the point T lies at the origin and is aligned with an x-axis. Then we scale so that the cusp C lies on a unit circle in the new

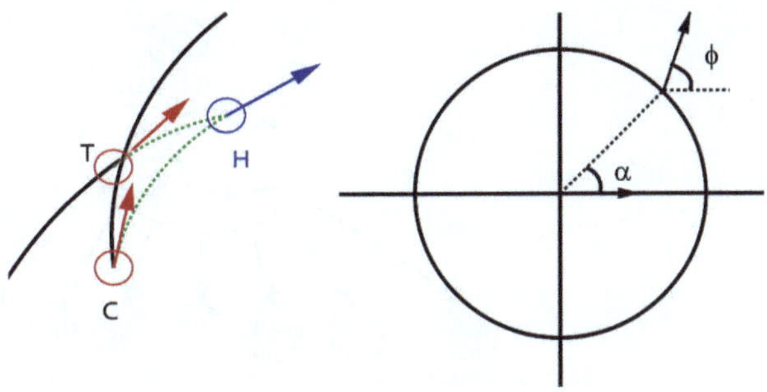

Fig. 12.11 (*Left*) Given a tee point T, a cusp C and tangent vectors at these points, we need to estimate the hidden cusp H and the tangent vector at H. (*Right*) Precomputing the table of hidden-cusp locations for a number of sampled locations and directions

coordinate system. We can then use the coordinates of these two points and two corresponding directions as an input to our table. After we get the resulting location and direction of "the best" hidden cusp for these two vectors, we rotate, translate and scale it back to the original coordinate system. This simple pre-calculation technique allows us to guess the locations of the hidden cusps interactively.

We connect the hidden cusp to the tee point and the visible cusp with Bézier curves, and compute E_{curve} for their union as described above.

12.5.2.2 Greedy Search for the Best Configuration

After a likelihood for each pair of endpoints is computed, we need to match up pairs to find the best total *configuration* (a configuration consists of endpoint pairs, where each endpoint appears in only one pair). For instance, if we have four endpoints numbered 1 to 4, the possible configurations are: $\{(1,2),(3,4)\}$, $\{(1,3),(2,4)\}$ and $\{(1,4),(2,3)\}$. The likelihood of a configuration is defined as the product of likelihoods of its pairs. It is not practical to compute the likelihoods of all possible configurations as the number of them grows exponentially in the number of tees and cusps. Instead, we do a greedy search similar to [24].

In particular, we perform a standard 'beam'-search technique [27] to reach an approximate solution. The procedure is not guaranteed to reach the globally optimal solution; in practice we find that it works well for a reasonable number (10–15) of nodes.

Consider the search procedure as being analogous to searching a tree. Each node of the tree contains a particular pair of endpoints and a set of all valid pairs available to the children of this node. Each pair has an associated energy (of the Bézier completion curve) computed as described above. We can choose the single pair that has the optimal energy at this point; note that the minimum energy is determined by taking a product of the energy of that pair with the energy of the path leading from the root of the tree to the node under consideration. If we choose to only explore the subtree corresponding to that pair we cannot know if the globally optimal value is indeed present in that subtree. Considering all possible pairs and exploring all possible subtrees at the node will result in exponentially many subtrees; making the procedure computationally intractable. 'Beam' search presents a compromise between the two extreme choices. At each level of the tree, there is finite budget of

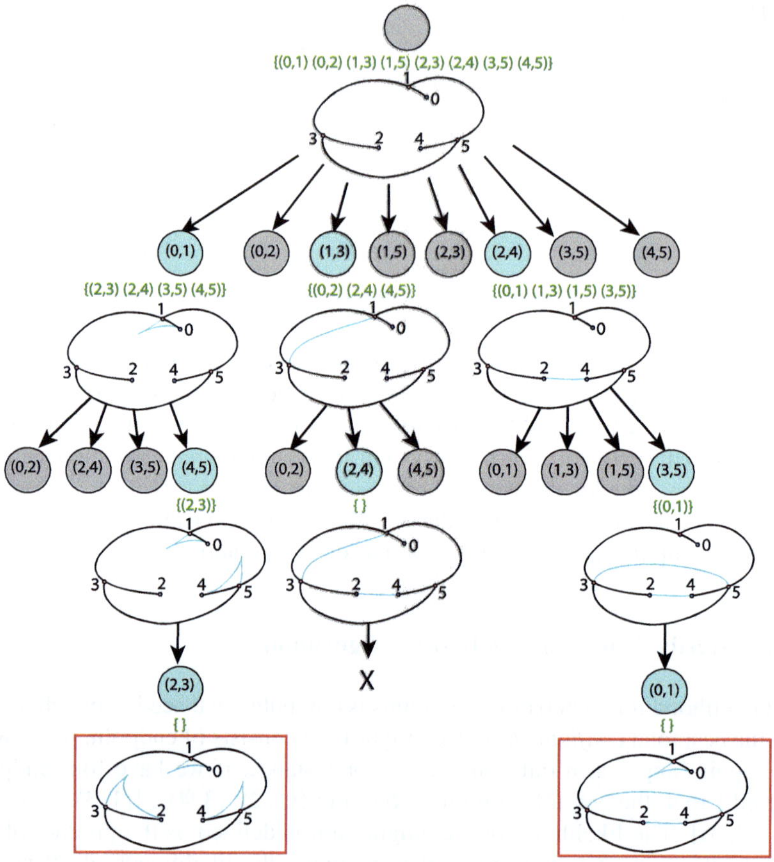

Fig. 12.12 The figure demonstrates the 'beam'-search procedure for choosing the best valid configuration on an example sketch that has six junctions. Two best configurations are shown in the *red rectangles*

m children (or possible pairs) that we can explore. m is called the *beam width* for the search procedure. We consider the set of all possible options at a certain level and choose m children with the least energy. Subsequently, only subtrees rooted at the m children will be searched for the optimal value.

Figure 12.12 demonstrates the 'beam'-search procedure for an example sketch that has six junctions numbered 0 to 5. First, we compute the list of all possible *available valid pairs* I_0. For each pair from the list, we check whether the pairing is valid and remove invalid pairs from the set I_0 (we explain validity checks in the next section). Each node in the tree has a list of *available valid pairs* I_k—pairs available to its children (shown in Fig. 12.12 in green font) and also every node except the root stores a pair chosen at the node (shown circled). In Fig. 12.12, $m = 3$ children are searched and expanded at every level (shown in blue circles). Once a particular optimal pair, say $(1, 3)$ is chosen, its node copies an array of available valid pairs from its parent and updates it to remove pairs that contain one of the indices of the pair. For example, for pair $(1, 3)$ we would remove all pairs from the array that contain indices 1 or 3. In the end, the algorithm finds two valid configurations outlined in red. The second configuration corresponds to two objects—a bean in front of an oval-like blob.

12.5.2.3 Checking the Consistency of the Pairing

We perform several consistency checks for a pair of endpoints before adding it to the configuration. The first three rules we describe come from Huffman's labeling scheme for contours of smooth objects in generic projections [9] (see Fig. 12.13, top row) and should hold true for both endpoints in the pairing.

Since we assumed that we only deal with configurations in which hidden contours do not intersect other visible or hidden contours except at the endpoints, we add two other Rules (4 and 5) to eliminate configurations for which it is not true. Please note that rules 4 and 5 will be substituted with different rules (checking the consistency of Huffman's depth labels) if the assumption is removed in the future work.

1. **Rule 1:** Let T be the T-junction location, $\overrightarrow{V_T}$ the tangent direction at the T, pointing away from the visible stroke, B the Bézier point lying on the hidden contour closest to T, and $\overrightarrow{V_B} = \overrightarrow{(T, B)}$. Then, Rule 1 says that $\text{dot}(\overrightarrow{V_T}, \overrightarrow{V_B}) \geq 0$ (see Fig. 12.13a, b).
2. **Rules 2 and 3:** Let C be the visible cusp, B the point on the hidden contour closest to C, $\overrightarrow{V_C}$ the tangent direction at the cusp, and $\overrightarrow{V_B} = \overrightarrow{(C, B)}$. Then, Rule 2 says that the cross-product of $\overrightarrow{V_C}$ and $\overrightarrow{V_B}$ should be equal to $(0, 0, -1)$ (assuming the z-axis is perpendicular to the screen pointing out of the screen). Rule 3 says that $\text{dot}(\overrightarrow{V_C}, \overrightarrow{V_B}) \leq 0$. (see Fig. 12.13c, d).
3. **Rule 4:** A pairing is invalid if the corresponding hidden contour intersects any visible stroke anywhere except at tee points or cusps it shares with this stroke.
4. **Rule 5:** Before adding any pairing to the beam search tree, check that the corresponding hidden contour does not intersect any hidden strokes of the nodes on the path to this one (except at tee points and cusps that the strokes share).

12.5.3 Gluing Segments and Assigning Huffman's Labels

After the optimal valid configuration is computed, we glue together regular points by filling in the Bézier curve between them. Now, these points belong to the same stroke and are removed from the list of endpoints. Then, we split visible strokes at tee junctions and assign orientations and Huffman's depth labels to all strokes. Since the optimal configuration does not have hidden contours that intersect each other or visible strokes, assigning depth labels is straightforward. We set the labels of all visible strokes to be 0, labels of hidden strokes connecting two tee points or a tee point and a hidden cusp to be 2, connecting cusps (visible or hidden) to be 1.

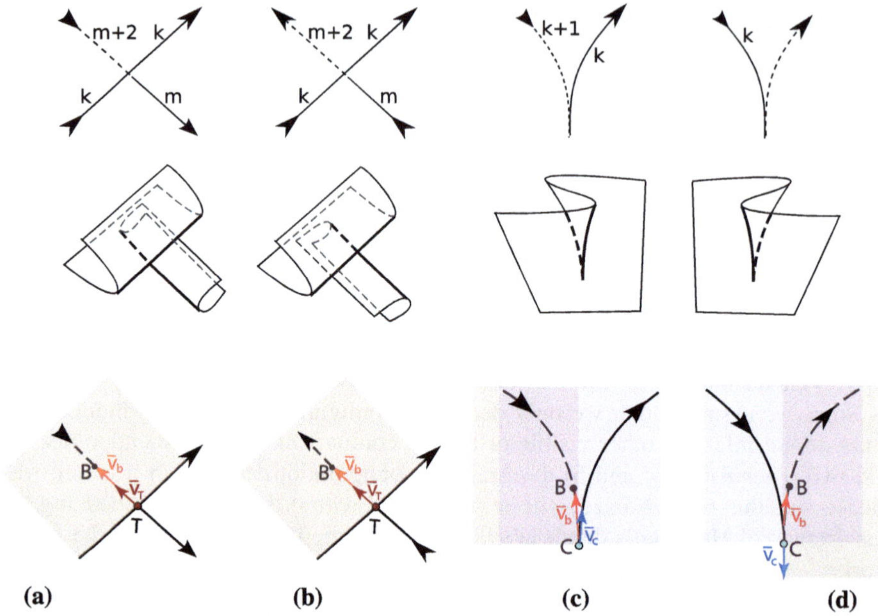

Fig. 12.13 Topological consistency checks near the endpoints. *Top row* shows four Huffman's labeling cases, middle row shows the surfaces corresponding to different cases of Huffman's labeling, bottom row—the corresponding validity checks. **a–b** Consistency check at the T-point. Let T be the T-junction location, V_T the tangent direction at the T, pointing away from the visible stroke, B the Bézier point lying on the hidden contour closest to T, and $V_B = (T, B)$. Then, Rule 1 says that $\text{dot}(V_T, V_B) \geq 0$. **c–d** Let C be the visible cusp, B the point on the hidden contour closest to C, V_C the tangent direction at the cusp, and $V_B = (C, B)$. Then, Rule 2 says that the cross-product of V_C and V_B should be equal to $(0, 0, -1)$ (assuming the z-axis is perpendicular to the screen pointing away from the screen). Rule 3 says that $\text{dot}(V_B, V_B) \leq 0$

12.5.4 Results and Limitations of the Figural Completion Algorithm

Some results of the hidden contour completion performed by SmoothSketch are shown in Fig. 12.14. Simple drawings took less than a second to complete, while the more complex one took about 5 seconds.

The figural completion approach that we presented has a number of limitations.

The location of a hidden cusp provided by the above method may be unsatisfactory. Indeed, in the bean-like case shown in Fig. 12.15, the hidden cusp is estimated to lie at a point that is not, in fact, hidden. Figure 12.15 (right) shows another example where the locations of hidden cusps are estimated incorrectly because of the simplifying assumption that the precomputed positions of hidden cusps are scale-invariant.

We assumed that hidden contours do not intersect visible and/or hidden contours which is a big simplification. In [14] we discuss how we might change the algorithm to eliminate this assumption.

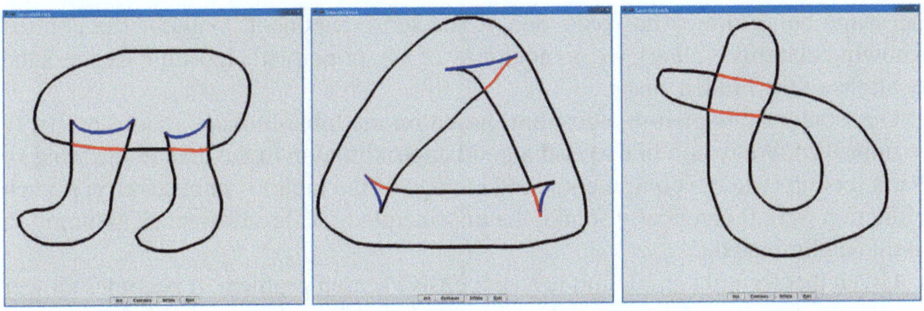

Fig. 12.14 Some of the results of the figural completion algorithm. Visible contours are shown in *black*, hidden contours with Huffman's depth 1 are shown in *blue* and with depth 2 in *red*

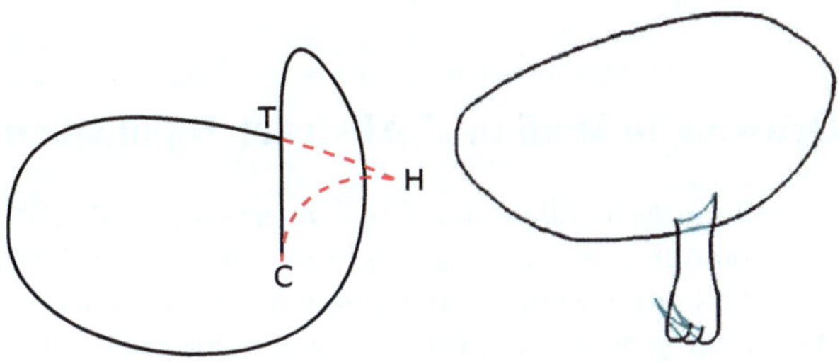

Fig. 12.15 Problem cases: our method can produce a contour completion which places the hidden cusps at impossible locations. This happens because our method only considers local probabilities, and not the shape of the remainder of the visible contour

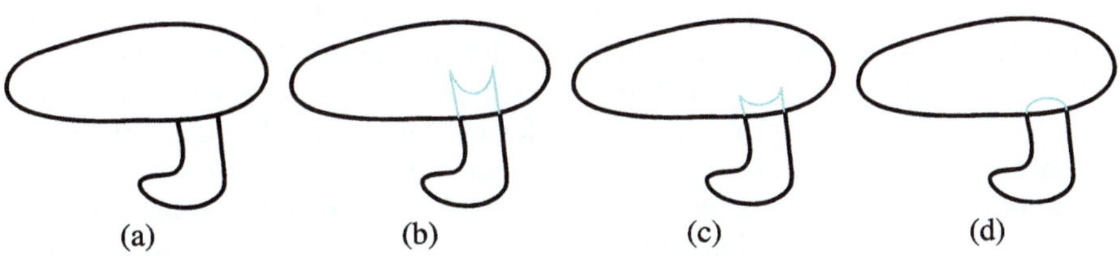

Fig. 12.16 **a** The back-leg drawing case; **b**, **c**, and **d** show possible completions; our system produces completion **d**

Consider a dog's body with one leg on the left hand side, seen from the right hand side (see Fig. 12.16). This is a case that our contour-completion algorithm cannot handle. The "completion" of the obscured contours consists of two hidden cusps connected by a U-shaped hidden contour, and two "straight" segments connecting the hidden cusps to two T-points. In the two-hidden-cusp completion, the location of the two cusps is ambiguous. The algorithm for finding a hidden cusp for a T-point/visible-cusp pair will not work for this case, because there are no visible cusps.

The figural completion for this case could equally well consist of just an arc joining the two T-points—there's no a priori reason for the system to assume that the shape being drawn has only one connected component. Without the context (knowing that this is a leg), we do not know of any principled algorithm to guess the locations of the hidden cusps.

Our contour-completion algorithm, based on the table-lookup, should probably be improved. We would like to find a good approximation to the data in the table so that a lookup (and the computation and storage of the table) is unnecessary; if such a function were theoretically sound, the unprincipled "scale-invariance" assumption could be eliminated.

Given that figural completion is an expensive search problem, it becomes slower for a large number of tee/cusps (say, more than 15) and is more likely to make incorrect inferences as the drawing gets more and more complicated (we only find an approximate solution to the optimization problem to make it tractable; as a result, the approximate minimum is not always the global minimum).

12.6 From Drawing to Williams' Abstract Topological Manifold

Figure 12.17 shows the steps involved in going from a completed contour drawing to Williams' abstract topological manifold that is homeomorphic to the surface we will eventually build. At this point we have a completed contour drawing, with a Huffman labeling. This drawing consists of directed arcs (which we call *edges*) between *vertices* corresponding to T-points and cusps. A set of strokes with orientations assigned to them together partition the plane into planar regions (for the kidney bean example, the inner regions are shown in green and yellow in Fig. 12.17). The outermost region is ignored; each of the inner ones (we call them "2D panels") needs to be computed from the input as a closed loop of consecutive strokes that form a boundary of the panel. We describe the solution to this graph problem in [15].

Each of these 2D panels is now triangulated to form a "3D panel" [30]. From now on, we will use the term "panel" to refer to a 3D panel. Williams' algorithm is then used to create multiple copies of each panel. Figure 12.17 shows 3D panels for the bean stacked up in random order along the projection direction. There are four copies of the small region and two copies of the big region in this example; intuitively, this has to do with how many times the view ray intersects the surface of the kidney bean for each region. Williams' algorithm also specifies which edges of these panels have to be glued to one another to form a topological manifold. In Fig. 12.17, the edges of each panel are colored; edges with identical colors will be identified to form the topological manifold. The paneling construction algorithm is formally described in Sect. 12.6.2.

12.6.1 Triangulating the Panels; The Issue of Two Distinct Points Having the Same 2D Location

Consider the stroke of the big panel for the kidney bean drawing—see Fig. 12.18. There are two distinct points at the bottom of the drawing and they should remain

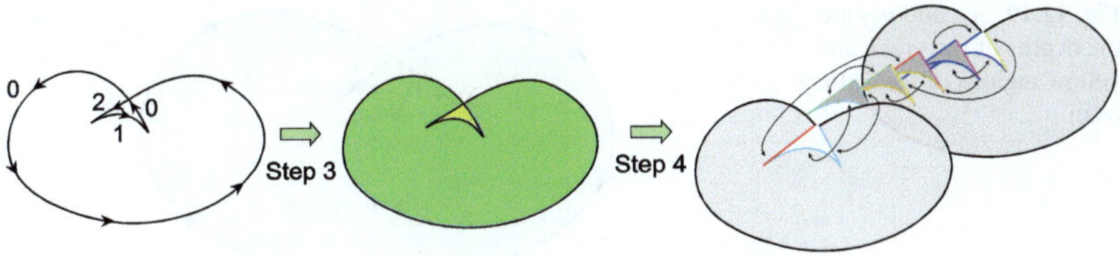

Fig. 12.17 Steps involved in creating a paneling construction from a completed and labeled contour drawing of a kidney bean

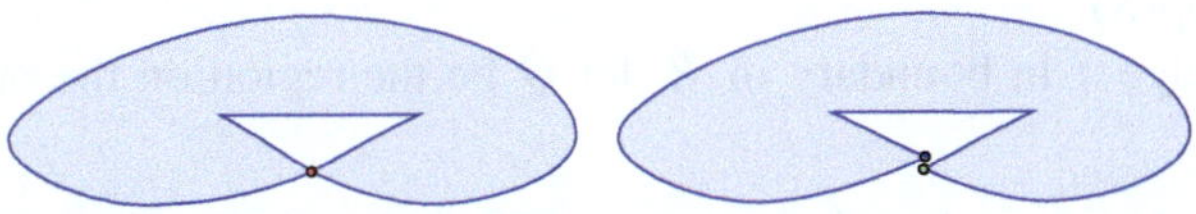

Fig. 12.18 (*Left*) A panel for a bean shape. (*Right*) There are actually two distinct points corresponding to the original red 2D vertex

distinct points in the mesh after the triangulation. We identify such cases at the figural completion stage and add extra information to the panel to be able to keep track of such points on the stroke. Then, before triangulating the panel, we move one of the points slightly toward the average of its neighbors (at this stage all points in the stroke are distinct), triangulate the panel, and then move the corresponding vertex back into its original position.

12.6.2 Paneling Construction

During Williams' paneling construction, multiple copies of each panel are created and correspondence is established between the edges of the panels.

12.6.2.1 Creating Multiple Copies of Each Panel

As mentioned above, panels correspond to the regions that the strokes partition the plane into (green and yellow regions in Fig. 12.19 for the kidney bean). The number of copies of each panel (region) depends on how many times the view ray intersects the surface of the object for each region. Thus this number is just the *depth complexity of each region*. Let n_R be the depth complexity of region R. We use the following algorithm to compute these depths (see Fig. 12.19):

1. Assign the exterior region depth 0 (i.e., a ray hitting this region passes through 0 panels). All other regions have unassigned depths.
2. Push the exterior region on a stack, S.

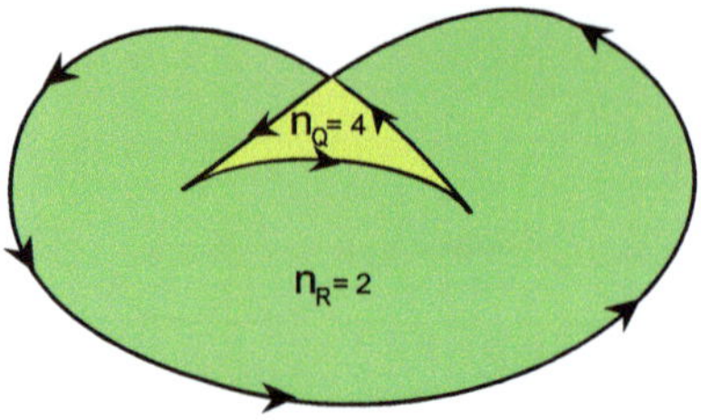

Fig. 12.19 n_R and n_Q are the depths of the green and yellow regions of the kidney bean

3. While S is not empty:
   Let $R = \text{pop}(S)$.
   For each edge q in boundary of R, let Q be the region on the other side of q from R.

- If n_Q is already assigned, then check if it differs from n_R by ± 2. If yes, just move on, otherwise return ERROR.
- If n_Q has not been assigned
  - if Q is to the left of the oriented edge, then $n_Q = n_R + 2$
  - if Q is to the right of the oriented edge, then $n_Q = n_R - 2$
  - push Q onto the stack.

The algorithm has complexity $O(E)$, where E is the number of edges of regions. Williams' algorithm [34] is very similar except he solves the $R \times R$ linear system of equations (where R is the number of regions).

Note that Huffman labels (*edge* labels) that were computed during the figural completion are not used for computing the depths above. They are needed in the next step, to establish correspondences between the edges of the panels.

12.6.2.2 Establishing Correspondences Between Edges of the Panels

We consider (see Figs. 12.20, 12.21) the disjoint copies of a region R as being of the form $R_i = R \times \{i\}$, where the index i never appears more than once in all copies of all regions. A typical identification in Williams' scheme is then that the point (r, i) is identified with (r, j), where r is a point on the boundary of region R, and (r, i) and (r, j) lie in R_i and R_j respectively; another might be that (r, i) is identified with (s, j), where R and S are adjacent regions in the plane both containing the point $r = s$ on their boundaries, $(r, i) \in R_i$ and $(s, j) \in S_j$. The disjoint union of all the copies of all the regions will be called U; there's a natural map $\pi : U \to \Re^2 : (r, i) \mapsto r$ in which the multiple copies of any point r are all mapped to r.

For a point P in the plane, the set $\pi^{-1}(P)$ is a set of points of the form (P, i); we call this the "stack over P." Similarly, we can consider the stack of edges over an edge in the plane, or the stack of panels over a panel in the plane. If an edge e in the plane goes from P to Q, we write $\partial e = (P, Q)$ to denote that the boundary of edge e consists of the points P and Q, in that order. If e_i is an edge in the stack over e, then $\partial e_i = (P_i, Q_i)$ as well.

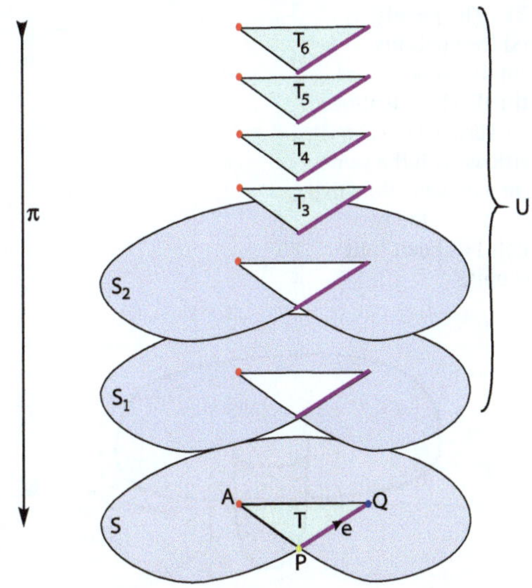

Fig. 12.20 Schematic view of the disjoint union of panels that are glued to form the topological manifold homeomorphic to the bean. Each copy of each panel lies in a different layer; the union of all these copies is called U. The map π is "projection back to $\Re^2$ along z." The collection of all points that project to A (the *red dots*) is called the "stack above A". The *magenta* edges are the stack above the edge e. Each panel is indexed by its height in z, so all panels have different indices

Williams identifies certain panel edges in pairs (see Fig. 12.21), that is, for certain i and j, he declares that e_i is to be identified with e_j, which means that the point $(x, i) \in e_i$, is identified with the point $(x, j) \in e_j$. This identification induces an identification on the stacks above vertices: if e_i is identified with e_j, and $\partial e = (P, Q)$, we declare $P_i \sim P_j$, and $Q_i \sim Q_j$. The transitive closure of the relation $\sim$ partitions stacks into equivalence classes that we call *clusters*; each cluster in each stack corresponds to a vertex in Williams' surface, which we will eventually embed.

Ordering the Clusters. Williams' construction gives a depth order to the panels in each panel-stack; this order is generally unrelated to the indices above. This order induces an order on the clusters as follows: if P_i and P_j are in two clusters, and R is a region containing $P = \pi(P_i) = \pi(P_j)$ consider all the faces in the stack over R that are adjacent to vertices in the first cluster, and all those adjacent to vertices in the second cluster. By Williams' construction, faces in the first group will either be all in front of or all behind the faces in the second group; we say that the first cluster is in front of or behind the second group accordingly. Again by construction, this order is independent of the adjacent region R that we choose.

Extra Vertices. One important issue remains: if two edges e and e' in the same edge-stack have the same clusters as their endpoints but are *not* identified in the topological manifold, these distinct edges would be assigned the same depth in the constructed surface, which would result in a non-embedding. Figure 12.22 shows two such edges in the lower portion of the leg case. In such cases, we add a new vertex at the midpoint of each of the edges e and e' of the contour (and to any other edges that are identified with these). The stacks and the clusters within these stacks are then created for these newly-inserted points in the same way we described above.

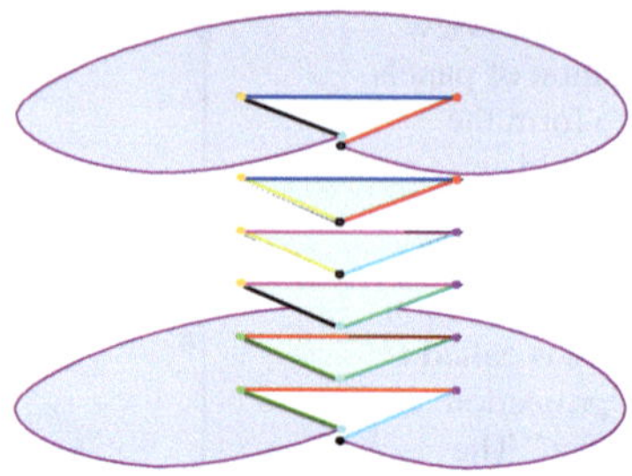

Fig. 12.21 The panels, re-ordered for visibility; edges with the same colors are identified. This identifies *clusters* of vertices in each stack; vertices with the same color form a cluster. Note that the near vertex in the two large panels has been split into two copies

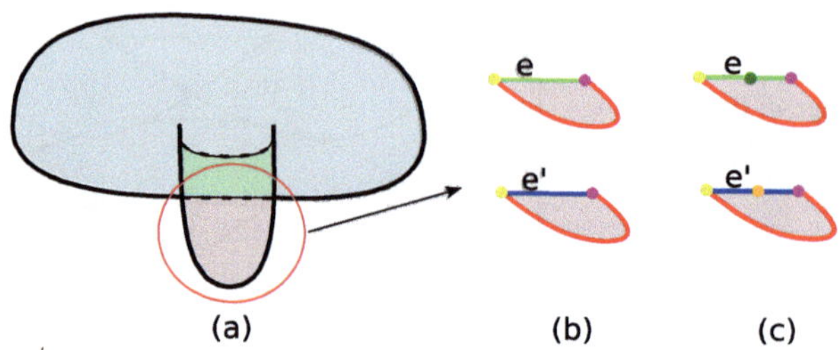

Fig. 12.22 **a** A contour-completed drawing of a leg attached to a body, with panels colored. **b** The two panels for the bottom of the leg, colored to show edge identifications and vertex clusters. Note that the top edges e and e' share endpoints but are not identified. **c** We add mid-edge vertices, sort, and cluster them as before

12.7 Constructing a Topological Embedding

We now present a novel algorithm that constructs a topological embedding from Williams' abstract manifold.

Embedding Vertices. To each cluster of the vertex stack over a vertex P, we associate a vertex whose xy-coordinates are those of P, and whose z coordinate is yet to be determined (we call these *cluster vertices*). We determine the z-placements using a mass–spring system. Suppose that the vertices corresponding to the clusters of one stack are X_α, where α ranges over the clusters. If cluster α is behind cluster β, we want the z-coordinate, z_α of X_α to be less than that of X_β. For each such order-relation between two of the Xs, we attach a spring whose rest-length z_0 is one, and for which the spring force follows the rule

$$F(d) = \begin{cases} 0 & d \geq 1, \\ Ce^{1-d} & d < 1 \end{cases}$$

which ensures that if the z-order is inverted, there is a substantial force pushing back toward the proper ordering.

This ordering and set of z-values could also be found by simply sorting the vertices; we use the mass–spring system as a way to relate the z-depths for vertices in separate stacks. In particular, if P and Q are distinct vertices joined by an edge e, then each cluster over P is joined to one or more clusters over Q by edges in the stack over e. For each such connection, we add a spring with rest-length zero between the corresponding cluster vertices; we use a sufficiently small spring constant that the intra-stack ordering is not disturbed. Our goal is to make each edge want to be somewhat parallel to the $z = 0$ plane, rather than having vertices associated with one stack be far in front of all others, for instance.

The mass–spring system acts on the points, which are constrained to move only in z. Clearly if the spring constant for the inter-stack springs is small enough, each stack will be ordered correctly. In our implementation, we use the constant 1.3, which seems to perform well on examples like the ones shown in this chapter and the associated video. The points of the drawings in our system lie in the bounding box of -1.0 to 1.0 in each direction.

Embedding edges. Having embedded the cluster vertices (i.e., the vertices of the manifold that Williams constructs), we can extend the embedding to edges by linearly interpolating depth along each edge. The ordering of edges in Williams' construction is generally sufficient to show that if e_i and e_j are distinct edges of the manifold corresponding to contour edge e, then they do not intersect except, perhaps, at endpoints which they share. In the event that e_i and e_j share *both* their endpoints, linear interpolation would assign them the same depths at all points, and our mapping would not be an embedding. Fortunately, the "extra vertices" step above inserts points exactly when necessary to prevent this; thus we have an embedding of both the vertices and the edges of Williams' manifold.

Embedding faces. We extend the embedding over the panel interiors using Poisson's formula to find a harmonic function on the panel whose values on the boundary are the given depth values that we've already assigned to the edges of the panel. Each interior point is assigned a depth that is a weighted average of the depths of points on the boundary edges. To prove that two panel interiors in the same stack never intersect, suppose that P is a point of some panel R, and that X and Y are points in the panel-stack over R, and that $\pi(X) = \pi(Y) = P$. Suppose that the panel to which X belongs, R_i, is in front of the panel to which Y belongs, R_j, so that the z-value for X should be larger than the z-value for Y. Then points on the edges of R_i are in front of (or equal to) the corresponding points on the edges of R_j. The z-coordinates of corresponding points cannot all be equal unless the boundaries of R_i and R_j are identical, in which case the union of R_i and R_j is a spherical connected component of the manifold, and is handled as a special case. In the remaining cases, since the z-values for R_i are greater than or equal to the corresponding values for R_j, and the z value for X is a weighted sum of these values *with all non-zero weights*, and the z-values for Y is the corresponding weighted sum of the other z-values, with the same weights, we find that the z value for X is strictly greater than that for Y. Thus the interiors of faces do not intersect. We have thus constructed a continuous 1-1 map from Williams' abstract manifold into $\mathfrak{R}^3$, i.e., a topological embedding.

12.8 Smoothing the Embedding Using the Mass–Spring System

Now that mesh vertices corresponding to each panel have been assigned depths, we "stitch" the meshes of individual panels into a single mesh. We start with the first panel, and stitch panels to it one at a time. If two panels are identified along an edge e, we alter the vertex indices on second to match those of the first. The edge correspondences for the stitched panel (excluding the edge we stitched along) come from the correspondence information of the two component panels. Although the resulting stitched mesh has the proper "contour projection" (for an appropriately modified definition of "contour"), its shape is generally unsatisfactory, as can be seen in the accompanying video. We therefore perform several optimization steps. During these steps, we constrain the vertices lying on the visible silhouette to remain on the silhouette so that the contours will match the drawing. That is, these vertices can only move in z, while others may move in x, y, and z.

First, we remesh the model using the algorithm proposed in [18] and apply ten iterations of Taubin's λ/μ smoothing [31] in order to create more regular triangles, as the behavior of the mass–spring system is sensitive to the quality of the triangulation. These operations are applied only to non-silhouette vertices and edges.

At this point, the mesh is smoother, but rather flat and sharp along the edges (because the silhouette constraints have not been incorporated smoothly). The next goal is to "inflate" the model, making it more rounded. To achieve this, we construct a mass–spring system on the initial mesh, with masses at the vertices and with two types of springs: length springs and what we call "pressure force" springs. The length springs try to keep the length of each edge as close to zero as possible, while the "pressure springs" simply push each triangle outward along its normal with a force proportional to the area of the triangle. We relax this mass–spring system and although the convergence in general is not guaranteed, in practice it converges quite fast. A model like the ones shown in the chapter inflates in several seconds on an AMD Athlon 64 3000+ processor.

Our mass–spring approach has several drawbacks; some of them are common to all mass–spring systems [4], others are particular to our choice of springs. First, most mass–spring systems approximate the physics of deformable models very crudely. Further, in our case, even the underlying "physical" model is quite *ad hoc*. We intuitively think of the current model as inflating the initial flat shape as a balloon, but with the restriction on the movement of silhouette points and disregard for surface curvature, it is a very weak analogy.

Secondly, our mass–spring system has several tuning constants that have to be chosen so that they work for most of the examples user draws.

Thirdly, there is currently no mechanism in the system to prevent self-penetrations of the surfaces. In fact, although different parts of the initial mesh are in the correct relative order, the mass–spring system could relax it into the configuration that is more or less planar (think of a worm example). We have not observed it in practice, but theoretically, the inflation algorithm does not prevent it from happening. Silhouette constraints prevent this issue to some degree: when we say that something is a cusp, the silhouette has to travel straight into the Z-direction at that

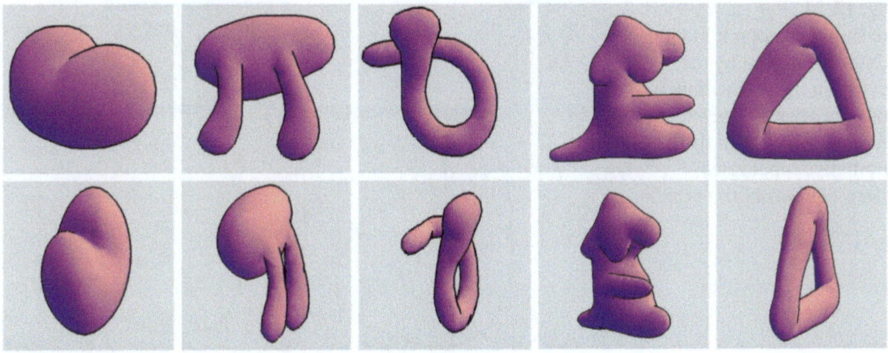

Fig. 12.23 The examples of the shapes created with our system from user drawings. The *top row* shows the shapes from the sketching viewpoint, and the *bottom row* shows them from a different view

point, which tends to mean that "bending back again to touch" is unlikely. This issue can be addressed by doing the relaxation in a way that does not allow silhouette vertices to move, or by inserting springs that preserve the relative order in the inflated mesh. Sometimes, though, we would like to allow self-penetrations: think of a body-with-two-legs example; there, the legs being slightly pushed inside the body is often more desirable than having them stick out far away from the body.

Having said all this, the mass–spring system we created seems to work reasonably well on most examples. The final results are shown in Fig. 12.23.

The smoothing process can be regarded as a kind of local search in probability space: if we assume that surfaces with sharp corners and high curvature are unlikely, and those that are smooth are more likely, then (returning to the probabilistic view of the problem mentioned in the introduction) our smoothing approach can be regarded as a local search for a more probable shape that matches the topological constraints that we have already established.

12.9 Editing Gestures

The system may return a different shape from the one that the user had in mind while drawing the sketch. We therefore let the user edit hidden contours or choose a better completion from the list of suggestions offered by the system. The user draws strokes by dragging the right mouse button; when he is finished drawing, he presses the middle mouse button and the sketch is inflated into a 3D model. The user can change the shape by pressing the "Contours" button at the bottom of SmoothSketch window. Then, in the main window, the system displays both visible and hidden contours inferred by the system. The hidden contours are shown in light blue and can be manipulated by dragging default Bézier control points for each hidden curve. In the second, smaller, window that shows up on top of the main one, the system shows up to three alternative hidden contour completions (see Fig. 12.24). If the

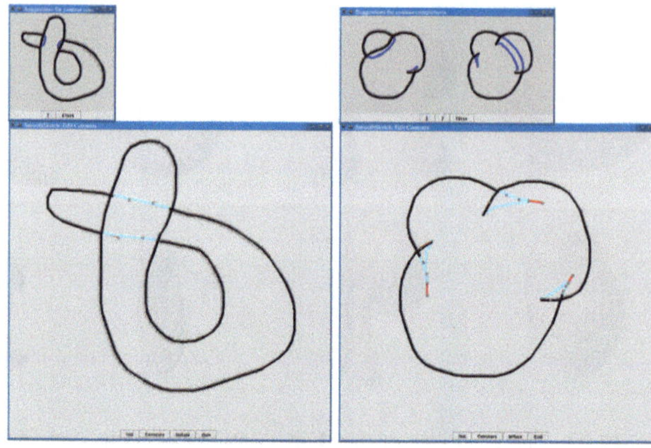

Fig. 12.24 For each sketch we show the default hidden contours inferred by the system in the main window and a smaller "suggestions window" with up to three alternative topological interpretations of the sketch

user selects one of the suggestions, the second window closes and the selection is shown in the main window where the user can edit it.

The list of suggestions lets the user change the topology of the model, while contour editing tool lets him change the shape of the hidden contours. Only valid contour completions are presented to the user, so the user can not use this tool to fix incorrect hidden-cusp locations like the ones shown in Fig. 12.15.

12.10 Limitations and Conclusions

Based on Williams' framework [33], we created a practical system that goes from a contour drawing to a fairly smooth surface with that drawing as its visible contour, one which works for a wide variety of useful cases.

As we indicated in the corresponding sections, both the hidden contour completion algorithm and the inflation algorithm for SmoothSketch have a number of limitations. The main limitation of the contour-completion approach is that it is local—the completed contour shape depends on the geometry of the starting and ending points, but ignores the remainder of the input shape; it will require a much deeper understanding of contour completion to address this.

The inflation algorithm based on relaxing the mass–spring system currently requires tuning constants; the constants that produce the most satisfactory-looking results actually produce self-intersecting surfaces, especially in locations like "armpits" (i.e., between a limb and a body). We would like to find an algorithm that produces embeddings instead.

We would like to extend our work to include minor surface discontinuities—things like ridges or creases on a surface, which often are perceptually significant. We have developed our system to be agnostic about shape, treating it purely geometrically, users *are* familiar with many shapes. We imagine the possibility of a hybrid system, in which the user's sketch is both inflated *and* matched against a large database of known forms, for possible suggestions ("You seem to be drawing a dog; would you like us to add the hidden legs for you?").

References

1. Alexe, A., Barthe, L., Cani, M.-P., Gaildrat, V.: Shape modeling by sketching using convolution surfaces. In: Pacific Graphics. Short Papers (2005)
2. Bellettini, G., Beorchia, V., Paolini, M.: Topological and variational properties of a model for the reconstruction of three-dimensional transparent images with self-occlusions. Journal of Mathematical Imaging and Vision **32**(3), 265–291 (2008)
3. Cordier, F., Seo, H.: Free-form sketching of self-occluding objects. IEEE Computer Graphics and Applications **27**(1), 50–59 (2007)
4. Gibson, S., Mirtich, B.: A survey of deformable modeling in computer graphics. Technical report TR-97-19, Mitsubishi Electric Research Lab., Cambridge, MA (1997)
5. Grenander, U.: Lectures in Pattern Theory, vols. 1–3. Springer, Berlin (1981)
6. Griffiths, H.B.: Surfaces. Cambridge University Press, Cambridge (1981)
7. Guillemin, V., Pollack, A.: Differential Topology. Prentice Hall, New York (1974)
8. Hoffman, D.D.: Visual Intelligence: How We Create What We See. Norton, New York (2000)
9. Huffman, D.A.: Impossible objects as nonsense sentences. In: Meltzer, B., Michie, D. (eds.) Machine Intelligence, vol. 6. American Elsevier, New York (1971)
10. Igarashi, T., Matsuoka, S., Tanaka, H.: Teddy: A sketching interface for 3D freeform design. In: Proceedings of SIGGRAPH 99, pp. 409–416 (1999)
11. Igarashi, T., Hughes, J.F.: Smooth meshes for sketch-based freeform modeling. In: Symposium on Interactive 3D Graphics, pp. 139–142 (2003)
12. Johnston, S.F.: Lumo: illumination for cel animation. In: Proceedings of the Symposium on Non-photorealistic Animation and Rendering, pp. 45–52 (2002)
13. Kanizsa, G.: Organization in Vision. Praeger, New York (1979)
14. Karpenko, O.: Algorithms and interfaces for sketch-based 3D modeling. Doctoral thesis, Brown University (2007)
15. Karpenko, O., Hughes, J.: Implementation sketch for SmoothSketch: 3D free-form shapes from complex sketches. In: Siggraph Sketches Program (2006)
16. Karpenko, O., Hughes, J.: SmoothSketch: 3D free-form shapes from complex sketches. ACM Transactions on Graphics **25**(3), 589–598 (2006)
17. Karpenko, O., Hughes, J., Raskar, R.: Free-form sketching with variational implicit surfaces. Eurographics Computer Graphics Forum **21**(3), 585–594 (2002)
18. Kobbelt, L.P., Bareuther, T., Seidel, H.-P.: Multiresolution shape deformations for meshes with dynamic vertex connectivity. Computer Graphics Forum **19**(3) (2000)
19. Koenderink, J.J.: What does the occluding contour tell us about solid shape. Perception **13**, 321–330 (1984)
20. Koenderink, J.J.: Solid Shape. MIT Press, Cambridge (1990)
21. Mumford, D.: Elastica and computer vision. In: Bajaj, C.L. (ed.) Algebraic Geometry and Its Applications. Springer, New York (1994)
22. Nealen, A., Sorkine, O., Alexa, M., Cohen-Or, D.: A sketch-based interface for detail-preserving mesh editing. In: ACM SIGGRAPH Transactions on Graphics, pp. 1142–1147 (2005)
23. Nealen, A., Igarashi, T., Sorkine, O., Alexa, M.: FiberMesh: Designing freeform surfaces with 3D curves. ACM Transactions on Computer Graphics (2007)
24. Nitzberg, M., Mumford, D., Shiota, T.: Filtering, Segmentation, and Depth. Springer, Berlin (1993)
25. Pentland, A., Kuo, J.: The artist at the interface. Technical Report 114, MIT Media Lab (1989)
26. Pereira, J.P., Branco, V.A., Jorge, J.A., Silva, N.F., Cardoso, T.D., Ferreira, F.N.: Cascading recognizers for ambiguous calligraphic interaction. In: Eurographics Workshop on Sketch-Based Interfaces and Modeling (2004)
27. Russel, S., Norvig, P.: Artificial Intelligence: A Modern Approach. Prentice Hall, New York (1995)
28. Schmidt, R., Wyvill, B., Sousa, M.C., Jorge, J.A.: ShapeShop: Sketch-based solid modeling with BlobTrees. In: Eurographics Workshop on Sketch-Based Interfaces and Modeling, pp. 53–62 (2005)

29. Shesh, A., Chen, B.: SMARTPAPER: An interactive and user-friendly sketching system. Eurographics Computer Graphics Forum **23**(3), 301–310 (2004)
30. Shewchuk, J.R.: Triangle: Engineering a 2D quality mesh generator and Delaunay triangulator. In: Lin, M.C., Manocha, D. (eds.) Applied Computational Geometry: Towards Geometric Engineering, vol. 1148 (1996)
31. Taubin, G.: A signal processing approach to fair surface design. Computer Graphics **29**, 351–358 (1995)
32. Williams, L.: Shading in two dimensions. In: Graphics Interface, pp. 143–151 (1991)
33. Williams, L.R.: Perceptual completion of occluded surfaces. Ph.D. thesis, University of Massachusetts (1994)
34. Williams, L.R.: Topological reconstruction of a smooth manifold-solid from its occluding contour. International Journal of Computer Vision **23**(1), 93–108 (1997)
35. Williams, L.R., Jacobs, D.W.: Stochastic completion fields: A neural model of illusory contour shape and salience. Neural Computation **9**(4), 837–858 (1997)
36. Zeleznik, R.C., Herndon, K., Hughes, J.: Sketch: An interface for sketching 3D scenes. ACM Transactions on Graphics 163–170 (1996)

Chapter 13
The Creation and Modification of 3D Models Using Sketches and Curves

Levent Burak Kara and Kenji Shimada

13.1 Introduction

While recent decades have seen significant progress in CAD software, the current state of the art still appears insufficient when it comes to the styling design of products. This is evidenced by the fact that a significant portion of early design activities such as concept development and style generation occurs almost exclusively in 2D environments—be it the traditional pen-and-paper environment or its digital equivalents. While part of this bias toward 2D tools in the early design stages comes from the undeniable convenience and familiarity of such media, we believe the lack of suitable software and interaction techniques to support 3D styling design has a significant role in the current bias.

In this chapter, we present our recent studies concerning pen-based modeling of 3D geometry for industrial product design. Our system allows users to create and edit 3D geometry through direct sketching on a pen-enabled tablet computer. A distinguishing feature of our system is that it is tailored toward the rapid and intuitive design of styling features such as free-form curves and surfaces, which is often a tedious, if not complicated, task using conventional software. A key commonality among the types of products we consider is that their aesthetic appeal is a central consideration. Additionally, given that the final aesthetic form usually evolves in time rather than simply occurring, it is important that users of our system are able to accurately reproduce their ideas, while having the ability to quickly explore alternatives. The main advantage of our system lies precisely here in that it supports the direct creation and editing of free-form curves and surfaces through an intuitive interface. Our system is intended to be used by a wide variety of designers rang-

L.B. Kara (✉) · K. Shimada
Mechanical Engineering Department, Carnegie Mellon University, Pittsburgh, PA 15213, USA
e-mail: lkara@cmu.edu

K. Shimada
e-mail: shimada@cmu.edu

J. Jorge, F. Samavati (eds.), *Sketch-based Interfaces and Modeling*,
DOI 10.1007/978-1-84882-812-4_13, © Springer-Verlag London Limited 2011

ing from those who prefer the traditional pen-and-paper interface, to those who are already familiar with existing CAD tools.

In Sect. 13.2 of this chapter, we describe a general purpose modeling system for designing a wide variety of 3D geometries. Our approach facilitates the creation of 3D geometry with arbitrary topology through the use of a simple underlying surface template. Early in the design process, this template serves as a convenient substrate allowing designers to quickly lay out a set of curves. These curves later form the constituent wireframe edges of the 3D object. Our curve creation and modification techniques allow the template be only roughly defined with no particular detail. Using this method, we illustrate the design of various consumer products.

Section 13.3 of this chapter is concerned specifically with automotive styling design. We describe a novel method based on camera calibration and elastic deformation that allows designers' rough, conceptual sketches to be quickly turned into 3D surface models, thereby facilitating a rapid design, evaluation and reuse of styling ideas directly in 3D. This approach closely relates to the first part of our chapter in that it provides a rapid and accurate means for generating an underlying surface model specifically for automotive design. The described techniques enhance the design process by producing 3D models readily commensurate with input sketches.

The content presented in this chapter has been summarized from our previous publications ([16–20]). We refer the reader to these references for the details not presented herein.

For more exploration of existing work on sketch-based 3D modeling, a rich body of literature is available. Such work can be categorized into five groups based on each work's characteristics:

- Gesture-based approach [4, 6, 7, 11, 39]: This approach uses designers' strokes primarily for geometric operations such as extrusion, bending and primitive deformation, rather than for directly depicting the target shape. While these methods allow a quick construction of rectilinear geometry, or a deformation of existing geometry, they are not targeted toward designing 3D space curves.
- Silhouette-based approach [1, 2, 12, 13, 22, 30–32]: In this approach, users' strokes are used to form a 2D silhouette representing an outline or a cross-section, which is then extruded, inflated or swept to give 3D form. The approach is suited for obtaining a reasonable 3D geometry quickly, rather than modeling a precise shape. Recently the silhouette drawing approach has been applied to the design of organic shapes such as plants, leaves and animal parts.
- Line-labeling and optimization [5, 9, 21, 24, 33–36]: In 3D interpretation from 2D input, the well-known issue of one-to-many mapping (thus the lack of a unique solution) has resulted in the development of various constraint and optimization-based methods. To date, much work has focused on interpreting line drawings of polyhedral objects. These methods typically use some form of a line-labeling algorithm, followed by an optimization step, to produce the most plausible interpretation.
- Template-based approach [16–20, 25, 34, 38]: In this approach, the desired 3D form is obtained by modifying an underlying 3D template. The effectiveness and applicability of the approach depends on the variety of target shapes—if target

shapes are akin to each other topologically and geometrically it is easy to define an effective underlying 3D template; otherwise the template may be too prohibitive to unleash the creativity of the designer. Note that our work presented in this chapter is an example of the template-based approach.

- Mesh editing [3, 23, 27]: Mesh-editing systems allow users to operate directly on existing surfaces to deform or add feature lines using a digital pen. The key difference of these methods compared to similar gesture-based approaches is that users' strokes are directly replicated on the resulting shape. Such systems let users add smoothly blended complex artifacts to an otherwise plain original geometry. A typical mesh-editing operation requires a specification of the target region, along with a specification of the desired deformation.

13.2 Sketch-based Creation and Modification of 3D Shapes

Consider the design of a computer mouse shown in Fig. 13.1. In a typical scenario, the user begins by constructing the base wireframe model of the design object. For this, the user first sketches the initial feature curves on a very rough and simplified 3D template model. In this particular case the template is defined as a polygonal mesh. This template acts as a platform that helps anchor users' initial strokes in 3D space. Once the initial curves comprising the wireframe are constructed, the base 3D template is removed, leaving the user with a set of 3D curves. Next, through

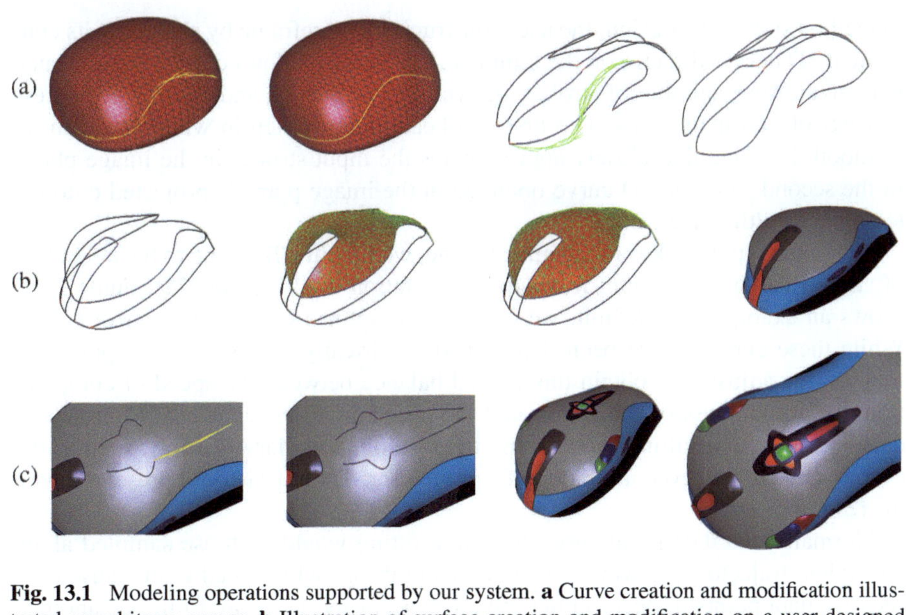

Fig. 13.1 Modeling operations supported by our system. **a** Curve creation and modification illustrated on arbitrary curves. **b** Illustration of surface creation and modification on a user-designed wireframe. **c** Further design is performed in a similar way. Curves of features are drawn, modified, and finally surfaced

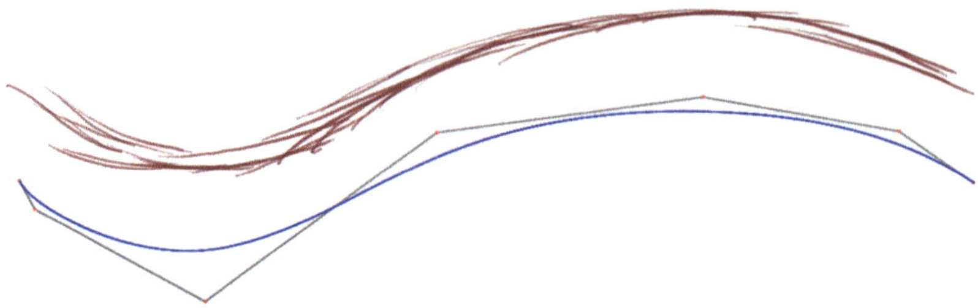

Fig. 13.2 B-spline fitting to raw strokes. *Top*: Input strokes. *Bottom*: Resulting B-spline and its control polygon

direct sketching, the user modifies the initially created curves to give them the precise desired shape. After the wireframe is obtained, the user constructs interpolating surfaces that cover the wireframe. Finally, using two physically based deformation tools, the user modifies the newly created surfaces to the desired shapes. Once the basic wireframe and surfaces are created, further details can be added using the same strategy of curve creation, curve modification, surface creation, and finally surface modification. The following sections detail these processes.

13.2.1 Constructing the 3D Wireframe

In the first step of the design, the user constructs the wireframe by sketching its constituent 3D curves directly on the template. Our system allows curves to be created with an arbitrary number of strokes, drawn in any direction and order. The process consists of two main steps. The first is a beautification step in which we identify a smooth B-spline that closely approximates the input strokes in the image plane. In the second step, the 2D curve obtained in the image plane is projected onto the template resulting in a 3D curve.

Given the input strokes in the image plane, we first fit a B-spline to the collection of strokes using a minimum least-squares criterion described in [28]. Figure 13.2 shows an example. By default, we use cubic B-splines with seven control points. While these choices have been determined empirically to best suit our purposes, they can be adjusted to obtain the desired balance between the speed of computation, the smoothness of the curve, and the approximation accuracy. Nevertheless, details of the curve fitting process and the resulting auxiliary features, such as the curve's control polygon, are hidden from the user. The user is only presented with the resulting curve.

Normally, the data points used for curve fitting would be those sampled along the stylus' trajectory. However, fluctuations in the drawing speed often cause consecutive data points to occur either too close to, or too far away from one another. This phenomenon, as evidenced by dense point clouds near the stroke ends (where drawing speed tends to be low) and large gaps in the middle of the stroke (where

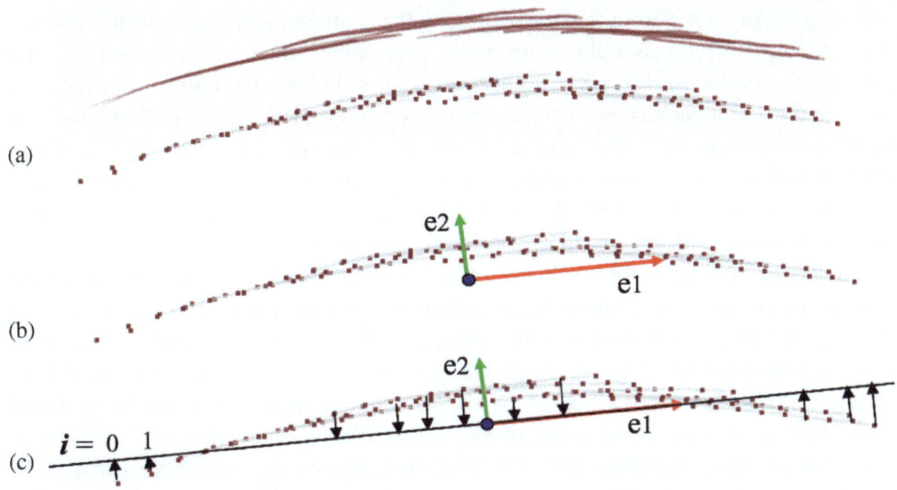

Fig. 13.3 Point ordering using principal component analysis. **a** Input strokes and extracted data points. **b** The two principal component directions are computed as the eigenvectors of the covariance matrix of the data points. The two direction vectors are positioned at the centroid of the data points. **c** Data points are projected onto the first principal direction e1, and sorted

speed is high), often adversely affects curve fitting. Hence, before curve fitting is applied, we resample each stroke to obtain data points equally spaced along the stroke's trajectory.

The main challenge in curve fitting, however, arises from the fact that a curve can be constructed using multiple strokes, drawn in arbitrary directions and orders. This arbitrariness often causes spatially adjacent data points to have markedly different indices in the vector storing the data points. An accurate organization of the data points based on spatial proximity, however, is a strict requirement of the curve fitting algorithm. Hence, prior to curve fitting, input points must be reorganized to convert the cloud of unordered points into an organized set of points. Note that this reorganization would only affect the points' indices in the storage vector, not their geometric locations.

To this goal, we use a principal component analysis as shown in Fig. 13.3. The main idea is that, by identifying the direction of maximum spread of the data points, one can obtain a straight line approximation to the points. Next, by projecting the original points onto this line and sorting the projected points, one can obtain a suitable ordering of the original points.

Given a set of 2D points, the two principal directions can be determined as the eigenvectors of the 2×2 covariance matrix Σ given as

$$\Sigma = \frac{1}{n}\sum_{k=1}^{n}(\mathbf{x}_k - \mu)(\mathbf{x}_k - \mu)^{\mathrm{T}}$$

Here, $\mathbf{x}_k$ represents the column vector containing the (x, y) coordinates of the kth data point, and μ is the centroid of the data points.

The principal direction we seek is the one that corresponds to maximum spread, and is the eigenvector associated with the larger eigenvalue. After identifying the principal direction, we form a straight line passing through the centroid of the data points and project each of the original points onto the principal line. Next, we sort the projected points according to their positions on the principal line. The resulting ordering is then used as the ordering of the original points. Note that one advantageous byproduct of this method is that it reveals the extremal points of the curve (i.e., its two ends), which would otherwise be difficult to identify.

In practice, we have found this approach to work well especially because the curves created with our system often stretch along a unique direction. Hence, the ordering of the projections along the principal direction often matches well with the expected ordering of the original data points. However, this method falls short when users' curves exhibit hooks at the ends, or contain nearly closed or fully closed loops. This is because these artifacts will cause folding or overlapping of the projected points along the principal direction, thus preventing a reliable sorting. To circumvent such peculiarities, we ask users to construct such curves in pieces consisting of simpler curves; our program allows separate curves to be later stitched together using a trim function.

Once the raw strokes are beautified into a B-spline, the resulting curve is projected onto the base template. This is trivially accomplished using the depth buffer of the graphics engine. At the end, a 3D curve is obtained that lies on the template, whose projection to the image plane matches with the user's strokes.

13.2.2 Modifying the Wireframe

After creating the initial wireframe, the user begins to modify its constituent curves to give them the precise desired shape. During this step, the base template can be removed, leaving the user with a set of 3D curves. We use an energy minimization algorithm to obtain the best modification of the curve in question.

To make matters simple, we designed our approach such that the curves of the wireframe are modified one at a time, with freedom to return to an earlier curve. At any point, the curve that the user intends to modify is determined automatically as explained below, thus allowing the user to modify edges in an arbitrary order. After each set of strokes, the user presses a button that processes accumulated strokes, and modifies the appropriate curve. To facilitate discussion, we shall call users' input strokes as *modifiers*, and the curve modified by those modifiers as the *target curve*.

Modification of the wireframe is performed in three steps. In the first step, curves of the wireframe are projected to the image plane resulting in a set of 2D curves. The curve that the user intends to modify is computed automatically by identifying the curve whose projection in the image plane lies closest to the modifier strokes. The proximity between a projected curve and the modifiers is computed by sampling a set of points from the curve and the modifiers, and calculating the aggregate

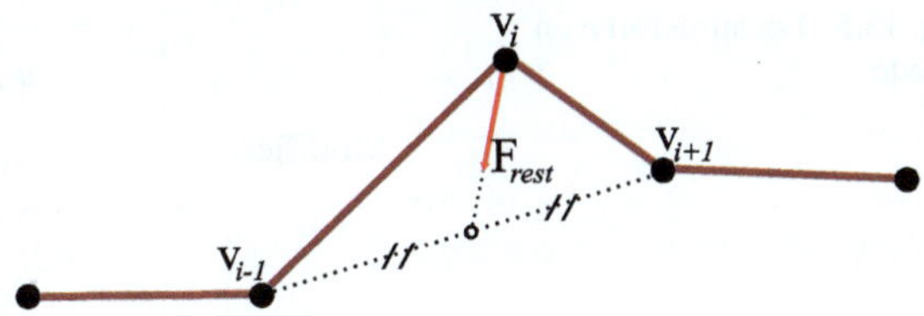

Fig. 13.4 Internal energy due to stretching and bending is minimized approximately by moving each snake node to the barycenter of its neighbors similar to Laplacian smoothing

minimum distance between the two point sets. In the second step, the target curve is deformed in the image plane until it matches well with the modifiers. In the third step, the modified target curve is projected back into 3D space.

13.2.2.1 Curve Modification in the Image Plane

We deform a projected target curve in the image plane using an energy minimizing algorithm based on active contour models [15]. Active contours (also known as snakes) have long been used in image processing applications such as segmentation, tracking, and registration. The principal idea is that a snake moves and conforms to certain features in an image, such as intensity gradient, while minimizing its internal energy due to bending and stretching. This approach allows an object to be extracted or tracked in the form of a continuous spline.

We adopt the above idea for curve manipulation. Here, the 2D target curve is modeled as a snake, whose nodes are sampled directly from the target curve. The nodes of the snakes are connected to one another with line segments making the snake geometrically equivalent to a polyline. The set of modifier strokes, on the other hand, is modeled as an unordered set of points (point cloud) extracted from the input strokes. As before, this allows for an arbitrary number of modifiers, drawn in arbitrary directions and order. With this formulation, the snake deforms and conforms to the modifiers, but locally resists excessive bending and stretching to maintain smoothness. Mathematically, this can be expressed as an energy functional to be minimized:

$$E_{\text{snake}} = \sum_i E_{\text{int}}(\mathbf{v}_i) + E_{\text{ext}}(\mathbf{v}_i)$$

where $\mathbf{v}_i = (x_i, y_i)$ is the ith node coordinate of the snake. E_{int} is the internal energy arising from the stretching and bending of the snake. Our solution of minimizing this term involves applying a restitutive force $\mathbf{F}_{\text{rest}}$ that simply moves each snake node toward the barycenter of its neighboring two nodes (Fig. 13.4).

External energy E_{ext} describes the potential energy of the snake due to external attractors, which arise in the presence of modifiers. The modifiers' influence on the snake consists of two components: (1) location forces, (2) pressure forces. The first component moves the snake toward the data points sampled from the modifiers. For each snake node $\mathbf{v}_i$, a force $\mathbf{F}_{\text{loc}}(\mathbf{v}_i)$ is computed corresponding to the influence of

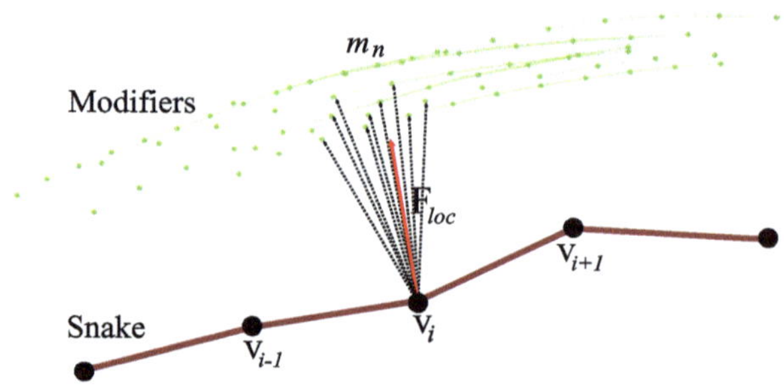

Fig. 13.5 Location force on a node

the location forces on $\mathbf{v}_i$:

$$\mathbf{F}_{\text{loc}}(\mathbf{v}_i) = \sum_{n \in k_{\text{neigh}}} \frac{\mathbf{m}_n - \mathbf{v}_i}{\|\mathbf{m}_n - \mathbf{v}_i\|} \cdot w(n)$$

where $\mathbf{m}_n$ is one of the k closest neighbors of $\mathbf{v}_i$ in the modifiers (Fig. 13.5). $w(n)$ is a weighting factor inversely proportional to the distance between $\mathbf{m}_n$ and $\mathbf{v}_i$. In other words, at any instant, a snake node $\mathbf{v}_i$ is pulled by k nearest modifier points. The force from each modifier point $\mathbf{m}_n$ is inversely proportional to its distance to $\mathbf{v}_i$, and points along the vector $\mathbf{m}_n - \mathbf{v}_i$.

The second component of E_{ext} is related to pressure with which strokes are drawn. The force created due to this energy pulls the snake toward sections of high pressure. The rationale behind considering the pressure effect is based on the observation that users typically press the pen harder to emphasize critical sections while sketching. The pressure term exploits this phenomenon by forcing the snake to favor sections drawn more emphatically. For each snake node $\mathbf{v}_i$, a force $\mathbf{F}_{\text{pres}}(\mathbf{v}_i)$ is computed as

$$\mathbf{F}_{\text{pres}}(\mathbf{v}_i) = \sum_{n \in k_{\text{neigh}}} \frac{\mathbf{m}_n - \mathbf{v}_i}{\|\mathbf{m}_n - \mathbf{v}_i\|} \cdot p(n)$$

where $p(n)$ is a weight factor proportional to the pen pressure recorded at point $\mathbf{m}_n$.

During modification, the snake moves under the influence of the two external forces while minimizing its internal energy through the restitutive force. In each iteration, the new position of $\mathbf{v}_i$ is determined by the vector sum of $\mathbf{F}_{\text{rest}}$, $\mathbf{F}_{\text{loc}}$ and $\mathbf{F}_{\text{pres}}$, whose relative weights can be adjusted to emphasize different components. For example, increasing the weight of $\mathbf{F}_{\text{rest}}$ will result in smoother curves with less bends. On the other hand, emphasizing $\mathbf{F}_{\text{pres}}$ will increase the sensitivity to pressure differences with the resulting curve favoring high pressure regions. Default weights are currently 30% for $\mathbf{F}_{\text{rest}}$, 40% for $\mathbf{F}_{\text{loc}}$, and 30% for $\mathbf{F}_{\text{pres}}$. We have determined these weights empirically such that we obtain subjectively the best outcomes in our test cases.

13.2.2.2 Unprojection to 3D

In this step, the newly designed 2D curve is projected back into 3D space. As mentioned previously, there is no unique solution because there are infinitely many 3D curves whose projections match the 2D curve. We therefore choose the best 3D configuration based on the following constraints:

- The 3D curve should appear right under the modifier strokes.
- If the modifier strokes appear precisely over the original target curve, i.e., the strokes do not alter the curve's 2D projection, the target curve should preserve its original 3D shape.
- If the curve is to change shape, it must maintain a reasonable 3D form. By "reasonable," we mean a solution that the designer would accept in many cases, while anticipating it in the worst case.

Based on these premises, we choose the optimal configuration as the one that minimizes the spatial deviation from the original target curve. That is, among the 3D curves whose projections match the newly designed 2D curve, we choose the one that lies nearest to the original target curve. This can be formulated as follows:

Let $\mathbf{C}$ be a curve in $\mathbb{R}^3$ constrained on a surface $\mathbf{S}$.[1] Let $\mathbf{C}^{\text{orig}}$ be the original target curve in $\mathbb{R}^3$ that the user is modifying. The new 3D configuration $\mathbf{C}^*$ of the modified curve is computed as:

$$\mathbf{C}^* = \underset{\mathbf{C}}{\operatorname{argmin}} \sum_i \left\| \mathbf{C}_i - \mathbf{C}_i^{\text{orig}} \right\|$$

where $\mathbf{C}_i$ denotes the ith vertex of $\mathbf{C}$. With this criterion, $\mathbf{C}^*$ is found by computing the minimum-distance projection points of $\mathbf{C}_i^{\text{orig}}$ onto $\mathbf{S}$ (Fig. 13.6(b)).

The rationale behind this choice is that, by remaining proximate to the original curve, the new curve can be thought to be "least surprising" when viewed from a different viewpoint. One advantage of this is that curves can be modified incrementally, with predictable outcomes in each step. That is, as the curve desirably conforms to the user's strokes in the current view, it still preserves most of its shape established in earlier steps as it deviates minimally from its previous configuration. This allows geometrically complex curves to be obtained by only a few successive modifications from different viewpoints.

During wireframe creation and modification, the user operates on the constituent curves one at a time, without regard to their connectivity. Hence, the curves in the resulting wireframe will likely be disconnected. To prepare the wireframe for surfacing, the user may invoke a "trim" command that merges curve ends that lie sufficiently close to one another. This command applies an appropriate set of translations, rotations and scalings to the entirety of a disconnected curve such that its

[1] $\mathbf{S}$ is the surface subtended by the rays emanating from the user's viewpoint and passing through the newly designed 2D curve, as illustrated in Fig. 13.6b. This surface extends into 3D space and is not visible from the original viewpoint.

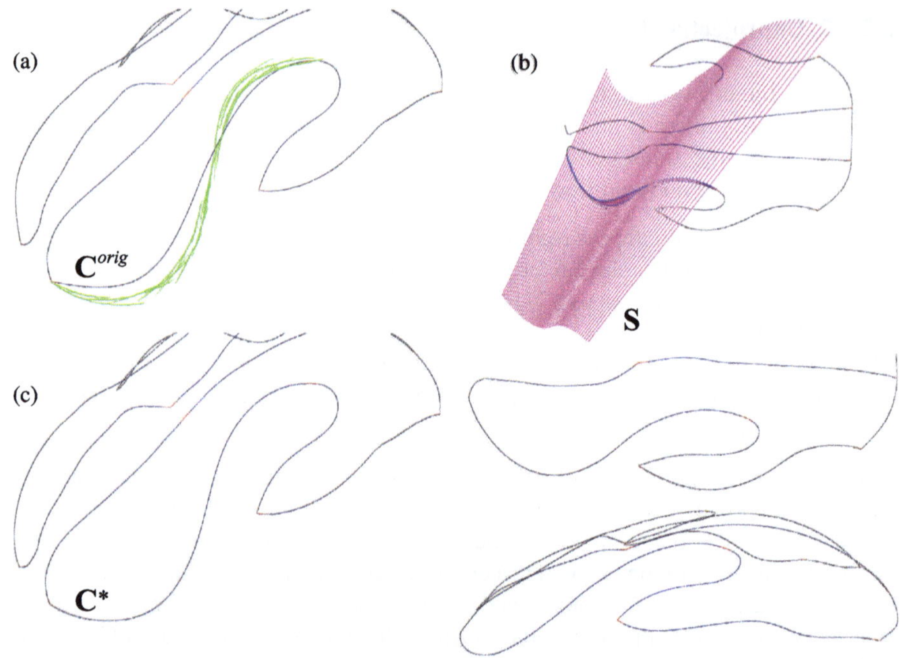

Fig. 13.6 Curve modification from a single view. **a** User's strokes. **b** Surface **S** created by the rays emanating from the user's eyes and passing through the strokes, and the minimum-distance lines from the original curve. **c** Resulting modification from three different views

ends meet with other curves. By transforming a curve as whole, rather than simply extending its ends, the shape established by the user is better preserved while eliminating the kinks that could otherwise occur at the curve ends. At the end, a well-connected wireframe is obtained that can be subsequently surfaced.

13.2.3 Surface Creation and Modification

In the last step, the newly designed wireframe model is surfaced to obtain a solid model. Once the initial surfaces are obtained, the user can modify them using simple deformation tools. The following sections detail these processes.

13.2.3.1 Initial Surface Creation

Given the wireframe model, this step creates a surface geometry for each of the face loops in the wireframe. In this work, it is assumed that the wireframe topology is already available with the template model and therefore all face loops are known a

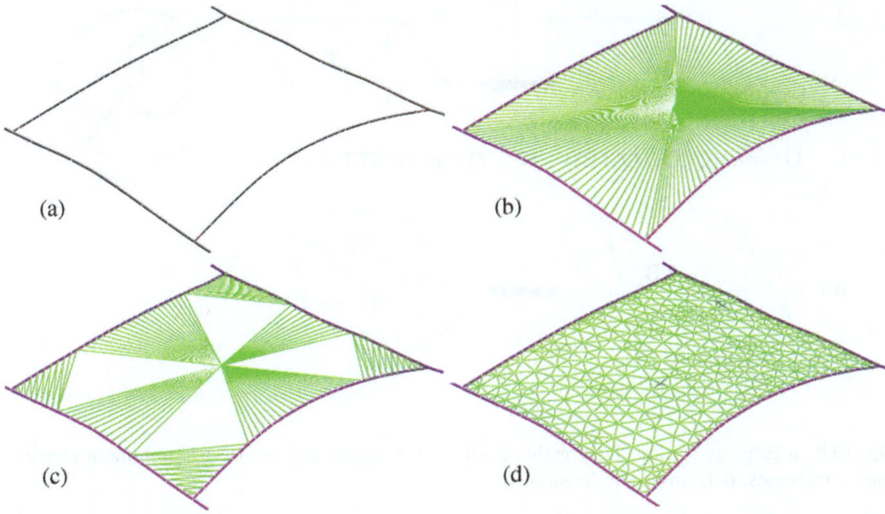

Fig. 13.7 Surface creation. **a** Initial boundary loop consisting of four curves. **b** Preliminary triangulation using a vertex created at the centroid. **c** Edge swapping **d** Final result after face splitting and mesh smoothing using V-spring method [37]

priori.[2] Each face loop may consist of an arbitrary number of edge curves. For each face loop, the surface geometry is constructed using the method proposed in [14]. In this method, each curve of the wireframe is represented as a polyline, and the resulting surfaces are polygonal surfaces consisting of purely triangular elements.

Figure 13.7 illustrates the creation of a surface geometry on a boundary loop. In the first step, a vertex is created at the centroid of the boundary vertices. Initial triangles are then created that use the new vertex as the apex, and have their bases at the boundary. Next, for each pair of adjacent triangular elements, edge swapping is performed. For two adjacent triangles, this operation seeks to improve the mesh quality by swapping their common edge (Fig. 13.8a). The mesh quality is based on the constituent triangles' quality. For a triangle, it is defined as the radius ratio, which is the radius of the inscribed circle divided by the radius of the circumscribed circle. Next, adjacent triangles are subdivided iteratively, until the longest edge length in the mesh is less than a threshold (Fig. 13.8b). Between each iteration, edge swapping and Laplacian smoothing is performed to maintain a regular vertex distribution with high quality elements. At the end, the resulting surface is smoothed using a physically based mesh deformation method, called the V-spring operator [37]. This method, which will be presented in detail in Sect. 13.2.3.2, iteratively adjusts the initial mesh so that the total variation of curvature is minimized. Once the initial surfaces are created in this way, new feature curves can be added to the model by direct sketching, as described in the previous section.

[2]If the topology is unknown, it has to be computed automatically, or it must be manually specified by the user. Currently, we are working toward automatically computing the wireframe topology.

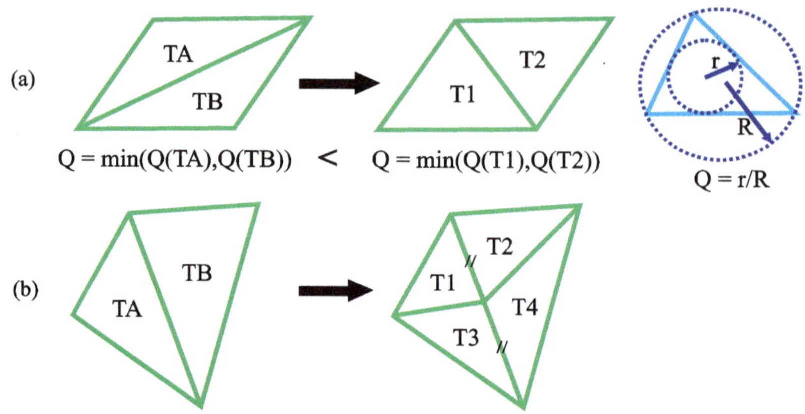

Fig. 13.8 **a** Edge swapping. Diagonals of adjacent triangles are swapped if minimum element quality increases. **b** Triangle subdivision

13.2.3.2 Surface Modification

Often times, the designer will need to modify the initial surfaces to give the model a more aesthetic look. In this work, we adopt a simple and intuitive modification scheme that allows users to explore different surface alternatives in a controllable and predictable way. Unlike most existing techniques, our approach operates directly on the polygonal surface without requiring the user to define a control grid or a lattice structure.

Our approach consists of two deformation methods. The first method uses pressure to deform a surface. With this tool, resulting surfaces look rounder and inflated, with more volume. The second method is based on the V-spring approach described by [37]. In this method, a network of springs work together to minimize the variation of surface curvature. A discussion of the practical utility of this type of surface can be found in [10]. In both methods, deformation is applied to the interior of the surface while keeping the boundaries fixed. This way, the underlying wireframe geometry is preserved, with no alterations to the designed curves.

Surface Modification Using Pressure Force This deformation tool simulates the effect of a pressure force on a thin membrane. The tool allows surfaces to be inflated or flattened in a predictable way. The extent of the deformation depends on the magnitude of the pressure, which is controlled by the user through a slider bar. Different pressure values can be specified for individual surfaces, thus giving the user a better control on the final shape of the solid model.

The equilibrium position of a pressurized surface is found iteratively. In each step, each vertex of the surface is moved by a small amount proportional to the pressure force applied to that vertex. The neighboring vertices, however, resist this displacement by pulling the vertex toward their barycenter akin to Laplacian smoothing. The equilibrium position is reached when the positive displacement for each

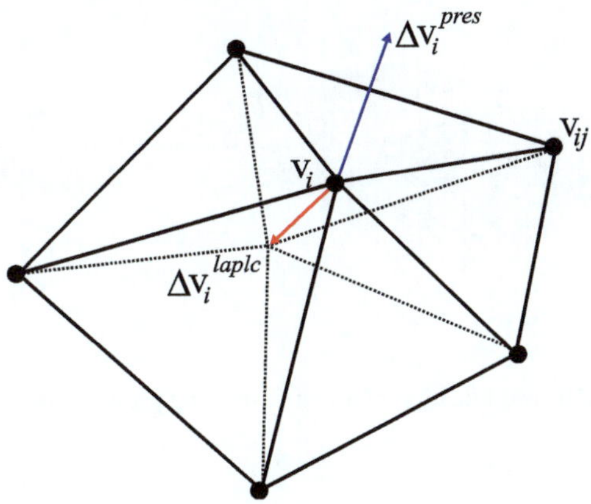

Fig. 13.9 A pressure force applied to a vertex moves the vertex along its normal direction. The neighboring vertices, however, pull the vertex back toward their barycenter. Equilibrium is reached when displacements due to the pressure force and the neighbors are balanced

node is balanced by the restitutive displacement caused by the neighboring vertices. Figure 13.9 illustrates the idea.

The algorithm can be outlined as follows. Let p be the pressure applied to the surface. Until convergence iterate:

for each vertex $\mathbf{v}_i$

Compute the unit normal $\mathbf{n}_i$ at vertex $\mathbf{v}_i$

Compute the pressure force on $\mathbf{v}_i$

$$F_i = p \cdot A_i^{\text{voronoi}}$$

$$\Delta \mathbf{v}_i^{\text{pres}} = F_i \cdot \mathbf{n}_i$$

$$\Delta \mathbf{v}_i^{\text{laplc}} = \left(\frac{1}{K} \sum_{j=1}^{K} \mathbf{v}_{ij} \right) - \mathbf{v}_i, \text{ where } \mathbf{v}_{ij} \text{ is one of the } K \text{ adjacent vertices of } \mathbf{v}_i$$

$$\mathbf{v}_i \leftarrow \mathbf{v}_i + \left((1 - \xi) \Delta \mathbf{v}_i^{\text{pres}} + \gamma \Delta \mathbf{v}_i^{\text{laplc}} \right)$$

end for

The vertex normal $\mathbf{n}_i$ is updated in each iteration and is computed as the average of the normals of the faces incident on $\mathbf{v}_i$, weighted by the area of each face. A_i^{voronoi} is the Voronoi area surrounding $\mathbf{v}_i$. It is obtained by connecting the circumcenters of the faces incident on $\mathbf{v}_i$ with the midpoints of the edges incident on $\mathbf{v}_i$. ξ and γ are damping coefficients that control the convergence rate. Too low values of ξ or γ may cause instability in convergence.

The above algorithm is applied to all surface vertices while keeping the boundary vertices fixed. Figure 13.10 shows an example on a seat model. If necessary, negative pressure can be applied to form concavities.

Surface Modification Using V-Spring Method This method creates surfaces of minimized curvature variation based on a discrete spring model. This scheme produces fair surfaces that vary smoothly, which is known to be an important criterion for aesthetic design purposes [29]. Additionally, when applied to a group of adja-

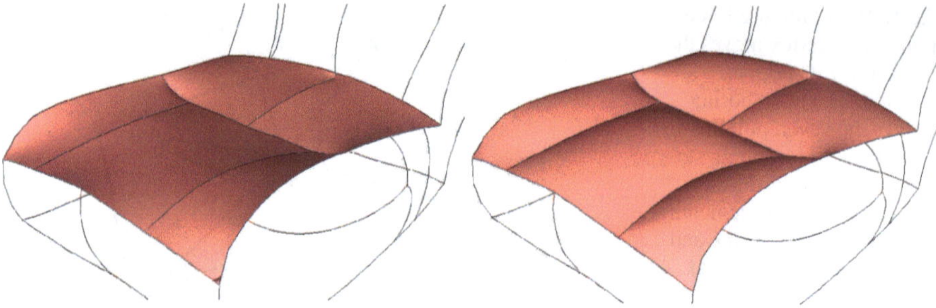

Fig. 13.10 Modification of a seat base using pressure force

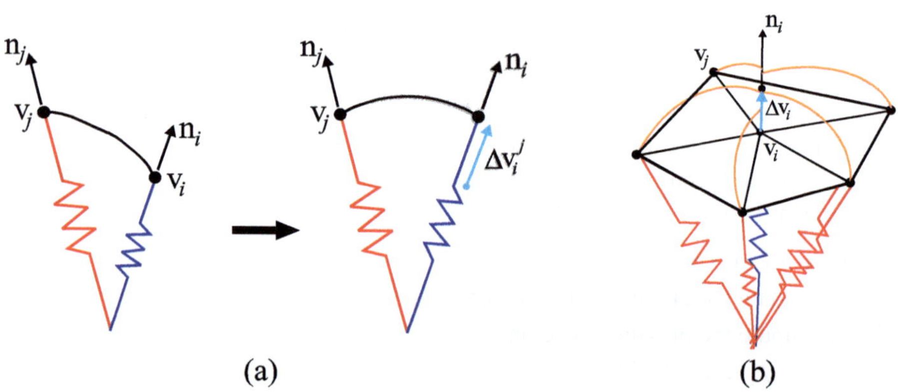

Fig. 13.11 V-spring. **a** Displacement of $\mathbf{v}_i$ due to $\mathbf{v}_j$. **b** Net displacement due to all neighbors

cent surfaces, it reduces sharp edges by smoothing the transition across the boundary curves.

In this method, a spring is attached to each surface vertex. Neighboring springs usually form a "V" shape, thus giving the name to the method. The spring length approximately represents the local curvature. During modification, the springs work together to keep their lengths equal, which is equal to minimizing the variation of curvature (Fig. 13.11). Each vertex thus moves under the influence of its neighbors until the vertices locally lie on a sphere.

Based on this model, the displacement of $\mathbf{v}_i$ due to a neighboring vertex $\mathbf{v}_j$ is given as follows (see [37] for details):

$$\Delta \mathbf{v}_i^j = \frac{1}{\|\mathbf{v}_j - \mathbf{v}_i\|}\left[\frac{(\mathbf{v}_j - \mathbf{v}_i)\cdot(\mathbf{n}_i + \mathbf{n}_j)}{1 + (\mathbf{n}_i \cdot \mathbf{n}_j)}\right]\mathbf{n}_i$$

where $\mathbf{n}_i$ and $\mathbf{n}_j$ are unit normal vectors at $\mathbf{v}_i$ and $\mathbf{v}_j$. The total displacement of $\mathbf{v}_i$ is computed as the average of displacements due to neighboring vertices. However, to maintain a regular vertex distribution throughout iterations, each vertex is also moved horizontally along its current tangent plane toward the barycenter of its neighbors. In each iteration, the positions and normals of the vertices are updated.

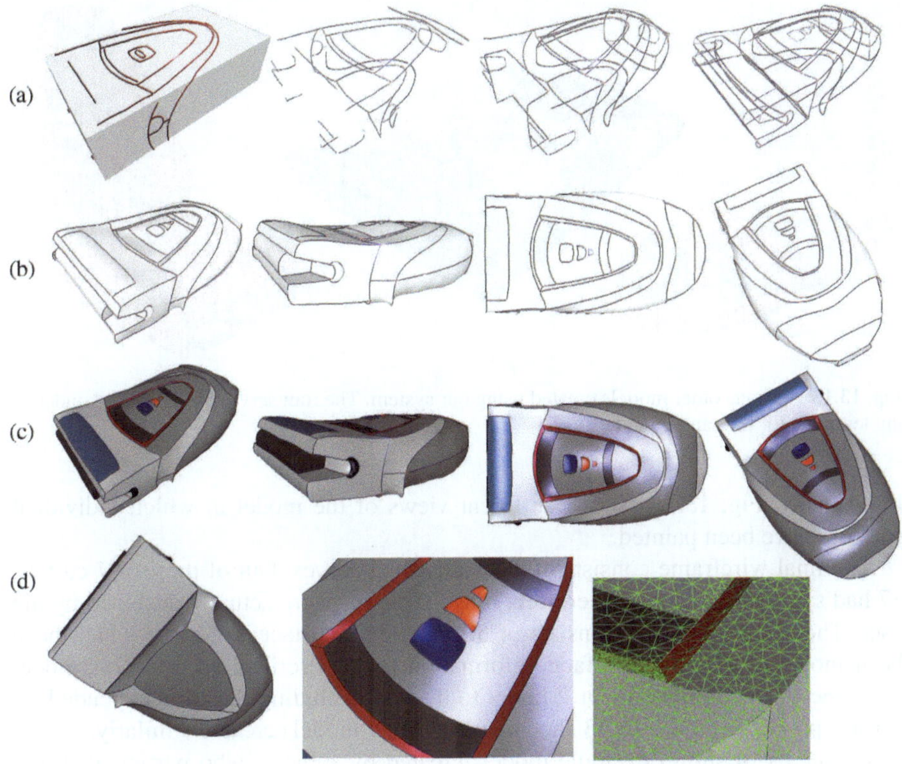

Fig. 13.12 Design of an electric shaver. **a** Wireframe creation. **b** Surfaced model rendered in *white*. **c** Surfaced model painted. **d** Bottom and top faces, and a detail view of the polygonal surfaces

The iterations are continued until the net displacement of each vertex is less than a threshold.

13.2.4 Examples

Figure 13.12 shows snapshots of our system in the design of an electric shaver. The base template used for this model is a rectangular prism as shown in Fig. 13.12a. The design begins by laying down several curves on this prism. Next, the initial curves are modified to give them the appropriate 3D shape. During the construction of the wireframe, curves are sometimes deleted if they are deemed premature at a given time. For instance, initially the part of the curves making up the three buttons on the top surface were drawn on the template prism, but were later removed in the early stages of curve modification. They were then introduced toward the end of the design process.

The last column of Fig. 13.12a shows the final wireframe designed via our system. Figure 13.12b shows different views of the solid model obtained after surfac-

Fig. 13.13 Various other models created using our system. The foot serves as the natural underlying template for the sandal model

ing. Finally, Fig. 13.12c shows different views of the model in which individual surfaces have been painted.

The final wireframe consists of 107 individual curves. Out of these 107 curves, 37 had symmetrical pairs. Therefore, only 70 curves were actually designed by the user. The surfaced model consists of 50 individual surfaces, most of which have been modified using the surface deformation tools described earlier. This model took one of the authors about 2 hours to design, excluding the time expended on surface painting. Figure 13.13 shows several other models created similarly.

Figure 13.14 shows example models created by subjects who participated in a user study ([20]). The results of this study show that our modeling techniques are effective in providing a natural and simple means to create 3D geometry. Most users found the ability to directly manipulate 3D curves using pen stokes to be a particularly powerful feature of our system. We observed that most users were comfortable adopting the new techniques and utilizing them effectively to complete their assignments. Despite having no prior experience with the system, most users quickly became adept at using the curve and surface creation techniques with little or no difficulty following a brief introductory tutorial. Given that none of the participants are routinely engaged in product design, we were pleased to see that many were able to produce satisfactory models in the allotted time frame.

13.3 Creating 3D Shape Templates from Sketches for Automotive Styling Design

In car industry, designers place huge emphasis on concept development and styling activities as the decisions made during these stages are key to the product's success. Most commonly, designers produce a multitude of rough sketches early in the design process as a way to explore different shapes and styles. While it would be desirable to seamlessly study a developing concept in 3D, the high fidelity, complex

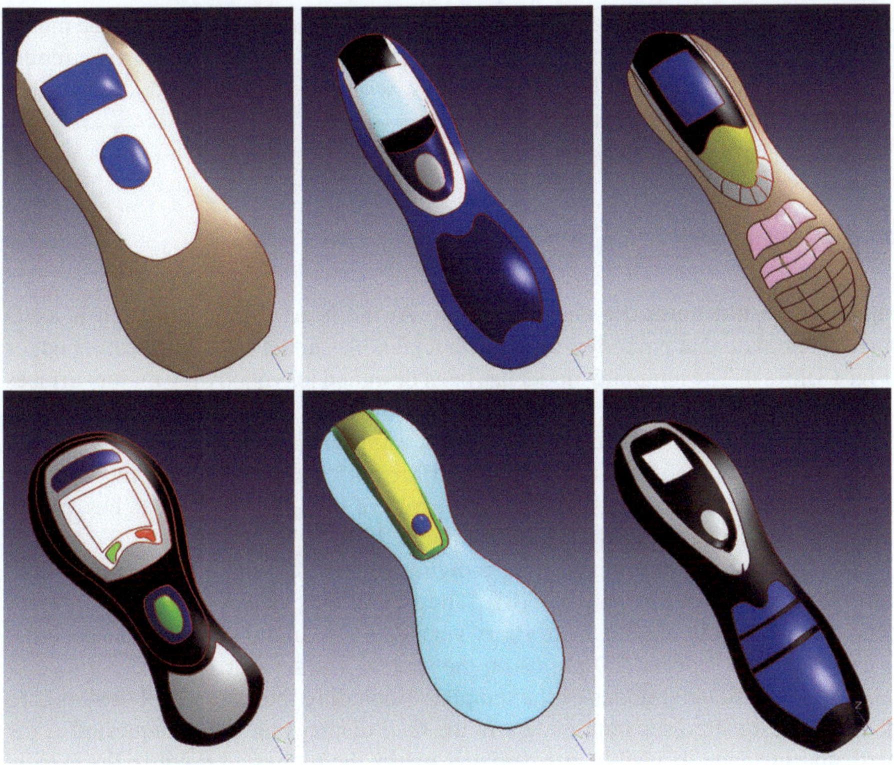

Fig. 13.14 Remote controllers designed by first-time users of our system

nature of existing 3D modeling tools typically precludes the use of such media early in the design. As a result, designers are restricted to 2D media for most of their early creative activities. Due to the significant effort and expertise required for 3D modeling, only a few select candidate concepts will typically pass to the next stage, while many others are prematurely abandoned.

The goal of this work is to improve current practice by helping the designer rapidly realize a 2D sketch in 3D and interact with the resulting geometry, without the need for complex modeling skills. With the proposed approach, we hope to enable 3D conceptual exploration early in the design cycle where constructing and interacting with the 3D model is, ideally, as easy as drawing on paper.

Our approach is based on a three-stage modeling framework that facilitates a rapid construction of a coarse 3D geometry followed by a progressive, sketch-based refinement. In the first stage, the user marks a set of fiducial points on the sketch. Using the fiducial points, our method first *aligns* an underlying template model with the sketch using a camera calibration algorithm. Next, an optimization algorithm *deforms* the template in 3D until the projection of its fiducial nodes match the fiducial points marked by the user. In the second stage, the user refines the template by tracing the car's key character lines. Input strokes modify the edges and surface patches of the template. At the end of this stage, the user obtains a smooth 3D surface model (devoid of details) that matches the car depicted in the sketch. This surface model is then used as a substrate for the final stage where the designer sketches further styling curves directly onto the model.

13.3.1 Overview

Figure 13.15 illustrates the design process. At the heart of our approach is a 3D surface template that embodies a set of fiducial nodes and a set of connecting edges (Fig. 13.15(a)). The template model has been designed to embody the major surfaces of a car body in the simplest, most abstract fashion. Aside from the overall shape that characterizes the class of the car (e.g., sedan vs. hatchback), the template is devoid of stylistic articulations that could later interfere with conceptual freedom. Note that this template model is represented by a network of bi-cubic surface patches, unlike the polygonal template mesh discussed in Sect. 13.2.

The designer begins by importing a digitally created or a scanned paper sketch into the user interface (Fig. 13.15(b)). The sketch may depict an orthographic or perspective projection, with an arbitrary vantage point. In the first step, the designer is asked to mark a set of 2D points on the sketch. The set of requested points correspond to the fiducial nodes of the template (including the four wheel centers). To guide the designer, a separate widget in the GUI displays the point requested at the particular instance. If visible, the designer marks the requested point in the sketch. Otherwise, the designer skips the point. At the completion of this process, the designer will have marked only a subset of the template's fiducial nodes as several of those points will be typically invisible in the sketch for marking. By monitoring which fiducial points have been marked and which ones have been skipped, our system establishes a one-to-one correspondence between template fiducials and the points marked by the designer.

Using the fiducial marks as input, a camera calibration algorithm first aligns the template with the sketch. This step adjusts the virtual camera properties such that the projection of the template in the image plane is similar to the view depicted in the sketch. Next, an optimization algorithm deforms the underlying template such that the projections of its fiducial nodes match closely with the designer's marker points (Fig. 13.15(c)). Although the fiducial points can be matched exactly via unrestrained deformations to the template, this will usually result in unrealistic 3D geometry. To maintain a sound 3D shape during deformation, our optimization algorithm thus seeks a deformation that deviates minimally from the original template.

Our data structure for the template model maintains a network of cubic curve edges connecting the fiducial nodes, and a set of bi-cubic surface patches for each of the associated face loops. Following fiducial point matching, the user refines the template by tracing its edges directly on the sketch (Fig. 13.15(d)). This process alters the template edge bodies in 3D to match the input strokes, while keeping the end nodes fixed. If edge modification from the current viewpoint is not satisfactory,

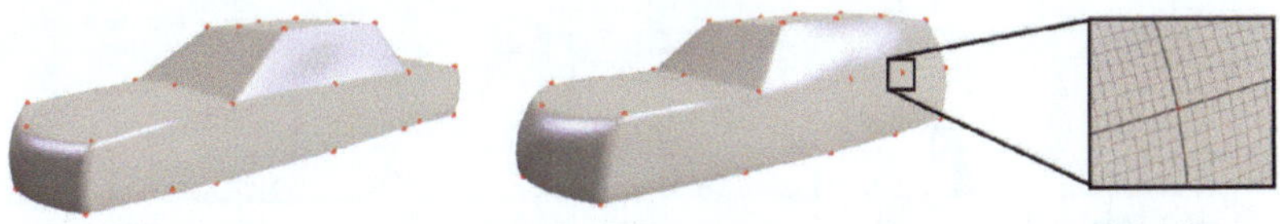

(a) Template models for sedan and hatchback class. Red dots are fiducial nodes.

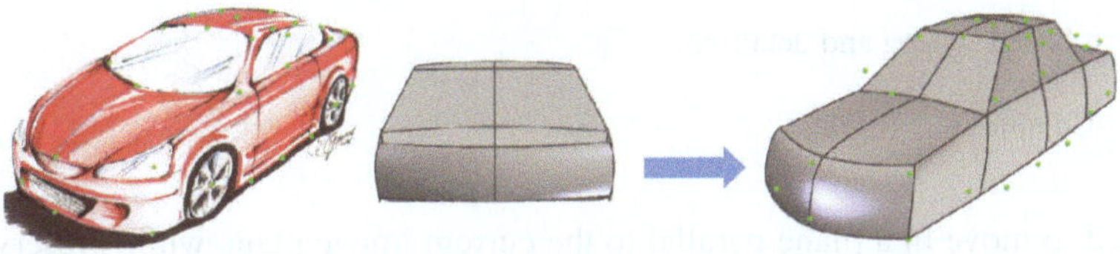

(b) Template alignment. Left: Input sketch with marked fiducial points. Middle: Initial template configuration. Right: Aligned template in relation to fiducial points.

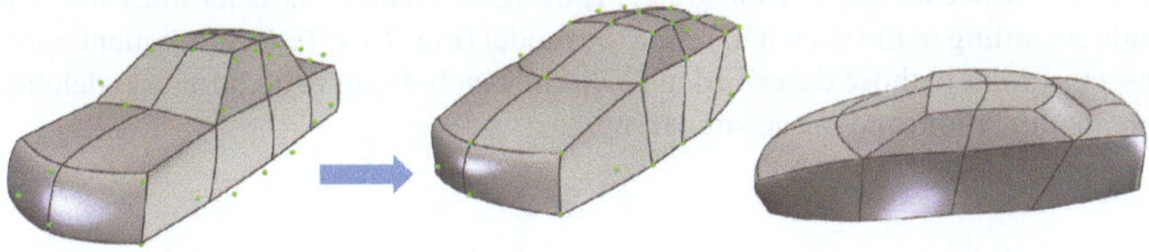

(c) Wireframe deformation. Left: Undeformed template. Middle: Deformed template. Right: Deformed template different view.

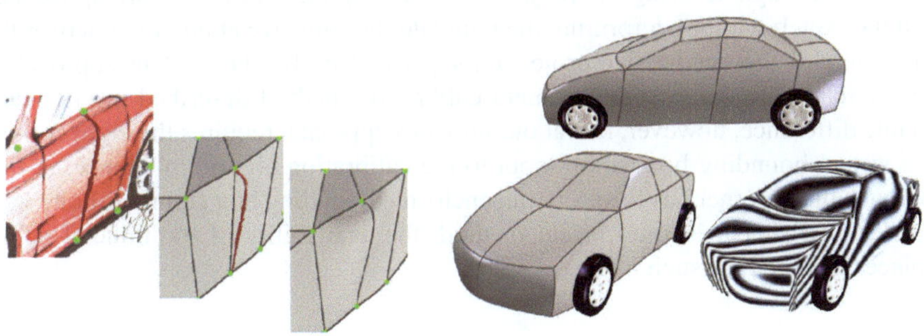

(d) Sketch-based edge modification. Left: Edge modification process. Right: Resulting template model after edge editing and node fine tuning.

Fig. 13.15 Car body design from sketches

the user may modify the template edges from other viewpoints very similar to the way described in Sect. 13.2.2. During edge modification, surface patches associated with the edges are updated instantly and automatically to match the deformed edges. When fine tuning is necessary, the designer can adjust individual node positions by a simple point-and-drag method. In the current implementation, the selected node is

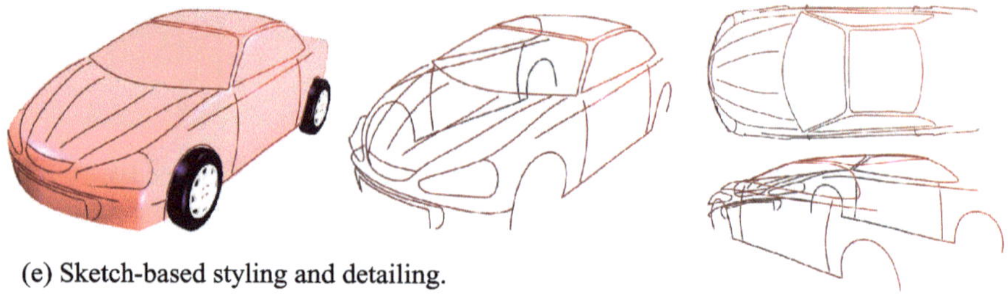

(e) Sketch-based styling and detailing.

Fig. 13.15 (Continued)

constrained to move in a plane parallel to the current image plane while preserving symmetry.

The resulting surface model provides a suitable basis for further development. Using the surface model as a substrate, the designer creates character lines and other details according to the sketch to refine the model (Fig. 13.15(e)). Subsequent operations are similar to those described in [20]. They include curve creation and deletion, curve modification, and curve smoothing.

13.3.2 Template Alignment

This step attempts to bring the projection of the template in close correspondence with the sketch without deforming the template. For this, we attempt to uncover the parameters of the perspective projection suggested in the sketch. Our approach is closely related to our previous camera calibration method described in [19]. One notable difference, however, is that our previous approach requires the eight corners of a virtual bounding box as the input to the calibration algorithm. Hence, in that approach the designer has to specify an enclosing bounding box commensurate with the sketched shape. In our current method, the availability of the fiducial points replaces the need for such a box.

13.3.3 Template Deformation Based on Fiducial Points

In this step, the fiducial nodes of the template are geometrically modified such that their projections to the image plane closely match the fiducial points marked by the designer. We model this problem as an elastic deformation problem subject to a set of constraints. The optimal 3D configuration is computed by minimizing the difference between the designer's marker points and the template fiducials, while maintaining an acceptable 3D form. We define the following optimization problem:

Let $\mathbf{V} = \{\mathbf{v}_1, \ldots, \mathbf{v}_n\} \in \mathbb{R}^3$, describe the geometric positions of the original, undeformed template nodes.

Let $\mathbf{V}' = \{\mathbf{v}'_1, \ldots, \mathbf{v}'_n\} \in \mathbb{R}^3$, describe the deformed positions of the same nodes. The goal is to compute $\mathbf{V}'$.

Let $\mathbf{F} = \{\mathbf{f}_1, \ldots, \mathbf{f}_m\} \in \mathbb{R}^2, m \leq n$, describe the screen coordinates of the fiducial points marked by the designer.

Let $\mathbf{V}'_\mathbf{s} = \{\mathbf{v}'_1, \ldots, \mathbf{v}'_m\} \subset \mathbf{V}'$, describe the corresponding set of template nodes that need to be matched to $\mathbf{F}$.

Let $\mathrm{P} : \mathbb{R}^3 \rightarrow \mathbb{R}^2$ be the mapping function that projects a point in world coordinates to screen coordinates using the current projection matrix.

We establish the following cost function to minimize:

$$H = \alpha \sum_{i=1}^{m} \|\mathbf{F}_i - \mathrm{P}(\mathbf{V}_{\mathbf{s}'_i})\| + \beta \sum_{j=1}^{n} \|\mathbf{V}_j - \mathbf{V}'_j\|.$$

The above cost function is composed of a weighted sum of (1) the cumulative 2D difference between user's fiducial points and the projections of the associated template nodes, and (2) the cumulative 3D difference between the original and deformed node positions. The first term ensures that the template is deformed into a shape that matches well with the fiducial points marked by the designer. The second term, on the other hand, ensures that the template deforms as little as possible from its original 3D configuration thus helping to maintain an acceptable geometry. The absence of the first term will fail to produce models that match the sketch since no deformation will be performed. The absence of the second term, on the other hand, can potentially result in unrealistic shapes as unnatural 3D deformations may be attempted in an effort to closely match the fiducial point in the image plane. Note that there are infinitely many deformations that would result in an exact match in the image plane. The above cost function thus helps deform the template in a way that closely matches the fiducial points, while maintaining a sound 3D shape.

Due to a difference of their domains, the two terms may differ by several orders of magnitudes and thus are not readily comparable. We thus normalize the two terms to achieve a congruent basis. Finally, the coefficients α and β control the relative weights of the terms and can be suitably adjusted. In our implementation we have found $\alpha = \beta = 0.5$ to produce satisfactory results.

Further details of the optimization problem including the optimization variables, equality and inequality constraints, and the solution technique can be found in [18].

13.3.4 Edge Representation and Manipulation

In this work, we use cubic splines as the base representation of our edges, unlike the polyline representation used in the template described in Sect. 13.2. Each edge is described in terms of its two end points and two corresponding tangent vectors. To modify an edge, the designer sketches the desired shape of the curve near the intended edge (Fig. 13.16). Using the same techniques presented in Sect. 13.2.2, an infinite virtual surface **S** originating from the eye, passing through designer's

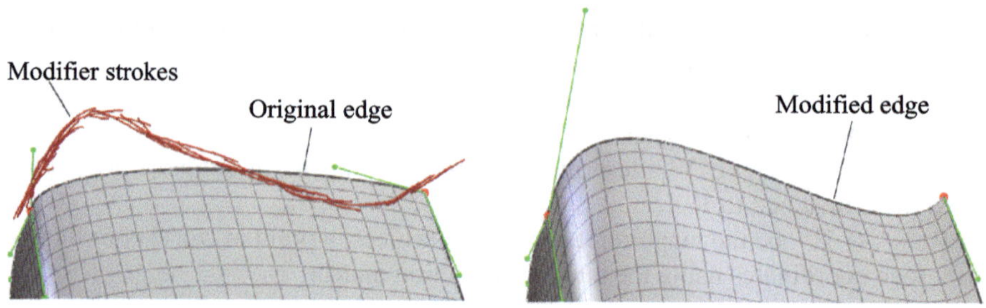

Fig. 13.16 Edge modification

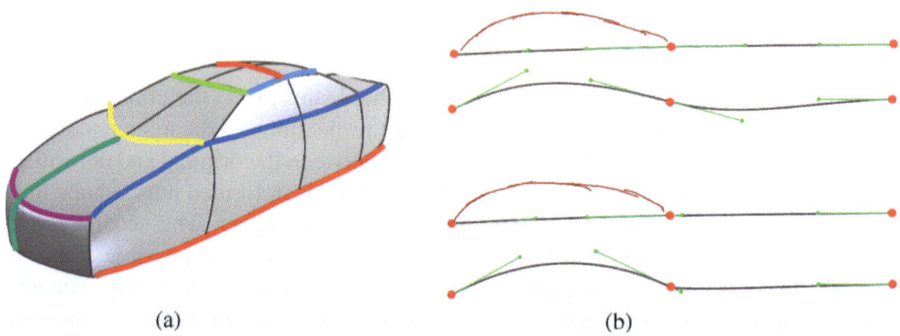

Fig. 13.17 **a** Examples of connected edges that form G^1 continuity. **b** *Top*: Edge modification causes significant changes to the neighboring edge. *Bottom*: Attenuating the influence on the neighboring edge by tangent reduction

strokes, and extending into the 3D space is constructed. This surface lies directly under the input strokes and is thus not visible from the current viewpoint.

The new edge is expected to lie on **S** while maintaining the two end points fixed. For this, we use a four-point cubic Hermite interpolation method [26]. We compute two interior edge points at parametric coordinates $u = 1/3$ and $2/3$ ($u : [0, 1]$) and project them onto **S**. The original end points and the two newly computed interior points define the new shape of the edge. The resulting cubic edge minimizes the deviation from the original edge due to the projection onto **S**. In most cases, this choice offers a reasonable solution to the inherently ill-defined problem of computing a 3D curve from 2D input. If necessary, the user may modify the edge from other viewpoints until the desired shape is achieved.

To preserve smoothness, we maintain a set of G^1 continuity constraints between edges that form the key character lines. Figure 13.17a shows example curves subject to these constraints. As a result, when the designer modifies an edge, neighboring edges will be automatically modified to reflect this continuity. During edge modification, our scheme preserves the magnitudes of neighboring edges' tangent vectors. As shown in Fig. 13.17b, this may have a notable effect on the neighboring edges if they have significantly large tangent vectors. While this can be desirable in many cases, it can also be a hindrance when the designer wants to minimize such effects

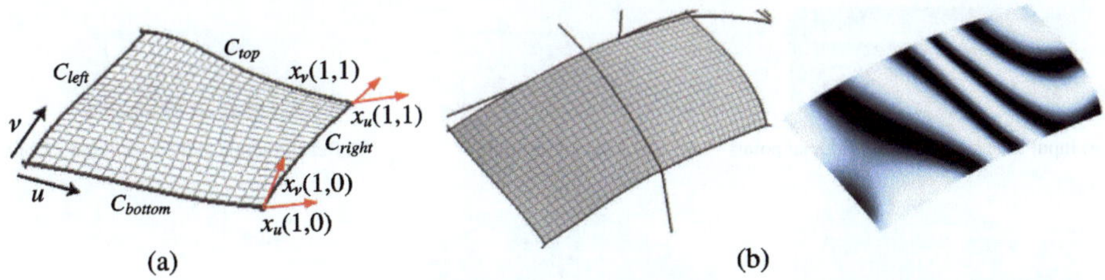

Fig. 13.18 **a** Coons patch surface representation. **b** Continuity between two surface patches

to create sharp transitions between neighboring edges. In such cases, the designer may explicitly interfere by revealing the tangent vector handles to adjust their magnitudes.

13.3.5 Surface Representation and Manipulation

The network of cubic edges gives rise to a set of face loops, which enables a natural surface representation based on parametric patches. For each face loop, we construct a bicubically blended Coons patch [8] using the four boundary edges. Figure 13.18 illustrates the idea. A key advantage of this representation is that, when a boundary edge is modified, neighboring surface patches are seamlessly adjusted with G^1 continuity to reflect the new edge shape. For further details, see [18].

The designer can use the resulting surface model as a substrate to explore specific styling ideas in 3D. For this, the designer can simply trace over the feature lines already in the sketch. The sketched curves are projected onto the underlying surface model using the techniques described in Sect. 13.2.1. The designer can then smooth or modify the newly created curves using the techniques described in Sect. 13.2.2 and those described in [20].

13.3.6 Examples

Figures 13.19 and 13.20 show example designs created using our system. In all cases, it took less than 20 minutes to obtain the displayed 3D geometry and create the styling curves.

Our experience has shown the accuracy of template alignment to be critical in the final result of 3D construction. We note that camera calibration becomes increasingly challenging for sketches that depict strong perspectives or exaggerated depictions. Additionally, the sensitivity of the optimization algorithm for points farther from the camera (where fiducial points pile together) typically causes corresponding 3D shape to be less accurate for those regions. However, this issue is often a consequence of insufficient information in the sketch, rather than a shortcoming

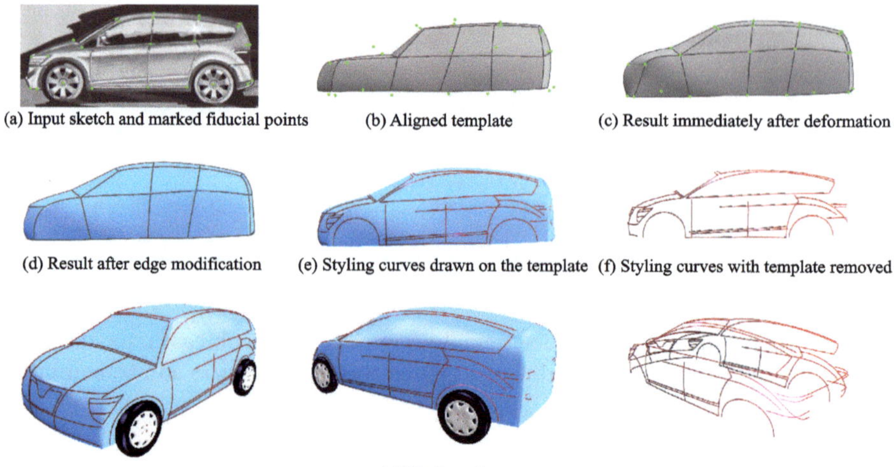

(a) Input sketch and marked fiducial points (b) Aligned template (c) Result immediately after deformation

(d) Result after edge modification (e) Styling curves drawn on the template (f) Styling curves with template removed

(g) Final results

Fig. 13.19 An example concept design

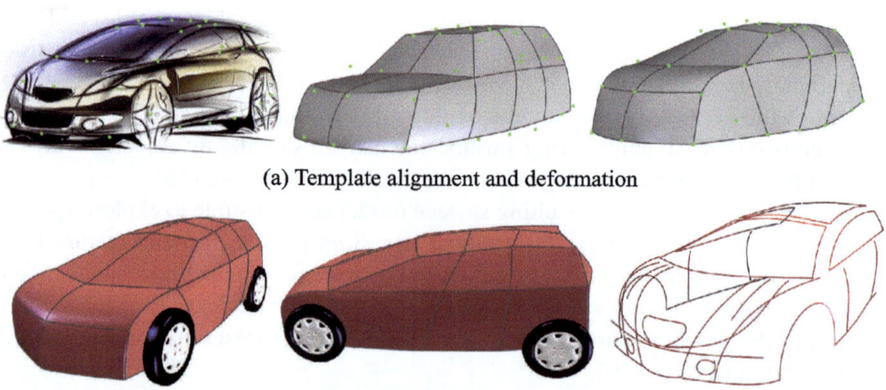

(a) Template alignment and deformation

(b) Final results

Fig. 13.20 Hatchback design

of the deformation algorithm. This can be remedied by allowing the designer to incorporate multiple sketches depicting different view of the concept, and judiciously combining the results into a single 3D geometry.

13.4 Conclusions

In this chapter, we demonstrated how a pen-based modeling system can be effectively applied to the styling design of 3D objects. Our template-based approach is tailored toward the rapid and natural design of styling features such as free-form curves and surfaces. In a typical scenario, the user first constructs the base wireframe model of the design object by sketching the initial feature curves on a very rough and simplified 3D template model. Once the initial curves comprising the wireframe are constructed, the base 3D template is removed, leaving the user with a set of 3D curves. Next, through direct sketching, the user modifies the initially created curves to give them the precise desired form. After the desired wireframe is obtained, the user constructs interpolating surfaces that cover the wireframe. Finally, using two physically based deformation tools, the user modifies the newly created surfaces to the desired shapes. Once the basic wireframe and surfaces are created, further details can be added using the same strategy of curve creation, curve modification, surface creation, and finally surface modification. The results of our user study indicate that our pen-based modeling framework is effective in providing a natural and simple means of creating 3D geometry. Most users found the ability to directly manipulate 3D curves using pen stokes to be a particularly powerful feature of our system. Our future goals include enhancing and expanding our current modeling techniques to enable a richer set of design tools for the user.

References

1. Bourguignon, D., Chaine, R., Cani, M.P., Drettakis, G.: Relief: a modeling by drawing tool. In: EUROGRAPHICS Workshop on Sketch-Based Interfaces and Modeling (2004)
2. Cherlin, J.J., Samavati, F., Sousa, M.C., Jorge, J.A.: Sketch-based modeling with few strokes. In: SCCG '05: Proceedings of the 21st Spring Conference on Computer graphics, pp. 137–145. ACM Press, New York (2005)
3. Cheutet, V., Catalano, C.E., Pernot, J.P., Falcidieno, B., Giannini, F., Léon, J.C.: 3d sketching for aesthetic design using fully free-form deformation features. Computers & Graphics **29**(6), 916–930 (2005)
4. Cohen, J.M., Markosian, L., Zeleznik, R.C., Hughes, J.F., Barzel, R.: An interface for sketching 3D curves. In: SI3D '99: Proceedings of the 1999 Symposium on Interactive 3D graphics, pp. 17–21. ACM Press, New York (1999)
5. Company, P., Contero, M., Conesa, J., Vicent, A.P.: An optimisation-based reconstruction engine for 3D modelling by sketching. Computers & Graphics **28**(6), 955–979 (2004)
6. Draper, G., Egbert, P.: A gestural interface to free-form deformation. In: Graphics Interface 2003, pp. 113–120 (2003)
7. Eggli, L., Bruderlin, B.D., Elber, G.: Sketching as a solid modeling tool. In: SMA '95: Proceedings of the Third ACM Symposium on Solid Modeling and Applications, pp. 313–322. ACM Press, New York (1995)
8. Farin, G.: Curves and Surfaces for CAGD: A Practical Guide. Morgan Kaufmann, San Francisco (2002)
9. Grimstead, I.J., Martin, R.R.: Creating solid models from single 2D sketches. In: SMA '95: Proceedings of the Third ACM Symposium on Solid Modeling and Applications, pp. 323–337. ACM Press, New York (1995)
10. Hou, K.H.: A computational method for mesh-based free-form functional surface design. Ph.D. thesis, Carnegie Mellon University (2002)
11. Hua, J., Qin, H.: Free-form deformations via sketching and manipulating scalar fields. In: SM '03: Proceedings of the Eighth ACM Symposium on Solid Modeling and Applications, pp. 328–333. ACM Press, New York (2003)
12. Igarashi, T., Matsuoka, S., Tanaka, H.: Teddy: a sketching interface for 3D freeform design. In: SIGGRAPH '99: Proceedings of the 26th Annual Conference on Computer Graphics and Interactive Techniques, pp. 409–416 (1999)

13. Ijiri, T., Owada, S., Igarashi, T.: Seamless integration of initial sketching and subsequent detail editing in flower modeling. Computer Graphics Forum **25**(3), 617–624 (2006)
14. Inoue, K.: Reconstruction of two-manifold geometry from wireframe CAD models. Ph.D. thesis, University of Tokyo (2003)
15. Kaas, M., Witkins, A., Terzopolus, D.: Snakes: active contour models. International Journal of Computer Vision **1**(4), 312–330 (1988)
16. Kara, L.B., Shimada, K.: Construction and modification of 3D geometry using a sketch-based interface. In: Eurographics Workshop on Sketch-Based Interfaces and Modeling (2006)
17. Kara, L.B., Shimada, K.: Sketch-based 3D shape creation for industrial styling design. IEEE Computer Graphics and Applications **27**(1), 60–71 (2007)
18. Kara, L.B., Shimada, K.: Supporting early styling design of automobiles using sketch-based 3D shape construction. Computer-Aided Design and Applications **5**(6), 867–876 (2008)
19. Kara, L.B., D'Eramo, C., Shimada, K.: Pen-based styling design of 3D geometry using concept sketches and template models. In: ACM Solid and Physical Modeling Conference (2006)
20. Kara, L.B., Shimada, K., Marmalefsky, S.D.: An evaluation of user experience with a sketch-based 3D modeling system. Computers and Graphics **31**(4), 580–597 (2007)
21. Karpenko, O., Hughes, J.F.: SmoothSketch: 3D free-form shapes from complex sketches. In: SIGGRAPH'06, pp. 589–598. ACM Press, Boston (2006)
22. Karpenko, O., Hughes, J.F., Raskar, R.: Free-form sketching with variational implicit surfaces. In: Eurographics (2002)
23. Kho, Y., Garland, M.: Sketching mesh deformations. In: SI3D '05: Proceedings of the 2005 Symposium on Interactive 3D Graphics and Games, pp. 147–154. ACM Press, New York (2005)
24. Masry, M., Kang, D.J., Lipson, H.: A freehand sketching interface for progressive construction of 3D objects. Computers and Graphics **29**(4), 563–575 (2005)
25. Mitani, J., Suzuki, H., Kimura, F.: 3D sketch: Sketch-based model reconstruction and rendering. In: Workshop on Geometric Modeling 2000, pp. 85–98 (2000)
26. Mortenson, M.E.: Geometric Modeling. Wiley, New York (1985)
27. Nealen, A., Sorkine, O., Alexa, M., Cohen-Or, D.: A sketch-based interface for detail-preserving mesh editing. ACM Transactions on Graphics **24**(3), 1142–1147 (2005)
28. Piegl, L., Tiller, W.: The NURBS Book, 2nd edn. Springer, New York (1997)
29. Sapidis, N.S. (ed.): Designing Fair Curves and Surfaces: Shape Quality in Geometric Modeling and Computer-Aided Design. Society for Industrial and Applied Mathematics, Philadelphia (1994)
30. Schmidt, R., Wyvill, B., Sousa, M.C., Jorge, J.A.: Shapeshop: sketch-based solid modeling with blobtrees. In: EUROGRAPHICS Workshop on Sketch-Based Interfaces and Modeling (2005)
31. Severn, A., Samavati, F., Sousa, M.C.: Transformation strokes. In: Eurographics Workshop on Sketch-Based Interfaces and Modeling, pp. 75–81. Eurographics, Vienna (2006)
32. Streit, L., Lapides, P., Sousa, M.C., Sharlin, E.: Modeling plant variations through 3D interactive sketches. In: Eurographics Workshop on Sketch-Based Interfaces and Modeling, pp. 99–106. Eurographics, Vienna (2006)
33. Turner, A., Chapman, D., Penn, A.: Sketching a virtual environment: modeling using line-drawing interpretation. In: VRST '99: Proceedings of the ACM Symposium on Virtual Reality Software and Technology, pp. 155–161. ACM Press, New York (1999)
34. Varley, P., Takahashi, Y., Mitani, J., Suzuki, H.: A two-stage approach for interpreting line drawings of curved objects. In: EUROGRAPHICS Workshop on Sketch-Based Interfaces and Modeling (2004)
35. Varley, P.A.C.: Automatic creation of boundary-representation models from single line drawings. Ph.D. thesis, Cardiff University (2003)
36. Varley, P.A.C.: Using depth reasoning to label line drawings of engineering objects. In: 9th ACM Symposium on Solid Modeling and Applications SM'04, pp. 191–202 (2004)

37. Yamada, A., Furuhata, T., Shimada, K., Hou, K.: A discrete spring model for generating fair curves and surfaces. In: PG '99: Proceedings of the 7th Pacific Conference on Computer Graphics and Applications (1999)
38. Yang, C., Sharon, D., Panne, M.v.d.: Sketch-based modeling of parameterized objects. In: EUROGRAPHICS Workshop on Sketch-Based Interfaces and Modeling (2005)
39. Zeleznik, R.C., Herndon, K.P., Hughes, J.F.: Sketch: an interface for sketching 3D scenes. In: SIGGRAPH '96: Proceedings of the 23rd Annual Conference on Computer Graphics and Interactive Techniques, pp. 163–170 (1996)

Chapter 14
Dressing and Hair-Styling Virtual Characters from a Sketch

Jamie Wither and Marie-Paule Cani

14.1 Introduction

Sketch-based modeling and edition of free form shapes has become popular in the past few years. The user typically sketches and refines a shape from different viewpoints and zoom factors. Usually assumptions are made on the nature of the resulting shape. For example: the surface generated should be a smooth, closed surface surrounding a volume of arbitrary topological genus. Inferring 3D from 2D is generally done by inflating the 2D contour of each shape component, guessing the depth of the shape in the third dimension or modifying it under the user's control.

This chapter presents a different application of sketch-based modeling: it illustrates the case when the nature of the object to be modeled is well known (modeling a mountain, a flower, a tree; or, using the examples from this chapter: modeling a garment or a hairstyle). Knowing the nature of the model the user wants to create makes things very different: all the prior knowledge we have of the object being modeled can be expressed, and used to infer the third dimension from 2D. This enables the extraction of much more information from a single sketch, which reduces the need for specifying the desired shape from several different viewpoints. In some cases, the technique can even be seen as designing a procedural model, and measuring its shape parameters on the user's sketch. 3D is then easily inferred, but the quality of the reconstruction depends on how well the sketch fits the potential outputs of the procedural model.

We illustrate the strength of these dedicated sketch-based interfaces by detailing the specific examples of designing clothing and hair for a virtual character. These

J. Wither · M.-P. Cani (✉)
Laboratoire Jean Kuntzmann, Grenoble Universities and INRIA, 655 avenus de l'Europe, 38330 Montbonnot, France
e-mail: marie-paule.cani@inrialpes.fr

Present address:
J. Wither
TTGames, Knutsford, UK
e-mail: jamie@wither.co.uk

J. Jorge, F. Samavati (eds.), *Sketch-based Interfaces and Modeling*,
DOI 10.1007/978-1-84882-812-4_14, © Springer-Verlag London Limited 2011

examples, for which several different sketch-based reconstruction techniques are presented, will help us characterize the prior knowledge that can be exploited when reconstructing a complex model from a sketch, from basic rules of thumb to more intricate geometric or physically-based properties. This will provide the basis for a general methodology for sketch-based interfaces for complex models.

Let us first emphasize the usefulness of sketch-based modeling for the specific applications described in this chapter. Modeling a garment or a hairstyle for a given character is tedious using a standard modeling system. Usually it is done in one of two ways:

- Geometrically: asking a computer artist to design the garment or hairstyle shape geometrically, such as manually modeling the shape of the garment mesh with all the folds that will make it look natural, or creating and shaping the hundreds of generalized cylinders representing the hair wisps of the character (a long process even with the multiresolution editing and style copy/past techniques of [12]). In these cases, the user gets no help from the system (the level of realism will only depend on his or her skill); animating this garment or hair will be difficult, since they are not the rest position of a physically-based model; and lastly, the same process will need to be started from scratch if another piece of clothing or another hairstyle needs to be modeled.
- Using physically-based modeling, which guarantees some degree of realism and eases subsequent animation: for garments, systems such as Maya nCloth [4] are based on the fact that a garment is a set of flat patterns sewn together, which fold due to gravity and due to collisions with the character's body. In this case the user requires some skill in tailoring in order to design and position the patterns, before a physically-based simulation is applied to compute the garment's shape; similarly for hair, using a physically-based model is possible [5] but then the designer requires hair-dressing skills since the hair will need to be wetted, cut, and shaped before obtaining the desired hairstyle.

Whichever method is used, computer artists typically spend hours designing a garment or a hairstyle. In contrast, the sketch-based interfaces presented below enable the creation of a variety of clothing and hairstyles in minutes, using intuitive sketching and annotation techniques which leverage the existing sketching skills of the artist.

The remainder of this chapter presents different solutions to sketch-based clothing and hairstyling, classified according to the nature of the prior knowledge they rely on: Sect. 14.2 presents a simple method for generating a plausible 3D garment from silhouettes and fold lines sketched over a front (and optionally back) view of a mannequin. The method for inferring 3D then simply expresses our basic understanding when we see such a sketch. Section 14.3 compares two solutions for incorporating some prior geometric knowledge, namely using the fact that a garment is a piecewise developable surface, made by assembling a set of 2D patterns; the associated folds can then be generated either procedurally or using physically-based simulation. Section 14.4 illustrates the case when a full procedural model of the object in question is available, here a static physically-based model for hair. The

Fig. 14.1 **a** A designers concept sketch. **b** The sketching interface. **c** Resulting garment

sketching interface can then be seen as a way to offer quick and intuitive control over the parameters that indirectly shape the model. Finally, Sect. 14.5 summarizes and discusses the general methodology used in these systems, namely combining procedural modeling with sketch-based interfaces to quickly design complex models.

14.2 Sketching in Distance Fields: Application to Garment Design

Clothes are as varied as the people who wear them, from a plain T-Shirt to an intricate a ball gown. An ideal sketch-based system for clothing should thus be as close as possible to the design process an artist would follow using paper and a pencil. Figure 14.1a is an image of a fashion designers concept sketch. The interface presented in this chapter [19] pictured in Fig. 14.1b closely matches this drawing process by allowing the artist to sketch the outlines and folds of a garment from a front (and optionally rear) view of a character model. The resulting inferred garment is shown in Fig. 14.1c. This section discusses the prior knowledge that can be incorporated in a sketch-based system dedicated to clothing, describes the interface and then details the method and implementation.

14.2.1 Expressing Prior Knowledge

The key to developing a simple yet expressive sketch-based interface is to carefully reduce the complexity of the problem by first asking: 'What prior knowledge of the problem domain do I possess?' and then following with 'How can I exploit this knowledge when designing the system?'. In the case of garments, the approach can be based on the simple observation they are designed relative to an underlying body. Designers often annotate a 2D view of a mannequin (see Fig. 14.1), so the interface can be based on the process of annotating a body model. One can easily observe that:

- The fit of the garment (tight/loose) from the front view is indicative of the fit from a side view.
- Garments consist of layers of cloth, and usually the cloth does not overlap itself within a layer.

Treating these observations as assumptions about the types of garments that can be modeled enables to reconstruct a whole garment from a single frontal sketch, at the price of only slightly reducing the variety of clothing that can be modeled. In particular the first assumption is the key to solving the main problem in any sketch-based interface: how to assign a third dimension (depth) to two-dimensional points along the sketched contours? The assumption above effectively states that once you know the offset of the garment from the body in the frontal plane, then you have the required offset from a side view—which is enough information to place the garment in 3D. The offset from the body at any point in space can be precalculated using a *distance field*, and then use this distance field to rapidly construct garments according to the current sketch. The second assumption gives us a hint about the type of data structures one can employ. If we assume a layer of cloth cannot overlap itself, the each layer can be represented using a *height field*.

14.2.2 The Sketch-based Interface

To keep the experience close to that of using paper and a pencil, the interface should be as unobtrusive as possible. This means minimizing the use of buttons, modifier keys and UI modes. The system uses only one mouse button (corresponding to the pen down event when using a tablet), two pen modes (drawing garment contours (the default mode) or drawing garment folds), and an optional time-saving vertical symmetry mode. Functionality while drawing is offered through gesture interpretation, which keeps the user focused on the design task.

14.2.2.1 Typical Garment Design Session

Let us now describe a typical user session in order to illustrate the whole process. An hypothetical designer, Lucy will sketch a skirt on a female model.

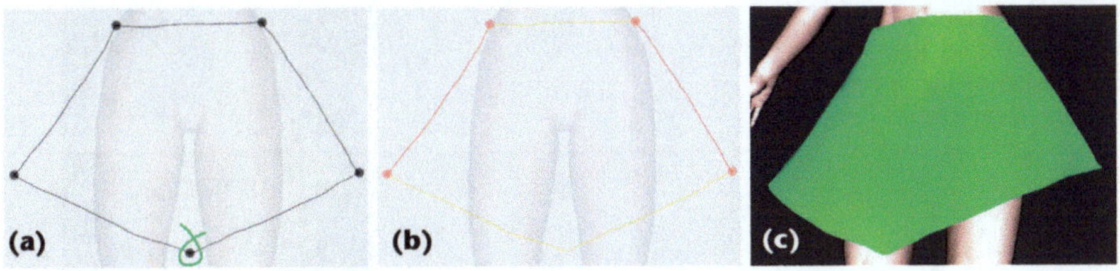

Fig. 14.2 **a** Lucy has drawn a few lines to indicate the shape of the skirt in *contour mode*; the corner-detector has detected a breakpoint that she does not want. Lucy makes a deletion gesture (a curve in the shape of an α enclosing the mistaken point) to delete it. **b** The breakpoint is deleted, and the lines have been classified: the *silhouettes* are in *red* and the *borders* in *yellow*. **c** The surface inferred by the system once Lucy requests a reconstruction

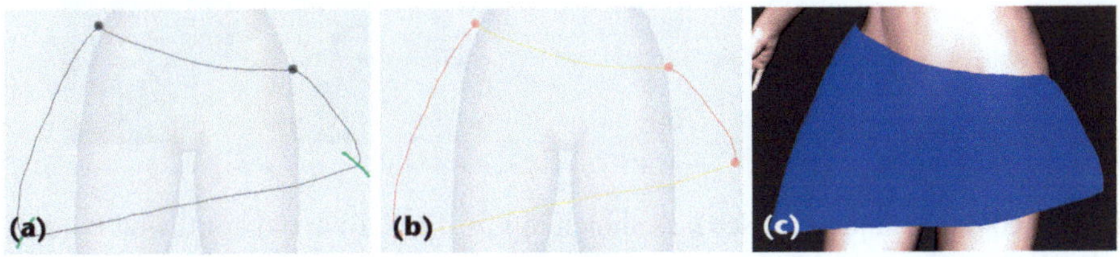

Fig. 14.3 **a** Lucy drew in *contour mode* the outline of the skirt without sharp corners at the bottom, and the corner-detector failed to put breakpoints there, she therefore gestures (overdrawn in *green* here) to indicate the need for new breakpoints, in the form of short strokes that cross the contour. **b** The new breakpoints have been inserted. **c** The reconstructed skirt

Contour Mode Lucy first draws a line across the waist (see Fig. 14.2a), indicating the top of the skirt, and then a line down the side, indicating the silhouette of the skirt, then a line across the bottom in a vee-shape indicating that she wants the front of the skirt to dip down, and finally the last side, forming a closed 2D boundary. A simple corner-detection process is applied to break the sketch into parts; one extra corner is detected by accident and Lucy can delete it with a deletion gesture. She may also add new breakpoints if required by drawing a small stroke crossing an existing contour (see Fig. 14.3). Breakpoints play an important role in the 3D positioning process (detailed later), since they determine the global 3D position of the garment with respect to the body. The two lines on the sides are classified as silhouettes, the others are classified as border lines.

Now Lucy asks to see the garment inferred by the system by pressing a button. A garment surface matching the drawn constraints and adapted to the shape of the underlying model appears almost instantly (Fig. 14.2c).

Front/Back Modes By default, the user's strokes affect both the front and back parts of the garment. Usually, most of the lines are shared by the two views. This is always the case for *silhouettes*, which by definition join the front and back parts, and it is true for the *borders* in many cases. It is, however, possible to edit front and back borders independently by toggling to the appropriate mode (with the constraint

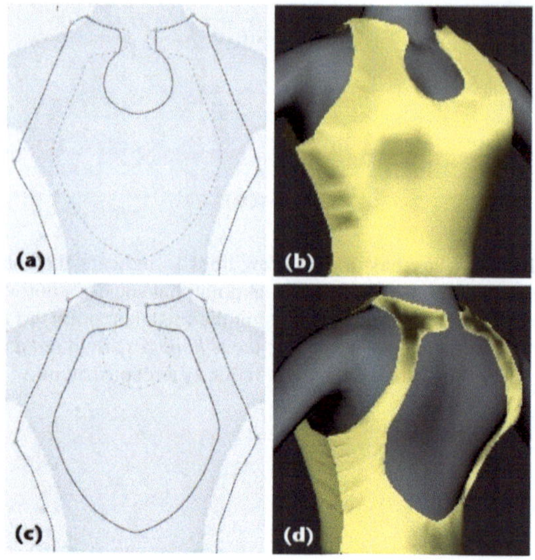

Fig. 14.4 Front (**a**, **b**) and back (**c**, **d**) of the garment. The borders of the opposite view are shown as *dashed line*

that the contour remains closed), as shown in Fig. 14.4. To avoid confusion borders belonging to the current view are rendered with a continuous stroke whereas the others appear dashed.

Vertical Symmetry. It is common for garments to exhibit vertical (i.e. left–right) symmetry. The system offers a *mirror mode* where only half the canvas is active: the other half automatically reproduces mirrored versions of the strokes.

Gestural Interface Components. The user's marks are interpreted as gestures; in *contour mode* the default stroke interpretation is to construct silhouette and border line segments. Other gestures add breakpoints for the classification process, delete breakpoints, delete a segment or an entire chain of segments, and clear all segments, as shown schematically in Fig. 14.5.

The breakpoint-deletion gesture is similar to the standard proof-reader's deletion-mark; the other deletion gestures require multiple intersections with existing strokes to prevent accidental deletions.

14.2.3 Construction of the Garment Surface in 3D

Given a set of closed 2D garment boundaries (such as the boundary in Fig. 14.5f, the technique used to generate a 3D surface consists of three main steps (described for one layer of the garment):

First, the garment boundary is segmented by classifying sections of the boundary as being one of two types:

- *Silhouette* sections exist in the same plane as the body model.

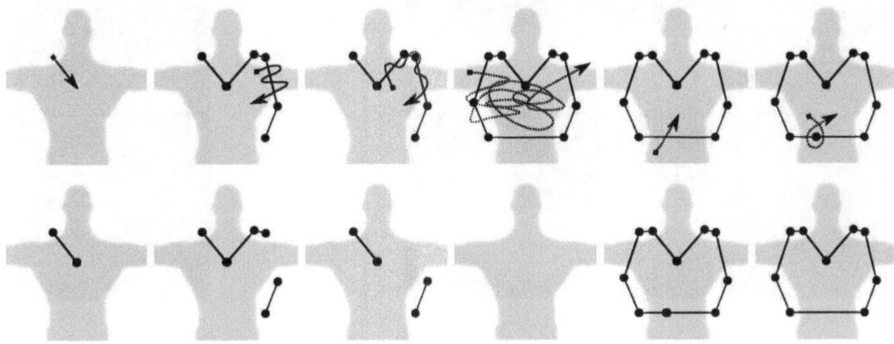

Fig. 14.5 The gestures in *contour mode*. (*Top row*) newly drawn strokes as dotted lines with an arrow. (*Bottom row*) result of stroke operation. *Black* dots are breakpoints in the boundary. **a** Adding a segment, **b** deleting a segment (intersecting scribble gesture), **c** deleting several segments, **d** clearing all segments (there must be many self-intersections), **e** adding a breakpoint, **f** deleting a breakpoint

- *Border* sections cross the projection of the body model.

Initially these sections are delimited by automatically detecting points of high curvature along the boundary and these points are denoted breakpoints (the black dots in the bottom row of Fig. 14.5), the user can add or delete them as required.

Second, these sections are placed in 3D by assigning depth information based on the basic understanding of garments already mentioned. As silhouette sections exist in the same plane as the body they are assigned a depth of zero along their interior ($z = 0$). Border sections must be assigned a depth that varies smoothly and in relation to the body. This is achieved by calculating the distance (d) of each breakpoint from the body and then interpolating this distance along the border between breakpoints. A depth that maintains this distance from the body at each point is then assigned along the interior of the section.

Third and finally, this depth information is propagated from the boundary to the interior of the garment by a diffusion process. We now have all the information required to generate a garment surface.

Many of these steps are accelerated by the use of a distance field, precalculated from the model. Let us now explain how this field is processed and then detail each step.

14.2.3.1 Distance Field

To accelerate the algorithm the distance field is precomputed when the model is first loaded. This field is a regular 3D grid which stores the closest distance to the model at each grid point (Fig. 14.6b). Distances from non-grid points can be calculated using tri-linear interpolation. The distance field is signed so that points inside the model have negative distances.

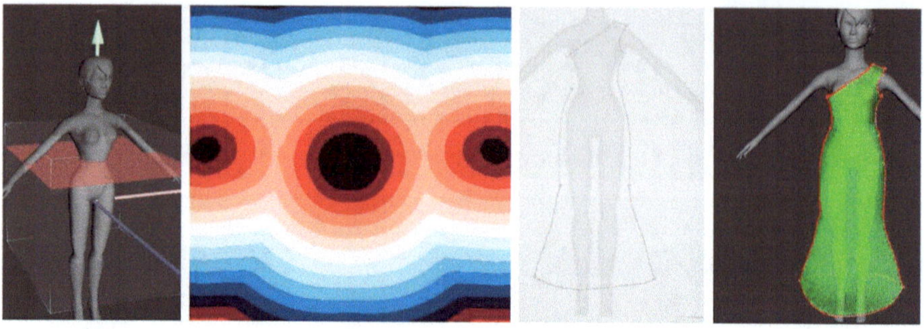

(a) (b) (c) (d)

Fig. 14.6 **a** A 2D slice through a model. **b** The corresponding isocontours of the 2D slice of the 3D distance field. **c** A garment sketch. **d** The corresponding garment surface calculated using the distance field

The system uses the distance field each time it needs to find the z-coordinate to assign to a point $p(x_0, y_0)$ to position it at a given distance from the model. This is accomplished by stepping along the ray $R(z) = (x_0, y_0, z)$ and stopping when the required distance value is reached.

14.2.3.2 Converting the 2D Contours into 3D

Once the boundary contour is complete the contour segments are classified as either *border lines* or *silhouettes* depending on whether the segments projection crosses the models projection in the xy-plane (border line) or not (silhouette). This is done efficiently using a projection mask of the body (body mask) stored in a buffer.

To position the silhouette lines in 3D the depth (z) is simply set to zero, as these lines exist in the same plane as the body, and act as seams joining the back and front layers of the garment. The d-values for interior points of the silhouette are then set to those stored in the distance field.

Having established the values of z and d along silhouette edges, this assignment is extended to the border lines. This can be done by simply interpolating d linearly along each border line, and then at each interior point search the distance field for a point with a z value which is that distance (d) from the model. All points along the contours are now in 3D, and have an associated distance to the model (d-value).

14.2.3.3 Surface Generation from 3D Contours

Just as with the contour lines, the main clue for inferring the 3D position of the interior of the garment is the interpolation of distances to the body. The process consists of propagating distance values from the boundary within the garment. A 2D buffer sized to the bounding box of the sketch is generated. Each pixel within the buffer is classified as *in*, *out* or *border* based on its position with respect to the

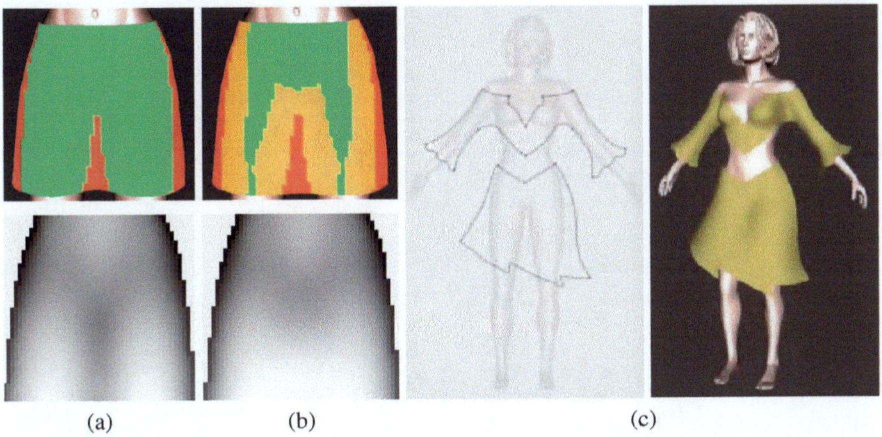

Fig. 14.7 **a** Surface reconstruction without accounting for tension. The *upper image* shows the part of the surface over the body mask in *green*. The *lower image* show the resulting z-buffer. **b** Surface reconstruction that takes tension into account. The body mask from (**a**) is eroded and the system uses Bézier curves to infer the z-values between the legs. **c** A smooth garment surface without folds

boundary. The border pixels are then assigned the distance values taken from the boundary. The goal is to minimize the distance variation inside the garment so that it fits as tightly as possible given the border constraints. The problem is posed as a Laplace equation with Dirichlet boundary conditions (see [19] for details). Let Ω be the set of inside and boundary pixels, with the boundary $\delta\Omega$. We already know $f_d^*|_{\delta\Omega}$, the pre-determined distance values on the boundary, and want to find an interpolant f_d without extrema over Ω. This interpolant satisfies the following Laplace equation:

$$\Delta f_d = 0 \quad \text{over } \Omega, \quad \text{with } f_d|_{\delta\Omega} = f_d^*|_{\delta\Omega}. \tag{1}$$

Equation (1) can be solved simply by iterating convolutions with a 3×3 neighbor averaging mask over Ω. We then convert the 2D grid to 3D by using the distance field to compute the z-values corresponding to the desired distances.

Mimicking Cloth Tension. A garment should not fit too tightly in the region between two limbs because the cloth has a tension of its own. In these cases we correct the garment surface by smoothly interpolating the limbs largest z-values, through a process of eroding the body mask and then using Bézier curves to interpolate the z-values (Fig. 14.7).

14.2.4 Drawing Folds

The garment models generated in Sect. 14.2.3 will appear artificially smooth, unlike real garments which exhibit folds under the effect of gravity. Folds may be

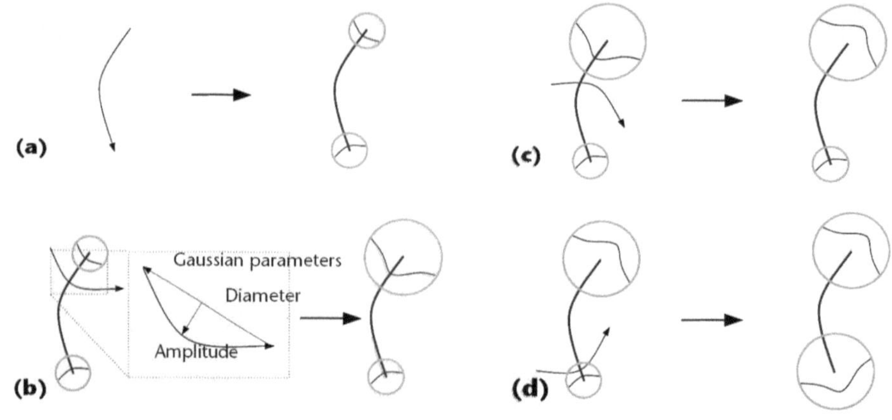

Fig. 14.8 The gestures in *folding mode*; new strokes are depicted as thin arrows. **a** adding a fold, by default a *valley*; **b** modifying the profile of the fold at one extremity (the closest to the intersection). The shape of the stroke defines both the amplitude and the width of the fold. A stroke that is convex with respect to the end point of the fold results in a *valley*; **c** conversely, a concave stroke results in a *ridge*; **d** changing the other extremity, making the fold a pure *ridge*

added automatically via physical simulation or a procedural method (discussed in Sect. 14.3.5), but an artist may wish to control precisely where folds appear. This motivates the addition of a sketch-based method for specifying such folds—a folding mode—described in this section. The fold strokes can be seen as being an annotation of another model, the newly generated garment surface model.

Folding Mode. Once satisfied with the global shape of the skirt, Lucy decides to add a few folds to obtain a more physically plausible 3D surface. To do this she simply switches to *folding mode* and draws strokes that mark the presence of either *ridges* or *valleys*, and can specify the width and amplitude of these folds in an intuitive way. The default fold type is a valley fold, but by drawing "u-shaped" gestures over either end of the stroke, the fold parameters at either end (width and amplitude) can be quickly altered (see Fig. 14.8). Fold strokes can be deleted using the same deletion gestures as used for other strokes. An example of the resulting interaction is depicted on Fig. 14.9).

To recompute the surface from the new user input, the folds are expressed as deformations to the underlying garment surface. The depth magnitude of the deformation is at a maximum along the fold stroke, and it decreases away from the stroke. The deformation's magnitude corresponds to a 2D Gaussian convolved along the stroke path. The support and the amplitude of the Gaussian at each end of the stroke are inferred from the "u-shaped" gestures and linearly interpolated along the length of the stroke. The deformations are applied to the garment surface depth map before the final mesh is created. Some final results are shown in Fig. 14.10.

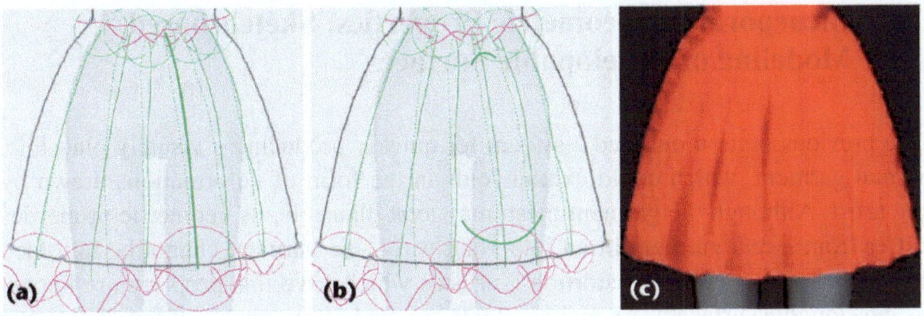

Fig. 14.9 **a** Lucy draws a few fold lines in *folding mode*, like the one highlighted in *thick green*, corresponding to *ridges* or *valleys* on the surface of the garment. **b** She may draw a "u-shaped" gesture crossing a fold line near either end. The width of the U determines the width of the fold; the depth determines the depth of the fold. The orientation of the U determines whether it is a ridge or a valley fold. These are indicated for the user at all times by a *pink* circled Gaussian profile at each end of the fold line, indicating both the width and the depth of the fold. **c** The system adds folds to the skirt

Fig. 14.10 Final results including sketched folds, each created by fashion designer Laurence Boissieux in less than five minutes

14.3 Incorporating Geometric Properties: Sketch-based Modeling of Developable Surfaces

The previous section outlined a system for quickly producing a visually plausible, virtual garment, which could exhibit folds in the form of deformations drawn by the artist. Although the garment mesh may look plausible, its geometric properties differ from a real garment in an important way—the garment cannot be unfolded flat onto a plane without distortion (surfaces which have this property are known as *developable* surfaces). As real garments are made from panels of flat cloth sewn together this geometric disparity has some implications for the virtual garment:

- Texture maps used for the garment will appear distorted.
- The behavior of the garment under a physically based simulation would appear strange. For examples folds may not fall as expected.
- It is not possible to produce a real version of the virtual garment using real cloth.

These drawbacks motivate an extension of the previous approach. In this section we present the work of [8, 17], which address these drawbacks by extending the approach in the previous section so that the produced garment model consists of a set of developable surfaces. Two different approaches are used. The first is to incrementally alter the existing garment mesh until it closely approximates a piecewise developable surface. The second is to generate a developable surface directly from sketched 3D contours. Both approaches have wider applicability than just clothing, for example they could be used in architectural modeling and engineering, where developability is an important surface property. Once the garment is finished, folds could be added in a post-process, as explained in Sect. 14.3.5.

14.3.1 Expressing Prior Knowledge

The prior knowledge in this case is that clothing is assembled from panels which have the specific geometric property of being developable. An important property of a developable surface is that when the surface normals are mapped onto a unit sphere (i.e. each surface normal is rendered as a point on the sphere) then this normal map forms a set of connected curves. This is because the normals cannot vary arbitrarily (Fig. 14.11). The generated garment surface should adhere to this additional constraint, while still respecting the user supplied boundary lines.

In order to decompose the garment into panels, some additional input is needed from the user, namely the location of seams and darts. Seams are the boundaries between the panels of cloth which assemble to form the garment. Darts are lines on the garment where different parts of the same panel were stitched together, effectively removing a section of material in order to improve the fit of the garment.

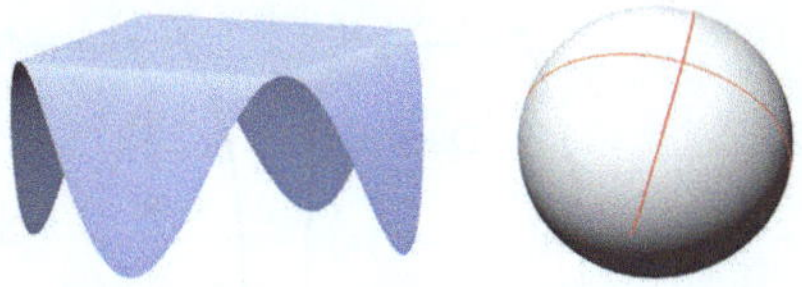

Fig. 14.11 A developable surface (*left*) and its normal map (*right*)

14.3.2 Sketching Seams and Darts

Seams and darts are a natural extension of the existing drawing method and do not require any additional modes. In the previous section breakpoints along the boundary of a garment panel would always have two associated boundary polylines (one incoming and one outgoing, we call this an order two breakpoint). With seams and darts, a breakpoint should be allowed to have one, two or three associated polylines (order one, two or three). A breakpoint with only one associated polyline can be considered to be the termination of a dart line. That dart line would have to begin at an order three breakpoint, somewhere on the panel boundary. Of course darts are only valid on the interior of a garment panel boundary. If a dart is extended to rejoin the panel boundary (so that it begins and ends with order three breakpoints) then that panel is split into two separate sub-panels, and the dart has become a seam (Fig. 14.12).

We now outline the two methods of producing a set of developable panels which respect the 3D boundaries, seams and darts inferred from the users sketch.

14.3.3 Creating a Developable Surface via Approximation

This method generates an initial surface using the same distance field method outlined in Sect. 14.2. This surface consists of a set of panels connected at the seams. The approach is to then incrementally modify each panel to bring it closer to being an ideal developable surface, without deviating too far from the input surface. The approach used is inspired by moving least squares approximation [14]. The algorithm follows a two-step procedure for each step of the iteration:

- For each triangle on the surface, find the best-fitting developable surface and move the triangle onto that surface. This breaks the triangle connectivity.
- Then reconnect the triangles, while trying to preserve the new triangle normals and positions.

Each pass of the algorithm further improves the developability of the approximation, at the price of deviating further from the original surface. With each pass the normal map of the garment onto the unit spheres moves closer to the ideal case of a network of curves (Fig. 14.13). Once the desired level of developability is reached, the surface panels are unfolded onto the plane to produce the garment patterns (Fig. 14.14). Unfolding is done using the angle-based flattening (ABF++, [18]) method which minimizes shearing.

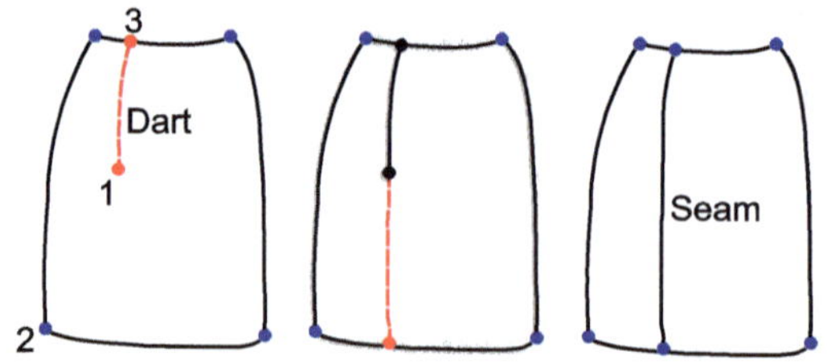

Fig. 14.12 The user extends an existing skirt outline with a dart (*left*). The numbers refer to the order of the adjacent breakpoint. The dart is extended to meet the outline again *(middle)* forming two panels joined by a seam (*right*)

14.3.4 Creating a Developable Surface Directly from the 3D Boundary Lines

The approximation method in the previous section produces reasonable results which suffice for non-distorted texture mapping, but the result will rarely be analytically developable, which is a problem when the results are to be used in manufacturing. A more elegant solution than generating a non-developable surface and then approximating it would be to generate the developable surface directly. The system we will now describe [17] models general developable surfaces using the 3D boundaries directly and so requires less user input and less user expertise than most existing techniques. The same input technique is used (annotating an existing model), except that the user may smooth and also deform existing 3D contours if desired by redrawing them from a different viewpoint.

The method of generating a developable surface from a 3D boundary assumes the input boundary is a piecewise smooth curve. This curve is sampled to produce a polyline. A *boundary triangulation* (a manifold triangulation with no interior vertices) is then generated, using this polyline as its boundary. By construction, any boundary triangulation is developable as the triangles can be unfolded onto the plane with no distortion. The system requires additionally that the majority of the boundary triangulations interior edges should be locally convex, to ensure a close approximation to a smooth developable surface (see [17] for details). This condition forms the basis of the method: since most edges of a desirable triangulation must be locally convex, a natural place to identify developable regions interpolating a boundary polyline is the *convex hull* of the boundary, where every edge is locally convex.

Hence the method proceeds recursively, by taking the convex hull of the polyline, dividing regions where the polyline lies on the convex hull into two *envelope triangulations* (Fig. 14.15a, b, c). When the polyline does not lie on the convex hull, the hull is subdivided into charts (sets of hull triangles having certain properties) and the algorithm proceeds recursively on these charts (see Fig. 14.16). This leads to a number of possible valid surfaces from which the desired result must be selected. The search is guided automatically by testing envelope triangulations for desirability using metrics such as smoothness and surface fairness. It can also be guided manually by the user who can choose between the visual representations of the results at

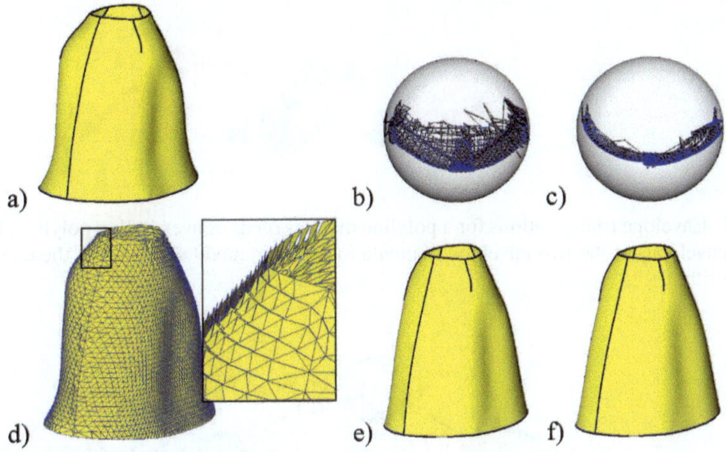

Fig. 14.13 Developable approximation stages: **a** input; **b** normal map of the front panel; **c** normal map after transformation; **d** mesh triangles after transformation, with a closed view showing the discontinuities temporarily created; **e** glued mesh after one iteration; **f** mesh after three iterations. Between one and three iterations the distortion decreases

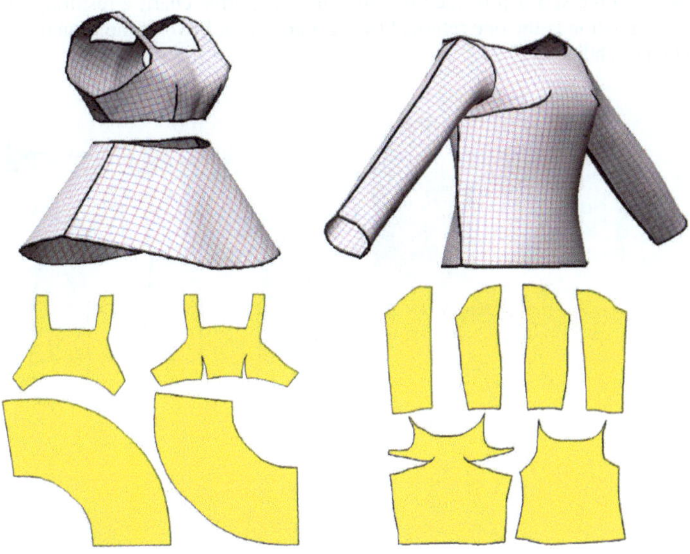

Fig. 14.14 Resulting texture mapped developable surfaces and corresponding patterns

each stage in the recursion. Results such as the shoe in Fig. 14.17 demonstrate the modeling complexity achievable via this approach.

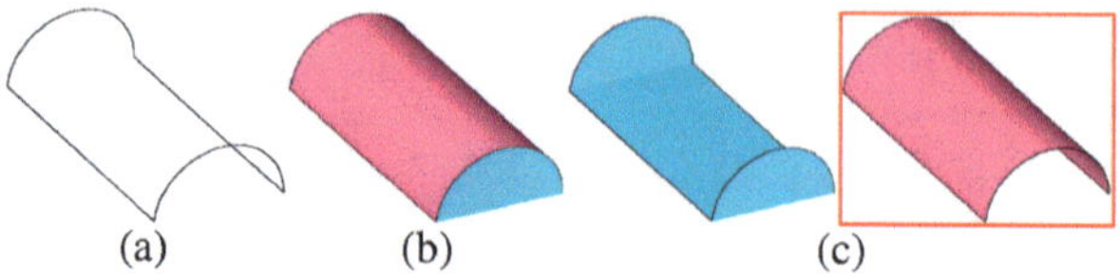

Fig. 14.15 Envelope triangulations for a polyline that lies on its convex hull: **a** polyline; **b** convex hull with envelopes; **c** the two envelope triangulations, the framed (*right*) one is the one selected by the algorithm

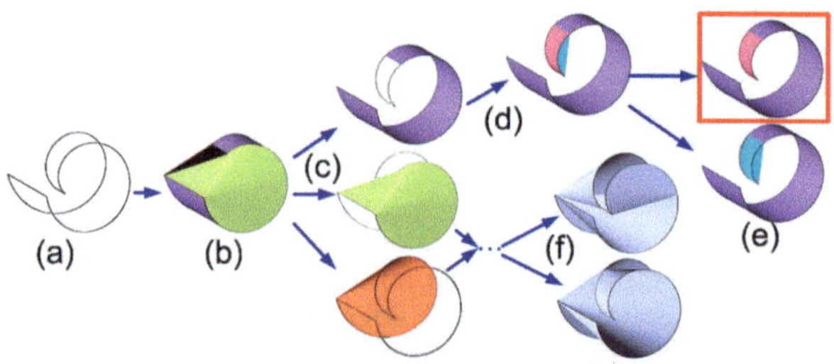

Fig. 14.16 Extracting a locally convex triangulation: **a** boundary; **b** convex hull with extracted charts (interior triangle shown in *black*) **c** individual charts and remaining subloops after subtraction; **d** recursing on the subloop formed by removing the purple chart; **e** resulting triangulations (the framed triangulation is the one returned by the algorithm); **f** two of the triangulations created with different chart choices

Fig. 14.17 Developable helmet, shoe and garments generated from their 3D boundaries

14.3.5 Automatic Generation of Folds

Once again the virtual clothing does not look realistic without folds. However using the sketching method of forming folds described in Sect. 14.2.4 would destroy the developable property of the garment surfaces. Fortunately the systems we just presented generate the 2D patterns for the garments, so automatic methods to generate folds can be used. We briefly outline two approaches: a time-consuming but realistic physically-based simulation, and a quicker but more limited procedural simulation of folds.

14.3.5.1 Physically-based Simulation of Folds

The dress in Fig. 14.17 is the result of taking the developable garment generated directly from the boundary curves and using a physical cloth simulation [3] to generate folds. Physical cloth simulations are usually based on modeling the garment as a grid of small masses interconnected by springs. Body collisions are taken into account as correcting forces acting on the cloth. The simulations can be time consuming, but with some expertise in setting the physical parameters very realistic results are possible.

14.3.5.2 Procedural Generation of Folds

The garments in Fig. 14.18 were generated using a procedural method based on prior knowledge [8]: the main observation is that when cloth is wrapped around a cylindrical object (such as a torso or an arm) and compressed or twisted, it exhibits characteristic buckling patterns, such as diamond shaped folds under compression. These patterns can be automatically reproduced by fitting a *buckling mesh* to the 2D garment patterns. This mesh embeds the diamond patterns and the diagonal folds formed by twisting. The buckling mesh is placed in 3D using the correspondence between the 3D garment model and its 2D patterns. When the 3D bucking mesh is deformed via compression or twisting it is constrained to buckle along its major directions, thus forming the desired folding patterns (Fig. 14.18). This efficient method can be implemented in realtime, and produces realistic looking folds, although it is limited to pre-determined types of fold.

14.4 Sketch-based Interface for a Physically-based System: Hairstyle Design from a Sketch

In the previous sections prior knowledge of the object being modeled was used to simplify the problem and guide the design of the interface. In this section some of the prior knowledge is already expressed concisely for us in the form of a physically-based model for a strand of hair. The problem becomes extracting the parameters

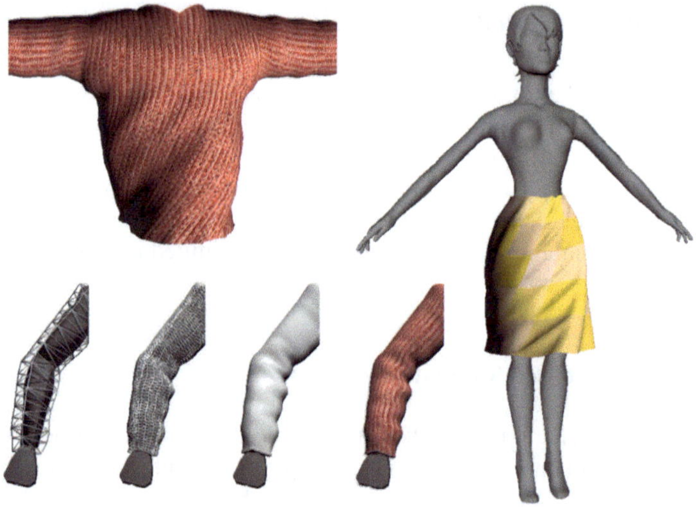

Fig. 14.18 Procedural folding of a developable garment [8]. The buckling control mesh is shown around the arm (*bottom left*)

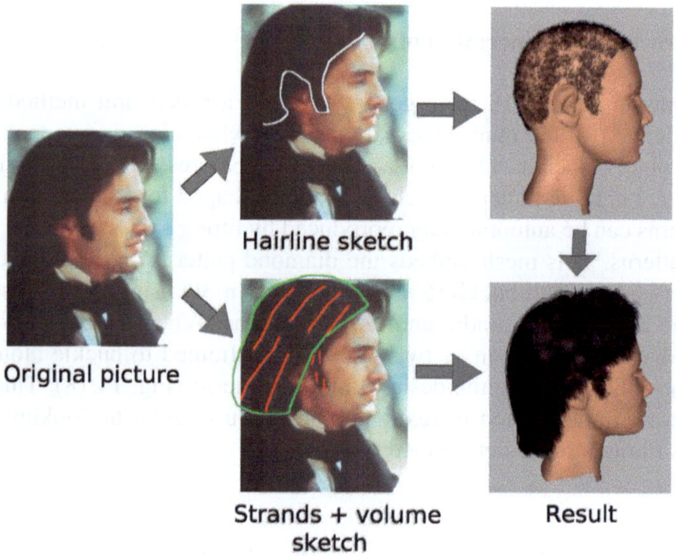

Fig. 14.19 An overview of the whole process

required to drive this model, and then to generalize to a whole head of hair. See Fig. 14.19.

14.4.1 Expressing Prior Knowledge

The work of [5, 6] presents a physically-based method for modeling a strand of human hair (called Super-Helices), a method of modeling a full head of hair using this model and a hair-styling methodology based on a simulated hair dressing process (wetting, cutting and drying). The model determines the shape of a hair by incorporating a number of geometrical shape constraints on a series of elastic rods. A simple way to visualize the model is to consider a strand of hair as consisting of a series of helical shapes. The model requires a number of parameters (detailed later) and can incorporate collisions and the effect of gravity due to being expressed in terms of an energy minimization problem. This combination of ideas produces convincing 3D virtual hairstyles, but the styling process is time consuming (at least 30 minutes per hairstyle, as each wisp of hair requires many parameters to be set by hand) and requires some hairdressing expertise from the user.

The aim is to simplify the hair-dressing process using a sketch-based interface. The problem becomes deriving the parameters needed to drive this physically-based model from a simple sketch. This can be done using the prior knowledge that:

- Hairs clump together in wisps, which can be modeled using a *guide strand.*
- A guide strand can be modeled as a series of helical shapes.
- Neighboring wisps tend to exhibit similar properties.
- Hairstyles are often symmetrical, and a side view displays most of the variety.

The first observation was used in [5]. The idea of an individual hair being modeled as a series of helical shapes leads to the approach of extracting helical parameters from a sketch of an example guide strand from a side view. The observation that neighboring wisps are similar leads to the use of interpolation between the parameters controlling each guide strand, so that the properties of the wisps can gradually vary across the head, and do not need to be explicitly specified for all wisps. Finally, because hairstyles are often symmetrical (when viewed from the front), and because a side view captures most of the detail of the style, the user can be allowed to sketch from a side view only. This limits the complexity of the interface while still enabling the user to draw strokes in the important regions of the head (fringe, side and back).

We now describe the interface and then detail the method and implementation.

14.4.2 The Sketch-based Interface

This work [21] represents the first sketch-based interface for physically-based hair styling. The user is presented with two views of a model head. The left view is the sketch input area which consists of a (zoomable) side projection of the head. The right view is the result area within which the camera can be moved freely. An image may be loaded as a background to be used as a guide for oversketching (Fig. 14.20). The color used to render the hair can be selected from the pixels in the photograph. The user progresses through three simple modeling stages:

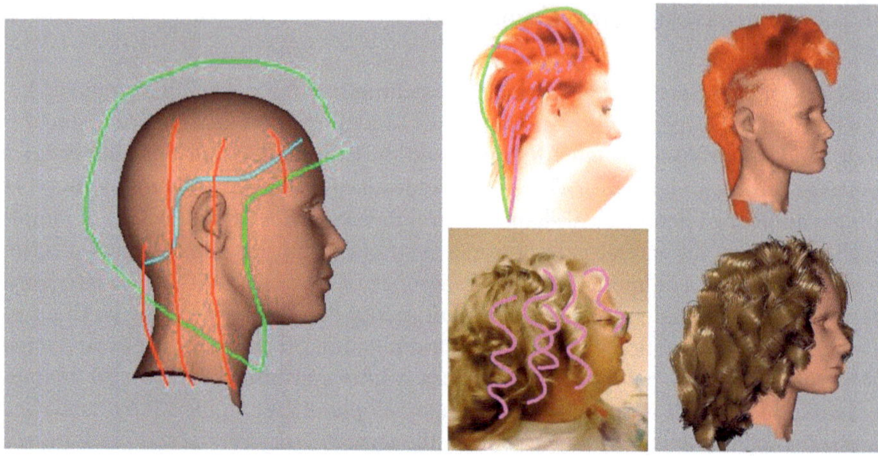

(a) (b)

Fig. 14.20 **a** The basic stroke types. Hairline (*blue*), example strands (*red*) and volume/cut (*green*). **b** Styles resulting from the annotation of photographs (photo 'Flaming Hair' ©DH Kong)

Hairline The user first defines the scalp area by drawing one stroke delimiting the scalp extent on one side of the head. The other side is deduced via symmetry. The user can redraw this stroke until happy with the resulting scalp shape, at which point the shape is fixed for the remainder of the modeling process. The scalp is initially covered with short, straight hair.

Example Strands The user may then draw example hair strands starting anywhere within the newly defined scalp area. These examples can be redrawn or deleted. Each time an example is drawn a similar physically modeled strand is immediately created or updated in the corresponding location on the head in the result viewport. At any point the user may calculate and render a full head of hair based on the example strands.

Volume and Cut Finally the user may draw a volume stroke, which is used to both alter the global volume of the style and to cut the hair if desired.

14.4.3 Shaping the Hair in 3D

This section details the process of extracting from a 2D sketch the parameters required to construct a full head of hair in 3D.

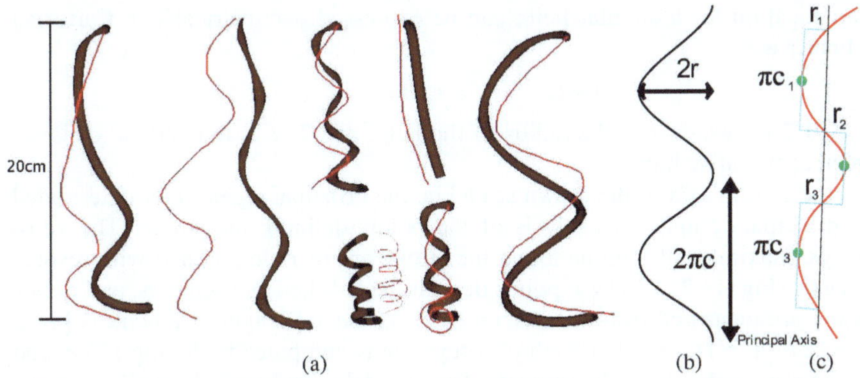

Fig. 14.21 **a** Single strands inferred from sketches (*thin lines*): the sketch is interpreted as an example of the desired shape, and the system generates similar, physically-based 3D strands (*thick lines*). **b** The orthogonal projection of a circular helix, and the measurements which can be made on it. **c** Inferring the length of a stroke using half helical segments

14.4.3.1 Determining Helical Parameters

The system makes the assumption that when a user draws an example hair strand, he is drawing the side view projection of a 3D strand of hair hanging from a head under the influence of gravity. The user is assumed to draw the stroke along a roughly straight axis. This idea is to generate 3D hair strands which 2D projection are *similar*, but not necessarily *exactly* the same as the sketched strand. In other words, the user input is interpreted as *examples* of the sort of hair strands he would like to see in the final model.

The strand parameters required by the physical model of [5] are length l, natural curvature κ_0, ellipticity e and stiffness k. The ellipticity stands for the shape of the strand's cross-section, which affects the distribution of curls along a strand hanging under gravity: elliptical cross-sections (non-zero ellipticity) produce curls evenly distributed along the strand (such as in African hair); circular cross-sections (zero ellipticity) produce strands which tend to be straight at the top and curly at the bottom. The last parameter, stiffness, controls how strongly the hair fiber tends to recover its natural curliness, and thus how much curliness balances the effect of gravity. Although this parameter value can be measured on natural hair, curls can be made stiffer using styling products, so stiffness needs to be inferred from the sketch to allow for this effect.

As shown in [5] and depicted in Fig. 14.21a, hair strands under gravity tend to take helical shapes at rest, where the helical parameters vary along the strand. This key observation can be used to infer parameters from a sketched 2D example of a hair strand. The idea is to divide the stroke into segments and model each segment as the projection of a half helix. Measurements are made on these small segments and the equations describing a helix is used to infer the length and curvature required by the strand model.

The equation for a circular helix can be expressed parametrically in Cartesian coordinates as:

$$x = r\cos(t) \qquad y = r\sin(t) \qquad z = ct$$

for $t \in [0, 2\pi)$, where r is the radius of the helix and $2\pi c$ is the vertical distance between consecutive loops.

Let the central axis of the drawn strand be the principal eigenvector determined using principal component analysis of the points defining the stroke. The zero-crossings, maxima and minima along the stroke are then determined with respect to this axis (Fig. 14.21c). These points delimit the half helical segments, and radius (r) and c are measured from these segments. As the arc length of a helix is given by $s = (\sqrt{r^2 + c^2})\,t$, the 3D length of a segment is computed by letting $t = \pi$ and using the r measured from the segment. Summing the arc length from all segments gives us an estimate for the length of the hair strand in 3D. The natural curvature κ_0 of the hairstrand is estimated as being $1/\max(r)$ measured from the set of all segments.

Ellipticity is set from the distribution of maxima and minima along the drawn strand. If they are to be positioned toward the end of the drawn strand then curls form at the end of the strand, which implies a low ellipticity. If they are more evenly distributed then it implies a high ellipticity.

The stiffness and mass of the strand are determined by solving an optimization problem. The span of a strand of hair is the distance between the root and the tip. Given the previously determined length and curvature and fixing a reasonable mass, stiffness is allowed to vary, in order to minimize the difference between the span of the drawn example and the span of the 3D model. This allows the user to set much higher values of stiffness than would be found in natural hair (but could be caused if hair spray was used, for example). Figure 14.21a shows the drawn examples and the resulting 3D models.

14.4.3.2 Generalizing to a Full Head of Hair

At least 30 wisps are required to generate a realistic looking head of hair, however the user should not be required to draw an example strand for every wisp. Instead, the information from the few examples the user provide is extrapolated. When only one example is provided, the same parameters are used everywhere. If two or more examples are provided an interpolation scheme is used. Consider a vertical plane bisecting the head model and passing through the nose. All wisp root positions are projected onto this plane (each wisp giving a point P_n).

If two examples are provided then a line is formed on this plane between the two projected example root positions. For each wisp the closest point on this line to P_n is found and used to linearly interpolate between the parameters of the two example strands.

If three examples are provided then a Delaunay triangulation of the projected example root positions is generated. Barycentric coordinates are then used to interpolate between example strand parameters. P_n outside the triangulation are projected to the nearest point on the triangulation.

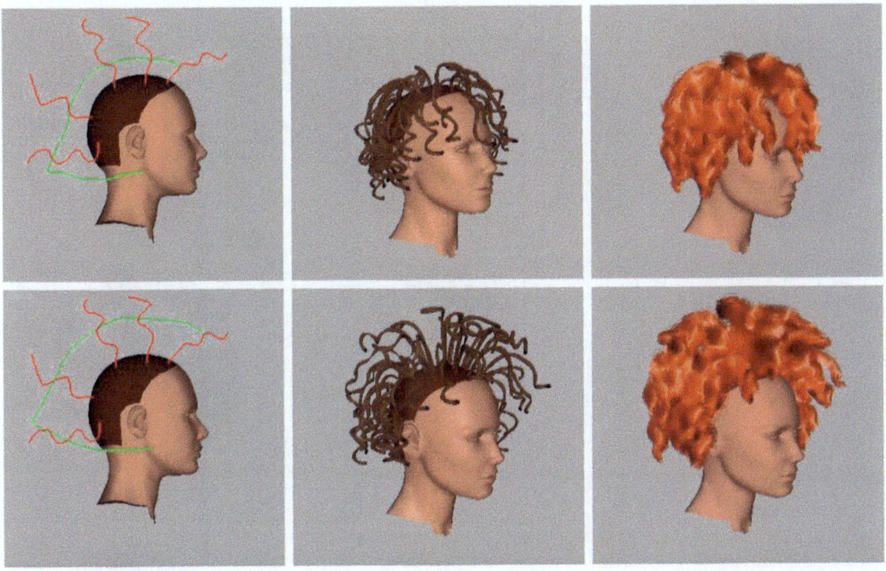

Fig. 14.22 The effect of increasing the size of the volume stroke. Note the hairs at the back of the head have been cut where they extend below the stroke

14.4.3.3 Setting the Volume, Adjusting the Cut

The volume of the overall hairstyle is a useful global parameter which should be simple to specify. The global shape of the hair is also often determined by the length of the 'cut'. To allow control over both these aspects with one simple stroke a 'volume stroke' is introduced (Fig. 14.22). With this stroke the user roughly indicates the outer boundary for the silhouette of the hairstyle. The part of the stroke above the scalp is used to determine the volume of the hairstyle, the part of the stroke below the scalp is used to trim hairs which intersect the stroke.

The hair volume is controlled using the multiple layer hulls model of [13]. In this model hair strands with roots higher up the head are tested for collisions against larger offsets of the head model. The volume is set via a hair volume scaling factor. This factor is determined by calculating the distance from the head model (using a precalculated distance field) of each point of the volume stroke above the lowest point of the scalp model. The maximum of these offsets is used to determine a suitable hair volume scaling factor.

To determine which hairs to cut, the sections of the volume stroke with normals pointing roughly upward are projected onto the modeled wisps. Any hairs which intersect are but back to their length at this intersection point. Some final results are depicted in Fig. 14.23.

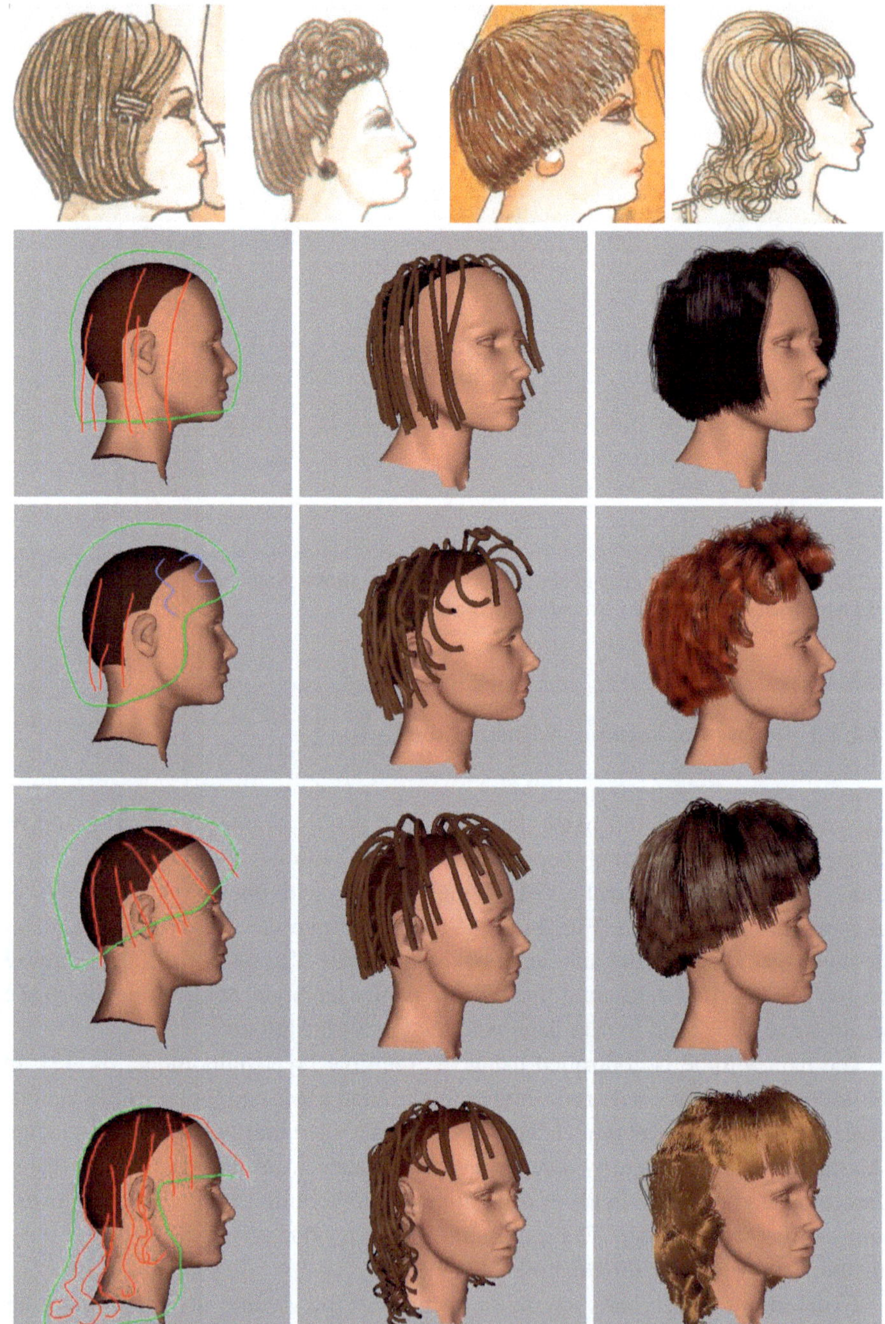

Fig. 14.23 Styles from 1927, 1945, 1965 and 1971. *Top*: Drawings from [16]

14.5 Discussion and Concluding Remarks

Modeling realistic cloth and hair for virtual characters is a burden with standard interfaces. In contrast, the sketching systems presented in this chapter enable to do it a very intuitive manner, through a single sketch similar to those used in fashion design. The process only takes a few minutes. Moreover, the method increases realism thanks to the a priori knowledge is used to infer 3D. To design garments and hair that fit a given mannequin, the systems we presented use annotation of 2D views of the mannequin model. The user quickly sketches the silhouette of garments over front or back views, with the options to sketch the folds as well or to generate them procedurally. The system results in both the 3D shape of the garment and the 2D patterns that can be used to sew it, or be input to a physically-based system for subsequent animation. In the case of hair modeling the user sketches a scalp contour and some example hair strands (varying from straight to curly), from which the parameters of the physically-based hair model are inferred; he may simply add a volume stroke to further specify the hair cut and volume. The resulting 3D head of hair is then ready to be animated.

More interestingly, these systems illustrate the fact that sketch-based modeling can effectively be used in very complex cases, granted that the right amount of prior knowledge is incorporated (similar to a human recognizing a garment or hairstyle from a sketch and inferring the full 3D shape). Note that a similar methodology for the rapid creation of 3D models has already been used in a number of other cases, from architectural sketching systems [9], to systems for sketching terrain [7, 20], trees [15, 22], plants and flowers [1, 2, 11] or human faces [10].

All these systems differ in the amount of prior knowledge they use. In the examples we discussed, several levels of knowledge were incorporated, from rules of thumb, to mathematical properties of surfaces (the piecewise developability of garments) and physical properties (expressed through a static strand model for hair). The associated sketching systems range between two extremes: starting from the way people would sketch the element in real life, and trying to incorporate just the necessary amount of knowledge to adequately infer 3D; or instead designing an intuitive interface for a standard generic, procedural model. Note that the latter requires some kind of inverse engineering to compute the parameters that indirectly control the shape of the model. In the system we presented for hair the sketch is seen as a rough example, and is not required to exactly match the results.

Can we identify a general methodology for creating sketch-based interfaces for complex models where some prior knowledge is available? Certainly there are some common themes:

Mapping to a Procedural Model Does an effective procedural model already exist for the thing you are modeling? Perhaps the parameters for this model can be extracted from a sketch. Which parameters have the largest effect on the resulting model? These are the ones which are most important, some of the others could perhaps be fixed (for example, mass per unit volume was fixed to an average natural value in the case of hair, length and curvature were the most important parameters).

Simplifying Assumptions Choose your assumptions carefully. You can often reduce the complexity of the problem by a large margin, while only slightly reducing the variety of results possible. For example deciding that layers of clothing may not self-overlap, or in the case of hair, limiting the drawing to a side projection only.

Non-intrusive Sketching Interface All tools which model themselves on the traditional pencil-and-paper workflow should try to hide the details of the interface, so as not to interrupt the user while they concentrate on the task in hand. For example minimizing the number of mode switches required, and making sure that when they are required they occur at a natural pause in the thought process. Switching from the front to back view of the garment does not interrupt the workflow, as the user naturally refocuses their attention at this stage—but requiring selection of a breakpoint and pressing the deletion key would be inappropriate for breakpoint deletion—hence the use of a gesture, which keeps the user focus on the virtual page.

Sketching vs. Annotation Finally, the sketching systems we presented not only illustrate sketching, but also the annotation of a 3D shape serving as a support for the sketch (here, a mannequin). Relying on the 3D information from the mannequin in addition to the prior knowledge makes sketching from a single viewpoint sufficient and thus makes the process much quicker, although other views can easily be added, for example to model the back and front of a garment, or a non-symmetric hairstyle. Further support shapes for annotation may be generated during the process. For example the initially generated garment surface served as a further support model for sketching folds. The method of successive 'coatings' of a base surface could be useful for other situations (such as sketching vegetation or features onto terrain).

Acknowledgements Thanks to all our collaborators on sketch-based interfaces for garments and hair: Florence Bertails, Laurence Boissieux, Philippe Decaudin, John Hughes, Dan Julius, Kenneth Rose, Boris Thibert, Emmanuel Turquin and Alla Sheffer. Thanks to the Marie-Curie Project *Visitor* for funding this research.

References

1. Anastacio, F., Sousa, M.C., Samavati, F., Jorge, J.: Modeling plant structures using concept sketches. In: Non Photorealistic Animation and Rendering (NPAR), Annecy, France (2006)
2. Anastacio, F., Prusinkiewicz, P., Sousa, M.C.: Sketch-based parameterization of l-systems using illustration-inspired construction lines. In: Eurographics Workshop on Sketch-Based Interfaces and Modeling, Annecy, France (2008)
3. Autodesk: 3dsmax (2008). http://autodesk.com/3dsmax
4. Autodesk: Maya nCloth (2008). http://autodesk.com/maya
5. Bertails, F., Audoly, B., Querleux, B., Leroy, F., Lévêque, J.L., Cani, M.P.: Predicting natural hair shapes by solving the statics of flexible rods. In: Dingliana, J., Ganovelli, F. (eds.) Eurographics (Short Papers). Eurographics (2005)
6. Bertails, F., Audoly, B., Cani, M.P., Querleux, B., Leroy, F., Lévêque, J.L.: Super-helices for predicting the dynamics of natural hair. In: Proceedings of SIGGRAPH (2006)
7. Cohen, J., Hughes, J., Zeleznik, R.: Harold: A world made of drawings. In: Non Photorealistic Animation and Rendering (NPAR), Annecy, France (2000)

8. Decaudin, P., Julius, D., Wither, J., Boissieux, L., Sheffer, A., Cani, M.P.: Virtual garments: A fully geometric approach for clothing design. Computer Graphics Forum (Eurographics'06 Proc.) **25**(3) (2006)
9. Google Sketchup (2008). http://sketchup.google.com/
10. Gunnarsson, O., Maddock, S.: Sketching faces. In: Eurographics Workshop on Sketch-Based Interfaces and Modeling (2008)
11. Ijiri, T., Owada, S., Okabe, M., Igarashi, T.: Floral diagrams and inflorescences: interactive flower modeling using botanical structural constraints. ACM Transactions on Graphics **24**(3), 720–726 (2005)
12. Kim, T.Y., Neumann, U.: Interactive multiresolution hair modeling and editing. ACM Transactions on Graphics **21**(3), 620–629 (2002) Proceedings of ACM SIGGRAPH 2002
13. Lee, D.W., Ko, H.S.: Natural hairstyle modeling and animation. Graphical Models **63**(2), 67–85 (2001)
14. Levin, D.: The approximation power of moving least-squares. Mathematics of Computation **67**(224), 1517–1531 (1998)
15. Okabe, M., Owada, S., Igarashi, T.: Interactive design of botanical trees using freehand sketches and example-based editing. Computer Graphics Forum (Proceedings of Eurographics) (2005)
16. Peacock, J.: La Mode du XX Siecle. Thames & Hudson (2003)
17. Rose, K., Sheffer, A., Wither, J., Cani, M.P., Thibert, B.: Developable surfaces from arbitrary sketched boundaries. In: Eurographics Symposium on Geometry Processing. Eurographics (2007)
18. Sheffer, A., Lévy, B., Mogilnitsky, M., Bogomyakov, A.: ABF++ : Fast and robust angle based flattening. ACM Transactions on Graphics (2005)
19. Turquin, E., Wither, J., Boissieux, L., Cani, M.P., Hughes, J.: A sketch-based interface for clothing virtual characters. IEEE Computer Graphics & Applications (2006)
20. Watanabe, N., Igarashi, T.: A sketching interface for terrain modeling. In: SIGGRAPH 2004 Posters. ACM, New York (2004)
21. Wither, J., Bertails, F., Cani, M.P.: Realistic hair from a sketch. In: Shape Modeling International (2007)
22. Wither, J., Boudon, F., Cani, M.P., Godin, C.: Structure from silhouettes: a new paradigm for fast sketch-based design of trees. Computer Graphics Forum **28**(2), 541–550 (2009) Special Issue: Eurographics 2009

Index

J. Jorge, F. Samavati (eds.), *Sketch-based Interfaces and Modeling*,
DOI 10.1007/978-1-84882-812-4, © Springer-Verlag London Limited 2011

MIX
Papier aus verantwortungsvollen Quellen
Paper from responsible sources
FSC® C105338

If you have any concerns about our products,
you can contact us on
ProductSafety@springernature.com

In case Publisher is established outside the EU,
the EU authorized representative is:
Springer Nature Customer Service Center GmbH
Europaplatz 3, 69115 Heidelberg, Germany

Printed by Libri Plureos GmbH
in Hamburg, Germany